Daniel Defoe
SELECTIONS

VOLUME I

THE LIFE AND ADVENTURES OF ROBINSON CRUSOE

●

THE FURTHER ADVENTURES OF ROBINSON CRUSOE

●

THE CONSOLIDATOR, OR MEMOIRS OF SUNDRY
TRANSACTIONS FROM THE WORLD IN THE MOON

●

THE LIFE ADVENTURES AND PIRACIES OF THE FAMOUS
CAPTAIN SINGLETON

From the editor

Like so many other outstanding English writers, Daniel Defoe (1659-1731) was not just a writer; he was also a spy. Like so many other men of talent, he died while hiding from his numerous creditors. A prolific author of novels and one of the creators of this genre itself, he lives in our memory as the author of *Robinson Crusoe* (1719). Meanwhile, there are many more works of Defoe — extravagant, full of adventures in exotic lands, and humourous - that deserve our attention. Three of them are presented in this volume.

The
Life and Adventures
of
Robinson Crusoe

The Life and Strange Surprising Adventures of Robinson Crusoe, of York, Mariner: Who lived Eight and Twenty Years, all alone in an un-inhabited Island on the Coast of America, near the Mouth of the Great River of Oroonoque; Having been cast on Shore by Shipwreck, wherein all the Men perished but himself. With An Account how he was at last as strangely deliver'd by Pyrates.

By
Daniel Defoe

CHAPTER I

START IN LIFE

I was born in the year 1632, in the city of York, of a good family, though not of that country, my father being a foreigner of Bremen, who settled first at Hull. He got a good estate by merchandise, and leaving off his trade, lived afterwards at York, from whence he had married my mother, whose relations were named Robinson, a very good family in that country, and from whom I was called Robinson Kreutznaer; but, by the usual corruption of words in England, we are now called—nay we call ourselves and write our name—Crusoe; and so my companions always called me.

I had two elder brothers, one of whom was lieutenant-colonel to an English regiment of foot in Flanders, formerly commanded by the famous Colonel Lockhart, and was killed at the battle near Dunkirk against the Spaniards. What became of my second brother I never knew, any more than my father or mother knew what became of me.

Being the third son of the family and not bred to any trade, my head began to be filled very early with rambling thoughts. My father, who was very ancient, had given me a competent share of learning, as far as house-education and a country free school generally go, and designed me for the law; but I would be satisfied with nothing but going to sea; and my inclination to this led me so strongly against the will, nay, the commands of my father, and against all the entreaties and persuasions of my mother and other friends, that there seemed to be something fatal in that propensity of nature, tending directly to the life of misery which was to befall me.

My father, a wise and grave man, gave me serious and excellent counsel against what he foresaw was my design. He called me one morning into his chamber, where he was confined by the gout, and expostulated very warmly with me upon this subject. He asked me what reasons, more than a mere wandering inclination, I had for leaving father's house and my native country, where I might be well introduced, and had a prospect of raising my fortune by application and industry, with a life of ease and pleasure. He told me it was men of desperate fortunes on one hand, or of aspiring, superior fortunes on the other, who went abroad upon adventures, to rise by enterprise, and make themselves famous in undertakings of a nature out of the common road;

that these things were all either too far above me or too far below me; that mine was the middle state, or what might be called the upper station of low life, which he had found, by long experience, was the best state in the world, the most suited to human happiness, not exposed to the miseries and hardships, the labour and sufferings of the mechanic part of mankind, and not embarrassed with the pride, luxury, ambition, and envy of the upper part of mankind. He told me I might judge of the happiness of this state by this one thing—viz. that this was the state of life which all other people envied; that kings have frequently lamented the miserable consequence of being born to great things, and wished they had been placed in the middle of the two extremes, between the mean and the great; that the wise man gave his testimony to this, as the standard of felicity, when he prayed to have neither poverty nor riches.

He bade me observe it, and I should always find that the calamities of life were shared among the upper and lower part of mankind, but that the middle station had the fewest disasters, and was not exposed to so many vicissitudes as the higher or lower part of mankind; nay, they were not subjected to so many distempers and uneasinesses, either of body or mind, as those were who, by vicious living, luxury, and extravagances on the one hand, or by hard labour, want of necessaries, and mean or insufficient diet on the other hand, bring distemper upon themselves by the natural consequences of their way of living; that the middle station of life was calculated for all kind of virtue and all kind of enjoyments; that peace and plenty were the handmaids of a middle fortune; that temperance, moderation, quietness, health, society, all agreeable diversions, and all desirable pleasures, were the blessings attending the middle station of life; that this way men went silently and smoothly through the world, and comfortably out of it, not embarrassed with the labours of the hands or of the head, not sold to a life of slavery for daily bread, nor harassed with perplexed circumstances, which rob the soul of peace and the body of rest, nor enraged with the passion of envy, or the secret burning lust of ambition for great things; but, in easy circumstances, sliding gently through the world, and sensibly tasting the sweets of living, without the bitter; feeling that they are happy, and learning by every day's experience to know it more sensibly.

After this he pressed me earnestly, and in the most affectionate manner, not to play the young man, nor to precipitate myself into miseries which nature, and the station of life I was born in, seemed to have provided against; that I was under no necessity of seeking my bread; that he would do well for me, and endeavour to enter me fairly into the station of life which he had just been recommending to me; and that if I was not very easy and happy in the world, it must be my mere fate or fault that must hinder it; and that he should have nothing to answer for, having thus discharged his duty in warning me against measures which he knew would be to my hurt; in a word, that as he would do very kind things for me if I would stay and settle at home as he directed, so he would not have so much hand in my misfortunes as to give me any encouragement to go away; and to close all, he told me I had my elder brother for an example, to whom he had used the same earnest persuasions to keep him from going into the Low Country wars, but could not prevail, his young desires prompting him to run into the army, where he was killed; and though he said he would not cease to pray for me, yet he would venture to say to me, that if I did take this foolish step, God would not bless me, and I should have leisure hereafter to reflect upon having neglected his counsel when there might be none to assist in my recovery.

I observed in this last part of his discourse, which was truly prophetic, though I suppose my father did not know it to be so himself—I say, I observed the tears run down his face very plentifully, especially when he spoke of my brother who was killed: and that when he spoke of my having leisure to repent, and none to assist me, he was so moved that he broke off the discourse, and told me his heart was so full he could say no more to me.

I was sincerely affected with this discourse, and, indeed, who could be otherwise? and I resolved not to think of going abroad any more, but to settle at home according to my father's desire. But alas! a few days wore it all off; and, in short, to prevent any of my father's further importunities, in a few weeks after I resolved to run quite away from him. However, I did not act quite so hastily as the first heat of my resolution prompted; but I took my mother at a time when I thought her a little more pleasant than ordinary, and told her that my thoughts were so entirely bent upon seeing the world that I should never settle to anything with resolution enough to go through with it, and my father had better give me his consent than force me to go without it; that I was now eighteen years old, which was too late to go apprentice to a trade or clerk to an attorney; that I was sure if I did I should never serve out my time, but I should certainly run away from my master before my time was out, and go to sea; and if she would speak to my father to let me go one voyage abroad, if I came home again, and did not like it, I would go no more; and I would promise, by a double diligence, to recover the time that I had lost.

This put my mother into a great passion; she told me she knew it would be to no purpose to speak to my father upon any such subject; that he knew too well what was my interest to give his consent to anything so much for my hurt; and that she wondered how I could think of any such thing after the discourse I had had with my father, and such kind and tender expressions as she knew my father had used to me; and that, in short, if I would ruin myself, there was no help for me; but I might depend I should never have their consent to it; that for her part she would not have so much hand in my destruction; and I should never have it to say that my mother was willing when my father was not.

Though my mother refused to move it to my father, yet I heard afterwards that she reported all the discourse to him, and that my father, after showing a great concern at it, said to her, with a sigh, "That boy might be happy if he would stay at home; but if he goes abroad, he will be the most miserable wretch that ever was born: I can give no consent to it."

It was not till almost a year after this that I broke loose, though, in the meantime, I continued obstinately deaf to all proposals of settling to business, and frequently expostulated with my father and mother about their being so positively determined against what they knew my inclinations prompted me to. But being one day at Hull, where I went casually, and without any purpose of making an elopement at that time; but, I say, being there, and one of my companions being about to sail to London in his father's ship, and prompting me to go with them with the common allurement of seafaring men, that it should cost me nothing for my passage, I consulted neither father nor mother any more, nor so much as sent them word of it; but leaving them to hear of it as they might, without asking God's blessing or my father's, without any consideration of circumstances or consequences, and in an ill hour, God knows, on the 1st of September 1651, I went on board a ship bound for London. Never any young adventurer's misfortunes, I believe, began sooner, or continued longer than mine. The ship was no sooner out of the Humber than the wind began to blow and the sea to rise in a most frightful manner; and, as I had never been at sea before, I was most inexpressibly sick in body and terrified in mind. I began now seriously to reflect upon what I had done, and how justly I was overtaken by the judgment of Heaven for my wicked leaving my father's house, and abandoning my duty. All the good counsels of my parents, my father's tears and my mother's entreaties, came now fresh into my mind; and my conscience, which was not yet come to the pitch of hardness to which it has since, reproached me with the contempt of advice, and the breach of my duty to God and my father.

All this while the storm increased, and the sea went very high, though nothing like what I have seen many times since; no, nor what I saw a few days after; but it was enough to affect me then, who was but a young sailor, and had never known anything of the matter. I expected every wave would have swallowed us up, and that every time the ship fell down, as I thought it did, in the trough or hollow of the sea, we should never rise more; in this agony of mind, I made many vows and resolutions that if it would please God to spare my life in this one voyage, if ever I got once my foot upon dry land again, I would go directly home to my father, and never set it into a ship again while I lived; that I would take his advice, and never run myself into such miseries as these any more. Now I saw plainly the goodness of his observations about the middle station of life, how easy, how comfortably he had lived all his days, and never had been exposed to tempests at sea or troubles on shore; and I resolved that I would, like a true repenting prodigal, go home to my father.

These wise and sober thoughts continued all the while the storm lasted, and indeed some time after; but the next day the wind was abated, and the sea calmer, and I began to be a little inured to it; however, I was very grave for all that day, being also a little sea-sick still; but towards night the weather cleared up, the wind was quite over, and a charming fine evening followed; the sun went down perfectly clear, and rose so the next morning; and having little or no wind, and a smooth sea, the sun shining upon it, the sight was, as I thought, the most delightful that ever I saw.

I had slept well in the night, and was now no more sea-sick, but very cheerful, looking with wonder upon the sea that was so rough and terrible the day before, and could be so calm and so pleasant in so little a time after. And now, lest my good resolutions should continue, my companion, who had enticed me away, comes to me; "Well, Bob," says he, clapping me upon the shoulder, "how do you do after it? I warrant you were frighted, wer'n't you, last night, when it blew but a capful of wind?" "A capful d'you call it?" said I; "'twas a terrible storm." "A storm, you fool you," replies he; "do you call that a storm? why, it was nothing at all; give us but a good ship and sea-room, and we think nothing of such a squall of wind as that; but you're but a fresh-water sailor, Bob. Come, let us make a bowl of punch, and we'll forget all that; d'ye see what charming weather 'tis now?" To make short this sad part of my story, we went the way of all sailors; the punch was made and I was made half drunk with it: and in that one night's wickedness I drowned all my repentance, all my reflections upon my past conduct, all my resolutions for the future. In a word, as the sea was returned to its smoothness of surface and settled calmness by the abatement of that storm, so the hurry of my thoughts being over, my fears and apprehensions of being swallowed up by the sea being forgotten, and the current of my former desires returned, I entirely forgot the vows and promises that I made in my distress. I found, indeed, some intervals of reflection; and the serious thoughts did, as it were, endeavour to return again sometimes; but I shook them off, and roused myself from them as it were from a distemper, and applying myself to drinking and company, soon mastered the return of those fits—for so I called them; and I had in five or six days got as complete a victory over conscience as any young fellow that resolved not to be troubled with it could desire. But I was to have another trial for it still; and Providence, as in such cases generally it does, resolved to leave me entirely without excuse; for if I would not take this for a deliverance, the next was to be such a one as the worst and most hardened wretch among us would confess both the danger and the mercy of.

The sixth day of our being at sea we came into Yarmouth Roads; the wind having been contrary and the weather calm, we had made but little way since the storm. Here we were obliged to come to an anchor, and here we lay, the wind continuing contrary—viz. at south-west—for seven or eight days, during which time a great many ships from Newcastle came into the same Roads, as the common harbour where the ships might wait for a wind for the river.

We had not, however, rid here so long but we should have tided it up the river, but that the wind blew too fresh, and after we had lain four or five days, blew very hard. However, the Roads being reckoned as good as a harbour, the anchorage good, and our ground-tackle very strong, our men were unconcerned, and not in the least apprehensive of danger, but spent the time in rest and mirth, after the manner of the sea; but the eighth day, in the morning, the wind increased, and we had all hands at work to strike our topmasts, and make everything snug and close, that the ship might ride as easy as possible. By noon the sea went very high indeed, and our ship rode forecastle in, shipped several seas, and we thought once or twice our anchor had come home; upon which our master ordered out the sheet-anchor, so that we rode with two anchors ahead, and the cables veered out to the bitter end.

By this time it blew a terrible storm indeed; and now I began to see terror and amazement in the faces even of the seamen themselves. The master, though vigilant in the business of preserving the ship, yet as he went in and out of his cabin by me, I could hear him softly to himself say, several times, "Lord be merciful to us! we shall be all lost! we shall be all undone!" and the like. During these first hurries I was stupid, lying still in my cabin, which was in the steerage, and cannot describe my temper: I could ill resume the first penitence which I had so apparently trampled upon and hardened myself against: I thought the bitterness of death had been past, and that this would be nothing like the first; but when the master himself came by me, as I said just now, and said we should be all lost, I was dreadfully frighted. I got up out of my cabin and looked out; but such a dismal sight I never saw: the sea ran mountains high, and broke upon us every three or four minutes; when I could look about, I could see nothing but distress round us; two ships that rode near us, we found, had cut their masts by the board, being deep laden; and our men cried out that a ship which rode about a mile ahead of us was foundered. Two more ships, being driven from their anchors, were run out of the Roads to sea, at all adventures, and that with not a mast standing. The light ships fared the best, as not so much labouring in the sea; but two or three of them drove, and came close by us, running away with only their spritsail out before the wind.

Towards evening the mate and boatswain begged the master of our ship to let them cut away the fore-mast, which he was very unwilling to do; but the boatswain protesting to him that if he did not the ship would founder, he consented; and when they had cut away the fore-mast, the main-mast stood so loose, and shook the ship so much, they were obliged to cut that away also, and make a clear deck.

Any one may judge what a condition I must be in at all this, who was but a young sailor, and who had been in such a fright before at but a little. But if I can express at this distance the thoughts I had about me at that time, I was in tenfold more horror of mind upon account of my former convictions, and the having returned from them to the resolutions I had wickedly taken at first, than I was at death itself; and these, added to the terror of the storm, put me into such a condition that I can by no words describe it. But the worst was not come yet; the storm continued with such fury that the seamen themselves acknowledged they had never seen a worse. We had a good ship, but she was deep laden, and wallowed in the sea, so that the seamen every now and then cried out she would founder. It was my advantage in one respect, that I did not know what they meant by *founder* till I inquired. However, the storm was so violent that I saw, what is not often seen, the master, the boatswain, and some others more sensible than the rest, at their prayers, and expecting every moment when the ship would go to the bottom. In the middle of the night, and under all the rest of our distresses, one of the men that had been down to see cried out we had sprung a leak; another said there was four feet water in the hold. Then all hands were called to the pump. At that word, my heart, as I thought, died within me: and I fell backwards upon the side of my bed where I sat, into the cabin. However, the men roused me, and told me that I, that was able to do nothing before, was as well able to pump as another; at which I stirred up and went to the pump, and worked very heartily. While this was doing the master, seeing some light colliers, who, not able to ride out the storm were obliged to slip and run away to sea, and would come near us, ordered to fire a gun as a signal of distress. I, who knew nothing what they meant, thought the ship had broken, or some dreadful thing happened. In a word, I was so surprised that I fell down in a swoon. As this was a time when everybody had his own life to think of, nobody minded me, or what was become of me; but another man stepped up to the pump, and thrusting me aside with his foot, let me lie, thinking I had been dead; and it was a great while before I came to myself.

We worked on; but the water increasing in the hold, it was apparent that the ship would founder; and though the storm began to abate a little, yet it was not possible she could swim till we might run into any port; so the master continued firing guns for help; and a light ship, who had rid it out just ahead of us, ventured a boat out to help us. It was with the utmost hazard the boat came near us; but it was impossible for us to get on board, or for the boat to lie near the ship's side, till at last the men rowing very heartily, and venturing their lives to save ours, our men cast them a rope over the stern with a buoy to it, and then veered it out a great length, which they, after much labour and hazard, took hold of, and we hauled them close under our stern, and got all into their boat. It was to no purpose for them or us, after we were in the boat, to think of reaching their own ship; so all agreed to let her drive, and only to pull her in towards shore as much as we could; and our master promised them, that if the boat was staved upon shore, he would make it good to their master: so partly rowing and partly driving, our boat went away to the northward, sloping towards the shore almost as far as Winterton Ness.

We were not much more than a quarter of an hour out of our ship till we saw her sink, and then I understood for the first time what was meant by a ship foundering in the sea. I must acknowledge I had hardly eyes to look up when the seamen told me she was sinking; for from the moment that they rather put me into the boat than that I might be said to go in, my heart was, as it were, dead within me, partly with fright, partly with horror of mind, and the thoughts of what was yet before me.

While we were in this condition—the men yet labouring at the oar to bring the boat near the shore—we could see (when, our boat mounting the waves, we were able to see the shore) a great many people running along the strand to assist us when we should come near; but we made but slow way towards the shore; nor were we able to reach the shore till, being past the lighthouse at Winterton, the shore falls off to the westward towards Cromer, and so the land broke off a little the violence of the wind. Here we got in, and though not without much difficulty, got all safe on shore, and walked afterwards on foot to Yarmouth, where, as unfortunate men, we were used with great humanity, as well by the magistrates of the town, who assigned us good quarters, as by particular merchants and owners of ships, and had money given us sufficient to carry us either to London or back to Hull as we thought fit.

Had I now had the sense to have gone back to Hull, and have gone home, I had been happy, and my father, as in our blessed Saviour's parable, had even killed the fatted calf for me; for hearing the ship I went away in was cast away in Yarmouth Roads, it was a great while before he had any assurances that I was not drowned.

But my ill fate pushed me on now with an obstinacy that nothing could resist; and though I had several times loud calls from my reason and my more composed judgment to go home, yet I had no power to do it. I know not what to call this, nor will I urge that it is a secret overruling decree, that hurries us on to be the instruments of our own destruction, even though it be before us, and that we rush upon it with our eyes open. Certainly, nothing but some such decreed unavoidable misery, which it was impossible for me to escape, could have pushed me forward against the calm reasonings and persuasions of my most retired thoughts, and against two such visible instructions as I had met with in my first attempt.

My comrade, who had helped to harden me before, and who was the master's son, was now less forward than I. The first time he spoke to me after we were at Yarmouth, which was not till two or three days, for we were separated in the town to several quarters; I say, the first time he saw me, it appeared his tone was altered; and, looking very melancholy, and shaking his head, he asked me how I did, and telling his father who I was, and how I had come this voyage only for a trial, in order to go further abroad, his father, turning to me with a very grave and concerned tone "Young man," says he, "you ought never to go to sea any more; you ought to take this for a plain and visible token that you are not to be a seafaring man." "Why, sir," said I, "will you go to sea no more?" "That is another case," said he; "it is my calling, and therefore my duty; but as you made this voyage on trial, you see what a taste Heaven has given you of what you are to expect if you persist. Perhaps this has all befallen us on your account, like Jonah in the ship of Tarshish. Pray," continues he, "what are you; and on what account did you go to sea?" Upon that I told him some of my story; at the end of which he burst out into a strange kind of passion: "What had I done," says he, "that such an unhappy wretch should come into my ship? I would not set my foot in the same ship with thee again for a thousand pounds." This indeed was, as I said, an excursion of his spirits, which were yet agitated by the sense of his loss, and was farther than he could have authority to go. However, he afterwards talked very gravely to me, exhorting me to go back to my father, and not tempt Providence to my ruin, telling me I might see a visible hand of Heaven against me. "And, young man," said he, "depend upon it, if you do not go back, wherever you go, you will meet with nothing but disasters and disappointments, till your father's words are fulfilled upon you."

We parted soon after; for I made him little answer, and I saw him no more; which way he went I knew not. As for me, having some money in my pocket, I travelled to London by land; and there, as well as on the road, had many struggles with myself what course of life I should take, and whether I should go home or to sea.

As to going home, shame opposed the best motions that offered to my thoughts, and it immediately occurred to me how I should be laughed at among the neighbours, and should be ashamed to see, not my father and mother only, but even everybody else; from whence I have since often observed, how incongruous and irrational the common temper of mankind is, especially of youth, to that reason which ought to guide them in such cases—viz. that they are not ashamed to sin, and yet are ashamed to repent; not ashamed of the action for which they ought justly to be esteemed fools, but are ashamed of the returning, which only can make them be esteemed wise men.

In this state of life, however, I remained some time, uncertain what measures to take, and what course of life to lead. An irresistible reluctance continued to going home; and as I stayed away a while, the remembrance of the distress I had been in wore off, and as that abated, the little motion I had in my desires to return wore off with it, till at last I quite laid aside the thoughts of it, and looked out for a voyage.

CHAPTER II

SLAVERY AND ESCAPE

That evil influence which carried me first away from my father's house—which hurried me into the wild and indigested notion of raising my fortune, and that impressed those conceits so forcibly upon me as to make me deaf to all good advice, and to the entreaties and even the commands of my father—I say, the same influence, whatever it was, presented the most unfortunate of all enterprises to my view; and I went on board a vessel bound to the coast of Africa; or, as our sailors vulgarly called it, a voyage to Guinea.

It was my great misfortune that in all these adventures I did not ship myself as a sailor; when, though I might indeed have worked a little harder than ordinary, yet at the same time I should have learnt the duty and office of a fore-mast man, and in time might have qualified myself for a mate or lieutenant, if not for a master. But as it was always my fate to choose for the worse, so I did here; for having money in my pocket and good clothes upon my back, I would always go on board in the habit of a gentleman; and so I neither had any business in the ship, nor learned to do any.

It was my lot first of all to fall into pretty good company in London, which does not always happen to such loose and misguided young fellows as I then was; the devil generally not omitting to lay some snare for them very early; but it was not so with me. I first got acquainted with the master of a ship who had been on the coast of Guinea; and who, having had very good success there, was resolved to go again. This captain taking a fancy to my conversation, which was not at all disagreeable at that time, hearing me say I had a mind to see the world, told me if I would go the voyage with him I should be at no expense; I should be his messmate and his companion; and if I could carry anything with me, I should have all the advantage of it that the trade would admit; and perhaps I might meet with some encouragement.

I embraced the offer; and entering into a strict friendship with this captain, who was an honest, plain-dealing man, I went the voyage with him, and carried a small adventure with me, which, by the disinterested honesty of my friend the captain, I increased very considerably; for I carried about £40 in such toys and trifles as the captain directed me to buy. These £40 I had mustered together by the assistance of some of

17

my relations whom I corresponded with; and who, I believe, got my father, or at least my mother, to contribute so much as that to my first adventure.

This was the only voyage which I may say was successful in all my adventures, which I owe to the integrity and honesty of my friend the captain; under whom also I got a competent knowledge of the mathematics and the rules of navigation, learned how to keep an account of the ship's course, take an observation, and, in short, to understand some things that were needful to be understood by a sailor; for, as he took delight to instruct me, I took delight to learn; and, in a word, this voyage made me both a sailor and a merchant; for I brought home five pounds nine ounces of gold-dust for my adventure, which yielded me in London, at my return, almost £300; and this filled me with those aspiring thoughts which have since so completed my ruin.

Yet even in this voyage I had my misfortunes too; particularly, that I was continually sick, being thrown into a violent calenture by the excessive heat of the climate; our principal trading being upon the coast, from latitude of 15 degrees north even to the line itself.

I was now set up for a Guinea trader; and my friend, to my great misfortune, dying soon after his arrival, I resolved to go the same voyage again, and I embarked in the same vessel with one who was his mate in the former voyage, and had now got the command of the ship. This was the unhappiest voyage that ever man made; for though I did not carry quite £100 of my new-gained wealth, so that I had £200 left, which I had lodged with my friend's widow, who was very just to me, yet I fell into terrible misfortunes. The first was this: our ship making her course towards the Canary Islands, or rather between those islands and the African shore, was surprised in the grey of the morning by a Turkish rover of Sallee, who gave chase to us with all the sail she could make. We crowded also as much canvas as our yards would spread, or our masts carry, to get clear; but finding the pirate gained upon us, and would certainly come up with us in a few hours, we prepared to fight; our ship having twelve guns, and the rogue eighteen. About three in the afternoon he came up with us, and bringing to, by mistake, just athwart our quarter, instead of athwart our stern, as he intended, we brought eight of our guns to bear on that side, and poured in a broadside upon him, which made him sheer off again, after returning our fire, and pouring in also his small shot from near two hundred men which he had on board. However, we had not a man touched, all our men keeping close. He prepared to attack us again, and we to defend ourselves. But laying us on board the next time upon our other quarter, he entered sixty men upon our decks, who immediately fell to cutting and hacking the sails and rigging. We plied them with small shot, half-pikes, powder-chests, and such like, and cleared our deck of them twice. However, to cut short this melancholy part of our story, our ship being disabled, and three of our men killed, and eight wounded, we were obliged to yield, and were carried all prisoners into Sallee, a port belonging to the Moors.

The usage I had there was not so dreadful as at first I apprehended; nor was I carried up the country to the emperor's court, as the rest of our men were, but was kept by the captain of the rover as his proper prize, and made his slave, being young and nimble, and fit for his business. At this surprising change of my circumstances, from a merchant to a miserable slave, I was perfectly overwhelmed; and now I looked back upon my father's prophetic discourse to me, that I should be miserable and have none to relieve me, which I thought was now so effectually brought to pass that I could not be worse; for now the hand of Heaven had overtaken me, and I was undone without redemption; but, alas! this was but a taste of the misery I was to go through, as will appear in the sequel of this story.

As my new patron, or master, had taken me home to his house, so I was in hopes that he would take me with him when he went to sea again, believing that it would some time or other be his fate to be taken by a Spanish or Portugal man-of-war; and that then I should be set at liberty. But this hope of mine was soon taken away; for when he went to sea, he left me on shore to look after his little garden, and do the common drudgery of slaves about his house; and when he came home again from his cruise, he ordered me to lie in the cabin to look after the ship.

Here I meditated nothing but my escape, and what method I might take to effect it, but found no way that had the least probability in it; nothing presented to make the supposition of it rational; for I had nobody to communicate it to that would embark with me—no fellow-slave, no Englishman, Irishman, or Scotchman there but myself; so that for two years, though I often pleased myself with the imagination, yet I never had the least encouraging prospect of putting it in practice.

After about two years, an odd circumstance presented itself, which put the old thought of making some attempt for my liberty again in my head. My patron lying at home longer than usual without fitting out his ship, which, as I heard, was for want of money, he used constantly, once or twice a week, sometimes oftener if the weather was fair, to take the ship's pinnace and go out into the road a-fishing; and as he always took me and young Maresco with him to row the boat, we made him very merry, and I proved very dexterous in catching fish; insomuch that sometimes he would send me with a Moor, one of his kinsmen, and the youth—the Maresco, as they called him—to catch a dish of fish for him.

It happened one time, that going a-fishing in a calm morning, a fog rose so thick that, though we were not half a league from the shore, we lost sight of it; and rowing we knew not whither or which way, we laboured all day, and all the next night; and when the morning came we found we had pulled off to sea instead of pulling in for the shore; and that we were at least two leagues from the shore. However, we got well in again, though with a great deal of labour and some danger; for the wind began to blow pretty fresh in the morning; but we were all very hungry.

But our patron, warned by this disaster, resolved to take more care of himself for the future; and having lying by him the longboat of our English ship that he had taken, he resolved he would not go a-fishing any more without a compass and some provision; so he ordered the carpenter of his ship, who also was an English slave, to build a little state-room, or cabin, in the middle of the long-boat, like that of a barge, with a place to stand behind it to steer, and haul home the main-sheet; the room before for a hand or two to stand and work the sails. She sailed with what we call a shoulder-of-mutton sail; and the boom jibed over the top of the cabin, which lay very snug and low, and had in it room for him to lie, with a slave or two, and a table to eat on, with some small lockers to put in some bottles of such liquor as he thought fit to drink; and his bread, rice, and coffee.

We went frequently out with this boat a-fishing; and as I was most dexterous to catch fish for him, he never went without me. It happened that he had appointed to go out in this boat, either for pleasure or for fish, with two or three Moors of some distinction in that place, and for whom he had provided extraordinarily, and had, therefore, sent on board the boat overnight a larger store of provisions than ordinary; and had ordered me to get ready three fusees with powder and shot, which were on board his ship, for that they designed some sport of fowling as well as fishing.

I got all things ready as he had directed, and waited the next morning with the boat washed clean, her ancient and pendants out, and everything to accommodate his guests; when by-and-by my patron came on board alone, and told me his guests had put off going from some business that fell out, and ordered me, with the man and boy, as usual, to go out with the boat and catch them some fish, for that his friends were to sup at his house, and commanded that as soon as I got some fish I should bring it home to his house; all which I prepared to do.

This moment my former notions of deliverance darted into my thoughts, for now I found I was likely to have a little ship at my command; and my master being gone, I prepared to furnish myself, not for fishing business, but for a voyage; though I knew not, neither did I so much as consider, whither I should steer—anywhere to get out of that place was my desire.

My first contrivance was to make a pretence to speak to this Moor, to get something for our subsistence on board; for I told him we must not presume to eat of our patron's bread. He said that was true; so he brought a large basket of rusk or biscuit, and three jars of fresh water, into the boat. I knew where my patron's case of bottles stood, which it was evident, by the make, were taken out of some English prize, and I conveyed them into the boat while the Moor was on shore, as if they had been there before for our master. I conveyed also a great lump of beeswax into the boat, which weighed about half a hundred-weight, with a parcel of twine or thread, a hatchet, a saw, and a hammer, all of which were of great use to us afterwards, especially the wax, to make candles. Another trick I tried upon him, which he innocently came into also: his name was Ismael, which they call Muley, or Moely; so I called to him—"Moely," said I, "our patron's guns are on board the boat; can you not get a little powder and shot? It may be we may kill some alcamies (a fowl like our curlews) for ourselves, for I know he keeps the gunner's stores in the ship." "Yes," says he, "I'll bring some;" and accordingly he brought a great leather pouch, which held a pound and a half of powder, or rather more; and another with shot, that had five or six pounds, with some bullets, and put all into the boat. At the same time I had found some powder of my master's in the great cabin, with which I filled one of the large bottles in the case, which was almost empty, pouring what was in it into another; and thus furnished with everything needful, we sailed out of the port to fish. The castle, which is at the entrance of the port, knew who we were, and took no notice of us; and we were not above a mile out of the port before we hauled in our sail and set us down to fish. The wind blew from the N.N.E., which was contrary to my desire, for had it blown southerly I had been sure to have made the coast of Spain, and at least reached to the bay of Cadiz; but my resolutions were, blow which way it would, I would be gone from that horrid place where I was, and leave the rest to fate.

After we had fished some time and caught nothing—for when I had fish on my hook I would not pull them up, that he might not see them—I said to the Moor, "This will not do; our master will not be thus served; we must stand farther off." He, thinking no harm, agreed, and being in the head of the boat, set the sails; and, as I had the helm, I ran the boat out near a league farther, and then brought her to, as if I would fish; when, giving the boy the helm, I stepped forward to where the Moor was, and making as if I stooped for something behind him, I took him by surprise with my arm under his waist, and tossed him clear overboard into the sea. He rose immediately, for he swam like a cork, and called to me, begged to be taken in, told me he would go all over the world with me. He swam so strong after the boat that he would have reached me very quickly, there being but little wind; upon which I stepped into the cabin, and fetching one of the fowling-pieces, I presented it at him, and told him I had done him no hurt, and if he would be quiet I would do him none. "But," said I, "you swim well enough to reach to the shore, and the sea is calm; make the best of your way to shore, and I will do you no harm; but if you come near the boat I'll shoot you through the head, for I am resolved to have my liberty;" so he turned himself about, and swam for the shore, and I make no doubt but he reached it with ease, for he was an excellent swimmer.

I could have been content to have taken this Moor with me, and have drowned the boy, but there was no venturing to trust him. When he was gone, I turned to the boy, whom they called Xury, and said to him, "Xury, if you will be faithful to me, I'll make you a great man; but if you will not stroke your face to be true to me"—that is, swear by Mahomet and his father's beard—"I must throw you into the sea too." The boy smiled in my face, and spoke so innocently that I could not distrust him, and swore to be faithful to me, and go all over the world with me.

While I was in view of the Moor that was swimming, I stood out directly to sea with the boat, rather stretching to windward, that they might think me gone towards the Straits' mouth (as indeed any one that had been in their wits must have been supposed to do): for who would have supposed we were sailed on to the southward, to the truly Barbarian coast, where whole nations of negroes were sure to surround us with their canoes and destroy us; where we could not go on shore but we should be devoured by savage beasts, or more merciless savages of human kind.

But as soon as it grew dusk in the evening, I changed my course, and steered directly south and by east, bending my course a little towards the east, that I might keep in with the shore; and having a fair, fresh gale of wind, and a smooth, quiet sea, I made such sail that I believe by the next day, at three o'clock in the afternoon, when I first made the land, I could not be less than one hundred and fifty miles south of Sallee; quite beyond the Emperor of Morocco's dominions, or indeed of any other king thereabouts, for we saw no people.

Yet such was the fright I had taken of the Moors, and the dreadful apprehensions I had of falling into their hands, that I would not stop, or go on shore, or come to an anchor; the wind continuing fair till I had sailed in that manner five days; and then the wind shifting to the southward, I concluded also that if any of our vessels were in chase of me, they also would now give over; so I ventured to make to the coast, and came to an anchor in the mouth of a little river, I knew not what, nor where, neither what latitude, what country, what nation, or what river. I neither saw, nor desired to see any people; the principal thing I wanted was fresh water. We came into this creek in the evening, resolving to swim on shore as soon as it was dark, and discover the country; but as soon as it was quite dark, we heard such dreadful noises of the barking, roaring, and howling of wild creatures, of we knew not what kinds, that the poor boy was ready to die with fear, and begged of me not to go on shore till day. "Well, Xury," said I, "then I won't; but it may be that we may see men by day, who will be as bad to us as those lions." "Then we give them the shoot gun," says Xury, laughing, "make them run wey." Such English Xury spoke by conversing among us slaves. However, I was glad to see the boy so cheerful, and I gave him a dram (out of our patron's case of bottles) to cheer him up. After all, Xury's advice was good, and I took it; we dropped our little anchor, and lay still all night; I say still, for we slept none; for in two or three hours we saw vast great creatures (we knew not what to call them) of many sorts, come down to the sea-shore and run into the water, wallowing and washing themselves for the pleasure of cooling themselves; and they made such hideous howlings and yellings, that I never indeed heard the like.

Xury was dreadfully frighted, and indeed so was I too; but we were both more frighted when we heard one of these mighty creatures come swimming towards our boat; we could not see him, but we might hear him by his blowing to be a monstrous huge and furious beast. Xury said it was a lion, and it might be so for aught I know; but poor Xury cried to me to weigh the anchor and row away; "No," says I, "Xury; we can slip our cable, with the buoy to it, and go off to sea; they cannot follow us far." I had no sooner said so, but I perceived the creature (whatever it was) within two oars' length, which something surprised me; however, I immediately stepped to the cabin door, and taking up my gun, fired at him; upon which he immediately turned about and swam towards the shore again.

But it is impossible to describe the horrid noises, and hideous cries and howlings that were raised, as well upon the edge of the shore as higher within the country, upon the noise or report of the gun, a thing I have some reason to believe those creatures had never heard before: this convinced me that there was no going on shore for us in the night on that coast, and how to venture on shore in the day was another question too; for to have fallen into the hands of any of the savages had been as bad as to have fallen into the hands of the lions and tigers; at least we were equally apprehensive of the danger of it.

Be that as it would, we were obliged to go on shore somewhere or other for water, for we had not a pint left in the boat; when and where to get to it was the point. Xury said, if I would let him go on shore with one of the jars, he would find if there was any water, and bring some to me. I asked him why he would go? why I should not go, and he stay in the boat? The boy answered with so much affection as made me love him ever after. Says he, "If wild mans come, they eat me, you go wey." "Well, Xury," said I, "we will both go and if the wild mans come, we will kill them, they shall eat neither of us." So I gave Xury a piece of rusk bread to eat, and a dram out of our patron's case of bottles which I mentioned before; and we hauled the boat in as near the shore as we thought was proper, and so waded on shore, carrying nothing but our arms and two jars for water.

I did not care to go out of sight of the boat, fearing the coming of canoes with savages down the river; but the boy seeing a low place about a mile up the country, rambled to it, and by-and-by I saw him come running towards me. I thought he was pursued by some savage, or frighted with some wild beast, and I ran forward towards him to help him; but when I came nearer to him I saw something hanging over his shoulders, which was a creature that he had shot, like a hare, but different in colour, and longer legs; however, we were very glad of it, and it was very good meat; but the great joy that poor Xury came with, was to tell me he had found good water and seen no wild mans.

But we found afterwards that we need not take such pains for water, for a little higher up the creek where we were we found the water fresh when the tide was out, which flowed but a little way up; so we filled our jars, and feasted on the hare he had killed, and prepared to go on our way, having seen no footsteps of any human creature in that part of the country.

As I had been one voyage to this coast before, I knew very well that the islands of the Canaries, and the Cape de Verde Islands also, lay not far off from the coast. But as I had no instruments to take an observation to know what latitude we were in, and not exactly knowing, or at least remembering, what latitude they were in, I knew not where to look for them, or when to stand off to sea towards them; otherwise I might now easily have found some of these islands. But my hope was, that if I stood along this coast till I came to that part where the English traded, I should find some of their vessels upon their usual design of trade, that would relieve and take us in.

By the best of my calculation, that place where I now was must be that country which, lying between the Emperor of Morocco's dominions and the negroes, lies waste and uninhabited, except by wild beasts; the negroes having abandoned it and gone farther south for fear of the Moors, and the Moors not thinking it worth inhabiting by reason of its barrenness; and indeed, both forsaking it because of the prodigious number of tigers, lions, leopards, and other furious creatures which harbour there; so that the Moors use it for their hunting only, where they go like an army, two or three thousand men at a time; and indeed for near a hundred miles together upon this coast we saw nothing but a waste, uninhabited country by day, and heard nothing but howlings and roaring of wild beasts by night.

Once or twice in the daytime I thought I saw the Pico of Teneriffe, being the high top of the Mountain Teneriffe in the Canaries, and had a great mind to venture out, in hopes of reaching thither; but having tried twice, I was forced in again by contrary winds, the sea also going too high for my little vessel; so, I resolved to pursue my first design, and keep along the shore.

Several times I was obliged to land for fresh water, after we had left this place; and once in particular, being early in morning, we came to an anchor under a little point of land, which was pretty high; and the tide beginning to flow, we lay still to go farther in. Xury, whose eyes

25

were more about him than it seems mine were, calls softly to me, and tells me that we had best go farther off the shore; "For," says he, "look, yonder lies a dreadful monster on the side of that hillock, fast asleep." I looked where he pointed, and saw a dreadful monster indeed, for it was a terrible, great lion that lay on the side of the shore, under the shade of a piece of the hill that hung as it were a little over him. "Xury," says I, "you shall on shore and kill him." Xury, looked frighted, and said, "Me kill! he eat me at one mouth!"—one mouthful he meant. However, I said no more to the boy, but bade him lie still, and I took our biggest gun, which was almost musket-bore, and loaded it with a good charge of powder, and with two slugs, and laid it down; then I loaded another gun with two bullets; and the third (for we had three pieces) I loaded with five smaller bullets. I took the best aim I could with the first piece to have shot him in the head, but he lay so with his leg raised a little above his nose, that the slugs hit his leg about the knee and broke the bone. He started up, growling at first, but finding his leg broken, fell down again; and then got upon three legs, and gave the most hideous roar that ever I heard. I was a little surprised that I had not hit him on the head; however, I took up the second piece immediately, and though he began to move off, fired again, and shot him in the head, and had the pleasure to see him drop and make but little noise, but lie struggling for life. Then Xury took heart, and would have me let him go on shore. "Well, go," said I: so the boy jumped into the water and taking a little gun in one hand, swam to shore with the other hand, and coming close to the creature, put the muzzle of the piece to his ear, and shot him in the head again, which despatched him quite.

This was game indeed to us, but this was no food; and I was very sorry to lose three charges of powder and shot upon a creature that was good for nothing to us. However, Xury said he would have some of him; so he comes on board, and asked me to give him the hatchet. "For what, Xury?" said I. "Me cut off his head," said he. However, Xury could not cut off his head, but he cut off a foot, and brought it with him, and it was a monstrous great one.

I bethought myself, however, that, perhaps the skin of him might, one way or other, be of some value to us; and I resolved to take off his skin if I could. So Xury and I went to work with him; but Xury was much the better workman at it, for I knew very ill how to do it. Indeed, it took us both up the whole day, but at last we got off the hide of him,

26

and spreading it on the top of our cabin, the sun effectually dried it in two days' time, and it afterwards served me to lie upon.

CHAPTER III

WRECKED ON A DESERT ISLAND

After this stop, we made on to the southward continually for ten or twelve days, living very sparingly on our provisions, which began to abate very much, and going no oftener to the shore than we were obliged to for fresh water. My design in this was to make the river Gambia or Senegal, that is to say anywhere about the Cape de Verde, where I was in hopes to meet with some European ship; and if I did not, I knew not what course I had to take, but to seek for the islands, or perish there among the negroes. I knew that all the ships from Europe, which sailed either to the coast of Guinea or to Brazil, or to the East Indies, made this cape, or those islands; and, in a word, I put the whole of my fortune upon this single point, either that I must meet with some ship or must perish.

When I had pursued this resolution about ten days longer, as I have said, I began to see that the land was inhabited; and in two or three places, as we sailed by, we saw people stand upon the shore to look at us; we could also perceive they were quite black and naked. I was once inclined to have gone on shore to them; but Xury was my better counsellor, and said to me, "No go, no go." However, I hauled in nearer the shore that I might talk to them, and I found they ran along the shore by me a good way. I observed they had no weapons in their hand, except one, who had a long slender stick, which Xury said was a lance, and that they could throw them a great way with good aim; so I kept at a distance, but talked with them by signs as well as I could; and particularly made signs for something to eat: they beckoned to me to stop my boat, and they would fetch me some meat. Upon this I lowered the top of my sail and lay by, and two of them ran up into the country, and in less than half-an-hour came back, and brought with them two pieces of dried flesh and some corn, such as is the produce of their country; but we neither knew what the one or the other was; however, we were willing to accept it, but how to come at it was our next dispute, for I would not venture on shore to them, and they were as much afraid of us; but they took a safe way for us all, for they brought it to the shore and laid it down, and went and stood a great way off till we fetched it on board, and then came close to us again.

We made signs of thanks to them, for we had nothing to make them amends; but an opportunity offered that very instant to oblige them wonderfully; for while we were lying by the shore came two mighty creatures, one pursuing the other (as we took it) with great fury from the mountains towards the sea; whether it was the male pursuing the female, or whether they were in sport or in rage, we could not tell, any more than we could tell whether it was usual or strange, but I believe it was the latter; because, in the first place, those ravenous creatures seldom appear but in the night; and, in the second place, we found the people terribly frighted, especially the women. The man that had the lance or dart did not fly from them, but the rest did; however, as the two creatures ran directly into the water, they did not offer to fall upon any of the negroes, but plunged themselves into the sea, and swam about, as if they had come for their diversion; at last one of them began to come nearer our boat than at first I expected; but I lay ready for him, for I had loaded my gun with all possible expedition, and bade Xury load both the others. As soon as he came fairly within my reach, I fired, and shot him directly in the head; immediately he sank down into the water, but rose instantly, and plunged up and down, as if he were struggling for life, and so indeed he was; he immediately made to the shore; but between the wound, which was his mortal hurt, and the strangling of the water, he died just before he reached the shore.

It is impossible to express the astonishment of these poor creatures at the noise and fire of my gun: some of them were even ready to die for fear, and fell down as dead with the very terror; but when they saw the creature dead, and sunk in the water, and that I made signs to them to come to the shore, they took heart and came, and began to search for the creature. I found him by his blood staining the water; and by the help of a rope, which I slung round him, and gave the negroes to haul, they dragged him on shore, and found that it was a most curious leopard, spotted, and fine to an admirable degree; and the negroes held up their hands with admiration, to think what it was I had killed him with.

The other creature, frighted with the flash of fire and the noise of the gun, swam on shore, and ran up directly to the mountains from whence they came; nor could I, at that distance, know what it was. I found quickly the negroes wished to eat the flesh of this creature, so I was willing to have them take it as a favour from me; which, when I made signs to them that they might take him, they were very thankful for. Immediately they fell to work with him; and though they had no knife, yet, with a sharpened piece of wood, they took off his skin as readily, and much more readily, than we could have done with a knife.

They offered me some of the flesh, which I declined, pointing out that I would give it them; but made signs for the skin, which they gave me very freely, and brought me a great deal more of their provisions, which, though I did not understand, yet I accepted. I then made signs to them for some water, and held out one of my jars to them, turning it bottom upward, to show that it was empty, and that I wanted to have it filled. They called immediately to some of their friends, and there came two women, and brought a great vessel made of earth, and burnt, as I supposed, in the sun, this they set down to me, as before, and I sent Xury on shore with my jars, and filled them all three. The women were as naked as the men.

I was now furnished with roots and corn, such as it was, and water; and leaving my friendly negroes, I made forward for about eleven days more, without offering to go near the shore, till I saw the land run out a great length into the sea, at about the distance of four or five leagues before me; and the sea being very calm, I kept a large offing to make this point. At length, doubling the point, at about two leagues from the land, I saw plainly land on the other side, to seaward; then I concluded, as it was most certain indeed, that this was the Cape de Verde, and those the islands called, from thence, Cape de Verde Islands. However, they were at a great distance, and I could not well tell what I had best to do; for if I should be taken with a fresh of wind, I might neither reach one or other.

In this dilemma, as I was very pensive, I stepped into the cabin and sat down, Xury having the helm; when, on a sudden, the boy cried out, "Master, master, a ship with a sail!" and the foolish boy was frighted out of his wits, thinking it must needs be some of his master's ships sent to pursue us, but I knew we were far enough out of their reach. I jumped out of the cabin, and immediately saw, not only the ship, but that it was a Portuguese ship; and, as I thought, was bound to the coast of Guinea, for negroes. But, when I observed the course she steered, I was soon convinced they were bound some other way, and did not design to come any nearer to the shore; upon which I stretched out to sea as much as I could, resolving to speak with them if possible.

With all the sail I could make, I found I should not be able to come in their way, but that they would be gone by before I could make any signal to them: but after I had crowded to the utmost, and began to despair, they, it seems, saw by the help of their glasses that it was some European boat, which they supposed must belong to some ship that was lost; so they shortened sail to let me come up. I was encouraged with this, and as I had my patron's ancient on board, I made a waft of it to them, for a signal of distress, and fired a gun, both which they saw; for they told me they saw the smoke, though they did not hear the gun. Upon these signals they very kindly brought to, and lay by for me; and in about three hours' time I came up with them.

They asked me what I was, in Portuguese, and in Spanish, and in French, but I understood none of them; but at last a Scotch sailor, who was on board, called to me: and I answered him, and told him I was an Englishman, that I had made my escape out of slavery from the Moors, at Sallee; they then bade me come on board, and very kindly took me in, and all my goods.

It was an inexpressible joy to me, which any one will believe, that I was thus delivered, as I esteemed it, from such a miserable and almost hopeless condition as I was in; and I immediately offered all I had to the captain of the ship, as a return for my deliverance; but he generously told me he would take nothing from me, but that all I had should be delivered safe to me when I came to the Brazils. "For," says he, "I have saved your life on no other terms than I would be glad to be saved myself: and it may, one time or other, be my lot to be taken up in the same condition. Besides," said he, "when I carry you to the Brazils, so great a way from your own country, if I should take from you what you have, you will be starved there, and then I only take away that life I have given. No, no," says he: "Seignior Inglese" (Mr. Englishman), "I will carry you thither in charity, and those things will help to buy your subsistence there, and your passage home again."

As he was charitable in this proposal, so he was just in the performance to a tittle; for he ordered the seamen that none should touch anything that I had: then he took everything into his own possession, and gave me back an exact inventory of them, that I might have them, even to my three earthen jars.

As to my boat, it was a very good one; and that he saw, and told me he would buy it of me for his ship's use; and asked me what I would have for it? I told him he had been so generous to me in everything that I could not offer to make any price of the boat, but left it entirely to him: upon which he told me he would give me a note of hand to pay me eighty pieces of eight for it at Brazil; and when it came there, if any one offered to give more, he would make it up. He offered me also sixty pieces of eight more for my boy Xury, which I was loth to take; not that I was unwilling to let the captain have him, but I was very loth to sell the poor boy's liberty, who had assisted me so faithfully in procuring my own. However, when I let him know my reason, he owned it to be just, and offered me this medium, that he would give the boy an obligation to set him free in ten years, if he turned Christian: upon this, and Xury saying he was willing to go to him, I let the captain have him.

We had a very good voyage to the Brazils, and I arrived in the Bay de Todos los Santos, or All Saints' Bay, in about twenty-two days after. And now I was once more delivered from the most miserable of all conditions of life; and what to do next with myself I was to consider.

The generous treatment the captain gave me I can never enough remember: he would take nothing of me for my passage, gave me twenty ducats for the leopard's skin, and forty for the lion's skin, which I had in my boat, and caused everything I had in the ship to be punctually delivered to me; and what I was willing to sell he bought of me, such as the case of bottles, two of my guns, and a piece of the lump of beeswax—for I had made candles of the rest: in a word, I made about two hundred and twenty pieces of eight of all my cargo; and with this stock I went on shore in the Brazils.

I had not been long here before I was recommended to the house of a good honest man like himself, who had an *ingenio*, as they call it (that is, a plantation and a sugar-house). I lived with him some time, and acquainted myself by that means with the manner of planting and making of sugar; and seeing how well the planters lived, and how they got rich suddenly, I resolved, if I could get a licence to settle there, I would turn planter among them: resolving in the meantime to find out some way to get my money, which I had left in London, remitted to me. To this purpose, getting a kind of letter of naturalisation, I purchased as much land that was uncured as my money would reach, and formed a plan for my plantation and settlement; such a one as might be suitable to the stock which I proposed to myself to receive from England.

I had a neighbour, a Portuguese, of Lisbon, but born of English parents, whose name was Wells, and in much such circumstances as I was. I call him my neighbour, because his plantation lay next to mine, and we went on very sociably together. My stock was but low, as well as his; and we rather planted for food than anything else, for about two years. However, we began to increase, and our land began to come into order; so that the third year we planted some tobacco, and made each of us a large piece of ground ready for planting canes in the year to come.

But we both wanted help; and now I found, more than before, I had done wrong in parting with my boy Xury.

But, alas! for me to do wrong that never did right, was no great wonder. I hail no remedy but to go on: I had got into an employment quite remote to my genius, and directly contrary to the life I delighted in, and for which I forsook my father's house, and broke through all his good advice. Nay, I was coming into the very middle station, or upper degree of low life, which my father advised me to before, and which, if I resolved to go on with, I might as well have stayed at home, and never have fatigued myself in the world as I had done; and I used often to say to myself, I could have done this as well in England, among my friends, as have gone five thousand miles off to do it among strangers and savages, in a wilderness, and at such a distance as never to hear from any part of the world that had the least knowledge of me.

In this manner I used to look upon my condition with the utmost regret. I had nobody to converse with, but now and then this neighbour; no work to be done, but by the labour of my hands; and I used to say, I lived just like a man cast away upon some desolate island, that had nobody there but himself. But how just has it been—and how should all men reflect, that when they compare their present conditions with others that are worse, Heaven may oblige them to make the exchange, and be convinced of their former felicity by their experience—I say, how just has it been, that the truly solitary life I reflected on, in an island of mere desolation, should be my lot, who had so often unjustly compared it with the life which I then led, in which, had I continued, I had in all probability been exceeding prosperous and rich.

I was in some degree settled in my measures for carrying on the plantation before my kind friend, the captain of the ship that took me up at sea, went back—for the ship remained there, in providing his lading and preparing for his voyage, nearly three months—when telling him what little stock I had left behind me in London, he gave me this friendly and sincere advice:—"Seignior Inglese," says he (for so he always called me), "if you will give me letters, and a procuration in form to me, with orders to the person who has your money in London to send your effects to Lisbon, to such persons as I shall direct, and in such goods as are proper for this country, I will bring you the produce of them, God willing, at my return; but, since human affairs are all subject to changes and disasters, I would have you give orders but for one hundred pounds sterling, which, you say, is half your stock, and let the hazard be run for the first; so that, if it come safe, you may order the rest the same way, and, if it miscarry, you may have the other half to have recourse to for your supply."

This was so wholesome advice, and looked so friendly, that I could not but be convinced it was the best course I could take; so I accordingly prepared letters to the gentlewoman with whom I had left my money, and a procuration to the Portuguese captain, as he desired.

I wrote the English captain's widow a full account of all my adventures—my slavery, escape, and how I had met with the Portuguese captain at sea, the humanity of his behaviour, and what condition I was now in, with all other necessary directions for my supply; and when this honest captain came to Lisbon, he found means, by some of the English merchants there, to send over, not the order only, but a full account of my story to a merchant in London, who represented it effectually to her; whereupon she not only delivered the money, but out of her own pocket sent the Portugal captain a very handsome present for his humanity and charity to me.

The merchant in London, vesting this hundred pounds in English goods, such as the captain had written for, sent them directly to him at Lisbon, and he brought them all safe to me to the Brazils; among which, without my direction (for I was too young in my business to think of them), he had taken care to have all sorts of tools, ironwork, and utensils necessary for my plantation, and which were of great use to me.

When this cargo arrived I thought my fortune made, for I was surprised with the joy of it; and my stood steward, the captain, had laid out the five pounds, which my friend had sent him for a present for himself, to purchase and bring me over a servant, under bond for six years' service, and would not accept of any consideration, except a little tobacco, which I would have him accept, being of my own produce.

Neither was this all; for my goods being all English manufacture, such as cloths, stuffs, baize, and things particularly valuable and desirable in the country, I found means to sell them to a very great advantage; so that I might say I had more than four times the value of my first cargo, and was now infinitely beyond my poor neighbour—I mean in the advancement of my plantation; for the first thing I did, I bought me a negro slave, and an European servant also—I mean another besides that which the captain brought me from Lisbon.

But as abused prosperity is oftentimes made the very means of our greatest adversity, so it was with me. I went on the next year with great success in my plantation: I raised fifty great rolls of tobacco on my own

34

ground, more than I had disposed of for necessaries among my neighbours; and these fifty rolls, being each of above a hundredweight, were well cured, and laid by against the return of the fleet from Lisbon: and now increasing in business and wealth, my head began to be full of projects and undertakings beyond my reach; such as are, indeed, often the ruin of the best heads in business. Had I continued in the station I was now in, I had room for all the happy things to have yet befallen me for which my father so earnestly recommended a quiet, retired life, and of which he had so sensibly described the middle station of life to be full of; but other things attended me, and I was still to be the wilful agent of all my own miseries; and particularly, to increase my fault, and double the reflections upon myself, which in my future sorrows I should have leisure to make, all these miscarriages were procured by my apparent obstinate adhering to my foolish inclination of wandering abroad, and pursuing that inclination, in contradiction to the clearest views of doing myself good in a fair and plain pursuit of those prospects, and those measures of life, which nature and Providence concurred to present me with, and to make my duty.

As I had once done thus in my breaking away from my parents, so I could not be content now, but I must go and leave the happy view I had of being a rich and thriving man in my new plantation, only to pursue a rash and immoderate desire of rising faster than the nature of the thing admitted; and thus I cast myself down again into the deepest gulf of human misery that ever man fell into, or perhaps could be consistent with life and a state of health in the world.

To come, then, by the just degrees to the particulars of this part of my story. You may suppose, that having now lived almost four years in the Brazils, and beginning to thrive and prosper very well upon my plantation, I had not only learned the language, but had contracted acquaintance and friendship among my fellow-planters, as well as among the merchants at St. Salvador, which was our port; and that, in my discourses among them, I had frequently given them an account of my two voyages to the coast of Guinea: the manner of trading with the negroes there, and how easy it was to purchase upon the coast for trifles—such as beads, toys, knives, scissors, hatchets, bits of glass, and the like—not only gold-dust, Guinea grains, elephants' teeth, &c., but negroes, for the service of the Brazils, in great numbers.

They listened always very attentively to my discourses on these heads, but especially to that part which related to the buying of negroes, which was a trade at that time, not only not far entered into, but, as far as it was, had been carried on by assientos, or permission of the kings of Spain and Portugal, and engrossed in the public stock: so that few negroes were bought, and these excessively dear.

It happened, being in company with some merchants and planters of my acquaintance, and talking of those things very earnestly, three of them came to me next morning, and told me they had been musing very much upon what I had discoursed with them of the last night, and they came to make a secret proposal to me; and, after enjoining me to secrecy, they told me that they had a mind to fit out a ship to go to Guinea; that they had all plantations as well as I, and were straitened for nothing so much as servants; that as it was a trade that could not be carried on, because they could not publicly sell the negroes when they came home, so they desired to make but one voyage, to bring the negroes on shore privately, and divide them among their own plantations; and, in a word, the question was whether I would go their supercargo in the ship, to manage the trading part upon the coast of Guinea; and they offered me that I should have my equal share of the negroes, without providing any part of the stock.

This was a fair proposal, it must be confessed, had it been made to any one that had not had a settlement and a plantation of his own to look after, which was in a fair way of coming to be very considerable, and with a good stock upon it; but for me, that was thus entered and established, and had nothing to do but to go on as I had begun, for three or four years more, and to have sent for the other hundred pounds from England; and who in that time, and with that little addition, could scarce have failed of being worth three or four thousand pounds sterling, and that increasing too—for me to think of such a voyage was the most preposterous thing that ever man in such circumstances could be guilty of.

But I, that was born to be my own destroyer, could no more resist the offer than I could restrain my first rambling designs when my father' good counsel was lost upon me. In a word, I told them I would go with all my heart, if they would undertake to look after my plantation in my absence, and would dispose of it to such as I should direct, if I miscarried. This they all engaged to do, and entered into writings or covenants to do so; and I made a formal will, disposing of my plantation and effects in case of my death, making the captain of the ship that had saved my life, as before, my universal heir, but obliging him to dispose of my effects as I had directed in my will; one half of the produce being to himself, and the other to be shipped to England.

36

In short, I took all possible caution to preserve my effects and to keep up my plantation. Had I used half as much prudence to have looked into my own interest, and have made a judgment of what I ought to have done and not to have done, I had certainly never gone away from so prosperous an undertaking, leaving all the probable views of a thriving circumstance, and gone upon a voyage to sea, attended with all its common hazards, to say nothing of the reasons I had to expect particular misfortunes to myself.

But I was hurried on, and obeyed blindly the dictates of my fancy rather than my reason; and, accordingly, the ship being fitted out, and the cargo furnished, and all things done, as by agreement, by my partners in the voyage, I went on board in an evil hour, the 1st September 1659, being the same day eight years that I went from my father and mother at Hull, in order to act the rebel to their authority, and the fool to my own interests.

Our ship was about one hundred and twenty tons burden, carried six guns and fourteen men, besides the master, his boy, and myself. We had on board no large cargo of goods, except of such toys as were fit for our trade with the negroes, such as beads, bits of glass, shells, and other trifles, especially little looking-glasses, knives, scissors, hatchets, and the like.

The same day I went on board we set sail, standing away to the northward upon our own coast, with design to stretch over for the African coast when we came about ten or twelve degrees of northern latitude, which, it seems, was the manner of course in those days. We had very good weather, only excessively hot, all the way upon our own coast, till we came to the height of Cape St. Augustino; from whence, keeping further off at sea, we lost sight of land, and steered as if we were bound for the isle Fernando de Noronha, holding our course N.E. by N., and leaving those isles on the east. In this course we passed the line in about twelve days' time, and were, by our last observation, in seven degrees twenty-two minutes northern latitude, when a violent tornado, or hurricane, took us quite out of our knowledge. It began from the south-east, came about to the north-west, and then settled in the north-east; from whence it blew in such a terrible manner, that for twelve days together we could do nothing but drive, and, scudding away before it, let it carry us whither fate and the fury of the winds directed; and, during these twelve days, I need not say that I expected every day to be swallowed up; nor, indeed, did any in the ship expect to save their lives.

In this distress we had, besides the terror of the storm, one of our men die of the calenture, and one man and the boy washed overboard. About the twelfth day, the weather abating a little, the master made an observation as well as he could, and found that he was in about eleven degrees north latitude, but that he was twenty-two degrees of longitude difference west from Cape St. Augustino; so that he found he was upon the coast of Guiana, or the north part of Brazil, beyond the river Amazon, toward that of the river Orinoco, commonly called the Great River; and began to consult with me what course he should take, for the ship was leaky, and very much disabled, and he was going directly back to the coast of Brazil.

I was positively against that; and looking over the charts of the sea-coast of America with him, we concluded there was no inhabited country for us to have recourse to till we came within the circle of the Caribbee Islands, and therefore resolved to stand away for Barbadoes; which, by keeping off at sea, to avoid the indraft of the Bay or Gulf of Mexico, we might easily perform, as we hoped, in about fifteen days' sail; whereas we could not possibly make our voyage to the coast of Africa without some assistance both to our ship and to ourselves.

With this design we changed our course, and steered away N.W. by W., in order to reach some of our English islands, where I hoped for relief. But our voyage was otherwise determined; for, being in the latitude of twelve degrees eighteen minutes, a second storm came upon us, which carried us away with the same impetuosity westward, and drove us so out of the way of all human commerce, that, had all our lives been saved as to the sea, we were rather in danger of being devoured by savages than ever returning to our own country.

In this distress, the wind still blowing very hard, one of our men early in the morning cried out, "Land!" and we had no sooner run out of the cabin to look out, in hopes of seeing whereabouts in the world we were, than the ship struck upon a sand, and in a moment her motion being so stopped, the sea broke over her in such a manner that we expected we should all have perished immediately; and we were immediately driven into our close quarters, to shelter us from the very foam and spray of the sea.

It is not easy for any one who has not been in the like condition to describe or conceive the consternation of men in such circumstances. We knew nothing where we were, or upon what land it was we were driven—whether an island or the main, whether inhabited or not inhabited. As the rage of the wind was still great, though rather less

38

than at first, we could not so much as hope to have the ship hold many minutes without breaking into pieces, unless the winds, by a kind of miracle, should turn immediately about. In a word, we sat looking upon one another, and expecting death every moment, and every man, accordingly, preparing for another world; for there was little or nothing more for us to do in this. That which was our present comfort, and all the comfort we had, was that, contrary to our expectation, the ship did not break yet, and that the master said the wind began to abate.

Now, though we thought that the wind did a little abate, yet the ship having thus struck upon the sand, and sticking too fast for us to expect her getting off, we were in a dreadful condition indeed, and had nothing to do but to think of saving our lives as well as we could. We had a boat at our stern just before the storm, but she was first staved by dashing against the ship's rudder, and in the next place she broke away, and either sunk or was driven off to sea; so there was no hope from her. We had another boat on board, but how to get her off into the sea was a doubtful thing. However, there was no time to debate, for we fancied that the ship would break in pieces every minute, and some told us she was actually broken already.

In this distress the mate of our vessel laid hold of the boat, and with the help of the rest of the men got her slung over the ship's side; and getting all into her, let go, and committed ourselves, being eleven in number, to God's mercy and the wild sea; for though the storm was abated considerably, yet the sea ran dreadfully high upon the shore, and might be well called *den wild zee*, as the Dutch call the sea in a storm.

And now our case was very dismal indeed; for we all saw plainly that the sea went so high that the boat could not live, and that we should be inevitably drowned. As to making sail, we had none, nor if we had could we have done anything with it; so we worked at the oar towards the land, though with heavy hearts, like men going to execution; for we all knew that when the boat came near the shore she would be dashed in a thousand pieces by the breach of the sea. However, we committed our souls to God in the most earnest manner; and the wind driving us towards the shore, we hastened our destruction with our own hands, pulling as well as we could towards land.

What the shore was, whether rock or sand, whether steep or shoal, we knew not. The only hope that could rationally give us the least shadow of expectation was, if we might find some bay or gulf, or the mouth of some river, where by great chance we might have run our boat in, or got under the lee of the land, and perhaps made smooth water.

But there was nothing like this appeared; but as we made nearer and nearer the shore, the land looked more frightful than the sea.

After we had rowed, or rather driven about a league and a half, as we reckoned it, a raging wave, mountain-like, came rolling astern of us, and plainly bade us expect the *coup de grâce*. It took us with such a fury, that it overset the boat at once; and separating us as well from the boat as from one another, gave us no time to say, "O God!" for we were all swallowed up in a moment.

Nothing can describe the confusion of thought which I felt when I sank into the water; for though I swam very well, yet I could not deliver myself from the waves so as to draw breath, till that wave having driven me, or rather carried me, a vast way on towards the shore, and having spent itself, went back, and left me upon the land almost dry, but half dead with the water I took in. I had so much presence of mind, as well as breath left, that seeing myself nearer the mainland than I expected, I got upon my feet, and endeavoured to make on towards the land as fast as I could before another wave should return and take me up again; but I soon found it was impossible to avoid it; for I saw the sea come after me as high as a great hill, and as furious as an enemy, which I had no means or strength to contend with: my business was to hold my breath, and raise myself upon the water if I could; and so, by swimming, to preserve my breathing, and pilot myself towards the shore, if possible, my greatest concern now being that the sea, as it would carry me a great way towards the shore when it came on, might not carry me back again with it when it gave back towards the sea.

The wave that came upon me again buried me at once twenty or thirty feet deep in its own body, and I could feel myself carried with a mighty force and swiftness towards the shore—a very great way; but I held my breath, and assisted myself to swim still forward with all my might. I was ready to burst with holding my breath, when, as I felt myself rising up, so, to my immediate relief, I found my head and hands shoot out above the surface of the water; and though it was not two seconds of time that I could keep myself so, yet it relieved me greatly, gave me breath, and new courage. I was covered again with water a good while, but not so long but I held it out; and finding the water had spent itself, and began to return, I struck forward against the return of the waves, and felt ground again with my feet. I stood still a few moments to recover breath, and till the waters went from me, and then took to my heels and ran with what strength I had further towards the shore. But neither would this deliver me from the fury of the sea, which came pouring in after me again; and twice more I was lifted up by the waves and carried forward as before, the shore being very flat.

The last time of these two had well-nigh been fatal to me, for the sea having hurried me along as before, landed me, or rather dashed me, against a piece of rock, and that with such force, that it left me senseless, and indeed helpless, as to my own deliverance; for the blow taking my side and breast, beat the breath as it were quite out of my body; and had it returned again immediately, I must have been strangled in the water; but I recovered a little before the return of the waves, and seeing I should be covered again with the water, I resolved to hold fast by a piece of the rock, and so to hold my breath, if possible, till the wave went back. Now, as the waves were not so high as at first, being nearer land, I held my hold till the wave abated, and then fetched another run, which brought me so near the shore that the next wave, though it went over me, yet did not so swallow me up as to carry me away; and the next run I took, I got to the mainland, where, to my great comfort, I clambered up the cliffs of the shore and sat me down upon the grass, free from danger and quite out of the reach of the water.

I was now landed and safe on shore, and began to look up and thank God that my life was saved, in a case wherein there was some minutes before scarce any room to hope. I believe it is impossible to express, to the life, what the ecstasies and transports of the soul are, when it is so saved, as I may say, out of the very grave: and I do not wonder now at the custom, when a malefactor, who has the halter about his neck, is tied up, and just going to be turned off, and has a reprieve brought to him—I say, I do not wonder that they bring a surgeon with it, to let him blood that very moment they tell him of it, that the surprise may not drive the animal spirits from the heart and overwhelm him.

"For sudden joys, like griefs, confound at first."

I walked about on the shore lifting up my hands, and my whole being, as I may say, wrapped up in a contemplation of my deliverance; making a thousand gestures and motions, which I cannot describe; reflecting upon all my comrades that were drowned, and that there should not be one soul saved but myself; for, as for them, I never saw them afterwards, or any sign of them, except three of their hats, one cap, and two shoes that were not fellows.

I cast my eye to the stranded vessel, when, the breach and froth of the sea being so big, I could hardly see it, it lay so far of; and considered, Lord! how was it possible I could get on shore?

After I had solaced my mind with the comfortable part of my condition, I began to look round me, to see what kind of place I was in, and what was next to be done; and I soon found my comforts abate, and that, in a word, I had a dreadful deliverance; for I was wet, had no clothes to shift me, nor anything either to eat or drink to comfort me; neither did I see any prospect before me but that of perishing with hunger or being devoured by wild beasts; and that which was particularly afflicting to me was, that I had no weapon, either to hunt and kill any creature for my sustenance, or to defend myself against any other creature that might desire to kill me for theirs. In a word, I had nothing about me but a knife, a tobacco-pipe, and a little tobacco in a box. This was all my provisions; and this threw me into such terrible agonies of mind, that for a while I ran about like a madman. Night coming upon me, I began with a heavy heart to consider what would be my lot if there were any ravenous beasts in that country, as at night they always come abroad for their prey.

All the remedy that offered to my thoughts at that time was to get up into a thick bushy tree like a fir, but thorny, which grew near me, and where I resolved to sit all night, and consider the next day what death I should die, for as yet I saw no prospect of life. I walked about a furlong from the shore, to see if I could find any fresh water to drink, which I did, to my great joy; and having drank, and put a little tobacco into my mouth to prevent hunger, I went to the tree, and getting up into it, endeavoured to place myself so that if I should sleep I might not fall. And having cut me a short stick, like a truncheon, for my defence, I took up my lodging; and having been excessively fatigued, I fell fast asleep, and slept as comfortably as, I believe, few could have done in my condition, and found myself more refreshed with it than, I think, I ever was on such an occasion.

CHAPTER IV

FIRST WEEKS ON THE ISLAND

When I waked it was broad day, the weather clear, and the storm abated, so that the sea did not rage and swell as before. But that which surprised me most was, that the ship was lifted off in the night from the sand where she lay by the swelling of the tide, and was driven up almost as far as the rock which I at first mentioned, where I had been so bruised by the wave dashing me against it. This being within about a mile from the shore where I was, and the ship seeming to stand upright still, I wished myself on board, that at least I might save some necessary things for my use.

When I came down from my apartment in the tree, I looked about me again, and the first thing I found was the boat, which lay, as the wind and the sea had tossed her up, upon the land, about two miles on my right hand. I walked as far as I could upon the shore to have got to her; but found a neck or inlet of water between me and the boat which was about half a mile broad; so I came back for the present, being more intent upon getting at the ship, where I hoped to find something for my present subsistence.

A little after noon I found the sea very calm, and the tide ebbed so far out that I could come within a quarter of a mile of the ship. And here I found a fresh renewing of my grief; for I saw evidently that if we had kept on board we had been all safe—that is to say, we had all got safe on shore, and I had not been so miserable as to be left entirely destitute of all comfort and company as I now was. This forced tears to my eyes again; but as there was little relief in that, I resolved, if possible, to get to the ship; so I pulled off my clothes—for the weather was hot to extremity—and took the water. But when I came to the ship my difficulty was still greater to know how to get on board; for, as she lay aground, and high out of the water, there was nothing within my reach to lay hold of. I swam round her twice, and the second time I spied a small piece of rope, which I wondered I did not see at first, hung down by the fore-chains so low, as that with great difficulty I got hold of it, and by the help of that rope I got up into the forecastle of the ship. Here I found that the ship was bulged, and had a great deal of water in her hold, but that she lay so on the side of a bank of hard sand, or, rather earth, that her stern lay lifted up upon the bank, and her head low, almost to the water. By this means all her quarter was free, and all that was in that part was dry; for you may be sure my first work was to search, and to see what was spoiled and what was free. And, first, I found that all the ship's provisions were dry and untouched by the water, and being very well disposed to eat, I went to the bread room and filled my pockets with biscuit, and ate it as I went about other things, for I had no time to lose. I also found some rum in the great cabin, of which I took a large dram, and which I had, indeed, need enough of to spirit me for what was before me. Now I wanted nothing but a boat to furnish myself with many things which I foresaw would be very necessary to me.

It was in vain to sit still and wish for what was not to be had; and this extremity roused my application. We had several spare yards, and two or three large spars of wood, and a spare topmast or two in the ship; I resolved to fall to work with these, and I flung as many of them overboard as I could manage for their weight, tying every one with a rope, that they might not drive away. When this was done I went down the ship's side, and pulling them to me, I tied four of them together at both ends as well as I could, in the form of a raft, and laying two or three short pieces of plank upon them crossways, I found I could walk upon it very well, but that it was not able to bear any great weight, the pieces being too light. So I went to work, and with a carpenter's saw I cut a spare topmast into three lengths, and added them to my raft, with a great deal of labour and pains. But the hope of furnishing myself with necessaries encouraged me to go beyond what I should have been able to have done upon another occasion.

My raft was now strong enough to bear any reasonable weight. My next care was what to load it with, and how to preserve what I laid upon it from the surf of the sea; but I was not long considering this. I first laid all the planks or boards upon it that I could get, and having considered well what I most wanted, I got three of the seamen's chests, which I had broken open, and emptied, and lowered them down upon my raft; the first of these I filled with provisions—viz. bread, rice, three Dutch cheeses, five pieces of dried goat's flesh (which we lived much upon), and a little remainder of European corn, which had been laid by for some fowls which we brought to sea with us, but the fowls were killed. There had been some barley and wheat together; but, to my great disappointment, I found afterwards that the rats had eaten or spoiled it all. As for liquors, I found several, cases of bottles belonging to our skipper, in which were some cordial waters; and, in all, about five or six gallons of rack. These I stowed by themselves, there being no need to put them into the chest, nor any room for them. While I was doing this, I found the tide begin to flow, though very calm; and I had the mortification to see my coat, shirt, and waistcoat, which I had left on the shore, upon the sand, swim away. As for my breeches, which were only linen, and open-kneed, I swam on board in them and my stockings. However, this set me on rummaging for clothes, of which I found enough, but took no more than I wanted for present use, for I had others things which my eye was more upon—as, first, tools to work with on shore. And it was after long searching that I found out the carpenter's chest, which was, indeed, a very useful prize to me, and much more valuable than a shipload of gold would have been at that time. I got it down to my raft, whole as it was, without losing time to look into it, for I knew in general what it contained.

My next care was for some ammunition and arms. There were two very good fowling-pieces in the great cabin, and two pistols. These I secured first, with some powder-horns and a small bag of shot, and two old rusty swords. I knew there were three barrels of powder in the ship, but knew not where our gunner had stowed them; but with much search I found them, two of them dry and good, the third had taken water. Those two I got to my raft with the arms. And now I thought myself pretty well freighted, and began to think how I should get to shore with them, having neither sail, oar, nor rudder; and the least capful of wind would have overset all my navigation.

I had three encouragements—1st, a smooth, calm sea; 2ndly, the tide rising, and setting in to the shore; 3rdly, what little wind there was blew me towards the land. And thus, having found two or three broken oars belonging to the boat—and, besides the tools which were in the chest, I found two saws, an axe, and a hammer; with this cargo I put to sea. For a mile or thereabouts my raft went very well, only that I found it drive a little distant from the place where I had landed before; by which I perceived that there was some indraft of the water, and consequently I hoped to find some creek or river there, which I might make use of as a port to get to land with my cargo.

As I imagined, so it was. There appeared before me a little opening of the land, and I found a strong current of the tide set into it; so I guided my raft as well as I could, to keep in the middle of the stream.

But here I had like to have suffered a second shipwreck, which, if I had, I think verily would have broken my heart; for, knowing nothing of the coast, my raft ran aground at one end of it upon a shoal, and not being aground at the other end, it wanted but a little that all my cargo had slipped off towards the end that was afloat, and to fallen into the water. I did my utmost, by setting my back against the chests, to keep them in their places, but could not thrust off the raft with all my strength; neither durst I stir from the posture I was in; but holding up the chests with all my might, I stood in that manner near half-an-hour, in which time the rising of the water brought me a little more upon a level; and a little after, the water still-rising, my raft floated again, and I thrust her off with the oar I had into the channel, and then driving up higher, I at length found myself in the mouth of a little river, with land on both sides, and a strong current of tide running up. I looked on both sides for a proper place to get to shore, for I was not willing to be driven too high up the river: hoping in time to see some ships at sea, and therefore resolved to place myself as near the coast as I could.

At length I spied a little cove on the right shore of the creek, to which with great pain and difficulty I guided my raft, and at last got so near that, reaching ground with my oar, I could thrust her directly in. But here I had like to have dipped all my cargo into the sea again; for that shore lying pretty steep—that is to say sloping—there was no place to land, but where one end of my float, if it ran on shore, would lie so high, and the other sink lower, as before, that it would endanger my cargo again. All that I could do was to wait till the tide was at the highest, keeping the raft with my oar like an anchor, to hold the side of it fast to the shore, near a flat piece of ground, which I expected the water would flow over; and so it did. As soon as I found water enough—for my raft drew about a foot of water—I thrust her upon that flat piece of ground, and there fastened or moored her, by sticking my two broken oars into the ground, one on one side near one end, and one on the other side near the other end; and thus I lay till the water ebbed away, and left my raft and all my cargo safe on shore.

My next work was to view the country, and seek a proper place for my habitation, and where to stow my goods to secure them from whatever might happen. Where I was, I yet knew not; whether on the continent or on an island; whether inhabited or not inhabited; whether in danger of wild beasts or not. There was a hill not above a mile from me, which rose up very steep and high, and which seemed to overtop some other hills, which lay as in a ridge from it northward. I took out one of the fowling-pieces, and one of the pistols, and a horn of powder; and thus armed, I travelled for discovery up to the top of that hill, where, after I had with great labour and difficulty got to the top, I saw my fate, to my great affliction—viz. that I was in an island environed every way with the sea: no land to be seen except some rocks, which lay a great way off; and two small islands, less than this, which lay about three leagues to the west.

I found also that the island I was in was barren, and, as I saw good reason to believe, uninhabited except by wild beasts, of whom, however, I saw none. Yet I saw abundance of fowls, but knew not their kinds; neither when I killed them could I tell what was fit for food, and what not. At my coming back, I shot at a great bird which I saw sitting upon a tree on the side of a great wood. I believe it was the first gun that had been fired there since the creation of the world. I had no sooner fired, than from all parts of the wood there arose an innumerable number of fowls, of many sorts, making a confused screaming and crying, and every one according to his usual note, but not one of them of any kind that I knew. As for the creature I killed, I took it to be a kind of hawk, its colour and beak resembling it, but it had no talons or claws more than common. Its flesh was carrion, and fit for nothing.

Contented with this discovery, I came back to my raft, and fell to work to bring my cargo on shore, which took me up the rest of that day. What to do with myself at night I knew not, nor indeed where to rest, for I was afraid to lie down on the ground, not knowing but some wild beast might devour me, though, as I afterwards found, there was really no need for those fears.

However, as well as I could, I barricaded myself round with the chest and boards that I had brought on shore, and made a kind of hut for that night's lodging. As for food, I yet saw not which way to supply myself, except that I had seen two or three creatures like hares run out of the wood where I shot the fowl.

I now began to consider that I might yet get a great many things out of the ship which would be useful to me, and particularly some of the rigging and sails, and such other things as might come to land; and I resolved to make another voyage on board the vessel, if possible. And as I knew that the first storm that blew must necessarily break her all in pieces, I resolved to set all other things apart till I had got everything out of the ship that I could get. Then I called a council—that is to say in my thoughts—whether I should take back the raft; but this appeared impracticable: so I resolved to go as before, when the tide was down; and I did so, only that I stripped before I went from my hut, having nothing on but my chequered shirt, a pair of linen drawers, and a pair of pumps on my feet.

I got on board the ship as before, and prepared a second raft; and, having had experience of the first, I neither made this so unwieldy, nor loaded it so hard, but yet I brought away several things very useful to me; as first, in the carpenters stores I found two or three bags full of nails and spikes, a great screw-jack, a dozen or two of hatchets, and, above all, that most useful thing called a grindstone. All these I secured, together with several things belonging to the gunner, particularly two or three iron crows, and two barrels of musket bullets, seven muskets, another fowling-piece, with some small quantity of powder more; a large bagful of small shot, and a great roll of sheet-lead; but this last was so heavy, I could not hoist it up to get it over the ship's side.

Besides these things, I took all the men's clothes that I could find, and a spare fore-topsail, a hammock, and some bedding; and with this I loaded my second raft, and brought them all safe on shore, to my very great comfort.

I was under some apprehension, during my absence from the land, that at least my provisions might be devoured on shore: but when I came back I found no sign of any visitor; only there sat a creature like a wild cat upon one of the chests, which, when I came towards it, ran away a little distance, and then stood still. She sat very composed and unconcerned, and looked full in my face, as if she had a mind to be acquainted with me. I presented my gun at her, but, as she did not understand it, she was perfectly unconcerned at it, nor did she offer to stir away; upon which I tossed her a bit of biscuit, though by the way, I was not very free of it, for my store was not great: however, I spared her a bit, I say, and she went to it, smelled at it, and ate it, and looked (as if pleased) for more; but I thanked her, and could spare no more: so she marched off.

Having got my second cargo on shore—though I was fain to open the barrels of powder, and bring them by parcels, for they were too heavy, being large casks—I went to work to make me a little tent with the sail and some poles which I cut for that purpose: and into this tent I brought everything that I knew would spoil either with rain or sun; and I piled all the empty chests and casks up in a circle round the tent, to fortify it from any sudden attempt, either from man or beast.

When I had done this, I blocked up the door of the tent with some boards within, and an empty chest set up on end without; and spreading one of the beds upon the ground, laying my two pistols just at my head, and my gun at length by me, I went to bed for the first time, and slept very quietly all night, for I was very weary and heavy; for the night before I had slept little, and had laboured very hard all day to fetch all those things from the ship, and to get them on shore.

I had the biggest magazine of all kinds now that ever was laid up, I believe, for one man: but I was not satisfied still, for while the ship sat upright in that posture, I thought I ought to get everything out of her that I could; so every day at low water I went on board, and brought away something or other; but particularly the third time I went I brought away as much of the rigging as I could, as also all the small ropes and rope-twine I could get, with a piece of spare canvas, which was to mend the sails upon occasion, and the barrel of wet gunpowder. In a word, I brought away all the sails, first and last; only that I was fain to cut them in pieces, and bring as much at a time as I could, for they were no more useful to be sails, but as mere canvas only.

But that which comforted me more still, was, that last of all, after I had made five or six such voyages as these, and thought I had nothing more to expect from the ship that was worth my meddling with—I say, after all this, I found a great hogshead of bread, three large runlets of rum, or spirits, a box of sugar, and a barrel of fine flour; this was surprising to me, because I had given over expecting any more provisions, except what was spoiled by the water. I soon emptied the hogshead of the bread, and wrapped it up, parcel by parcel, in pieces of the sails, which I cut out; and, in a word, I got all this safe on shore also.

The next day I made another voyage, and now, having plundered the ship of what was portable and fit to hand out, I began with the cables. Cutting the great cable into pieces, such as I could move, I got two cables and a hawser on shore, with all the ironwork I could get; and having cut down the spritsail-yard, and the mizzen-yard, and everything I could, to make a large raft, I loaded it with all these heavy goods, and came away. But my good luck began now to leave me; for this raft was so unwieldy, and so overladen, that, after I had entered the little cove where I had landed the rest of my goods, not being able to guide it so handily as I did the other, it overset, and threw me and all my cargo into the water. As for myself, it was no great harm, for I was near the shore; but as to my cargo, it was a great part of it lost, especially the iron, which I expected would have been of great use to me; however, when the tide was out, I got most of the pieces of the cable ashore, and some of the iron, though with infinite labour; for I was fain to dip for it into the water, a work which fatigued me very much. After this, I went every day on board, and brought away what I could get.

I had been now thirteen days on shore, and had been eleven times on board the ship, in which time I had brought away all that one pair of hands could well be supposed capable to bring; though I believe verily, had the calm weather held, I should have brought away the whole ship, piece by piece. But preparing the twelfth time to go on board, I found the wind began to rise: however, at low water I went on board, and though I thought I had rummaged the cabin so effectually that nothing more could be found, yet I discovered a locker with drawers in it, in one of which I found two or three razors, and one pair of large scissors, with some ten or a dozen of good knives and forks: in another I found about thirty-six pounds value in money—some European coin, some Brazil, some pieces of eight, some gold, and some silver.

I smiled to myself at the sight of this money: "O drug!" said I, aloud, "what art thou good for? Thou art not worth to me—no, not the taking off the ground; one of those knives is worth all this heap; I have no manner of use for thee—e'en remain where thou art, and go to the bottom as a creature whose life is not worth saying." However, upon second thoughts I took it away; and wrapping all this in a piece of canvas, I began to think of making another raft; but while I was preparing this, I found the sky overcast, and the wind began to rise, and in a quarter of an hour it blew a fresh gale from the shore. It presently occurred to me that it was in vain to pretend to make a raft with the wind offshore; and that it was my business to be gone before the tide of flood began, otherwise I might not be able to reach the shore at all. Accordingly, I let myself down into the water, and swam across the channel, which lay between the ship and the sands, and even that with difficulty enough, partly with the weight of the things I had about me, and partly the roughness of the water; for the wind rose very hastily, and before it was quite high water it blew a storm.

But I had got home to my little tent, where I lay, with all my wealth about me, very secure. It blew very hard all night, and in the morning, when I looked out, behold, no more ship was to be seen! I was a little surprised, but recovered myself with the satisfactory reflection that I had lost no time, nor abated any diligence, to get everything out of her that could be useful to me; and that, indeed, there was little left in her that I was able to bring away, if I had had more time.

I now gave over any more thoughts of the ship, or of anything out of her, except what might drive on shore from her wreck; as, indeed, divers pieces of her afterwards did; but those things were of small use to me.

My thoughts were now wholly employed about securing myself against either savages, if any should appear, or wild beasts, if any were in the island; and I had many thoughts of the method how to do this, and what kind of dwelling to make—whether I should make me a cave in the earth, or a tent upon the earth; and, in short, I resolved upon both; the manner and description of which, it may not be improper to give an account of.

I soon found the place I was in was not fit for my settlement, because it was upon a low, moorish ground, near the sea, and I believed it would not be wholesome, and more particularly because there was no fresh water near it; so I resolved to find a more healthy and more convenient spot of ground.

I consulted several things in my situation, which I found would he proper for me: 1st, health and fresh water, I just now mentioned; 2ndly, shelter from the heat of the sun; 3rdly, security from ravenous creatures, whether man or beast; 4thly, a view to the sea, that if God sent any ship in sight, I might not lose any advantage for my deliverance, of which I was not willing to banish all my expectation yet.

In search of a place proper for this, I found a little plain on the side of a rising hill, whose front towards this little plain was steep as a house-side, so that nothing could come down upon me from the top. On the one side of the rock there was a hollow place, worn a little way in, like the entrance or door of a cave but there was not really any cave or way into the rock at all.

On the flat of the green, just before this hollow place, I resolved to pitch my tent. This plain was not above a hundred yards broad, and about twice as long, and lay like a green before my door; and, at the end of it, descended irregularly every way down into the low ground by the seaside. It was on the N.N.W. side of the hill; so that it was sheltered from the heat every day, till it came to a W. and by S. sun, or thereabouts, which, in those countries, is near the setting.

Before I set up my tent I drew a half-circle before the hollow place, which took in about ten yards in its semi-diameter from the rock, and twenty yards in its diameter from its beginning and ending.

In this half-circle I pitched two rows of strong stakes, driving them into the ground till they stood very firm like piles, the biggest end being out of the ground above five feet and a half, and sharpened on the top. The two rows did not stand above six inches from one another.

Then I took the pieces of cable which I had cut in the ship, and laid them in rows, one upon another, within the circle, between these two rows of stakes, up to the top, placing other stakes in the inside, leaning against them, about two feet and a half high, like a spur to a post; and this fence was so strong, that neither man nor beast could get into it or over it. This cost me a great deal of time and labour, especially to cut the piles in the woods, bring them to the place, and drive them into the earth.

The entrance into this place I made to be, not by a door, but by a short ladder to go over the top; which ladder, when I was in, I lifted over after me; and so I was completely fenced in and fortified, as I thought, from all the world, and consequently slept secure in the night, which otherwise I could not have done; though, as it appeared afterwards, there was no need of all this caution from the enemies that I apprehended danger from.

Into this fence or fortress, with infinite labour, I carried all my riches, all my provisions, ammunition, and stores, of which you have the account above; and I made a large tent, which to preserve me from the rains that in one part of the year are very violent there, I made double— one smaller tent within, and one larger tent above it; and covered the uppermost with a large tarpaulin, which I had saved among the sails.

And now I lay no more for a while in the bed which I had brought on shore, but in a hammock, which was indeed a very good one, and belonged to the mate of the ship.

Into this tent I brought all my provisions, and everything that would spoil by the wet; and having thus enclosed all my goods, I made up the entrance, which till now I had left open, and so passed and repassed, as I said, by a short ladder.

When I had done this, I began to work my way into the rock, and bringing all the earth and stones that I dug down out through my tent, I laid them up within my fence, in the nature of a terrace, so that it raised the ground within about a foot and a half; and thus I made me a cave, just behind my tent, which served me like a cellar to my house.

It cost me much labour and many days before all these things were brought to perfection; and therefore I must go back to some other things which took up some of my thoughts. At the same time it happened, after I had laid my scheme for the setting up my tent, and making the cave, that a storm of rain falling from a thick, dark cloud, a sudden flash of lightning happened, and after that a great clap of thunder, as is naturally the effect of it. I was not so much surprised with the lightning as I was with the thought which darted into my mind as swift as the lightning itself—Oh, my powder! My very heart sank within me when I thought that, at one blast, all my powder might be destroyed; on which, not my defence only, but the providing my food, as I thought, entirely depended. I was nothing near so anxious about my own danger, though, had the powder took fire, I should never have known who had hurt me.

Such impression did this make upon me, that after the storm was over I laid aside all my works, my building and fortifying, and applied myself to make bags and boxes, to separate the powder, and to keep it a little and a little in a parcel, in the hope that, whatever might come, it might not all take fire at once; and to keep it so apart that it should not be possible to make one part fire another. I finished this work in about a fortnight; and I think my powder, which in all was about two hundred and forty pounds weight, was divided in not less than a hundred parcels. As to the barrel that had been wet, I did not apprehend any danger from that; so I placed it in my new cave, which, in my fancy, I called my kitchen; and the rest I hid up and down in holes among the rocks, so that no wet might come to it, marking very carefully where I laid it.

In the interval of time while this was doing, I went out once at least every day with my gun, as well to divert myself as to see if I could kill anything fit for food; and, as near as I could, to acquaint myself with what the island produced. The first time I went out, I presently discovered that there were goats in the island, which was a great satisfaction to me; but then it was attended with this misfortune to me—viz. that they were so shy, so subtle, and so swift of foot, that it was the most difficult thing in the world to come at them; but I was not discouraged at this, not doubting but I might now and then shoot one, as it soon happened; for after I had found their haunts a little, I laid wait in this manner for them: I observed if they saw me in the valleys, though they were upon the rocks, they would run away, as in a terrible fright; but if they were feeding in the valleys, and I was upon the rocks, they took no notice of me; from whence I concluded that, by the position of their optics, their sight was so directed downward that they did not readily see objects that were above them; so afterwards I took this method—I always climbed the rocks first, to get above them, and then had frequently a fair mark.

The first shot I made among these creatures, I killed a she-goat, which had a little kid by her, which she gave suck to, which grieved me heartily; for when the old one fell, the kid stood stock still by her, till I came and took her up; and not only so, but when I carried the old one with me, upon my shoulders, the kid followed me quite to my enclosure; upon which I laid down the dam, and took the kid in my arms, and carried it over my pale, in hopes to have bred it up tame; but it would not eat; so I was forced to kill it and eat it myself. These two supplied me with flesh a great while, for I ate sparingly, and saved my provisions, my bread especially, as much as possibly I could.

Having now fixed my habitation, I found it absolutely necessary to provide a place to make a fire in, and fuel to burn: and what I did for that, and also how I enlarged my cave, and what conveniences I made, I shall give a full account of in its place; but I must now give some little account of myself, and of my thoughts about living, which, it may well be supposed, were not a few.

I had a dismal prospect of my condition; for as I was not cast away upon that island without being driven, as is said, by a violent storm, quite out of the course of our intended voyage, and a great way, viz. some hundreds of leagues, out of the ordinary course of the trade of mankind, I had great reason to consider it as a determination of Heaven, that in this desolate place, and in this desolate manner, I should end my life. The tears would run plentifully down my face when I made these reflections; and sometimes I would expostulate with myself why Providence should thus completely ruin His creatures, and render them so absolutely miserable; so without help, abandoned, so entirely depressed, that it could hardly be rational to be thankful for such a life.

But something always returned swift upon me to check these thoughts, and to reprove me; and particularly one day, walking with my gun in my hand by the seaside, I was very pensive upon the subject of my present condition, when reason, as it were, expostulated with me the other way, thus: "Well, you are in a desolate condition, it is true; but, pray remember, where are the rest of you? Did not you come, eleven of you in the boat? Where are the ten? Why were they not saved, and you lost? Why were you singled out? Is it better to be here or there?" And then I pointed to the sea. All evils are to be considered with the good that is in them, and with what worse attends them.

Then it occurred to me again, how well I was furnished for my subsistence, and what would have been my case if it had not happened (which was a hundred thousand to one) that the ship floated from the place where she first struck, and was driven so near to the shore that I had time to get all these things out of her; what would have been my case, if I had been forced to have lived in the condition in which I at first came on shore, without necessaries of life, or necessaries to supply and procure them? "Particularly," said I, aloud (though to myself), "what should I have done without a gun, without ammunition, without any tools to make anything, or to work with, without clothes, bedding, a tent, or any manner of covering?" and that now I had all these to sufficient quantity, and was in a fair way to provide myself in such a manner as to live without my gun, when my ammunition was spent: so that I had a tolerable view of subsisting, without any want, as long as I lived; for I considered from the beginning how I would provide for the accidents that might happen, and for the time that was to come, even not only after my ammunition should be spent, but even after my health and strength should decay.

I confess I had not entertained any notion of my ammunition being destroyed at one blast—I mean my powder being blown up by lightning; and this made the thoughts of it so surprising to me, when it lightened and thundered, as I observed just now.

And now being about to enter into a melancholy relation of a scene of silent life, such, perhaps, as was never heard of in the world before, I shall take it from its beginning, and continue it in its order. It was by my account the 30th of September, when, in the manner as above said, I first set foot upon this horrid island; when the sun, being to us in its autumnal equinox, was almost over my head; for I reckoned myself, by observation, to be in the latitude of nine degrees twenty-two minutes north of the line.

After I had been there about ten or twelve days, it came into my thoughts that I should lose my reckoning of time for want of books, and pen and ink, and should even forget the Sabbath days; but to prevent this, I cut with my knife upon a large post, in capital letters— and making it into a great cross, I set it up on the shore where I first landed—"I came on shore here on the 30th September 1659."

Upon the sides of this square post I cut every day a notch with my knife, and every seventh notch was as long again as the rest, and every first day of the month as long again as that long one; and thus I kept my calendar, or weekly, monthly, and yearly reckoning of time.

In the next place, we are to observe that among the many things which I brought out of the ship, in the several voyages which, as above mentioned, I made to it, I got several things of less value, but not at all less useful to me, which I omitted setting down before; as, in particular, pens, ink, and paper, several parcels in the captain's, mate's, gunner's and carpenter's keeping; three or four compasses, some mathematical instruments, dials, perspectives, charts, and books of navigation, all which I huddled together, whether I might want them or no; also, I found three very good Bibles, which came to me in my cargo from England, and which I had packed up among my things; some Portuguese books also; and among them two or three Popish prayer-books, and several other books, all which I carefully secured. And I must not forget that we had in the ship a dog and two cats, of whose eminent history I may have occasion to say something in its place; for I carried both the cats with me; and as for the dog, he jumped out of the ship of himself, and swam on shore to me the day after I went on shore with my first cargo, and was a trusty servant to me many years; I wanted nothing that he could fetch me, nor any company that he could make up to me; I only wanted to have him talk to me, but that would not do. As I observed before, I found pens, ink, and paper, and I husbanded them to the utmost; and I shall show that while my ink lasted, I kept things very exact, but after that was gone I could not, for I could not make any ink by any means that I could devise.

And this put me in mind that I wanted many things notwithstanding all that I had amassed together; and of these, ink was one; as also a spade, pickaxe, and shovel, to dig or remove the earth; needles, pins, and thread; as for linen, I soon learned to want that without much difficulty.

This want of tools made every work I did go on heavily; and it was near a whole year before I had entirely finished my little pale, or surrounded my habitation. The piles, or stakes, which were as heavy as I could well lift, were a long time in cutting and preparing in the woods, and more, by far, in bringing home; so that I spent sometimes two days in cutting and bringing home one of those posts, and a third day in driving it into the ground; for which purpose I got a heavy piece of wood at first, but at last bethought myself of one of the iron crows; which, however, though I found it, made driving those posts or piles very laborious and tedious work. But what need I have been concerned at the tediousness of anything I had to do, seeing I had time enough to do it in? nor had I any other employment, if that had been over, at least that I could foresee, except the ranging the island to seek for food, which I did, more or less, every day.

I now began to consider seriously my condition, and the circumstances I was reduced to; and I drew up the state of my affairs in writing, not so much to leave them to any that were to come after me—for I was likely to have but few heirs—as to deliver my thoughts from daily poring over them, and afflicting my mind; and as my reason began now to master my despondency, I began to comfort myself as well as I could, and to set the good against the evil, that I might have something to distinguish my case from worse; and I stated very impartially, like debtor and creditor, the comforts I enjoyed against the miseries I suffered, thus:—

Evil.	*Good.*
I am cast upon a horrible, desolate island, void of all hope of recovery.	But I am alive; and not drowned, as all my ship's company were.
I am singled out and separated, as it were, from all the world, to be miserable.	But I am singled out, too, from all the ship's crew, to be spared from death; and He that miraculously saved me from death can deliver me from this condition.
I am divided from mankind—a solitaire; one banished from human society.	But I am not starved, and perishing on a barren place, affording no sustenance.
I have no clothes to cover me.	But I am in a hot climate, where, if I had clothes, I could hardly wear them.
I am without any defence, or means to resist any violence of man or beast.	But I am cast on an island where I see no wild beasts to hurt me, as I saw on the coast of Africa; and what if I had been shipwrecked there?
I have no soul to speak to or relieve me.	But God wonderfully sent the ship in near enough to the shore, that I have got out as many necessary things as will either supply my wants or

enable me to supply myself,
even as long as I live.

Upon the whole, here was an undoubted testimony that there was scarce any condition in the world so miserable but there was something negative or something positive to be thankful for in it; and let this stand as a direction from the experience of the most miserable of all conditions in this world: that we may always find in it something to comfort ourselves from, and to set, in the description of good and evil, on the credit side of the account.

Having now brought my mind a little to relish my condition, and given over looking out to sea, to see if I could spy a ship—I say, giving over these things, I began to apply myself to arrange my way of living, and to make things as easy to me as I could.

I have already described my habitation, which was a tent under the side of a rock, surrounded with a strong pale of posts and cables: but I might now rather call it a wall, for I raised a kind of wall up against it of turfs, about two feet thick on the outside; and after some time (I think it was a year and a half) I raised rafters from it, leaning to the rock, and thatched or covered it with boughs of trees, and such things as I could get, to keep out the rain; which I found at some times of the year very violent.

I have already observed how I brought all my goods into this pale, and into the cave which I had made behind me. But I must observe, too, that at first this was a confused heap of goods, which, as they lay in no order, so they took up all my place; I had no room to turn myself: so I set myself to enlarge my cave, and work farther into the earth; for it was a loose sandy rock, which yielded easily to the labour I bestowed on it: and so when I found I was pretty safe as to beasts of prey, I worked sideways, to the right hand, into the rock; and then, turning to the right again, worked quite out, and made me a door to come out on the outside of my pale or fortification. This gave me not only egress and regress, as it was a back way to my tent and to my storehouse, but gave me room to store my goods.

And now I began to apply myself to make such necessary things as I found I most wanted, particularly a chair and a table; for without these I was not able to enjoy the few comforts I had in the world; I could not write or eat, or do several things, with so much pleasure without a table: so I went to work. And here I must needs observe, that as reason is the substance and origin of the mathematics, so by stating and squaring everything by reason, and by making the most rational judgment of things, every man may be, in time, master of every mechanic art. I had never handled a tool in my life; and yet, in time, by labour, application, and contrivance, I found at last that I wanted nothing but I could have made it, especially if I had had tools. However, I made abundance of things, even without tools; and some with no more tools than an adze and a hatchet, which perhaps were never made that way before, and that with infinite labour. For example, if I wanted a board, I had no other way but to cut down a tree, set it on an edge before me, and hew it flat on either side with my axe, till I brought it to be thin as a plank, and then dub it smooth with my adze. It is true, by this method I could make but one board out of a whole tree; but this I had no remedy for but patience, any more than I had for the prodigious deal of time and labour which it took me up to make a plank or board: but my time or labour was little worth, and so it was as well employed one way as another.

However, I made me a table and a chair, as I observed above, in the first place; and this I did out of the short pieces of boards that I brought on my raft from the ship. But when I had wrought out some boards as above, I made large shelves, of the breadth of a foot and a half, one over another all along one side of my cave, to lay all my tools, nails and ironwork on; and, in a word, to separate everything at large into their places, that I might come easily at them. I knocked pieces into the wall of the rock to hang my guns and all things that would hang up; so that, had my cave been to be seen, it looked like a general magazine of all necessary things; and had everything so ready at my hand, that it was a great pleasure to me to see all my goods in such order, and especially to find my stock of all necessaries so great.

And now it was that I began to keep a journal of every day's employment; for, indeed, at first I was in too much hurry, and not only hurry as to labour, but in too much discomposure of mind; and my journal would have been full of many dull things; for example, I must have said thus: "30*th*.—After I had got to shore, and escaped drowning, instead of being thankful to God for my deliverance, having first vomited, with the great quantity of salt water which had got into my stomach, and recovering myself a little, I ran about the shore wringing my hands and beating my head and face, exclaiming at my misery, and crying out, 'I was undone, undone!' till, tired and faint, I was forced to lie down on the ground to repose, but durst not sleep for fear of being devoured."

Some days after this, and after I had been on board the ship, and got all that I could out of her, yet I could not forbear getting up to the top of a little mountain and looking out to sea, in hopes of seeing a ship; then fancy at a vast distance I spied a sail, please myself with the hopes of it, and then after looking steadily, till I was almost blind, lose it quite, and sit down and weep like a child, and thus increase my misery by my folly.

But having gotten over these things in some measure, and having settled my household staff and habitation, made me a table and a chair, and all as handsome about me as I could, I began to keep my journal; of which I shall here give you the copy (though in it will be told all these particulars over again) as long as it lasted; for having no more ink, I was forced to leave it off.

CHAPTER V

BUILDS A HOUSE—THE JOURNAL

September 30, 1659.—I, poor miserable Robinson Crusoe, being shipwrecked during a dreadful storm in the offing, came on shore on this dismal, unfortunate island, which I called "The Island of Despair"; all the rest of the ship's company being drowned, and myself almost dead.

All the rest of the day I spent in afflicting myself at the dismal circumstances I was brought to—viz. I had neither food, house, clothes, weapon, nor place to fly to; and in despair of any relief, saw nothing but death before me—either that I should be devoured by wild beasts, murdered by savages, or starved to death for want of food. At the approach of night I slept in a tree, for fear of wild creatures; but slept soundly, though it rained all night.

October 1.—In the morning I saw, to my great surprise, the ship had floated with the high tide, and was driven on shore again much nearer the island; which, as it was some comfort, on one hand—for, seeing her set upright, and not broken to pieces, I hoped, if the wind abated, I might get on board, and get some food and necessaries out of her for my relief—so, on the other hand, it renewed my grief at the loss of my comrades, who, I imagined, if we had all stayed on board, might have saved the ship, or, at least, that they would not have been all drowned as they were; and that, had the men been saved, we might perhaps have built us a boat out of the ruins of the ship to have carried us to some other part of the world. I spent great part of this day in perplexing myself on these things; but at length, seeing the ship almost dry, I went upon the sand as near as I could, and then swam on board. This day also it continued raining, though with no wind at all.

From the 1st of October to the 24th.—All these days entirely spent in many several voyages to get all I could out of the ship, which I brought on shore every tide of flood upon rafts. Much rain also in the days, though with some intervals of fair weather; but it seems this was the rainy season.

Oct. 20.—I overset my raft, and all the goods I had got upon it; but, being in shoal water, and the things being chiefly heavy, I recovered many of them when the tide was out.

Oct. 25.—It rained all night and all day, with some gusts of wind; during which time the ship broke in pieces, the wind blowing a little harder than before, and was no more to be seen, except the wreck of her, and that only at low water. I spent this day in covering and securing the goods which I had saved, that the rain might not spoil them.

Oct. 26.—I walked about the shore almost all day, to find out a place to fix my habitation, greatly concerned to secure myself from any attack in the night, either from wild beasts or men. Towards night, I fixed upon a proper place, under a rock, and marked out a semicircle for my encampment; which I resolved to strengthen with a work, wall, or fortification, made of double piles, lined within with cables, and without with turf.

From the 26th to the 30th I worked very hard in carrying all my goods to my new habitation, though some part of the time it rained exceedingly hard.

The 31st, in the morning, I went out into the island with my gun, to seek for some food, and discover the country; when I killed a she-goat, and her kid followed me home, which I afterwards killed also, because it would not feed.

November 1.—I set up my tent under a rock, and lay there for the first night; making it as large as I could, with stakes driven in to swing my hammock upon.

Nov. 2.—I set up all my chests and boards, and the pieces of timber which made my rafts, and with them formed a fence round me, a little within the place I had marked out for my fortification.

Nov. 3.—I went out with my gun, and killed two fowls like ducks, which were very good food. In the afternoon went to work to make me a table.

Nov. 4.—This morning I began to order my times of work, of going out with my gun, time of sleep, and time of diversion—viz. every morning I walked out with my gun for two or three hours, if it did not rain; then employed myself to work till about eleven o'clock; then eat what I had to live on; and from twelve to two I lay down to sleep, the weather being excessively hot; and then, in the evening, to work again. The working part of this day and of the next were wholly employed in making my table, for I was yet but a very sorry workman, though time and necessity made me a complete natural mechanic soon after, as I believe they would do any one else.

Nov. 5.—This day went abroad with my gun and my dog, and killed a wild cat; her skin pretty soft, but her flesh good for nothing; every creature that I killed I took of the skins and preserved them.

Coming back by the sea-shore, I saw many sorts of sea-fowls, which I did not understand; but was surprised, and almost frightened, with two or three seals, which, while I was gazing at, not well knowing what they were, got into the sea, and escaped me for that time.

Nov. 6.—After my morning walk I went to work with my table again, and finished it, though not to my liking; nor was it long before I learned to mend it.

Nov. 7.—Now it began to be settled fair weather. The 7th, 8th, 9th, 10th, and part of the 12th (for the 11th was Sunday) I took wholly up to make me a chair, and with much ado brought it to a tolerable shape, but never to please me; and even in the making I pulled it in pieces several times.

Note.—I soon neglected my keeping Sundays; for, omitting my mark for them on my post, I forgot which was which.

Nov. 13.—This day it rained, which refreshed me exceedingly, and cooled the earth; but it was accompanied with terrible thunder and lightning, which frightened me dreadfully, for fear of my powder. As soon as it was over, I resolved to separate my stock of powder into as many little parcels as possible, that it might not be in danger.

Nov. 14, 15, 16.—These three days I spent in making little square chests, or boxes, which might hold about a pound, or two pounds at most, of powder; and so, putting the powder in, I stowed it in places as secure and remote from one another as possible. On one of these three days I killed a large bird that was good to eat, but I knew not what to call it.

Nov. 17.—This day I began to dig behind my tent into the rock, to make room for my further conveniency.

Note.—Three things I wanted exceedingly for this work—viz. a pickaxe, a shovel, and a wheelbarrow or basket; so I desisted from my work, and began to consider how to supply that want, and make me some tools. As for the pickaxe, I made use of the iron crows, which were proper enough, though heavy; but the next thing was a shovel or spade; this was so absolutely necessary, that, indeed, I could do nothing effectually without it; but what kind of one to make I knew not.

Nov. 18.—The next day, in searching the woods, I found a tree of that wood, or like it, which in the Brazils they call the iron-tree, for its exceeding hardness. Of this, with great labour, and almost spoiling my axe, I cut a piece, and brought it home, too, with difficulty enough, for it was exceeding heavy. The excessive hardness of the wood, and my having no other way, made me a long while upon this machine, for I worked it effectually by little and little into the form of a shovel or spade; the handle exactly shaped like ours in England, only that the board part having no iron shod upon it at bottom, it would not last me so long; however, it served well enough for the uses which I had occasion to put it to; but never was a shovel, I believe, made after that fashion, or so long in making.

I was still deficient, for I wanted a basket or a wheelbarrow. A basket I could not make by any means, having no such things as twigs that would bend to make wicker-ware—at least, none yet found out; and as to a wheelbarrow, I fancied I could make all but the wheel; but that I had no notion of; neither did I know how to go about it; besides, I had no possible way to make the iron gudgeons for the spindle or axis of the wheel to run in; so I gave it over, and so, for carrying away the earth which I dug out of the cave, I made me a thing like a hod which the labourers carry mortar in when they serve the bricklayers. This was not so difficult to me as the making the shovel: and yet this and the shovel, and the attempt which I made in vain to make a wheelbarrow, took me up no less than four days—I mean always excepting my morning walk with my gun, which I seldom failed, and very seldom failed also bringing home something fit to eat.

Nov. 23.—My other work having now stood still, because of my making these tools, when they were finished I went on, and working every day, as my strength and time allowed, I spent eighteen days entirely in widening and deepening my cave, that it might hold my goods commodiously.

Note.—During all this time I worked to make this room or cave spacious enough to accommodate me as a warehouse or magazine, a kitchen, a dining-room, and a cellar. As for my lodging, I kept to the tent; except that sometimes, in the wet season of the year, it rained so hard that I could not keep myself dry, which caused me afterwards to cover all my place within my pale with long poles, in the form of rafters, leaning against the rock, and load them with flags and large leaves of trees, like a thatch.

December 10.—I began now to think my cave or vault finished, when on a sudden (it seems I had made it too large) a great quantity of earth fell down from the top on one side; so much that, in short, it frighted me, and not without reason, too, for if I had been under it, I had never wanted a gravedigger. I had now a great deal of work to do over again, for I had the loose earth to carry out; and, which was of more importance, I had the ceiling to prop up, so that I might be sure no more would come down.

Dec. 11.—This day I went to work with it accordingly, and got two shores or posts pitched upright to the top, with two pieces of boards across over each post; this I finished the next day; and setting more posts up with boards, in about a week more I had the roof secured, and the posts, standing in rows, served me for partitions to part off the house.

Dec. 17.—From this day to the 20th I placed shelves, and knocked up nails on the posts, to hang everything up that could be hung up; and now I began to be in some order within doors.

Dec. 20.—Now I carried everything into the cave, and began to furnish my house, and set up some pieces of boards like a dresser, to order my victuals upon; but boards began to be very scarce with me; also, I made me another table.

Dec. 24.—Much rain all night and all day. No stirring out.

Dec. 25.—Rain all day.

Dec. 26.—No rain, and the earth much cooler than before, and pleasanter.

Dec. 27.—Killed a young goat, and lamed another, so that I caught it and led it home in a string; when I had it at home, I bound and splintered up its leg, which was broke.

N.B.—I took such care of it that it lived, and the leg grew well and as strong as ever; but, by my nursing it so long, it grew tame, and fed upon the little green at my door, and would not go away. This was the first time that I entertained a thought of breeding up some tame creatures, that I might have food when my powder and shot was all spent.

Dec. 28,29,30,31.—Great heats, and no breeze, so that there was no stirring abroad, except in the evening, for food; this time I spent in putting all my things in order within doors.

January 1.—Very hot still: but I went abroad early and late with my gun, and lay still in the middle of the day. This evening, going farther into the valleys which lay towards the centre of the island, I found there were plenty of goats, though exceedingly shy, and hard to come at; however, I resolved to try if I could not bring my dog to hunt them down.

Jan. 2.—Accordingly, the next day I went out with my dog, and set him upon the goats, but I was mistaken, for they all faced about upon the dog, and he knew his danger too well, for he would not come near them.

Jan. 3.—I began my fence or wall; which, being still jealous of my being attacked by somebody, I resolved to make very thick and strong.

N.B.—This wall being described before, I purposely omit what was said in the journal; it is sufficient to observe, that I was no less time than from the 2nd of January to the 14th of April working, finishing, and perfecting this wall, though it was no more than about twenty-four yards in length, being a half-circle from one place in the rock to another place, about eight yards from it, the door of the cave being in the centre behind it.

All this time I worked very hard, the rains hindering me many days, nay, sometimes weeks together; but I thought I should never be perfectly secure till this wall was finished; and it is scarce credible what inexpressible labour everything was done with, especially the bringing piles out of the woods and driving them into the ground; for I made them much bigger than I needed to have done.

When this wall was finished, and the outside double fenced, with a turf wall raised up close to it, I perceived myself that if any people were to come on shore there, they would not perceive anything like a habitation; and it was very well I did so, as may be observed hereafter, upon a very remarkable occasion.

During this time I made my rounds in the woods for game every day when the rain permitted me, and made frequent discoveries in these walks of something or other to my advantage; particularly, I found a kind of wild pigeons, which build, not as wood-pigeons in a tree, but rather as house-pigeons, in the holes of the rocks; and taking some young ones, I endeavoured to breed them up tame, and did so; but when they grew older they flew away, which perhaps was at first for want of feeding them, for I had nothing to give them; however, I frequently found their nests, and got their young ones, which were very good meat. And now, in the managing my household affairs, I found myself wanting in many things, which I thought at first it was impossible for me to make; as, indeed, with some of them it was: for instance, I could never make a cask to be hooped. I had a small runlet or two, as I observed before; but I could never arrive at the capacity of making one by them, though I spent many weeks about it; I could neither put in the heads, or join the staves so true to one another as to make them hold water; so I gave that also over. In the next place, I was at a great loss for candles; so that as soon as ever it was dark, which was generally by seven o'clock, I was obliged to go to bed. I remembered the lump of beeswax with which I made candles in my African adventure; but I had none of that now; the only remedy I had was, that when I had killed a goat I saved the tallow, and with a little dish made of clay, which I baked in the sun, to which I added a wick of some oakum, I made me a lamp; and this gave me light, though not a clear, steady light, like a candle. In the middle of all my labours it happened that, rummaging my things, I found a little bag which, as I hinted before, had been filled with corn for the feeding of poultry—not for this voyage, but before, as I suppose, when the ship came from Lisbon. The little remainder of corn that had been in the bag was all devoured by the rats, and I saw nothing in the bag but husks and dust; and being willing to have the bag for some other use (I think it was to put powder in, when I divided it for fear of the lightning, or some such use), I shook the husks of corn out of it on one side of my fortification, under the rock.

It was a little before the great rains just now mentioned that I threw this stuff away, taking no notice, and not so much as remembering that I had thrown anything there, when, about a month after, or thereabouts, I saw some few stalks of something green shooting out of the ground, which I fancied might be some plant I had not seen; but I was surprised, and perfectly astonished, when, after a little longer time, I saw about ten or twelve ears come out, which were perfect green barley, of the same kind as our European—nay, as our English barley.

It is impossible to express the astonishment and confusion of my thoughts on this occasion. I had hitherto acted upon no religious foundation at all; indeed, I had very few notions of religion in my head, nor had entertained any sense of anything that had befallen me otherwise than as chance, or, as we lightly say, what pleases God, without so much as inquiring into the end of Providence in these things, or His order in governing events for the world. But after I saw barley grow there, in a climate which I knew was not proper for corn, and especially that I knew not how it came there, it startled me strangely, and I began to suggest that God had miraculously caused His grain to grow without any help of seed sown, and that it was so directed purely for my sustenance on that wild, miserable place.

This touched my heart a little, and brought tears out of my eyes, and I began to bless myself that such a prodigy of nature should happen upon my account; and this was the more strange to me, because I saw near it still, all along by the side of the rock, some other straggling stalks, which proved to be stalks of rice, and which I knew, because I had seen it grow in Africa when I was ashore there.

I not only thought these the pure productions of Providence for my support, but not doubting that there was more in the place, I went all over that part of the island, where I had been before, peering in every corner, and under every rock, to see for more of it, but I could not find any. At last it occurred to my thoughts that I shook a bag of chickens' meat out in that place; and then the wonder began to cease; and I must confess my religious thankfulness to God's providence began to abate, too, upon the discovering that all this was nothing but what was common; though I ought to have been as thankful for so strange and unforeseen a providence as if it had been miraculous; for it was really the work of Providence to me, that should order or appoint that ten or twelve grains of corn should remain unspoiled, when the rats had destroyed all the rest, as if it had been dropped from heaven; as also, that I should throw it out in that particular place, where, it being in the shade of a high rock, it sprang up immediately; whereas, if I had thrown it anywhere else at that time, it had been burnt up and destroyed.

I carefully saved the ears of this corn, you may be sure, in their season, which was about the end of June; and, laying up every corn, I resolved to sow them all again, hoping in time to have some quantity sufficient to supply me with bread. But it was not till the fourth year that I could allow myself the least grain of this corn to eat, and even then but sparingly, as I shall say afterwards, in its order; for I lost all that I sowed the first season by not observing the proper time; for I sowed it just before the dry season, so that it never came up at all, at least not as it would have done; of which in its place.

Besides this barley, there were, as above, twenty or thirty stalks of rice, which I preserved with the same care and for the same use, or to the same purpose—to make me bread, or rather food; for I found ways to cook it without baking, though I did that also after some time.

But to return to my Journal.

I worked excessive hard these three or four months to get my wall done; and the 14th of April I closed it up, contriving to go into it, not by a door but over the wall, by a ladder, that there might be no sign on the outside of my habitation.

April 16.—I finished the ladder; so I went up the ladder to the top, and then pulled it up after me, and let it down in the inside. This was a complete enclosure to me; for within I had room enough, and nothing could come at me from without, unless it could first mount my wall.

The very next day after this wall was finished I had almost had all my labour overthrown at once, and myself killed. The case was thus: As I was busy in the inside, behind my tent, just at the entrance into my cave, I was terribly frighted with a most dreadful, surprising thing indeed; for all on a sudden I found the earth come crumbling down from the roof of my cave, and from the edge of the hill over my head, and two of the posts I had set up in the cave cracked in a frightful manner. I was heartily scared; but thought nothing of what was really the cause, only thinking that the top of my cave was fallen in, as some of it had done before: and for fear I should be buried in it I ran forward to my ladder, and not thinking myself safe there neither, I got over my wall for fear of the pieces of the hill, which I expected might roll down upon me. I had no sooner stepped do ground, than I plainly saw it was a terrible earthquake, for the ground I stood on shook three times at about eight minutes' distance, with three such shocks as would have overturned the strongest building that could be supposed to have stood on the earth; and a great piece of the top of a rock which stood about half a mile from me next the sea fell down with such a terrible noise as I never heard in all my life. I perceived also the very sea was put into violent motion by it; and I believe the shocks were stronger under the water than on the island.

I was so much amazed with the thing itself, having never felt the like, nor discoursed with any one that had, that I was like one dead or stupefied; and the motion of the earth made my stomach sick, like one that was tossed at sea; but the noise of the falling of the rock awakened me, as it were, and rousing me from the stupefied condition I was in, filled me with horror; and I thought of nothing then but the hill falling upon my tent and all my household goods, and burying all at once; and this sunk my very soul within me a second time.

After the third shock was over, and I felt no more for some time, I began to take courage; and yet I had not heart enough to go over my wall again, for fear of being buried alive, but sat still upon the ground greatly cast down and disconsolate, not knowing what to do. All this while I had not the least serious religious thought; nothing but the common "Lord have mercy upon me!" and when it was over that went away too.

While I sat thus, I found the air overcast and grow cloudy, as if it would rain. Soon after that the wind arose by little and little, so that in less than half-an-hour it blew a most dreadful hurricane; the sea was all on a sudden covered over with foam and froth; the shore was covered with the breach of the water, the trees were torn up by the roots, and a terrible storm it was. This held about three hours, and then began to abate; and in two hours more it was quite calm, and began to rain very hard. All this while I sat upon the ground very much terrified and dejected; when on a sudden it came into my thoughts, that these winds and rain being the consequences of the earthquake, the earthquake itself was spent and over, and I might venture into my cave again. With this thought my spirits began to revive; and the rain also helping to persuade me, I went in and sat down in my tent. But the rain was so violent that my tent was ready to be beaten down with it; and I was forced to go into my cave, though very much afraid and uneasy, for fear it should fall on my head. This violent rain forced me to a new work—viz. to cut a hole through my new fortification, like a sink, to let the water go out, which would else have flooded my cave. After I had been in my cave for some time, and found still no more shocks of the earthquake follow, I began to be more composed. And now, to support my spirits, which indeed wanted it very much, I went to my little store, and took a small sup of rum; which, however, I did then and always very sparingly, knowing I could have no more when that was gone. It continued raining all that night and great part of the next day, so that I could not stir abroad; but my mind being more composed, I began to think of what I had best do; concluding that if the island was subject to these earthquakes, there would be no living for me in a cave, but I must consider of building a little hut in an open place which I might surround with a wall, as I had done here, and so make myself secure from wild beasts or men; for I concluded, if I stayed where I was, I should certainly one time or other be buried alive.

With these thoughts, I resolved to remove my tent from the place where it stood, which was just under the hanging precipice of the hill; and which, if it should be shaken again, would certainly fall upon my tent; and I spent the two next days, being the 19th and 20th of April, in contriving where and how to remove my habitation. The fear of being swallowed up alive made me that I never slept in quiet; and yet the apprehension of lying abroad without any fence was almost equal to it; but still, when I looked about, and saw how everything was put in order, how pleasantly concealed I was, and how safe from danger, it made me very loath to remove. In the meantime, it occurred to me that it would require a vast deal of time for me to do this, and that I must be contented to venture where I was, till I had formed a camp for myself, and had secured it so as to remove to it. So with this resolution I composed myself for a time, and resolved that I would go to work with all speed to build me a wall with piles and cables, &c., in a circle, as before, and set my tent up in it when it was finished; but that I would venture to stay where I was till it was finished, and fit to remove. This was the 21st.

April 22.—The next morning I begin to consider of means to put this resolve into execution; but I was at a great loss about my tools. I had three large axes, and abundance of hatchets (for we carried the hatchets for traffic with the Indians); but with much chopping and cutting knotty hard wood, they were all full of notches, and dull; and though I had a grindstone, I could not turn it and grind my tools too. This cost me as much thought as a statesman would have bestowed upon a grand point of politics, or a judge upon the life and death of a man. At length I contrived a wheel with a string, to turn it with my foot, that I might have both my hands at liberty. *Note.*—I had never seen any such thing in England, or at least, not to take notice how it was done, though since I have observed, it is very common there; besides that, my grindstone was very large and heavy. This machine cost me a full week's work to bring it to perfection.

April 28, 29.—These two whole days I took up in grinding my tools, my machine for turning my grindstone performing very well.

April 30.—Having perceived my bread had been low a great while, now I took a survey of it, and reduced myself to one biscuit cake a day, which made my heart very heavy.

May 1.—In the morning, looking towards the sea side, the tide being low, I saw something lie on the shore bigger than ordinary, and it looked like a cask; when I came to it, I found a small barrel, and two or three pieces of the wreck of the ship, which were driven on shore by the late hurricane; and looking towards the wreck itself, I thought it seemed to lie higher out of the water than it used to do. I examined the barrel which was driven on shore, and soon found it was a barrel of gunpowder; but it had taken water, and the powder was caked as hard as a stone; however, I rolled it farther on shore for the present, and went on upon the sands, as near as I could to the wreck of the ship, to look for more.

CHAPTER VI

ILL AND CONSCIENCE-STRICKEN

When I came down to the ship I found it strangely removed. The forecastle, which lay before buried in sand, was heaved up at least six feet, and the stern, which was broke in pieces and parted from the rest by the force of the sea, soon after I had left rummaging her, was tossed as it were up, and cast on one side; and the sand was thrown so high on that side next her stern, that whereas there was a great place of water before, so that I could not come within a quarter of a mile of the wreck without swimming I could now walk quite up to her when the tide was out. I was surprised with this at first, but soon concluded it must be done by the earthquake; and as by this violence the ship was more broke open than formerly, so many things came daily on shore, which the sea had loosened, and which the winds and water rolled by degrees to the land.

This wholly diverted my thoughts from the design of removing my habitation, and I busied myself mightily, that day especially, in searching whether I could make any way into the ship; but I found nothing was to be expected of that kind, for all the inside of the ship was choked up with sand. However, as I had learned not to despair of anything, I resolved to pull everything to pieces that I could of the ship, concluding that everything I could get from her would be of some use or other to me.

May 3.—I began with my saw, and cut a piece of a beam through, which I thought held some of the upper part or quarter-deck together, and when I had cut it through, I cleared away the sand as well as I could from the side which lay highest; but the tide coming in, I was obliged to give over for that time.

May 4.—I went a-fishing, but caught not one fish that I durst eat of, till I was weary of my sport; when, just going to leave off, I caught a young dolphin. I had made me a long line of some rope-yarn, but I had no hooks; yet I frequently caught fish enough, as much as I cared to eat; all which I dried in the sun, and ate them dry.

May 5.—Worked on the wreck; cut another beam asunder, and brought three great fir planks off from the decks, which I tied together, and made to float on shore when the tide of flood came on.

May 6.—Worked on the wreck; got several iron bolts out of her and other pieces of ironwork. Worked very hard, and came home very much tired, and had thoughts of giving it over.

May 7.—Went to the wreck again, not with an intent to work, but found the weight of the wreck had broke itself down, the beams being cut; that several pieces of the ship seemed to lie loose, and the inside of the hold lay so open that I could see into it; but it was almost full of water and sand.

May 8.—Went to the wreck, and carried an iron crow to wrench up the deck, which lay now quite clear of the water or sand. I wrenched open two planks, and brought them on shore also with the tide. I left the iron crow in the wreck for next day.

May 9.—Went to the wreck, and with the crow made way into the body of the wreck, and felt several casks, and loosened them with the crow, but could not break them up. I felt also a roll of English lead, and could stir it, but it was too heavy to remove.

May 10–14.—Went every day to the wreck; and got a great many pieces of timber, and boards, or plank, and two or three hundredweight of iron.

May 15.—I carried two hatchets, to try if I could not cut a piece off the roll of lead by placing the edge of one hatchet and driving it with the other; but as it lay about a foot and a half in the water, I could not make any blow to drive the hatchet.

May 16.—It had blown hard in the night, and the wreck appeared more broken by the force of the water; but I stayed so long in the woods, to get pigeons for food, that the tide prevented my going to the wreck that day.

May 17.—I saw some pieces of the wreck blown on shore, at a great distance, near two miles off me, but resolved to see what they were, and found it was a piece of the head, but too heavy for me to bring away.

May 24.—Every day, to this day, I worked on the wreck; and with hard labour I loosened some things so much with the crow, that the first flowing tide several casks floated out, and two of the seamen's chests; but the wind blowing from the shore, nothing came to land that day but pieces of timber, and a hogshead, which had some Brazil pork in it; but the salt water and the sand had spoiled it. I continued this work every day to the 15th of June, except the time necessary to get food, which I always appointed, during this part of my employment, to be when the tide was up, that I might be ready when it was ebbed out;

and by this time I had got timber and plank and ironwork enough to have built a good boat, if I had known how; and also I got, at several times and in several pieces, near one hundredweight of the sheet lead.

June 16.—Going down to the seaside, I found a large tortoise or turtle. This was the first I had seen, which, it seems, was only my misfortune, not any defect of the place, or scarcity; for had I happened to be on the other side of the island, I might have had hundreds of them every day, as I found afterwards; but perhaps had paid dear enough for them.

June 17.—I spent in cooking the turtle. I found in her three-score eggs; and her flesh was to me, at that time, the most savoury and pleasant that ever I tasted in my life, having had no flesh, but of goats and fowls, since I landed in this horrid place.

June 18.—Rained all day, and I stayed within. I thought at this time the rain felt cold, and I was something chilly; which I knew was not usual in that latitude.

June 19.—Very ill, and shivering, as if the weather had been cold.

June 20.—No rest all night; violent pains in my head, and feverish.

June 21.—Very ill; frighted almost to death with the apprehensions of my sad condition—to be sick, and no help. Prayed to God, for the first time since the storm off Hull, but scarce knew what I said, or why, my thoughts being all confused.

June 22.—A little better; but under dreadful apprehensions of sickness.

June 23.—Very bad again; cold and shivering, and then a violent headache.

June 24.—Much better.

June 25.—An ague very violent; the fit held me seven hours; cold fit and hot, with faint sweats after it.

June 26.—Better; and having no victuals to eat, took my gun, but found myself very weak. However, I killed a she-goat, and with much difficulty got it home, and broiled some of it, and ate, I would fain have stewed it, and made some broth, but had no pot.

June 27.—The ague again so violent that I lay a-bed all day, and neither ate nor drank. I was ready to perish for thirst; but so weak, I had not strength to stand up, or to get myself any water to drink. Prayed to God again, but was light-headed; and when I was not, I was so ignorant that I knew not what to say; only I lay and cried, "Lord, look upon me! Lord, pity me! Lord, have mercy upon me!" I suppose

I did nothing else for two or three hours; till, the fit wearing off, I fell asleep, and did not wake till far in the night. When I awoke, I found myself much refreshed, but weak, and exceeding thirsty. However, as I had no water in my habitation, I was forced to lie till morning, and went to sleep again. In this second sleep I had this terrible dream: I thought that I was sitting on the ground, on the outside of my wall, where I sat when the storm blew after the earthquake, and that I saw a man descend from a great black cloud, in a bright flame of fire, and light upon the ground. He was all over as bright as a flame, so that I could but just bear to look towards him; his countenance was most inexpressibly dreadful, impossible for words to describe. When he stepped upon the ground with his feet, I thought the earth trembled, just as it had done before in the earthquake, and all the air looked, to my apprehension, as if it had been filled with flashes of fire. He was no sooner landed upon the earth, but he moved forward towards me, with a long spear or weapon in his hand, to kill me; and when he came to a rising ground, at some distance, he spoke to me—or I heard a voice so terrible that it is impossible to express the terror of it. All that I can say I understood was this: "Seeing all these things have not brought thee to repentance, now thou shalt die;" at which words, I thought he lifted up the spear that was in his hand to kill me.

No one that shall ever read this account will expect that I should be able to describe the horrors of my soul at this terrible vision. I mean, that even while it was a dream, I even dreamed of those horrors. Nor is it any more possible to describe the impression that remained upon my mind when I awaked, and found it was but a dream.

I had, alas! no divine knowledge. What I had received by the good instruction of my father was then worn out by an uninterrupted series, for eight years, of seafaring wickedness, and a constant conversation with none but such as were, like myself, wicked and profane to the last degree. I do not remember that I had, in all that time, one thought that so much as tended either to looking upwards towards God, or inwards towards a reflection upon my own ways; but a certain stupidity of soul, without desire of good, or conscience of evil, had entirely overwhelmed me; and I was all that the most hardened, unthinking, wicked creature among our common sailors can be supposed to be; not having the least sense, either of the fear of God in danger, or of thankfulness to God in deliverance.

In the relating what is already past of my story, this will be the more easily believed when I shall add, that through all the variety of miseries that had to this day befallen me, I never had so much as one thought of it being the hand of God, or that it was a just punishment for my sin—my rebellious behaviour against my father—or my present sins, which were great—or so much as a punishment for the general course of my wicked life. When I was on the desperate expedition on the desert shores of Africa, I never had so much as one thought of what would become of me, or one wish to God to direct me whither I should go, or to keep me from the danger which apparently surrounded me, as well from voracious creatures as cruel savages. But I was merely thoughtless of a God or a Providence, acted like a mere brute, from the principles of nature, and by the dictates of common sense only, and, indeed, hardly that. When I was delivered and taken up at sea by the Portugal captain, well used, and dealt justly and honourably with, as well as charitably, I had not the least thankfulness in my thoughts. When, again, I was shipwrecked, ruined, and in danger of drowning on this island, I was as far from remorse, or looking on it as a judgment. I only said to myself often, that I was an unfortunate dog, and born to be always miserable.

It is true, when I got on shore first here, and found all my ship's crew drowned and myself spared, I was surprised with a kind of ecstasy, and some transports of soul, which, had the grace of God assisted, might have come up to true thankfulness; but it ended where it began, in a mere common flight of joy, or, as I may say, being glad I was alive, without the least reflection upon the distinguished goodness of the hand which had preserved me, and had singled me out to be preserved when all the rest were destroyed, or an inquiry why Providence had been thus merciful unto me. Even just the same common sort of joy which seamen generally have, after they are got safe ashore from a shipwreck, which they drown all in the next bowl of punch, and forget almost as soon as it is over; and all the rest of my life was like it. Even when I was afterwards, on due consideration, made sensible of my condition, how I was cast on this dreadful place, out of the reach of human kind, out of all hope of relief, or prospect of redemption, as soon as I saw but a prospect of living and that I should not starve and perish for hunger, all the sense of my affliction wore off; and I began to be very easy, applied myself to the works proper for my preservation and supply, and was far enough from being afflicted at my condition, as a judgment from heaven, or as the hand of God against me: these were thoughts which very seldom entered my head.

The growing up of the corn, as is hinted in my Journal, had at first some little influence upon me, and began to affect me with seriousness, as long as I thought it had something miraculous in it; but as soon as ever that part of the thought was removed, all the impression that was raised from it wore off also, as I have noted already. Even the earthquake, though nothing could be more terrible in its nature, or more immediately directing to the invisible Power which alone directs such things, yet no sooner was the first fright over, but the impression it had made went off also. I had no more sense of God or His judgments—much less of the present affliction of my circumstances being from His hand—than if I had been in the most prosperous condition of life. But now, when I began to be sick, and a leisurely view of the miseries of death came to place itself before me; when my spirits began to sink under the burden of a strong distemper, and nature was exhausted with the violence of the fever; conscience, that had slept so long, began to awake, and I began to reproach myself with my past life, in which I had so evidently, by uncommon wickedness, provoked the justice of God to lay me under uncommon strokes, and to deal with me in so vindictive a manner. These reflections oppressed me for the second or third day of my distemper; and in the violence, as well of the fever as of the dreadful reproaches of my conscience, extorted some words from me like praying to God, though I cannot say they were either a prayer attended with desires or with hopes: it was rather the voice of mere fright and distress. My thoughts were confused, the convictions great upon my mind, and the horror of dying in such a miserable condition raised vapours into my head with the mere apprehensions; and in these hurries of my soul I knew not what my tongue might express. But it was rather exclamation, such as, "Lord, what a miserable creature am I! If I should be sick, I shall certainly die for want of help; and what will become of me!" Then the tears burst out of my eyes, and I could say no more for a good while. In this interval the good advice of my father came to my mind, and presently his prediction, which I mentioned at the beginning of this story—viz. that if I did take this foolish step, God would not bless me, and I would have leisure hereafter to reflect upon having neglected his counsel when there might be none to assist in my recovery. "Now," said I, aloud, "my dear father's words are come to pass; God's justice has overtaken me, and I have none to help or hear me. I rejected the voice of Providence, which had mercifully put me in a posture or station of life wherein I might have been happy and easy; but I would neither see it

77

myself nor learn to know the blessing of it from my parents. I left them to mourn over my folly, and now I am left to mourn under the consequences of it. I abused their help and assistance, who would have lifted me in the world, and would have made everything easy to me; and now I have difficulties to struggle with, too great for even nature itself to support, and no assistance, no help, no comfort, no advice." Then I cried out, "Lord, be my help, for I am in great distress." This was the first prayer, if I may call it so, that I had made for many years.

But to return to my Journal.

June 28.—Having been somewhat refreshed with the sleep I had had, and the fit being entirely off, I got up; and though the fright and terror of my dream was very great, yet I considered that the fit of the ague would return again the next day, and now was my time to get something to refresh and support myself when I should be ill; and the first thing I did, I filled a large square case-bottle with water, and set it upon my table, in reach of my bed; and to take off the chill or aguish disposition of the water, I put about a quarter of a pint of rum into it, and mixed them together. Then I got me a piece of the goat's flesh and broiled it on the coals, but could eat very little. I walked about, but was very weak, and withal very sad and heavy-hearted under a sense of my miserable condition, dreading, the return of my distemper the next day. At night I made my supper of three of the turtle's eggs, which I roasted in the ashes, and ate, as we call it, in the shell, and this was the first bit of meat I had ever asked God's blessing to, that I could remember, in my whole life. After I had eaten I tried to walk, but found myself so weak that I could hardly carry a gun, for I never went out without that; so I went but a little way, and sat down upon the ground, looking out upon the sea, which was just before me, and very calm and smooth. As I sat here some such thoughts as these occurred to me: What is this earth and sea, of which I have seen so much? Whence is it produced? And what am I, and all the other creatures wild and tame, human and brutal? Whence are we? Sure we are all made by some secret Power, who formed the earth and sea, the air and sky. And who is that? Then it followed most naturally, it is God that has made all. Well, but then it came on strangely, if God has made all these things, He guides and governs them all, and all things that concern them; for the Power that could make all things must certainly have power to guide and direct them. If so, nothing can happen in the great circuit of His works, either without His knowledge or appointment.

And if nothing happens without His knowledge, He knows that I am here, and am in this dreadful condition; and if nothing happens without His appointment, He has appointed all this to befall me. Nothing occurred to my thought to contradict any of these conclusions, and therefore it rested upon me with the greater force, that it must needs be that God had appointed all this to befall me; that I was brought into this miserable circumstance by His direction, He having the sole power, not of me only, but of everything that happened in the world. Immediately it followed: Why has God done this to me? What have I done to be thus used? My conscience presently checked me in that inquiry, as if I had blasphemed, and methought it spoke to me like a voice: "Wretch! dost *thou* ask what thou hast done? Look back upon a dreadful misspent life, and ask thyself what thou hast *not* done? Ask, why is it that thou wert not long ago destroyed? Why wert thou not drowned in Yarmouth Roads; killed in the fight when the ship was taken by the Sallee man-of-war; devoured by the wild beasts on the coast of Africa; or drowned *here*, when all the crew perished but thyself? Dost *thou* ask, what have I done?" I was struck dumb with these reflections, as one astonished, and had not a word to say—no, not to answer to myself, but rose up pensive and sad, walked back to my retreat, and went up over my wall, as if I had been going to bed; but my thoughts were sadly disturbed, and I had no inclination to sleep; so I sat down in my chair, and lighted my lamp, for it began to be dark. Now, as the apprehension of the return of my distemper terrified me very much, it occurred to my thought that the Brazilians take no physic but their tobacco for almost all distempers, and I had a piece of a roll of tobacco in one of the chests, which was quite cured, and some also that was green, and not quite cured.

I went, directed by Heaven no doubt; for in this chest I found a cure both for soul and body. I opened the chest, and found what I looked for, the tobacco; and as the few books I had saved lay there too, I took out one of the Bibles which I mentioned before, and which to this time I had not found leisure or inclination to look into. I say, I took it out, and brought both that and the tobacco with me to the table. What use to make of the tobacco I knew not, in my distemper, or whether it was good for it or no: but I tried several experiments with it, as if I was resolved it should hit one way or other. I first took a piece of leaf, and chewed it in my mouth, which, indeed, at first almost stupefied my brain, the tobacco being green and strong, and that I had not been much used to. Then I took some and steeped it an hour or two in some rum, and resolved to take a dose of it when I lay down; and lastly, I burnt some upon a pan of coals, and held my nose close over the smoke of it as long as I could bear it, as well for the heat as almost for suffocation. In the interval of this operation I took up the Bible and began to read; but my head was too much disturbed with the tobacco to bear reading, at least at that time; only, having opened the book casually, the first words that occurred to me were these, "Call on Me in the day of trouble, and I will deliver thee, and thou shalt glorify Me." These words were very apt to my case, and made some impression upon my thoughts at the time of reading them, though not so much as they did afterwards; for, as for being *delivered*, the word had no sound, as I may say, to me; the thing was so remote, so impossible in my apprehension of things, that I began to say, as the children of Israel did when they were promised flesh to eat, "Can God spread a table in the wilderness?" so I began to say, "Can God Himself deliver me from this place?" And as it was not for many years that any hopes appeared, this prevailed very often upon my thoughts; but, however, the words made a great impression upon me, and I mused upon them very often. It grew now late, and the tobacco had, as I said, dozed my head so much that I inclined to sleep; so I left my lamp burning in the cave, lest I should want anything in the night, and went to bed. But before I lay down, I did what I never had done in all my life—I kneeled down, and prayed to God to fulfil the promise to me, that if I called upon Him in the day of trouble, He would deliver me. After my broken and imperfect prayer was over, I drank the rum in which I had steeped the tobacco, which was so strong and rank of the tobacco that I could scarcely get it down; immediately upon this I went to bed. I found presently it flew up into my head violently; but I fell into a sound sleep, and waked no more till, by the sun, it must necessarily be near three o'clock in the afternoon the next day—nay, to this hour I am partly of opinion that I slept all the next day and night, and till almost three the day after; for otherwise I know not how I should lose a day out of my reckoning in the days of the week, as it appeared some years after I had done; for if I had lost it by crossing and recrossing the line, I should have lost more than one day; but certainly I lost a day in my account, and never knew which way. Be that, however, one way or the other, when I awaked I found myself exceedingly refreshed, and my spirits lively and cheerful; when I got up I was stronger than I was the day before, and my stomach better, for I was hungry; and, in short, I had no fit the next day, but continued much altered for the better. This was the 29th.

The 30th was my well day, of course, and I went abroad with my gun, but did not care to travel too far. I killed a sea-fowl or two, something like a brandgoose, and brought them home, but was not very forward to eat them; so I ate some more of the turtle's eggs, which were very good. This evening I renewed the medicine, which I had supposed did me good the day before—the tobacco steeped in rum; only I did not take so much as before, nor did I chew any of the leaf, or hold my head over the smoke; however, I was not so well the next day, which was the first of July, as I hoped I should have been; for I had a little spice of the cold fit, but it was not much.

July 2.—I renewed the medicine all the three ways; and dosed myself with it as at first, and doubled the quantity which I drank.

July 3.—I missed the fit for good and all, though I did not recover my full strength for some weeks after. While I was thus gathering strength, my thoughts ran exceedingly upon this Scripture, "I will deliver thee"; and the impossibility of my deliverance lay much upon my mind, in bar of my ever expecting it; but as I was discouraging myself with such thoughts, it occurred to my mind that I pored so much upon my deliverance from the main affliction, that I disregarded the deliverance I had received, and I was as it were made to ask myself such questions as these—viz. Have I not been delivered, and wonderfully too, from sickness—from the most distressed condition that could be, and that was so frightful to me? and what notice had I taken of it? Had I done my part? God had delivered me, but I had not glorified Him—that is to say, I had not owned and been thankful for that as a deliverance; and how could I expect greater deliverance? This touched my heart very much; and immediately I knelt down and gave God thanks aloud for my recovery from my sickness.

July 4.—In the morning I took the Bible; and beginning at the New Testament, I began seriously to read it, and imposed upon myself to read a while every morning and every night; not tying myself to the number of chapters, but long as my thoughts should engage me. It was not long after I set seriously to this work till I found my heart more deeply and sincerely affected with the wickedness of my past life. The impression of my dream revived; and the words, "All these things have not brought thee to repentance," ran seriously through my thoughts. I was earnestly begging of God to give me repentance, when it happened providentially, the very day, that, reading the Scripture, I came to these words: "He is exalted a Prince and a Saviour, to give repentance and to give remission." I threw down the book; and with my heart as well as my hands lifted up to heaven, in a kind of ecstasy of joy, I cried out aloud, "Jesus, thou son of David! Jesus, thou exalted Prince and Saviour! give me repentance!" This was the first time I could say, in the true sense of the words, that I prayed in all my life; for now I prayed with a sense of my condition, and a true Scripture view of hope, founded on the encouragement of the Word of God; and from this time, I may say, I began to hope that God would hear me.

Now I began to construe the words mentioned above, "Call on Me, and I will deliver thee," in a different sense from what I had ever done before; for then I had no notion of anything being called *deliverance*, but my being delivered from the captivity I was in; for though I was indeed at large in the place, yet the island was certainly a prison to me, and that in the worse sense in the world. But now I learned to take it in another sense: now I looked back upon my past life with such horror, and my sins appeared so dreadful, that my soul sought nothing of God but deliverance from the load of guilt that bore down all my comfort. As for my solitary life, it was nothing. I did not so much as pray to be delivered from it or think of it; it was all of no consideration in comparison to this. And I add this part here, to hint to whoever shall read it, that whenever they come to a true sense of things, they will find deliverance from sin a much greater blessing than deliverance from affliction.

But, leaving this part, I return to my Journal.

My condition began now to be, though not less miserable as to my way of living, yet much easier to my mind: and my thoughts being directed, by a constant reading the Scripture and praying to God, to things of a higher nature, I had a great deal of comfort within, which till now I knew nothing of; also, my health and strength returned, I bestirred myself to furnish myself with everything that I wanted, and make my way of living as regular as I could.

From the 4th of July to the 14th I was chiefly employed in walking about with my gun in my hand, a little and a little at a time, as a man that was gathering up his strength after a fit of sickness; for it is hardly to be imagined how low I was, and to what weakness I was reduced. The application which I made use of was perfectly new, and perhaps which had never cured an ague before; neither can I recommend it to any to practise, by this experiment: and though it did carry off the fit, yet it rather contributed to weakening me; for I had frequent

82

convulsions in my nerves and limbs for some time. I learned from it also this, in particular, that being abroad in the rainy season was the most pernicious thing to my health that could be, especially in those rains which came attended with storms and hurricanes of wind; for as the rain which came in the dry season was almost always accompanied with such storms, so I found that rain was much more dangerous than the rain which fell in September and October.

CHAPTER VII

AGRICULTURAL EXPERIENCE

I had now been in this unhappy island above ten months. All possibility of deliverance from this condition seemed to be entirely taken from me; and I firmly believe that no human shape had ever set foot upon that place. Having now secured my habitation, as I thought, fully to my mind, I had a great desire to make a more perfect discovery of the island, and to see what other productions I might find, which I yet knew nothing of.

It was on the 15th of July that I began to take a more particular survey of the island itself. I went up the creek first, where, as I hinted, I brought my rafts on shore. I found after I came about two miles up, that the tide did not flow any higher, and that it was no more than a little brook of running water, very fresh and good; but this being the dry season, there was hardly any water in some parts of it—at least not enough to run in any stream, so as it could be perceived. On the banks of this brook I found many pleasant savannahs or meadows, plain, smooth, and covered with grass; and on the rising parts of them, next to the higher grounds, where the water, as might be supposed, never overflowed, I found a great deal of tobacco, green, and growing to a great and very strong stalk. There were divers other plants, which I had no notion of or understanding about, that might, perhaps, have virtues of their own, which I could not find out. I searched for the cassava root, which the Indians, in all that climate, make their bread of, but I could find none. I saw large plants of aloes, but did not understand them. I saw several sugar-canes, but wild, and, for want of cultivation, imperfect. I contented myself with these discoveries for this time, and came back, musing with myself what course I might take to know the virtue and goodness of any of the fruits or plants which I should discover, but could bring it to no conclusion; for, in short, I had made so little observation while I was in the Brazils, that I knew little of the plants in the field; at least, very little that might serve to any purpose now in my distress.

The next day, the sixteenth, I went up the same way again; and after going something further than I had gone the day before, I found the brook and the savannahs cease, and the country become more woody than before. In this part I found different fruits, and particularly I found melons upon the ground, in great abundance, and

84

grapes upon the trees. The vines had spread, indeed, over the trees, and the clusters of grapes were just now in their prime, very ripe and rich. This was a surprising discovery, and I was exceeding glad of them; but I was warned by my experience to eat sparingly of them; remembering that when I was ashore in Barbary, the eating of grapes killed several of our Englishmen, who were slaves there, by throwing them into fluxes and fevers. But I found an excellent use for these grapes; and that was, to cure or dry them in the sun, and keep them as dried grapes or raisins are kept, which I thought would be, as indeed they were, wholesome and agreeable to eat when no grapes could be had.

I spent all that evening there, and went not back to my habitation; which, by the way, was the first night, as I might say, I had lain from home. In the night, I took my first contrivance, and got up in a tree, where I slept well; and the next morning proceeded upon my discovery; travelling nearly four miles, as I might judge by the length of the valley, keeping still due north, with a ridge of hills on the south and north side of me. At the end of this march I came to an opening where the country seemed to descend to the west; and a little spring of fresh water, which issued out of the side of the hill by me, ran the other way, that is, due east; and the country appeared so fresh, so green, so flourishing, everything being in a constant verdure or flourish of spring that it looked like a planted garden. I descended a little on the side of that delicious vale, surveying it with a secret kind of pleasure, though mixed with my other afflicting thoughts, to think that this was all my own; that I was king and lord of all this country indefensibly, and had a right of possession; and if I could convey it, I might have it in inheritance as completely as any lord of a manor in England. I saw here abundance of cocoa trees, orange, and lemon, and citron trees; but all wild, and very few bearing any fruit, at least not then. However, the green limes that I gathered were not only pleasant to eat, but very wholesome; and I mixed their juice afterwards with water, which made it very wholesome, and very cool and refreshing. I found now I had business enough to gather and carry home; and I resolved to lay up a store as well of grapes as limes and lemons, to furnish myself for the wet season, which I knew was approaching. In order to do this, I gathered a great heap of grapes in one place, a lesser heap in another place, and a great parcel of limes and lemons in another place; and taking a few of each with me, I travelled homewards; resolving to come again, and bring a bag or sack, or what I could make, to carry the rest home. Accordingly, having spent three days in this journey, I came home (so I must now call my tent and my cave); but before I got thither the grapes were spoiled; the richness of the fruit and the weight of the juice having broken them and bruised them, they were good for little or nothing; as to the limes, they were good, but I could bring but a few.

The next day, being the nineteenth, I went back, having made me two small bags to bring home my harvest; but I was surprised, when coming to my heap of grapes, which were so rich and fine when I gathered them, to find them all spread about, trod to pieces, and dragged about, some here, some there, and abundance eaten and devoured. By this I concluded there were some wild creatures thereabouts, which had done this; but what they were I knew not. However, as I found there was no laying them up on heaps, and no carrying them away in a sack, but that one way they would be destroyed, and the other way they would be crushed with their own weight, I took another course; for I gathered a large quantity of the grapes, and hung upon the out-branches of the trees, that they might cure and dry in the sun; and as for the limes and lemons, I carried as many back as I could well stand under.

When I came home from this journey, I contemplated with great pleasure the fruitfulness of that valley, and the pleasantness of the situation; the security from storms on that side of the water, and the wood: and concluded that I had pitched upon a place to fix my abode which was by far the worst part of the country. Upon the whole, I began to consider of removing my habitation, and looking out for a place equally safe as where now I was situate, if possible, in that pleasant, fruitful part of the island.

This thought ran long in my head, and I was exceeding fond of it for some time, the pleasantness of the place tempting me; but when I came to a nearer view of it, I considered that I was now by the seaside, where it was at least possible that something might happen to my advantage, and, by the same ill fate that brought me hither might bring some other unhappy wretches to the same place; and though it was scarce probable that any such thing should ever happen, yet to enclose myself among the hills and woods in the centre of the island was to anticipate my bondage, and to render such an affair not only improbable, but impossible; and that therefore I ought not by any means to remove. However, I was so enamoured of this place, that I spent much of my time there for the whole of the remaining part of the month of July; and though upon second thoughts, I resolved not to remove, yet I built me a little kind of a bower, and surrounded it at a distance with a strong fence, being a double hedge, as high as I could reach, well staked and filled between with brushwood; and here I lay very secure, sometimes two or three nights together; always going over it with a ladder; so that I fancied now I had my country house and my sea-coast house; and this work took me up to the beginning of August.

I had but newly finished my fence, and began to enjoy my labour, when the rains came on, and made me stick close to my first habitation; for though I had made me a tent like the other, with a piece of a sail, and spread it very well, yet I had not the shelter of a hill to keep me from storms, nor a cave behind me to retreat into when the rains were extraordinary.

About the beginning of August, as I said, I had finished my bower, and began to enjoy myself. The 3rd of August, I found the grapes I had hung up perfectly dried, and, indeed, were excellent good raisins of the sun; so I began to take them down from the trees, and it was very happy that I did so, for the rains which followed would have spoiled them, and I had lost the best part of my winter food; for I had above two hundred large bunches of them. No sooner had I taken them all down, and carried the most of them home to my cave, than it began to rain; and from hence, which was the 14th of August, it rained, more or less, every day till the middle of October; and sometimes so violently, that I could not stir out of my cave for several days.

In this season I was much surprised with the increase of my family; I had been concerned for the loss of one of my cats, who ran away from me, or, as I thought, had been dead, and I heard no more tidings of her till, to my astonishment, she came home about the end of August with three kittens. This was the more strange to me because, though I had killed a wild cat, as I called it, with my gun, yet I thought it was quite a different kind from our European cats; but the young cats were the same kind of house-breed as the old one; and both my cats being females, I thought it very strange. But from these three cats I afterwards came to be so pestered with cats that I was forced to kill them like vermin or wild beasts, and to drive them from my house as much as possible.

From the 14th of August to the 26th, incessant rain, so that I could not stir, and was now very careful not to be much wet. In this confinement, I began to be straitened for food: but venturing out twice, I one day killed a goat; and the last day, which was the 26th, found a very large tortoise, which was a treat to me, and my food was regulated thus: I ate a bunch of raisins for my breakfast; a piece of the goat's flesh, or of the turtle, for my dinner, broiled—for, to my great misfortune, I had no vessel to boil or stew anything; and two or three of the turtle's eggs for my supper.

During this confinement in my cover by the rain, I worked daily two or three hours at enlarging my cave, and by degrees worked it on towards one side, till I came to the outside of the hill, and made a door or way out, which came beyond my fence or wall; and so I came in and out this way. But I was not perfectly easy at lying so open; for, as I had managed myself before, I was in a perfect enclosure; whereas now I thought I lay exposed, and open for anything to come in upon me; and yet I could not perceive that there was any living thing to fear, the biggest creature that I had yet seen upon the island being a goat.

Sept. 30.—I was now come to the unhappy anniversary of my landing. I cast up the notches on my post, and found I had been on shore three hundred and sixty-five days. I kept this day as a solemn fast, setting it apart for religious exercise, prostrating myself on the ground with the most serious humiliation, confessing my sins to God, acknowledging His righteous judgments upon me, and praying to Him to have mercy on me through Jesus Christ; and not having tasted the least refreshment for twelve hours, even till the going down of the sun, I then ate a biscuit-cake and a bunch of grapes, and went to bed, finishing the day as I began it. I had all this time observed no Sabbath day; for as at first I had no sense of religion upon my mind, I had, after some time, omitted to distinguish the weeks, by making a longer notch than ordinary for the Sabbath day, and so did not really know what any of the days were; but now, having cast up the days as above, I found I had been there a year; so I divided it into weeks, and set apart every seventh day for a Sabbath; though I found at the end of my account I had lost a day or two in my reckoning. A little after this, my ink began to fail me, and so I contented myself to use it more sparingly, and to write down only the most remarkable events of my life, without continuing a daily memorandum of other things.

The rainy season and the dry season began now to appear regular to me, and I learned to divide them so as to provide for them accordingly; but I bought all my experience before I had it, and this I am going to relate was one of the most discouraging experiments that I made.

I have mentioned that I had saved the few ears of barley and rice, which I had so surprisingly found spring up, as I thought, of themselves, and I believe there were about thirty stalks of rice, and about twenty of barley; and now I thought it a proper time to sow it, after the rains, the sun being in its southern position, going from me. Accordingly, I dug up a piece of ground as well as I could with my wooden spade, and dividing it into two parts, I sowed my grain; but as I was sowing, it casually occurred to my thoughts that I would not sow it all at first, because I did not know when was the proper time for it, so I sowed about two-thirds of the seed, leaving about a handful of each. It was a great comfort to me afterwards that I did so, for not one grain of what I sowed this time came to anything: for the dry months following, the earth having had no rain after the seed was sown, it had no moisture to assist its growth, and never came up at all till the wet season had come again, and then it grew as if it had been but newly sown. Finding my first seed did not grow, which I easily imagined was by the drought, I sought for a moister piece of ground to make another trial in, and I dug up a piece of ground near my new bower, and sowed the rest of my seed in February, a little before the vernal equinox; and this having the rainy months of March and April to water it, sprung up very pleasantly, and yielded a very good crop; but having part of the seed left only, and not daring to sow all that I had, I had but a small quantity at last, my whole crop not amounting to above half a peck of each kind. But by this experiment I was made master of my business, and knew exactly when the proper season was to sow, and that I might expect two seed-times and two harvests every year.

While this corn was growing I made a little discovery, which was of use to me afterwards. As soon as the rains were over, and the weather began to settle, which was about the month of November, I made a visit up the country to my bower, where, though I had not been some months, yet I found all things just as I left them. The circle or double hedge that I had made was not only firm and entire, but the stakes which I had cut out of some trees that grew thereabouts were all shot out and grown with long branches, as much as a willow-tree usually shoots the first year after lopping its head. I could not tell what tree to call it that these stakes were cut from. I was surprised, and yet very well pleased, to see the young trees grow; and I pruned them, and led them up to grow as much alike as I could; and it is scarce credible how beautiful a figure they grew into in three years; so that though the hedge made a circle of about twenty-five yards in diameter, yet the trees, for such I might now call them, soon covered it, and it was a complete shade, sufficient to lodge under all the dry season. This made me resolve to cut some more stakes, and make me a hedge like this, in a semi-circle round my wall (I mean that of my first dwelling), which I did; and placing the trees or stakes in a double row, at about eight yards distance from my first fence, they grew presently, and were at first a fine cover to my habitation, and afterwards served for a defence also, as I shall observe in its order.

I found now that the seasons of the year might generally be divided, not into summer and winter, as in Europe, but into the rainy seasons and the dry seasons, which were generally thus:—The half of February, the whole of March, and the half of April—rainy, the sun being then on or near the equinox.

The half of April, the whole of May, June, and July, and the half of August—dry, the sun being then to the north of the line.

The half of August, the whole of September, and the half of October—rainy, the sun being then come back.

The half of October, the whole of November, December, and January, and the half of February—dry, the sun being then to the south of the line.

The rainy seasons sometimes held longer or shorter as the winds happened to blow, but this was the general observation I made. After I had found by experience the ill consequences of being abroad in the rain, I took care to furnish myself with provisions beforehand, that I might not be obliged to go out, and I sat within doors as much as possible during the wet months. This time I found much employment, and very suitable also to the time, for I found great occasion for many things which I had no way to furnish myself with but by hard labour and constant application; particularly I tried many ways to make myself a basket, but all the twigs I could get for the purpose proved so brittle that they would do nothing. It proved of excellent advantage to me now, that when I was a boy, I used to take great delight in standing at a basket-maker's, in the town where my father lived, to see them make their wicker-ware; and being, as boys usually are, very officious to help, and a great observer of the manner in which they worked those things, and sometimes lending a hand, I had by these means full knowledge of the methods of it, and I wanted nothing but the materials, when it came into my mind that the twigs of that tree from whence I cut my stakes that grew might possibly be as tough as the sallows, willows, and osiers in England, and I resolved to try. Accordingly, the next day I went to my country house, as I called it, and cutting some of the smaller twigs, I found them to my purpose as much as I could desire; whereupon I came the next time prepared with a hatchet to cut down a quantity, which I soon found, for there was great plenty of them. These I set up to dry within my circle or hedge, and when they were fit for use I carried them to my cave; and here, during the next season, I employed myself in making, as well as I could, a great many baskets, both to carry earth or to carry or lay up anything, as I had occasion; and though I did not finish them very handsomely, yet I made them sufficiently serviceable for my purpose; thus, afterwards, I took care never to be without them; and as my wicker-ware decayed, I made more, especially strong, deep baskets to place my corn in, instead of sacks, when I should come to have any quantity of it.

Having mastered this difficulty, and employed a world of time about it, I bestirred myself to see, if possible, how to supply two wants. I had no vessels to hold anything that was liquid, except two runlets, which were almost full of rum, and some glass bottles—some of the common size, and others which were case bottles, square, for the holding of water, spirits, &c. I had not so much as a pot to boil anything, except a great kettle, which I saved out of the ship, and which was too big for such as I desired it—viz. to make broth, and stew a bit of meat by itself. The second thing I fain would have had was a tobacco-pipe, but it was impossible to me to make one; however, I found a contrivance for that, too, at last. I employed myself in planting my second rows of stakes or piles, and in this wicker-working all the summer or dry season, when another business took me up more time than it could be imagined I could spare.

CHAPTER VIII

SURVEYS HIS POSITION

I mentioned before that I had a great mind to see the whole island, and that I had travelled up the brook, and so on to where I built my bower, and where I had an opening quite to the sea, on the other side of the island. I now resolved to travel quite across to the sea-shore on that side; so, taking my gun, a hatchet, and my dog, and a larger quantity of powder and shot than usual, with two biscuit-cakes and a great bunch of raisins in my pouch for my store, I began my journey. When I had passed the vale where my bower stood, as above, I came within view of the sea to the west, and it being a very clear day, I fairly descried land— whether an island or a continent I could not tell; but it lay very high, extending from the W. to the W.S.W. at a very great distance; by my guess it could not be less than fifteen or twenty leagues off.

I could not tell what part of the world this might be, otherwise than that I knew it must be part of America, and, as I concluded by all my observations, must be near the Spanish dominions, and perhaps was all inhabited by savages, where, if I had landed, I had been in a worse condition than I was now; and therefore I acquiesced in the dispositions of Providence, which I began now to own and to believe ordered everything for the best; I say I quieted my mind with this, and left off afflicting myself with fruitless wishes of being there.

Besides, after some thought upon this affair, I considered that if this land was the Spanish coast, I should certainly, one time or other, see some vessel pass or repass one way or other; but if not, then it was the savage coast between the Spanish country and Brazils, where are found the worst of savages; for they are cannibals or men-eaters, and fail not to murder and devour all the human bodies that fall into their hands.

With these considerations, I walked very leisurely forward. I found that side of the island where I now was much pleasanter than mine—the open or savannah fields sweet, adorned with flowers and grass, and full of very fine woods. I saw abundance of parrots, and fain I would have caught one, if possible, to have kept it to be tame, and taught it to speak to me. I did, after some painstaking, catch a young parrot, for I knocked it down with a stick, and having recovered it, I brought it home; but it was some years before I could make him speak; however, at last I taught him to call me by name very familiarly. But the accident that followed, though it be a trifle, will be very diverting in its place.

I was exceedingly diverted with this journey. I found in the low grounds hares (as I thought them to be) and foxes; but they differed greatly from all the other kinds I had met with, nor could I satisfy myself to eat them, though I killed several. But I had no need to be venturous, for I had no want of food, and of that which was very good too, especially these three sorts, viz. goats, pigeons, and turtle, or tortoise, which added to my grapes, Leadenhall market could not have furnished a table better than I, in proportion to the company; and though my case was deplorable enough, yet I had great cause for thankfulness that I was not driven to any extremities for food, but had rather plenty, even to dainties.

I never travelled in this journey above two miles outright in a day, or thereabouts; but I took so many turns and re-turns to see what discoveries I could make, that I came weary enough to the place where I resolved to sit down all night; and then I either reposed myself in a tree, or surrounded myself with a row of stakes set upright in the ground, either from one tree to another, or so as no wild creature could come at me without waking me.

As soon as I came to the sea-shore, I was surprised to see that I had taken up my lot on the worst side of the island, for here, indeed, the shore was covered with innumerable turtles, whereas on the other side I had found but three in a year and a half. Here was also an infinite number of fowls of many kinds, some which I had seen, and some which I had not seen before, and many of them very good meat, but such as I knew not the names of, except those called penguins.

I could have shot as many as I pleased, but was very sparing of my powder and shot, and therefore had more mind to kill a she-goat if I could, which I could better feed on; and though there were many goats here, more than on my side the island, yet it was with much more difficulty that I could come near them, the country being flat and even, and they saw me much sooner than when I was on the hills.

I confess this side of the country was much pleasanter than mine; but yet I had not the least inclination to remove, for as I was fixed in my habitation it became natural to me, and I seemed all the while I was here to be as it were upon a journey, and from home. However, I travelled along the shore of the sea towards the east, I suppose about twelve miles, and then setting up a great pole upon the shore for a mark, I concluded I would go home again, and that the next journey I took should be on the other side of the island east from my dwelling, and so round till I came to my post again.

I took another way to come back than that I went, thinking I could easily keep all the island so much in my view that I could not miss finding my first dwelling by viewing the country; but I found myself mistaken, for being come about two or three miles, I found myself descended into a very large valley, but so surrounded with hills, and those hills covered with wood, that I could not see which was my way by any direction but that of the sun, nor even then, unless I knew very well the position of the sun at that time of the day. It happened, to my further misfortune, that the weather proved hazy for three or four days while I was in the valley, and not being able to see the sun, I wandered about very uncomfortably, and at last was obliged to find the seaside, look for my post, and come back the same way I went: and then, by easy journeys, I turned homeward, the weather being exceeding hot, and my gun, ammunition, hatchet, and other things very heavy.

In this journey my dog surprised a young kid, and seized upon it; and I, running in to take hold of it, caught it, and saved it alive from the dog. I had a great mind to bring it home if I could, for I had often been musing whether it might not be possible to get a kid or two, and so raise a breed of tame goats, which might supply me when my powder and shot should be all spent. I made a collar for this little creature, and with a string, which I made of some rope-yam, which I always carried about me, I led him along, though with some difficulty, till I came to my bower, and there I enclosed him and left him, for I was very impatient to be at home, from whence I had been absent above a month.

I cannot express what a satisfaction it was to me to come into my old hutch, and lie down in my hammock-bed. This little wandering journey, without settled place of abode, had been so unpleasant to me, that my own house, as I called it to myself, was a perfect settlement to me compared to that; and it rendered everything about me so comfortable, that I resolved I would never go a great way from it again while it should be my lot to stay on the island.

I reposed myself here a week, to rest and regale myself after my long journey; during which most of the time was taken up in the weighty affair of making a cage for my Poll, who began now to be a mere domestic, and to be well acquainted with me. Then I began to think of the poor kid which I had penned in within my little circle, and resolved to go and fetch it home, or give it some food; accordingly I went, and found it where I left it, for indeed it could not get out, but was almost starved for want of food. I went and cut boughs of trees, and branches of such shrubs as I could find, and threw it over, and having fed it, I tied it as I did before, to lead it away; but it was so tame with being hungry, that I had no need to have tied it, for it followed me like a dog: and as I continually fed it, the creature became so loving, so gentle, and so fond, that it became from that time one of my domestics also, and would never leave me afterwards.

The rainy season of the autumnal equinox was now come, and I kept the 30th of September in the same solemn manner as before, being the anniversary of my landing on the island, having now been there two years, and no more prospect of being delivered than the first day I came there, I spent the whole day in humble and thankful acknowledgments of the many wonderful mercies which my solitary condition was attended with, and without which it might have been infinitely more miserable. I gave humble and hearty thanks that God had been pleased to discover to me that it was possible I might be more happy in this solitary condition than I should have been in the liberty of society, and in all the pleasures of the world; that He could fully make up to me the deficiencies of my solitary state, and the want of human society, by His presence and the communications of His grace to my soul; supporting, comforting, and encouraging me to depend upon His providence here, and hope for His eternal presence hereafter.

It was now that I began sensibly to feel how much more happy this life I now led was, with all its miserable circumstances, than the wicked, cursed, abominable life I led all the past part of my days; and now I changed both my sorrows and my joys; my very desires altered, my affections changed their gusts, and my delights were perfectly new from what they were at my first coming, or, indeed, for the two years past.

Before, as I walked about, either on my hunting or for viewing the country, the anguish of my soul at my condition would break out upon me on a sudden, and my very heart would die within me, to think of the woods, the mountains, the deserts I was in, and how I was a prisoner, locked up with the eternal bars and bolts of the ocean, in an uninhabited wilderness, without redemption. In the midst of the greatest composure of my mind, this would break out upon me like a storm, and make me wring my hands and weep like a child. Sometimes it would take me in the middle of my work, and I would immediately sit down and sigh, and look upon the ground for an hour or two together; and this was still worse to me, for if I could burst out into tears, or vent myself by words, it would go off, and the grief, having exhausted itself, would abate.

But now I began to exercise myself with new thoughts: I daily read the word of God, and applied all the comforts of it to my present state. One morning, being very sad, I opened the Bible upon these words, "I will never, never leave thee, nor forsake thee." Immediately it occurred that these words were to me; why else should they be directed in such a manner, just at the moment when I was mourning over my condition, as one forsaken of God and man? "Well, then," said I, "if God does not forsake me, of what ill consequence can it be, or what matters it, though the world should all forsake me, seeing on the other hand, if I had all the world, and should lose the favour and blessing of God, there would be no comparison in the loss?"

From this moment I began to conclude in my mind that it was possible for me to be more happy in this forsaken, solitary condition than it was probable I should ever have been in any other particular state in the world; and with this thought I was going to give thanks to God for bringing me to this place. I know not what it was, but something shocked my mind at that thought, and I durst not speak the words. "How canst thou become such a hypocrite," said I, even audibly, "to pretend to be thankful for a condition which, however thou mayest endeavour to be contented with, thou wouldst rather pray heartily to be delivered from?" So I stopped there; but though I could not say I thanked God for being there, yet I sincerely gave thanks to God for opening my eyes, by whatever afflicting providences, to see the former condition of my life, and to mourn for my wickedness, and repent. I never opened the Bible, or shut it, but my very soul within me blessed God for directing my friend in England, without any order of mine, to pack it up among my goods, and for assisting me afterwards to save it out of the wreck of the ship.

Thus, and in this disposition of mind, I began my third year; and though I have not given the reader the trouble of so particular an account of my works this year as the first, yet in general it may be observed that I was very seldom idle, but having regularly divided my time according to the several daily employments that were before me, such as: first, my duty to God, and the reading the Scriptures, which I constantly set apart some time for thrice every day; secondly, the going abroad with my gun for food, which generally took me up three hours in every morning, when it did not rain; thirdly, the ordering, cutting, preserving, and cooking what I had killed or caught for my supply; these took up great part of the day. Also, it is to be considered, that in the middle of the day, when the sun was in the zenith, the violence of the heat was too great to stir out; so that about four hours in the evening was all the time I could be supposed to work in, with this exception, that sometimes I changed my hours of hunting and working, and went to work in the morning, and abroad with my gun in the afternoon.

To this short time allowed for labour I desire may be added the exceeding laboriousness of my work; the many hours which, for want of tools, want of help, and want of skill, everything I did took up out of my time. For example, I was full two and forty days in making a board for a long shelf, which I wanted in my cave; whereas, two sawyers, with their tools and a saw-pit, would have cut six of them out of the same tree in half a day.

My case was this: it was to be a large tree which was to be cut down, because my board was to be a broad one. This tree I was three days in cutting down, and two more cutting off the boughs, and reducing it to a log or piece of timber. With inexpressible hacking and hewing I reduced both the sides of it into chips till it began to be light enough to move; then I turned it, and made one side of it smooth and flat as a board from end to end; then, turning that side downward, cut the other side til I brought the plank to be about three inches thick, and smooth on both sides. Any one may judge the labour of my hands in such a piece of work; but labour and patience carried me through that, and many other things. I only observe this in particular, to show the reason why so much of my time went away with so little work—viz. that what might be a little to be done with help and tools, was a vast labour and required a prodigious time to do alone, and by hand. But notwithstanding this, with patience and labour I got through everything that my circumstances made necessary to me to do, as will appear by what follows.

I was now, in the months of November and December, expecting my crop of barley and rice. The ground I had manured and dug up for them was not great; for, as I observed, my seed of each was not above the quantity of half a peck, for I had lost one whole crop by sowing in the dry season. But now my crop promised very well, when on a sudden I found I was in danger of losing it all again by enemies of several sorts, which it was scarcely possible to keep from it; as, first, the goats, and wild creatures which I called hares, who, tasting the sweetness of the blade, lay in it night and day, as soon as it came up, and eat it so close, that it could get no time to shoot up into stalk.

This I saw no remedy for but by making an enclosure about it with a hedge; which I did with a great deal of toil, and the more, because it required speed. However, as my arable land was but small, suited to my crop, I got it totally well fenced in about three weeks' time; and shooting some of the creatures in the daytime, I set my dog to guard it in the night, tying him up to a stake at the gate, where he would stand and bark all night long; so in a little time the enemies forsook the place, and the corn grew very strong and well, and began to ripen apace.

But as the beasts ruined me before, while my corn was in the blade, so the birds were as likely to ruin me now, when it was in the ear; for, going along by the place to see how it throve, I saw my little crop surrounded with fowls, of I know not how many sorts, who stood, as it were, watching till I should be gone. I immediately let fly among them, for I always had my gun with me. I had no sooner shot, but there rose up a little cloud of fowls, which I had not seen at all, from among the corn itself.

This touched me sensibly, for I foresaw that in a few days they would devour all my hopes; that I should be starved, and never be able to raise a crop at all; and what to do I could not tell; however, I resolved not to lose my corn, if possible, though I should watch it night and day. In the first place, I went among it to see what damage was already done, and found they had spoiled a good deal of it; but that as it was yet too green for them, the loss was not so great but that the remainder was likely to be a good crop if it could be saved.

I stayed by it to load my gun, and then coming away, I could easily see the thieves sitting upon all the trees about me, as if they only waited till I was gone away, and the event proved it to be so; for as I walked off, as if I was gone, I was no sooner out of their sight than they dropped down one by one into the corn again. I was so provoked, that I could not have patience to stay till more came on, knowing that every grain that they ate now was, as it might be said, a peck-loaf to me in the consequence; but coming up to the hedge, I fired again, and killed three of them. This was what I wished for; so I took them up, and served them as we serve notorious thieves in England—hanged them in chains, for a terror to others. It is impossible to imagine that this should have such an effect as it had, for the fowls would not only not come at the corn, but, in short, they forsook all that part of the island, and I could never see a bird near the place as long as my scarecrows hung there. This I was very glad of, you may be sure, and about the latter end of December, which was our second harvest of the year, I reaped my corn.

I was sadly put to it for a scythe or sickle to cut it down, and all I could do was to make one, as well as I could, out of one of the broadswords, or cutlasses, which I saved among the arms out of the ship. However, as my first crop was but small, I had no great difficulty to cut it down; in short, I reaped it in my way, for I cut nothing off but the ears, and carried it away in a great basket which I had made, and so rubbed it out with my hands; and at the end of all my harvesting, I found that out of my half-peck of seed I had near two bushels of rice, and about two bushels and a half of barley; that is to say, by my guess, for I had no measure at that time.

However, this was a great encouragement to me, and I foresaw that, in time, it would please God to supply me with bread. And yet here I was perplexed again, for I neither knew how to grind or make meal of my corn, or indeed how to clean it and part it; nor, if made into meal, how to make bread of it; and if how to make it, yet I knew not how to bake it. These things being added to my desire of having a good quantity for store, and to secure a constant supply, I resolved not to taste any of this crop but to preserve it all for seed against the next season; and in the meantime to employ all my study and hours of working to accomplish this great work of providing myself with corn and bread.

It might be truly said, that now I worked for my bread. I believe few people have thought much upon the strange multitude of little things necessary in the providing, producing, curing, dressing, making, and finishing this one article of bread.

I, that was reduced to a mere state of nature, found this to my daily discouragement; and was made more sensible of it every hour, even after I had got the first handful of seed-corn, which, as I have said, came up unexpectedly, and indeed to a surprise.

First, I had no plough to turn up the earth—no spade or shovel to dig it. Well, this I conquered by making me a wooden spade, as I observed before; but this did my work but in a wooden manner; and though it cost me a great many days to make it, yet, for want of iron, it not only wore out soon, but made my work the harder, and made it be performed much worse. However, this I bore with, and was content to work it out with patience, and bear with the badness of the performance. When the corn was sown, I had no harrow, but was forced to go over it myself, and drag a great heavy bough of a tree over it, to scratch it, as it may be called, rather than rake or harrow it. When it was growing, and grown, I have observed already how many things I wanted to fence it, secure it, mow or reap it, cure and carry it home, thrash, part it from the chaff, and save it. Then I wanted a mill to grind it sieves to dress it, yeast and salt to make it into bread, and an oven to bake it; but all these things I did without, as shall be observed; and yet the corn was an inestimable comfort and advantage to me too. All this, as I said, made everything laborious and tedious to me; but that there was no help for. Neither was my time so much loss to me, because, as I had divided it, a certain part of it was every day appointed to these works; and as I had resolved to use none of the corn for bread till I had a greater quantity by me, I had the next six months to apply myself wholly, by labour and invention, to furnish myself with utensils proper for the performing all the operations necessary for making the corn, when I had it, fit for my use.

CHAPTER IX

A BOAT

But first I was to prepare more land, for I had now seed enough to sow above an acre of ground. Before I did this, I had a week's work at least to make me a spade, which, when it was done, was but a sorry one indeed, and very heavy, and required double labour to work with it. However, I got through that, and sowed my seed in two large flat pieces of ground, as near my house as I could find them to my mind, and fenced them in with a good hedge, the stakes of which were all cut off that wood which I had set before, and knew it would grow; so that, in a year's time, I knew I should have a quick or living hedge, that would want but little repair. This work did not take me up less than three months, because a great part of that time was the wet season, when I could not go abroad. Within-doors, that is when it rained and I could not go out, I found employment in the following occupations—always observing, that all the while I was at work I diverted myself with talking to my parrot, and teaching him to speak; and I quickly taught him to know his own name, and at last to speak it out pretty loud, "Poll," which was the first word I ever heard spoken in the island by any mouth but my own. This, therefore, was not my work, but an assistance to my work; for now, as I said, I had a great employment upon my hands, as follows: I had long studied to make, by some means or other, some earthen vessels, which, indeed, I wanted sorely, but knew not where to come at them. However, considering the heat of the climate, I did not doubt but if I could find out any clay, I might make some pots that might, being dried in the sun, be hard enough and strong enough to bear handling, and to hold anything that was dry, and required to be kept so; and as this was necessary in the preparing corn, meal, &c., which was the thing I was doing, I resolved to make some as large as I could, and fit only to stand like jars, to hold what should be put into them.

It would make the reader pity me, or rather laugh at me, to tell how many awkward ways I took to raise this paste; what odd, misshapen, ugly things I made; how many of them fell in and how many fell out, the clay not being stiff enough to bear its own weight; how many cracked by the over-violent heat of the sun, being set out too hastily; and how many fell in pieces with only removing, as well before as after they were dried; and, in a word, how, after having laboured hard to find the clay—to dig it, to temper it, to bring it home, and work it—I could not make above two large earthen ugly things (I cannot call them jars) in about two months' labour.

However, as the sun baked these two very dry and hard, I lifted them very gently up, and set them down again in two great wicker baskets, which I had made on purpose for them, that they might not break; and as between the pot and the basket there was a little room to spare, I stuffed it full of the rice and barley straw; and these two pots being to stand always dry I thought would hold my dry corn, and perhaps the meal, when the corn was bruised.

Though I miscarried so much in my design for large pots, yet I made several smaller things with better success; such as little round pots, flat dishes, pitchers, and pipkins, and any things my hand turned to; and the heat of the sun baked them quite hard.

But all this would not answer my end, which was to get an earthen pot to hold what was liquid, and bear the fire, which none of these could do. It happened after some time, making a pretty large fire for cooking my meat, when I went to put it out after I had done with it, I found a broken piece of one of my earthenware vessels in the fire, burnt as hard as a stone, and red as a tile. I was agreeably surprised to see it, and said to myself, that certainly they might be made to burn whole, if they would burn broken.

This set me to study how to order my fire, so as to make it burn some pots. I had no notion of a kiln, such as the potters burn in, or of glazing them with lead, though I had some lead to do it with; but I placed three large pipkins and two or three pots in a pile, one upon another, and placed my firewood all round it, with a great heap of embers under them. I plied the fire with fresh fuel round the outside and upon the top, till I saw the pots in the inside red-hot quite through, and observed that they did not crack at all. When I saw them clear red, I let them stand in that heat about five or six hours, till I found one of them, though it did not crack, did melt or run; for the sand which was mixed with the clay melted by the violence of the heat, and would have run into glass if I had gone on; so I slacked my fire gradually till the pots began to abate of the red colour; and watching them all night, that I might not let the fire abate too fast, in the morning I had three very good (I will not say handsome) pipkins, and two other earthen pots, as hard burnt as could be desired, and one of them perfectly glazed with the running of the sand.

After this experiment, I need not say that I wanted no sort of earthenware for my use; but I must needs say as to the shapes of them, they were very indifferent, as any one may suppose, when I had no way of making them but as the children make dirt pies, or as a woman would make pies that never learned to raise paste.

No joy at a thing of so mean a nature was ever equal to mine, when I found I had made an earthen pot that would bear the fire; and I had hardly patience to stay till they were cold before I set one on the fire again with some water in it to boil me some meat, which it did admirably well; and with a piece of a kid I made some very good broth, though I wanted oatmeal, and several other ingredients requisite to make it as good as I would have had it been.

My next concern was to get me a stone mortar to stamp or beat some corn in; for as to the mill, there was no thought of arriving at that perfection of art with one pair of hands. To supply this want, I was at a great loss; for, of all the trades in the world, I was as perfectly unqualified for a stone-cutter as for any whatever; neither had I any tools to go about it with. I spent many a day to find out a great stone big enough to cut hollow, and make fit for a mortar, and could find none at all, except what was in the solid rock, and which I had no way to dig or cut out; nor indeed were the rocks in the island of hardness sufficient, but were all of a sandy, crumbling stone, which neither would bear the weight of a heavy pestle, nor would break the corn without filling it with sand. So, after a great deal of time lost in searching for a stone, I gave it over, and resolved to look out for a great block of hard wood, which I found, indeed, much easier; and getting one as big as I had strength to stir, I rounded it, and formed it on the outside with my axe and hatchet, and then with the help of fire and infinite labour, made a hollow place in it, as the Indians in Brazil make their canoes. After this, I made a great heavy pestle or beater of the wood called the iron-wood; and this I prepared and laid by against I had my next crop of corn, which I proposed to myself to grind, or rather pound into meal to make bread.

My next difficulty was to make a sieve or searce, to dress my meal, and to part it from the bran and the husk; without which I did not see it possible I could have any bread. This was a most difficult thing even to think on, for to be sure I had nothing like the necessary thing to make it—I mean fine thin canvas or stuff to searce the meal through. And here I was at a full stop for many months; nor did I really know what to do. Linen I had none left but what was mere rags; I had goat's hair, but neither knew how to weave it or spin it; and had I known how, here were no tools to work it with. All the remedy that I found for this was, that at last I did remember I had, among the seamen's clothes which were saved out of the ship, some neckcloths of calico or muslin; and with some pieces of these I made three small sieves proper enough for the work; and thus I made shift for some years: how I did afterwards, I shall show in its place.

The baking part was the next thing to be considered, and how I should make bread when I came to have corn; for first, I had no yeast. As to that part, there was no supplying the want, so I did not concern myself much about it. But for an oven I was indeed in great pain. At length I found out an experiment for that also, which was this: I made some earthen-vessels very broad but not deep, that is to say, about two feet diameter, and not above nine inches deep. These I burned in the fire, as I had done the other, and laid them by; and when I wanted to bake, I made a great fire upon my hearth, which I had paved with some square tiles of my own baking and burning also; but I should not call them square.

When the firewood was burned pretty much into embers or live coals, I drew them forward upon this hearth, so as to cover it all over, and there I let them lie till the hearth was very hot. Then sweeping away all the embers, I set down my loaf or loaves, and whelming down the earthen pot upon them, drew the embers all round the outside of the pot, to keep in and add to the heat; and thus as well as in the best oven in the world, I baked my barley-loaves, and became in little time a good pastrycook into the bargain; for I made myself several cakes and puddings of the rice; but I made no pies, neither had I anything to put into them supposing I had, except the flesh either of fowls or goats.

It need not be wondered at if all these things took me up most part of the third year of my abode here; for it is to be observed that in the intervals of these things I had my new harvest and husbandry to manage; for I reaped my corn in its season, and carried it home as well as I could, and laid it up in the ear, in my large baskets, till I had time to rub it out, for I had no floor to thrash it on, or instrument to thrash it with.

And now, indeed, my stock of corn increasing, I really wanted to build my barns bigger; I wanted a place to lay it up in, for the increase of the corn now yielded me so much, that I had of the barley about twenty bushels, and of the rice as much or more; insomuch that now I resolved to begin to use it freely; for my bread had been quite gone a great while; also I resolved to see what quantity would be sufficient for me a whole year, and to sow but once a year.

Upon the whole, I found that the forty bushels of barley and rice were much more than I could consume in a year; so I resolved to sow just the same quantity every year that I sowed the last, in hopes that such a quantity would fully provide me with bread, &c.

All the while these things were doing, you may be sure my thoughts ran many times upon the prospect of land which I had seen from the other side of the island; and I was not without secret wishes that I were on shore there, fancying that, seeing the mainland, and an inhabited country, I might find some way or other to convey myself further, and perhaps at last find some means of escape.

But all this while I made no allowance for the dangers of such an undertaking, and how I might fall into the hands of savages, and perhaps such as I might have reason to think far worse than the lions and tigers of Africa: that if I once came in their power, I should run a hazard of more than a thousand to one of being killed, and perhaps of being eaten; for I had heard that the people of the Caribbean coast were cannibals or man-eaters, and I knew by the latitude that I could not be far from that shore. Then, supposing they were not cannibals, yet they might kill me, as many Europeans who had fallen into their hands had been served, even when they had been ten or twenty together—much more I, that was but one, and could make little or no defence; all these things, I say, which I ought to have considered well; and did come into my thoughts afterwards, yet gave me no apprehensions at first, and my head ran mightily upon the thought of getting over to the shore.

Now I wished for my boy Xury, and the long-boat with shoulder-of-mutton sail, with which I sailed above a thousand miles on the coast of Africa; but this was in vain: then I thought I would go and look at our ship's boat, which, as I have said, was blown up upon the shore a great way, in the storm, when we were first cast away. She lay almost where she did at first, but not quite; and was turned, by the force of the waves and the winds, almost bottom upward, against a high ridge of beachy, rough sand, but no water about her. If I had had hands to have refitted her, and to have launched her into the water, the boat would have done well enough, and I might have gone back into the Brazils with her easily enough; but I might have foreseen that I could no more turn her and set her upright upon her bottom than I could remove the island; however, I went to the woods, and cut levers and rollers, and brought them to the boat resolving to try what I could do; suggesting to myself that if I could but turn her down, I might repair the damage she had received, and she would be a very good boat, and I might go to sea in her very easily.

I spared no pains, indeed, in this piece of fruitless toil, and spent, I think, three or four weeks about it; at last finding it impossible to heave it up with my little strength, I fell to digging away the sand, to undermine it, and so to make it fall down, setting pieces of wood to thrust and guide it right in the fall.

But when I had done this, I was unable to stir it up again, or to get under it, much less to move it forward towards the water; so I was forced to give it over; and yet, though I gave over the hopes of the boat, my desire to venture over for the main increased, rather than decreased, as the means for it seemed impossible.

This at length put me upon thinking whether it was not possible to make myself a canoe, or periagua, such as the natives of those climates make, even without tools, or, as I might say, without hands, of the trunk of a great tree. This I not only thought possible, but easy, and pleased myself extremely with the thoughts of making it, and with my having much more convenience for it than any of the negroes or Indians; but not at all considering the particular inconveniences which I lay under more than the Indians did—viz. want of hands to move it, when it was made, into the water—a difficulty much harder for me to surmount than all the consequences of want of tools could be to them; for what was it to me, if when I had chosen a vast tree in the woods, and with much trouble cut it down, if I had been able with my tools to hew and dub the outside into the proper shape of a boat, and burn or cut out the inside to make it hollow, so as to make a boat of it—if, after all this, I must leave it just there where I found it, and not be able to launch it into the water?

One would have thought I could not have had the least reflection upon my mind of my circumstances while I was making this boat, but I should have immediately thought how I should get it into the sea; but my thoughts were so intent upon my voyage over the sea in it, that I never once considered how I should get it off the land: and it was really, in its own nature, more easy for me to guide it over forty-five miles of sea than about forty-five fathoms of land, where it lay, to set it afloat in the water.

I went to work upon this boat the most like a fool that ever man did who had any of his senses awake. I pleased myself with the design, without determining whether I was ever able to undertake it; not but that the difficulty of launching my boat came often into my head; but I put a stop to my inquiries into it by this foolish answer which I gave myself—"Let me first make it; I warrant I will find some way or other to get it along when it is done."

This was a most preposterous method; but the eagerness of my fancy prevailed, and to work I went. I felled a cedar-tree, and I question much whether Solomon ever had such a one for the building of the Temple of Jerusalem; it was five feet ten inches diameter at the lower part next the stump, and four feet eleven inches diameter at the end of twenty-two feet; after which it lessened for a while, and then parted into branches. It was not without infinite labour that I felled this tree; I was twenty days hacking and hewing at it at the bottom; I was fourteen more getting the branches and limbs and the vast spreading head cut off, which I hacked and hewed through with axe and hatchet, and inexpressible labour; after this, it cost me a month to shape it and dub it to a proportion, and to something like the bottom of a boat, that it might swim upright as it ought to do. It cost me near three months more to clear the inside, and work it out so as to make an exact boat of it; this I did, indeed, without fire, by mere mallet and chisel, and by the dint of hard labour, till I had brought it to be a very handsome periagua, and big enough to have carried six-and-twenty men, and consequently big enough to have carried me and all my cargo.

When I had gone through this work I was extremely delighted with it. The boat was really much bigger than ever I saw a canoe or periagua, that was made of one tree, in my life. Many a weary stroke it had cost, you may be sure; and had I gotten it into the water, I make no question, but I should have begun the maddest voyage, and the most unlikely to be performed, that ever was undertaken.

But all my devices to get it into the water failed me; though they cost me infinite labour too. It lay about one hundred yards from the water, and not more; but the first inconvenience was, it was up hill towards the creek. Well, to take away this discouragement, I resolved to dig into the surface of the earth, and so make a declivity: this I began, and it cost me a prodigious deal of pains (but who grudge pains who have their deliverance in view?); but when this was worked through, and this difficulty managed, it was still much the same, for I could no more stir the canoe than I could the other boat. Then I measured the distance of ground, and resolved to cut a dock or canal, to bring the water up to the canoe, seeing I could not bring the canoe down to the water. Well, I began this work; and when I began to enter upon it, and calculate how deep it was to be dug, how broad, how the stuff was to be thrown out, I found that, by the number of hands I had, being none but my own, it must have been ten or twelve years before I could have gone through with it; for the shore lay so high, that at the upper end it must have been at least twenty feet deep; so at length, though with great reluctancy, I gave this attempt over also.

This grieved me heartily; and now I saw, though too late, the folly of beginning a work before we count the cost, and before we judge rightly of our own strength to go through with it.

In the middle of this work I finished my fourth year in this place, and kept my anniversary with the same devotion, and with as much comfort as ever before; for, by a constant study and serious application to the Word of God, and by the assistance of His grace, I gained a different knowledge from what I had before. I entertained different notions of things. I looked now upon the world as a thing remote, which I had nothing to do with, no expectations from, and, indeed, no desires about: in a word, I had nothing indeed to do with it, nor was ever likely to have, so I thought it looked, as we may perhaps look upon it hereafter—viz. as a place I had lived in, but was come out of it; and well might I say, as Father Abraham to Dives, "Between me and thee is a great gulf fixed."

In the first place, I was removed from all the wickedness of the world here; I had neither the lusts of the flesh, the lusts of the eye, nor the pride of life. I had nothing to covet, for I had all that I was now capable of enjoying; I was lord of the whole manor; or, if I pleased, I might call myself king or emperor over the whole country which I had possession of: there were no rivals; I had no competitor, none to dispute sovereignty or command with me: I might have raised ship-loadings of corn, but I had no use for it; so I let as little grow as I thought enough for my occasion. I had tortoise or turtle enough, but now and then one was as much as I could put to any use: I had timber enough to have built a fleet of ships; and I had grapes enough to have made wine, or to have cured into raisins, to have loaded that fleet when it had been built.

But all I could make use of was all that was valuable: I had enough to eat and supply my wants, and what was all the rest to me? If I killed more flesh than I could eat, the dog must eat it, or vermin; if I sowed more corn than I could eat, it must be spoiled; the trees that I cut down were lying to rot on the ground; I could make no more use of them but for fuel, and that I had no occasion for but to dress my food.

In a word, the nature and experience of things dictated to me, upon just reflection, that all the good things of this world are no farther good to us than they are for our use; and that, whatever we may heap up to give others, we enjoy just as much as we can use, and no more. The most covetous, griping miser in the world would have been cured of the vice of covetousness if he had been in my case; for I possessed infinitely more than I knew what to do with. I had no room for desire, except it was of things which I had not, and they were but trifles, though, indeed, of great use to me. I had, as I hinted before, a parcel of money, as well gold as silver, about thirty-six pounds sterling. Alas! there the sorry, useless stuff lay; I had no more manner of business for it; and often thought with myself that I would have given a handful of it for a gross of tobacco-pipes; or for a hand-mill to grind my corn; nay, I would have given it all for a sixpenny-worth of turnip and carrot seed out of England, or for a handful of peas and beans, and a bottle of ink. As it was, I had not the least advantage by it or benefit from it; but there it lay in a drawer, and grew mouldy with the damp of the cave in the wet seasons; and if I had had the drawer full of diamonds, it had been the same case—they had been of no manner of value to me, because of no use.

I had now brought my state of life to be much easier in itself than it was at first, and much easier to my mind, as well as to my body. I frequently sat down to meat with thankfulness, and admired the hand of God's providence, which had thus spread my table in the wilderness. I learned to look more upon the bright side of my condition, and less upon the dark side, and to consider what I enjoyed rather than what I wanted; and this gave me sometimes such secret comforts, that I cannot express them; and which I take notice of here, to put those discontented people in mind of it, who cannot enjoy comfortably what God has given them, because they see and covet something that He has not given them. All our discontents about what we want appeared to me to spring from the want of thankfulness for what we have.

Another reflection was of great use to me, and doubtless would be so to any one that should fall into such distress as mine was; and this was, to compare my present condition with what I at first expected it would be; nay, with what it would certainly have been, if the good providence of God had not wonderfully ordered the ship to be cast up nearer to the shore, where I not only could come at her, but could bring what I got out of her to the shore, for my relief and comfort; without which, I had wanted for tools to work, weapons for defence, and gunpowder and shot for getting my food.

I spent whole hours, I may say whole days, in representing to myself, in the most lively colours, how I must have acted if I had got nothing out of the ship. How I could not have so much as got any food, except fish and turtles; and that, as it was long before I found any of them, I must have perished first; that I should have lived, if I had not perished, like a mere savage; that if I had killed a goat or a fowl, by any contrivance, I had no way to flay or open it, or part the flesh from the skin and the bowels, or to cut it up; but must gnaw it with my teeth, and pull it with my claws, like a beast.

These reflections made me very sensible of the goodness of Providence to me, and very thankful for my present condition, with all its hardships and misfortunes; and this part also I cannot but recommend to the reflection of those who are apt, in their misery, to say, "Is any affliction like mine?" Let them consider how much worse the cases of some people are, and their case might have been, if Providence had thought fit.

I had another reflection, which assisted me also to comfort my mind with hopes; and this was comparing my present situation with what I had deserved, and had therefore reason to expect from the hand of Providence. I had lived a dreadful life, perfectly destitute of the knowledge and fear of God. I had been well instructed by father and mother; neither had they been wanting to me in their early endeavours to infuse a religious awe of God into my mind, a sense of my duty, and what the nature and end of my being required of me. But, alas! falling early into the seafaring life, which of all lives is the most destitute of the fear of God, though His terrors are always before them; I say, falling early into the seafaring life, and into seafaring company, all that little sense of religion which I had entertained was laughed out of me by my messmates; by a hardened despising of dangers, and the views of death, which grew habitual to me by my long absence from all manner of opportunities to converse with anything but what was like myself, or to hear anything that was good or tended towards it.

So void was I of everything that was good, or the least sense of what I was, or was to be, that, in the greatest deliverances I enjoyed— such as my escape from Sallee; my being taken up by the Portuguese master of the ship; my being planted so well in the Brazils; my receiving the cargo from England, and the like—I never had once the words "Thank God!" so much as on my mind, or in my mouth; nor in the greatest distress had I so much as a thought to pray to Him, or so much as to say, "Lord, have mercy upon me!" no, nor to mention the name of God, unless it was to swear by, and blaspheme it.

I had terrible reflections upon my mind for many months, as I have already observed, on account of my wicked and hardened life past; and when I looked about me, and considered what particular providences had attended me since my coming into this place, and how God had dealt bountifully with me—had not only punished me less than my iniquity had deserved, but had so plentifully provided for me—this gave me great hopes that my repentance was accepted, and that God had yet mercy in store for me.

With these reflections I worked my mind up, not only to a resignation to the will of God in the present disposition of my circumstances, but even to a sincere thankfulness for my condition; and that I, who was yet a living man, ought not to complain, seeing I had not the due punishment of my sins; that I enjoyed so many mercies which I had no reason to have expected in that place; that I ought never more to repine at my condition, but to rejoice, and to give daily thanks for that daily bread, which nothing but a crowd of wonders could have brought; that I ought to consider I had been fed even by a miracle, even as great as that of feeding Elijah by ravens, nay, by a long series of miracles; and that I could hardly have named a place in the uninhabitable part of the world where I could have been cast more to my advantage; a place where, as I had no society, which was my affliction on one hand, so I found no ravenous beasts, no furious wolves or tigers, to threaten my life; no venomous creatures, or poisons, which I might feed on to my hurt; no savages to murder and devour me. In a word, as my life was a life of sorrow one way, so it was a life of mercy another; and I wanted nothing to make it a life of comfort but to be able to make my sense of God's goodness to me, and care over me in this condition, be my daily consolation; and after I did make a just improvement on these things, I went away, and was no more sad. I had now been here so long that many things which I had brought on shore for my help were either quite gone, or very much wasted and near spent.

My ink, as I observed, had been gone some time, all but a very little, which I eked out with water, a little and a little, till it was so pale, it scarce left any appearance of black upon the paper. As long as it lasted I made use of it to minute down the days of the month on which any remarkable thing happened to me; and first, by casting up times past, I remembered that there was a strange concurrence of days in the various providences which befell me, and which, if I had been superstitiously inclined to observe days as fatal or fortunate, I might have had reason to have looked upon with a great deal of curiosity.

First, I had observed that the same day that I broke away from my father and friends and ran away to Hull, in order to go to sea, the same day afterwards I was taken by the Sallee man-of-war, and made a slave; the same day of the year that I escaped out of the wreck of that ship in Yarmouth Roads, that same day-year afterwards I made my escape from Sallee in a boat; the same day of the year I was born on—viz. the 30th of September, that same day I had my life so miraculously saved twenty-six years after, when I was cast on shore in this island; so that my wicked life and my solitary life began both on a day.

The next thing to my ink being wasted was that of my bread—I mean the biscuit which I brought out of the ship; this I had husbanded to the last degree, allowing myself but one cake of bread a-day for above a year; and yet I was quite without bread for near a year before I got any corn of my own, and great reason I had to be thankful that I had any at all, the getting it being, as has been already observed, next to miraculous.

My clothes, too, began to decay; as to linen, I had had none a good while, except some chequered shirts which I found in the chests of the other seamen, and which I carefully preserved; because many times I could bear no other clothes on but a shirt; and it was a very great help to me that I had, among all the men's clothes of the ship, almost three dozen of shirts. There were also, indeed, several thick watch-coats of the seamen's which were left, but they were too hot to wear; and though it is true that the weather was so violently hot that there was no need of clothes, yet I could not go quite naked—no, though I had been inclined to it, which I was not—nor could I abide the thought of it, though I was alone. The reason why I could not go naked was, I could not bear the heat of the sun so well when quite naked as with some clothes on; nay, the very heat frequently blistered my skin: whereas, with a shirt on, the air itself made some motion, and whistling under the shirt, was twofold cooler than without it. No more could I ever bring myself to go out in the heat of the sun without a cap or a hat; the heat of the sun, beating with such violence as it does in that place, would give me the headache presently, by darting so directly on my head, without a cap or hat on, so that I could not bear it; whereas, if I put on my hat it would presently go away.

Upon these views I began to consider about putting the few rags I had, which I called clothes, into some order; I had worn out all the waistcoats I had, and my business was now to try if I could not make jackets out of the great watch-coats which I had by me, and with such other materials as I had; so I set to work, tailoring, or rather, indeed, botching, for I made most piteous work of it. However, I made shift to make two or three new waistcoats, which I hoped would serve me a great while: as for breeches or drawers, I made but a very sorry shift indeed till afterwards.

I have mentioned that I saved the skins of all the creatures that I killed, I mean four-footed ones, and I had them hung up, stretched out with sticks in the sun, by which means some of them were so dry and hard that they were fit for little, but others were very useful. The first thing I made of these was a great cap for my head, with the hair on the outside, to shoot off the rain; and this I performed so well, that after I made me a suit of clothes wholly of these skins—that is to say, a waistcoat, and breeches open at the knees, and both loose, for they were rather wanting to keep me cool than to keep me warm. I must not omit to acknowledge that they were wretchedly made; for if I was a bad carpenter, I was a worse tailor. However, they were such as I made very good shift with, and when I was out, if it happened to rain, the hair of my waistcoat and cap being outermost, I was kept very dry.

After this, I spent a great deal of time and pains to make an umbrella; I was, indeed, in great want of one, and had a great mind to make one; I had seen them made in the Brazils, where they are very useful in the great heats there, and I felt the heats every jot as great here, and greater too, being nearer the equinox; besides, as I was obliged to be much abroad, it was a most useful thing to me, as well for the rains as the heats. I took a world of pains with it, and was a great while before I could make anything likely to hold: nay, after I had thought I had hit the way, I spoiled two or three before I made one to my mind: but at last I made one that answered indifferently well: the main difficulty I found was to make it let down. I could make it spread, but if it did not let down too, and draw in, it was not portable for me any way but just over my head, which would not do. However, at last, as I said, I made one to answer, and covered it with skins, the hair upwards, so that it cast off the rain like a pent-house, and kept off the sun so effectually, that I could walk out in the hottest of the weather with greater advantage than I could before in the coolest, and when I had no need of it could close it, and carry it under my arm.

Thus I lived mighty comfortably, my mind being entirely composed by resigning myself to the will of God, and throwing myself wholly upon the disposal of His providence. This made my life better than sociable, for when I began to regret the want of conversation I would ask myself, whether thus conversing mutually with my own thoughts, and (as I hope I may say) with even God Himself, by ejaculations, was not better than the utmost enjoyment of human society in the world?

CHAPTER X

TAMES GOATS

I cannot say that after this, for five years, any extraordinary thing happened to me, but I lived on in the same course, in the same posture and place, as before; the chief things I was employed in, besides my yearly labour of planting my barley and rice, and curing my raisins, of both which I always kept up just enough to have sufficient stock of one year's provisions beforehand; I say, besides this yearly labour, and my daily pursuit of going out with my gun, I had one labour, to make a canoe, which at last I finished: so that, by digging a canal to it of six feet wide and four feet deep, I brought it into the creek, almost half a mile. As for the first, which was so vastly big, for I made it without considering beforehand, as I ought to have done, how I should be able to launch it, so, never being able to bring it into the water, or bring the water to it, I was obliged to let it lie where it was as a memorandum to teach me to be wiser the next time: indeed, the next time, though I could not get a tree proper for it, and was in a place where I could not get the water to it at any less distance than, as I have said, near half a mile, yet, as I saw it was practicable at last, I never gave it over; and though I was near two years about it, yet I never grudged my labour, in hopes of having a boat to go off to sea at last.

However, though my little periagua was finished, yet the size of it was not at all answerable to the design which I had in view when I made the first; I mean of venturing over to the *terra firma*, where it was above forty miles broad; accordingly, the smallness of my boat assisted to put an end to that design, and now I thought no more of it. As I had a boat, my next design was to make a cruise round the island; for as I had been on the other side in one place, crossing, as I have already described it, over the land, so the discoveries I made in that little journey made me very eager to see other parts of the coast; and now I had a boat, I thought of nothing but sailing round the island.

For this purpose, that I might do everything with discretion and consideration, I fitted up a little mast in my boat, and made a sail too out of some of the pieces of the ship's sails which lay in store, and of which I had a great stock by me. Having fitted my mast and sail, and tried the boat, I found she would sail very well; then I made little lockers or boxes at each end of my boat, to put provisions, necessaries, ammunition, &c., into, to be kept dry, either from rain or the spray of the sea; and a little, long, hollow place I cut in the inside of the boat, where I could lay my gun, making a flap to hang down over it to keep it dry.

I fixed my umbrella also in the step at the stern, like a mast, to stand over my head, and keep the heat of the sun off me, like an awning; and thus I every now and then took a little voyage upon the sea, but never went far out, nor far from the little creek. At last, being eager to view the circumference of my little kingdom, I resolved upon my cruise; and accordingly I victualled my ship for the voyage, putting in two dozen of loaves (cakes I should call them) of barley-bread, an earthen pot full of parched rice (a food I ate a good deal of), a little bottle of rum, half a goat, and powder and shot for killing more, and two large watch-coats, of those which, as I mentioned before, I had saved out of the seamen's chests; these I took, one to lie upon, and the other to cover me in the night.

It was the 6th of November, in the sixth year of my reign—or my captivity, which you please—that I set out on this voyage, and I found it much longer than I expected; for though the island itself was not very large, yet when I came to the east side of it, I found a great ledge of rocks lie out about two leagues into the sea, some above water, some under it; and beyond that a shoal of sand, lying dry half a league more, so that I was obliged to go a great way out to sea to double the point.

When I first discovered them, I was going to give over my enterprise, and come back again, not knowing how far it might oblige me to go out to sea; and above all, doubting how I should get back again: so I came to an anchor; for I had made a kind of an anchor with a piece of a broken grappling which I got out of the ship.

Having secured my boat, I took my gun and went on shore, climbing up a hill, which seemed to overlook that point where I saw the full extent of it, and resolved to venture.

In my viewing the sea from that hill where I stood, I perceived a strong, and indeed a most furious current, which ran to the east, and even came close to the point; and I took the more notice of it because I saw there might be some danger that when I came into it I might be carried out to sea by the strength of it, and not be able to make the island again; and indeed, had I not got first upon this hill, I believe it would have been so; for there was the same current on the other side the island, only that it set off at a further distance, and I saw there was a strong eddy under the shore; so I had nothing to do but to get out of the first current, and I should presently be in an eddy.

I lay here, however, two days, because the wind blowing pretty fresh at ESE., and that being just contrary to the current, made a great breach of the sea upon the point: so that it was not safe for me to keep too close to the shore for the breach, nor to go too far off, because of the stream.

The third day, in the morning, the wind having abated overnight, the sea was calm, and I ventured: but I am a warning to all rash and ignorant pilots; for no sooner was I come to the point, when I was not even my boat's length from the shore, but I found myself in a great depth of water, and a current like the sluice of a mill; it carried my boat along with it with such violence that all I could do could not keep her so much as on the edge of it; but I found it hurried me farther and farther out from the eddy, which was on my left hand. There was no wind stirring to help me, and all I could do with my paddles signified nothing: and now I began to give myself over for lost; for as the current was on both sides of the island, I knew in a few leagues distance they must join again, and then I was irrecoverably gone; nor did I see any possibility of avoiding it; so that I had no prospect before me but of perishing, not by the sea, for that was calm enough, but of starving from hunger. I had, indeed, found a tortoise on the shore, as big almost as I could lift, and had tossed it into the boat; and I had a great jar of fresh water, that is to say, one of my earthen pots; but what was all this to being driven into the vast ocean, where, to be sure, there was no shore, no mainland or island, for a thousand leagues at least?

And now I saw how easy it was for the providence of God to make even the most miserable condition of mankind worse. Now I looked back upon my desolate, solitary island as the most pleasant place in the world and all the happiness my heart could wish for was to be but there again. I stretched out my hands to it, with eager wishes—"O happy desert!" said I, "I shall never see thee more. O miserable creature! whither am going?" Then I reproached myself with my unthankful temper, and that I had repined at my solitary condition; and now what would I give to be on shore there again! Thus, we never see the true state of our condition till it is illustrated to us by its contraries, nor know how to value what we enjoy, but by the want of it. It is scarcely possible to imagine the consternation I was now in, being driven from my beloved island (for so it appeared to me now to be) into the wide ocean, almost two leagues, and in the utmost despair of ever recovering it again. However, I worked hard till, indeed, my strength was almost exhausted, and kept my boat as much to the northward, that is, towards the side of the current which the eddy lay on, as possibly I could; when about noon, as the sun passed the meridian, I thought I felt a little breeze of wind in my face, springing up from SSE. This cheered my heart a little, and especially when, in about half-an-hour more, it blew a pretty gentle gale. By this time I had got at a frightful distance from the island, and had the least cloudy or hazy weather intervened, I had been undone another way, too; for I had no compass on board, and should never have known how to have steered towards the island, if I had but once lost sight of it; but the weather continuing clear, I applied myself to get up my mast again, and spread my sail, standing away to the north as much as possible, to get out of the current.

Just as I had set my mast and sail, and the boat began to stretch away, I saw even by the clearness of the water some alteration of the current was near; for where the current was so strong the water was foul; but perceiving the water clear, I found the current abate; and presently I found to the east, at about half a mile, a breach of the sea upon some rocks: these rocks I found caused the current to part again, and as the main stress of it ran away more southerly, leaving the rocks to the north-east, so the other returned by the repulse of the rocks, and made a strong eddy, which ran back again to the north-west, with a very sharp stream.

They who know what it is to have a reprieve brought to them upon the ladder, or to be rescued from thieves just going to murder them, or who have been in such extremities, may guess what my present surprise of joy was, and how gladly I put my boat into the stream of this eddy; and the wind also freshening, how gladly I spread my sail to it, running cheerfully before the wind, and with a strong tide or eddy underfoot.

This eddy carried me about a league on my way back again, directly towards the island, but about two leagues more to the northward than the current which carried me away at first; so that when I came near the island, I found myself open to the northern shore of it, that is to say, the other end of the island, opposite to that which I went out from.

When I had made something more than a league of way by the help of this current or eddy, I found it was spent, and served me no further. However, I found that being between two great currents—viz. that on the south side, which had hurried me away, and that on the north, which lay about a league on the other side; I say, between these two, in the wake of the island, I found the water at least still, and running no way; and having still a breeze of wind fair for me, I kept on steering directly for the island, though not making such fresh way as I did before.

About four o'clock in the evening, being then within a league of the island, I found the point of the rocks which occasioned this disaster stretching out, as is described before, to the southward, and casting off the current more southerly, had, of course, made another eddy to the north; and this I found very strong, but not directly setting the way my course lay, which was due west, but almost full north. However, having a fresh gale, I stretched across this eddy, slanting north-west; and in about an hour came within about a mile of the shore, where, it being smooth water, I soon got to land.

When I was on shore, God I fell on my knees and gave God thanks for my deliverance, resolving to lay aside all thoughts of my deliverance by my boat; and refreshing myself with such things as I had, I brought my boat close to the shore, in a little cove that I had spied under some trees, and laid me down to sleep, being quite spent with the labour and fatigue of the voyage.

I was now at a great loss which way to get home with my boat! I had run so much hazard, and knew too much of the case, to think of attempting it by the way I went out; and what might be at the other side (I mean the west side) I knew not, nor had I any mind to run any more ventures; so I resolved on the next morning to make my way westward along the shore, and to see if there was no creek where I might lay up my frigate in safety, so as to have her again if I wanted her. In about three miles or thereabouts, coasting the shore, I came to a very good inlet or bay, about a mile over, which narrowed till it came to a very little rivulet or brook, where I found a very convenient harbour for my boat, and where she lay as if she had been in a little dock made on purpose for her. Here I put in, and having stowed my boat very safe, I went on shore to look about me, and see where I was.

I soon found I had but a little passed by the place where I had been before, when I travelled on foot to that shore; so taking nothing out of my boat but my gun and umbrella, for it was exceedingly hot, I began my march. The way was comfortable enough after such a voyage as I had been upon, and I reached my old bower in the evening, where I found everything standing as I left it; for I always kept it in good order, being, as I said before, my country house.

I got over the fence, and laid me down in the shade to rest my limbs, for I was very weary, and fell asleep; but judge you, if you can, that read my story, what a surprise I must be in when I was awaked out of my sleep by a voice calling me by my name several times, "Robin, Robin, Robin Crusoe: poor Robin Crusoe! Where are you, Robin Crusoe? Where are you? Where have you been?"

I was so dead asleep at first, being fatigued with rowing, or part of the day, and with walking the latter part, that I did not wake thoroughly; but dozing thought I dreamed that somebody spoke to me; but as the voice continued to repeat, "Robin Crusoe, Robin Crusoe," at last I began to wake more perfectly, and was at first dreadfully frightened, and started up in the utmost consternation; but no sooner were my eyes open, but I saw my Poll sitting on the top of the hedge; and immediately knew that it was he that spoke to me; for just in such bemoaning language I had used to talk to him and teach him; and he had learned it so perfectly that he would sit upon my finger, and lay his bill close to my face and cry, "Poor Robin Crusoe! Where are you? Where have you been? How came you here?" and such things as I had taught him.

However, even though I knew it was the parrot, and that indeed it could be nobody else, it was a good while before I could compose myself. First, I was amazed how the creature got thither; and then, how he should just keep about the place, and nowhere else; but as I was well satisfied it could be nobody but honest Poll, I got over it; and holding out my hand, and calling him by his name, "Poll," the sociable creature came to me, and sat upon my thumb, as he used to do, and continued talking to me, "Poor Robin Crusoe! and how did I come here? and where had I been?" just as if he had been overjoyed to see me again; and so I carried him home along with me.

I had now had enough of rambling to sea for some time, and had enough to do for many days to sit still and reflect upon the danger I had been in. I would have been very glad to have had my boat again on my side of the island; but I knew not how it was practicable to get it about. As to the east side of the island, which I had gone round, I knew well enough there was no venturing that way; my very heart would shrink, and my very blood run chill, but to think of it; and as to the other side of the island, I did not know how it might be there; but supposing the current ran with the same force against the shore at the east as it passed by it on the other, I might run the same risk of being driven down the stream, and carried by the island, as I had been before of being carried away from it: so with these thoughts, I contented myself to be without any boat, though it had been the product of so many months' labour to make it, and of so many more to get it into the sea.

In this government of my temper I remained near a year; and lived a very sedate, retired life, as you may well suppose; and my thoughts being very much composed as to my condition, and fully comforted in resigning myself to the dispositions of Providence, I thought I lived really very happily in all things except that of society.

I improved myself in this time in all the mechanic exercises which my necessities put me upon applying myself to; and I believe I should, upon occasion, have made a very good carpenter, especially considering how few tools I had.

Besides this, I arrived at an unexpected perfection in my earthenware, and contrived well enough to make them with a wheel, which I found infinitely easier and better; because I made things round and shaped, which before were filthy things indeed to look on. But I think I was never more vain of my own performance, or more joyful for anything I found out, than for my being able to make a tobacco-pipe; and though it was a very ugly, clumsy thing when it was done, and only burned red, like other earthenware, yet as it was hard and firm, and would draw the smoke, I was exceedingly comforted with it, for I had been always used to smoke; and there were pipes in the ship, but I forgot them at first, not thinking there was tobacco in the island; and afterwards, when I searched the ship again, I could not come at any pipes.

In my wicker-ware also I improved much, and made abundance of necessary baskets, as well as my invention showed me; though not very handsome, yet they were such as were very handy and convenient for laying things up in, or fetching things home. For example, if I killed a goat abroad, I could hang it up in a tree, flay it, dress it, and cut it in pieces, and bring it home in a basket; and the like by a turtle; I could cut it up, take out the eggs and a piece or two of the flesh, which was enough for me, and bring them home in a basket, and leave the rest behind me. Also, large deep baskets were the receivers of my corn, which I always rubbed out as soon as it was dry and cured, and kept it in great baskets.

I began now to perceive my powder abated considerably; this was a want which it was impossible for me to supply, and I began seriously to consider what I must do when I should have no more powder; that is to say, how I should kill any goats. I had, as is observed in the third year of my being here, kept a young kid, and bred her up tame, and I was in hopes of getting a he-goat; but I could not by any means bring it to pass, till my kid grew an old goat; and as I could never find in my heart to kill her, she died at last of mere age.

But being now in the eleventh year of my residence, and, as I have said, my ammunition growing low, I set myself to study some art to trap and snare the goats, to see whether I could not catch some of them alive; and particularly I wanted a she-goat great with young. For this purpose I made snares to hamper them; and I do believe they were more than once taken in them; but my tackle was not good, for I had no wire, and I always found them broken and my bait devoured. At length I resolved to try a pitfall; so I dug several large pits in the earth, in places where I had observed the goats used to feed, and over those pits I placed hurdles of my own making too, with a great weight upon them; and several times I put ears of barley and dry rice without setting the trap; and I could easily perceive that the goats had gone in and eaten up the corn, for I could see the marks of their feet. At length I set three traps in one night, and going the next morning I found them, all standing, and yet the bait eaten and gone; this was very discouraging. However, I altered my traps; and not to trouble you with particulars, going one morning to see my traps, I found in one of them a large old he-goat; and in one of the others three kids, a male and two females.

As to the old one, I knew not what to do with him; he was so fierce I durst not go into the pit to him; that is to say, to bring him away alive, which was what I wanted. I could have killed him, but that was not my business, nor would it answer my end; so I even let him out, and he ran away as if he had been frightened out of his wits. But I did not then know what I afterwards learned, that hunger will tame a lion. If I had let him stay three or four days without food, and then have carried him some water to drink and then a little corn, he would have been as tame as one of the kids; for they are mighty sagacious, tractable creatures, where they are well used.

However, for the present I let him go, knowing no better at that time: then I went to the three kids, and taking them one by one, I tied them with strings together, and with some difficulty brought them all home.

It was a good while before they would feed; but throwing them some sweet corn, it tempted them, and they began to be tame. And now I found that if I expected to supply myself with goats' flesh, when I had no powder or shot left, breeding some up tame was my only way, when, perhaps, I might have them about my house like a flock of sheep. But then it occurred to me that I must keep the tame from the wild, or else they would always run wild when they grew up; and the only way for this was to have some enclosed piece of ground, well fenced either with hedge or pale, to keep them in so effectually, that those within might not break out, or those without break in.

This was a great undertaking for one pair of hands yet, as I saw there was an absolute necessity for doing it, my first work was to find out a proper piece of ground, where there was likely to be herbage for them to eat, water for them to drink, and cover to keep them from the sun.

Those who understand such enclosures will think I had very little contrivance when I pitched upon a place very proper for all these (being a plain, open piece of meadow land, or savannah, as our people call it in the western colonies), which had two or three little drills of fresh water in it, and at one end was very woody—I say, they will smile at my forecast, when I shall tell them I began by enclosing this piece of ground in such a manner that, my hedge or pale must have been at least two miles about. Nor was the madness of it so great as to the compass, for if it was ten miles about, I was like to have time enough to do it in; but I did not consider that my goats would be as wild in so much compass as if they had had the whole island, and I should have so much room to chase them in that I should never catch them.

My hedge was begun and carried on, I believe, about fifty yards when this thought occurred to me; so I presently stopped short, and, for the beginning, I resolved to enclose a piece of about one hundred and fifty yards in length, and one hundred yards in breadth, which, as it would maintain as many as I should have in any reasonable time, so, as my stock increased, I could add more ground to my enclosure.

This was acting with some prudence, and I went to work with courage. I was about three months hedging in the first piece; and, till I had done it, I tethered the three kids in the best part of it, and used them to feed as near me as possible, to make them familiar; and very often I would go and carry them some ears of barley, or a handful of rice, and feed them out of my hand; so that after my enclosure was finished and I let them loose, they would follow me up and down, bleating after me for a handful of corn.

This answered my end, and in about a year and a half I had a flock of about twelve goats, kids and all; and in two years more I had three-and-forty, besides several that I took and killed for my food. After that, I enclosed five several pieces of ground to feed them in, with little pens to drive them to take them as I wanted, and gates out of one piece of ground into another.

But this was not all; for now I not only had goat's flesh to feed on when I pleased, but milk too—a thing which, indeed, in the beginning, I did not so much as think of, and which, when it came into my thoughts, was really an agreeable surprise, for now I set up my dairy, and had sometimes a gallon or two of milk in a day. And as Nature, who gives supplies of food to every creature, dictates even naturally how to make use of it, so I, that had never milked a cow, much less a goat, or seen butter or cheese made only when I was a boy, after a great many essays and miscarriages, made both butter and cheese at last, also salt (though I found it partly made to my hand by the heat of the sun upon some of the rocks of the sea), and never wanted it afterwards. How mercifully can our Creator treat His creatures, even in those conditions in which they seemed to be overwhelmed in destruction! How can He sweeten the bitterest providences, and give us cause to praise Him for dungeons and prisons! What a table was here spread for me in the wilderness, where I saw nothing at first but to perish for hunger!

CHAPTER XI

FINDS PRINT OF MAN'S FOOT ON THE SAND

It would have made a Stoic smile to have seen me and my little family sit down to dinner. There was my majesty the prince and lord of the whole island; I had the lives of all my subjects at my absolute command; I could hang, draw, give liberty, and take it away, and no rebels among all my subjects. Then, to see how like a king I dined, too, all alone, attended by my servants! Poll, as if he had been my favourite, was the only person permitted to talk to me. My dog, who was now grown old and crazy, and had found no species to multiply his kind upon, sat always at my right hand; and two cats, one on one side of the table and one on the other, expecting now and then a bit from my hand, as a mark of especial favour.

But these were not the two cats which I brought on shore at first, for they were both of them dead, and had been interred near my habitation by my own hand; but one of them having multiplied by I know not what kind of creature, these were two which I had preserved tame; whereas the rest ran wild in the woods, and became indeed troublesome to me at last, for they would often come into my house, and plunder me too, till at last I was obliged to shoot them, and did kill a great many; at length they left me. With this attendance and in this plentiful manner I lived; neither could I be said to want anything but society; and of that, some time after this, I was likely to have too much.

I was something impatient, as I have observed, to have the use of my boat, though very loath to run any more hazards; and therefore sometimes I sat contriving ways to get her about the island, and at other times I sat myself down contented enough without her. But I had a strange uneasiness in my mind to go down to the point of the island where, as I have said in my last ramble, I went up the hill to see how the shore lay, and how the current set, that I might see what I had to do: this inclination increased upon me every day, and at length I resolved to travel thither by land, following the edge of the shore. I did so; but had any one in England met such a man as I was, it must either have frightened him, or raised a great deal of laughter; and as I frequently stood still to look at myself, I could not but smile at the notion of my travelling through Yorkshire with such an equipage, and in such a dress. Be pleased to take a sketch of my figure, as follows.

I had a great high shapeless cap, made of a goat's skin, with a flap hanging down behind, as well to keep the sun from me as to shoot the rain off from running into my neck, nothing being so hurtful in these climates as the rain upon the flesh under the clothes.

I had a short jacket of goat's skin, the skirts coming down to about the middle of the thighs, and a pair of open-kneed breeches of the same; the breeches were made of the skin of an old he-goat, whose hair hung down such a length on either side that, like pantaloons, it reached to the middle of my legs; stockings and shoes I had none, but had made me a pair of somethings, I scarce knew what to call them, like buskins, to flap over my legs, and lace on either side like spatterdashes, but of a most barbarous shape, as indeed were all the rest of my clothes.

I had on a broad belt of goat's skin dried, which I drew together with two thongs of the same instead of buckles, and in a kind of a frog on either side of this, instead of a sword and dagger, hung a little saw and a hatchet, one on one side and one on the other. I had another belt not so broad, and fastened in the same manner, which hung over my shoulder, and at the end of it, under my left arm, hung two pouches, both made of goat's skin too, in one of which hung my powder, in the other my shot. At my back I carried my basket, and on my shoulder my gun, and over my head a great clumsy, ugly, goat's-skin umbrella, but which, after all, was the most necessary thing I had about me next to my gun. As for my face, the colour of it was really not so mulatto-like as one might expect from a man not at all careful of it, and living within nine or ten degrees of the equinox. My beard I had once suffered to grow till it was about a quarter of a yard long; but as I had both scissors and razors sufficient, I had cut it pretty short, except what grew on my upper lip, which I had trimmed into a large pair of Mahometan whiskers, such as I had seen worn by some Turks at Sallee, for the Moors did not wear such, though the Turks did; of these moustachios, or whiskers, I will not say they were long enough to hang my hat upon them, but they were of a length and shape monstrous enough, and such as in England would have passed for frightful.

But all this is by-the-bye; for as to my figure, I had so few to observe me that it was of no manner of consequence, so I say no more of that. In this kind of dress I went my new journey, and was out five or six days. I travelled first along the sea-shore, directly to the place where I first brought my boat to an anchor to get upon the rocks; and having no boat now to take care of, I went over the land a nearer way to the same height that I was upon before, when, looking forward to the points of the rocks which lay out, and which I was obliged to double with my boat, as is said above, I was surprised to see the sea all smooth and quiet—no rippling, no motion, no current, any more there than in other places. I was at a strange loss to understand this, and resolved to spend some time in the observing it, to see if nothing from the sets of the tide had occasioned it; but I was presently convinced how it was— viz. that the tide of ebb setting from the west, and joining with the current of waters from some great river on the shore, must be the occasion of this current, and that, according as the wind blew more forcibly from the west or from the north, this current came nearer or went farther from the shore; for, waiting thereabouts till evening, I went up to the rock again, and then the tide of ebb being made, I plainly saw the current again as before, only that it ran farther off, being near half a league from the shore, whereas in my case it set close upon the shore, and hurried me and my canoe along with it, which at another time it would not have done.

This observation convinced me that I had nothing to do but to observe the ebbing and the flowing of the tide, and I might very easily bring my boat about the island again; but when I began to think of putting it in practice, I had such terror upon my spirits at the remembrance of the danger I had been in, that I could not think of it again with any patience, but, on the contrary, I took up another resolution, which was more safe, though more laborious—and this was, that I would build, or rather make, me another periagua or canoe, and so have one for one side of the island, and one for the other.

You are to understand that now I had, as I may call it, two plantations in the island—one my little fortification or tent, with the wall about it, under the rock, with the cave behind me, which by this time I had enlarged into several apartments or caves, one within another. One of these, which was the driest and largest, and had a door out beyond my wall or fortification—that is to say, beyond where my wall joined to the rock—was all filled up with the large earthen pots of which I have given an account, and with fourteen or fifteen great baskets, which would hold five or six bushels each, where I laid up my stores of provisions, especially my corn, some in the ear, cut off short from the straw, and the other rubbed out with my hand.

As for my wall, made, as before, with long stakes or piles, those piles grew all like trees, and were by this time grown so big, and spread so very much, that there was not the least appearance, to any one's view, of any habitation behind them.

Near this dwelling of mine, but a little farther within the land, and upon lower ground, lay my two pieces of corn land, which I kept duly cultivated and sowed, and which duly yielded me their harvest in its season; and whenever I had occasion for more corn, I had more land adjoining as fit as that.

Besides this, I had my country seat, and I had now a tolerable plantation there also; for, first, I had my little bower, as I called it, which I kept in repair—that is to say, I kept the hedge which encircled it in constantly fitted up to its usual height, the ladder standing always in the inside. I kept the trees, which at first were no more than stakes, but were now grown very firm and tall, always cut, so that they might spread and grow thick and wild, and make the more agreeable shade, which they did effectually to my mind. In the middle of this I had my tent always standing, being a piece of a sail spread over poles, set up for that purpose, and which never wanted any repair or renewing; and under this I had made me a squab or couch with the skins of the creatures I had killed, and with other soft things, and a blanket laid on them, such as belonged to our sea-bedding, which I had saved; and a great watch-coat to cover me. And here, whenever I had occasion to be absent from my chief seat, I took up my country habitation.

Adjoining to this I had my enclosures for my cattle, that is to say my goats, and I had taken an inconceivable deal of pains to fence and enclose this ground. I was so anxious to see it kept entire, lest the goats should break through, that I never left off till, with infinite labour, I had stuck the outside of the hedge so full of small stakes, and so near to one another, that it was rather a pale than a hedge, and there was scarce room to put a hand through between them; which afterwards, when those stakes grew, as they all did in the next rainy season, made the enclosure strong like a wall, indeed stronger than any wall.

This will testify for me that I was not idle, and that I spared no pains to bring to pass whatever appeared necessary for my comfortable support, for I considered the keeping up a breed of tame creatures thus at my hand would be a living magazine of flesh, milk, butter, and cheese for me as long as I lived in the place, if it were to be forty years; and that keeping them in my reach depended entirely upon my perfecting my enclosures to such a degree that I might be sure of keeping them together; which by this method, indeed, I so effectually secured, that when these little stakes began to grow, I had planted them so very thick that I was forced to pull some of them up again.

In this place also I had my grapes growing, which I principally depended on for my winter store of raisins, and which I never failed to preserve very carefully, as the best and most agreeable dainty of my whole diet; and indeed they were not only agreeable, but medicinal, wholesome, nourishing, and refreshing to the last degree.

As this was also about half-way between my other habitation and the place where I had laid up my boat, I generally stayed and lay here in my way thither, for I used frequently to visit my boat; and I kept all things about or belonging to her in very good order. Sometimes I went out in her to divert myself, but no more hazardous voyages would I go, scarcely ever above a stone's cast or two from the shore, I was so apprehensive of being hurried out of my knowledge again by the currents or winds, or any other accident. But now I come to a new scene of my life. It happened one day, about noon, going towards my boat, I was exceedingly surprised with the print of a man's naked foot on the shore, which was very plain to be seen on the sand. I stood like one thunderstruck, or as if I had seen an apparition. I listened, I looked round me, but I could hear nothing, nor see anything; I went up to a rising ground to look farther; I went up the shore and down the shore, but it was all one; I could see no other impression but that one. I went to it again to see if there were any more, and to observe if it might not be my fancy; but there was no room for that, for there was exactly the print of a foot—toes, heel, and every part of a foot. How it came thither I knew not, nor could I in the least imagine; but after innumerable fluttering thoughts, like a man perfectly confused and out of myself, I came home to my fortification, not feeling, as we say, the ground I went on, but terrified to the last degree, looking behind me at every two or three steps, mistaking every bush and tree, and fancying every stump at a distance to be a man. Nor is it possible to describe how many various shapes my affrighted imagination represented things to me in, how many wild ideas were found every moment in my fancy, and what strange, unaccountable whimsies came into my thoughts by the way.

When I came to my castle (for so I think I called it ever after this), I fled into it like one pursued. Whether I went over by the ladder, as first contrived, or went in at the hole in the rock, which I had called a door, I cannot remember; no, nor could I remember the next morning, for never frightened hare fled to cover, or fox to earth, with more terror of mind than I to this retreat.

I slept none that night; the farther I was from the occasion of my fright, the greater my apprehensions were, which is something contrary to the nature of such things, and especially to the usual practice of all creatures in fear; but I was so embarrassed with my own frightful ideas of the thing, that I formed nothing but dismal imaginations to myself, even though I was now a great way off. Sometimes I fancied it must be the devil, and reason joined in with me in this supposition, for how should any other thing in human shape come into the place? Where was the vessel that brought them? What marks were there of any other footstep? And how was it possible a man should come there? But then, to think that Satan should take human shape upon him in such a place, where there could be no manner of occasion for it, but to leave the print of his foot behind him, and that even for no purpose too, for he could not be sure I should see it—this was an amusement the other way. I considered that the devil might have found out abundance of other ways to have terrified me than this of the single print of a foot; that as I lived quite on the other side of the island, he would never have been so simple as to leave a mark in a place where it was ten thousand to one whether I should ever see it or not, and in the sand too, which the first surge of the sea, upon a high wind, would have defaced entirely. All this seemed inconsistent with the thing itself and with all the notions we usually entertain of the subtlety of the devil.

Abundance of such things as these assisted to argue me out of all apprehensions of its being the devil; and I presently concluded then that it must be some more dangerous creature—viz. that it must be some of the savages of the mainland opposite who had wandered out to sea in their canoes, and either driven by the currents or by contrary winds, had made the island, and had been on shore, but were gone away again to sea; being as loath, perhaps, to have stayed in this desolate island as I would have been to have had them.

While these reflections were rolling in my mind, I was very thankful in my thoughts that I was so happy as not to be thereabouts at that time, or that they did not see my boat, by which they would have concluded that some inhabitants had been in the place, and perhaps have searched farther for me. Then terrible thoughts racked my imagination about their having found out my boat, and that there were people here; and that, if so, I should certainly have them come again in greater numbers and devour me; that if it should happen that they should not find me, yet they would find my enclosure, destroy all my corn, and carry away all my flock of tame goats, and I should perish at last for mere want.

Thus my fear banished all my religious hope, all that former confidence in God, which was founded upon such wonderful experience as I had had of His goodness; as if He that had fed me by miracle hitherto could not preserve, by His power, the provision which He had made for me by His goodness. I reproached myself with my laziness, that would not sow any more corn one year than would just serve me till the next season, as if no accident could intervene to prevent my enjoying the crop that was upon the ground; and this I thought so just a reproof, that I resolved for the future to have two or three years' corn beforehand; so that, whatever might come, I might not perish for want of bread.

How strange a chequer-work of Providence is the life of man! and by what secret different springs are the affections hurried about, as different circumstances present! To-day we love what to-morrow we hate; to-day we seek what to-morrow we shun; to-day we desire what to-morrow we fear, nay, even tremble at the apprehensions of. This was exemplified in me, at this time, in the most lively manner imaginable; for I, whose only affliction was that I seemed banished from human society, that I was alone, circumscribed by the boundless ocean, cut off from mankind, and condemned to what I call silent life; that I was as one whom Heaven thought not worthy to be numbered among the living, or to appear among the rest of His creatures; that to have seen one of my own species would have seemed to me a raising me from death to life, and the greatest blessing that Heaven itself, next to the supreme blessing of salvation, could bestow; I say, that I should now tremble at the very apprehensions of seeing a man, and was ready to sink into the ground at but the shadow or silent appearance of a man having set his foot in the island.

Such is the uneven state of human life; and it afforded me a great many curious speculations afterwards, when I had a little recovered my first surprise. I considered that this was the station of life the infinitely wise and good providence of God had determined for me; that as I could not foresee what the ends of Divine wisdom might be in all this, so I was not to dispute His sovereignty; who, as I was His creature, had an undoubted right, by creation, to govern and dispose of me absolutely as He thought fit; and who, as I was a creature that had offended Him, had likewise a judicial right to condemn me to what punishment He thought fit; and that it was my part to submit to bear His indignation, because I had sinned against Him. I then reflected, that as God, who was not only righteous but omnipotent, had thought fit thus to punish and afflict me, so He was able to deliver me: that if He did not think fit to do so, it was my unquestioned duty to resign myself absolutely and entirely to His will; and, on the other hand, it was my duty also to hope in Him, pray to Him, and quietly to attend to the dictates and directions of His daily providence.

These thoughts took me up many hours, days, nay, I may say weeks and months: and one particular effect of my cogitations on this occasion I cannot omit. One morning early, lying in my bed, and filled with thoughts about my danger from the appearances of savages, I found it discomposed me very much; upon which these words of the Scripture came into my thoughts, "Call upon Me in the day of trouble, and I will deliver thee, and thou shalt glorify Me." Upon this, rising cheerfully out of my bed, my heart was not only comforted, but I was guided and encouraged to pray earnestly to God for deliverance: when I had done praying I took up my Bible, and opening it to read, the first words that presented to me were, "Wait on the Lord, and be of good cheer, and He shall strengthen thy heart; wait, I say, on the Lord." It is impossible to express the comfort this gave me. In answer, I thankfully laid down the book, and was no more sad, at least on that occasion.

In the middle of these cogitations, apprehensions, and reflections, it came into my thoughts one day that all this might be a mere chimera of my own, and that this foot might be the print of my own foot, when I came on shore from my boat: this cheered me up a little, too, and I began to persuade myself it was all a delusion; that it was nothing else but my own foot; and why might I not come that way from the boat, as well as I was going that way to the boat? Again, I considered also that I could by no means tell for certain where I had trod, and where I had not; and that if, at last, this was only the print of my own foot, I had played the part of those fools who try to make stories of spectres and apparitions, and then are frightened at them more than anybody.

Now I began to take courage, and to peep abroad again, for I had not stirred out of my castle for three days and nights, so that I began to starve for provisions; for I had little or nothing within doors but some barley-cakes and water; then I knew that my goats wanted to be milked too, which usually was my evening diversion: and the poor creatures were in great pain and inconvenience for want of it; and, indeed, it almost spoiled some of them, and almost dried up their milk. Encouraging myself, therefore, with the belief that this was nothing but the print of one of my own feet, and that I might be truly said to start at my own shadow, I began to go abroad again, and went to my country house to milk my flock: but to see with what fear I went forward, how often I looked behind me, how I was ready every now and then to lay down my basket and run for my life, it would have made any one have thought I was haunted with an evil conscience, or that I had been lately most terribly frightened; and so, indeed, I had. However, I went down thus two or three days, and having seen nothing, I began to be a little bolder, and to think there was really nothing in it but my own imagination; but I could not persuade myself fully of this till I should go down to the shore again, and see this print of a foot, and measure it by my own, and see if there was any similitude or fitness, that I might be assured it was my own foot: but when I came to the place, first, it appeared evidently to me, that when I laid up my boat I could not possibly be on shore anywhere thereabouts; secondly, when I came to measure the mark with my own foot, I found my foot not so large by a great deal. Both these things filled my head with new imaginations, and gave me the vapours again to the highest degree, so that I shook with cold like one in an ague; and I went home again, filled with the belief that some man or men had been on shore there; or, in short, that the island was inhabited, and I might be surprised before I was aware; and what course to take for my security I knew not.

Oh, what ridiculous resolutions men take when possessed with fear! It deprives them of the use of those means which reason offers for their relief. The first thing I proposed to myself was, to throw down my enclosures, and turn all my tame cattle wild into the woods, lest the enemy should find them, and then frequent the island in prospect of the same or the like booty: then the simple thing of digging up my two corn-fields, lest they should find such a grain there, and still be prompted to frequent the island: then to demolish my bower and tent, that they might not see any vestiges of habitation, and be prompted to look farther, in order to find out the persons inhabiting.

These were the subject of the first night's cogitations after I was come home again, while the apprehensions which had so overrun my mind were fresh upon me, and my head was full of vapours. Thus, fear of danger is ten thousand times more terrifying than danger itself, when apparent to the eyes; and we find the burden of anxiety greater, by much, than the evil which we are anxious about: and what was worse than all this, I had not that relief in this trouble that from the resignation I used to practise I hoped to have. I looked, I thought, like

Saul, who complained not only that the Philistines were upon him, but that God had forsaken him; for I did not now take due ways to compose my mind, by crying to God in my distress, and resting upon His providence, as I had done before, for my defence and deliverance; which, if I had done, I had at least been more cheerfully supported under this new surprise, and perhaps carried through it with more resolution.

This confusion of my thoughts kept me awake all night; but in the morning I fell asleep; and having, by the amusement of my mind, been as it were tired, and my spirits exhausted, I slept very soundly, and waked much better composed than I had ever been before. And now I began to think sedately; and, upon debate with myself, I concluded that this island (which was so exceedingly pleasant, fruitful, and no farther from the mainland than as I had seen) was not so entirely abandoned as I might imagine; that although there were no stated inhabitants who lived on the spot, yet that there might sometimes come boats off from the shore, who, either with design, or perhaps never but when they were driven by cross winds, might come to this place; that I had lived there fifteen years now and had not met with the least shadow or figure of any people yet; and that, if at any time they should be driven here, it was probable they went away again as soon as ever they could, seeing they had never thought fit to fix here upon any occasion; that the most I could suggest any danger from was from any casual accidental landing of straggling people from the main, who, as it was likely, if they were driven hither, were here against their wills, so they made no stay here, but went off again with all possible speed; seldom staying one night on shore, lest they should not have the help of the tides and daylight back again; and that, therefore, I had nothing to do but to consider of some safe retreat, in case I should see any savages land upon the spot.

Now, I began sorely to repent that I had dug my cave so large as to bring a door through again, which door, as I said, came out beyond where my fortification joined to the rock: upon maturely considering this, therefore, I resolved to draw me a second fortification, in the manner of a semicircle, at a distance from my wall, just where I had planted a double row of trees about twelve years before, of which I made mention: these trees having been planted so thick before, they wanted but few piles to be driven between them, that they might be thicker and stronger, and my wall would be soon finished. So that I had now a double wall; and my outer wall was thickened with pieces of timber, old cables, and everything I could think of, to make it strong;

having in it seven little holes, about as big as I might put my arm out at. In the inside of this I thickened my wall to about ten feet thick with continually bringing earth out of my cave, and laying it at the foot of the wall, and walking upon it; and through the seven holes I contrived to plant the muskets, of which I took notice that I had got seven on shore out of the ship; these I planted like my cannon, and fitted them into frames, that held them like a carriage, so that I could fire all the seven guns in two minutes' time; this wall I was many a weary month in finishing, and yet never thought myself safe till it was done.

When this was done I stuck all the ground without my wall, for a great length every way, as full with stakes or sticks of the osier-like wood, which I found so apt to grow, as they could well stand; insomuch that I believe I might set in near twenty thousand of them, leaving a pretty large space between them and my wall, that I might have room to see an enemy, and they might have no shelter from the young trees, if they attempted to approach my outer wall.

Thus in two years' time I had a thick grove; and in five or six years' time I had a wood before my dwelling, growing so monstrously thick and strong that it was indeed perfectly impassable: and no men, of what kind soever, could ever imagine that there was anything beyond it, much less a habitation. As for the way which I proposed to myself to go in and out (for I left no avenue), it was by setting two ladders, one to a part of the rock which was low, and then broke in, and left room to place another ladder upon that; so when the two ladders were taken down no man living could come down to me without doing himself mischief; and if they had come down, they were still on the outside of my outer wall.

Thus I took all the measures human prudence could suggest for my own preservation; and it will be seen at length that they were not altogether without just reason; though I foresaw nothing at that time more than my mere fear suggested to me.

CHAPTER XII

A CAVE RETREAT

While this was doing, I was not altogether careless of my other affairs; for I had a great concern upon me for my little herd of goats: they were not only a ready supply to me on every occasion, and began to be sufficient for me, without the expense of powder and shot, but also without the fatigue of hunting after the wild ones; and I was loath to lose the advantage of them, and to have them all to nurse up over again.

For this purpose, after long consideration, I could think of but two ways to preserve them: one was, to find another convenient place to dig a cave underground, and to drive them into it every night; and the other was to enclose two or three little bits of land, remote from one another, and as much concealed as I could, where I might keep about half-a-dozen young goats in each place; so that if any disaster happened to the flock in general, I might be able to raise them again with little trouble and time: and this though it would require a good deal of time and labour, I thought was the most rational design.

Accordingly, I spent some time to find out the most retired parts of the island; and I pitched upon one, which was as private, indeed, as my heart could wish: it was a little damp piece of ground in the middle of the hollow and thick woods, where, as is observed, I almost lost myself once before, endeavouring to come back that way from the eastern part of the island. Here I found a clear piece of land, near three acres, so surrounded with woods that it was almost an enclosure by nature; at least, it did not want near so much labour to make it so as the other piece of ground I had worked so hard at.

I immediately went to work with this piece of ground; and in less than a month's time I had so fenced it round that my flock, or herd, call it which you please, which were not so wild now as at first they might be supposed to be, were well enough secured in it: so, without any further delay, I removed ten young she-goats and two he-goats to this piece, and when they were there I continued to perfect the fence till I had made it as secure as the other; which, however, I did at more leisure, and it took me up more time by a great deal. All this labour I was at the expense of, purely from my apprehensions on account of the print of a man's foot; for as yet I had never seen any human creature come near the island; and I had now lived two years under this uneasiness, which, indeed, made my life much less comfortable than it was before, as may be well imagined by any who know what it is to live in the constant snare of the fear of man. And this I must observe, with grief, too, that the discomposure of my mind had great impression also upon the religious part of my thoughts; for the dread and terror of falling into the hands of savages and cannibals lay so upon my spirits, that I seldom found myself in a due temper for application to my Maker; at least, not with the sedate calmness and resignation of soul which I was wont to do: I rather prayed to God as under great affliction and pressure of mind, surrounded with danger, and in expectation every night of being murdered and devoured before morning; and I must testify, from my experience, that a temper of peace, thankfulness, love, and affection, is much the more proper frame for prayer than that of terror and discomposure: and that under the dread of mischief impending, a man is no more fit for a comforting performance of the duty of praying to God than he is for a repentance on a sick-bed; for these discomposures affect the mind, as the others do the body; and the discomposure of the mind must necessarily be as great a disability as that of the body, and much greater; praying to God being properly an act of the mind, not of the body.

But to go on. After I had thus secured one part of my little living stock, I went about the whole island, searching for another private place to make such another deposit; when, wandering more to the west point of the island than I had ever done yet, and looking out to sea, I thought I saw a boat upon the sea, at a great distance. I had found a perspective glass or two in one of the seamen's chests, which I saved out of our ship, but I had it not about me; and this was so remote that I could not tell what to make of it, though I looked at it till my eyes were not able to hold to look any longer; whether it was a boat or not I do not know, but as I descended from the hill I could see no more of it, so I gave it over; only I resolved to go no more out without a perspective glass in my pocket. When I was come down the hill to the end of the island, where, indeed, I had never been before, I was presently convinced that the seeing the print of a man's foot was not such a strange thing in the island as I imagined: and but that it was a special providence that I was cast upon the side of the island where the savages never came, I should easily have known that nothing was more frequent than for the canoes from the main, when they happened to be a little too far out at sea, to shoot over to that side of the island for harbour: likewise, as they often met and fought in their canoes, the victors, having taken any prisoners, would bring them over to this shore, where, according to their dreadful customs, being all cannibals, they would kill and eat them; of which hereafter.

When I was come down the hill to the shore, as I said above, being the SW. point of the island, I was perfectly confounded and amazed; nor is it possible for me to express the horror of my mind at seeing the shore spread with skulls, hands, feet, and other bones of human bodies; and particularly I observed a place where there had been a fire made, and a circle dug in the earth, like a cockpit, where I supposed the savage wretches had sat down to their human feastings upon the bodies of their fellow-creatures.

I was so astonished with the sight of these things, that I entertained no notions of any danger to myself from it for a long while: all my apprehensions were buried in the thoughts of such a pitch of inhuman, hellish brutality, and the horror of the degeneracy of human nature, which, though I had heard of it often, yet I never had so near a view of before; in short, I turned away my face from the horrid spectacle; my stomach grew sick, and I was just at the point of fainting, when nature discharged the disorder from my stomach; and having vomited with uncommon violence, I was a little relieved, but could not bear to stay in the place a moment; so I got up the hill again with all the speed I could, and walked on towards my own habitation.

When I came a little out of that part of the island I stood still awhile, as amazed, and then, recovering myself, I looked up with the utmost affection of my soul, and, with a flood of tears in my eyes, gave God thanks, that had cast my first lot in a part of the world where I was distinguished from such dreadful creatures as these; and that, though I had esteemed my present condition very miserable, had yet given me so many comforts in it that I had still more to give thanks for than to complain of: and this, above all, that I had, even in this miserable condition, been comforted with the knowledge of Himself, and the hope of His blessing: which was a felicity more than sufficiently equivalent to all the misery which I had suffered, or could suffer.

In this frame of thankfulness I went home to my castle, and began to be much easier now, as to the safety of my circumstances, than ever I was before: for I observed that these wretches never came to this island in search of what they could get; perhaps not seeking, not wanting, or not expecting anything here; and having often, no doubt, been up the covered, woody part of it without finding anything to their purpose. I knew I had been here now almost eighteen years, and never saw the least footsteps of human creature there before; and I might be eighteen years more as entirely concealed as I was now, if I did not discover myself to them, which I had no manner of occasion to do; it being my only business to keep myself entirely concealed where I was, unless I found a better sort of creatures than cannibals to make myself known to. Yet I entertained such an abhorrence of the savage wretches that I have been speaking of, and of the wretched, inhuman custom of their devouring and eating one another up, that I continued pensive and sad, and kept close within my own circle for almost two years after this: when I say my own circle, I mean by it my three plantations—viz. my castle, my country seat (which I called my bower), and my enclosure in the woods: nor did I look after this for any other use than an enclosure for my goats; for the aversion which nature gave me to these hellish wretches was such, that I was as fearful of seeing them as of seeing the devil himself. I did not so much as go to look after my boat all this time, but began rather to think of making another; for I could not think of ever making any more attempts to bring the other boat round the island to me, lest I should meet with some of these creatures at sea; in which case, if I had happened to have fallen into their hands, I knew what would have been my lot.

Time, however, and the satisfaction I had that I was in no danger of being discovered by these people, began to wear off my uneasiness about them; and I began to live just in the same composed manner as before, only with this difference, that I used more caution, and kept my eyes more about me than I did before, lest I should happen to be seen by any of them; and particularly, I was more cautious of firing my gun, lest any of them, being on the island, should happen to hear it. It was, therefore, a very good providence to me that I had furnished myself with a tame breed of goats, and that I had no need to hunt any more about the woods, or shoot at them; and if I did catch any of them after this, it was by traps and snares, as I had done before; so that for two years after this I believe I never fired my gun once off, though I never went out without it; and what was more, as I had saved three pistols out of the ship, I always carried them out with me, or at least two of them, sticking them in my goat-skin belt. I also furbished up one of the great cutlasses that I had out of the ship, and made me a belt to hang it on also; so that I was now a most formidable fellow to look at when I went abroad, if you add to the former description of myself the particular of two pistols, and a broadsword hanging at my side in a belt, but without a scabbard.

Things going on thus, as I have said, for some time, I seemed, excepting these cautions, to be reduced to my former calm, sedate way of living. All these things tended to show me more and more how far my condition was from being miserable, compared to some others; nay, to many other particulars of life which it might have pleased God to have made my lot. It put me upon reflecting how little repining there would be among mankind at any condition of life if people would rather compare their condition with those that were worse, in order to be thankful, than be always comparing them with those which are better, to assist their murmurings and complainings.

As in my present condition there were not really many things which I wanted, so indeed I thought that the frights I had been in about these savage wretches, and the concern I had been in for my own preservation, had taken off the edge of my invention, for my own conveniences; and I had dropped a good design, which I had once bent my thoughts upon, and that was to try if I could not make some of my barley into malt, and then try to brew myself some beer. This was really a whimsical thought, and I reproved myself often for the simplicity of it: for I presently saw there would be the want of several things necessary to the making my beer that it would be impossible for me to supply; as, first, casks to preserve it in, which was a thing that, as I have observed already, I could never compass: no, though I spent not only many days, but weeks, nay months, in attempting it, but to no purpose. In the next place, I had no hops to make it keep, no yeast to make it work, no copper or kettle to make it boil; and yet with all these things wanting, I verily believe, had not the frights and terrors I was in about the savages intervened, I had undertaken it, and perhaps brought it to pass too; for I seldom gave anything over without accomplishing it, when once I had it in my head to began it. But my invention now ran quite another way; for night and day I could think of nothing but how I might destroy some of the monsters in their cruel, bloody entertainment, and if possible save the victim they should bring hither to destroy. It would take up a larger volume than this whole work is intended to be to set down all the contrivances I hatched, or rather brooded upon, in my thoughts, for the destroying these creatures, or at least frightening them so as to prevent their coming hither any more: but all this was abortive; nothing could be possible to take effect, unless I was to be there to do it myself: and what could one man do among them, when perhaps there might be twenty or thirty of them together with their darts, or their bows and arrows, with which they could shoot as true to a mark as I could with my gun?

Sometimes I thought if digging a hole under the place where they made their fire, and putting in five or six pounds of gunpowder, which, when they kindled their fire, would consequently take fire, and blow up all that was near it: but as, in the first place, I should be unwilling to waste so much powder upon them, my store being now within the quantity of one barrel, so neither could I be sure of its going off at any certain time, when it might surprise them; and, at best, that it would do little more than just blow the fire about their ears and fright them, but not sufficient to make them forsake the place: so I laid it aside; and then proposed that I would place myself in ambush in some convenient place, with my three guns all double-loaded, and in the middle of their bloody ceremony let fly at them, when I should be sure to kill or wound perhaps two or three at every shot; and then falling in upon them with my three pistols and my sword, I made no doubt but that, if there were twenty, I should kill them all. This fancy pleased my thoughts for some weeks, and I was so full of it that I often dreamed of it, and, sometimes, that I was just going to let fly at them in my sleep. I went so far with it in my imagination that I employed myself several days to find out proper places to put myself in ambuscade, as I said, to watch for them, and I went frequently to the place itself, which was now grown more familiar to me; but while my mind was thus filled with thoughts of revenge and a bloody putting twenty or thirty of them to the sword, as I may call it, the horror I had at the place, and at the signals of the barbarous wretches devouring one another, abetted my malice. Well, at length I found a place in the side of the hill where I was satisfied I might securely wait till I saw any of their boats coming; and might then, even before they would be ready to come on shore, convey myself unseen into some thickets of trees, in one of which there was a hollow large enough to conceal me entirely; and there I might sit and observe all their bloody doings, and take my full aim at their heads, when they were so close together as that it would be next to impossible that I should miss my shot, or that I could fail wounding three or four of them at the first shot. In this place, then, I resolved to fulfil my design; and accordingly I prepared two muskets and my ordinary fowling-piece. The two muskets I loaded with a brace of slugs each, and four or five smaller bullets, about the size of pistol bullets; and the fowling-piece I loaded with near a handful of swan-shot of the largest size; I also loaded my pistols with about four bullets each; and, in this posture, well provided with ammunition for a second and third charge, I prepared myself for my expedition.

After I had thus laid the scheme of my design, and in my imagination put it in practice, I continually made my tour every morning to the top of the hill, which was from my castle, as I called it, about three miles or more, to see if I could observe any boats upon the sea, coming near the island, or standing over towards it; but I began to tire of this hard duty, after I had for two or three months constantly kept my watch, but came always back without any discovery; there having not, in all that time, been the least appearance, not only on or near the shore, but on the whole ocean, so far as my eye or glass could reach every way.

As long as I kept my daily tour to the hill, to look out, so long also I kept up the vigour of my design, and my spirits seemed to be all the while in a suitable frame for so outrageous an execution as the killing twenty or thirty naked savages, for an offence which I had not at all entered into any discussion of in my thoughts, any farther than my passions were at first fired by the horror I conceived at the unnatural custom of the people of that country, who, it seems, had been suffered by Providence, in His wise disposition of the world, to have no other guide than that of their own abominable and vitiated passions; and consequently were left, and perhaps had been so for some ages, to act such horrid things, and receive such dreadful customs, as nothing but nature, entirely abandoned by Heaven, and actuated by some hellish degeneracy, could have run them into. But now, when, as I have said, I began to be weary of the fruitless excursion which I had made so long and so far every morning in vain, so my opinion of the action itself began to alter; and I began, with cooler and calmer thoughts, to consider what I was going to engage in; what authority or call I had to pretend to be judge and executioner upon these men as criminals, whom Heaven had thought fit for so many ages to suffer unpunished to go on, and to be as it were the executioners of His judgments one upon another; how far these people were offenders against me, and what right I had to engage in the quarrel of that blood which they shed promiscuously upon one another. I debated this very often with myself thus: "How do I know what God Himself judges in this particular case? It is certain these people do not commit this as a crime; it is not against their own consciences reproving, or their light reproaching them; they do not know it to be an offence, and then commit it in defiance of divine justice, as we do in almost all the sins we commit.

They think it no more a crime to kill a captive taken in war than we do to kill an ox; or to eat human flesh than we do to eat mutton."

When I considered this a little, it followed necessarily that I was certainly in the wrong; that these people were not murderers, in the sense that I had before condemned them in my thoughts, any more than those Christians were murderers who often put to death the prisoners taken in battle; or more frequently, upon many occasions, put whole troops of men to the sword, without giving quarter, though they threw down their arms and submitted. In the next place, it occurred to me that although the usage they gave one another was thus brutish and inhuman, yet it was really nothing to me: these people had done me no injury: that if they attempted, or I saw it necessary, for my immediate preservation, to fall upon them, something might be said for it: but that I was yet out of their power, and they really had no knowledge of me, and consequently no design upon me; and therefore it could not be just for me to fall upon them; that this would justify the conduct of the Spaniards in all their barbarities practised in America, where they destroyed millions of these people; who, however they were idolators and barbarians, and had several bloody and barbarous rites in their customs, such as sacrificing human bodies to their idols, were yet, as to the Spaniards, very innocent people; and that the rooting them out of the country is spoken of with the utmost abhorrence and detestation by even the Spaniards themselves at this time, and by all other Christian nations of Europe, as a mere butchery, a bloody and unnatural piece of cruelty, unjustifiable either to God or man; and for which the very name of a Spaniard is reckoned to be frightful and terrible, to all people of humanity or of Christian compassion; as if the kingdom of Spain were particularly eminent for the produce of a race of men who were without principles of tenderness, or the common bowels of pity to the miserable, which is reckoned to be a mark of generous temper in the mind.

These considerations really put me to a pause, and to a kind of a full stop; and I began by little and little to be off my design, and to conclude I had taken wrong measures in my resolution to attack the savages; and that it was not my business to meddle with them, unless they first attacked me; and this it was my business, if possible, to prevent: but that, if I were discovered and attacked by them, I knew my duty. On the other hand, I argued with myself that this really was the way not to deliver myself, but entirely to ruin and destroy myself; for unless I was sure to kill every one that not only should be on shore at that time, but that should ever come on shore afterwards, if but one of them escaped to tell their country-people what had happened, they would come over again by thousands to revenge the death of their fellows, and I should only bring upon myself a certain destruction, which, at present, I had no manner of occasion for. Upon the whole, I concluded that I ought, neither in principle nor in policy, one way or other, to concern myself in this affair: that my business was, by all possible means to conceal myself from them, and not to leave the least sign for them to guess by that there were any living creatures upon the island—I mean of human shape. Religion joined in with this prudential resolution; and I was convinced now, many ways, that I was perfectly out of my duty when I was laying all my bloody schemes for the destruction of innocent creatures—I mean innocent as to me. As to the crimes they were guilty of towards one another, I had nothing to do with them; they were national, and I ought to leave them to the justice of God, who is the Governor of nations, and knows how, by national punishments, to make a just retribution for national offences, and to bring public judgments upon those who offend in a public manner, by such ways as best please Him. This appeared so clear to me now, that nothing was a greater satisfaction to me than that I had not been suffered to do a thing which I now saw so much reason to believe would have been no less a sin than that of wilful murder if I had committed it; and I gave most humble thanks on my knees to God, that He had thus delivered me from blood-guiltiness; beseeching Him to grant me the protection of His providence, that I might not fall into the hands of the barbarians, or that I might not lay my hands upon them, unless I had a more clear call from Heaven to do it, in defence of my own life.

In this disposition I continued for near a year after this; and so far was I from desiring an occasion for falling upon these wretches, that in all that time I never once went up the hill to see whether there were any of them in sight, or to know whether any of them had been on shore there or not, that I might not be tempted to renew any of my contrivances against them, or be provoked by any advantage that might present itself to fall upon them; only this I did: I went and removed my boat, which I had on the other side of the island, and carried it down to the east end of the whole island, where I ran it into a little cove, which I found under some high rocks, and where I knew, by reason of the currents, the savages durst not, at least would not, come with their boats upon any account whatever. With my boat I carried away everything that I had left there belonging to her, though not necessary for the bare going thither—viz. a mast and sail which I had made for her, and a thing like an anchor, but which, indeed, could not be called either anchor or grapnel; however, it was the best I could make of its kind: all these I removed, that there might not be the least shadow for discovery, or appearance of any boat, or of any human habitation upon the island. Besides this, I kept myself, as I said, more retired than ever, and seldom went from my cell except upon my constant employment, to milk my she-goats, and manage my little flock in the wood, which, as it was quite on the other part of the island, was out of danger; for certain, it is that these savage people, who sometimes haunted this island, never came with any thoughts of finding anything here, and consequently never wandered off from the coast, and I doubt not but they might have been several times on shore after my apprehensions of them had made me cautious, as well as before. Indeed, I looked back with some horror upon the thoughts of what my condition would have been if I had chopped upon them and been discovered before that; when, naked and unarmed, except with one gun, and that loaded often only with small shot, I walked everywhere, peeping and peering about the island, to see what I could get; what a surprise should I have been in if, when I discovered the print of a man's foot, I had, instead of that, seen fifteen or twenty savages, and found them pursuing me, and by the swiftness of their running no possibility of my escaping them! The thoughts of this sometimes sank my very soul within me, and distressed my mind so much that I could not soon recover it, to think what I should have done, and how I should not only have been unable to resist them, but even should not have had presence of mind enough to do what I might have done; much less what now, after so much consideration and preparation, I might be able to do. Indeed, after serious thinking of these things, I would be melancholy, and sometimes it would last a great while; but I resolved it all at last into thankfulness to that Providence which had delivered me from so many unseen dangers, and had kept me from those mischiefs which I could have no way been the agent in delivering myself from, because I had not the least notion of any such thing depending, or the least supposition of its being possible. This renewed a contemplation which often had come into my thoughts in former times, when first I began to see the merciful dispositions of Heaven, in the dangers we run through in this life; how wonderfully we are delivered when we know nothing of it; how, when we are in a quandary as we call it, a doubt or hesitation whether to go this way or that way, a secret hint shall direct us this way, when we intended to go that way: nay, when sense, our own inclination, and perhaps business has called us to go the other way, yet a strange impression upon the mind, from we know not what springs, and by we know not what power, shall overrule us to go this way; and it shall afterwards appear that had we gone that way, which we should have gone, and even to our imagination ought to have gone, we should have been ruined and lost. Upon these and many like reflections I afterwards made it a certain rule with me, that whenever I found those secret hints or pressings of mind to doing or not doing anything that presented, or going this way or that way, I never failed to obey the secret dictate; though I knew no other reason for it than such a pressure or such a hint hung upon my mind. I could give many examples of the success of this conduct in the course of my life, but more especially in the latter part of my inhabiting this unhappy island; besides many occasions which it is very likely I might have taken notice of, if I had seen with the same eyes then that I see with now. But it is never too late to be wise; and I cannot but advise all considering men, whose lives are attended with such extraordinary incidents as mine, or even though not so extraordinary, not to slight such secret intimations of Providence, let them come from what invisible intelligence they will. That I shall not discuss, and perhaps cannot account for; but certainly they are a proof of the converse of spirits, and a secret communication between those embodied and those unembodied, and such a proof as can never be withstood; of which I shall have occasion to give some remarkable instances in the remainder of my solitary residence in this dismal place.

I believe the reader of this will not think it strange if I confess that these anxieties, these constant dangers I lived in, and the concern that was now upon me, put an end to all invention, and to all the contrivances that I had laid for my future accommodations and conveniences. I had the care of my safety more now upon my hands than that of my food. I cared not to drive a nail, or chop a stick of wood now, for fear the noise I might make should be heard: much less would I fire a gun for the same reason: and above all I was intolerably uneasy at making any fire, lest the smoke, which is visible at a great distance in the day, should betray me. For this reason, I removed that part of my business which required fire, such as burning of pots and pipes, &c., into my new apartment in the woods; where, after I had been some time, I found, to my unspeakable consolation, a mere natural cave in the earth, which went in a vast way, and where, I daresay, no savage, had he been at the mouth of it, would be so hardy as to venture in; nor, indeed, would any man else, but one who, like me, wanted nothing so much as a safe retreat.

The mouth of this hollow was at the bottom of a great rock, where, by mere accident (I would say, if I did not see abundant reason to ascribe all such things now to Providence), I was cutting down some thick branches of trees to make charcoal; and before I go on I must observe the reason of my making this charcoal, which was this—I was afraid of making a smoke about my habitation, as I said before; and yet I could not live there without baking my bread, cooking my meat, &c.; so I contrived to burn some wood here, as I had seen done in England, under turf, till it became chark or dry coal: and then putting the fire out, I preserved the coal to carry home, and perform the other services for which fire was wanting, without danger of smoke. But this is by-the-bye. While I was cutting down some wood here, I perceived that, behind a very thick branch of low brushwood or underwood, there was a kind of hollow place: I was curious to look in it; and getting with difficulty into the mouth of it, I found it was pretty large, that is to say, sufficient for me to stand upright in it, and perhaps another with me: but I must confess to you that I made more haste out than I did in, when looking farther into the place, and which was perfectly dark, I saw two broad shining eyes of some creature, whether devil or man I knew not, which twinkled like two stars; the dim light from the cave's mouth shining directly in, and making the reflection. However, after some pause I recovered myself, and began to call myself a thousand fools, and to think that he that was afraid to see the devil was not fit to live twenty years in an island all alone; and that I might well think there was nothing in this cave that was more frightful than myself. Upon this, plucking up my courage, I took up a firebrand, and in I rushed again, with the stick flaming in my hand: I had not gone three steps in before I was almost as frightened as before; for I heard a very loud sigh, like that of a man in some pain, and it was followed by a broken noise, as of words half expressed, and then a deep sigh again. I stepped back, and was indeed struck with such a surprise that it put me into a cold sweat, and if I had had a hat on my head, I will not answer for it that my hair might not have lifted it off. But still plucking up my spirits as well as I could, and encouraging myself a little with considering that the power and presence of God was everywhere, and was able to protect me, I stepped forward again, and by the light of the firebrand, holding it up a little over my head, I saw lying on the ground a monstrous, frightful old he-goat, just making his will, as we say, and gasping for life, and, dying, indeed, of mere old age. I stirred him a little to see if I could get him out, and he essayed to get up, but was not able to raise himself; and I thought with myself he might even lie there—for if he had frightened me, so he would certainly fright any of the savages, if any of them should be so hardy as to come in there while he had any life in him.

I was now recovered from my surprise, and began to look round me, when I found the cave was but very small—that is to say, it might be about twelve feet over, but in no manner of shape, neither round nor square, no hands having ever been employed in making it but those of mere Nature. I observed also that there was a place at the farther side of it that went in further, but was so low that it required me to creep upon my hands and knees to go into it, and whither it went I knew not; so, having no candle, I gave it over for that time, but resolved to go again the next day provided with candles and a tinder-box, which I had made of the lock of one of the muskets, with some wildfire in the pan.

Accordingly, the next day I came provided with six large candles of my own making (for I made very good candles now of goat's tallow, but was hard set for candle-wick, using sometimes rags or rope-yarn, and sometimes the dried rind of a weed like nettles); and going into this low place I was obliged to creep upon all-fours as I have said, almost ten yards—which, by the way, I thought was a venture bold enough, considering that I knew not how far it might go, nor what was beyond it. When I had got through the strait, I found the roof rose higher up, I believe near twenty feet; but never was such a glorious sight seen in the island, I daresay, as it was to look round the sides and roof of this vault or cave—the wall reflected a hundred thousand lights to me from my two candles. What it was in the rock—whether diamonds or any other precious stones, or gold which I rather supposed it to be—I knew not. The place I was in was a most delightful cavity, or grotto, though perfectly dark; the floor was dry and level, and had a sort of a small loose gravel upon it, so that there was no nauseous or venomous creature to be seen, neither was there any damp or wet on the sides or roof. The only difficulty in it was the entrance—which, however, as it was a place of security, and such a retreat as I wanted; I thought was a convenience; so that I was really rejoiced at the discovery, and resolved, without any delay, to bring some of those things which I was most anxious about to this place: particularly, I resolved to bring hither my magazine of powder, and all my spare arms—viz. two fowling-pieces—for I had three in all—and three muskets—for of them I had eight in all; so I kept in my castle only five, which stood ready mounted like pieces of cannon on my outmost fence, and were ready also to take out upon any expedition. Upon this occasion of removing my ammunition I happened to open the barrel of powder which I took up out of the sea, and which had been wet, and I found that the water had penetrated about three or four inches into the powder on every side, which caking and growing hard, had preserved the inside like a kernel in the shell, so that I had near sixty pounds of very good powder in the centre of the cask. This was a very agreeable discovery to me at that time; so I carried all away thither, never keeping above two or three pounds of powder with me in my castle, for fear of a surprise of any kind; I also carried thither all the lead I had left for bullets.

I fancied myself now like one of the ancient giants who were said to live in caves and holes in the rocks, where none could come at them; for I persuaded myself, while I was here, that if five hundred savages were to hunt me, they could never find me out—or if they did, they would not venture to attack me here. The old goat whom I found expiring died in the mouth of the cave the next day after I made this discovery; and I found it much easier to dig a great hole there, and throw him in and cover him with earth, than to drag him out; so I interred him there, to prevent offence to my nose.

CHAPTER XIII

WRECK OF A SPANISH SHIP

I was now in the twenty-third year of my residence in this island, and was so naturalised to the place and the manner of living, that, could I but have enjoyed the certainty that no savages would come to the place to disturb me, I could have been content to have capitulated for spending the rest of my time there, even to the last moment, till I had laid me down and died, like the old goat in the cave. I had also arrived to some little diversions and amusements, which made the time pass a great deal more pleasantly with me than it did before—first, I had taught my Poll, as I noted before, to speak; and he did it so familiarly, and talked so articulately and plain, that it was very pleasant to me; and he lived with me no less than six-and-twenty years. How long he might have lived afterwards I know not, though I know they have a notion in the Brazils that they live a hundred years. My dog was a pleasant and loving companion to me for no less than sixteen years of my time, and then died of mere old age. As for my cats, they multiplied, as I have observed, to that degree that I was obliged to shoot several of them at first, to keep them from devouring me and all I had; but at length, when the two old ones I brought with me were gone, and after some time continually driving them from me, and letting them have no provision with me, they all ran wild into the woods, except two or three favourites, which I kept tame, and whose young, when they had any, I always drowned; and these were part of my family. Besides these I always kept two or three household kids about me, whom I taught to feed out of my hand; and I had two more parrots, which talked pretty well, and would all call "Robin Crusoe," but none like my first; nor, indeed, did I take the pains with any of them that I had done with him. I had also several tame sea-fowls, whose name I knew not, that I caught upon the shore, and cut their wings; and the little stakes which I had planted before my castle-wall being now grown up to a good thick grove, these fowls all lived among these low trees, and bred there, which was very agreeable to me; so that, as I said above, I began to be very well contented with the life I led, if I could have been secured from the dread of the savages. But it was otherwise directed; and it may not be amiss for all people who shall meet with my story to make this just observation from it: How frequently, in the course of our lives, the evil which in itself we seek most to shun, and which, when we are fallen into, is the most dreadful to us, is oftentimes the very means or door of our deliverance, by which alone we can be raised again from the affliction we are fallen into. I could give many examples of this in the course of my unaccountable life; but in nothing was it more particularly remarkable than in the circumstances of my last years of solitary residence in this island.

It was now the month of December, as I said above, in my twenty-third year; and this, being the southern solstice (for winter I cannot call it), was the particular time of my harvest, and required me to be pretty much abroad in the fields, when, going out early in the morning, even before it was thorough daylight, I was surprised with seeing a light of some fire upon the shore, at a distance from me of about two miles, toward that part of the island where I had observed some savages had been, as before, and not on the other side; but, to my great affliction, it was on my side of the island.

I was indeed terribly surprised at the sight, and stopped short within my grove, not daring to go out, lest I might be surprised; and yet I had no more peace within, from the apprehensions I had that if these savages, in rambling over the island, should find my corn standing or cut, or any of my works or improvements, they would immediately conclude that there were people in the place, and would then never rest till they had found me out. In this extremity I went back directly to my castle, pulled up the ladder after me, and made all things without look as wild and natural as I could.

Then I prepared myself within, putting myself in a posture of defence. I loaded all my cannon, as I called them—that is to say, my muskets, which were mounted upon my new fortification—and all my pistols, and resolved to defend myself to the last gasp—not forgetting seriously to commend myself to the Divine protection, and earnestly to pray to God to deliver me out of the hands of the barbarians. I continued in this posture about two hours, and began to be impatient for intelligence abroad, for I had no spies to send out. After sitting a while longer, and musing what I should do in this case, I was not able to bear sitting in ignorance longer; so setting up my ladder to the side of the hill, where there was a flat place, as I observed before, and then pulling the ladder after me, I set it up again and mounted the top of the hill, and pulling out my perspective glass, which I had taken on purpose, I laid me down flat on my belly on the ground, and began to look for the place. I presently found there were no less than nine naked savages sitting round a small fire they had made, not to warm them, for they had no need of that, the weather being extremely hot, but, as I supposed, to dress some of their barbarous diet of human flesh which they had brought with them, whether alive or dead I could not tell.

They had two canoes with them, which they had hauled up upon the shore; and as it was then ebb of tide, they seemed to me to wait for the return of the flood to go away again. It is not easy to imagine what confusion this sight put me into, especially seeing them come on my side of the island, and so near to me; but when I considered their coming must be always with the current of the ebb, I began afterwards to be more sedate in my mind, being satisfied that I might go abroad with safety all the time of the flood of tide, if they were not on shore before; and having made this observation, I went abroad about my harvest work with the more composure.

As I expected, so it proved; for as soon as the tide made to the westward I saw them all take boat and row (or paddle as we call it) away. I should have observed, that for an hour or more before they went off they were dancing, and I could easily discern their postures and gestures by my glass. I could not perceive, by my nicest observation, but that they were stark naked, and had not the least covering upon them; but whether they were men or women I could not distinguish.

As soon as I saw them shipped and gone, I took two guns upon my shoulders, and two pistols in my girdle, and my great sword by my side without a scabbard, and with all the speed I was able to make went away to the hill where I had discovered the first appearance of all; and as soon as I get thither, which was not in less than two hours (for I could not go quickly, being so loaded with arms as I was), I perceived there had been three canoes more of the savages at that place; and looking out farther, I saw they were all at sea together, making over for the main. This was a dreadful sight to me, especially as, going down to the shore, I could see the marks of horror which the dismal work they had been about had left behind it—viz. the blood, the bones, and part of the flesh of human bodies eaten and devoured by those wretches with merriment and sport. I was so filled with indignation at the sight, that I now began to premeditate the destruction of the next that I saw there, let them be whom or how many soever. It seemed evident to me that the visits which they made thus to this island were not very frequent, for it was above fifteen months before any more of them came on shore there again—that is to say, I neither saw them nor any footsteps or signals of them in all that time; for as to the rainy seasons, then they are sure not to come abroad, at least not so far. Yet all this while I lived uncomfortably, by reason of the constant apprehensions of their coming upon me by surprise: from whence I observe, that the expectation of evil is more bitter than the suffering, especially if there is no room to shake off that expectation or those apprehensions.

During all this time I was in a murdering humour, and spent most of my hours, which should have been better employed, in contriving how to circumvent and fall upon them the very next time I should see them—especially if they should be divided, as they were the last time, into two parties; nor did I consider at all that if I killed one party— suppose ten or a dozen—I was still the next day, or week, or month, to kill another, and so another, even *ad infinitum*, till I should be, at length, no less a murderer than they were in being man-eaters—and perhaps much more so. I spent my days now in great perplexity and anxiety of mind, expecting that I should one day or other fall, into the hands of these merciless creatures; and if I did at any time venture abroad, it was not without looking around me with the greatest care and caution imaginable. And now I found, to my great comfort, how happy it was that I had provided a tame flock or herd of goats, for I durst not upon any account fire my gun, especially near that side of the island where they usually came, lest I should alarm the savages; and if they had fled from me now, I was sure to have them come again with perhaps two or three hundred canoes with them in a few days, and then I knew what to expect. However, I wore out a year and three months more before I ever saw any more of the savages, and then I found them again, as I shall soon observe. It is true they might have been there once or twice; but either they made no stay, or at least I did not see them; but in the month of May, as near as I could calculate, and in my four-and-twentieth year, I had a very strange encounter with them; of which in its place.

The perturbation of my mind during this fifteen or sixteen months' interval was very great; I slept unquietly, dreamed always frightful dreams, and often started out of my sleep in the night. In the day great troubles overwhelmed my mind; and in the night I dreamed often of killing the savages and of the reasons why I might justify doing it.

But to waive all this for a while. It was in the middle of May, on the sixteenth day, I think, as well as my poor wooden calendar would reckon, for I marked all upon the post still; I say, it was on the sixteenth of May that it blew a very great storm of wind all day, with a great deal of lightning and thunder, and; a very foul night it was after it. I knew

153

not what was the particular occasion of it, but as I was reading in the Bible, and taken up with very serious thoughts about my present condition, I was surprised with the noise of a gun, as I thought, fired at sea. This was, to be sure, a surprise quite of a different nature from any I had met with before; for the notions this put into my thoughts were quite of another kind. I started up in the greatest haste imaginable; and, in a trice, clapped my ladder to the middle place of the rock, and pulled it after me; and mounting it the second time, got to the top of the hill the very moment that a flash of fire bid me listen for a second gun, which, accordingly, in about half a minute I heard; and by the sound, knew that it was from that part of the sea where I was driven down the current in my boat. I immediately considered that this must be some ship in distress, and that they had some comrade, or some other ship in company, and fired these for signals of distress, and to obtain help. I had the presence of mind at that minute to think, that though I could not help them, it might be that they might help me; so I brought together all the dry wood I could get at hand, and making a good handsome pile, I set it on fire upon the hill. The wood was dry, and blazed freely; and, though the wind blew very hard, yet it burned fairly out; so that I was certain, if there was any such thing as a ship, they must needs see it. And no doubt they did; for as soon as ever my fire blazed up, I heard another gun, and after that several others, all from the same quarter. I plied my fire all night long, till daybreak: and when it was broad day, and the air cleared up, I saw something at a great distance at sea, full east of the island, whether a sail or a hull I could not distinguish—no, not with my glass: the distance was so great, and the weather still something hazy also; at least, it was so out at sea.

I looked frequently at it all that day, and soon perceived that it did not move; so I presently concluded that it was a ship at anchor; and being eager, you may be sure, to be satisfied, I took my gun in my hand, and ran towards the south side of the island to the rocks where I had formerly been carried away by the current; and getting up there, the weather by this time being perfectly clear, I could plainly see, to my great sorrow, the wreck of a ship, cast away in the night upon those concealed rocks which I found when I was out in my boat; and which rocks, as they checked the violence of the stream, and made a kind of counter-stream, or eddy, were the occasion of my recovering from the most desperate, hopeless condition that ever I had been in in all my life. Thus, what is one man's safety is another man's destruction; for it seems these men, whoever they were, being out of their knowledge, and the rocks being wholly under water, had been driven upon them in the night, the wind blowing hard at ENE. Had they seen the island, as I must necessarily suppose they did not, they must, as I thought, have endeavoured to have saved themselves on shore by the help of their boat; but their firing off guns for help, especially when they saw, as I imagined, my fire, filled me with many thoughts. First, I imagined that upon seeing my light they might have put themselves into their boat, and endeavoured to make the shore: but that the sea running very high, they might have been cast away. Other times I imagined that they might have lost their boat before, as might be the case many ways; particularly by the breaking of the sea upon their ship, which many times obliged men to stave, or take in pieces, their boat, and sometimes to throw it overboard with their own hands. Other times I imagined they had some other ship or ships in company, who, upon the signals of distress they made, had taken them up, and carried them off. Other times I fancied they were all gone off to sea in their boat, and being hurried away by the current that I had been formerly in, were carried out into the great ocean, where there was nothing but misery and perishing: and that, perhaps, they might by this time think of starving, and of being in a condition to eat one another.

As all these were but conjectures at best, so, in the condition I was in, I could do no more than look on upon the misery of the poor men, and pity them; which had still this good effect upon my side, that it gave me more and more cause to give thanks to God, who had so happily and comfortably provided for me in my desolate condition; and that of two ships' companies, who were now cast away upon this part of the world, not one life should be spared but mine. I learned here again to observe, that it is very rare that the providence of God casts us into any condition so low, or any misery so great, but we may see something or other to be thankful for, and may see others in worse circumstances than our own. Such certainly was the case of these men, of whom I could not so much as see room to suppose any were saved; nothing could make it rational so much as to wish or expect that they did not all perish there, except the possibility only of their being taken up by another ship in company; and this was but mere possibility indeed, for I saw not the least sign or appearance of any such thing. I cannot explain, by any possible energy of words, what a strange longing I felt in my soul upon this sight, breaking out sometimes thus: "Oh that there had been but one or two, nay, or but one soul saved out of this ship, to have escaped to me, that I might but have had one companion, one fellow-creature, to have spoken to me and to have conversed with!" In all the time of my solitary life I never felt so earnest, so strong a desire after the society of my fellow-creatures, or so deep a regret at the want of it.

There are some secret springs in the affections which, when they are set a-going by some object in view, or, though not in view, yet rendered present to the mind by the power of imagination, that motion carries out the soul, by its impetuosity, to such violent, eager embracings of the object, that the absence of it is insupportable. Such were these earnest wishings that but one man had been saved. I believe I repeated the words, "Oh that it had been but one!" a thousand times; and my desires were so moved by it, that when I spoke the words my hands would clinch together, and my fingers would press the palms of my hands, so that if I had had any soft thing in my hand I should have crushed it involuntarily; and the teeth in my head would strike together, and set against one another so strong, that for some time I could not part them again. Let the naturalists explain these things, and the reason and manner of them. All I can do is to describe the fact, which was even surprising to me when I found it, though I knew not from whence it proceeded; it was doubtless the effect of ardent wishes, and of strong ideas formed in my mind, realising the comfort which the conversation of one of my fellow-Christians would have been to me. But it was not to be; either their fate or mine, or both, forbade it; for, till the last year of my being on this island, I never knew whether any were saved out of that ship or no; and had only the affliction, some days after, to see the corpse of a drowned boy come on shore at the end of the island which was next the shipwreck. He had no clothes on but a seaman's waistcoat, a pair of open-kneed linen drawers, and a blue linen shirt; but nothing to direct me so much as to guess what nation he was of. He had nothing in his pockets but two pieces of eight and a tobacco pipe—the last was to me of ten times more value than the first.

It was now calm, and I had a great mind to venture out in my boat to this wreck, not doubting but I might find something on board that might be useful to me. But that did not altogether press me so much as the possibility that there might be yet some living creature on board, whose life I might not only save, but might, by saving that life, comfort my own to the last degree; and this thought clung so to my heart that I could not be quiet night or day, but I must venture out in my boat on board this wreck; and committing the rest to God's providence, I thought the impression was so strong upon my mind that it could not be resisted—that it must come from some invisible direction, and that I should be wanting to myself if I did not go.

Under the power of this impression, I hastened back to my castle, prepared everything for my voyage, took a quantity of bread, a great pot of fresh water, a compass to steer by, a bottle of rum (for I had still a great deal of that left), and a basket of raisins; and thus, loading myself with everything necessary. I went down to my boat, got the water out of her, got her afloat, loaded all my cargo in her, and then went home again for more. My second cargo was a great bag of rice, the umbrella to set up over my head for a shade, another large pot of water, and about two dozen of small loaves, or barley cakes, more than before, with a bottle of goat's milk and a cheese; all which with great labour and sweat I carried to my boat; and praying to God to direct my voyage, I put out, and rowing or paddling the canoe along the shore, came at last to the utmost point of the island on the north-east side. And now I was to launch out into the ocean, and either to venture or not to venture. I looked on the rapid currents which ran constantly on both sides of the island at a distance, and which were very terrible to me from the remembrance of the hazard I had been in before, and my heart began to fail me; for I foresaw that if I was driven into either of those currents, I should be carried a great way out to sea, and perhaps out of my reach or sight of the island again; and that then, as my boat was but small, if any little gale of wind should rise, I should be inevitably lost.

These thoughts so oppressed my mind that I began to give over my enterprise; and having hauled my boat into a little creek on the shore, I stepped out, and sat down upon a rising bit of ground, very pensive and anxious, between fear and desire, about my voyage; when, as I was musing, I could perceive that the tide was turned, and the flood come on; upon which my going was impracticable for so many hours. Upon this, presently it occurred to me that I should go up to the highest piece of ground I could find, and observe, if I could, how the sets of the tide or currents lay when the flood came in, that I might judge whether, if I was driven one way out, I might not expect to be driven another way home, with the same rapidity of the currents. This thought was no sooner in my head than I cast my eye upon a little hill which sufficiently overlooked the sea both ways, and from whence I had a clear view of the currents or sets of the tide, and which way I was to guide myself in my return. Here I found, that as the current of ebb set out close by the south point of the island, so the current of the flood set in close by the shore of the north side; and that I had nothing to do but to keep to the north side of the island in my return, and I should do well enough.

Encouraged by this observation, I resolved the next morning to set out with the first of the tide; and reposing myself for the night in my canoe, under the watch-coat I mentioned, I launched out. I first made a little out to sea, full north, till I began to feel the benefit of the current, which set eastward, and which carried me at a great rate; and yet did not so hurry me as the current on the south side had done before, so as to take from me all government of the boat; but having a strong steerage with my paddle, I went at a great rate directly for the wreck, and in less than two hours I came up to it. It was a dismal sight to look at; the ship, which by its building was Spanish, stuck fast, jammed in between two rocks. All the stern and quarter of her were beaten to pieces by the sea; and as her forecastle, which stuck in the rocks, had run on with great violence, her mainmast and foremast were brought by the board—that is to say, broken short off; but her bowsprit was sound, and the head and bow appeared firm. When I came close to her, a dog appeared upon her, who, seeing me coming, yelped and cried; and as soon as I called him, jumped into the sea to come to me. I took him into the boat, but found him almost dead with hunger and thirst. I gave him a cake of my bread, and he devoured it like a ravenous wolf that had been starving a fortnight in the snow; I then gave the poor creature some fresh water, with which, if I would have let him, he would have burst himself. After this I went on board; but the first sight I met with was two men drowned in the cook-room, or forecastle of the ship, with their arms fast about one another. I concluded, as is indeed probable, that when the ship struck, it being in a storm, the sea broke so high and so continually over her, that the men were not able to bear it, and were strangled with the constant rushing in of the water, as much as if they had been under water. Besides the dog, there was nothing left in the ship that had life; nor any goods, that I could see, but what were spoiled by the water. There were some casks of liquor, whether wine or brandy I knew not, which lay lower in the hold, and which, the water being ebbed out, I could see; but they were too big to meddle with. I saw several chests, which I believe belonged to some of the seamen; and I got two of them into the boat, without examining what was in them. Had the stern of the ship been fixed, and the forepart broken off, I am persuaded I might have made a good voyage; for by what I found in those two chests I had room to suppose the ship had a great deal of wealth on board; and, if I may guess from the course she steered, she must have been bound from Buenos Ayres, or the Rio de la Plata, in the south part of America, beyond the Brazils to the Havannah, in the Gulf of Mexico, and so perhaps to Spain. She had, no doubt, a great treasure in her, but of no use, at that time, to anybody; and what became of the crew I then knew not.

I found, besides these chests, a little cask full of liquor, of about twenty gallons, which I got into my boat with much difficulty. There were several muskets in the cabin, and a great powder-horn, with about four pounds of powder in it; as for the muskets, I had no occasion for them, so I left them, but took the powder-horn. I took a fire-shovel and tongs, which I wanted extremely, as also two little brass kettles, a copper pot to make chocolate, and a gridiron; and with this cargo, and the dog, I came away, the tide beginning to make home again—and the same evening, about an hour within night, I reached the island again, weary and fatigued to the last degree. I reposed that night in the boat and in the morning I resolved to harbour what I had got in my new cave, and not carry it home to my castle. After refreshing myself, I got all my cargo on shore, and began to examine the particulars. The cask of liquor I found to be a kind of rum, but not such as we had at the Brazils; and, in a word, not at all good; but when I came to open the chests, I found several things of great use to me—for example, I found in one a fine case of bottles, of an extraordinary kind, and filled with cordial waters, fine and very good; the bottles held about three pints each, and were tipped with silver. I found two pots of very good succades, or sweetmeats, so fastened also on the top that the salt-water had not hurt them; and two more of the same, which the water had spoiled. I found some very good shirts, which were very welcome to me; and about a dozen and a half of white linen handkerchiefs and coloured neckcloths; the former were also very welcome, being exceedingly refreshing to wipe my face in a hot day. Besides this, when I came to the till in the chest, I found there three great bags of pieces of eight, which held about eleven hundred pieces in all; and in one of them, wrapped up in a paper, six doubloons of gold, and some small bars or wedges of gold; I suppose they might all weigh near a pound. In the other chest were some clothes, but of little value; but, by the circumstances, it must have belonged to the gunner's mate; though there was no powder in it, except two pounds of fine glazed powder, in three flasks, kept, I suppose, for charging their fowling-pieces on occasion. Upon the whole, I got very little by this voyage that was of any use to me; for, as to the money, I had no manner of occasion for it; it was to me as the dirt under my feet, and I would have given it all for three or four pair of English shoes and stockings, which were things I greatly wanted, but had had none on my feet for many years. I had, indeed, got two pair of shoes now, which I took off the feet of two drowned men whom I saw in the wreck, and I found two pair more in one of the chests, which were very welcome to me; but they were not like our English shoes, either for ease or service, being rather what we call pumps than shoes. I found in this seaman's chest about fifty pieces of eight, in rials, but no gold: I supposed this belonged to a poorer man than the other, which seemed to belong to some officer. Well, however, I lugged this money home to my cave, and laid it up, as I had done that before which I had brought from our own ship; but it was a great pity, as I said, that the other part of this ship had not come to my share: for I am satisfied I might have loaded my canoe several times over with money; and, thought I, if I ever escape to England, it might lie here safe enough till I come again and fetch it.

CHAPTER XIV

A DREAM REALISED

Having now brought all my things on shore and secured them, I went back to my boat, and rowed or paddled her along the shore to her old harbour, where I laid her up, and made the best of my way to my old habitation, where I found everything safe and quiet. I began now to repose myself, live after my old fashion, and take care of my family affairs; and for a while I lived easy enough, only that I was more vigilant than I used to be, looked out oftener, and did not go abroad so much; and if at any time I did stir with any freedom, it was always to the east part of the island, where I was pretty well satisfied the savages never came, and where I could go without so many precautions, and such a load of arms and ammunition as I always carried with me if I went the other way. I lived in this condition near two years more; but my unlucky head, that was always to let me know it was born to make my body miserable, was all these two years filled with projects and designs how, if it were possible, I might get away from this island: for sometimes I was for making another voyage to the wreck, though my reason told me that there was nothing left there worth the hazard of my voyage; sometimes for a ramble one way, sometimes another—and I believe verily, if I had had the boat that I went from Sallee in, I should have ventured to sea, bound anywhere, I knew not whither. I have been, in all my circumstances, a memento to those who are touched with the general plague of mankind, whence, for aught I know, one half of their miseries flow: I mean that of not being satisfied with the station wherein God and Nature hath placed them—for, not to look back upon my primitive condition, and the excellent advice of my father, the opposition to which was, as I may call it, my *original sin*, my subsequent mistakes of the same kind had been the means of my coming into this miserable condition; for had that Providence which so happily seated me at the Brazils as a planter blessed me with confined desires, and I could have been contented to have gone on gradually, I might have been by this time—I mean in the time of my being in this island—one of the most considerable planters in the Brazils—nay, I am persuaded, that by the improvements I had made in that little time I lived there, and the increase I should probably have made if I had remained, I might have been worth a hundred thousand moidores—and what business had I to leave a settled fortune, a well-stocked plantation, improving and increasing, to turn supercargo to Guinea to fetch negroes, when patience and time would have so increased our stock at home, that we could have bought them at our own door from those whose business it was to fetch them? and though it had cost us something more, yet the difference of that price was by no means worth saving at so great a hazard. But as this is usually the fate of young heads, so reflection upon the folly of it is as commonly the exercise of more years, or of the dear-bought experience of time—so it was with me now; and yet so deep had the mistake taken root in my temper, that I could not satisfy myself in my station, but was continually poring upon the means and possibility of my escape from this place; and that I may, with greater pleasure to the reader, bring on the remaining part of my story, it may not be improper to give some account of my first conceptions on the subject of this foolish scheme for my escape, and how, and upon what foundation, I acted.

I am now to be supposed retired into my castle, after my late voyage to the wreck, my frigate laid up and secured under water, as usual, and my condition restored to what it was before: I had more wealth, indeed, than I had before, but was not at all the richer; for I had no more use for it than the Indians of Peru had before the Spaniards came there.

It was one of the nights in the rainy season in March, the four-and-twentieth year of my first setting foot in this island of solitude, I was lying in my bed or hammock, awake, very well in health, had no pain, no distemper, no uneasiness of body, nor any uneasiness of mind more than ordinary, but could by no means close my eyes, that is, so as to sleep; no, not a wink all night long, otherwise than as follows: It is impossible to set down the innumerable crowd of thoughts that whirled through that great thoroughfare of the brain, the memory, in this night's time. I ran over the whole history of my life in miniature, or by abridgment, as I may call it, to my coming to this island, and also of that part of my life since I came to this island. In my reflections upon the state of my case since I came on shore on this island, I was comparing the happy posture of my affairs in the first years of my habitation here, with the life of anxiety, fear, and care which I had lived in ever since I had seen the print of a foot in the sand. Not that I did not believe the savages had frequented the island even all the while, and might have been several hundreds of them at times on shore there; but I had never known it, and was incapable of any apprehensions about it; my satisfaction was perfect, though my danger was the same, and I was as happy in not knowing my danger as if I had never really been exposed to it. This furnished my thoughts with many very profitable reflections, and particularly this one: How infinitely good that Providence is, which has provided, in its government of mankind, such narrow bounds to his sight and knowledge of things; and though he walks in the midst of so many thousand dangers, the sight of which, if discovered to him, would distract his mind and sink his spirits, he is kept serene and calm, by having the events of things hid from his eyes, and knowing nothing of the dangers which surround him.

After these thoughts had for some time entertained me, I came to reflect seriously upon the real danger I had been in for so many years in this very island, and how I had walked about in the greatest security, and with all possible tranquillity, even when perhaps nothing but the brow of a hill, a great tree, or the casual approach of night, had been between me and the worst kind of destruction—viz. that of falling into the hands of cannibals and savages, who would have seized on me with the same view as I would on a goat or turtle; and have thought it no more crime to kill and devour me than I did of a pigeon or a curlew. I would unjustly slander myself if I should say I was not sincerely thankful to my great Preserver, to whose singular protection I acknowledged, with great humanity, all these unknown deliverances were due, and without which I must inevitably have fallen into their merciless hands.

When these thoughts were over, my head was for some time taken up in considering the nature of these wretched creatures, I mean the savages, and how it came to pass in the world that the wise Governor of all things should give up any of His creatures to such inhumanity—nay, to something so much below even brutality itself—as to devour its own kind: but as this ended in some (at that time) fruitless speculations, it occurred to me to inquire what part of the world these wretches lived in? how far off the coast was from whence they came? what they ventured over so far from home for? what kind of boats they had? and why I might not order myself and my business so that I might be able to go over thither, as they were to come to me?

I never so much as troubled myself to consider what I should do with myself when I went thither; what would become of me if I fell into the hands of these savages; or how I should escape them if they attacked me; no, nor so much as how it was possible for me to reach the coast, and not to be attacked by some or other of them, without any possibility of delivering myself: and if I should not fall into their hands, what I should do for provision, or whither I should bend my course: none of these thoughts, I say, so much as came in my way; but my mind was wholly bent upon the notion of my passing over in my boat to the mainland. I looked upon my present condition as the most miserable that could possibly be; that I was not able to throw myself into anything but death, that could be called worse; and if I reached the shore of the main I might perhaps meet with relief, or I might coast along, as I did on the African shore, till I came to some inhabited country, and where I might find some relief; and after all, perhaps I might fall in with some Christian ship that might take me in: and if the worst came to the worst, I could but die, which would put an end to all these miseries at once. Pray note, all this was the fruit of a disturbed mind, an impatient temper, made desperate, as it were, by the long continuance of my troubles, and the disappointments I had met in the wreck I had been on board of, and where I had been so near obtaining what I so earnestly longed for—somebody to speak to, and to learn some knowledge from them of the place where I was, and of the probable means of my deliverance. I was agitated wholly by these thoughts; all my calm of mind, in my resignation to Providence, and waiting the issue of the dispositions of Heaven, seemed to be suspended; and I had as it were no power to turn my thoughts to anything but to the project of a voyage to the main, which came upon me with such force, and such an impetuosity of desire, that it was not to be resisted.

When this had agitated my thoughts for two hours or more, with such violence that it set my very blood into a ferment, and my pulse beat as if I had been in a fever, merely with the extraordinary fervour of my mind about it, Nature—as if I had been fatigued and exhausted with the very thoughts of it—threw me into a sound sleep. One would have thought I should have dreamed of it, but I did not, nor of anything relating to it, but I dreamed that as I was going out in the morning as usual from my castle, I saw upon the shore two canoes and eleven savages coming to land, and that they brought with them another savage whom they were going to kill in order to eat him; when, on a sudden, the savage that they were going to kill jumped away, and ran for his life; and I thought in my sleep that he came running into my little thick grove before my fortification, to hide himself; and that I seeing him alone, and not perceiving that the others sought him that way, showed myself to him, and smiling upon him, encouraged him: that he kneeled down to me, seeming to pray me to assist him; upon which I showed him my ladder, made him go up, and carried him into my cave, and he became my servant; and that as soon as I had got this man, I said to myself, "Now I may certainly venture to the mainland, for this fellow will serve me as a pilot, and will tell me what to do, and whither to go for provisions, and whither not to go for fear of being devoured; what places to venture into, and what to shun." I waked with this thought; and was under such inexpressible impressions of joy at the prospect of my escape in my dream, that the disappointments which I felt upon coming to myself, and finding that it was no more than a dream, were equally extravagant the other way, and threw me into a very great dejection of spirits.

Upon this, however, I made this conclusion: that my only way to go about to attempt an escape was, to endeavour to get a savage into my possession: and, if possible, it should be one of their prisoners, whom they had condemned to be eaten, and should bring hither to kill. But these thoughts still were attended with this difficulty: that it was impossible to effect this without attacking a whole caravan of them, and killing them all; and this was not only a very desperate attempt, and might miscarry, but, on the other hand, I had greatly scrupled the lawfulness of it to myself; and my heart trembled at the thoughts of shedding so much blood, though it was for my deliverance. I need not repeat the arguments which occurred to me against this, they being the same mentioned before; but though I had other reasons to offer now— viz. that those men were enemies to my life, and would devour me if they could; that it was self-preservation, in the highest degree, to deliver myself from this death of a life, and was acting in my own defence as much as if they were actually assaulting me, and the like; I say though these things argued for it, yet the thoughts of shedding human blood for my deliverance were very terrible to me, and such as I could by no means reconcile myself to for a great while. However, at last, after many secret disputes with myself, and after great perplexities about it (for all these arguments, one way and another, struggled in my head a long time), the eager prevailing desire of deliverance at length mastered all the rest; and I resolved, if possible, to get one of these savages into my hands, cost what it would. My next thing was to contrive how to do it, and this, indeed, was very difficult to resolve on; but as I could pitch upon no probable means for it, so I resolved to put myself upon the watch, to see them when they came on shore, and leave the rest to the event; taking such measures as the opportunity should present, let what would be.

With these resolutions in my thoughts, I set myself upon the scout as often as possible, and indeed so often that I was heartily tired of it; for it was above a year and a half that I waited; and for great part of that time went out to the west end, and to the south-west corner of the island almost every day, to look for canoes, but none appeared. This was very discouraging, and began to trouble me much, though I cannot say that it did in this case (as it had done some time before) wear off the edge of my desire to the thing; but the longer it seemed to be delayed, the more eager I was for it: in a word, I was not at first so careful to shun the sight of these savages, and avoid being seen by them, as I was now eager to be upon them. Besides, I fancied myself able to manage one, nay, two or three savages, if I had them, so as to make them entirely slaves to me, to do whatever I should direct them, and to prevent their being able at any time to do me any hurt. It was a great while that I pleased myself with this affair; but nothing still presented itself; all my fancies and schemes came to nothing, for no savages came near me for a great while.

About a year and a half after I entertained these notions (and by long musing had, as it were, resolved them all into nothing, for want of an occasion to put them into execution), I was surprised one morning by seeing no less than five canoes all on shore together on my side the island, and the people who belonged to them all landed and out of my sight. The number of them broke all my measures; for seeing so many, and knowing that they always came four or six, or sometimes more in a boat, I could not tell what to think of it, or how to take my measures to attack twenty or thirty men single-handed; so lay still in my castle, perplexed and discomforted. However, I put myself into the same position for an attack that I had formerly provided, and was just ready for action, if anything had presented. Having waited a good while, listening to hear if they made any noise, at length, being very impatient, I set my guns at the foot of my ladder, and clambered up to the top of the hill, by my two stages, as usual; standing so, however, that my head did not appear above the hill, so that they could not perceive me by any means. Here I observed, by the help of my perspective glass, that they were no less than thirty in number; that they had a fire kindled, and that they had meat dressed. How they had cooked it I knew not, or what it was; but they were all dancing, in I know not how many barbarous gestures and figures, their own way, round the fire.

While I was thus looking on them, I perceived, by my perspective, two miserable wretches dragged from the boats, where, it seems, they were laid by, and were now brought out for the slaughter. I perceived one of them immediately fall; being knocked down, I suppose, with a club or wooden sword, for that was their way; and two or three others were at work immediately, cutting him open for their cookery, while the other victim was left standing by himself, till they should be ready for him. In that very moment this poor wretch, seeing himself a little at liberty and unbound, Nature inspired him with hopes of life, and he started away from them, and ran with incredible swiftness along the sands, directly towards me; I mean towards that part of the coast where my habitation was. I was dreadfully frightened, I must acknowledge, when I perceived him run my way; and especially when, as I thought, I saw him pursued by the whole body: and now I expected that part of my dream was coming to pass, and that he would certainly take shelter in my grove; but I could not depend, by any means, upon my dream, that the other savages would not pursue him thither and find him there. However, I kept my station, and my spirits began to recover when I found that there was not above three men that followed him; and still more was I encouraged, when I found that he outstripped them exceedingly in running, and gained ground on them; so that, if he could but hold out for half-an-hour, I saw easily he would fairly get away from them all.

There was between them and my castle the creek, which I mentioned often in the first part of my story, where I landed my cargoes out of the ship; and this I saw plainly he must necessarily swim over, or the poor wretch would be taken there; but when the savage escaping came thither, he made nothing of it, though the tide was then up; but plunging in, swam through in about thirty strokes, or thereabouts, landed, and ran with exceeding strength and swiftness. When the three persons came to the creek, I found that two of them could swim, but the third could not, and that, standing on the other side, he looked at the others, but went no farther, and soon after went softly back again; which, as it happened, was very well for him in the end. I observed that the two who swam were yet more than twice as strong swimming over the creek as the fellow was that fled from them. It came very warmly upon my thoughts, and indeed irresistibly, that now was the time to get me a servant, and, perhaps, a companion or assistant; and that I was plainly called by Providence to save this poor creature's life. I immediately ran down the ladders with all possible expedition, fetched my two guns, for they were both at the foot of the ladders, as I observed before, and getting up again with the same haste

167

to the top of the hill, I crossed towards the sea; and having a very short cut, and all down hill, placed myself in the way between the pursuers and the pursued, hallowing aloud to him that fled, who, looking back, was at first perhaps as much frightened at me as at them; but I beckoned with my hand to him to come back; and, in the meantime, I slowly advanced towards the two that followed; then rushing at once upon the foremost, I knocked him down with the stock of my piece. I was loath to fire, because I would not have the rest hear; though, at that distance, it would not have been easily heard, and being out of sight of the smoke, too, they would not have known what to make of it. Having knocked this fellow down, the other who pursued him stopped, as if he had been frightened, and I advanced towards him: but as I came nearer, I perceived presently he had a bow and arrow, and was fitting it to shoot at me: so I was then obliged to shoot at him first, which I did, and killed him at the first shot. The poor savage who fled, but had stopped, though he saw both his enemies fallen and killed, as he thought, yet was so frightened with the fire and noise of my piece that he stood stock still, and neither came forward nor went backward, though he seemed rather inclined still to fly than to come on. I hallooed again to him, and made signs to come forward, which he easily understood, and came a little way; then stopped again, and then a little farther, and stopped again; and I could then perceive that he stood trembling, as if he had been taken prisoner, and had just been to be killed, as his two enemies were. I beckoned to him again to come to me, and gave him all the signs of encouragement that I could think of; and he came nearer and nearer, kneeling down every ten or twelve steps, in token of acknowledgment for saving his life. I smiled at him, and looked pleasantly, and beckoned to him to come still nearer; at length he came close to me; and then he kneeled down again, kissed the ground, and laid his head upon the ground, and taking me by the foot, set my foot upon his head; this, it seems, was in token of swearing to be my slave for ever. I took him up and made much of him, and encouraged him all I could. But there was more work to do yet; for I perceived the savage whom I had knocked down was not killed, but stunned with the blow, and began to come to himself: so I pointed to him, and showed him the savage, that he was not dead; upon this he spoke some words to me, and though I could not understand them, yet I thought they were pleasant to hear; for they were the first sound of a man's voice that I had heard, my own excepted, for above twenty-five years. But there was no time for such reflections now; the savage who was knocked down recovered himself so far as to sit up upon the ground, and I perceived that my savage began to be afraid; but when I saw that, I presented my other piece at the man, as if I would shoot him: upon this my savage, for so I call him now, made a motion to me to lend him my sword, which hung naked in a belt by my side, which I did. He no sooner had it, but he runs to his enemy, and at one blow cut off his head so cleverly, no executioner in Germany could have done it sooner or better; which I thought very strange for one who, I had reason to believe, never saw a sword in his life before, except their own wooden swords: however, it seems, as I learned afterwards, they make their wooden swords so sharp, so heavy, and the wood is so hard, that they will even cut off heads with them, ay, and arms, and that at one blow, too. When he had done this, he comes laughing to me in sign of triumph, and brought me the sword again, and with abundance of gestures which I did not understand, laid it down, with the head of the savage that he had killed, just before me. But that which astonished him most was to know how I killed the other Indian so far off; so, pointing to him, he made signs to me to let him go to him; and I bade him go, as well as I could. When he came to him, he stood like one amazed, looking at him, turning him first on one side, then on the other; looked at the wound the bullet had made, which it seems was just in his breast, where it had made a hole, and no great quantity of blood had followed; but he had bled inwardly, for he was quite dead. He took up his bow and arrows, and came back; so I turned to go away, and beckoned him to follow me, making signs to him that more might come after them. Upon this he made signs to me that he should bury them with sand, that they might not be seen by the rest, if they followed; and so I made signs to him again to do so. He fell to work; and in an instant he had scraped a hole in the sand with his hands big enough to bury the first in, and then dragged him into it, and covered him; and did so by the other also; I believe he had him buried them both in a quarter of an hour. Then, calling away, I carried him, not to my castle, but quite away to my cave, on the farther part of the island: so I did not let my dream come to pass in that part, that he came into my grove for shelter. Here I gave him bread and a bunch of raisins to eat, and a draught of water, which I found he was indeed in great distress for, from his running: and having refreshed him, I made signs for him to go and lie down to sleep, showing him a place where I had laid some rice-straw, and a blanket upon it, which I used to sleep upon myself sometimes; so the poor creature lay down, and went to sleep.

He was a comely, handsome fellow, perfectly well made, with straight, strong limbs, not too large; tall, and well-shaped; and, as I reckon, about twenty-six years of age. He had a very good countenance, not a fierce and surly aspect, but seemed to have something very manly in his face; and yet he had all the sweetness and softness of a European in his countenance, too, especially when he smiled. His hair was long and black, not curled like wool; his forehead very high and large; and a great vivacity and sparkling sharpness in his eyes. The colour of his skin was not quite black, but very tawny; and yet not an ugly, yellow, nauseous tawny, as the Brazilians and Virginians, and other natives of America are, but of a bright kind of a dun olive-colour, that had in it something very agreeable, though not very easy to describe. His face was round and plump; his nose small, not flat, like the negroes; a very good mouth, thin lips, and his fine teeth well set, and as white as ivory.

After he had slumbered, rather than slept, about half-an-hour, he awoke again, and came out of the cave to me: for I had been milking my goats which I had in the enclosure just by: when he espied me he came running to me, laying himself down again upon the ground, with all the possible signs of an humble, thankful disposition, making a great many antic gestures to show it. At last he lays his head flat upon the ground, close to my foot, and sets my other foot upon his head, as he had done before; and after this made all the signs to me of subjection, servitude, and submission imaginable, to let me know how he would serve me so long as he lived. I understood him in many things, and let him know I was very well pleased with him. In a little time I began to speak to him; and teach him to speak to me: and first, I let him know his name should be Friday, which was the day I saved his life: I called him so for the memory of the time. I likewise taught him to say Master; and then let him know that was to be my name: I likewise taught him to say Yes and No and to know the meaning of them. I gave him some milk in an earthen pot, and let him see me drink it before him, and sop my bread in it; and gave him a cake of bread to do the like, which he quickly complied with, and made signs that it was very good for him. I kept there with him all that night; but as soon as it was day I beckoned to him to come with me, and let him know I would give him some clothes; at which he seemed very glad, for he was stark naked. As we went by the place where he had buried the two men, he pointed exactly to the place, and showed me the marks that he had made to find them again, making signs to me that we should dig them up again and eat them. At this I appeared very angry, expressed my abhorrence of it, made as if I would vomit at the thoughts of it, and beckoned with my hand to him to come away, which he did immediately, with great submission. I then led him up to the top of the hill, to see if his enemies were gone; and pulling out my glass I looked, and saw plainly the place where they had been, but no appearance of them or their canoes; so that it was plain they were gone, and had left their two comrades behind them, without any search after them.

But I was not content with this discovery; but having now more courage, and consequently more curiosity, I took my man Friday with me, giving him the sword in his hand, with the bow and arrows at his back, which I found he could use very dexterously, making him carry one gun for me, and I two for myself; and away we marched to the place where these creatures had been; for I had a mind now to get some further intelligence of them. When I came to the place my very blood ran chill in my veins, and my heart sunk within me, at the horror of the spectacle; indeed, it was a dreadful sight, at least it was so to me, though Friday made nothing of it. The place was covered with human bones, the ground dyed with their blood, and great pieces of flesh left here and there, half-eaten, mangled, and scorched; and, in short, all the tokens of the triumphant feast they had been making there, after a victory over their enemies. I saw three skulls, five hands, and the bones of three or four legs and feet, and abundance of other parts of the bodies; and Friday, by his signs, made me understand that they brought over four prisoners to feast upon; that three of them were eaten up, and that he, pointing to himself, was the fourth; that there had been a great battle between them and their next king, of whose subjects, it seems, he had been one, and that they had taken a great number of prisoners; all which were carried to several places by those who had taken them in the fight, in order to feast upon them, as was done here by these wretches upon those they brought hither.

I caused Friday to gather all the skulls, bones, flesh, and whatever remained, and lay them together in a heap, and make a great fire upon it, and burn them all to ashes. I found Friday had still a hankering stomach after some of the flesh, and was still a cannibal in his nature; but I showed so much abhorrence at the very thoughts of it, and at the least appearance of it, that he durst not discover it: for I had, by some means, let him know that I would kill him if he offered it.

When he had done this, we came back to our castle; and there I fell to work for my man Friday; and first of all, I gave him a pair of linen drawers, which I had out of the poor gunner's chest I mentioned, which I found in the wreck, and which, with a little alteration, fitted him very well; and then I made him a jerkin of goat's skin, as well as my skill would allow (for I was now grown a tolerably good tailor); and I gave him a cap which I made of hare's skin, very convenient, and fashionable enough; and thus he was clothed, for the present, tolerably well, and was mighty well pleased to see himself almost as well clothed as his master. It is true he went awkwardly in these clothes at first: wearing the drawers was very awkward to him, and the sleeves of the waistcoat galled his shoulders and the inside of his arms; but a little easing them where he complained they hurt him, and using himself to them, he took to them at length very well.

The next day, after I came home to my hutch with him, I began to consider where I should lodge him: and that I might do well for him and yet be perfectly easy myself, I made a little tent for him in the vacant place between my two fortifications, in the inside of the last, and in the outside of the first. As there was a door or entrance there into my cave, I made a formal framed door-case, and a door to it, of boards, and set it up in the passage, a little within the entrance; and, causing the door to open in the inside, I barred it up in the night, taking in my ladders, too; so that Friday could no way come at me in the inside of my innermost wall, without making so much noise in getting over that it must needs awaken me; for my first wall had now a complete roof over it of long poles, covering all my tent, and leaning up to the side of the hill; which was again laid across with smaller sticks, instead of laths, and then thatched over a great thickness with the rice-straw, which was strong, like reeds; and at the hole or place which was left to go in or out by the ladder I had placed a kind of trap-door, which, if it had been attempted on the outside, would not have opened at all, but would have fallen down and made a great noise—as to weapons, I took them all into my side every night. But I needed none of all this precaution; for never man had a more faithful, loving, sincere servant than Friday was to me: without passions, sullenness, or designs, perfectly obliged and engaged; his very affections were tied to me, like those of a child to a father; and I daresay he would have sacrificed his life to save mine upon any occasion whatsoever—the many testimonies he gave me of this put it out of doubt, and soon convinced me that I needed to use no precautions for my safety on his account.

This frequently gave me occasion to observe, and that with wonder, that however it had pleased God in His providence, and in the government of the works of His hands, to take from so great a part of the world of His creatures the best uses to which their faculties and the powers of their souls are adapted, yet that He has bestowed upon them the same powers, the same reason, the same affections, the same sentiments of kindness and obligation, the same passions and resentments of wrongs, the same sense of gratitude, sincerity, fidelity, and all the capacities of doing good and receiving good that He has given to us; and that when He pleases to offer them occasions of exerting these, they are as ready, nay, more ready, to apply them to the right uses for which they were bestowed than we are. This made me very melancholy sometimes, in reflecting, as the several occasions presented, how mean a use we make of all these, even though we have these powers enlightened by the great lamp of instruction, the Spirit of God, and by the knowledge of His word added to our understanding; and why it has pleased God to hide the like saving knowledge from so many millions of souls, who, if I might judge by this poor savage, would make a much better use of it than we did. From hence I sometimes was led too far, to invade the sovereignty of Providence, and, as it were, arraign the justice of so arbitrary a disposition of things, that should hide that sight from some, and reveal it to others, and yet expect a like duty from both; but I shut it up, and checked my thoughts with this conclusion: first, that we did not know by what light and law these should be condemned; but that as God was necessarily, and by the nature of His being, infinitely holy and just, so it could not be, but if these creatures were all sentenced to absence from Himself, it was on account of sinning against that light which, as the Scripture says, was a law to themselves, and by such rules as their consciences would acknowledge to be just, though the foundation was not discovered to us; and secondly, that still as we all are the clay in the hand of the potter, no vessel could say to him, "Why hast thou formed me thus?"

But to return to my new companion. I was greatly delighted with him, and made it my business to teach him everything that was proper to make him useful, handy, and helpful; but especially to make him speak, and understand me when I spoke; and he was the aptest scholar that ever was; and particularly was so merry, so constantly diligent, and so pleased when he could but understand me, or make me understand him, that it was very pleasant for me to talk to him. Now my life began to be so easy that I began to say to myself that could I but have been safe from more savages, I cared not if I was never to remove from the place where I lived.

173

CHAPTER XV

FRIDAY'S EDUCATION

After I had been two or three days returned to my castle, I thought that, in order to bring Friday off from his horrid way of feeding, and from the relish of a cannibal's stomach, I ought to let him taste other flesh; so I took him out with me one morning to the woods. I went, indeed, intending to kill a kid out of my own flock; and bring it home and dress it; but as I was going I saw a she-goat lying down in the shade, and two young kids sitting by her. I catched hold of Friday. "Hold," said I, "stand still;" and made signs to him not to stir: immediately I presented my piece, shot, and killed one of the kids. The poor creature, who had at a distance, indeed, seen me kill the savage, his enemy, but did not know, nor could imagine how it was done, was sensibly surprised, trembled, and shook, and looked so amazed that I thought he would have sunk down. He did not see the kid I shot at, or perceive I had killed it, but ripped up his waistcoat to feel whether he was not wounded; and, as I found presently, thought I was resolved to kill him: for he came and kneeled down to me, and embracing my knees, said a great many things I did not understand; but I could easily see the meaning was to pray me not to kill him.

I soon found a way to convince him that I would do him no harm; and taking him up by the hand, laughed at him, and pointing to the kid which I had killed, beckoned to him to run and fetch it, which he did: and while he was wondering, and looking to see how the creature was killed, I loaded my gun again. By-and-by I saw a great fowl, like a hawk, sitting upon a tree within shot; so, to let Friday understand a little what I would do, I called him to me again, pointed at the fowl, which was indeed a parrot, though I thought it had been a hawk; I say, pointing to the parrot, and to my gun, and to the ground under the parrot, to let him see I would make it fall, I made him understand that I would shoot and kill that bird; accordingly, I fired, and bade him look, and immediately he saw the parrot fall. He stood like one frightened again, notwithstanding all I had said to him; and I found he was the more amazed, because he did not see me put anything into the gun, but thought that there must be some wonderful fund of death and destruction in that thing, able to kill man, beast, bird, or anything near or far off; and the astonishment this created in him was such as could not wear off for a long time; and I believe, if I would have let him, he

174

would have worshipped me and my gun. As for the gun itself, he would not so much as touch it for several days after; but he would speak to it and talk to it, as if it had answered him, when he was by himself; which, as I afterwards learned of him, was to desire it not to kill him. Well, after his astonishment was a little over at this, I pointed to him to run and fetch the bird I had shot, which he did, but stayed some time; for the parrot, not being quite dead, had fluttered away a good distance from the place where she fell: however, he found her, took her up, and brought her to me; and as I had perceived his ignorance about the gun before, I took this advantage to charge the gun again, and not to let him see me do it, that I might be ready for any other mark that might present; but nothing more offered at that time: so I brought home the kid, and the same evening I took the skin off, and cut it out as well as I could; and having a pot fit for that purpose, I boiled or stewed some of the flesh, and made some very good broth. After I had begun to eat some I gave some to my man, who seemed very glad of it, and liked it very well; but that which was strangest to him was to see me eat salt with it. He made a sign to me that the salt was not good to eat; and putting a little into his own mouth, he seemed to nauseate it, and would spit and sputter at it, washing his mouth with fresh water after it: on the other hand, I took some meat into my mouth without salt, and I pretended to spit and sputter for want of salt, as much as he had done at the salt; but it would not do; he would never care for salt with meat or in his broth; at least, not for a great while, and then but a very little.

Having thus fed him with boiled meat and broth, I was resolved to feast him the next day by roasting a piece of the kid: this I did by hanging it before the fire on a string, as I had seen many people do in England, setting two poles up, one on each side of the fire, and one across the top, and tying the string to the cross stick, letting the meat turn continually. This Friday admired very much; but when he came to taste the flesh, he took so many ways to tell me how well he liked it, that I could not but understand him: and at last he told me, as well as he could, he would never eat man's flesh any more, which I was very glad to hear.

The next day I set him to work beating some corn out, and sifting it in the manner I used to do, as I observed before; and he soon understood how to do it as well as I, especially after he had seen what the meaning of it was, and that it was to make bread of; for after that I let him see me make my bread, and bake it too; and in a little time Friday was able to do all the work for me as well as I could do it myself.

I began now to consider, that having two mouths to feed instead of one, I must provide more ground for my harvest, and plant a larger quantity of corn than I used to do; so I marked out a larger piece of land, and began the fence in the same manner as before, in which Friday worked not only very willingly and very hard, but did it very cheerfully: and I told him what it was for; that it was for corn to make more bread, because he was now with me, and that I might have enough for him and myself too. He appeared very sensible of that part, and let me know that he thought I had much more labour upon me on his account than I had for myself; and that he would work the harder for me if I would tell him what to do.

This was the pleasantest year of all the life I led in this place. Friday began to talk pretty well, and understand the names of almost everything I had occasion to call for, and of every place I had to send him to, and talked a great deal to me; so that, in short, I began now to have some use for my tongue again, which, indeed, I had very little occasion for before. Besides the pleasure of talking to him, I had a singular satisfaction in the fellow himself: his simple, unfeigned honesty appeared to me more and more every day, and I began really to love the creature; and on his side I believe he loved me more than it was possible for him ever to love anything before.

I had a mind once to try if he had any inclination for his own country again; and having taught him English so well that he could answer me almost any question, I asked him whether the nation that he belonged to never conquered in battle? At which he smiled, and said—"Yes, yes, we always fight the better;" that is, he meant always get the better in fight; and so we began the following discourse:—

Master.—You always fight the better; how came you to be taken prisoner, then, Friday?

Friday.—My nation beat much for all that.

Master.—How beat? If your nation beat them, how came you to be taken?

Friday.—They more many than my nation, in the place where me was; they take one, two, three, and me: my nation over-beat them in the yonder place, where me no was; there my nation take one, two, great thousand.

Master.—But why did not your side recover you from the hands of your enemies, then?

Friday.—They run, one, two, three, and me, and make go in the canoe; my nation have no canoe that time.

Master.—Well, Friday, and what does your nation do with the men they take? Do they carry them away and eat them, as these did?

Friday.—Yes, my nation eat mans too; eat all up.

Master.—Where do they carry them?

Friday.—Go to other place, where they think.

Master.—Do they come hither?

Friday.—Yes, yes, they come hither; come other else place.

Master.—Have you been here with them?

Friday.—Yes, I have been here (points to the NW. side of the island, which, it seems, was their side).

By this I understood that my man Friday had formerly been among the savages who used to come on shore on the farther part of the island, on the same man-eating occasions he was now brought for; and some time after, when I took the courage to carry him to that side, being the same I formerly mentioned, he presently knew the place, and told me he was there once, when they ate up twenty men, two women, and one child; he could not tell twenty in English, but he numbered them by laying so many stones in a row, and pointing to me to tell them over.

I have told this passage, because it introduces what follows: that after this discourse I had with him, I asked him how far it was from our island to the shore, and whether the canoes were not often lost. He told me there was no danger, no canoes ever lost: but that after a little way out to sea, there was a current and wind, always one way in the morning, the other in the afternoon. This I understood to be no more than the sets of the tide, as going out or coming in; but I afterwards understood it was occasioned by the great draft and reflux of the mighty river Orinoco, in the mouth or gulf of which river, as I found afterwards, our island lay; and that this land, which I perceived to be W. and NW., was the great island Trinidad, on the north point of the mouth of the river. I asked Friday a thousand questions about the country, the inhabitants, the sea, the coast, and what nations were near; he told me all he knew with the greatest openness imaginable. I asked him the names of the several nations of his sort of people, but could get no other name than Caribs; from whence I easily understood that these were the Caribbees, which our maps place on the part of America which reaches from the mouth of the river Orinoco to Guiana, and onwards to St. Martha. He told me that up a great way beyond the moon, that was beyond the setting of the moon, which must be west from their country, there dwelt white bearded men, like me, and pointed to my great whiskers, which I mentioned before; and that they had killed much mans, that was his word: by all which I understood he meant the Spaniards, whose cruelties in America had been spread over the whole country, and were remembered by all the nations from father to son.

I inquired if he could tell me how I might go from this island, and get among those white men. He told me, "Yes, yes, you may go in two canoe." I could not understand what he meant, or make him describe to me what he meant by two canoe, till at last, with great difficulty, I found he meant it must be in a large boat, as big as two canoes. This part of Friday's discourse I began to relish very well; and from this time I entertained some hopes that, one time or other, I might find an opportunity to make my escape from this place, and that this poor savage might be a means to help me.

During the long time that Friday had now been with me, and that he began to speak to me, and understand me, I was not wanting to lay a foundation of religious knowledge in his mind; particularly I asked him one time, who made him. The creature did not understand me at all, but thought I had asked who was his father—but I took it up by another handle, and asked him who made the sea, the ground we walked on, and the hills and woods. He told me, "It was one Benamuckee, that lived beyond all;" he could describe nothing of this great person, but that he was very old, "much older," he said, "than the sea or land, than the moon or the stars." I asked him then, if this old person had made all things, why did not all things worship him? He looked very grave, and, with a perfect look of innocence, said, "All things say O to him." I asked him if the people who die in his country went away anywhere? He said, "Yes; they all went to Benamuckee." Then I asked him whether those they eat up went thither too. He said, "Yes."

From these things, I began to instruct him in the knowledge of the true God; I told him that the great Maker of all things lived up there, pointing up towards heaven; that He governed the world by the same power and providence by which He made it; that He was omnipotent, and could do everything for us, give everything to us, take everything from us; and thus, by degrees, I opened his eyes. He listened with great attention, and received with pleasure the notion of Jesus Christ being sent to redeem us; and of the manner of making our prayers to God, and His being able to hear us, even in heaven. He told me one day, that if our God could hear us, up beyond the sun, he must needs be a greater God than their Benamuckee, who lived but a little way off, and yet could not hear till they went up to the great mountains where he dwelt to speak to them. I asked him if ever he went thither to speak to him. He said, "No; they never went that were young men; none went thither but the old men," whom he called their Oowokakee; that is, as I made him explain to me, their religious, or clergy; and that they went to say O (so he called saying prayers), and then came back and told them what Benamuckee said. By this I observed, that there is priestcraft even among the most blinded, ignorant pagans in the world; and the policy of making a secret of religion, in order to preserve the veneration of the people to the clergy, not only to be found in the Roman, but, perhaps, among all religions in the world, even among the most brutish and barbarous savages.

I endeavoured to clear up this fraud to my man Friday; and told him that the pretence of their old men going up to the mountains to say O to their god Benamuckee was a cheat; and their bringing word from thence what he said was much more so; that if they met with any answer, or spake with any one there, it must be with an evil spirit; and then I entered into a long discourse with him about the devil, the origin of him, his rebellion against God, his enmity to man, the reason of it, his setting himself up in the dark parts of the world to be worshipped instead of God, and as God, and the many stratagems he made use of to delude mankind to their ruin; how he had a secret access to our passions and to our affections, and to adapt his snares to our inclinations, so as to cause us even to be our own tempters, and run upon our destruction by our own choice.

I found it was not so easy to imprint right notions in his mind about the devil as it was about the being of a God. Nature assisted all my arguments to evidence to him even the necessity of a great First Cause, an overruling, governing Power, a secret directing Providence, and of the equity and justice of paying homage to Him that made us, and the like; but there appeared nothing of this kind in the notion of an evil spirit, of his origin, his being, his nature, and above all, of his inclination to do evil, and to draw us in to do so too; and the poor creature puzzled me once in such a manner, by a question merely natural and innocent, that I scarce knew what to say to him. I had been talking a great deal to him of the power of God, His omnipotence, His aversion to sin, His being a consuming fire to the workers of iniquity; how, as He had made us all, He could destroy us and all the world in a moment; and he listened with great seriousness to me all the while. After this I had been telling him how the devil was God's enemy in the hearts of men, and used all his malice and skill to defeat the good designs of Providence, and to ruin the kingdom of Christ in the world, and the like. "Well," says Friday, "but you say God is so strong, so great; is He not much strong, much might as the devil?" "Yes, yes," says I, "Friday; God is stronger than the devil—God is above the devil, and therefore we pray to God to tread him down under our feet, and enable us to resist his temptations and quench his fiery darts." "But," says he again, "if God much stronger, much might as the wicked devil, why God no kill the devil, so make him no more do wicked?" I was strangely surprised at this question; and, after all, though I was now an old man, yet I was but a young doctor, and ill qualified for a casuist or a solver of difficulties; and at first I could not tell what to say; so I pretended not to hear him, and asked him what he said; but he was too earnest for an answer to forget his question, so that he repeated it in the very same broken words as above. By this time I had recovered myself a little, and I said, "God will at last punish him severely; he is reserved for the judgment, and is to be cast into the bottomless pit, to dwell with everlasting fire." This did not satisfy Friday; but he returns upon me, repeating my words, "'*Reserve at last*!' me no understand—but why not kill the devil now; not kill great ago?" "You may as well ask me," said I, "why God does not kill you or me, when we do wicked things here that offend Him—we are preserved to repent and be pardoned." He mused some time on this. "Well, well," says he, mighty affectionately, "that well—so you, I, devil, all wicked, all preserve, repent, God pardon all." Here I was run down again by him to the last degree; and it was a testimony to me, how the mere notions of nature, though they will guide reasonable creatures to the knowledge of a God, and of a worship or homage due to the supreme being of God, as the consequence of our nature, yet nothing but divine revelation can form the knowledge of Jesus Christ, and of redemption purchased for us; of a Mediator of the new covenant, and of an Intercessor at the footstool of God's throne; I say, nothing but a revelation from Heaven can form these in the soul; and that, therefore, the gospel of our Lord and Saviour Jesus Christ, I mean the Word of God, and the Spirit of God, promised for the guide and sanctifier of His people, are the absolutely necessary instructors of the souls of men in the saving knowledge of God and the means of salvation.

I therefore diverted the present discourse between me and my man, rising up hastily, as upon some sudden occasion of going out; then sending him for something a good way off, I seriously prayed to God that He would enable me to instruct savingly this poor savage; assisting, by His Spirit, the heart of the poor ignorant creature to receive the light of the knowledge of God in Christ, reconciling him to Himself, and would guide me so to speak to him from the Word of God that his conscience might be convinced, his eyes opened, and his soul saved. When he came again to me, I entered into a long discourse with him upon the subject of the redemption of man by the Saviour of the world, and of the doctrine of the gospel preached from Heaven, viz. of repentance towards God, and faith in our blessed Lord Jesus. I then explained to him as well as I could why our blessed Redeemer took not on Him the nature of angels but the seed of Abraham; and how, for that reason, the fallen angels had no share in the redemption; that He came only to the lost sheep of the house of Israel, and the like.

I had, God knows, more sincerity than knowledge in all the methods I took for this poor creature's instruction, and must acknowledge, what I believe all that act upon the same principle will find, that in laying things open to him, I really informed and instructed myself in many things that either I did not know or had not fully considered before, but which occurred naturally to my mind upon searching into them, for the information of this poor savage; and I had more affection in my inquiry after things upon this occasion than ever I felt before: so that, whether this poor wild wretch was better for me or no, I had great reason to be thankful that ever he came to me; my grief sat lighter, upon me; my habitation grew comfortable to me beyond measure: and when I reflected that in this solitary life which I have been confined to, I had not only been moved to look up to heaven myself, and to seek the Hand that had brought me here, but was now to be made an instrument, under Providence, to save the life, and, for aught I knew, the soul of a poor savage, and bring him to the true knowledge of religion and of the Christian doctrine, that he might know Christ Jesus, in whom is life eternal; I say, when I reflected upon all these things, a secret joy ran through every part of My soul, and I frequently rejoiced that ever I was brought to this place, which I had so often thought the most dreadful of all afflictions that could possibly have befallen me.

I continued in this thankful frame all the remainder of my time; and the conversation which employed the hours between Friday and me was such as made the three years which we lived there together perfectly and completely happy, if any such thing as complete happiness can be formed in a sublunary state. This savage was now a good Christian, a much better than I; though I have reason to hope, and bless God for it, that we were equally penitent, and comforted, restored penitents. We had here the Word of God to read, and no farther off from His Spirit to instruct than if we had been in England. I always applied myself, in reading the Scripture, to let him know, as well as I could, the meaning of what I read; and he again, by his serious inquiries and questionings, made me, as I said before, a much better scholar in the Scripture knowledge than I should ever have been by my own mere private reading. Another thing I cannot refrain from observing here also, from experience in this retired part of my life, viz. how infinite and inexpressible a blessing it is that the knowledge of God, and of the doctrine of salvation by Christ Jesus, is so plainly laid down in the Word of God, so easy to be received and understood, that, as the bare reading the Scripture made me capable of understanding enough of my duty to carry me directly on to the great work of sincere repentance for my sins, and laying hold of a Saviour for life and salvation, to a stated reformation in practice, and obedience to all God's commands, and this without any teacher or instructor, I mean human; so the same plain instruction sufficiently served to the enlightening this savage creature, and bringing him to be such a Christian as I have known few equal to him in my life.

As to all the disputes, wrangling, strife, and contention which have happened in the world about religion, whether niceties in doctrines or schemes of church government, they were all perfectly useless to us, and, for aught I can yet see, they have been so to the rest of the world. We had the sure guide to heaven, viz. the Word of God; and we had, blessed be God, comfortable views of the Spirit of God teaching and instructing by His word, leading us into all truth, and making us both willing and obedient to the instruction of His word. And I cannot see the least use that the greatest knowledge of the disputed points of religion, which have made such confusion in the world, would have been to us, if we could have obtained it. But I must go on with the historical part of things, and take every part in its order.

After Friday and I became more intimately acquainted, and that he could understand almost all I said to him, and speak pretty fluently, though in broken English, to me, I acquainted him with my own history, or at least so much of it as related to my coming to this place: how I had lived there, and how long; I let him into the mystery, for such it was to him, of gunpowder and bullet, and taught him how to shoot. I gave him a knife, which he was wonderfully delighted with; and I made him a belt, with a frog hanging to it, such as in England we wear hangers in; and in the frog, instead of a hanger, I gave him a hatchet, which was not only as good a weapon in some cases, but much more useful upon other occasions.

I described to him the country of Europe, particularly England, which I came from; how we lived, how we worshipped God, how we behaved to one another, and how we traded in ships to all parts of the world. I gave him an account of the wreck which I had been on board of, and showed him, as near as I could, the place where she lay; but she was all beaten in pieces before, and gone. I showed him the ruins of our boat, which we lost when we escaped, and which I could not stir with my whole strength then; but was now fallen almost all to pieces. Upon seeing this boat, Friday stood, musing a great while, and said nothing. I asked him what it was he studied upon. At last says he, "Me see such boat like come to place at my nation." I did not understand him a good while; but at last, when I had examined further into it, I understood by him that a boat, such as that had been, came on shore upon the country where he lived: that is, as he explained it, was driven thither by stress of weather. I presently imagined that some European ship must have been cast away upon their coast, and the boat might get loose and drive ashore; but was so dull that I never once thought of men making their escape from a wreck thither, much less whence they might come: so I only inquired after a description of the boat.

Friday described the boat to me well enough; but brought me better to understand him when he added with some warmth, "We save the white mans from drown." Then I presently asked if there were any white mans, as he called them, in the boat. "Yes," he said; "the boat full of white mans." I asked him how many. He told upon his fingers seventeen. I asked him then what became of them. He told me, "They live, they dwell at my nation."

This put new thoughts into my head; for I presently imagined that these might be the men belonging to the ship that was cast away in the sight of my island, as I now called it; and who, after the ship was struck on the rock, and they saw her inevitably lost, had saved themselves in their boat, and were landed upon that wild shore among the savages. Upon this I inquired of him more critically what was become of them. He assured me they lived still there; that they had been there about four years; that the savages left them alone, and gave them victuals to live on. I asked him how it came to pass they did not kill them and eat them. He said, "No, they make brother with them;" that is, as I understood him, a truce; and then he added, "They no eat mans but

183

when make the war fight;" that is to say, they never eat any men but such as come to fight with them and are taken in battle.

It was after this some considerable time, that being upon the top of the hill at the east side of the island, from whence, as I have said, I had, in a clear day, discovered the main or continent of America, Friday, the weather being very serene, looks very earnestly towards the mainland, and, in a kind of surprise, falls a jumping and dancing, and calls out to me, for I was at some distance from him. I asked him what was the matter. "Oh, joy!" says he; "Oh, glad! there see my country, there my nation!" I observed an extraordinary sense of pleasure appeared in his face, and his eyes sparkled, and his countenance discovered a strange eagerness, as if he had a mind to be in his own country again. This observation of mine put a great many thoughts into me, which made me at first not so easy about my new man Friday as I was before; and I made no doubt but that, if Friday could get back to his own nation again, he would not only forget all his religion but all his obligation to me, and would be forward enough to give his countrymen an account of me, and come back, perhaps with a hundred or two of them, and make a feast upon me, at which he might be as merry as he used to be with those of his enemies when they were taken in war. But I wronged the poor honest creature very much, for which I was very sorry afterwards. However, as my jealousy increased, and held some weeks, I was a little more circumspect, and not so familiar and kind to him as before: in which I was certainly wrong too; the honest, grateful creature having no thought about it but what consisted with the best principles, both as a religious Christian and as a grateful friend, as appeared afterwards to my full satisfaction.

While my jealousy of him lasted, you may be sure I was every day pumping him to see if he would discover any of the new thoughts which I suspected were in him; but I found everything he said was so honest and so innocent, that I could find nothing to nourish my suspicion; and in spite of all my uneasiness, he made me at last entirely his own again; nor did he in the least perceive that I was uneasy, and therefore I could not suspect him of deceit.

One day, walking up the same hill, but the weather being hazy at sea, so that we could not see the continent, I called to him, and said, "Friday, do not you wish yourself in your own country, your own nation?" "Yes," he said, "I be much O glad to be at my own nation." "What would you do there?" said I. "Would you turn wild again, eat men's flesh again, and be a savage as you were before?" He looked full

184

of concern, and shaking his head, said, "No, no, Friday tell them to live good; tell them to pray God; tell them to eat corn-bread, cattle flesh, milk; no eat man again." "Why, then," said I to him, "they will kill you." He looked grave at that, and then said, "No, no, they no kill me, they willing love learn." He meant by this, they would be willing to learn. He added, they learned much of the bearded mans that came in the boat. Then I asked him if he would go back to them. He smiled at that, and told me that he could not swim so far. I told him I would make a canoe for him. He told me he would go if I would go with him. "I go!" says I; "why, they will eat me if I come there." "No, no," says he, "me make they no eat you; me make they much love you." He meant, he would tell them how I had killed his enemies, and saved his life, and so he would make them love me. Then he told me, as well as he could, how kind they were to seventeen white men, or bearded men, as he called them who came on shore there in distress.

From this time, I confess, I had a mind to venture over, and see if I could possibly join with those bearded men, who I made no doubt were Spaniards and Portuguese; not doubting but, if I could, we might find some method to escape from thence, being upon the continent, and a good company together, better than I could from an island forty miles off the shore, alone and without help. So, after some days, I took Friday to work again by way of discourse, and told him I would give him a boat to go back to his own nation; and, accordingly, I carried him to my frigate, which lay on the other side of the island, and having cleared it of water (for I always kept it sunk in water), I brought it out, showed it him, and we both went into it. I found he was a most dexterous fellow at managing it, and would make it go almost as swift again as I could. So when he was in, I said to him, "Well, now, Friday, shall we go to your nation?" He looked very dull at my saying so; which it seems was because he thought the boat was too small to go so far. I then told him I had a bigger; so the next day I went to the place where the first boat lay which I had made, but which I could not get into the water. He said that was big enough; but then, as I had taken no care of it, and it had lain two or three and twenty years there, the sun had so split and dried it, that it was rotten. Friday told me such a boat would do very well, and would carry "much enough vittle, drink, bread;" this was his way of talking.

CHAPTER XVI

RESCUE OF PRISONERS FROM CANNIBALS

Upon the whole, I was by this time so fixed upon my design of going over with him to the continent that I told him we would go and make one as big as that, and he should go home in it. He answered not one word, but looked very grave and sad. I asked him what was the matter with him. He asked me again, "Why you angry mad with Friday?—what me done?" I asked him what he meant. I told him I was not angry with him at all. "No angry!" says he, repeating the words several times; "why send Friday home away to my nation?" "Why," says I, "Friday, did not you say you wished you were there?" "Yes, yes," says he, "wish we both there; no wish Friday there, no master there." In a word, he would not think of going there without me. "I go there, Friday?" says I; "what shall I do there?" He turned very quick upon me at this. "You do great deal much good," says he; "you teach wild mans be good, sober, tame mans; you tell them know God, pray God, and live new life." "Alas, Friday!" says I, "thou knowest not what thou sayest; I am but an ignorant man myself." "Yes, yes," says he, "you teachee me good, you teachee them good." "No, no, Friday," says I, "you shall go without me; leave me here to live by myself, as I did before." He looked confused again at that word; and running to one of the hatchets which he used to wear, he takes it up hastily, and gives it to me. "What must I do with this?" says I to him. "You take kill Friday," says he. "What must kill you for?" said I again. He returns very quick—"What you send Friday away for? Take kill Friday, no send Friday away." This he spoke so earnestly that I saw tears stand in his eyes. In a word, I so plainly discovered the utmost affection in him to me, and a firm resolution in him, that I told him then and often after, that I would never send him away from me if he was willing to stay with me.

Upon the whole, as I found by all his discourse a settled affection to me, and that nothing could part him from me, so I found all the foundation of his desire to go to his own country was laid in his ardent affection to the people, and his hopes of my doing them good; a thing which, as I had no notion of myself, so I had not the least thought or intention, or desire of undertaking it. But still I found a strong inclination to attempting my escape, founded on the supposition gathered from the discourse, that there were seventeen bearded men there; and therefore, without any more delay, I went to work with

Friday to find out a great tree proper to fell, and make a large periagua, or canoe, to undertake the voyage. There were trees enough in the island to have built a little fleet, not of periaguas or canoes, but even of good, large vessels; but the main thing I looked at was, to get one so near the water that we might launch it when it was made, to avoid the mistake I committed at first. At last Friday pitched upon a tree; for I found he knew much better than I what kind of wood was fittest for it; nor can I tell to this day what wood to call the tree we cut down, except that it was very like the tree we call fustic, or between that and the Nicaragua wood, for it was much of the same colour and smell. Friday wished to burn the hollow or cavity of this tree out, to make it for a boat, but I showed him how to cut it with tools; which, after I had showed him how to use, he did very handily; and in about a month's hard labour we finished it and made it very handsome; especially when, with our axes, which I showed him how to handle, we cut and hewed the outside into the true shape of a boat. After this, however, it cost us near a fortnight's time to get her along, as it were inch by inch, upon great rollers into the water; but when she was in, she would have carried twenty men with great ease.

When she was in the water, though she was so big, it amazed me to see with what dexterity and how swift my man Friday could manage her, turn her, and paddle her along. So I asked him if he would, and if we might venture over in her. "Yes," he said, "we venture over in her very well, though great blow wind." However I had a further design that he knew nothing of, and that was, to make a mast and a sail, and to fit her with an anchor and cable. As to a mast, that was easy enough to get; so I pitched upon a straight young cedar-tree, which I found near the place, and which there were great plenty of in the island, and I set Friday to work to cut it down, and gave him directions how to shape and order it. But as to the sail, that was my particular care. I knew I had old sails, or rather pieces of old sails, enough; but as I had had them now six-and-twenty years by me, and had not been very careful to preserve them, not imagining that I should ever have this kind of use for them, I did not doubt but they were all rotten; and, indeed, most of them were so. However, I found two pieces which appeared pretty good, and with these I went to work; and with a great deal of pains, and awkward stitching, you may be sure, for want of needles, I at length made a three-cornered ugly thing, like what we call in England a shoulder-of-mutton sail, to go with a boom at bottom, and a little short sprit at the top, such as usually our ships' long-boats sail with, and such as I best knew how to manage, as it was such a one as I had to the boat in which I made my escape from Barbary, as related in the first part of my story.

I was near two months performing this last work, viz. rigging and fitting my masts and sails; for I finished them very complete, making a small stay, and a sail, or foresail, to it, to assist if we should turn to windward; and, what was more than all, I fixed a rudder to the stern of her to steer with. I was but a bungling shipwright, yet as I knew the usefulness and even necessity of such a thing, I applied myself with so much pains to do it, that at last I brought it to pass; though, considering the many dull contrivances I had for it that failed, I think it cost me almost as much labour as making the boat.

After all this was done, I had my man Friday to teach as to what belonged to the navigation of my boat; though he knew very well how to paddle a canoe, he knew nothing of what belonged to a sail and a rudder; and was the most amazed when he saw me work the boat to and again in the sea by the rudder, and how the sail jibed, and filled this way or that way as the course we sailed changed; I say when he saw this he stood like one astonished and amazed. However, with a little use, I made all these things familiar to him, and he became an expert sailor, except that of the compass I could make him understand very little. On the other hand, as there was very little cloudy weather, and seldom or never any fogs in those parts, there was the less occasion for a compass, seeing the stars were always to be seen by night, and the shore by day, except in the rainy seasons, and then nobody cared to stir abroad either by land or sea.

I was now entered on the seven-and-twentieth year of my captivity in this place; though the three last years that I had this creature with me ought rather to be left out of the account, my habitation being quite of another kind than in all the rest of the time. I kept the anniversary of my landing here with the same thankfulness to God for His mercies as at first: and if I had such cause of acknowledgment at first, I had much more so now, having such additional testimonies of the care of Providence over me, and the great hopes I had of being effectually and speedily delivered; for I had an invincible impression upon my thoughts that my deliverance was at hand, and that I should not be another year in this place. I went on, however, with my husbandry; digging, planting, and fencing as usual. I gathered and cured my grapes, and did every necessary thing as before.

The rainy season was in the meantime upon me, when I kept more within doors than at other times. We had stowed our new vessel as secure as we could, bringing her up into the creek, where, as I said in the beginning, I landed my rafts from the ship; and hauling her up to the shore at high-water mark, I made my man Friday dig a little dock, just big enough to hold her, and just deep enough to give her water enough to float in; and then, when the tide was out, we made a strong dam across the end of it, to keep the water out; and so she lay, dry as to the tide from the sea: and to keep the rain off we laid a great many boughs of trees, so thick that she was as well thatched as a house; and thus we waited for the months of November and December, in which I designed to make my adventure.

When the settled season began to come in, as the thought of my design returned with the fair weather, I was preparing daily for the voyage. And the first thing I did was to lay by a certain quantity of provisions, being the stores for our voyage; and intended in a week or a fortnight's time to open the dock, and launch out our boat. I was busy one morning upon something of this kind, when I called to Friday, and bid him to go to the sea-shore and see if he could find a turtle or a tortoise, a thing which we generally got once a week, for the sake of the eggs as well as the flesh. Friday had not been long gone when he came running back, and flew over my outer wall or fence, like one that felt not the ground or the steps he set his foot on; and before I had time to speak to him he cries out to me, "O master! O master! O sorrow! O bad!"—"What's the matter, Friday?" says I. "O yonder there," says he, "one, two, three canoes; one, two, three!" By this way of speaking I concluded there were six; but on inquiry I found there were but three. "Well, Friday," says I, "do not be frightened." So I heartened him up as well as I could. However, I saw the poor fellow was most terribly scared, for nothing ran in his head but that they were come to look for him, and would cut him in pieces and eat him; and the poor fellow trembled so that I scarcely knew what to do with him. I comforted him as well as I could, and told him I was in as much danger as he, and that they would eat me as well as him. "But," says I, "Friday, we must resolve to fight them. Can you fight, Friday?" "Me shoot," says he, "but there come many great number." "No matter for that," said I again; "our guns will fright them that we do not kill." So I asked him whether, if I resolved to defend him, he would defend me, and stand by me, and do just as I bid him. He said, "Me die when you bid die, master." So I went and fetched a good dram of rum and gave him; for I had been so good a husband of my rum that I had a great deal left. When we had drunk it, I made him take the two fowling-pieces, which we always carried, and loaded them with large swan-shot, as big as small pistol-bullets. Then I took four muskets, and loaded them with two slugs and five small bullets each; and my two pistols I loaded with a brace of bullets each. I hung my great sword, as usual, naked by my side, and gave Friday his hatchet. When I had thus prepared myself, I took my perspective glass, and went up to the side of the hill, to see what I could discover; and I found quickly by my glass that there were one-and-twenty savages, three prisoners, and three canoes; and that their whole business seemed to be the triumphant banquet upon these three human bodies: a barbarous feast, indeed! but nothing more than, as I had observed, was usual with them. I observed also that they had landed, not where they had done when Friday made his escape, but nearer to my creek, where the shore was low, and where a thick wood came almost close down to the sea. This, with the abhorrence of the inhuman errand these wretches came about, filled me with such indignation that I came down again to Friday, and told him I was resolved to go down to them and kill them all; and asked him if he would stand by me. He had now got over his fright, and his spirits being a little raised with the dram I had given him, he was very cheerful, and told me, as before, he would die when I bid die.

In this fit of fury I divided the arms which I had charged, as before, between us; I gave Friday one pistol to stick in his girdle, and three guns upon his shoulder, and I took one pistol and the other three guns myself; and in this posture we marched out. I took a small bottle of rum in my pocket, and gave Friday a large bag with more powder and bullets; and as to orders, I charged him to keep close behind me, and not to stir, or shoot, or do anything till I bid him, and in the meantime not to speak a word. In this posture I fetched a compass to my right hand of near a mile, as well to get over the creek as to get into the wood, so that I could come within shot of them before I should be discovered, which I had seen by my glass it was easy to do.

While I was making this march, my former thoughts returning, I began to abate my resolution: I do not mean that I entertained any fear of their number, for as they were naked, unarmed wretches, it is certain I was superior to them—nay, though I had been alone. But it occurred to my thoughts, what call, what occasion, much less what necessity I was in to go and dip my hands in blood, to attack people who had neither done or intended me any wrong? who, as to me, were innocent, and whose barbarous customs were their own disaster, being in them a token, indeed, of God's having left them, with the other nations of that part of the world, to such stupidity, and to such inhuman courses, but did not call me to take upon me to be a judge of their actions, much less an executioner of His justice—that whenever He thought fit He would take the cause into His own hands, and by national vengeance punish them as a people for national crimes, but that, in the meantime, it was none of my business—that it was true Friday might justify it, because he was a declared enemy and in a state of war with those very particular people, and it was lawful for him to attack them—but I could not say the same with regard to myself. These things were so warmly pressed upon my thoughts all the way as I went, that I resolved I would only go and place myself near them that I might observe their barbarous feast, and that I would act then as God should direct; but that unless something offered that was more a call to me than yet I knew of, I would not meddle with them.

With this resolution I entered the wood, and, with all possible wariness and silence, Friday following close at my heels, I marched till I came to the skirts of the wood on the side which was next to them, only that one corner of the wood lay between me and them. Here I called softly to Friday, and showing him a great tree which was just at the corner of the wood, I bade him go to the tree, and bring me word if he could see there plainly what they were doing. He did so, and came immediately back to me, and told me they might be plainly viewed there—that they were all about their fire, eating the flesh of one of their prisoners, and that another lay bound upon the sand a little from them, whom he said they would kill next; and this fired the very soul within me. He told me it was not one of their nation, but one of the bearded men he had told me of, that came to their country in the boat. I was filled with horror at the very naming of the white bearded man; and going to the tree, I saw plainly by my glass a white man, who lay upon the beach of the sea with his hands and his feet tied with flags, or things like rushes, and that he was an European, and had clothes on.

There was another tree and a little thicket beyond it, about fifty yards nearer to them than the place where I was, which, by going a little way about, I saw I might come at undiscovered, and that then I should be within half a shot of them; so I withheld my passion, though I was indeed enraged to the highest degree; and going back about twenty paces, I got behind some bushes, which held all the way till I came to the other tree, and then came to a little rising ground, which gave me a full view of them at the distance of about eighty yards.

I had now not a moment to lose, for nineteen of the dreadful wretches sat upon the ground, all close huddled together, and had just sent the other two to butcher the poor Christian, and bring him perhaps limb by limb to their fire, and they were stooping down to untie the bands at his feet. I turned to Friday. "Now, Friday," said I, "do as I bid thee." Friday said he would. "Then, Friday," says I, "do exactly as you see me do; fail in nothing." So I set down one of the muskets and the fowling-piece upon the ground, and Friday did the like by his, and with the other musket I took my aim at the savages, bidding him to do the like; then asking him if he was ready, he said, "Yes." "Then fire at them," said I; and at the same moment I fired also.

Friday took his aim so much better than I, that on the side that he shot he killed two of them, and wounded three more; and on my side I killed one, and wounded two. They were, you may be sure, in a dreadful consternation: and all of them that were not hurt jumped upon their feet, but did not immediately know which way to run, or which way to look, for they knew not from whence their destruction came. Friday kept his eyes close upon me, that, as I had bid him, he might observe what I did; so, as soon as the first shot was made, I threw down the piece, and took up the fowling-piece, and Friday did the like; he saw me cock and present; he did the same again. "Are you ready, Friday?" said I. "Yes," says he. "Let fly, then," says I, "in the name of God!" and with that I fired again among the amazed wretches, and so did Friday; and as our pieces were now loaded with what I call swan-shot, or small pistol-bullets, we found only two drop; but so many were wounded that they ran about yelling and screaming like mad creatures, all bloody, and most of them miserably wounded; whereof three more fell quickly after, though not quite dead.

"Now, Friday," says I, laying down the discharged pieces, and taking up the musket which was yet loaded, "follow me," which he did with a great deal of courage; upon which I rushed out of the wood and showed myself, and Friday close at my foot. As soon as I perceived they saw me, I shouted as loud as I could, and bade Friday do so too, and running as fast as I could, which, by the way, was not very fast, being loaded with arms as I was, I made directly towards the poor victim, who was, as I said, lying upon the beach or shore, between the place where they sat and the sea. The two butchers who were just going to work with him had left him at the surprise of our first fire, and fled in a terrible fright to the seaside, and had jumped into a canoe, and three more of the rest made the same way. I turned to Friday, and bade him step forwards and fire at them; he understood me immediately, and running about forty yards, to be nearer them, he shot at them; and I thought he had killed them all, for I saw them all fall of a heap into the boat, though I saw two of them up again quickly; however, he killed two of them, and wounded the third, so that he lay down in the bottom of the boat as if he had been dead.

While my man Friday fired at them, I pulled out my knife and cut the flags that bound the poor victim; and loosing his hands and feet, I lifted him up, and asked him in the Portuguese tongue what he was. He answered in Latin, Christianus; but was so weak and faint that he could scarce stand or speak. I took my bottle out of my pocket and gave it him, making signs that he should drink, which he did; and I gave him a piece of bread, which he ate. Then I asked him what countryman he was: and he said, Espagniole; and being a little recovered, let me know, by all the signs he could possibly make, how much he was in my debt for his deliverance. "Seignior," said I, with as much Spanish as I could make up, "we will talk afterwards, but we must fight now: if you have any strength left, take this pistol and sword, and lay about you." He took them very thankfully; and no sooner had he the arms in his hands, but, as if they had put new vigour into him, he flew upon his murderers like a fury, and had cut two of them in pieces in an instant; for the truth is, as the whole was a surprise to them, so the poor creatures were so much frightened with the noise of our pieces that they fell down for mere amazement and fear, and had no more power to attempt their own escape than their flesh had to resist our shot; and that was the case of those five that Friday shot at in the boat; for as three of them fell with the hurt they received, so the other two fell with the fright.

I kept my piece in my hand still without firing, being willing to keep my charge ready, because I had given the Spaniard my pistol and sword: so I called to Friday, and bade him run up to the tree from whence we first fired, and fetch the arms which lay there that had been discharged, which he did with great swiftness; and then giving him my musket, I sat down myself to load all the rest again, and bade them come to me when they wanted. While I was loading these pieces, there happened a fierce engagement between the Spaniard and one of the savages, who made at him with one of their great wooden swords, the weapon that was to have killed him before, if I had not prevented it. The Spaniard, who was as bold and brave as could be imagined, though

193

weak, had fought the Indian a good while, and had cut two great wounds on his head; but the savage being a stout, lusty fellow, closing in with him, had thrown him down, being faint, and was wringing my sword out of his hand; when the Spaniard, though undermost, wisely quitting the sword, drew the pistol from his girdle, shot the savage through the body, and killed him upon the spot, before I, who was running to help him, could come near him.

Friday, being now left to his liberty, pursued the flying wretches, with no weapon in his hand but his hatchet: and with that he despatched those three who as I said before, were wounded at first, and fallen, and all the rest he could come up with: and the Spaniard coming to me for a gun, I gave him one of the fowling-pieces, with which he pursued two of the savages, and wounded them both; but as he was not able to run, they both got from him into the wood, where Friday pursued them, and killed one of them, but the other was too nimble for him; and though he was wounded, yet had plunged himself into the sea, and swam with all his might off to those two who were left in the canoe; which three in the canoe, with one wounded, that we knew not whether he died or no, were all that escaped our hands of one-and-twenty. The account of the whole is as follows: Three killed at our first shot from the tree; two killed at the next shot; two killed by Friday in the boat; two killed by Friday of those at first wounded; one killed by Friday in the wood; three killed by the Spaniard; four killed, being found dropped here and there, of the wounds, or killed by Friday in his chase of them; four escaped in the boat, whereof one wounded, if not dead—twenty-one in all.

Those that were in the canoe worked hard to get out of gun-shot, and though Friday made two or three shots at them, I did not find that he hit any of them. Friday would fain have had me take one of their canoes, and pursue them; and indeed I was very anxious about their escape, lest, carrying the news home to their people, they should come back perhaps with two or three hundred of the canoes and devour us by mere multitude; so I consented to pursue them by sea, and running to one of their canoes, I jumped in and bade Friday follow me: but when I was in the canoe I was surprised to find another poor creature lie there, bound hand and foot, as the Spaniard was, for the slaughter, and almost dead with fear, not knowing what was the matter; for he had not been able to look up over the side of the boat, he was tied so hard neck and heels, and had been tied so long that he had really but little life in him.

I immediately cut the twisted flags or rushes which they had bound him with, and would have helped him up; but he could not stand or speak, but groaned most piteously, believing, it seems, still, that he was only unbound in order to be killed. When Friday came to him I bade him speak to him, and tell him of his deliverance; and pulling out my bottle, made him give the poor wretch a dram, which, with the news of his being delivered, revived him, and he sat up in the boat. But when Friday came to hear him speak, and look in his face, it would have moved any one to tears to have seen how Friday kissed him, embraced him, hugged him, cried, laughed, hallooed, jumped about, danced, sang; then cried again, wrung his hands, beat his own face and head; and then sang and jumped about again like a distracted creature. It was a good while before I could make him speak to me or tell me what was the matter; but when he came a little to himself he told me that it was his father.

It is not easy for me to express how it moved me to see what ecstasy and filial affection had worked in this poor savage at the sight of his father, and of his being delivered from death; nor indeed can I describe half the extravagances of his affection after this: for he went into the boat and out of the boat a great many times: when he went in to him he would sit down by him, open his breast, and hold his father's head close to his bosom for many minutes together, to nourish it; then he took his arms and ankles, which were numbed and stiff with the binding, and chafed and rubbed them with his hands; and I, perceiving what the case was, gave him some rum out of my bottle to rub them with, which did them a great deal of good.

This affair put an end to our pursuit of the canoe with the other savages, who were now almost out of sight; and it was happy for us that we did not, for it blew so hard within two hours after, and before they could be got a quarter of their way, and continued blowing so hard all night, and that from the north-west, which was against them, that I could not suppose their boat could live, or that they ever reached their own coast.

But to return to Friday; he was so busy about his father that I could not find in my heart to take him off for some time; but after I thought he could leave him a little, I called him to me, and he came jumping and laughing, and pleased to the highest extreme: then I asked him if he had given his father any bread. He shook his head, and said, "None; ugly dog eat all up self." I then gave him a cake of bread out of a little pouch I carried on purpose; I also gave him a dram for himself;

but he would not taste it, but carried it to his father. I had in my pocket two or three bunches of raisins, so I gave him a handful of them for his father. He had no sooner given his father these raisins but I saw him come out of the boat, and run away as if he had been bewitched, for he was the swiftest fellow on his feet that ever I saw: I say, he ran at such a rate that he was out of sight, as it were, in an instant; and though I called, and hallooed out too after him, it was all one—away he went; and in a quarter of an hour I saw him come back again, though not so fast as he went; and as he came nearer I found his pace slacker, because he had something in his hand. When he came up to me I found he had been quite home for an earthen jug or pot, to bring his father some fresh water, and that he had got two more cakes or loaves of bread: the bread he gave me, but the water he carried to his father; however, as I was very thirsty too, I took a little of it. The water revived his father more than all the rum or spirits I had given him, for he was fainting with thirst.

When his father had drunk, I called to him to know if there was any water left. He said, "Yes"; and I bade him give it to the poor Spaniard, who was in as much want of it as his father; and I sent one of the cakes that Friday brought to the Spaniard too, who was indeed very weak, and was reposing himself upon a green place under the shade of a tree; and whose limbs were also very stiff, and very much swelled with the rude bandage he had been tied with. When I saw that upon Friday's coming to him with the water he sat up and drank, and took the bread and began to eat, I went to him and gave him a handful of raisins. He looked up in my face with all the tokens of gratitude and thankfulness that could appear in any countenance; but was so weak, notwithstanding he had so exerted himself in the fight, that he could not stand up upon his feet—he tried to do it two or three times, but was really not able, his ankles were so swelled and so painful to him; so I bade him sit still, and caused Friday to rub his ankles, and bathe them with rum, as he had done his father's.

I observed the poor affectionate creature, every two minutes, or perhaps less, all the while he was here, turn his head about to see if his father was in the same place and posture as he left him sitting; and at last he found he was not to be seen; at which he started up, and, without speaking a word, flew with that swiftness to him that one could scarce perceive his feet to touch the ground as he went; but when he came, he only found he had laid himself down to ease his limbs, so Friday came back to me presently; and then I spoke to the Spaniard to let Friday help him up if he could, and lead him to the boat, and then he should carry him to our dwelling, where I would take care of him. But Friday, a lusty, strong fellow, took the Spaniard upon his back, and carried him away to the boat, and set him down softly upon the side or gunnel of the canoe, with his feet in the inside of it; and then lifting him quite in, he set him close to his father; and presently stepping out again, launched the boat off, and paddled it along the shore faster than I could walk, though the wind blew pretty hard too; so he brought them both safe into our creek, and leaving them in the boat, ran away to fetch the other canoe. As he passed me I spoke to him, and asked him whither he went. He told me, "Go fetch more boat;" so away he went like the wind, for sure never man or horse ran like him; and he had the other canoe in the creek almost as soon as I got to it by land; so he wafted me over, and then went to help our new guests out of the boat, which he did; but they were neither of them able to walk; so that poor Friday knew not what to do.

To remedy this, I went to work in my thought, and calling to Friday to bid them sit down on the bank while he came to me, I soon made a kind of hand-barrow to lay them on, and Friday and I carried them both up together upon it between us.

But when we got them to the outside of our wall, or fortification, we were at a worse loss than before, for it was impossible to get them over, and I was resolved not to break it down; so I set to work again, and Friday and I, in about two hours' time, made a very handsome tent, covered with old sails, and above that with boughs of trees, being in the space without our outward fence and between that and the grove of young wood which I had planted; and here we made them two beds of such things as I had—viz. of good rice-straw, with blankets laid upon it to lie on, and another to cover them, on each bed.

My island was now peopled, and I thought myself very rich in subjects; and it was a merry reflection, which I frequently made, how like a king I looked. First of all, the whole country was my own property, so that I had an undoubted right of dominion. Secondly, my people were perfectly subjected—I was absolutely lord and lawgiver—they all owed their lives to me, and were ready to lay down their lives, if there had been occasion for it, for me. It was remarkable, too, I had but three subjects, and they were of three different religions—my man Friday was a Protestant, his father was a Pagan and a cannibal, and the Spaniard was a Papist. However, I allowed liberty of conscience throughout my dominions. But this is by the way.

197

As soon as I had secured my two weak, rescued prisoners, and given them shelter, and a place to rest them upon, I began to think of making some provision for them; and the first thing I did, I ordered Friday to take a yearling goat, betwixt a kid and a goat, out of my particular flock, to be killed; when I cut off the hinder-quarter, and chopping it into small pieces, I set Friday to work to boiling and stewing, and made them a very good dish, I assure you, of flesh and broth; and as I cooked it without doors, for I made no fire within my inner wall, so I carried it all into the new tent, and having set a table there for them, I sat down, and ate my own dinner also with them, and, as well as I could, cheered them and encouraged them. Friday was my interpreter, especially to his father, and, indeed, to the Spaniard too; for the Spaniard spoke the language of the savages pretty well.

After we had dined, or rather supped, I ordered Friday to take one of the canoes, and go and fetch our muskets and other firearms, which, for want of time, we had left upon the place of battle; and the next day I ordered him to go and bury the dead bodies of the savages, which lay open to the sun, and would presently be offensive. I also ordered him to bury the horrid remains of their barbarous feast, which I could not think of doing myself; nay, I could not bear to see them if I went that way; all which he punctually performed, and effaced the very appearance of the savages being there; so that when I went again, I could scarce know where it was, otherwise than by the corner of the wood pointing to the place.

I then began to enter into a little conversation with my two new subjects; and, first, I set Friday to inquire of his father what he thought of the escape of the savages in that canoe, and whether we might expect a return of them, with a power too great for us to resist. His first opinion was, that the savages in the boat never could live out the storm which blew that night they went off, but must of necessity be drowned, or driven south to those other shores, where they were as sure to be devoured as they were to be drowned if they were cast away; but, as to what they would do if they came safe on shore, he said he knew not; but it was his opinion that they were so dreadfully frightened with the manner of their being attacked, the noise, and the fire, that he believed they would tell the people they were all killed by thunder and lightning, not by the hand of man; and that the two which appeared—viz. Friday and I—were two heavenly spirits, or furies, come down to destroy them, and not men with weapons. This, he said, he knew; because he heard them all cry out so, in their language, one to another; for it was impossible for them to conceive that a man could dart fire, and speak thunder, and kill at a distance, without lifting up the hand, as was done now: and this old savage was in the right; for, as I understood since, by other hands, the savages never attempted to go over to the island afterwards, they were so terrified with the accounts given by those four men (for it seems they did escape the sea), that they believed whoever went to that enchanted island would be destroyed with fire from the gods. This, however, I knew not; and therefore was under continual apprehensions for a good while, and kept always upon my guard, with all my army: for, as there were now four of us, I would have ventured upon a hundred of them, fairly in the open field, at any time.

CHAPTER XVII

VISIT OF MUTINEERS

In a little time, however, no more canoes appearing, the fear of their coming wore off; and I began to take my former thoughts of a voyage to the main into consideration; being likewise assured by Friday's father that I might depend upon good usage from their nation, on his account, if I would go. But my thoughts were a little suspended when I had a serious discourse with the Spaniard, and when I understood that there were sixteen more of his countrymen and Portuguese, who having been cast away and made their escape to that side, lived there at peace, indeed, with the savages, but were very sore put to it for necessaries, and, indeed, for life. I asked him all the particulars of their voyage, and found they were a Spanish ship, bound from the Rio de la Plata to the Havanna, being directed to leave their loading there, which was chiefly hides and silver, and to bring back what European goods they could meet with there; that they had five Portuguese seamen on board, whom they took out of another wreck; that five of their own men were drowned when first the ship was lost, and that these escaped through infinite dangers and hazards, and arrived, almost starved, on the cannibal coast, where they expected to have been devoured every moment. He told me they had some arms with them, but they were perfectly useless, for that they had neither powder nor ball, the washing of the sea having spoiled all their powder but a little, which they used at their first landing to provide themselves with some food.

I asked him what he thought would become of them there, and if they had formed any design of making their escape. He said they had many consultations about it; but that having neither vessel nor tools to build one, nor provisions of any kind, their councils always ended in tears and despair. I asked him how he thought they would receive a proposal from me, which might tend towards an escape; and whether, if they were all here, it might not be done. I told him with freedom, I feared mostly their treachery and ill-usage of me, if I put my life in their hands; for that gratitude was no inherent virtue in the nature of man, nor did men always square their dealings by the obligations they had received so much as they did by the advantages they expected. I told him it would be very hard that I should be made the instrument of their deliverance, and that they should afterwards make me their prisoner in

New Spain, where an Englishman was certain to be made a sacrifice, what necessity or what accident soever brought him thither; and that I had rather be delivered up to the savages, and be devoured alive, than fall into the merciless claws of the priests, and be carried into the Inquisition. I added that, otherwise, I was persuaded, if they were all here, we might, with so many hands, build a barque large enough to carry us all away, either to the Brazils southward, or to the islands or Spanish coast northward; but that if, in requital, they should, when I had put weapons into their hands, carry me by force among their own people, I might be ill-used for my kindness to them, and make my case worse than it was before.

He answered, with a great deal of candour and ingenuousness, that their condition was so miserable, and that they were so sensible of it, that he believed they would abhor the thought of using any man unkindly that should contribute to their deliverance; and that, if I pleased, he would go to them with the old man, and discourse with them about it, and return again and bring me their answer; that he would make conditions with them upon their solemn oath, that they should be absolutely under my direction as their commander and captain; and they should swear upon the holy sacraments and gospel to be true to me, and go to such Christian country as I should agree to, and no other; and to be directed wholly and absolutely by my orders till they were landed safely in such country as I intended, and that he would bring a contract from them, under their hands, for that purpose. Then he told me he would first swear to me himself that he would never stir from me as long as he lived till I gave him orders; and that he would take my side to the last drop of his blood, if there should happen the least breach of faith among his countrymen. He told me they were all of them very civil, honest men, and they were under the greatest distress imaginable, having neither weapons nor clothes, nor any food, but at the mercy and discretion of the savages; out of all hopes of ever returning to their own country; and that he was sure, if I would undertake their relief, they would live and die by me.

Upon these assurances, I resolved to venture to relieve them, if possible, and to send the old savage and this Spaniard over to them to treat. But when we had got all things in readiness to go, the Spaniard himself started an objection, which had so much prudence in it on one hand, and so much sincerity on the other hand, that I could not but be very well satisfied in it; and, by his advice, put off the deliverance of his comrades for at least half a year. The case was thus: he had been with us now about a month, during which time I had let him see in what manner I had provided, with the assistance of Providence, for my support; and he saw evidently what stock of corn and rice I had laid up; which, though it was more than sufficient for myself, yet it was not sufficient, without good husbandry, for my family, now it was increased to four; but much less would it be sufficient if his countrymen, who were, as he said, sixteen, still alive, should come over; and least of all would it be sufficient to victual our vessel, if we should build one, for a voyage to any of the Christian colonies of America; so he told me he thought it would be more advisable to let him and the other two dig and cultivate some more land, as much as I could spare seed to sow, and that we should wait another harvest, that we might have a supply of corn for his countrymen, when they should come; for want might be a temptation to them to disagree, or not to think themselves delivered, otherwise than out of one difficulty into another. "You know," says he, "the children of Israel, though they rejoiced at first for their being delivered out of Egypt, yet rebelled even against God Himself, that delivered them, when they came to want bread in the wilderness."

His caution was so seasonable, and his advice so good, that I could not but be very well pleased with his proposal, as well as I was satisfied with his fidelity; so we fell to digging, all four of us, as well as the wooden tools we were furnished with permitted; and in about a month's time, by the end of which it was seed-time, we had got as much land cured and trimmed up as we sowed two-and-twenty bushels of barley on, and sixteen jars of rice, which was, in short, all the seed we had to spare: indeed, we left ourselves barely sufficient, for our own food for the six months that we had to expect our crop; that is to say reckoning from the time we set our seed aside for sowing; for it is not to be supposed it is six months in the ground in that country.

Having now society enough, and our numbers being sufficient to put us out of fear of the savages, if they had come, unless their number had been very great, we went freely all over the island, whenever we found occasion; and as we had our escape or deliverance upon our thoughts, it was impossible, at least for me, to have the means of it out of mine. For this purpose I marked out several trees, which I thought fit for our work, and I set Friday and his father to cut them down; and then I caused the Spaniard, to whom I imparted my thoughts on that affair, to oversee and direct their work. I showed them with what indefatigable pains I had hewed a large tree into single planks, and I caused them to do the like, till they made about a dozen large planks, of good oak, near two feet broad, thirty-five feet long, and from two inches to four inches thick: what prodigious labour it took up any one may imagine.

At the same time I contrived to increase my little flock of tame goats as much as I could; and for this purpose I made Friday and the Spaniard go out one day, and myself with Friday the next day (for we took our turns), and by this means we got about twenty young kids to breed up with the rest; for whenever we shot the dam, we saved the kids, and added them to our flock. But above all, the season for curing the grapes coming on, I caused such a prodigious quantity to be hung up in the sun, that, I believe, had we been at Alicant, where the raisins of the sun are cured, we could have filled sixty or eighty barrels; and these, with our bread, formed a great part of our food—very good living too, I assure you, for they are exceedingly nourishing.

It was now harvest, and our crop in good order: it was not the most plentiful increase I had seen in the island, but, however, it was enough to answer our end; for from twenty-two bushels of barley we brought in and thrashed out above two hundred and twenty bushels; and the like in proportion of the rice; which was store enough for our food to the next harvest, though all the sixteen Spaniards had been on shore with me; or, if we had been ready for a voyage, it would very plentifully have victualled our ship to have carried us to any part of the world; that is to say, any part of America. When we had thus housed and secured our magazine of corn, we fell to work to make more wicker-ware, viz. great baskets, in which we kept it; and the Spaniard was very handy and dexterous at this part, and often blamed me that I did not make some things for defence of this kind of work; but I saw no need of it.

And now, having a full supply of food for all the guests I expected, I gave the Spaniard leave to go over to the main, to see what he could do with those he had left behind him there. I gave him a strict charge not to bring any man who would not first swear in the presence of himself and the old savage that he would in no way injure, fight with, or attack the person he should find in the island, who was so kind as to send for them in order to their deliverance; but that they would stand by him and defend him against all such attempts, and wherever they went would be entirely under and subjected to his command; and that this should be put in writing, and signed in their hands. How they were to have done this, when I knew they had neither pen nor ink, was a question which we never asked. Under these instructions, the Spaniard and the old savage, the father of Friday, went away in one of the canoes which they might be said to have come in, or rather were brought in, when they came as prisoners to be devoured by the savages. I gave each of them a musket, with a firelock on it, and about eight charges of powder and ball, charging them to be very good husbands of both, and not to use either of them but upon urgent occasions.

This was a cheerful work, being the first measures used by me in view of my deliverance for now twenty-seven years and some days. I gave them provisions of bread and of dried grapes, sufficient for themselves for many days, and sufficient for all the Spaniards—for about eight days' time; and wishing them a good voyage, I saw them go, agreeing with them about a signal they should hang out at their return, by which I should know them again when they came back, at a distance, before they came on shore. They went away with a fair gale on the day that the moon was at full, by my account in the month of October; but as for an exact reckoning of days, after I had once lost it I could never recover it again; nor had I kept even the number of years so punctually as to be sure I was right; though, as it proved when I afterwards examined my account, I found I had kept a true reckoning of years.

It was no less than eight days I had waited for them, when a strange and unforeseen accident intervened, of which the like has not, perhaps, been heard of in history. I was fast asleep in my hutch one morning, when my man Friday came running in to me, and called aloud, "Master, master, they are come, they are come!" I jumped up, and regardless of danger I went, as soon as I could get my clothes on, through my little grove, which, by the way, was by this time grown to be a very thick wood; I say, regardless of danger I went without my arms, which was not my custom to do; but I was surprised when, turning my eyes to the sea, I presently saw a boat at about a league and a half distance, standing in for the shore, with a shoulder-of-mutton sail, as they call it, and the wind blowing pretty fair to bring them in: also I observed, presently, that they did not come from that side which the shore lay on, but from the southernmost end of the island. Upon this I called Friday in, and bade him lie close, for these were not the people we looked for, and that we might not know yet whether they were friends or enemies. In the next place I went in to fetch my perspective glass to see what I could make of them; and having taken the ladder out, I climbed up to the top of the hill, as I used to do when I was apprehensive of anything, and to take my view the plainer without being discovered. I had scarce set my foot upon the hill when my eye plainly discovered a ship lying at anchor, at about two leagues and a half distance from me, SSE., but not above a league and a half from the shore. By my observation it appeared plainly to be an English ship, and the boat appeared to be an English long-boat.

I cannot express the confusion I was in, though the joy of seeing a ship, and one that I had reason to believe was manned by my own countrymen, and consequently friends, was such as I cannot describe; but yet I had some secret doubts hung about me—I cannot tell from whence they came—bidding me keep upon my guard. In the first place, it occurred to me to consider what business an English ship could have in that part of the world, since it was not the way to or from any part of the world where the English had any traffic; and I knew there had been no storms to drive them in there in distress; and that if they were really English it was most probable that they were here upon no good design; and that I had better continue as I was than fall into the hands of thieves and murderers.

Let no man despise the secret hints and notices of danger which sometimes are given him when he may think there is no possibility of its being real. That such hints and notices are given us I believe few that have made any observation of things can deny; that they are certain discoveries of an invisible world, and a converse of spirits, we cannot doubt; and if the tendency of them seems to be to warn us of danger, why should we not suppose they are from some friendly agent (whether supreme, or inferior and subordinate, is not the question), and that they are given for our good?

The present question abundantly confirms me in the justice of this reasoning; for had I not been made cautious by this secret admonition, come it from whence it will, I had been done inevitably, and in a far worse condition than before, as you will see presently. I had not kept myself long in this posture till I saw the boat draw near the shore, as if they looked for a creek to thrust in at, for the convenience of landing; however, as they did not come quite far enough, they did not see the little inlet where I formerly landed my rafts, but ran their boat on shore upon the beach, at about half a mile from me, which was very happy for me; for otherwise they would have landed just at my door, as I may say, and would soon have beaten me out of my castle, and perhaps have plundered me of all I had. When they were on shore I was fully satisfied they were Englishmen, at least most of them; one or two I thought were Dutch, but it did not prove so; there were in all eleven men, whereof three of them I found were unarmed and, as I thought, bound; and when the first four or five of them were jumped on shore, they took those three out of the boat as prisoners: one of the three I could perceive using the most passionate gestures of entreaty, affliction, and despair, even to a kind of extravagance; the other two, I could perceive, lifted up their hands sometimes, and appeared concerned indeed, but not to such a degree as the first. I was perfectly confounded at the sight, and knew not what the meaning of it should be. Friday called out to me in English, as well as he could, "O master! you see English mans eat prisoner as well as savage mans." "Why, Friday," says I, "do you think they are going to eat them, then?" "Yes," says Friday, "they will eat them." "No no," says I, "Friday; I am afraid they will murder them, indeed; but you may be sure they will not eat them."

All this while I had no thought of what the matter really was, but stood trembling with the horror of the sight, expecting every moment when the three prisoners should be killed; nay, once I saw one of the villains lift up his arm with a great cutlass, as the seamen call it, or sword, to strike one of the poor men; and I expected to see him fall every moment; at which all the blood in my body seemed to run chill in my veins. I wished heartily now for the Spaniard, and the savage that had gone with him, or that I had any way to have come undiscovered within shot of them, that I might have secured the three men, for I saw no firearms they had among them; but it fell out to my mind another way. After I had observed the outrageous usage of the three men by the insolent seamen, I observed the fellows run scattering about the island, as if they wanted to see the country. I observed that the three other men had liberty to go also where they pleased; but they sat down all three upon the ground, very pensive, and looked like men in despair. This put me in mind of the first time when I came on shore, and began to look about me; how I gave myself over for lost; how wildly I looked round me; what dreadful apprehensions I had; and how I lodged in the tree all night for fear of being devoured by wild beasts. As I knew nothing that night of the supply I was to receive by the providential driving of the ship nearer the land by the storms and tide, by which I have since been so long nourished and supported; so these three poor desolate men knew nothing how certain of deliverance and supply they were, how near it was to them, and how effectually and really they were in a condition of safety, at the same time that they thought themselves lost and their case desperate. So little do we see before us in the world, and so much reason have we to depend cheerfully upon the great Maker of the world, that He does not leave His creatures so absolutely destitute, but that in the worst circumstances they have always something to be thankful for, and sometimes are nearer deliverance than they imagine; nay, are even brought to their deliverance by the means by which they seem to be brought to their destruction.

It was just at high-water when these people came on shore; and while they rambled about to see what kind of a place they were in, they had carelessly stayed till the tide was spent, and the water was ebbed considerably away, leaving their boat aground. They had left two men in the boat, who, as I found afterwards, having drunk a little too much brandy, fell asleep; however, one of them waking a little sooner than the other and finding the boat too fast aground for him to stir it, hallooed out for the rest, who were straggling about: upon which they all soon came to the boat: but it was past all their strength to launch her, the boat being very heavy, and the shore on that side being a soft oozy sand, almost like a quicksand. In this condition, like true seamen, who are, perhaps, the least of all mankind given to forethought, they gave it over, and away they strolled about the country again; and I heard one of them say aloud to another, calling them off from the boat, "Why, let her alone, Jack, can't you? she'll float next tide;" by which I was fully confirmed in the main inquiry of what countrymen they were. All this while I kept myself very close, not once daring to stir out of my castle any farther than to my place of observation near the top of the hill: and very glad I was to think how well it was fortified. I knew it was no less than ten hours before the boat could float again, and by that time it would be dark, and I might be at more liberty to see their motions, and to hear their discourse, if they had any. In the meantime I fitted myself up for a battle as before, though with more caution, knowing I had to do with another kind of enemy than I had at first. I ordered Friday also, whom I had made an excellent marksman with his gun, to load himself with arms. I took myself two fowling-pieces, and I gave him three muskets. My figure, indeed, was very fierce; I had my formidable goat-skin coat on, with the great cap I have mentioned, a naked sword by my side, two pistols in my belt, and a gun upon each shoulder.

It was my design, as I said above, not to have made any attempt till it was dark; but about two o'clock, being the heat of the day, I found that they were all gone straggling into the woods, and, as I thought, laid down to sleep. The three poor distressed men, too anxious for their condition to get any sleep, had, however, sat down under the shelter of a great tree, at about a quarter of a mile from me, and, as I thought, out of sight of any of the rest. Upon this I resolved to discover myself to them, and learn something of their condition; immediately I marched as above, my man Friday at a good distance behind me, as formidable for his arms as I, but not making quite so staring a spectre-like figure as I did. I came as near them undiscovered as I could, and then, before any of them saw me, I called aloud to them in Spanish, "What are ye, gentlemen?" They started up at the noise, but were ten times more confounded when they saw me, and the uncouth figure that I made. They made no answer at all, but I thought I perceived them just going to fly from me, when I spoke to them in English. "Gentlemen," said I, "do not be surprised at me; perhaps you may have a friend near when you did not expect it." "He must be sent directly from heaven then," said one of them very gravely to me, and pulling off his hat at the same time to me; "for our condition is past the help of man." "All help is from heaven, sir," said I, "but can you put a stranger in the way to help you? for you seem to be in some great distress. I saw you when you landed; and when you seemed to make application to the brutes that came with you, I saw one of them lift up his sword to kill you."

The poor man, with tears running down his face, and trembling, looking like one astonished, returned, "Am I talking to God or man? Is it a real man or an angel?" "Be in no fear about that, sir," said I; "if God had sent an angel to relieve you, he would have come better clothed, and armed after another manner than you see me; pray lay aside your fears; I am a man, an Englishman, and disposed to assist you; you see I have one servant only; we have arms and ammunition; tell us freely, can we serve you? What is your case?" "Our case, sir," said he, "is too long to tell you while our murderers are so near us; but, in short, sir, I was commander of that ship—my men have mutinied against me; they have been hardly prevailed on not to murder me, and, at last, have set me on shore in this desolate place, with these two men with me—one my mate, the other a passenger—where we expected to perish, believing the place to be uninhabited, and know not yet what to think of it." "Where are these brutes, your enemies?" said I; "do you know where they are gone? There they lie, sir," said he, pointing to a thicket of trees; "my heart trembles for fear they have seen us and heard you speak; if they have, they will certainly murder us all." "Have they any firearms?" said I. He answered, "They had only two pieces, one of which they left in the boat." "Well, then," said I, "leave the rest to me; I see they are all asleep; it is an easy thing to kill them all; but shall we rather take them prisoners?" He told me there were two desperate

208

villains among them that it was scarce safe to show any mercy to; but if they were secured, he believed all the rest would return to their duty. I asked him which they were. He told me he could not at that distance distinguish them, but he would obey my orders in anything I would direct. "Well," says I, "let us retreat out of their view or hearing, lest they awake, and we will resolve further." So they willingly went back with me, till the woods covered us from them.

"Look you, sir," said I, "if I venture upon your deliverance, are you willing to make two conditions with me?" He anticipated my proposals by telling me that both he and the ship, if recovered, should be wholly directed and commanded by me in everything; and if the ship was not recovered, he would live and die with me in what part of the world soever I would send him; and the two other men said the same. "Well," says I, "my conditions are but two; first, that while you stay in this island with me, you will not pretend to any authority here; and if I put arms in your hands, you will, upon all occasions, give them up to me, and do no prejudice to me or mine upon this island, and in the meantime be governed by my orders; secondly, that if the ship is or may be recovered, you will carry me and my man to England passage free."

He gave me all the assurances that the invention or faith of man could devise that he would comply with these most reasonable demands, and besides would owe his life to me, and acknowledge it upon all occasions as long as he lived. "Well, then," said I, "here are three muskets for you, with powder and ball; tell me next what you think is proper to be done." He showed all the testimonies of his gratitude that he was able, but offered to be wholly guided by me. I told him I thought it was very hard venturing anything; but the best method I could think of was to fire on them at once as they lay, and if any were not killed at the first volley, and offered to submit, we might save them, and so put it wholly upon God's providence to direct the shot. He said, very modestly, that he was loath to kill them if he could help it; but that those two were incorrigible villains, and had been the authors of all the mutiny in the ship, and if they escaped, we should be undone still, for they would go on board and bring the whole ship's company, and destroy us all. "Well, then," says I, "necessity legitimates my advice, for it is the only way to save our lives." However, seeing him still cautious of shedding blood, I told him they should go themselves, and manage as they found convenient.

In the middle of this discourse we heard some of them awake, and soon after we saw two of them on their feet. I asked him if either of them were the heads of the mutiny? He said, "No." "Well, then," said I, "you may let them escape; and Providence seems to have awakened them on purpose to save themselves. Now," says I, "if the rest escape you, it is your fault." Animated with this, he took the musket I had given him in his hand, and a pistol in his belt, and his two comrades with him, with each a piece in his hand; the two men who were with him going first made some noise, at which one of the seamen who was awake turned about, and seeing them coming, cried out to the rest; but was too late then, for the moment he cried out they fired—I mean the two men, the captain wisely reserving his own piece. They had so well aimed their shot at the men they knew, that one of them was killed on the spot, and the other very much wounded; but not being dead, he started up on his feet, and called eagerly for help to the other; but the captain stepping to him, told him it was too late to cry for help, he should call upon God to forgive his villainy, and with that word knocked him down with the stock of his musket, so that he never spoke more; there were three more in the company, and one of them was slightly wounded. By this time I was come; and when they saw their danger, and that it was in vain to resist, they begged for mercy. The captain told them he would spare their lives if they would give him an assurance of their abhorrence of the treachery they had been guilty of, and would swear to be faithful to him in recovering the ship, and afterwards in carrying her back to Jamaica, from whence they came. They gave him all the protestations of their sincerity that could be desired; and he was willing to believe them, and spare their lives, which I was not against, only that I obliged him to keep them bound hand and foot while they were on the island.

While this was doing, I sent Friday with the captain's mate to the boat with orders to secure her, and bring away the oars and sails, which they did; and by-and-by three straggling men, that were (happily for them) parted from the rest, came back upon hearing the guns fired; and seeing the captain, who was before their prisoner, now their conqueror, they submitted to be bound also; and so our victory was complete.

It now remained that the captain and I should inquire into one another's circumstances. I began first, and told him my whole history, which he heard with an attention even to amazement—and particularly at the wonderful manner of my being furnished with provisions and ammunition; and, indeed, as my story is a whole collection of wonders, it affected him deeply. But when he reflected from thence upon himself, and how I seemed to have been preserved there on purpose to save his life, the tears ran down his face, and he could not speak a word more. After this communication was at an end, I carried him and his two men into my apartment, leading them in just where I came out, viz. at the top of the house, where I refreshed them with such provisions as I had, and showed them all the contrivances I had made during my long, long inhabiting that place.

All I showed them, all I said to them, was perfectly amazing; but above all, the captain admired my fortification, and how perfectly I had concealed my retreat with a grove of trees, which having been now planted nearly twenty years, and the trees growing much faster than in England, was become a little wood, so thick that it was impassable in any part of it but at that one side where I had reserved my little winding passage into it. I told him this was my castle and my residence, but that I had a seat in the country, as most princes have, whither I could retreat upon occasion, and I would show him that too another time; but at present our business was to consider how to recover the ship. He agreed with me as to that, but told me he was perfectly at a loss what measures to take, for that there were still six-and-twenty hands on board, who, having entered into a cursed conspiracy, by which they had all forfeited their lives to the law, would be hardened in it now by desperation, and would carry it on, knowing that if they were subdued they would be brought to the gallows as soon as they came to England, or to any of the English colonies, and that, therefore, there would be no attacking them with so small a number as we were.

I mused for some time on what he had said, and found it was a very rational conclusion, and that therefore something was to be resolved on speedily, as well to draw the men on board into some snare for their surprise as to prevent their landing upon us, and destroying us. Upon this, it presently occurred to me that in a little while the ship's crew, wondering what was become of their comrades and of the boat, would certainly come on shore in their other boat to look for them, and that then, perhaps, they might come armed, and be too strong for us: this he allowed to be rational. Upon this, I told him the first thing we had to do was to stave the boat which lay upon the beach, so that they might not carry her of, and taking everything out of her, leave her so far useless as not to be fit to swim. Accordingly, we went on board, took the arms which were left on board out of her, and whatever else we found there—which was a bottle of brandy, and another of rum, a few biscuit-cakes, a horn of powder, and a great lump of sugar in a piece of canvas (the sugar was five or six pounds): all which was very welcome to me, especially the brandy and sugar, of which I had had none left for many years.

When we had carried all these things on shore (the oars, mast, sail, and rudder of the boat were carried away before), we knocked a great hole in her bottom, that if they had come strong enough to master us, yet they could not carry off the boat. Indeed, it was not much in my thoughts that we could be able to recover the ship; but my view was, that if they went away without the boat, I did not much question to make her again fit to carry as to the Leeward Islands, and call upon our friends the Spaniards in my way, for I had them still in my thoughts.

CHAPTER XVIII

THE SHIP RECOVERED

While we were thus preparing our designs, and had first, by main strength, heaved the boat upon the beach, so high that the tide would not float her off at high-water mark, and besides, had broke a hole in her bottom too big to be quickly stopped, and were set down musing what we should do, we heard the ship fire a gun, and make a waft with her ensign as a signal for the boat to come on board—but no boat stirred; and they fired several times, making other signals for the boat. At last, when all their signals and firing proved fruitless, and they found the boat did not stir, we saw them, by the help of my glasses, hoist another boat out and row towards the shore; and we found, as they approached, that there were no less than ten men in her, and that they had firearms with them.

As the ship lay almost two leagues from the shore, we had a full view of them as they came, and a plain sight even of their faces; because the tide having set them a little to the east of the other boat, they rowed up under shore, to come to the same place where the other had landed, and where the boat lay; by this means, I say, we had a full view of them, and the captain knew the persons and characters of all the men in the boat, of whom, he said, there were three very honest fellows, who, he was sure, were led into this conspiracy by the rest, being over-powered and frightened; but that as for the boatswain, who it seems was the chief officer among them, and all the rest, they were as outrageous as any of the ship's crew, and were no doubt made desperate in their new enterprise; and terribly apprehensive he was that they would be too powerful for us. I smiled at him, and told him that men in our circumstances were past the operation of fear; that seeing almost every condition that could be was better than that which we were supposed to be in, we ought to expect that the consequence, whether death or life, would be sure to be a deliverance. I asked him what he thought of the circumstances of my life, and whether a deliverance were not worth venturing for? "And where, sir," said I, "is your belief of my being preserved here on purpose to save your life, which elevated you a little while ago? For my part," said I, "there seems to be but one thing amiss in all the prospect of it." "What is that?" say he. "Why," said I, "it is, that as you say there are three or four honest fellows among them which should be spared, had they been all of the wicked part of the crew I should have thought God's providence had singled them out to deliver them into your hands; for depend upon it, every man that comes ashore is our own, and shall die or live as they behave to us." As I spoke this with a raised voice and cheerful countenance, I found it greatly encouraged him; so we set vigorously to our business.

We had, upon the first appearance of the boat's coming from the ship, considered of separating our prisoners; and we had, indeed, secured them effectually. Two of them, of whom the captain was less assured than ordinary, I sent with Friday, and one of the three delivered men, to my cave, where they were remote enough, and out of danger of being heard or discovered, or of finding their way out of the woods if they could have delivered themselves. Here they left them bound, but gave them provisions; and promised them, if they continued there quietly, to give them their liberty in a day or two; but that if they attempted their escape they should be put to death without mercy. They promised faithfully to bear their confinement with patience, and were very thankful that they had such good usage as to have provisions and light left them; for Friday gave them candles (such as we made ourselves) for their comfort; and they did not know but that he stood sentinel over them at the entrance.

The other prisoners had better usage; two of them were kept pinioned, indeed, because the captain was not able to trust them; but the other two were taken into my service, upon the captain's recommendation, and upon their solemnly engaging to live and die with us; so with them and the three honest men we were seven men, well armed; and I made no doubt we should be able to deal well enough with the ten that were coming, considering that the captain had said there were three or four honest men among them also. As soon as they got to the place where their other boat lay, they ran their boat into the beach and came all on shore, hauling the boat up after them, which I was glad to see, for I was afraid they would rather have left the boat at an anchor some distance from the shore, with some hands in her to guard her, and so we should not be able to seize the boat. Being on shore, the first thing they did, they ran all to their other boat; and it was easy to see they were under a great surprise to find her stripped, as above, of all that was in her, and a great hole in her bottom. After they had mused a while upon this, they set up two or three great shouts, hallooing with all their might, to try if they could make their companions hear; but all was to no purpose. Then they came all close in a ring, and fired a volley of their small arms, which indeed we heard, and the echoes made the woods ring. But it was all one; those in the cave, we were sure, could not hear; and those in our keeping, though they heard it well enough, yet durst give no answer to them. They were so astonished at the surprise of this, that, as they told us afterwards, they resolved to go all on board again to their ship, and let them know that the men were all murdered, and the long-boat staved; accordingly, they immediately launched their boat again, and got all of them on board.

The captain was terribly amazed, and even confounded, at this, believing they would go on board the ship again and set sail, giving their comrades over for lost, and so he should still lose the ship, which he was in hopes we should have recovered; but he was quickly as much frightened the other way.

They had not been long put off with the boat, when we perceived them all coming on shore again; but with this new measure in their conduct, which it seems they consulted together upon, viz. to leave three men in the boat, and the rest to go on shore, and go up into the country to look for their fellows. This was a great disappointment to us, for now we were at a loss what to do, as our seizing those seven men on shore would be no advantage to us if we let the boat escape; because they would row away to the ship, and then the rest of them would be sure to weigh and set sail, and so our recovering the ship would be lost. However we had no remedy but to wait and see what the issue of things might present. The seven men came on shore, and the three who remained in the boat put her off to a good distance from the shore, and came to an anchor to wait for them; so that it was impossible for us to come at them in the boat. Those that came on shore kept close together, marching towards the top of the little hill under which my habitation lay; and we could see them plainly, though they could not perceive us. We should have been very glad if they would have come nearer us, so that we might have fired at them, or that they would have gone farther off, that we might come abroad. But when they were come to the brow of the hill where they could see a great way into the valleys and woods, which lay towards the north-east part, and where the island lay lowest, they shouted and hallooed till they were weary; and not caring, it seems, to venture far from the shore, nor far from one another, they sat down together under a tree to consider it. Had they thought fit to have gone to sleep there, as the other part of them had done, they had done the job for us; but they were too full of apprehensions of danger to venture to go to sleep, though they could not tell what the danger was they had to fear.

The captain made a very just proposal to me upon this consultation of theirs, viz. that perhaps they would all fire a volley again, to endeavour to make their fellows hear, and that we should all sally upon them just at the juncture when their pieces were all discharged, and they would certainly yield, and we should have them without bloodshed. I liked this proposal, provided it was done while we were near enough to come up to them before they could load their pieces again. But this event did not happen; and we lay still a long time, very irresolute what course to take. At length I told them there would be nothing done, in my opinion, till night; and then, if they did not return to the boat, perhaps we might find a way to get between them and the shore, and so might use some stratagem with them in the boat to get them on shore. We waited a great while, though very impatient for their removing; and were very uneasy when, after long consultation, we saw them all start up and march down towards the sea; it seems they had such dreadful apprehensions of the danger of the place that they resolved to go on board the ship again, give their companions over for lost, and so go on with their intended voyage with the ship.

As soon as I perceived them go towards the shore, I imagined it to be as it really was that they had given over their search, and were going back again; and the captain, as soon as I told him my thoughts, was ready to sink at the apprehensions of it; but I presently thought of a stratagem to fetch them back again, and which answered my end to a tittle. I ordered Friday and the captain's mate to go over the little creek westward, towards the place where the savages came on shore, when Friday was rescued, and so soon as they came to a little rising round, at about half a mile distant, I bid them halloo out, as loud as they could, and wait till they found the seamen heard them; that as soon as ever they heard the seamen answer them, they should return it again; and then, keeping out of sight, take a round, always answering when the others hallooed, to draw them as far into the island and among the woods as possible, and then wheel about again to me by such ways as I directed them.

They were just going into the boat when Friday and the mate hallooed; and they presently heard them, and answering, ran along the shore westward, towards the voice they heard, when they were stopped by the creek, where the water being up, they could not get over, and called for the boat to come up and set them over; as, indeed, I expected. When they had set themselves over, I observed that the boat being gone a good way into the creek, and, as it were, in a harbour within the land, they took one of the three men out of her, to go along with them, and left only two in the boat, having fastened her to the stump of a little tree on the shore. This was what I wished for; and immediately leaving Friday and the captain's mate to their business, I took the rest with me; and, crossing the creek out of their sight, we surprised the two men before they were aware—one of them lying on the shore, and the other being in the boat. The fellow on shore was between sleeping and waking, and going to start up; the captain, who was foremost, ran in upon him, and knocked him down; and then called out to him in the boat to yield, or he was a dead man. They needed very few arguments to persuade a single man to yield, when he saw five men upon him and his comrade knocked down: besides, this was, it seems, one of the three who were not so hearty in the mutiny as the rest of the crew, and therefore was easily persuaded not only to yield, but afterwards to join very sincerely with us. In the meantime, Friday and the captain's mate so well managed their business with the rest that they drew them, by hallooing and answering, from one hill to another, and from one wood to another, till they not only heartily tired them, but left them where they were, very sure they could not reach back to the boat before it was dark; and, indeed, they were heartily tired themselves also, by the time they came back to us.

We had nothing now to do but to watch for them in the dark, and to fall upon them, so as to make sure work with them. It was several hours after Friday came back to me before they came back to their boat; and we could hear the foremost of them, long before they came quite up, calling to those behind to come along; and could also hear them answer, and complain how lame and tired they were, and not able to come any faster: which was very welcome news to us. At length they came up to the boat: but it is impossible to express their confusion when they found the boat fast aground in the creek, the tide ebbed out, and their two men gone. We could hear them call one to another in a most lamentable manner, telling one another they were got into an enchanted island; that either there were inhabitants in it, and they should all be murdered, or else there were devils and spirits in it, and they should be all carried away and devoured. They hallooed again, and called their two comrades by their names a great many times; but no answer. After some time we could see them, by the little light there was, run about, wringing their hands like men in despair, and sometimes they would go and sit down in the boat to rest themselves: then come ashore again, and walk about again, and so the same thing over again. My men would fain have had me give them leave to fall upon them at once in the dark; but I was willing to take them at some advantage, so as to spare them, and kill as few of them as I could; and especially I was unwilling to hazard the killing of any of our men, knowing the others were very well armed. I resolved to wait, to see if they did not separate; and therefore, to make sure of them, I drew my ambuscade nearer, and ordered Friday and the captain to creep upon their hands and feet, as close to the ground as they could, that they might not be discovered, and get as near them as they could possibly before they offered to fire.

They had not been long in that posture when the boatswain, who was the principal ringleader of the mutiny, and had now shown himself the most dejected and dispirited of all the rest, came walking towards them, with two more of the crew; the captain was so eager at having this principal rogue so much in his power, that he could hardly have patience to let him come so near as to be sure of him, for they only heard his tongue before: but when they came nearer, the captain and Friday, starting up on their feet, let fly at them. The boatswain was killed upon the spot: the next man was shot in the body, and fell just by him, though he did not die till an hour or two after; and the third ran for it. At the noise of the fire I immediately advanced with my whole army, which was now eight men, viz. myself, generalissimo; Friday, my lieutenant-general; the captain and his two men, and the three prisoners of war whom we had trusted with arms. We came upon them, indeed, in the dark, so that they could not see our number; and I made the man they had left in the boat, who was now one of us, to call them by name, to try if I could bring them to a parley, and so perhaps might reduce them to terms; which fell out just as we desired: for indeed it was easy to think, as their condition then was, they would be very willing to capitulate. So he calls out as loud as he could to one of them, "Tom Smith! Tom Smith!" Tom Smith answered immediately, "Is that Robinson?" for it seems he knew the voice. The other answered, "Ay, ay; for God's sake, Tom Smith, throw down your arms and yield, or you are all dead men this moment." "Who must we yield to? Where are they?" says Smith again. "Here they are," says he; "here's our captain and fifty men with him, have been hunting you these two hours; the boatswain is killed; Will Fry is wounded, and I am a prisoner; and if you do not yield you are all lost." "Will they give us quarter, then?" says Tom Smith, "and we will yield." "I'll go and ask, if you promise to yield," said Robinson: so he asked the captain, and the captain himself then calls out, "You, Smith, you know my voice; if you lay down your arms immediately and submit, you shall have your lives, all but Will Atkins."

Upon this Will Atkins cried out, "For God's sake, captain, give me quarter; what have I done? They have all been as bad as I:" which, by the way, was not true; for it seems this Will Atkins was the first man that laid hold of the captain when they first mutinied, and used him barbarously in tying his hands and giving him injurious language. However, the captain told him he must lay down his arms at discretion, and trust to the governor's mercy: by which he meant me, for they all called me governor. In a word, they all laid down their arms and begged their lives; and I sent the man that had parleyed with them, and two more, who bound them all; and then my great army of fifty men, which, with those three, were in all but eight, came up and seized upon them, and upon their boat; only that I kept myself and one more out of sight for reasons of state.

Our next work was to repair the boat, and think of seizing the ship: and as for the captain, now he had leisure to parley with them, he expostulated with them upon the villainy of their practices with him, and upon the further wickedness of their design, and how certainly it must bring them to misery and distress in the end, and perhaps to the gallows. They all appeared very penitent, and begged hard for their lives. As for that, he told them they were not his prisoners, but the commander's of the island; that they thought they had set him on shore in a barren, uninhabited island; but it had pleased God so to direct them that it was inhabited, and that the governor was an Englishman; that he might hang them all there, if he pleased; but as he had given them all quarter, he supposed he would send them to England, to be dealt with there as justice required, except Atkins, whom he was commanded by the governor to advise to prepare for death, for that he would be hanged in the morning.

Though this was all but a fiction of his own, yet it had its desired effect; Atkins fell upon his knees to beg the captain to intercede with the governor for his life; and all the rest begged of him, for God's sake, that they might not be sent to England.

It now occurred to me that the time of our deliverance was come, and that it would be a most easy thing to bring these fellows in to be hearty in getting possession of the ship; so I retired in the dark from them, that they might not see what kind of a governor they had, and called the captain to me; when I called, at a good distance, one of the men was ordered to speak again, and say to the captain, "Captain, the commander calls for you;" and presently the captain replied, "Tell his excellency I am just coming." This more perfectly amazed them, and they all believed that the commander was just by, with his fifty men. Upon the captain coming to me, I told him my project for seizing the ship, which he liked wonderfully well, and resolved to put it in execution the next morning. But, in order to execute it with more art, and to be secure of success, I told him we must divide the prisoners, and that he should go and take Atkins, and two more of the worst of them, and send them pinioned to the cave where the others lay. This was committed to Friday and the two men who came on shore with the captain. They conveyed them to the cave as to a prison: and it was, indeed, a dismal place, especially to men in their condition. The others I ordered to my bower, as I called it, of which I have given a full description: and as it was fenced in, and they pinioned, the place was secure enough, considering they were upon their behaviour.

To these in the morning I sent the captain, who was to enter into a parley with them; in a word, to try them, and tell me whether he thought they might be trusted or not to go on board and surprise the ship. He talked to them of the injury done him, of the condition they were brought to, and that though the governor had given them quarter for their lives as to the present action, yet that if they were sent to England they would all be hanged in chains; but that if they would join in so just an attempt as to recover the ship, he would have the governor's engagement for their pardon.

Any one may guess how readily such a proposal would be accepted by men in their condition; they fell down on their knees to the captain, and promised, with the deepest imprecations, that they would be faithful to him to the last drop, and that they should owe their lives to him, and would go with him all over the world; that they would own him as a father to them as long as they lived. "Well," says the captain, "I must go and tell the governor what you say, and see what I can do to bring him to consent to it." So he brought me an account of the temper he found them in, and that he verily believed they would be faithful. However, that we might be very secure, I told him he should go back again and choose out those five, and tell them, that they might see he did not want men, that he would take out those five to be his assistants, and that the governor would keep the other two, and the three that were sent prisoners to the castle (my cave), as hostages for the fidelity of those five; and that if they proved unfaithful in the execution, the five hostages should be hanged in chains alive on the shore. This looked severe, and convinced them that the governor was in earnest; however, they had no way left them but to accept it; and it was now the business of the prisoners, as much as of the captain, to persuade the other five to do their duty.

Our strength was now thus ordered for the expedition: first, the captain, his mate, and passenger; second, the two prisoners of the first gang, to whom, having their character from the captain, I had given their liberty, and trusted them with arms; third, the other two that I had kept till now in my bower, pinioned, but on the captain's motion had now released; fourth, these five released at last; so that there were twelve in all, besides five we kept prisoners in the cave for hostages.

I asked the captain if he was willing to venture with these hands on board the ship; but as for me and my man Friday, I did not think it was proper for us to stir, having seven men left behind; and it was employment enough for us to keep them asunder, and supply them with victuals. As to the five in the cave, I resolved to keep them fast, but Friday went in twice a day to them, to supply them with necessaries; and I made the other two carry provisions to a certain distance, where Friday was to take them.

When I showed myself to the two hostages, it was with the captain, who told them I was the person the governor had ordered to look after them; and that it was the governor's pleasure they should not stir anywhere but by my direction; that if they did, they would be fetched into the castle, and be laid in irons: so that as we never suffered them to see me as governor, I now appeared as another person, and spoke of the governor, the garrison, the castle, and the like, upon all occasions.

The captain now had no difficulty before him, but to furnish his two boats, stop the breach of one, and man them. He made his passenger captain of one, with four of the men; and himself, his mate, and five more, went in the other; and they contrived their business very well, for they came up to the ship about midnight. As soon as they came within call of the ship, he made Robinson hail them, and tell them they had brought off the men and the boat, but that it was a long time before they had found them, and the like, holding them in a chat till they came to the ship's side; when the captain and the mate entering first with their arms, immediately knocked down the second mate and carpenter with the butt-end of their muskets, being very faithfully seconded by their men; they secured all the rest that were upon the main and quarter decks, and began to fasten the hatches, to keep them down that were below; when the other boat and their men, entering at the forechains, secured the forecastle of the ship, and the scuttle which went down into the cook-room, making three men they found there prisoners. When this was done, and all safe upon deck, the captain ordered the mate, with three men, to break into the round-house, where the new rebel captain lay, who, having taken the alarm, had got up, and with two men and a boy had got firearms in their hands; and when the mate, with a crow, split open the door, the new captain and his men fired boldly among them, and wounded the mate with a musket ball, which broke his arm, and wounded two more of the men, but killed nobody. The mate, calling for help, rushed, however, into the round-house, wounded as he was, and, with his pistol, shot the new captain through the head, the bullet entering at his mouth, and came out again behind one of his ears, so that he never spoke a word more: upon which the rest yielded, and the ship was taken effectually, without any more lives lost.

As soon as the ship was thus secured, the captain ordered seven guns to be fired, which was the signal agreed upon with me to give me notice of his success, which, you may be sure, I was very glad to hear, having sat watching upon the shore for it till near two o'clock in the morning. Having thus heard the signal plainly, I laid me down; and it having been a day of great fatigue to me, I slept very sound, till I was surprised with the noise of a gun; and presently starting up, I heard a man call me by the name of "Governor! Governor!" and presently I knew the captain's voice; when, climbing up to the top of the hill, there he stood, and, pointing to the ship, he embraced me in his arms, "My dear friend and deliverer," says he, "there's your ship; for she is all yours, and so are we, and all that belong to her." I cast my eyes to the ship, and there she rode, within little more than half a mile of the shore; for they had weighed her anchor as soon as they were masters of her, and, the weather being fair, had brought her to an anchor just against the mouth of the little creek; and the tide being up, the captain had brought the pinnace in near the place where I had first landed my rafts, and so landed just at my door. I was at first ready to sink down with the surprise; for I saw my deliverance, indeed, visibly put into my hands, all things easy, and a large ship just ready to carry me away whither I pleased to go. At first, for some time, I was not able to answer him one word; but as he had taken me in his arms I held fast by him, or I should have fallen to the ground. He perceived the surprise, and immediately pulled a bottle out of his pocket and gave me a dram of cordial, which he had brought on purpose for me. After I had drunk it, I sat down upon the ground; and though it brought me to myself, yet it was a good while before I could speak a word to him. All this time the poor man was in as great an ecstasy as I, only not under any surprise as I was; and he said a thousand kind and tender things to me, to compose and bring me to myself; but such was the flood of joy in my breast, that it put all my spirits into confusion: at last it broke out into tears, and in a little while after I recovered my speech; I then took my turn, and embraced him as my deliverer, and we rejoiced together. I told him I looked upon him as a man sent by Heaven to deliver me, and that the whole transaction seemed to be a chain of wonders; that such things as these were the testimonies we had of a secret hand of Providence governing the world, and an evidence that the eye of an infinite Power could search into the remotest corner of the world, and send help to the miserable whenever He pleased. I forgot not to lift up my heart in thankfulness to Heaven; and what heart could forbear to bless Him, who had not only in a miraculous manner provided for me in such a wilderness, and in such a desolate condition, but from whom every deliverance must always be acknowledged to proceed.

When we had talked a while, the captain told me he had brought me some little refreshment, such as the ship afforded, and such as the wretches that had been so long his masters had not plundered him of. Upon this, he called aloud to the boat, and bade his men bring the things ashore that were for the governor; and, indeed, it was a present as if I had been one that was not to be carried away with them, but as if I had been to dwell upon the island still. First, he had brought me a case of bottles full of excellent cordial waters, six large bottles of Madeira wine (the bottles held two quarts each), two pounds of excellent good tobacco, twelve good pieces of the ship's beef, and six pieces of pork, with a bag of peas, and about a hundred-weight of biscuit; he also brought me a box of sugar, a box of flour, a bag full of lemons, and two bottles of lime-juice, and abundance of other things. But besides these, and what was a thousand times more useful to me, he brought me six new clean shirts, six very good neckcloths, two pair of gloves, one pair of shoes, a hat, and one pair of stockings, with a very good suit of clothes of his own, which had been worn but very little: in a word, he clothed me from head to foot. It was a very kind and agreeable present, as any one may imagine, to one in my circumstances, but never was anything in the world of that kind so unpleasant, awkward, and uneasy as it was to me to wear such clothes at first.

After these ceremonies were past, and after all his good things were brought into my little apartment, we began to consult what was to be done with the prisoners we had; for it was worth considering whether we might venture to take them with us or no, especially two of them, whom he knew to be incorrigible and refractory to the last degree; and the captain said he knew they were such rogues that there was no obliging them, and if he did carry them away, it must be in irons, as malefactors, to be delivered over to justice at the first English colony he could come to; and I found that the captain himself was very anxious about it. Upon this, I told him that, if he desired it, I would undertake to bring the two men he spoke of to make it their own request that he should leave them upon the island. "I should be very glad of that," says the captain, "with all my heart." "Well," says I, "I will send for them up and talk with them for you." So I caused Friday and the two hostages, for they were now discharged, their comrades having performed their promise; I say, I caused them to go to the cave, and bring up the five men, pinioned as they were, to the bower, and keep them there till I came. After some time, I came thither dressed in my new habit; and now I was called governor again. Being all met, and the captain with me, I caused the men to be brought before me, and I told them I had got a full account of their villainous behaviour to the captain, and how they had run away with the ship, and were preparing to commit further robberies, but that Providence had ensnared them in their own ways, and that they were fallen into the pit which they had dug for others. I let them know that by my direction the ship had been seized; that she lay now in the road; and they might see by-and-by that their new captain had received the reward of his villainy, and that they would see him hanging at the yard-arm; that, as to them, I wanted to know what they had to say why I should not execute them as pirates taken in the fact, as by my commission they could not doubt but I had authority so to do.

One of them answered in the name of the rest, that they had nothing to say but this, that when they were taken the captain promised them their lives, and they humbly implored my mercy. But I told them I knew not what mercy to show them; for as for myself, I had resolved to quit the island with all my men, and had taken passage with the captain to go to England; and as for the captain, he could not carry them to England other than as prisoners in irons, to be tried for mutiny and running away with the ship; the consequence of which, they must needs know, would be the gallows; so that I could not tell what was best for them, unless they had a mind to take their fate in the island. If they desired that, as I had liberty to leave the island, I had some inclination to give them their lives, if they thought they could shift on shore. They seemed very thankful for it, and said they would much rather venture to stay there than be carried to England to be hanged. So I left it on that issue.

However, the captain seemed to make some difficulty of it, as if he durst not leave them there. Upon this I seemed a little angry with the captain, and told him that they were my prisoners, not his; and that seeing I had offered them so much favour, I would be as good as my word; and that if he did not think fit to consent to it I would set them at liberty, as I found them: and if he did not like it he might take them again if he could catch them. Upon this they appeared very thankful, and I accordingly set them at liberty, and bade them retire into the woods, to the place whence they came, and I would leave them some firearms, some ammunition, and some directions how they should live very well if they thought fit. Upon this I prepared to go on board the ship; but told the captain I would stay that night to prepare my things, and desired him to go on board in the meantime, and keep all right in the ship, and send the boat on shore next day for me; ordering him, at all events, to cause the new captain, who was killed, to be hanged at the yard-arm, that these men might see him.

When the captain was gone I sent for the men up to me to my apartment, and entered seriously into discourse with them on their circumstances. I told them I thought they had made a right choice; that if the captain had carried them away they would certainly be hanged. I showed them the new captain hanging at the yard-arm of the ship, and told them they had nothing less to expect.

When they had all declared their willingness to stay, I then told them I would let them into the story of my living there, and put them into the way of making it easy to them. Accordingly, I gave them the whole history of the place, and of my coming to it; showed them my fortifications, the way I made my bread, planted my corn, cured my grapes; and, in a word, all that was necessary to make them easy. I told them the story also of the seventeen Spaniards that were to be expected, for whom I left a letter, and made them promise to treat them in common with themselves. Here it may be noted that the captain, who had ink on board, was greatly surprised that I never hit upon a way of making ink of charcoal and water, or of something else, as I had done things much more difficult.

I left them my firearms—viz. five muskets, three fowling-pieces, and three swords. I had above a barrel and a half of powder left; for after the first year or two I used but little, and wasted none. I gave them a description of the way I managed the goats, and directions to milk and fatten them, and to make both butter and cheese. In a word, I gave them every part of my own story; and told them I should prevail with the captain to leave them two barrels of gunpowder more, and some garden-seeds, which I told them I would have been very glad of. Also, I gave them the bag of peas which the captain had brought me to eat, and bade them be sure to sow and increase them.

CHAPTER XIX

RETURN TO ENGLAND

Having done all this I left them the next day, and went on board the ship. We prepared immediately to sail, but did not weigh that night. The next morning early, two of the five men came swimming to the ship's side, and making the most lamentable complaint of the other three, begged to be taken into the ship for God's sake, for they should be murdered, and begged the captain to take them on board, though he hanged them immediately. Upon this the captain pretended to have no power without me; but after some difficulty, and after their solemn promises of amendment, they were taken on board, and were, some time after, soundly whipped and pickled; after which they proved very honest and quiet fellows.

Some time after this, the boat was ordered on shore, the tide being up, with the things promised to the men; to which the captain, at my intercession, caused their chests and clothes to be added, which they took, and were very thankful for. I also encouraged them, by telling them that if it lay in my power to send any vessel to take them in, I would not forget them.

When I took leave of this island, I carried on board, for relics, the great goat-skin cap I had made, my umbrella, and one of my parrots; also, I forgot not to take the money I formerly mentioned, which had lain by me so long useless that it was grown rusty or tarnished, and could hardly pass for silver till it had been a little rubbed and handled, as also the money I found in the wreck of the Spanish ship. And thus I left the island, the 19th of December, as I found by the ship's account, in the year 1686, after I had been upon it eight-and-twenty years, two months, and nineteen days; being delivered from this second captivity the same day of the month that I first made my escape in the long-boat from among the Moors of Sallee. In this vessel, after a long voyage, I arrived in England the 11th of June, in the year 1687, having been thirty-five years absent.

When I came to England I was as perfect a stranger to all the world as if I had never been known there. My benefactor and faithful steward, whom I had left my money in trust with, was alive, but had had great misfortunes in the world; was become a widow the second time, and very low in the world. I made her very easy as to what she owed me, assuring her I would give her no trouble; but, on the contrary, in gratitude for her former care and faithfulness to me, I relieved her as my little stock would afford; which at that time would, indeed, allow me to do but little for her; but I assured her I would never forget her former kindness to me; nor did I forget her when I had sufficient to help her, as shall be observed in its proper place. I went down afterwards into Yorkshire; but my father was dead, and my mother and all the family extinct, except that I found two sisters, and two of the children of one of my brothers; and as I had been long ago given over for dead, there had been no provision made for me; so that, in a word, I found nothing to relieve or assist me; and that the little money I had would not do much for me as to settling in the world.

I met with one piece of gratitude indeed, which I did not expect; and this was, that the master of the ship, whom I had so happily delivered, and by the same means saved the ship and cargo, having given a very handsome account to the owners of the manner how I had saved the lives of the men and the ship, they invited me to meet them and some other merchants concerned, and all together made me a very handsome compliment upon the subject, and a present of almost £200 sterling.

But after making several reflections upon the circumstances of my life, and how little way this would go towards settling me in the world, I resolved to go to Lisbon, and see if I might not come at some information of the state of my plantation in the Brazils, and of what was become of my partner, who, I had reason to suppose, had some years past given me over for dead. With this view I took shipping for Lisbon, where I arrived in April following, my man Friday accompanying me very honestly in all these ramblings, and proving a most faithful servant upon all occasions. When I came to Lisbon, I found out, by inquiry, and to my particular satisfaction, my old friend, the captain of the ship who first took me up at sea off the shore of Africa. He was now grown old, and had left off going to sea, having put his son, who was far from a young man, into his ship, and who still used the Brazil trade. The old man did not know me, and indeed I hardly knew him. But I soon brought him to my remembrance, and as soon brought myself to his remembrance, when I told him who I was.

After some passionate expressions of the old acquaintance between us, I inquired, you may be sure, after my plantation and my partner. The old man told me he had not been in the Brazils for about nine years; but that he could assure me that when he came away my partner was living, but the trustees whom I had joined with him to take cognisance of my part were both dead: that, however, he believed I would have a very good account of the improvement of the plantation; for that, upon the general belief of my being cast away and drowned, my trustees had given in the account of the produce of my part of the plantation to the procurator-fiscal, who had appropriated it, in case I never came to claim it, one-third to the king, and two-thirds to the monastery of St. Augustine, to be expended for the benefit of the poor, and for the conversion of the Indians to the Catholic faith: but that, if I appeared, or any one for me, to claim the inheritance, it would be restored; only that the improvement, or annual production, being distributed to charitable uses, could not be restored: but he assured me that the steward of the king's revenue from lands, and the providore, or steward of the monastery, had taken great care all along that the incumbent, that is to say my partner, gave every year a faithful account of the produce, of which they had duly received my moiety. I asked him if he knew to what height of improvement he had brought the plantation, and whether he thought it might be worth looking after; or whether, on my going thither, I should meet with any obstruction to my possessing my just right in the moiety. He told me he could not tell exactly to what degree the plantation was improved; but this he knew, that my partner was grown exceeding rich upon the enjoying his part of it; and that, to the best of his remembrance, he had heard that the king's third of my part, which was, it seems, granted away to some other monastery or religious house, amounted to above two hundred moidores a year: that as to my being restored to a quiet possession of it, there was no question to be made of that, my partner being alive to witness my title, and my name being also enrolled in the register of the country; also he told me that the survivors of my two trustees were very fair, honest people, and very wealthy; and he believed I would not only have their assistance for putting me in possession, but would find a very considerable sum of money in their hands for my account, being the produce of the farm while their fathers held the trust, and before it was given up, as above; which, as he remembered, was for about twelve years.

I showed myself a little concerned and uneasy at this account, and inquired of the old captain how it came to pass that the trustees should thus dispose of my effects, when he knew that I had made my will, and had made him, the Portuguese captain, my universal heir, &c.

He told me that was true; but that as there was no proof of my being dead, he could not act as executor until some certain account should come of my death; and, besides, he was not willing to intermeddle with a thing so remote: that it was true he had registered my will, and put in his claim; and could he have given any account of my being dead or alive, he would have acted by procuration, and taken possession of the ingenio (so they call the sugar-house), and have given his son, who was now at the Brazils, orders to do it. "But," says the old man, "I have one piece of news to tell you, which perhaps may not be so acceptable to you as the rest; and that is, believing you were lost, and all the world believing so also, your partner and trustees did offer to account with me, in your name, for the first six or eight years' profits, which I received. There being at that time great disbursements for increasing the works, building an ingenio, and buying slaves, it did not amount to near so much as afterwards it produced; however," says the old man, "I shall give you a true account of what I have received in all, and how I have disposed of it."

After a few days' further conference with this ancient friend, he brought me an account of the first six years' income of my plantation, signed by my partner and the merchant-trustees, being always delivered in goods, viz. tobacco in roll, and sugar in chests, besides rum, molasses, &c., which is the consequence of a sugar-work; and I found by this account, that every year the income considerably increased; but, as above, the disbursements being large, the sum at first was small: however, the old man let me see that he was debtor to me four hundred and seventy moidores of gold, besides sixty chests of sugar and fifteen double rolls of tobacco, which were lost in his ship; he having been shipwrecked coming home to Lisbon, about eleven years after my having the place. The good man then began to complain of his misfortunes, and how he had been obliged to make use of my money to recover his losses, and buy him a share in a new ship. "However, my old friend," says he, "you shall not want a supply in your necessity; and as soon as my son returns you shall be fully satisfied." Upon this he pulls out an old pouch, and gives me one hundred and sixty Portugal moidores in gold; and giving the writings of his title to the ship, which his son was gone to the Brazils in, of which he was quarter-part owner, and his son another, he puts them both into my hands for security of the rest.

I was too much moved with the honesty and kindness of the poor man to be able to bear this; and remembering what he had done for me, how he had taken me up at sea, and how generously he had used me on all occasions, and particularly how sincere a friend he was now to me, I could hardly refrain weeping at what he had said to me; therefore I asked him if his circumstances admitted him to spare so much money at that time, and if it would not straiten him? He told me he could not say but it might straiten him a little; but, however, it was my money, and I might want it more than he.

Everything the good man said was full of affection, and I could hardly refrain from tears while he spoke; in short, I took one hundred of the moidores, and called for a pen and ink to give him a receipt for them: then I returned him the rest, and told him if ever I had possession of the plantation I would return the other to him also (as, indeed, I afterwards did); and that as to the bill of sale of his part in his son's ship, I would not take it by any means; but that if I wanted the money, I found he was honest enough to pay me; and if I did not, but came to receive what he gave me reason to expect, I would never have a penny more from him.

When this was past, the old man asked me if he should put me into a method to make my claim to my plantation. I told him I thought to go over to it myself. He said I might do so if I pleased, but that if I did not, there were ways enough to secure my right, and immediately to appropriate the profits to my use: and as there were ships in the river of Lisbon just ready to go away to Brazil, he made me enter my name in a public register, with his affidavit, affirming, upon oath, that I was alive, and that I was the same person who took up the land for the planting the said plantation at first. This being regularly attested by a notary, and a procuration affixed, he directed me to send it, with a letter of his writing, to a merchant of his acquaintance at the place; and then proposed my staying with him till an account came of the return.

Never was anything more honourable than the proceedings upon this procuration; for in less than seven months I received a large packet from the survivors of my trustees, the merchants, for whose account I went to sea, in which were the following, particular letters and papers enclosed:—

First, there was the account-current of the produce of my farm or plantation, from the year when their fathers had balanced with my old Portugal captain, being for six years; the balance appeared to be one thousand one hundred and seventy-four moidores in my favour.

Secondly, there was the account of four years more, while they kept the effects in their hands, before the government claimed the administration, as being the effects of a person not to be found, which they called civil death; and the balance of this, the value of the plantation increasing, amounted to nineteen thousand four hundred and forty-six crusadoes, being about three thousand two hundred and forty moidores.

Thirdly, there was the Prior of St. Augustine's account, who had received the profits for above fourteen years; but not being able to account for what was disposed of by the hospital, very honestly declared he had eight hundred and seventy-two moidores not distributed, which he acknowledged to my account: as to the king's part, that refunded nothing.

There was a letter of my partner's, congratulating me very affectionately upon my being alive, giving me an account how the estate was improved, and what it produced a year; with the particulars of the number of squares, or acres that it contained, how planted, how many slaves there were upon it: and making two-and-twenty crosses for blessings, told me he had said so many *Ave Marias* to thank the Blessed Virgin that I was alive; inviting me very passionately to come over and take possession of my own, and in the meantime to give him orders to whom he should deliver my effects if I did not come myself; concluding with a hearty tender of his friendship, and that of his family; and sent me as a present seven fine leopards' skins, which he had, it seems, received from Africa, by some other ship that he had sent thither, and which, it seems, had made a better voyage than I. He sent me also five chests of excellent sweetmeats, and a hundred pieces of gold uncoined, not quite so large as moidores. By the same fleet my two merchant-trustees shipped me one thousand two hundred chests of sugar, eight hundred rolls of tobacco, and the rest of the whole account in gold.

I might well say now, indeed, that the latter end of Job was better than the beginning. It is impossible to express the flutterings of my very heart when I found all my wealth about me; for as the Brazil ships come all in fleets, the same ships which brought my letters brought my goods: and the effects were safe in the river before the letters came to my hand. In a word, I turned pale, and grew sick; and, had not the old man run and fetched me a cordial, I believe the sudden surprise of joy had overset nature, and I had died upon the spot: nay, after that I continued very ill, and was so some hours, till a physician being sent for, and something of the real cause of my illness being known, he ordered me to be let blood; after which I had relief, and grew well: but I verily believe, if I had not been eased by a vent given in that manner to the spirits, I should have died.

I was now master, all on a sudden, of above five thousand pounds sterling in money, and had an estate, as I might well call it, in the Brazils, of above a thousand pounds a year, as sure as an estate of lands in England: and, in a word, I was in a condition which I scarce knew how to understand, or how to compose myself for the enjoyment of it. The first thing I did was to recompense my original benefactor, my good old captain, who had been first charitable to me in my distress, kind to me in my beginning, and honest to me at the end. I showed him all that was sent to me; I told him that, next to the providence of Heaven, which disposed all things, it was owing to him; and that it now lay on me to reward him, which I would do a hundred-fold: so I first returned to him the hundred moidores I had received of him; then I sent for a notary, and caused him to draw up a general release or discharge from the four hundred and seventy moidores, which he had acknowledged he owed me, in the fullest and firmest manner possible. After which I caused a procuration to be drawn, empowering him to be the receiver of the annual profits of my plantation: and appointing my partner to account with him, and make the returns, by the usual fleets, to him in my name; and by a clause in the end, made a grant of one hundred moidores a year to him during his life, out of the effects, and fifty moidores a year to his son after him, for his life: and thus I requited my old man.

I had now to consider which way to steer my course next, and what to do with the estate that Providence had thus put into my hands; and, indeed, I had more care upon my head now than I had in my state of life in the island where I wanted nothing but what I had, and had nothing but what I wanted; whereas I had now a great charge upon me, and my business was how to secure it. I had not a cave now to hide my money in, or a place where it might lie without lock or key, till it grew mouldy and tarnished before anybody would meddle with it; on the contrary, I knew not where to put it, or whom to trust with it. My old patron, the captain, indeed, was honest, and that was the only refuge I had. In the next place, my interest in the Brazils seemed to summon me thither; but now I could not tell how to think of going thither till I had settled my affairs, and left my effects in some safe hands behind me. At first I thought of my old friend the widow, who I knew was honest, and would be just to me; but then she was in years, and but poor, and, for aught I knew, might be in debt: so that, in a word, I had no way but to go back to England myself and take my effects with me.

It was some months, however, before I resolved upon this; and, therefore, as I had rewarded the old captain fully, and to his satisfaction, who had been my former benefactor, so I began to think of the poor widow, whose husband had been my first benefactor, and she, while it was in her power, my faithful steward and instructor. So, the first thing I did, I got a merchant in Lisbon to write to his correspondent in London, not only to pay a bill, but to go find her out, and carry her, in money, a hundred pounds from me, and to talk with her, and comfort her in her poverty, by telling her she should, if I lived, have a further supply: at the same time I sent my two sisters in the country a hundred pounds each, they being, though not in want, yet not in very good circumstances; one having been married and left a widow; and the other having a husband not so kind to her as he should be. But among all my relations or acquaintances I could not yet pitch upon one to whom I durst commit the gross of my stock, that I might go away to the Brazils, and leave things safe behind me; and this greatly perplexed me.

I had once a mind to have gone to the Brazils and have settled myself there, for I was, as it were, naturalised to the place; but I had some little scruple in my mind about religion, which insensibly drew me back. However, it was not religion that kept me from going there for the present; and as I had made no scruple of being openly of the religion of the country all the while I was among them, so neither did I yet; only that, now and then, having of late thought more of it than formerly, when I began to think of living and dying among them, I began to regret having professed myself a Papist, and thought it might not be the best religion to die with.

But, as I have said, this was not the main thing that kept me from going to the Brazils, but that really I did not know with whom to leave my effects behind me; so I resolved at last to go to England, where, if I arrived, I concluded that I should make some acquaintance, or find some relations, that would be faithful to me; and, accordingly, I prepared to go to England with all my wealth.

In order to prepare things for my going home, I first (the Brazil fleet being just going away) resolved to give answers suitable to the just and faithful account of things I had from thence; and, first, to the Prior of St. Augustine I wrote a letter full of thanks for his just dealings, and the offer of the eight hundred and seventy-two moidores which were undisposed of, which I desired might be given, five hundred to the monastery, and three hundred and seventy-two to the poor, as the prior should direct; desiring the good padre's prayers for me, and the like. I wrote next a letter of thanks to my two trustees, with all the acknowledgment that so much justice and honesty called for: as for sending them any present, they were far above having any occasion of it. Lastly, I wrote to my partner, acknowledging his industry in the improving the plantation, and his integrity in increasing the stock of the works; giving him instructions for his future government of my part, according to the powers I had left with my old patron, to whom I desired him to send whatever became due to me, till he should hear from me more particularly; assuring him that it was my intention not only to come to him, but to settle myself there for the remainder of my life. To this I added a very handsome present of some Italian silks for his wife and two daughters, for such the captain's son informed me he had; with two pieces of fine English broadcloth, the best I could get in Lisbon, five pieces of black baize, and some Flanders lace of a good value.

Having thus settled my affairs, sold my cargo, and turned all my effects into good bills of exchange, my next difficulty was which way to go to England: I had been accustomed enough to the sea, and yet I had a strange aversion to go to England by the sea at that time, and yet I could give no reason for it, yet the difficulty increased upon me so much, that though I had once shipped my baggage in order to go, yet I altered my mind, and that not once but two or three times.

It is true I had been very unfortunate by sea, and this might be one of the reasons; but let no man slight the strong impulses of his own thoughts in cases of such moment: two of the ships which I had singled out to go in, I mean more particularly singled out than any other, having put my things on board one of them, and in the other having agreed with the captain; I say two of these ships miscarried. One was taken by the Algerines, and the other was lost on the Start, near Torbay, and all the people drowned except three; so that in either of those vessels I had been made miserable.

Having been thus harassed in my thoughts, my old pilot, to whom I communicated everything, pressed me earnestly not to go by sea, but either to go by land to the Groyne, and cross over the Bay of Biscay to Rochelle, from whence it was but an easy and safe journey by land to Paris, and so to Calais and Dover; or to go up to Madrid, and so all the way by land through France. In a word, I was so prepossessed against my going by sea at all, except from Calais to Dover, that I resolved to travel all the way by land; which, as I was not in haste, and did not value the charge, was by much the pleasanter way: and to make it more so, my old captain brought an English gentleman, the son of a merchant in Lisbon, who was willing to travel with me; after which we picked up two more English merchants also, and two young Portuguese gentlemen, the last going to Paris only; so that in all there were six of us and five servants; the two merchants and the two Portuguese, contenting themselves with one servant between two, to save the charge; and as for me, I got an English sailor to travel with me as a servant, besides my man Friday, who was too much a stranger to be capable of supplying the place of a servant on the road.

In this manner I set out from Lisbon; and our company being very well mounted and armed, we made a little troop, whereof they did me the honour to call me captain, as well because I was the oldest man, as because I had two servants, and, indeed, was the origin of the whole journey.

As I have troubled you with none of my sea journals, so I shall trouble you now with none of my land journals; but some adventures that happened to us in this tedious and difficult journey I must not omit.

When we came to Madrid, we, being all of us strangers to Spain, were willing to stay some time to see the court of Spain, and what was worth observing; but it being the latter part of the summer, we hastened away, and set out from Madrid about the middle of October; but when we came to the edge of Navarre, we were alarmed, at several towns on the way, with an account that so much snow was falling on the French side of the mountains, that several travellers were obliged to come back to Pampeluna, after having attempted at an extreme hazard to pass on.

When we came to Pampeluna itself, we found it so indeed; and to me, that had been always used to a hot climate, and to countries where I could scarce bear any clothes on, the cold was insufferable; nor, indeed, was it more painful than surprising to come but ten days before out of Old Castile, where the weather was not only warm but very hot, and immediately to feel a wind from the Pyrenean Mountains so very keen, so severely cold, as to be intolerable and to endanger benumbing and perishing of our fingers and toes.

Poor Friday was really frightened when he saw the mountains all covered with snow, and felt cold weather, which he had never seen or felt before in his life. To mend the matter, when we came to Pampeluna it continued snowing with so much violence and so long, that the people said winter was come before its time; and the roads, which were difficult before, were now quite impassable; for, in a word, the snow lay in some places too thick for us to travel, and being not hard frozen, as is the case in the northern countries, there was no going without being in danger of being buried alive every step. We stayed no less than twenty days at Pampeluna; when (seeing the winter coming on, and no likelihood of its being better, for it was the severest winter all over Europe that had been known in the memory of man) I proposed that we should go away to Fontarabia, and there take shipping for Bordeaux, which was a very little voyage. But, while I was considering this, there came in four French gentlemen, who, having been stopped on the French side of the passes, as we were on the Spanish, had found out a guide, who, traversing the country near the head of Languedoc, had brought them over the mountains by such ways that they were not much incommoded with the snow; for where they met with snow in any quantity, they said it was frozen hard enough to bear them and their horses. We sent for this guide, who told us he would undertake to carry us the same way, with no hazard from the snow, provided we were armed sufficiently to protect ourselves from wild beasts; for, he said, in these great snows it was frequent for some wolves to show themselves at the foot of the mountains, being made ravenous for want of food, the ground being covered with snow. We told him we were well enough prepared for such creatures as they were, if he would insure us from a kind of two-legged wolves, which we were told we were in most danger from, especially on the French side of the mountains. He satisfied us that there was no danger of that kind in the way that we were to go; so we readily agreed to follow him, as did also twelve other gentlemen with their servants, some French, some Spanish, who, as I said, had attempted to go, and were obliged to come back again.

Accordingly, we set out from Pampeluna with our guide on the 15th of November; and indeed I was surprised when, instead of going forward, he came directly back with us on the same road that we came from Madrid, about twenty miles; when, having passed two rivers, and come into the plain country, we found ourselves in a warm climate again, where the country was pleasant, and no snow to be seen; but, on a sudden, turning to his left, he approached the mountains another way; and though it is true the hills and precipices looked dreadful, yet he made so many tours, such meanders, and led us by such winding ways, that we insensibly passed the height of the mountains without being much encumbered with the snow; and all on a sudden he showed us the pleasant and fruitful provinces of Languedoc and Gascony, all green and flourishing, though at a great distance, and we had some rough way to pass still.

We were a little uneasy, however, when we found it snowed one whole day and a night so fast that we could not travel; but he bid us be easy; we should soon be past it all: we found, indeed, that we began to descend every day, and to come more north than before; and so, depending upon our guide, we went on.

It was about two hours before night when, our guide being something before us, and not just in sight, out rushed three monstrous wolves, and after them a bear, from a hollow way adjoining to a thick wood; two of the wolves made at the guide, and had he been far before us, he would have been devoured before we could have helped him; one of them fastened upon his horse, and the other attacked the man with such violence, that he had not time, or presence of mind enough, to draw his pistol, but hallooed and cried out to us most lustily. My man Friday being next me, I bade him ride up and see what was the matter. As soon as Friday came in sight of the man, he hallooed out as loud as the other, "O master! O master!" but like a bold fellow, rode directly up to the poor man, and with his pistol shot the wolf in the head that attacked him.

It was happy for the poor man that it was my man Friday; for, having been used to such creatures in his country, he had no fear upon him, but went close up to him and shot him; whereas, any other of us would have fired at a farther distance, and have perhaps either missed the wolf or endangered shooting the man.

But it was enough to have terrified a bolder man than I; and, indeed, it alarmed all our company, when, with the noise of Friday's pistol, we heard on both sides the most dismal howling of wolves; and the noise, redoubled by the echo of the mountains, appeared to us as if there had been a prodigious number of them; and perhaps there was not such a few as that we had no cause of apprehension: however, as Friday had killed this wolf, the other that had fastened upon the horse left him immediately, and fled, without doing him any damage, having happily fastened upon his head, where the bosses of the bridle had stuck in his teeth. But the man was most hurt; for the raging creature had bit him twice, once in the arm, and the other time a little above his knee; and though he had made some defence, he was just tumbling down by the disorder of his horse, when Friday came up and shot the wolf.

It is easy to suppose that at the noise of Friday's pistol we all mended our pace, and rode up as fast as the way, which was very difficult, would give us leave, to see what was the matter. As soon as we came clear of the trees, which blinded us before, we saw clearly what had been the case, and how Friday had disengaged the poor guide, though we did not presently discern what kind of creature it was he had killed.

CHAPTER XX

FIGHT BETWEEN FRIDAY AND A BEAR

But never was a fight managed so hardily, and in such a surprising manner as that which followed between Friday and the bear, which gave us all, though at first we were surprised and afraid for him, the greatest diversion imaginable. As the bear is a heavy, clumsy creature, and does not gallop as the wolf does, who is swift and light, so he has two particular qualities, which generally are the rule of his actions; first, as to men, who are not his proper prey (he does not usually attempt them, except they first attack him, unless he be excessively hungry, which it is probable might now be the case, the ground being covered with snow), if you do not meddle with him, he will not meddle with you; but then you must take care to be very civil to him, and give him the road, for he is a very nice gentleman; he will not go a step out of his way for a prince; nay, if you are really afraid, your best way is to look another way and keep going on; for sometimes if you stop, and stand still, and look steadfastly at him, he takes it for an affront; but if you throw or toss anything at him, though it were but a bit of stick as big as your finger, he thinks himself abused, and sets all other business aside to pursue his revenge, and will have satisfaction in point of honour—that is his first quality: the next is, if he be once affronted, he will never leave you, night or day, till he has his revenge, but follows at a good round rate till he overtakes you.

My man Friday had delivered our guide, and when we came up to him he was helping him off his horse, for the man was both hurt and frightened, when on a sudden we espied the bear come out of the wood; and a monstrous one it was, the biggest by far that ever I saw. We were all a little surprised when we saw him; but when Friday saw him, it was easy to see joy and courage in the fellow's countenance. "O! O! O!" says Friday, three times, pointing to him; "O master, you give me te leave, me shakee te hand with him; me makee you good laugh."

I was surprised to see the fellow so well pleased. "You fool," says I, "he will eat you up."—"Eatee me up! eatee me up!" says Friday, twice over again; "me eatee him up; me makee you good laugh; you all stay here, me show you good laugh." So down he sits, and gets off his boots in a moment, and puts on a pair of pumps (as we call the flat shoes they wear, and which he had in his pocket), gives my other servant his horse, and with his gun away he flew, swift like the wind.

The bear was walking softly on, and offered to meddle with nobody, till Friday coming pretty near, calls to him, as if the bear could understand him. "Hark ye, hark ye," says Friday, "me speakee with you." We followed at a distance, for now being down on the Gascony side of the mountains, we were entered a vast forest, where the country was plain and pretty open, though it had many trees in it scattered here and there. Friday, who had, as we say, the heels of the bear, came up with him quickly, and took up a great stone, and threw it at him, and hit him just on the head, but did him no more harm than if he had thrown it against a wall; but it answered Friday's end, for the rogue was so void of fear that he did it purely to make the bear follow him, and show us some laugh as he called it. As soon as the bear felt the blow, and saw him, he turns about and comes after him, taking very long strides, and shuffling on at a strange rate, so as would have put a horse to a middling gallop; away reins Friday, and takes his course as if he ran towards us for help; so we all resolved to fire at once upon the bear, and deliver my man; though I was angry at him for bringing the bear back upon us, when he was going about his own business another way; and especially I was angry that he had turned the bear upon us, and then ran away; and I called out, "You dog! is this your making us laugh? Come away, and take your horse, that we may shoot the creature." He heard me, and cried out, "No shoot, no shoot; stand still, and you get much laugh:" and as the nimble creature ran two feet for the bear's one, he turned on a sudden on one side of us, and seeing a great oak-tree fit for his purpose, he beckoned to us to follow; and doubling his pace, he got nimbly up the tree, laying his gun down upon the ground, at about five or six yards from the bottom of the tree. The bear soon came to the tree, and we followed at a distance: the first thing he did he stopped at the gun, smelt at it, but let it lie, and up he scrambles into the tree, climbing like a cat, though so monstrous heavy. I was amazed at the folly, as I thought it, of my man, and could not for my life see anything to laugh at, till seeing the bear get up the tree, we all rode near to him.

When we came to the tree, there was Friday got out to the small end of a large branch, and the bear got about half-way to him. As soon as the bear got out to that part where the limb of the tree was weaker, "Ha!" says he to us, "now you see me teachee the bear dance:" so he began jumping and shaking the bough, at which the bear began to totter, but stood still, and began to look behind him, to see how he should get back; then, indeed, we did laugh heartily. But Friday had not done with him by a great deal; when seeing him stand still, he called out to him again, as if he had supposed the bear could speak English, "What, you come no farther? pray you come farther;" so he left jumping and shaking the tree; and the bear, just as if he understood what he said, did come a little farther; then he began jumping again, and the bear stopped again. We thought now was a good time to knock him in the head, and called to Friday to stand still and we should shoot the bear: but he cried out earnestly, "Oh, pray! Oh, pray! no shoot, me shoot by and then:" he would have said by-and-by. However, to shorten the story, Friday danced so much, and the bear stood so ticklish, that we had laughing enough, but still could not imagine what the fellow would do: for first we thought he depended upon shaking the bear off; and we found the bear was too cunning for that too; for he would not go out far enough to be thrown down, but clung fast with his great broad claws and feet, so that we could not imagine what would be the end of it, and what the jest would be at last. But Friday put us out of doubt quickly: for seeing the bear cling fast to the bough, and that he would not be persuaded to come any farther, "Well, well," says Friday, "you no come farther, me go; you no come to me, me come to you;" and upon this he went out to the smaller end, where it would bend with his weight, and gently let himself down by it, sliding down the bough till he came near enough to jump down on his feet, and away he ran to his gun, took it up, and stood still. "Well," said I to him, "Friday, what will you do now? Why don't you shoot him?" "No shoot," says Friday, "no yet; me shoot now, me no kill; me stay, give you one more laugh:" and, indeed, so he did; for when the bear saw his enemy gone, he came back from the bough, where he stood, but did it very cautiously, looking behind him every step, and coming backward till he got into the body of the tree, then, with the same hinder end foremost, he came down the tree, grasping it with his claws, and moving one foot at a time, very leisurely. At this juncture, and just before he could set his hind foot on the ground, Friday stepped up close to him, clapped the muzzle of his piece into his ear, and shot him dead. Then the rogue turned about to see if we did not laugh; and when he saw we were pleased by our looks, he began to laugh very loud. "So we kill bear in my country," says Friday. "So you kill them?" says I; "why, you have no guns."—"No," says he, "no gun, but shoot great much long arrow." This was a good diversion to us; but we were still in a wild place, and our guide very much hurt, and what to do we hardly knew; the howling of wolves ran much in my head; and, indeed, except the noise I once heard on the shore of Africa, of which I have said something already, I never heard anything that filled me with so much horror.

These things, and the approach of night, called us off, or else, as Friday would have had us, we should certainly have taken the skin of this monstrous creature off, which was worth saving; but we had near three leagues to go, and our guide hastened us; so we left him, and went forward on our journey.

The ground was still covered with snow, though not so deep and dangerous as on the mountains; and the ravenous creatures, as we heard afterwards, were come down into the forest and plain country, pressed by hunger, to seek for food, and had done a great deal of mischief in the villages, where they surprised the country people, killed a great many of their sheep and horses, and some people too. We had one dangerous place to pass, and our guide told us if there were more wolves in the country we should find them there; and this was a small plain, surrounded with woods on every side, and a long, narrow defile, or lane, which we were to pass to get through the wood, and then we should come to the village where we were to lodge. It was within half-an-hour of sunset when we entered the wood, and a little after sunset when we came into the plain: we met with nothing in the first wood, except that in a little plain within the wood, which was not above two furlongs over, we saw five great wolves cross the road, full speed, one after another, as if they had been in chase of some prey, and had it in view; they took no notice of us, and were gone out of sight in a few moments. Upon this, our guide, who, by the way, was but a fainthearted fellow, bid us keep in a ready posture, for he believed there were more wolves a-coming. We kept our arms ready, and our eyes about us; but we saw no more wolves till we came through that wood, which was near half a league, and entered the plain. As soon as we came into the plain, we had occasion enough to look about us. The first object we met with was a dead horse; that is to say, a poor horse which the wolves had killed, and at least a dozen of them at work, we could not say eating him, but picking his bones rather; for they had eaten up all the flesh before. We did not think fit to disturb them at their feast, neither did they take much notice of us. Friday would have let fly at them, but I would not suffer him by any means; for I found we were like to have more business upon our hands than we were aware of. We had not gone half over the plain when we began to hear the wolves howl in the wood on our left in a frightful manner, and presently after we saw about a hundred coming on directly towards us, all in a body, and most of them in a line, as regularly as an army drawn up by experienced officers. I scarce knew in what manner to receive them, but found to draw ourselves in a close line was the only way; so we formed in a moment; but that we might not have too much interval, I ordered that only every other man should fire, and that the others, who had not fired, should stand ready to give them a second volley immediately, if they continued to advance upon us; and then that those that had fired at first should not pretend to load their fusees again, but stand ready, every one with a pistol, for we were all armed with a fusee and a pair of pistols each man; so we were, by this method, able to fire six volleys, half of us at a time; however, at present we had no necessity; for upon firing the first volley, the enemy made a full stop, being terrified as well with the noise as with the fire. Four of them being shot in the head, dropped; several others were wounded, and went bleeding off, as we could see by the snow. I found they stopped, but did not immediately retreat; whereupon, remembering that I had been told that the fiercest creatures were terrified at the voice of a man, I caused all the company to halloo as loud as they could; and I found the notion not altogether mistaken; for upon our shout they began to retire and turn about. I then ordered a second volley to be fired in their rear, which put them to the gallop, and away they went to the woods. This gave us leisure to charge our pieces again; and that we might lose no time, we kept going; but we had but little more than loaded our fusees, and put ourselves in readiness, when we heard a terrible noise in the same wood on our left, only that it was farther onward, the same way we were to go.

The night was coming on, and the light began to be dusky, which made it worse on our side; but the noise increasing, we could easily perceive that it was the howling and yelling of those hellish creatures; and on a sudden we perceived three troops of wolves, one on our left, one behind us, and one in our front, so that we seemed to be surrounded with them: however, as they did not fall upon us, we kept our way forward, as fast as we could make our horses go, which, the way being very rough, was only a good hard trot. In this manner, we came in view of the entrance of a wood, through which we were to pass, at the farther side of the plain; but we were greatly surprised, when coming nearer the lane or pass, we saw a confused number of wolves standing just at the entrance. On a sudden, at another opening of the wood, we heard the noise of a gun, and looking that way, out rushed a horse, with a saddle and a bridle on him, flying like the wind, and sixteen or seventeen wolves after him, full speed: the horse had the advantage of them; but as we supposed that he could not hold it at that rate, we doubted not but they would get up with him at last: no question but they did.

But here we had a most horrible sight; for riding up to the entrance where the horse came out, we found the carcasses of another horse and of two men, devoured by the ravenous creatures; and one of the men was no doubt the same whom we heard fire the gun, for there lay a gun just by him fired off; but as to the man, his head and the upper part of his body was eaten up. This filled us with horror, and we knew not what course to take; but the creatures resolved us soon, for they gathered about us presently, in hopes of prey; and I verily believe there were three hundred of them. It happened, very much to our advantage, that at the entrance into the wood, but a little way from it, there lay some large timber-trees, which had been cut down the summer before, and I suppose lay there for carriage. I drew my little troop in among those trees, and placing ourselves in a line behind one long tree, I advised them all to alight, and keeping that tree before us for a breastwork, to stand in a triangle, or three fronts, enclosing our horses in the centre. We did so, and it was well we did; for never was a more furious charge than the creatures made upon us in this place. They came on with a growling kind of noise, and mounted the piece of timber, which, as I said, was our breastwork, as if they were only rushing upon their prey; and this fury of theirs, it seems, was principally occasioned by their seeing our horses behind us. I ordered our men to fire as before, every other man; and they took their aim so sure that they killed several of the wolves at the first volley; but there was a necessity to keep a continual firing, for they came on like devils, those behind pushing on those before.

When we had fired a second volley of our fusees, we thought they stopped a little, and I hoped they would have gone off, but it was but a moment, for others came forward again; so we fired two volleys of our pistols; and I believe in these four firings we had killed seventeen or eighteen of them, and lamed twice as many, yet they came on again. I was loth to spend our shot too hastily; so I called my servant, not my man Friday, for he was better employed, for, with the greatest dexterity imaginable, he had charged my fusee and his own while we were engaged—but, as I said, I called my other man, and giving him a horn of powder, I had him lay a train all along the piece of timber, and let it be a large train. He did so, and had but just time to get away, when the wolves came up to it, and some got upon it, when I, snapping an unchanged pistol close to the powder, set it on fire; those that were upon the timber were scorched with it, and six or seven of them fell; or rather jumped in among us with the force and fright of the fire; we despatched these in an instant, and the rest were so frightened with the light, which the night—for it was now very near dark—made more terrible that they drew back a little; upon which I ordered our last pistols to be fired off in one volley, and after that we gave a shout; upon this the wolves turned tail, and we sallied immediately upon near twenty lame ones that we found struggling on the ground, and fell to cutting them with our swords, which answered our expectation, for the crying and howling they made was better understood by their fellows; so that they all fled and left us.

We had, first and last, killed about threescore of them, and had it been daylight we had killed many more. The field of battle being thus cleared, we made forward again, for we had still near a league to go. We heard the ravenous creatures howl and yell in the woods as we went several times, and sometimes we fancied we saw some of them; but the snow dazzling our eyes, we were not certain. In about an hour more we came to the town where we were to lodge, which we found in a terrible fright and all in arms; for, it seems, the night before the wolves and some bears had broken into the village, and put them in such terror that they were obliged to keep guard night and day, but especially in the night, to preserve their cattle, and indeed their people.

The next morning our guide was so ill, and his limbs swelled so much with the rankling of his two wounds, that he could go no farther; so we were obliged to take a new guide here, and go to Toulouse, where we found a warm climate, a fruitful, pleasant country, and no snow, no wolves, nor anything like them; but when we told our story at Toulouse, they told us it was nothing but what was ordinary in the great forest at the foot of the mountains, especially when the snow lay on the ground; but they inquired much what kind of guide we had got who would venture to bring us that way in such a severe season, and told us it was surprising we were not all devoured. When we told them how we placed ourselves and the horses in the middle, they blamed us exceedingly, and told us it was fifty to one but we had been all destroyed, for it was the sight of the horses which made the wolves so furious, seeing their prey, and that at other times they are really afraid of a gun; but being excessively hungry, and raging on that account, the eagerness to come at the horses had made them senseless of danger, and that if we had not by the continual fire, and at last by the stratagem of the train of powder, mastered them, it had been great odds but that we had been torn to pieces; whereas, had we been content to have sat still on horseback, and fired as horsemen, they would not have taken the horses so much for their own, when men were on their backs, as otherwise; and withal, they told us that at last, if we had stood altogether, and left our horses, they would have been so eager to have devoured them, that we might have come off safe, especially having our firearms in our hands, being so many in number. For my part, I was never so sensible of danger in my life; for, seeing above three hundred devils come roaring and open-mouthed to devour us, and having nothing to shelter us or retreat to, I gave myself over for lost; and, as it was, I believe I shall never care to cross those mountains again: I think I would much rather go a thousand leagues by sea, though I was sure to meet with a storm once a-week.

I have nothing uncommon to take notice of in my passage through France—nothing but what other travellers have given an account of with much more advantage than I can. I travelled from Toulouse to Paris, and without any considerable stay came to Calais, and landed safe at Dover the 14th of January, after having had a severe cold season to travel in.

I was now come to the centre of my travels, and had in a little time all my new-discovered estate safe about me, the bills of exchange which I brought with me having been currently paid.

My principal guide and privy-counsellor was my good ancient widow, who, in gratitude for the money I had sent her, thought no pains too much nor care too great to employ for me; and I trusted her so entirely that I was perfectly easy as to the security of my effects; and, indeed, I was very happy from the beginning, and now to the end, in the unspotted integrity of this good gentlewoman.

And now, having resolved to dispose of my plantation in the Brazils, I wrote to my old friend at Lisbon, who, having offered it to the two merchants, the survivors of my trustees, who lived in the Brazils, they accepted the offer, and remitted thirty-three thousand pieces of eight to a correspondent of theirs at Lisbon to pay for it.

In return, I signed the instrument of sale in the form which they sent from Lisbon, and sent it to my old man, who sent me the bills of exchange for thirty-two thousand eight hundred pieces of eight for the estate, reserving the payment of one hundred moidores a year to him (the old man) during his life, and fifty moidores afterwards to his son for his life, which I had promised them, and which the plantation was to make good as a rent-charge. And thus I have given the first part of a life of fortune and adventure—a life of Providence's chequer-work, and of a variety which the world will seldom be able to show the like of; beginning foolishly, but closing much more happily than any part of it ever gave me leave so much as to hope for.

Any one would think that in this state of complicated good fortune I was past running any more hazards—and so, indeed, I had been, if other circumstances had concurred; but I was inured to a wandering life, had no family, nor many relations; nor, however rich, had I contracted fresh acquaintance; and though I had sold my estate in the Brazils, yet I could not keep that country out of my head, and had a great mind to be upon the wing again; especially I could not resist the strong inclination I had to see my island, and to know if the poor Spaniards were in being there. My true friend, the widow, earnestly dissuaded me from it, and so far prevailed with me, that for almost seven years she prevented my running abroad, during which time I took my two nephews, the children of one of my brothers, into my care; the eldest, having something of his own, I bred up as a gentleman, and gave him a settlement of some addition to his estate after my decease. The other I placed with the captain of a ship; and after five years, finding him a sensible, bold, enterprising young fellow, I put him into a good ship, and sent him to sea; and this young fellow afterwards drew me in, as old as I was, to further adventures myself.

In the meantime, I in part settled myself here; for, first of all, I married, and that not either to my disadvantage or dissatisfaction, and had three children, two sons and one daughter; but my wife dying, and my nephew coming home with good success from a voyage to Spain, my inclination to go abroad, and his importunity, prevailed, and engaged me to go in his ship as a private trader to the East Indies; this was in the year 1694.

In this voyage I visited my new colony in the island, saw my successors the Spaniards, had the old story of their lives and of the villains I left there; how at first they insulted the poor Spaniards, how they afterwards agreed, disagreed, united, separated, and how at last the Spaniards were obliged to use violence with them; how they were subjected to the Spaniards, how honestly the Spaniards used them—a history, if it were entered into, as full of variety and wonderful accidents as my own part—particularly, also, as to their battles with the Caribbeans, who landed several times upon the island, and as to the improvement they made upon the island itself, and how five of them made an attempt upon the mainland, and brought away eleven men and five women prisoners, by which, at my coming, I found about twenty young children on the island.

Here I stayed about twenty days, left them supplies of all necessary things, and particularly of arms, powder, shot, clothes, tools, and two workmen, which I had brought from England with me, viz. a carpenter and a smith.

Besides this, I shared the lands into parts with them, reserved to myself the property of the whole, but gave them such parts respectively as they agreed on; and having settled all things with them, and engaged them not to leave the place, I left them there.

From thence I touched at the Brazils, from whence I sent a bark, which I bought there, with more people to the island; and in it, besides other supplies, I sent seven women, being such as I found proper for service, or for wives to such as would take them. As to the Englishmen, I promised to send them some women from England, with a good cargo of necessaries, if they would apply themselves to planting—which I afterwards could not perform. The fellows proved very honest and diligent after they were mastered and had their properties set apart for them. I sent them, also, from the Brazils, five cows, three of them being big with calf, some sheep, and some hogs, which when I came again were considerably increased.

But all these things, with an account how three hundred Caribbees came and invaded them, and ruined their plantations, and how they fought with that whole number twice, and were at first defeated, and one of them killed; but at last, a storm destroying their enemies' canoes, they famished or destroyed almost all the rest, and renewed and recovered the possession of their plantation, and still lived upon the island.

All these things, with some very surprising incidents in some new adventures of my own, for ten years more, I shall give a farther account of in the Second Part of my Story.

THE FURTHER ADVENTURES OF ROBINSON CRUSOE

CHAPTER I. REVISITS ISLAND

That homely proverb, used on so many occasions in England, viz. "That what is bred in the bone will not go out of the flesh," was never more verified than in the story of my Life. Any one would think that after thirty-five years' affliction, and a variety of unhappy circumstances, which few men, if any, ever went through before, and after near seven years of peace and enjoyment in the fullness of all things; grown old, and when, if ever, it might be allowed me to have had experience of every state of middle life, and to know which was most adapted to make a man completely happy; I say, after all this, any one would have thought that the native propensity to rambling which I gave an account of in my first setting out in the world to have been so predominant in my thoughts, should be worn out, and I might, at sixty one years of age, have been a little inclined to stay at home, and have done venturing life and fortune any more.

Nay, farther, the common motive of foreign adventures was taken away in me, for I had no fortune to make; I had nothing to seek: if I had gained ten thousand pounds I had been no richer; for I had already sufficient for me, and for those I had to leave it to; and what I had was visibly increasing; for, having no great family, I could not spend the income of what I had unless I would set up for an expensive way of living, such as a great family, servants, equipage, gaiety, and the like, which were things I had no notion of, or inclination to; so that I had nothing, indeed, to do but to sit still, and fully enjoy what I had got, and see it increase daily upon my hands. Yet all these things had no effect upon me, or at least not enough to resist the strong inclination I had to go abroad again, which hung about me like a chronic distemper. In particular, the desire of seeing my new plantation in the island, and the colony I left there, ran in my head continually. I dreamed of it all night, and my imagination ran upon it all day: it was uppermost in all my thoughts, and my fancy worked so steadily and strongly upon it that I talked of it in my sleep; in short, nothing could remove it out of my mind: it even broke so violently into all my discourses that it made my conversation tiresome, for I could talk of nothing else; all my discourse ran into it, even to impertinence; and I saw it myself.

I have often heard persons of good judgment say that all the stir that people make in the world about ghosts and apparitions is owing to the strength of imagination, and the powerful operation of fancy in their minds; that there is no such thing as a spirit appearing, or a ghost walking; that people's poring affectionately upon the past conversation of their deceased friends so realizes it to them that they are capable of fancying, upon some extraordinary circumstances, that they see them, talk to them, and are answered by them, when, in truth, there is nothing but shadow and vapour in the thing, and they really know nothing of the matter.

For my part, I know not to this hour whether there are any such things as real apparitions, spectres, or walking of people after they are dead; or whether there is anything in the stories they tell us of that kind more than the product of vapours, sick minds, and wandering fancies: but this I know, that my imagination worked up to such a height, and brought me into such excess of vapours, or what else I may call it, that I actually supposed myself often upon the spot, at my old castle, behind the trees; saw my old Spaniard, Friday's father, and the reprobate sailors I left upon the island; nay, I fancied I talked with them, and looked at them steadily, though I was broad awake, as at persons just before me; and this I did till I often frightened myself with the images my fancy represented to me. One time, in my sleep, I had the villainy of the three pirate sailors so lively related to me by the first Spaniard, and Friday's father, that it was surprising: they told me how they barbarously attempted to murder all the Spaniards, and that they set fire to the provisions they had laid up, on purpose to distress and starve them; things that I had never heard of, and that, indeed, were never all of them true in fact: but it was so warm in my imagination, and so realized to me, that, to the hour I saw them, I could not be persuaded but that it was or would be true; also how I resented it, when the Spaniard complained to me; and how I brought them to justice, tried them, and ordered them all three to be hanged. What there was really in this shall be seen in its place; for however I came to form such things in my dream, and what secret converse of spirits injected it, yet there was, I say, much of it true. I own that this dream had nothing in it literally and specifically true; but the general part was so true — the base, villainous behaviour of these three hardened rogues was such, and had been so much worse than all I can describe, that the dream had too much similitude of the fact; and as I would afterwards have punished them severely, so, if I had hanged them all, I had been much in the right, and even should have been justified both by the laws of God and man.

But to return to my story. In this kind of temper I lived some years; I had no enjoyment of my life, no pleasant hours, no agreeable diversion but what had something or other of this in it; so that my wife, who saw my mind wholly bent upon it, told me very seriously one night that she believed there was some secret, powerful impulse of Providence upon me, which had determined me to go thither again; and that she found nothing hindered me going but my being engaged to a wife and children. She told me that it was true she could not think of parting with me: but as she was assured that if she was dead it would be the first thing I would do, so, as it seemed to her that the thing was determined above, she would not be the only obstruction; for, if I thought fit and resolved to go — (Here she found me very intent upon her words, and that I looked very earnestly at her, so that it a little disordered her, and she stopped. I asked her why she did not go on, and say out what she was going to say? But I perceived that her heart was too full, and some tears stood in her eyes.) "Speak out, my dear," said I; "are you willing I should go?" — "No," says she, very affectionately, "I am far from willing; but if you are resolved to go," says she, "rather than I would be the only hindrance, I will go with you: for though I think it a most preposterous thing for one of your years, and in your condition, yet, if it must be," said she, again weeping, "I would not leave you; for if it be of Heaven you must do it, there is no resisting it; and if Heaven make it your duty to go, He will also make it mine to go with you, or otherwise dispose of me, that I may not obstruct it."

This affectionate behaviour of my wife's brought me a little out of the vapours, and I began to consider what I was doing; I corrected my wandering fancy, and began to argue with myself sedately what business I had after threescore years, and after such a life of tedious sufferings and disasters, and closed in so happy and easy a manner; I, say, what business had I to rush into new hazards, and put myself upon adventures fit only for youth and poverty to run into?

With those thoughts I considered my new engagement; that I had a wife, one child born, and my wife then great with child of another; that I had all the world could give me, and had no need to seek hazard for gain; that I was declining in years, and ought to think rather of leaving what I had gained than of seeking to increase it; that as to what my wife had said of its being an impulse from Heaven, and that it should be my duty to go, I had no notion of that; so, after many of these cogitations, I struggled with the power of my imagination, reasoned myself out of it, as I believe people may always do in like cases if they will: in a word, I conquered it, composed myself with such arguments as occurred to my thoughts, and which my present condition furnished me plentifully with; and particularly, as the most effectual method, I resolved to divert myself with other things, and to engage in some business that might effectually tie me up from any more excursions of this kind; for I found that thing return upon me chiefly when I was idle, and had nothing to do, nor anything of moment immediately before me. To this purpose, I bought a little farm in the county of Bedford, and resolved to remove myself thither. I had a little convenient house upon it, and the land about it, I found, was capable of great improvement; and it was many ways suited to my inclination, which delighted in cultivating, managing, planting, and improving of land; and particularly, being an inland country, I was removed from conversing among sailors and things relating to the remote parts of the world. I went down to my farm, settled my family, bought ploughs, harrows, a cart, wagon-horses, cows, and sheep, and, setting seriously to work, became in one half-year a mere country gentleman. My thoughts were entirely taken up in managing my servants, cultivating the ground, enclosing, planting, &c.; and I lived, as I thought, the most agreeable life that nature was capable of directing, or that a man always bred to misfortunes was capable of retreating to.

I farmed upon my own land; I had no rent to pay, was limited by no articles; I could pull up or cut down as I pleased; what I planted was for myself, and what I improved was for my family; and having thus left off the thoughts of wandering, I had not the least discomfort in any part of life as to this world. Now I thought, indeed, that I enjoyed the middle state of life which my father so earnestly recommended to me, and lived a kind of heavenly life, something like what is described by the poet, upon the subject of a country life: —

"Free from vices, free from care,   Age has no pain, and youth no snare."

But in the middle of all this felicity, one blow from unseen Providence unhinged me at once; and not only made a breach upon me inevitable and incurable, but drove me, by its consequences, into a deep relapse of the wandering disposition, which, as I may say, being born in my very blood, soon recovered its hold of me; and, like the returns of a violent distemper, came on with an irresistible force upon me. This blow was the loss of my wife. It is not my business here to write an elegy upon my wife, give a character of her particular virtues, and make

254

my court to the sex by the flattery of a funeral sermon. She was, in a few words, the stay of all my affairs; the centre of all my enterprises; the engine that, by her prudence, reduced me to that happy compass I was in, from the most extravagant and ruinous project that filled my head, and did more to guide my rambling genius than a mother's tears, a father's instructions, a friend's counsel, or all my own reasoning powers could do. I was happy in listening to her, and in being moved by her entreaties; and to the last degree desolate and dislocated in the world by the loss of her.

When she was gone, the world looked awkwardly round me. I was as much a stranger in it, in my thoughts, as I was in the Brazils, when I first went on shore there; and as much alone, except for the assistance of servants, as I was in my island. I knew neither what to think nor what to do. I saw the world busy around me: one part labouring for bread, another part squandering in vile excesses or empty pleasures, but equally miserable because the end they proposed still fled from them; for the men of pleasure every day surfeited of their vice, and heaped up work for sorrow and repentance; and the men of labour spent their strength in daily struggling for bread to maintain the vital strength they laboured with: so living in a daily circulation of sorrow, living but to work, and working but to live, as if daily bread were the only end of wearisome life, and a wearisome life the only occasion of daily bread.

This put me in mind of the life I lived in my kingdom, the island; where I suffered no more corn to grow, because I did not want it; and bred no more goats, because I had no more use for them; where the money lay in the drawer till it grew mouldy, and had scarce the favour to be looked upon in twenty years. All these things, had I improved them as I ought to have done, and as reason and religion had dictated to me, would have taught me to search farther than human enjoyments for a full felicity; and that there was something which certainly was the reason and end of life superior to all these things, and which was either to be possessed, or at least hoped for, on this side of the grave.

But my sage counselor was gone; I was like a ship without a pilot, that could only run afore the wind. My thoughts ran all away again into the old affair; my head was quite turned with the whimsies of foreign adventures; and all the pleasant, innocent amusements of my farm, my garden, my cattle, and my family, which before entirely possessed me, were nothing to me, had no relish, and were like music to one that has no ear, or food to one that has no taste. In a word, I resolved to leave off housekeeping, let my farm, and return to London; and in a few months after I did so.

When I came to London, I was still as uneasy as I was before; I had no relish for the place, no employment in it, nothing to do but to saunter about like an idle person, of whom it may be said he is perfectly useless in God's creation, and it is not one farthing's matter to the rest of his kind whether he be dead or alive. This also was the thing which, of all circumstances of life, was the most my aversion, who had been all my days used to an active life; and I would often say to myself, "A state of idleness is the very dregs of life;" and, indeed, I thought I was much more suitably employed when I was twenty-six days making a deal board.

It was now the beginning of the year 1693, when my nephew, whom, as I have observed before, I had brought up to the sea, and had made him commander of a ship, was come home from a short voyage to Bilbao, being the first he had made. He came to me, and told me that some merchants of his acquaintance had been proposing to him to go a voyage for them to the East Indies, and to China, as private traders. "And now, uncle," says he, "if you will go to sea with me, I will engage to land you upon your old habitation in the island; for we are to touch at the Brazils."

Nothing can be a greater demonstration of a future state, and of the existence of an invisible world, than the concurrence of second causes with the idea of things which we form in our minds, perfectly reserved, and not communicated to any in the world.

My nephew knew nothing how far my distemper of wandering was returned upon me, and I knew nothing of what he had in his thought to say, when that very morning, before he came to me, I had, in a great deal of confusion of thought, and revolving every part of my circumstances in my mind, come to this resolution, that I would go to Lisbon, and consult with my old sea-captain; and if it was rational and practicable, I would go and see the island again, and what was become of my people there. I had pleased myself with the thoughts of peopling the place, and carrying inhabitants from hence, getting a patent for the possession and I know not what; when, in the middle of all this, in comes my nephew, as I have said, with his project of carrying me thither in his way to the East Indies.

I paused a while at his words, and looking steadily at him, "What devil," said I, "sent you on this unlucky errand?" My nephew stared as if he had been frightened at first; but perceiving that I was not much displeased at the proposal, he recovered himself. "I hope it may not be an unlucky proposal, sir," says he. "I daresay you would be pleased to see your new colony there, where you once reigned with more felicity than most of your brother monarchs in the world." In a word, the scheme hit so exactly with my temper, that is to say, the prepossession I was under, and of which I have said so much, that I told him, in a few words, if he agreed with the merchants, I would go with him; but I told him I would not promise to go any further than my own island. "Why, sir," says he, "you don't want to be left there again, I hope?" "But," said I, "can you not take me up again on your return?" He told me it would not be possible to do so; that the merchants would never allow him to come that way with a laden ship of such value, it being a month's sail out of his way, and might be three or four. "Besides, sir, if I should miscarry," said he, "and not return at all, then you would be just reduced to the condition you were in before."

This was very rational; but we both found out a remedy for it, which was to carry a framed sloop on board the ship, which, being taken in pieces, might, by the help of some carpenters, whom we agreed to carry with us, be set up again in the island, and finished fit to go to sea in a few days. I was not long resolving, for indeed the importunities of my nephew joined so effectually with my inclination that nothing could oppose me; on the other hand, my wife being dead, none concerned themselves so much for me as to persuade me one way or the other, except my ancient good friend the widow, who earnestly struggled with me to consider my years, my easy circumstances, and the needless hazards of a long voyage; and above all, my young children. But it was all to no purpose, I had an irresistible desire for the voyage; and I told her I thought there was something so uncommon in the impressions I had upon my mind, that it would be a kind of resisting Providence if I should attempt to stay at home; after which she ceased her expostulations, and joined with me, not only in making provision for my voyage, but also in settling my family affairs for my absence, and providing for the education of my children. In order to do this, I made my will, and settled the estate I had in such a manner for my children, and placed in such hands, that I was perfectly easy and satisfied they would have justice done them, whatever might befall me; and for their education, I left it wholly to the widow, with a sufficient maintenance to herself for her care: all which she richly deserved; for no mother could have taken more care in their education, or understood it better; and as she lived till I came home, I also lived to thank her for it.

My nephew was ready to sail about the beginning of January 1694-5; and I, with my man Friday, went on board, in the Downs, the 8th; having, besides that sloop which I mentioned above, a very considerable cargo of all kinds of necessary things for my colony, which, if I did not find in good condition, I resolved to leave so.

First, I carried with me some servants whom I purposed to place there as inhabitants, or at least to set on work there upon my account while I stayed, and either to leave them there or carry them forward, as they should appear willing; particularly, I carried two carpenters, a smith, and a very handy, ingenious fellow, who was a cooper by trade, and was also a general mechanic; for he was dexterous at making wheels and hand-mills to grind corn, was a good turner and a good pot-maker; he also made anything that was proper to make of earth or of wood: in a word, we called him our Jack-of-all-trades. With these I carried a tailor, who had offered himself to go a passenger to the East Indies with my nephew, but afterwards consented to stay on our new plantation, and who proved a most necessary handy fellow as could be desired in many other businesses besides that of his trade; for, as I observed formerly, necessity arms us for all employments.

My cargo, as near as I can recollect, for I have not kept account of the particulars, consisted of a sufficient quantity of linen, and some English thin stuffs, for clothing the Spaniards that I expected to find there; and enough of them, as by my calculation might comfortably supply them for seven years; if I remember right, the materials I carried for clothing them, with gloves, hats, shoes, stockings, and all such things as they could want for wearing, amounted to about two hundred pounds, including some beds, bedding, and household stuff, particularly kitchen utensils, with pots, kettles, pewter, brass, &c.; and near a hundred pounds more in ironwork, nails, tools of every kind, staples, hooks, hinges, and every necessary thing I could think of.

I carried also a hundred spare arms, muskets, and fusées; besides some pistols, a considerable quantity of shot of all sizes, three or four tons of lead, and two pieces of brass cannon; and, because I knew not what time and what extremities I was providing for, I carried a hundred barrels of powder, besides swords, cutlasses, and the iron part of some pikes and halberds. In short, we had a large magazine of all sorts of store; and I made my nephew carry two small quarter-deck guns more than he wanted for his ship, to leave behind if there was occasion; so that when we came there we might build a fort and man it against all sorts of enemies. Indeed, I at first thought there would be need enough for all, and much more, if we hoped to maintain our possession of the island, as shall be seen in the course of that story.

I had not such bad luck in this voyage as I had been used to meet with, and therefore shall have the less occasion to interrupt the reader, who perhaps may be impatient to hear how matters went with my colony; yet some odd accidents, cross winds and bad weather happened on this first setting out, which made the voyage longer than I expected it at first; and I, who had never made but one voyage, my first voyage to Guinea, in which I might be said to come back again, as the voyage was at first designed, began to think the same ill fate attended me, and that I was born to be never contented with being on shore, and yet to be always unfortunate at sea. Contrary winds first put us to the northward, and we were obliged to put in at Galway, in Ireland, where we lay wind-bound two-and-twenty days; but we had this satisfaction with the disaster, that provisions were here exceeding cheap, and in the utmost plenty; so that while we lay here we never touched the ship's stores, but rather added to them. Here, also, I took in several live hogs, and two cows with their calves, which I resolved, if I had a good passage, to put on shore in my island; but we found occasion to dispose otherwise of them.

We set out on the 5th of February from Ireland, and had a very fair gale of wind for some days. As I remember, it might be about the 20th of February in the evening late, when the mate, having the watch, came into the round-house and told us he saw a flash of fire, and heard a gun fired; and while he was telling us of it, a boy came in and told us the boatswain heard another. This made us all run out upon the quarter-deck, where for a while we heard nothing; but in a few minutes we saw a very great light, and found that there was some very terrible fire at a distance; immediately we had recourse to our reckonings, in which we all agreed that there could be no land that way in which the fire showed itself, no, not for five hundred leagues, for it appeared at WNW. Upon this, we concluded it must be some ship on fire at sea; and as, by our hearing the noise of guns just before, we concluded that it could not be far off, we stood directly towards it, and were presently satisfied we should discover it, because the further we sailed, the greater the light appeared; though, the weather being hazy, we could not perceive anything but the light for a while. In about half-an-hour's sailing, the wind being fair for us, though not much of it, and the weather clearing up a little, we could plainly discern that it was a great ship on fire in the middle of the sea.

I was most sensibly touched with this disaster, though not at all acquainted with the persons engaged in it; I presently recollected my former circumstances, and what condition I was in when taken up by the Portuguese captain; and how much more deplorable the circumstances of the poor creatures belonging to that ship must be, if they had no other ship in company with them. Upon this I immediately ordered that five guns should be fired, one soon after another, that, if possible, we might give notice to them that there was help for them at hand and that they might endeavour to save themselves in their boat; for though we could see the flames of the ship, yet they, it being night, could see nothing of us.

We lay by some time upon this, only driving as the burning ship drove, waiting for daylight; when, on a sudden, to our great terror, though we had reason to expect it, the ship blew up in the air; and in a few minutes all the fire was out, that is to say, the rest of the ship sunk. This was a terrible, and indeed an afflicting sight, for the sake of the poor men, who, I concluded, must be either all destroyed in the ship, or be in the utmost distress in their boat, in the middle of the ocean; which, at present, as it was dark, I could not see. However, to direct them as well as I could, I caused lights to be hung out in all parts of the ship where we could, and which we had lanterns for, and kept firing guns all the night long, letting them know by this that there was a ship not far off.

About eight o'clock in the morning we discovered the ship's boats by the help of our perspective glasses, and found there were two of them, both thronged with people, and deep in the water. We perceived they rowed, the wind being against them; that they saw our ship, and did their utmost to make us see them. We immediately spread our ancient, to let them know we saw them, and hung a waft out, as a signal for them to come on board, and then made more sail, standing directly to them. In little more than half-an-hour we came up with them; and took them all in, being no less than sixty-four men, women, and children; for there were a great many passengers.

Upon inquiry we found it was a French merchant ship of three-hundred tons, home-bound from Quebec. The master gave us a long account of the distress of his ship; how the fire began in the steerage by the negligence of the steersman, which, on his crying out for help, was, as everybody thought, entirely put out; but they soon found that some sparks of the first fire had got into some part of the ship so difficult to come at that they could not effectually quench it; and afterwards getting in between the timbers, and within the ceiling of the ship, it proceeded into the hold, and mastered all the skill and all the application they were able to exert.

They had no more to do then but to get into their boats, which, to their great comfort, were pretty large; being their long-boat, and a great shallop, besides a small skiff, which was of no great service to them, other than to get some fresh water and provisions into her, after they had secured their lives from the fire. They had, indeed, small hopes of their lives by getting into these boats at that distance from any land; only, as they said, that they thus escaped from the fire, and there was a possibility that some ship might happen to be at sea, and might take them in. They had sails, oars, and a compass; and had as much provision and water as, with sparing it so as to be next door to starving, might support them about twelve days, in which, if they had no bad weather and no contrary winds, the captain said he hoped he might get to the banks of Newfoundland, and might perhaps take some fish, to sustain them till they might go on shore. But there were so many chances against them in all these cases, such as storms, to overset and founder them; rains and cold, to benumb and perish their limbs; contrary winds, to keep them out and starve them; that it must have been next to miraculous if they had escaped.

In the midst of their consternation, every one being hopeless and ready to despair, the captain, with tears in his eyes, told me they were on a sudden surprised with the joy of hearing a gun fire, and after that four more: these were the five guns which I caused to be fired at first seeing the light. This revived their hearts, and gave them the notice, which, as above, I desired it should, that there was a ship at hand for their help. It was upon the hearing of these guns that they took down their masts and sails: the sound coming from the windward, they resolved to lie by till morning. Some time after this, hearing no more guns, they fired three muskets, one a considerable while after another; but these, the wind being contrary, we never heard. Some time after that again they were still more agreeably surprised with seeing our lights, and hearing the guns, which, as I have said, I caused to be fired all the rest of the night. This set them to work with their oars, to keep their boats ahead, at least that we might the sooner come up with them; and at last, to their inexpressible joy, they found we saw them.

It is impossible for me to express the several gestures, the strange ecstasies, the variety of postures which these poor delivered people ran into, to express the joy of their souls at so unexpected a deliverance.

Grief and fear are easily described: sighs, tears, groans, and a very few motions of the head and hands, make up the sum of its variety; but an excess of joy, a surprise of joy, has a thousand extravagances in it. There were some in tears; some raging and tearing themselves, as if they had been in the greatest agonies of sorrow; some stark raving and downright lunatic; some ran about the ship stamping with their feet, others wringing their hands; some were dancing, some singing, some laughing, more crying, many quite dumb, not able to speak a word; others sick and vomiting; several swooning and ready to faint; and a few were crossing themselves and giving God thanks.

I would not wrong them either; there might be many that were thankful afterwards; but the passion was too strong for them at first, and they were not able to master it: then were thrown into ecstasies, and a kind of frenzy, and it was but a very few that were composed and serious in their joy. Perhaps also, the case may have some addition to it from the particular circumstance of that nation they belonged to: I mean the French, whose temper is allowed to be more volatile, more passionate, and more sprightly, and their spirits more fluid than in other nations. I am not philosopher enough to determine the cause; but nothing I had ever seen before came up to it. The ecstasies poor Friday, my trusty savage, was in when he found his father in the boat came the nearest to it; and the surprise of the master and his two companions, whom I delivered from the villains that set them on shore in the island, came a little way towards it; but nothing was to compare to this, either that I saw in Friday, or anywhere else in my life.

It is further observable, that these extravagances did not show themselves in that different manner I have mentioned, in different persons only; but all the variety would appear, in a short succession of moments, in one and the same person. A man that we saw this minute dumb, and, as it were, stupid and confounded, would the next minute be dancing and hallooing like an antic; and the next moment be tearing his hair, or pulling his clothes to pieces, and stamping them under his feet like a madman; in a few moments after that we would have him all in tears, then sick, swooning, and, had not immediate help been had, he would in a few moments have been dead. Thus it was, not with one or two, or ten or twenty, but with the greatest part of them; and, if I remember right, our surgeon was obliged to let blood of about thirty persons.

There were two priests among them: one an old man, and the other a young man; and that which was strangest was, the oldest man was the worst. As soon as he set his foot on board our ship, and saw himself safe, he dropped down stone dead to all appearance. Not the least sign of life could be perceived in him; our surgeon immediately applied proper remedies to recover him, and was the only man in the ship that believed he was not dead. At length he opened a vein in his arm, having first chafed and rubbed the part, so as to warm it as much as possible. Upon this the blood, which only dropped at first, flowing freely, in three minutes after the man opened his eyes; a quarter of an hour after that he spoke, grew better, and after the blood was stopped, he walked about, told us he was perfectly well, and took a dram of cordial which the surgeon gave him. About a quarter of an hour after this they came running into the cabin to the surgeon, who was bleeding a Frenchwoman that had fainted, and told him the priest was gone stark mad. It seems he had begun to revolve the change of his circumstances in his mind, and again this put him into an ecstasy of joy. His spirits whirled about faster than the vessels could convey them, the blood grew hot and feverish, and the man was as fit for Bedlam as any creature that ever was in it. The surgeon would not bleed him again in that condition, but gave him something to doze and put him to sleep; which, after some time, operated upon him, and he awoke next morning perfectly composed and well. The younger priest behaved with great command of his passions, and was really an example of a serious, well-governed mind. At his first coming on board the ship he threw himself flat on his face, prostrating himself in thankfulness for his deliverance, in which I unhappily and unseasonably disturbed him, really thinking he had been in a swoon; but he spoke calmly, thanked me, told me he was giving God thanks for his deliverance, begged me to leave him a few moments, and that, next to his Maker, he would give me thanks also. I was heartily sorry that I disturbed him, and not only left him, but kept others from interrupting him also. He continued in that posture about three minutes, or little more, after I left him, then came to me, as he had said he would, and with a great deal of seriousness and affection, but with tears in his eyes, thanked me, that had, under God, given him and so many miserable creatures their lives. I told him I had no need to tell him to thank God for it, rather than me, for I had seen that he had done that already; but I added that it was nothing but what reason and humanity dictated to all men, and that we had as much reason as he to give thanks to God, who had blessed us so far as to make us the instruments of His mercy to so many of His creatures. After this the young priest applied himself to his countrymen, and laboured to

263

compose them: he persuaded, entreated, argued, reasoned with them, and did his utmost to keep them within the exercise of their reason; and with some he had success, though others were for a time out of all government of themselves.

I cannot help committing this to writing, as perhaps it may be useful to those into whose hands it may fall, for guiding themselves in the extravagances of their passions; for if an excess of joy can carry men out to such a length beyond the reach of their reason, what will not the extravagances of anger, rage, and a provoked mind carry us to? And, indeed, here I saw reason for keeping an exceeding watch over our passions of every kind, as well those of joy and satisfaction as those of sorrow and anger.

We were somewhat disordered by these extravagances among our new guests for the first day; but after they had retired to lodgings provided for them as well as our ship would allow, and had slept heartily — as most of them did, being fatigued and frightened — they were quite another sort of people the next day. Nothing of good manners, or civil acknowledgments for the kindness shown them, was wanting; the French, it is known, are naturally apt enough to exceed that way. The captain and one of the priests came to me the next day, and desired to speak with me and my nephew; the commander began to consult with us what should be done with them; and first, they told us we had saved their lives, so all they had was little enough for a return to us for that kindness received. The captain said they had saved some money and some things of value in their boats, caught hastily out of the flames, and if we would accept it they were ordered to make an offer of it all to us; they only desired to be set on shore somewhere in our way, where, if possible, they might get a passage to France. My nephew wished to accept their money at first word, and to consider what to do with them afterwards; but I overruled him in that part, for I knew what it was to be set on shore in a strange country; and if the Portuguese captain that took me up at sea had served me so, and taken all I had for my deliverance, I must have been starved, or have been as much a slave at the Brazils as I had been at Barbary, the mere being sold to a Mahometan excepted; and perhaps a Portuguese is not a much better master than a Turk, if not in some cases much worse.

I therefore told the French captain that we had taken them up in their distress, it was true, but that it was our duty to do so, as we were fellow-creatures; and we would desire to be so delivered if we were in the like or any other extremity; that we had done nothing for them but what we believed they would have done for us if we had been in their case and they in ours; but that we took them up to save them, not to plunder them; and it would be a most barbarous thing to take that little from them which they had saved out of the fire, and then set them on shore and leave them; that this would be first to save them from death, and then kill them ourselves: save them from drowning, and abandon them to starving; and therefore I would not let the least thing be taken from them. As to setting them on shore, I told them indeed that was an exceeding difficulty to us, for that the ship was bound to the East Indies; and though we were driven out of our course to the westward a very great way, and perhaps were directed by Heaven on purpose for their deliverance, yet it was impossible for us willfully to change our voyage on their particular account; nor could my nephew, the captain, answer it to the freighters, with whom he was under charter to pursue his voyage by way of Brazil; and all I knew we could do for them was to put ourselves in the way of meeting with other ships homeward bound from the West Indies, and get them a passage, if possible, to England or France.

The first part of the proposal was so generous and kind they could not but be very thankful for it; but they were in very great consternation, especially the passengers, at the notion of being carried away to the East Indies; they then entreated me that as I was driven so far to the westward before I met with them, I would at least keep on the same course to the banks of Newfoundland, where it was probable I might meet with some ship or sloop that they might hire to carry them back to Canada.

I thought this was but a reasonable request on their part, and therefore I inclined to agree to it; for indeed I considered that to carry this whole company to the East Indies would not only be an intolerable severity upon the poor people, but would be ruining our whole voyage by devouring all our provisions; so I thought it no breach of charter-party, but what an unforeseen accident made absolutely necessary to us, and in which no one could say we were to blame; for the laws of God and nature would have forbid that we should refuse to take up two boats full of people in such a distressed condition; and the nature of the thing, as well respecting ourselves as the poor people, obliged us to set them on shore somewhere or other for their deliverance. So I consented that we would carry them to Newfoundland, if wind and weather would permit: and if not, I would carry them to Martinico, in the West Indies.

The wind continued fresh easterly, but the weather pretty good; and as the winds had continued in the points between NE. and SE. a long time, we missed several opportunities of sending them to France; for we met several ships bound to Europe, whereof two were French, from St. Christopher's, but they had been so long beating up against the wind that they durst take in no passengers, for fear of wanting provisions for the voyage, as well for themselves as for those they should take in; so we were obliged to go on. It was about a week after this that we made the banks of Newfoundland; where, to shorten my story, we put all our French people on board a bark, which they hired at sea there, to put them on shore, and afterwards to carry them to France, if they could get provisions to victual themselves with. When I say all the French went on shore, I should remember that the young priest I spoke of, hearing we were bound to the East Indies, desired to go the voyage with us, and to be set on shore on the coast of Coromandel; which I readily agreed to, for I wonderfully liked the man, and had very good reason, as will appear afterwards; also four of the seamen entered themselves on our ship, and proved very useful fellows.

From hence we directed our course for the West Indies, steering away S. and S. by E. for about twenty days together, sometimes little or no wind at all; when we met with another subject for our humanity to work upon, almost as deplorable as that before.

CHAPTER II. INTERVENING HISTORY OF COLONY

It was in the latitude of 27 degrees 5 minutes N., on the 19th day of March 1694-95, when we spied a sail, our course SE. and by S. We soon perceived it was a large vessel, and that she bore up to us, but could not at first know what to make of her, till, after coming a little nearer, we found she had lost her main-topmast, fore-mast, and bowsprit; and presently she fired a gun as a signal of distress. The weather was pretty good, wind at NNW. a fresh gale, and we soon came to speak with her. We found her a ship of Bristol, bound home from Barbados, but had been blown out of the road at Barbados a few days before she was ready to sail, by a terrible hurricane, while the captain and chief mate were both gone on shore; so that, besides the terror of the storm, they were in an indifferent case for good mariners to bring the ship home. They had been already nine weeks at sea, and had met with another terrible storm, after the hurricane was over, which had blown them quite out of their knowledge to the westward, and in which they lost their masts. They told us they expected to have seen the Bahama Islands, but were then driven away again to the south-east, by a strong gale of wind at NNW., the same that blew now: and having no sails to work the ship with but a main course, and a kind of square sail upon a jury fore-mast, which they had set up, they could not lie near the wind, but were endeavouring to stand away for the Canaries.

But that which was worst of all was, that they were almost starved for want of provisions, besides the fatigues they had undergone; their bread and flesh were quite gone — they had not one ounce left in the ship, and had had none for eleven days. The only relief they had was, their water was not all spent, and they had about half a barrel of flour left; they had sugar enough; some succades, or sweetmeats, they had at first, but these were all devoured; and they had seven casks of rum. There was a youth and his mother and a maid-servant on board, who were passengers, and thinking the ship was ready to sail, unhappily came on board the evening before the hurricane began; and having no provisions of their own left, they were in a more deplorable condition than the rest: for the seamen being reduced to such an extreme necessity themselves, had no compassion, we may be sure, for the poor passengers; and they were, indeed, in such a condition that their misery is very hard to describe.

I had perhaps not known this part, if my curiosity had not led me, the weather being fair and the wind abated, to go on board the ship.

The second mate, who upon this occasion commanded the ship, had been on board our ship, and he told me they had three passengers in the great cabin that were in a deplorable condition. "Nay," says he, "I believe they are dead, for I have heard nothing of them for above two days; and I was afraid to inquire after them," said he, "for I had nothing to relieve them with." We immediately applied ourselves to give them what relief we could spare; and indeed I had so far overruled things with my nephew, that I would have victualled them though we had gone away to Virginia, or any other part of the coast of America, to have supplied ourselves; but there was no necessity for that.

But now they were in a new danger; for they were afraid of eating too much, even of that little we gave them. The mate, or commander, brought six men with him in his boat; but these poor wretches looked like skeletons, and were so weak that they could hardly sit to their oars. The mate himself was very ill, and half starved; for he declared he had reserved nothing from the men, and went share and share alike with them in every bit they ate. I cautioned him to eat sparingly, and set meat before him immediately, but he had not eaten three mouthfuls before he began to be sick and out of order; so he stopped a while, and our surgeon mixed him up something with some broth, which he said would be to him both food and physic; and after he had taken it he grew better. In the meantime I forgot not the men. I ordered victuals to be given them, and the poor creatures rather devoured than ate it: they were so exceedingly hungry that they were in a manner ravenous, and had no command of themselves; and two of them ate with so much greediness that they were in danger of their lives the next morning. The sight of these people's distress was very moving to me, and brought to mind what I had a terrible prospect of at my first coming on shore in my island, where I had not the least mouthful of food, or any prospect of procuring any; besides the hourly apprehensions I had of being made the food of other creatures. But all the while the mate was thus relating to me the miserable condition of the ship's company, I could not put out of my thought the story he had told me of the three poor creatures in the great cabin, viz. the mother, her son, and the maid-servant, whom he had heard nothing of for two or three days, and whom, he seemed to confess, they had wholly neglected, their own extremities being so great; by which I understood that they had really given them no food at all, and that therefore they must be perished, and be all lying dead, perhaps, on the floor or deck of the cabin.

As I therefore kept the mate, whom we then called captain, on board with his men, to refresh them, so I also forgot not the starving crew that were left on board, but ordered my own boat to go on board the ship, and, with my mate and twelve men, to carry them a sack of bread, and four or five pieces of beef to boil. Our surgeon charged the men to cause the meat to be boiled while they stayed, and to keep guard in the cook-room, to prevent the men taking it to eat raw, or taking it out of the pot before it was well boiled, and then to give every man but a very little at a time: and by this caution he preserved the men, who would otherwise have killed themselves with that very food that was given them on purpose to save their lives.

At the same time I ordered the mate to go into the great cabin, and see what condition the poor passengers were in; and if they were alive, to comfort them, and give them what refreshment was proper: and the surgeon gave him a large pitcher, with some of the prepared broth which he had given the mate that was on board, and which he did not question would restore them gradually. I was not satisfied with this; but, as I said above, having a great mind to see the scene of misery which I knew the ship itself would present me with, in a more lively manner than I could have it by report, I took the captain of the ship, as we now called him, with me, and went myself, a little after, in their boat.

I found the poor men on board almost in a tumult to get the victuals out of the boiler before it was ready; but my mate observed his orders, and kept a good guard at the cook-room door, and the man he placed there, after using all possible persuasion to have patience, kept them off by force; however, he caused some biscuit-cakes to be dipped in the pot, and softened with the liquor of the meat, which they called brewis, and gave them every one some to stay their stomachs, and told them it was for their own safety that he was obliged to give them but little at a time. But it was all in vain; and had I not come on board, and their own commander and officers with me, and with good words, and some threats also of giving them no more, I believe they would have broken into the cook-room by force, and torn the meat out of the furnace — for words are indeed of very small force to a hungry belly; however, we pacified them, and fed them gradually and cautiously at first, and the next time gave them more, and at last filled their bellies, and the men did well enough.

But the misery of the poor passengers in the cabin was of another nature, and far beyond the rest; for as, first, the ship's company had so little for themselves, it was but too true that they had at first kept them very low, and at last totally neglected them: so that for six or seven days it might be said they had really no food at all, and for several days before very little. The poor mother, who, as the men reported, was a woman of sense and good breeding, had spared all she could so affectionately for her son, that at last she entirely sank under it; and when the mate of our ship went in, she sat upon the floor on deck, with her back up against the sides, between two chairs, which were lashed fast, and her head sunk between her shoulders like a corpse, though not quite dead. My mate said all he could to revive and encourage her, and with a spoon put some broth into her mouth. She opened her lips, and lifted up one hand, but could not speak: yet she understood what he said, and made signs to him, intimating, that it was too late for her, but pointed to her child, as if she would have said they should take care of him. However, the mate, who was exceedingly moved at the sight, endeavoured to get some of the broth into her mouth, and, as he said, got two or three spoonfuls down — though I question whether he could be sure of it or not; but it was too late, and she died the same night.

The youth, who was preserved at the price of his most affectionate mother's life, was not so far gone; yet he lay in a cabin bed, as one stretched out, with hardly any life left in him. He had a piece of an old glove in his mouth, having eaten up the rest of it; however, being young, and having more strength than his mother, the mate got something down his throat, and he began sensibly to revive; though by giving him, some time after, but two or three spoonfuls extraordinary, he was very sick, and brought it up again.

But the next care was the poor maid: she lay all along upon the deck, hard by her mistress, and just like one that had fallen down in a fit of apoplexy, and struggled for life. Her limbs were distorted; one of her hands was clasped round the frame of the chair, and she gripped it so hard that we could not easily make her let it go; her other arm lay over her head, and her feet lay both together, set fast against the frame of the cabin table: in short, she lay just like one in the agonies of death, and yet she was alive too. The poor creature was not only starved with hunger, and terrified with the thoughts of death, but, as the men told us afterwards, was broken-hearted for her mistress, whom she saw dying for two or three days before, and whom she loved most tenderly. We knew not what to do with this poor girl; for when our surgeon, who was a man of very great knowledge and experience, had, with great application, recovered her as to life, he had her upon his hands still; for she was little less than distracted for a considerable time after.

Whoever shall read these memorandums must be desired to consider that visits at sea are not like a journey into the country, where sometimes people stay a week or a fortnight at a place. Our business was to relieve this distressed ship's crew, but not lie by for them; and though they were willing to steer the same course with us for some days, yet we could carry no sail to keep pace with a ship that had no masts. However, as their captain begged of us to help him to set up a main-topmast, and a kind of a topmast to his jury fore-mast, we did, as it were, lie by him for three or four days; and then, having given him five barrels of beef, a barrel of pork, two hogsheads of biscuit, and a proportion of peas, flour, and what other things we could spare; and taking three casks of sugar, some rum, and some pieces of eight from them for satisfaction, we left them, taking on board with us, at their own earnest request, the youth and the maid, and all their goods.

The young lad was about seventeen years of age, a pretty, well-bred, modest, and sensible youth, greatly dejected with the loss of his mother, and also at having lost his father but a few months before, at Barbados. He begged of the surgeon to speak to me to take him out of the ship; for he said the cruel fellows had murdered his mother: and indeed so they had, that is to say, passively; for they might have spared a small sustenance to the poor helpless widow, though it had been but just enough to keep her alive; but hunger knows no friend, no relation, no justice, no right, and therefore is remorseless, and capable of no compassion.

The surgeon told him how far we were going, and that it would carry him away from all his friends, and put him, perhaps, in as bad circumstances almost as those we found him in, that is to say, starving in the world. He said it mattered not whither he went, if he was but delivered from the terrible crew that he was among; that the captain (by which he meant me, for he could know nothing of my nephew) had saved his life, and he was sure would not hurt him; and as for the maid, he was sure, if she came to herself, she would be very thankful for it, let us carry them where we would. The surgeon represented the case so affectionately to me that I yielded, and we took them both on board, with all their goods, except eleven hogsheads of sugar, which could not be removed or come at; and as the youth had a bill of lading for them, I made his commander sign a writing, obliging himself to go, as soon as he came to Bristol, to one Mr. Rogers, a merchant there, to whom the

271

youth said he was related, and to deliver a letter which I wrote to him, and all the goods he had belonging to the deceased widow; which, I suppose, was not done, for I could never learn that the ship came to Bristol, but was, as is most probable, lost at sea, being in so disabled a condition, and so far from any land, that I am of opinion the first storm she met with afterwards she might founder, for she was leaky, and had damage in her hold when we met with her.

I was now in the latitude of 19 degrees 32 minutes, and had hitherto a tolerable voyage as to weather, though at first the winds had been contrary. I shall trouble nobody with the little incidents of wind, weather, currents, &c., on the rest of our voyage; but to shorten my story, shall observe that I came to my old habitation, the island, on the 10th of April 1695. It was with no small difficulty that I found the place; for as I came to it and went to it before on the south and east side of the island, coming from the Brazils, so now, coming in between the main and the island, and having no chart for the coast, nor any landmark, I did not know it when I saw it, or, know whether I saw it or not. We beat about a great while, and went on shore on several islands in the mouth of the great river Orinoco, but none for my purpose; only this I learned by my coasting the shore, that I was under one great mistake before, viz. that the continent which I thought I saw from the island I lived in was really no continent, but a long island, or rather a ridge of islands, reaching from one to the other side of the extended mouth of that great river; and that the savages who came to my island were not properly those which we call Caribbees, but islanders, and other barbarians of the same kind, who inhabited nearer to our side than the rest.

In short, I visited several of these islands to no purpose; some I found were inhabited, and some were not; on one of them I found some Spaniards, and thought they had lived there; but speaking with them, found they had a sloop lying in a small creek hard by, and came thither to make salt, and to catch some pearl-mussels if they could; but that they belonged to the Isle de Trinidad, which lay farther north, in the latitude of 10 and 11 degrees.

Thus coasting from one island to another, sometimes with the ship, sometimes with the Frenchman's shallop, which we had found a convenient boat, and therefore kept her with their very good will, at length I came fair on the south side of my island, and presently knew the very countenance of the place: so I brought the ship safe to an anchor, broadside with the little creek where my old habitation was. As soon as I saw the place I called for Friday, and asked him if he knew where he was? He looked about a little, and presently clapping his hands, cried, "Oh yes, Oh there, Oh yes, Oh there!" pointing to our old habitation, and fell dancing and capering like a mad fellow; and I had much ado to keep him from jumping into the sea to swim ashore to the place.

"Well, Friday," says I, "do you think we shall find anybody here or no? and do you think we shall see your father?" The fellow stood mute as a stock a good while; but when I named his father, the poor affectionate creature looked dejected, and I could see the tears run down his face very plentifully. "What is the matter, Friday? are you troubled because you may see your father?" "No, no," says he, shaking his head, "no see him more: no, never more see him again." "Why so, Friday? how do you know that?" "Oh no, Oh no," says Friday, "he long ago die, long ago; he much old man." "Well, well, Friday, you don't know; but shall we see any one else, then?" The fellow, it seems, had better eyes than I, and he points to the hill just above my old house; and though we lay half a league off, he cries out, "We see! we see! yes, we see much man there, and there, and there." I looked, but I saw nobody, no, not with a perspective glass, which was, I suppose, because I could not hit the place: for the fellow was right, as I found upon inquiry the next day; and there were five or six men all together, who stood to look at the ship, not knowing what to think of us.

As soon as Friday told me he saw people, I caused the English ancient to be spread, and fired three guns, to give them notice we were friends; and in about a quarter of an hour after we perceived a smoke arise from the side of the creek; so I immediately ordered the boat out, taking Friday with me, and hanging out a white flag, I went directly on shore, taking with me the young friar I mentioned, to whom I had told the story of my living there, and the manner of it, and every particular both of myself and those I left there, and who was on that account extremely desirous to go with me. We had, besides, about sixteen men well armed, if we had found any new guests there which we did not know of; but we had no need of weapons.

As we went on shore upon the tide of flood, near high water, we rowed directly into the creek; and the first man I fixed my eye upon was the Spaniard whose life I had saved, and whom I knew by his face perfectly well: as to his habit, I shall describe it afterwards. I ordered nobody to go on shore at first but myself; but there was no keeping Friday in the boat, for the affectionate creature had spied his father at a

273

distance, a good way off the Spaniards, where, indeed, I saw nothing of him; and if they had not let him go ashore, he would have jumped into the sea. He was no sooner on shore, but he flew away to his father like an arrow out of a bow. It would have made any man shed tears, in spite of the firmest resolution, to have seen the first transports of this poor fellow's joy when he came to his father: how he embraced him, kissed him, stroked his face, took him up in his arms, set him down upon a tree, and lay down by him; then stood and looked at him, as any one would look at a strange picture, for a quarter of an hour together; then lay down on the ground, and stroked his legs, and kissed them, and then got up again and stared at him; one would have thought the fellow bewitched. But it would have made a dog laugh the next day to see how his passion ran out another way: in the morning he walked along the shore with his father several hours, always leading him by the hand, as if he had been a lady; and every now and then he would come to the boat to fetch something or other for him, either a lump of sugar, a dram, a biscuit, or something or other that was good. In the afternoon his frolics ran another way; for then he would set the old man down upon the ground, and dance about him, and make a thousand antic gestures; and all the while he did this he would be talking to him, and telling him one story or another of his travels, and of what had happened to him abroad to divert him. In short, if the same filial affection was to be found in Christians to their parents in our part of the world, one would be tempted to say there would hardly have been any need of the fifth commandment.

But this is a digression: I return to my landing. It would be needless to take notice of all the ceremonies and civilities that the Spaniards received me with. The first Spaniard, whom, as I said, I knew very well, was he whose life I had saved. He came towards the boat, attended by one more, carrying a flag of truce also; and he not only did not know me at first, but he had no thoughts, no notion of its being me that was come, till I spoke to him. "Seignior," said I, in Portuguese, "do you not know me?" At which he spoke not a word, but giving his musket to the man that was with him, threw his arms abroad, saying something in Spanish that I did not perfectly hear, came forward and embraced me, telling me he was inexcusable not to know that face again that he had once seen, as of an angel from heaven sent to save his life; he said abundance of very handsome things, as a well-bred Spaniard always knows how, and then, beckoning to the person that attended him, bade him go and call out his comrades. He then asked me if I would walk to my old habitation, where he would give me possession of my own house again, and where I should see they had made but mean improvements. I walked along with him, but, alas! I could no more find the place than if I had never been there; for they had planted so many trees, and placed them in such a position, so thick and close to one another, and in ten years' time they were grown so big, that the place was inaccessible, except by such windings and blind ways as they themselves only, who made them, could find.

I asked them what put them upon all these fortifications; he told me I would say there was need enough of it when they had given me an account how they had passed their time since their arriving in the island, especially after they had the misfortune to find that I was gone. He told me he could not but have some pleasure in my good fortune, when he heard that I was gone in a good ship, and to my satisfaction; and that he had oftentimes a strong persuasion that one time or other he should see me again, but nothing that ever befell him in his life, he said, was so surprising and afflicting to him at first as the disappointment he was under when he came back to the island and found I was not there.

As to the three barbarians (so he called them) that were left behind, and of whom, he said, he had a long story to tell me, the Spaniards all thought themselves much better among the savages, only that their number was so small: "And," says he, "had they been strong enough, we had been all long ago in purgatory;" and with that he crossed himself on the breast. "But, sir," says he, "I hope you will not be displeased when I shall tell you how, forced by necessity, we were obliged for our own preservation to disarm them, and make them our subjects, as they would not be content with being moderately our masters, but would be our murderers." I answered I was afraid of it when I left them there, and nothing troubled me at my parting from the island but that they were not come back, that I might have put them in possession of everything first, and left the others in a state of subjection, as they deserved; but if they had reduced them to it I was very glad, and should be very far from finding any fault with it; for I knew they were a parcel of refractory, ungoverned villains, and were fit for any manner of mischief.

While I was saying this, the man came whom he had sent back, and with him eleven more. In the dress they were in it was impossible to guess what nation they were of; but he made all clear, both to them and to me. First, he turned to me, and pointing to them, said, "These, sir, are some of the gentlemen who owe their lives to you;" and then turning to them, and pointing to me, he let them know who I was; upon which they all came up, one by one, not as if they had been sailors, and ordinary fellows, and the like, but really as if they had been ambassadors or noblemen, and I a monarch or great conqueror: their behaviour was, to the last degree, obliging and courteous, and yet mixed with a manly, majestic gravity, which very well became them; and, in short, they had so much more manners than I, that I scarce knew how to receive their civilities, much less how to return them in kind.

The history of their coming to, and conduct in, the island after my going away is so very remarkable, and has so many incidents which the former part of my relation will help to understand, and which will in most of the particulars, refer to the account I have already given, that I cannot but commit them, with great delight, to the reading of those that come after me.

In order to do this as intelligibly as I can, I must go back to the circumstances in which I left the island, and the persons on it, of whom I am to speak. And first, it is necessary to repeat that I had sent away Friday's father and the Spaniard (the two whose lives I had rescued from the savages) in a large canoe to the main, as I then thought it, to fetch over the Spaniard's companions that he left behind him, in order to save them from the like calamity that he had been in, and in order to succour them for the present; and that, if possible, we might together find some way for our deliverance afterwards. When I sent them away I had no visible appearance of, or the least room to hope for, my own deliverance, any more than I had twenty years before — much less had I any foreknowledge of what afterwards happened, I mean, of an English ship coming on shore there to fetch me off; and it could not be but a very great surprise to them, when they came back, not only to find that I was gone, but to find three strangers left on the spot, possessed of all that I had left behind me, which would otherwise have been their own.

The first thing, however, which I inquired into, that I might begin where I left off, was of their own part; and I desired the Spaniard would give me a particular account of his voyage back to his countrymen with the boat, when I sent him to fetch them over. He told me there was little variety in that part, for nothing remarkable happened to them on the way, having had very calm weather and a smooth sea. As for his countrymen, it could not be doubted, he said, but that they were overjoyed to see him (it seems he was the principal man among them, the captain of the vessel they had been shipwrecked in having been dead some time): they were, he said, the more surprised to see him, because they knew that he was fallen into the hands of the savages, who, they were satisfied, would devour him as they did all the rest of their prisoners; that when he told them the story of his deliverance, and in what manner he was furnished for carrying them away, it was like a dream to them, and their astonishment, he said, was somewhat like that of Joseph's brethren when he told them who he was, and the story of his exaltation in Pharaoh's court; but when he showed them the arms, the powder, the ball, the provisions that he brought them for their journey or voyage, they were restored to themselves, took a just share of the joy of their deliverance, and immediately prepared to come away with him.

Their first business was to get canoes; and in this they were obliged not to stick so much upon the honesty of it, but to trespass upon their friendly savages, and to borrow two large canoes, or periaguas, on pretence of going out a-fishing, or for pleasure. In these they came away the next morning. It seems they wanted no time to get themselves ready; for they had neither clothes nor provisions, nor anything in the world but what they had on them, and a few roots to eat, of which they used to make their bread. They were in all three weeks absent; and in that time, unluckily for them, I had the occasion offered for my escape, as I mentioned in the other part, and to get off from the island, leaving three of the most impudent, hardened, ungoverned, disagreeable villains behind me that any man could desire to meet with — to the poor Spaniards' great grief and disappointment.

The only just thing the rogues did was, that when the Spaniards came ashore, they gave my letter to them, and gave them provisions, and other relief, as I had ordered them to do; also they gave them the long paper of directions which I had left with them, containing the particular methods which I took for managing every part of my life there; the way I baked my bread, bred up tame goats, and planted my corn; how I cured my grapes, made my pots, and, in a word, everything I did. All this being written down, they gave to the Spaniards (two of them understood English well enough): nor did they refuse to accommodate the Spaniards with anything else, for they agreed very well for some time. They gave them an equal admission into the house or cave, and they began to live very sociably; and the head Spaniard, who had seen pretty much of my methods, together with Friday's father, managed all their affairs; but as for the Englishmen, they did nothing but ramble about the island, shoot parrots, and catch tortoises; and when they came home at night, the Spaniards provided their suppers for them.

277

The Spaniards would have been satisfied with this had the others but let them alone, which, however, they could not find in their hearts to do long: but, like the dog in the manger, they would not eat themselves, neither would they let the others eat. The differences, nevertheless, were at first but trivial, and such as are not worth relating, but at last it broke out into open war: and it began with all the rudeness and insolence that can be imagined — without reason, without provocation, contrary to nature, and indeed to common sense; and though, it is true, the first relation of it came from the Spaniards themselves, whom I may call the accusers, yet when I came to examine the fellows they could not deny a word of it.

But before I come to the particulars of this part, I must supply a defect in my former relation; and this was, I forgot to set down among the rest, that just as we were weighing the anchor to set sail, there happened a little quarrel on board of our ship, which I was once afraid would have turned to a second mutiny; nor was it appeased till the captain, rousing up his courage, and taking us all to his assistance, parted them by force, and making two of the most refractory fellows prisoners, he laid them in irons: and as they had been active in the former disorders, and let fall some ugly, dangerous words the second time, he threatened to carry them in irons to England, and have them hanged there for mutiny and running away with the ship. This, it seems, though the captain did not intend to do it, frightened some other men in the ship; and some of them had put it into the head of the rest that the captain only gave them good words for the present, till they should come to same English port, and that then they should be all put into jail, and tried for their lives. The mate got intelligence of this, and acquainted us with it, upon which it was desired that I, who still passed for a great man among them, should go down with the mate and satisfy the men, and tell them that they might be assured, if they behaved well the rest of the voyage, all they had done for the time past should be pardoned. So I went, and after passing my honour's word to them they appeared easy, and the more so when I caused the two men that were in irons to be released and forgiven.

But this mutiny had brought us to an anchor for that night; the wind also falling calm next morning, we found that our two men who had been laid in irons had stolen each of them a musket and some other weapons (what powder or shot they had we knew not), and had taken the ship's pinnace, which was not yet hauled up, and run away with her to their companions in roguery on shore. As soon as we found this, I ordered the long-boat on shore, with twelve men and the mate, and away they went to seek the rogues; but they could neither find them nor any of the rest, for they all fled into the woods when they saw the boat coming on shore. The mate was once resolved, in justice to their roguery, to have destroyed their plantations, burned all their household stuff and furniture, and left them to shift without it; but having no orders, he let it all alone, left everything as he found it, and bringing the pinnace way, came on board without them. These two men made their number five; but the other three villains were so much more wicked than they, that after they had been two or three days together they turned the two newcomers out of doors to shift for themselves, and would have nothing to do with them; nor could they for a good while be persuaded to give them any food: as for the Spaniards, they were not yet come.

When the Spaniards came first on shore, the business began to go forward: the Spaniards would have persuaded the three English brutes to have taken in their countrymen again, that, as they said, they might be all one family; but they would not hear of it, so the two poor fellows lived by themselves; and finding nothing but industry and application would make them live comfortably, they pitched their tents on the north shore of the island, but a little more to the west, to be out of danger of the savages, who always landed on the east parts of the island. Here they built them two huts, one to lodge in, and the other to lay up their magazines and stores in; and the Spaniards having given them some corn for seed, and some of the peas which I had left them, they dug, planted, and enclosed, after the pattern I had set for them all, and began to live pretty well. Their first crop of corn was on the ground; and though it was but a little bit of land which they had dug up at first, having had but a little time, yet it was enough to relieve them, and find them with bread and other eatables; and one of the fellows being the cook's mate of the ship, was very ready at making soup, puddings, and such other preparations as the rice and the milk, and such little flesh as they got, furnished him to do.

They were going on in this little thriving position when the three unnatural rogues, their own countrymen too, in mere humour, and to insult them, came and bullied them, and told them the island was theirs: that the governor, meaning me, had given them the possession of it, and nobody else had any right to it; and that they should build no houses upon their ground unless they would pay rent for them. The two men, thinking they were jesting at first, asked them to come in and sit down, and see what fine houses they were that they had built, and to tell them what rent they demanded; and one of them merrily said if they were the ground-landlords, he hoped if they built tenements upon their land, and made improvements, they would, according to the custom of landlords, grant a long lease: and desired they would get a scrivener to draw the writings. One of the three, cursing and raging, told them they should see they were not in jest; and going to a little place at a distance, where the honest men had made a fire to dress their victuals, he takes a firebrand, and claps it to the outside of their hut, and set it on fire: indeed, it would have been all burned down in a few minutes if one of the two had not run to the fellow, thrust him away, and trod the fire out with his feet, and that not without some difficulty too.

The fellow was in such a rage at the honest man's thrusting him away, that he returned upon him, with a pole he had in his hand, and had not the man avoided the blow very nimbly, and run into the hut, he had ended his days at once. His comrade, seeing the danger they were both in, ran after him, and immediately they came both out with their muskets, and the man that was first struck at with the pole knocked the fellow down that began the quarrel with the stock of his musket, and that before the other two could come to help him; and then, seeing the rest come at them, they stood together, and presenting the other ends of their pieces to them, bade them stand off.

The others had firearms with them too; but one of the two honest men, bolder than his comrade, and made desperate by his danger, told them if they offered to move hand or foot they were dead men, and boldly commanded them to lay down their arms. They did not, indeed, lay down their arms, but seeing him so resolute, it brought them to a parley, and they consented to take their wounded man with them and be gone: and, indeed, it seems the fellow was wounded sufficiently with the blow. However, they were much in the wrong, since they had the advantage, that they did not disarm them effectually, as they might have done, and have gone immediately to the Spaniards, and given them an account how the rogues had treated them; for the three villains studied nothing but revenge, and every day gave them some intimation that they did so.

CHAPTER III. FIGHT WITH CANNIBALS

But not to crowd this part with an account of the lesser part of the rogueries with which they plagued them continually, night and day, it forced the two men to such a desperation that they resolved to fight them all three, the first time they had a fair opportunity. In order to do this they resolved to go to the castle (as they called my old dwelling), where the three rogues and the Spaniards all lived together at that time, intending to have a fair battle, and the Spaniards should stand by to see fair play: so they got up in the morning before day, and came to the place, and called the Englishmen by their names telling a Spaniard that answered that they wanted to speak with them.

It happened that the day before two of the Spaniards, having been in the woods, had seen one of the two Englishmen, whom, for distinction, I called the honest men, and he had made a sad complaint to the Spaniards of the barbarous usage they had met with from their three countrymen, and how they had ruined their plantation, and destroyed their corn, that they had laboured so hard to bring forward, and killed the milch-goat and their three kids, which was all they had provided for their sustenance, and that if he and his friends, meaning the Spaniards, did not assist them again, they should be starved. When the Spaniards came home at night, and they were all at supper, one of them took the freedom to reprove the three Englishmen, though in very gentle and mannerly terms, and asked them how they could be so cruel, they being harmless, inoffensive fellows: that they were putting themselves in a way to subsist by their labour, and that it had cost them a great deal of pains to bring things to such perfection as they were then in.

One of the Englishmen returned very briskly, "What had they to do there? that they came on shore without leave; and that they should not plant or build upon the island; it was none of their ground." "Why," says the Spaniard, very calmly, "Seignior Inglese, they must not starve." The Englishman replied, like a rough tarpaulin, "They might starve; they should not plant nor build in that place." "But what must they do then, seignior?" said the Spaniard. Another of the brutes returned, "Do? they should be servants, and work for them." "But how can you expect that of them?" says the Spaniard; "they are not bought with your money; you have no right to make them servants." The Englishman answered, "The island was theirs; the governor had given it to them, and no man had anything to do there but themselves;" and with that he swore that he would go and burn all their new huts; they should build none upon their land. "Why, seignior," says the Spaniard, "by the same rule, we must be your servants, too." "Ay," returned the bold dog, "and so you shall, too, before we have done with you;" mixing two or three oaths in the proper intervals of his speech. The Spaniard only smiled at that, and made him no answer. However, this little discourse had heated them; and starting up, one says to the other. (I think it was he they called Will Atkins), "Come, Jack, let's go and have t'other brush with them; we'll demolish their castle, I'll warrant you; they shall plant no colony in our dominions."

Upon this they were all trooping away, with every man a gun, a pistol, and a sword, and muttered some insolent things among themselves of what they would do to the Spaniards, too, when opportunity offered; but the Spaniards, it seems, did not so perfectly understand them as to know all the particulars, only that in general they threatened them hard for taking the two Englishmen's part. Whither they went, or how they bestowed their time that evening, the Spaniards said they did not know; but it seems they wandered about the country part of the night, and them lying down in the place which I used to call my bower, they were weary and overslept themselves. The case was this: they had resolved to stay till midnight, and so take the two poor men when they were asleep, and as they acknowledged afterwards, intended to set fire to their huts while they were in them, and either burn them there or murder them as they came out. As malice seldom sleeps very sound, it was very strange they should not have been kept awake. However, as the two men had also a design upon them, as I have said, though a much fairer one than that of burning and murdering, it happened, and very luckily for them all, that they were up and gone abroad before the bloody-minded rogues came to their huts.

When they came there, and found the men gone, Atkins, who it seems was the forwardest man, called out to his comrade, "Ha, Jack, here's the nest, but the birds are flown." They mused a while, to think what should be the occasion of their being gone abroad so soon, and suggested presently that the Spaniards had given them notice of it; and with that they shook hands, and swore to one another that they would be revenged of the Spaniards. As soon as they had made this bloody bargain they fell to work with the poor men's habitation; they did not set fire, indeed, to anything, but they pulled down both their houses, and left not the least stick standing, or scarce any sign on the ground where they stood; they tore all their household stuff in pieces, and

282

threw everything about in such a manner, that the poor men afterwards found some of their things a mile off. When they had done this, they pulled up all the young trees which the poor men had planted; broke down an enclosure they had made to secure their cattle and their corn; and, in a word, sacked and plundered everything as completely as a horde of Tartars would have done.

The two men were at this juncture gone to find them out, and had resolved to fight them wherever they had been, though they were but two to three; so that, had they met, there certainly would have been blood shed among them, for they were all very stout, resolute fellows, to give them their due.

But Providence took more care to keep them asunder than they themselves could do to meet; for, as if they had dogged one another, when the three were gone thither, the two were here; and afterwards, when the two went back to find them, the three were come to the old habitation again: we shall see their different conduct presently. When the three came back like furious creatures, flushed with the rage which the work they had been about had put them into, they came up to the Spaniards, and told them what they had done, by way of scoff and bravado; and one of them stepping up to one of the Spaniards, as if they had been a couple of boys at play, takes hold of his hat as it was upon his head, and giving it a twirl about, fleering in his face, says to him, "And you, Seignior Jack Spaniard, shall have the same sauce if you do not mend your manners." The Spaniard, who, though a quiet civil man, was as brave a man as could be, and withal a strong, well-made man, looked at him for a good while, and then, having no weapon in his hand, stepped gravely up to him, and, with one blow of his fist, knocked him down, as an ox is felled with a pole-axe; at which one of the rogues, as insolent as the first, fired his pistol at the Spaniard immediately; he missed his body, indeed, for the bullets went through his hair, but one of them touched the tip of his ear, and he bled pretty much. The blood made the Spaniard believe he was more hurt than he really was, and that put him into some heat, for before he acted all in a perfect calm; but now resolving to go through with his work, he stooped, and taking the fellow's musket whom he had knocked down, was just going to shoot the man who had fired at him, when the rest of the Spaniards, being in the cave, came out, and calling to him not to shoot, they stepped in, secured the other two, and took their arms from them.

When they were thus disarmed, and found they had made all the Spaniards their enemies, as well as their own countrymen, they began to cool, and giving the Spaniards better words, would have their arms again; but the Spaniards, considering the feud that was between them and the other two Englishmen, and that it would be the best method they could take to keep them from killing one another, told them they would do them no harm, and if they would live peaceably, they would be very willing to assist and associate with them as they did before; but that they could not think of giving them their arms again, while they appeared so resolved to do mischief with them to their own countrymen, and had even threatened them all to make them their servants.

The rogues were now quite deaf to all reason, and being refused their arms, they raved away like madmen, threatening what they would do, though they had no firearms. But the Spaniards, despising their threatening, told them they should take care how they offered any injury to their plantation or cattle; for if they did they would shoot them as they would ravenous beasts, wherever they found them; and if they fell into their hands alive, they should certainly be hanged. However, this was far from cooling them, but away they went, raging and swearing like furies. As soon as they were gone, the two men came back, in passion and rage enough also, though of another kind; for having been at their plantation, and finding it all demolished and destroyed, as above mentioned, it will easily be supposed they had provocation enough. They could scarce have room to tell their tale, the Spaniards were so eager to tell them theirs: and it was strange enough to find that three men should thus bully nineteen, and receive no punishment at all.

The Spaniards, indeed, despised them, and especially, having thus disarmed them, made light of their threatenings; but the two Englishmen resolved to have their remedy against them, what pains so ever it cost to find them out. But the Spaniards interposed here too, and told them that as they had disarmed them, they could not consent that they (the two) should pursue them with firearms, and perhaps kill them. "But," said the grave Spaniard, who was their governor, "we will endeavour to make them do you justice, if you will leave it to us: for there is no doubt but they will come to us again, when their passion is over, being not able to subsist without our assistance. We promise you to make no peace with them without having full satisfaction for you; and upon this condition we hope you will promise to use no violence with them, other than in your own defence." The two Englishmen yielded to this very awkwardly, and with great reluctance; but the Spaniards protested that they did it only to keep them from bloodshed, and to make them all easy at last. "For," said they, "we are not so many of us; here is room enough for us all, and it is a great pity that we should not be all good friends." At length they did consent, and waited for the issue of the thing, living for some days with the Spaniards; for their own habitation was destroyed.

In about five days' time the vagrants, tired with wandering, and almost starved with hunger, having chiefly lived on turtles' eggs all that while, came back to the grove; and finding my Spaniard, who, as I have said, was the governor, and two more with him, walking by the side of the creek, they came up in a very submissive, humble manner, and begged to be received again into the society. The Spaniards used them civilly, but told them they had acted so unnaturally to their countrymen, and so very grossly to themselves, that they could not come to any conclusion without consulting the two Englishmen and the rest; but, however, they would go to them and discourse about it, and they should know in half-an-hour. It may be guessed that they were very hard put to it; for, as they were to wait this half-hour for an answer, they begged they would send them out some bread in the meantime, which they did, sending at the same time a large piece of goat's flesh and a boiled parrot, which they ate very eagerly.

After half-an-hour's consultation they were called in, and a long debate ensued, their two countrymen charging them with the ruin of all their labour, and a design to murder them; all which they owned before, and therefore could not deny now. Upon the whole, the Spaniards acted the moderators between them; and as they had obliged the two Englishmen not to hurt the three while they were naked and unarmed, so they now obliged the three to go and rebuild their fellows' two huts, one to be of the same and the other of larger dimensions than they were before; to fence their ground again, plant trees in the room of those pulled up, dig up the land again for planting corn, and, in a word, to restore everything to the same state as they found it, that is, as near as they could.

Well, they submitted to all this; and as they had plenty of provisions given them all the while, they grew very orderly, and the whole society began to live pleasantly and agreeably together again; only that these three fellows could never be persuaded to work — I mean for themselves — except now and then a little, just as they pleased.

285

However, the Spaniards told them plainly that if they would but live sociably and friendly together, and study the good of the whole plantation, they would be content to work for them, and let them walk about and be as idle as they pleased; and thus, having lived pretty well together for a month or two, the Spaniards let them have arms again, and gave them liberty to go abroad with them as before.

It was not above a week after they had these arms, and went abroad, before the ungrateful creatures began to be as insolent and troublesome as ever. However, an accident happened presently upon this, which endangered the safety of them all, and they were obliged to lay by all private resentments, and look to the preservation of their lives.

It happened one night that the governor, the Spaniard whose life I had saved, who was now the governor of the rest, found himself very uneasy in the night, and could by no means get any sleep: he was perfectly well in body, only found his thoughts tumultuous; his mind ran upon men fighting and killing one another; but he was broad awake, and could not by any means get any sleep; in short, he lay a great while, but growing more and more uneasy, he resolved to rise. As they lay, being so many of them, on goat-skins laid thick upon such couches and pads as they made for themselves, so they had little to do, when they were willing to rise, but to get upon their feet, and perhaps put on a coat, such as it was, and their pumps, and they were ready for going any way that their thoughts guided them. Being thus got up, he looked out; but being dark, he could see little or nothing, and besides, the trees which I had planted, and which were now grown tall, intercepted his sight, so that he could only look up, and see that it was a starlight night, and hearing no noise, he returned and lay down again; but to no purpose; he could not compose himself to anything like rest; but his thoughts were to the last degree uneasy, and he knew not for what. Having made some noise with rising and walking about, going out and coming in, another of them waked, and asked who it was that was up. The governor told him how it had been with him. "Say you so?" says the other Spaniard; "such things are not to be slighted, I assure you; there is certainly some mischief working near us;" and presently he asked him, "Where are the Englishmen?" "They are all in their huts," says he, "safe enough." It seems the Spaniards had kept possession of the main apartment, and had made a place for the three Englishmen, who, since their last mutiny, were always quartered by themselves, and could not come at the rest. "Well," says the Spaniard, "there is something in it, I am persuaded, from my own experience. I am satisfied that our spirits embodied have a converse with and receive intelligence from the spirits unembodied, and inhabiting the invisible world; and this friendly notice is given for our advantage, if we knew how to make use of it. Come, let us go and look abroad; and if we find nothing at all in it to justify the trouble, I'll tell you a story to the purpose, that shall convince you of the justice of my proposing it."

They went out presently to go up to the top of the hill, where I used to go; but they being strong, and a good company, nor alone, as I was, used none of my cautions to go up by the ladder, and pulling it up after them, to go up a second stage to the top, but were going round through the grove unwarily, when they were surprised with seeing a light as of fire, a very little way from them, and hearing the voices of men, not of one or two, but of a great number.

Among the precautions I used to take on the savages landing on the island, it was my constant care to prevent them making the least discovery of there being any inhabitant upon the place: and when by any occasion they came to know it, they felt it so effectually that they that got away were scarce able to give any account of it; for we disappeared as soon as possible, nor did ever any that had seen me escape to tell any one else, except it was the three savages in our last encounter who jumped into the boat; of whom, I mentioned, I was afraid they should go home and bring more help. Whether it was the consequence of the escape of those men that so great a number came now together, or whether they came ignorantly, and by accident, on their usual bloody errand, the Spaniards could not understand; but whatever it was, it was their business either to have concealed themselves or not to have seen them at all, much less to have let the savages have seen there were any inhabitants in the place; or to have fallen upon them so effectually as not a man of them should have escaped, which could only have been by getting in between them and their boats; but this presence of mind was wanting to them, which was the ruin of their tranquility for a great while.

We need not doubt but that the governor and the man with him, surprised with this sight, ran back immediately and raised their fellows, giving them an account of the imminent danger they were all in, and they again as readily took the alarm; but it was impossible to persuade them to stay close within where they were, but they must all run out to see how things stood. While it was dark, indeed, they were safe, and they had opportunity enough for some hours to view the savages by the light of three fires they had made at a distance from one another; what they were doing they knew not, neither did they know what to do themselves. For, first, the enemy were too many; and secondly, they did not keep together, but were divided into several parties, and were on shore in several places.

The Spaniards were in no small consternation at this sight; and, as they found that the fellows went straggling all over the shore, they made no doubt but, first or last, some of them would chop in upon their habitation, or upon some other place where they would see the token of inhabitants; and they were in great perplexity also for fear of their flock of goats, which, if they should be destroyed, would have been little less than starving them. So the first thing they resolved upon was to dispatch three men away before it was light, two Spaniards and one Englishman, to drive away all the goats to the great valley where the cave was, and, if need were, to drive them into the very cave itself. Could they have seen the savages all together in one body, and at a distance from their canoes, they were resolved, if there had been a hundred of them, to attack them; but that could not be done, for they were some of them two miles off from the other, and, as it appeared afterwards, were of two different nations.

After having mused a great while on the course they should take, they resolved at last, while it was still dark, to send the old savage, Friday's father, out as a spy, to learn, if possible, something concerning them, as what they came for, what they intended to do, and the like. The old man readily undertook it; and stripping himself quite naked, as most of the savages were, away he went. After he had been gone an hour or two, he brings word that he had been among them undiscovered, that he found they were two parties, and of two several nations, who had war with one another, and had a great battle in their own country; and that both sides having had several prisoners taken in the fight, they were, by mere chance, landed all on the same island, for the devouring their prisoners and making merry; but their coming so by chance to the same place had spoiled all their mirth — that they were in a great rage at one another, and were so near that he believed they would fight again as soon as daylight began to appear; but he did not perceive that they had any notion of anybody being on the island but themselves. He had hardly made an end of telling his story, when they could perceive, by the unusual noise they made, that the two little armies were engaged in a bloody fight. Friday's father used all the arguments he could to persuade our people to lie close, and not be seen; he told them their safety consisted in it, and that they had nothing to do but lie still, and the savages would kill one another to their hands, and then the rest would go away; and it was so to a tittle. But it was impossible to prevail, especially upon the Englishmen; their curiosity was so importunate that they must run out and see the battle. However, they used some caution too: they did not go openly, just by their own dwelling, but went farther into the woods, and placed themselves to advantage, where they might securely see them manage the fight, and, as they thought, not be seen by them; but the savages did see them, as we shall find hereafter.

The battle was very fierce, and, if I might believe the Englishmen, one of them said he could perceive that some of them were men of great bravery, of invincible spirit, and of great policy in guiding the fight. The battle, they said, held two hours before they could guess which party would be beaten; but then that party which was nearest our people's habitation began to appear weakest, and after some time more some of them began to fly; and this put our men again into a great consternation, lest any one of those that fled should run into the grove before their dwelling for shelter, and thereby involuntarily discover the place; and that, by consequence, the pursuers would also do the like in search of them. Upon this, they resolved that they would stand armed within the wall, and whoever came into the grove, they resolved to sally out over the wall and kill them, so that, if possible, not one should return to give an account of it; they ordered also that it should be done with their swords, or by knocking them down with the stocks of their muskets, but not by shooting them, for fear of raising an alarm by the noise.

As they expected it fell out; three of the routed army fled for life, and crossing the creek, ran directly into the place, not in the least knowing whither they went, but running as into a thick wood for shelter. The scout they kept to look abroad gave notice of this within, with this comforting addition, that the conquerors had not pursued them, or seen which way they were gone; upon this the Spanish governor, a man of humanity, would not suffer them to kill the three fugitives, but sending three men out by the top of the hill, ordered them to go round, come in behind them, and surprise and take them prisoners, which was done. The residue of the conquered people fled to their canoes, and got off to sea; the victors retired, made no pursuit, or very little, but drawing themselves into a body together, gave two great screaming shouts, most likely by way of triumph, and so the fight ended; the same day, about three o'clock in the afternoon, they also marched to their canoes. And thus the Spaniards had the island again free to themselves, their fright was over, and they saw no savages for several years after.

After they were all gone, the Spaniards came out of their den, and viewing the field of battle, they found about two-and-thirty men dead on the spot; some were killed with long arrows, which were found sticking in their bodies; but most of them were killed with great wooden swords, sixteen or seventeen of which they found in the field of battle, and as many bows, with a great many arrows. These swords were strange, unwieldy things, and they must be very strong men that used them; most of those that were killed with them had their heads smashed to pieces, as we may say, or, as we call it in English, their brains knocked out, and several their arms and legs broken; so that it is evident they fight with inexpressible rage and fury. We found not one man that was not stone dead; for either they stay by their enemy till they have killed him, or they carry all the wounded men that are not quite dead away with them.

This deliverance tamed our ill-disposed Englishmen for a great while; the sight had filled them with horror, and the consequences appeared terrible to the last degree, especially upon supposing that some time or other they should fall into the hands of those creatures, who would not only kill them as enemies, but for food, as we kill our cattle; and they professed to me that the thoughts of being eaten up like beef and mutton, though it was supposed it was not to be till they were dead, had something in it so horrible that it nauseated their very stomachs, made them sick when they thought of it, and filled their minds with such unusual terror, that they were not themselves for some weeks after. This, as I said, tamed even the three English brutes I have been speaking of; and for a great while after they were tractable, and went about the common business of the whole society well enough — planted, sowed, reaped, and began to be all naturalized to the country. But some time after this they fell into such simple measures again as brought them into a great deal of trouble.

They had taken three prisoners, as I observed; and these three being stout young fellows, they made them servants, and taught them to work for them, and as slaves they did well enough; but they did not take their measures as I did by my man Friday, viz. to begin with them upon the principle of having saved their lives, and then instruct them in the rational principles of life; much less did they think of teaching them religion, or attempt civilizing and reducing them by kind usage and

affectionate arguments. As they gave them their food every day, so they gave them their work too, and kept them fully employed in drudgery enough; but they failed in this by it, that they never had them to assist them and fight for them as I had my man Friday, who was as true to me as the very flesh upon my bones.

But to come to the family part. Being all now good friends — for common danger, as I said above, had effectually reconciled them — they began to consider their general circumstances; and the first thing that came under consideration was whether, seeing the savages particularly haunted that side of the island, and that there were more remote and retired parts of it equally adapted to their way of living, and manifestly to their advantage, they should not rather move their habitation, and plant in some more proper place for their safety, and especially for the security of their cattle and corn.

Upon this, after long debate, it was concluded that they would not remove their habitation; because that, some time or other, they thought they might hear from their governor again, meaning me; and if I should send any one to seek them, I should be sure to direct them to that side, where, if they should find the place demolished, they would conclude the savages had killed us all, and we were gone, and so our supply would go too. But as to their corn and cattle, they agreed to remove them into the valley where my cave was, where the land was as proper for both, and where indeed there was land enough. However, upon second thoughts they altered one part of their resolution too, and resolved only to remove part of their cattle thither, and part of their corn there; so that if one part was destroyed the other might be saved. And one part of prudence they luckily used: they never trusted those three savages which they had taken prisoners with knowing anything of the plantation they had made in that valley, or of any cattle they had there, much less of the cave at that place, which they kept, in case of necessity, as a safe retreat; and thither they carried also the two barrels of powder which I had sent them at my coming away. They resolved, however, not to change their habitation; yet, as I had carefully covered it first with a wall or fortification, and then with a grove of trees, and as they were now fully convinced their safety consisted entirely in their being concealed, they set to work to cover and conceal the place yet more effectually than before. For this purpose, as I planted trees, or rather thrust in stakes, which in time all grew up to be trees, for some good distance before the entrance into my apartments, they went on in the same manner, and filled up the rest of that whole space of ground from the trees I had set quite down to the side of the creek, where I landed my floats, and even into the very ooze where the tide flowed, not so much as leaving any place to land, or any sign that there had been any landing thereabouts: these stakes also being of a wood very forward to grow, they took care to have them generally much larger and taller than those which I had planted. As they grew apace, they planted them so very thick and close together, that when they had been three or four years grown there was no piercing with the eye any considerable way into the plantation. As for that part which I had planted, the trees were grown as thick as a man's thigh, and among them they had placed so many other short ones, and so thick, that it stood like a palisado a quarter of a mile thick, and it was next to impossible to penetrate it, for a little dog could hardly get between the trees, they stood so close.

But this was not all; for they did the same by all the ground to the right hand and to the left, and round even to the side of the hill, leaving no way, not so much as for themselves, to come out but by the ladder placed up to the side of the hill, and then lifted up, and placed again from the first stage up to the top: so that when the ladder was taken down, nothing but what had wings or witchcraft to assist it could come at them. This was excellently well contrived: nor was it less than what they afterwards found occasion for, which served to convince me, that as human prudence has the authority of Providence to justify it, so it has doubtless the direction of Providence to set it to work; and if we listened carefully to the voice of it, I am persuaded we might prevent many of the disasters which our lives are now, by our own negligence, subjected to.

They lived two years after this in perfect retirement, and had no more visits from the savages. They had, indeed, an alarm given them one morning, which put them into a great consternation; for some of the Spaniards being out early one morning on the west side or end of the island (which was that end where I never went, for fear of being discovered), they were surprised with seeing about twenty canoes of Indians just coming on shore. They made the best of their way home in hurry enough; and giving the alarm to their comrades, they kept close all that day and the next, going out only at night to make their observation: but they had the good luck to be undiscovered, for wherever the savages went, they did not land that time on the island, but pursued some other design.

CHAPTER IV. RENEWED INVASION OF SAVAGES

And now they had another broil with the three Englishmen; one of whom, a most turbulent fellow, being in a rage at one of the three captive slaves, because the fellow had not done something right which he bade him do, and seemed a little intractable in his showing him, drew a hatchet out of a frog-belt which he wore by his side, and fell upon the poor savage, not to correct him, but to kill him. One of the Spaniards who was by, seeing him give the fellow a barbarous cut with the hatchet, which he aimed at his head, but stuck into his shoulder, so that he thought he had cut the poor creature's arm off, ran to him, and entreating him not to murder the poor man, placed himself between him and the savage, to prevent the mischief. The fellow, being enraged the more at this, struck at the Spaniard with his hatchet, and swore he would serve him as he intended to serve the savage; which the Spaniard perceiving, avoided the blow, and with a shovel, which he had in his hand (for they were all working in the field about their corn land), knocked the brute down. Another of the Englishmen, running up at the same time to help his comrade, knocked the Spaniard down; and then two Spaniards more came in to help their man, and a third Englishman fell in upon them. They had none of them any firearms or any other weapons but hatchets and other tools, except this third Englishman; he had one of my rusty cutlasses, with which he made at the two last Spaniards, and wounded them both. This fray set the whole family in an uproar, and more help coming in they took the three Englishmen prisoners. The next question was, what should be done with them? They had been so often mutinous, and were so very furious, so desperate, and so idle withal, they knew not what course to take with them, for they were mischievous to the highest degree, and cared not what hurt they did to any man; so that, in short, it was not safe to live with them.

The Spaniard who was governor told them, in so many words, that if they had been of his own country he would have hanged them; for all laws and all governors were to preserve society, and those who were dangerous to the society ought to be expelled out of it; but as they were Englishmen, and that it was to the generous kindness of an Englishman that they all owed their preservation and deliverance, he would use them with all possible lenity, and would leave them to the judgment of the other two Englishmen, who were their countrymen. One of the two honest Englishmen stood up, and said they desired it might not be left to them. "For," says he, "I am sure we ought to sentence them to the gallows;" and with that he gives an account how Will Atkins, one of the three, had proposed to have all the five Englishmen join together and murder all the Spaniards when they were in their sleep.

When the Spanish governor heard this, he calls to Will Atkins, "How, Seignior Atkins, would you murder us all? What have you to say to that?" The hardened villain was so far from denying it, that he said it was true, and swore they would do it still before they had done with them. "Well, but Seignior Atkins," says the Spaniard, "what have we done to you that you will kill us? What would you get by killing us? And what must we do to prevent you killing us? Must we kill you, or you kill us? Why will you put us to the necessity of this, Seignior Atkins?" says the Spaniard very calmly, and smiling. Seignior Atkins was in such a rage at the Spaniard's making a jest of it, that, had he not been held by three men, and withal had no weapon near him, it was thought he would have attempted to kill the Spaniard in the middle of all the company. This hare-brained carriage obliged them to consider seriously what was to be done. The two Englishmen and the Spaniard who saved the poor savage were of the opinion that they should hang one of the three for an example to the rest, and that particularly it should be he that had twice attempted to commit murder with his hatchet; indeed, there was some reason to believe he had done it, for the poor savage was in such a miserable condition with the wound he had received that it was thought he could not live. But the governor Spaniard still said No; it was an Englishman that had saved all their lives, and he would never consent to put an Englishman to death, though he had murdered half of them; nay, he said if he had been killed himself by an Englishman, and had time left to speak, it should be that they should pardon him.

This was so positively insisted on by the governor Spaniard, that there was no gainsaying it; and as merciful counsels are most apt to prevail where they are so earnestly pressed, so they all came into it. But then it was to be considered what should be done to keep them from doing the mischief they designed; for all agreed, governor and all, that means were to be used for preserving the society from danger. After a long debate, it was agreed that they should be disarmed, and not permitted to have either gun, powder, shot, sword, or any weapon; that they should be turned out of the society, and left to live where they would and how they would, by themselves; but that none of the rest, either Spaniards or English, should hold any kind of converse with them, or have anything to do with them; that they should be forbid to come within a certain distance of the place where the rest dwelt; and if they offered to commit any disorder, so as to spoil, burn, kill, or destroy any of the corn, plantings, buildings, fences, or cattle belonging to the society, they should die without mercy, and they would shoot them wherever they could find them.

The humane governor, musing upon the sentence, considered a little upon it; and turning to the two honest Englishmen, said, "Hold; you must reflect that it will be long ere they can raise corn and cattle of their own, and they must not starve; we must therefore allow them provisions." So he caused to be added, that they should have a proportion of corn given them to last them eight months, and for seed to sow, by which time they might be supposed to raise some of their own; that they should have six milch-goats, four he-goats, and six kids given them, as well for present subsistence as for a store; and that they should have tools given them for their work in the fields, but they should have none of these tools or provisions unless they would swear solemnly that they would not hurt or injure any of the Spaniards with them, or of their fellow-Englishmen.

Thus they dismissed them the society, and turned them out to shift for themselves. They went away sullen and refractory, as neither content to go away nor to stay: but, as there was no remedy, they went, pretending to go and choose a place where they would settle themselves; and some provisions were given them, but no weapons. About four or five days after, they came again for some victuals, and gave the governor an account where they had pitched their tents, and marked themselves out a habitation and plantation; and it was a very convenient place indeed, on the remotest part of the island, NE., much about the place where I providentially landed in my first voyage, when I was driven out to sea in my foolish attempt to sail round the island.

Here they built themselves two handsome huts, and contrived them in a manner like my first habitation, being close under the side of a hill, having some trees already growing on three sides of it, so that by planting others it would be very easily covered from the sight, unless narrowly searched for. They desired some dried goat-skins for beds and covering, which were given them; and upon giving their words that they would not disturb the rest, or injure any of their plantations, they gave them hatchets, and what other tools they could spare; some peas, barley, and rice, for sowing; and, in a word, anything they wanted, except arms and ammunition.

They lived in this separate condition about six months, and had got in their first harvest, though the quantity was but small, the parcel of land they had planted being but little. Indeed, having all their plantation to form, they had a great deal of work upon their hands; and when they came to make boards and pots, and such things, they were quite out of their element, and could make nothing of it; therefore when the rainy season came on, for want of a cave in the earth, they could not keep their grain dry, and it was in great danger of spoiling. This humbled them much: so they came and begged the Spaniards to help them, which they very readily did; and in four days worked a great hole in the side of the hill for them, big enough to secure their corn and other things from the rain: but it was a poor place at best compared to mine, and especially as mine was then, for the Spaniards had greatly enlarged it, and made several new apartments in it.

About three quarters of a year after this separation, a new frolic took these rogues, which, together with the former villainy they had committed, brought mischief enough upon them, and had very near been the ruin of the whole colony. The three new associates began, it seems, to be weary of the laborious life they led, and that without hope of bettering their circumstances: and a whim took them that they would make a voyage to the continent, from whence the savages came, and would try if they could seize upon some prisoners among the natives there, and bring them home, so as to make them do the laborious part of the work for them.

The project was not so preposterous, if they had gone no further. But they did nothing, and proposed nothing, but had either mischief in the design, or mischief in the event. And if I may give my opinion, they seemed to be under a blast from Heaven: for if we will not allow a visible curse to pursue visible crimes, how shall we reconcile the events of things with the divine justice? It was certainly an apparent vengeance on their crime of mutiny and piracy that brought them to the state they were in; and they showed not the least remorse for the crime, but added new villainies to it, such as the piece of monstrous cruelty of wounding a poor slave because he did not, or perhaps could not, understand to do what he was directed, and to wound him in such a manner as made him a cripple all his life, and in a place where no surgeon or medicine could be had for his cure; and, what was still worse, the intentional murder, for such to be sure it was, as was afterwards the formed design they all laid to murder the Spaniards in cold blood, and in their sleep.

The three fellows came down to the Spaniards one morning, and in very humble terms desired to be admitted to speak with them. The Spaniards very readily heard what they had to say, which was this: that they were tired of living in the manner they did, and that they were not handy enough to make the necessaries they wanted, and that having no help, they found they should be starved; but if the Spaniards would give them leave to take one of the canoes which they came over in, and give them arms and ammunition proportioned to their defence, they would go over to the main, and seek their fortunes, and so deliver them from the trouble of supplying them with any other provisions.

The Spaniards were glad enough to get rid of them, but very honestly represented to them the certain destruction they were running into; told them they had suffered such hardships upon that very spot, that they could, without any spirit of prophecy, tell them they would be starved or murdered, and bade them consider of it. The men replied audaciously, they should be starved if they stayed here, for they could not work, and would not work, and they could but be starved abroad; and if they were murdered, there was an end of them; they had no wives or children to cry after them; and, in short, insisted importunately upon their demand, declaring they would go, whether they gave them any arms or not.

The Spaniards told them, with great kindness, that if they were resolved to go they should not go like naked men, and be in no condition to defend themselves; and that though they could ill spare firearms, not having enough for themselves, yet they would let them have two muskets, a pistol, and a cutlass, and each man a hatchet, which they thought was sufficient for them. In a word, they accepted the offer; and having baked bread enough to serve them a month given them, and as much goats' flesh as they could eat while it was sweet, with a great basket of dried grapes, a pot of fresh water, and a young kid alive, they boldly set out in the canoe for a voyage over the sea, where it was at least forty miles broad. The boat, indeed, was a large one, and would very well have carried fifteen or twenty men, and therefore was rather too big for them to manage; but as they had a fair breeze and flood-tide with them, they did well enough. They had made a mast of a long pole, and a sail of four large goat-skins dried, which they had sewed or laced together; and away they went merrily together. The

Spaniards called after them "*Bon voyajo*," and no man ever thought of seeing them any more.

The Spaniards were often saying to one another, and to the two honest Englishmen who remained behind, how quietly and comfortably they lived, now these three turbulent fellows were gone. As for their coming again, that was the remotest thing from their thoughts that could be imagined; when, behold, after two-and-twenty days' absence, one of the Englishmen being abroad upon his planting work, sees three strange men coming towards him at a distance, with guns upon their shoulders.

Away runs the Englishman, frightened and amazed, as if he was bewitched, to the governor Spaniard, and tells him they were all undone, for there were strangers upon the island, but he could not tell who they were. The Spaniard, pausing a while, says to him, "How do you mean — you cannot tell who? They are the savages, to be sure." "No, no," says the Englishman, "they are men in clothes, with arms." "Nay, then," says the Spaniard, "why are you so concerned! If they are not savages they must be friends; for there is no Christian nation upon earth but will do us good rather than harm." While they were debating thus, came up the three Englishmen, and standing without the wood, which was new planted, hallooed to them. They presently knew their voices, and so all the wonder ceased. But now the admiration was turned upon another question — What could be the matter, and what made them come back again?

It was not long before they brought the men in, and inquiring where they had been, and what they had been doing, they gave them a full account of their voyage in a few words: that they reached the land in less than two days, but finding the people alarmed at their coming, and preparing with bows and arrows to fight them, they durst not go on, shore, but sailed on to the northward six or seven hours, till they came to a great opening, by which they perceived that the land they saw from our island was not the main, but an island: that upon entering that opening of the sea they saw another island on the right hand north, and several more west; and being resolved to land somewhere, they put over to one of the islands which lay west, and went boldly on shore; that they found the people very courteous and friendly to them; and they gave them several roots and some dried fish, and appeared very sociable; and that the women, as well as the men, were very forward to supply them with anything they could get for them to eat, and brought it to them a great way, on their heads. They continued here for four days, and inquired as well as they could of them by signs, what nations were this way, and that way, and were told of several fierce and terrible people that lived almost every way, who, as they made known by signs to them, used to eat men; but, as for themselves, they said they never ate men or women, except only such as they took in the wars; and then they owned they made a great feast, and ate their prisoners.

The Englishmen inquired when they had had a feast of that kind; and they told them about two moons ago, pointing to the moon and to two fingers; and that their great king had two hundred prisoners now, which he had taken in his war, and they were feeding them to make them fat for the next feast. The Englishmen seemed mighty desirous of seeing those prisoners; but the others mistaking them, thought they were desirous to have some of them to carry away for their own eating. So they beckoned to them, pointing to the setting of the sun, and then to the rising; which was to signify that the next morning at sunrising they would bring some for them; and accordingly the next morning they brought down five women and eleven men, and gave them to the Englishmen to carry with them on their voyage, just as we would bring so many cows and oxen down to a seaport town to victual a ship.

As brutish and barbarous as these fellows were at home, their stomachs turned at this sight, and they did not know what to do. To refuse the prisoners would have been the highest affront to the savage gentry that could be offered them, and what to do with them they knew not. However, after some debate, they resolved to accept of them: and, in return, they gave the savages that brought them one of their hatchets, an old key, a knife, and six or seven of their bullets; which, though they did not understand their use, they seemed particularly pleased with; and then tying the poor creatures' hands behind them, they dragged the prisoners into the boat for our men.

The Englishmen were obliged to come away as soon as they had them, or else they that gave them this noble present would certainly have expected that they should have gone to work with them, have killed two or three of them the next morning, and perhaps have invited the donors to dinner. But having taken their leave, with all the respect and thanks that could well pass between people, where on either side they understood not one word they could say, they put off with their boat, and came back towards the first island; where, when they arrived, they set eight of their prisoners at liberty, there being too many of them for their occasion. In their voyage they endeavoured to have some communication with their prisoners; but it was impossible to make them understand anything. Nothing they could say to them, or give them, or do for them, but was looked upon as going to murder them. They first of all unbound them; but the poor creatures screamed at that, especially the women, as if they had just felt the knife at their throats; for they immediately concluded they were unbound on purpose to be killed. If they gave them thing to eat, it was the same thing; they then concluded it was for fear they should sink in flesh, and so not be fat enough to kill. If they looked at one of them more particularly, the party presently concluded it was to see whether he or she was fattest, and fittest to kill first; nay, after they had brought them quite over, and began to use them kindly, and treat them well, still they expected every day to make a dinner or supper for their new masters.

When the three wanderers had give this unaccountable history or journal of their voyage, the Spaniard asked them where their new family was; and being told that they had brought them on shore, and put them into one of their huts, and were come up to beg some victuals for them, they (the Spaniards) and the other two Englishmen, that is to say, the whole colony, resolved to go all down to the place and see them; and did so, and Friday's father with them. When they came into the hut, there they sat, all bound; for when they had brought them on shore they bound their hands that they might not take the boat and make their escape; there, I say, they sat, all of them stark naked. First, there were three comely fellows, well shaped, with straight limbs, about thirty to thirty-five years of age; and five women, whereof two might be from thirty to forty, two more about four or five and twenty; and the fifth, a tall, comely maiden, about seventeen. The women were well-favoured, agreeable persons, both in shape and features, only tawny; and two of them, had they been perfect white, would have passed for very handsome women, even in London, having pleasant countenances, and of a very modest behaviour; especially when they came afterwards to be clothed and dressed, though that dress was very indifferent, it must be confessed.

The sight, you may be sure, was something uncouth to our Spaniards, who were, to give them a just character, men of the most calm, sedate tempers, and perfect good humour, that ever I met with: and, in particular, of the utmost modesty: I say, the sight was very uncouth, to see three naked men and five naked women, all together bound, and in the most miserable circumstances that human nature could be supposed to be, viz. to be expecting every moment to be dragged out and have their brains knocked out, and then to be eaten up like a calf that is killed for a dainty.

The first thing they did was to cause the old Indian, Friday's father, to go in, and see first if he knew any of them, and then if he understood any of their speech. As soon as the old man came in, he looked seriously at them, but knew none of them; neither could any of them understand a word he said, or a sign he could make, except one of the women. However, this was enough to answer the end, which was to satisfy them that the men into whose hands they were fallen were Christians; that they abhorred eating men or women; and that they might be sure they would not be killed. As soon as they were assured of this, they discovered such a joy, and by such awkward gestures, several ways, as is hard to describe; for it seems they were of several nations. The woman who was their interpreter was bid, in the next place, to ask them if they were willing to be servants, and to work for the men who had brought them away, to save their lives; at which they all fell a-dancing; and presently one fell to taking up this, and another that, anything that lay next, to carry on their shoulders, to intimate they were willing to work.

The governor, who found that the having women among them would presently be attended with some inconvenience, and might occasion some strife, and perhaps blood, asked the three men what they intended to do with these women, and how they intended to use them, whether as servants or as wives? One of the Englishmen answered, very boldly and readily, that they would use them as both; to which the governor said: "I am not going to restrain you from it — you are your own masters as to that; but this I think is but just, for avoiding disorders and quarrels among you, and I desire it of you for that reason only, viz. that you will all engage, that if any of you take any of these women as a wife, he shall take but one; and that having taken one, none else shall touch her; for though we cannot marry any one of you, yet it is but reasonable that, while you stay here, the woman any of you takes shall be maintained by the man that takes her, and should be his wife — I mean," says he, "while he continues here, and that none else shall have anything to do with her." All this appeared so just, that every one agreed to it without any difficulty.

Then the Englishmen asked the Spaniards if they designed to take any of them? But every one of them answered "No." Some of them said they had wives in Spain, and the others did not like women that were not Christians; and all together declared that they would not touch one of them, which was an instance of such virtue as I have not met with in all my travels. On the other hand, the five Englishmen took them every one a wife, that is to say, a temporary wife; and so they set up a new form of living; for the Spaniards and Friday's father lived in my old habitation, which they had enlarged exceedingly within. The three servants which were taken in the last battle of the savages lived with them; and these carried on the main part of the colony, supplied all the rest with food, and assisted them in anything as they could, or as they found necessity required.

But the wonder of the story was, how five such refractory, ill-matched fellows should agree about these women, and that some two of them should not choose the same woman, especially seeing two or three of them were, without comparison, more agreeable than the others; but they took a good way enough to prevent quarrelling among themselves, for they set the five women by themselves in one of their huts, and they went all into the other hut, and drew lots among them who should choose first.

Him that drew to choose first went away by himself to the hut where the poor naked creatures were, and fetched out her he chose; and it was worth observing, that he that chose first took her that was reckoned the homeliest and oldest of the five, which made mirth enough amongst the rest; and even the Spaniards laughed at it; but the fellow considered better than any of them, that it was application and business they were to expect assistance in, as much as in anything else; and she proved the best wife of all the parcel.

When the poor women saw themselves set in a row thus, and fetched out one by one, the terrors of their condition returned upon them again, and they firmly believed they were now going to be devoured. Accordingly, when the English sailor came in and fetched out one of them, the rest set up a most lamentable cry, and hung about her, and took their leave of her with such agonies and affection as would have grieved the hardest heart in the world: nor was it possible for the Englishmen to satisfy them that they were not to be immediately murdered, till they fetched the old man, Friday's father, who immediately let them know that the five men, who were to fetch them out one by one, had chosen them for their wives. When they had done, and the fright the women were in was a little over, the men went to work, and the Spaniards came and helped them: and in a few hours they had built them every one a new hut or tent for their lodging apart; for those they had already were crowded with their tools, household stuff, and provisions. The three wicked ones had pitched farthest off, and the two honest ones nearer, but both on the north shore of the island, so that they continued separated as before; and thus my island was peopled in three places, and, as I might say, three towns were begun to be built.

And here it is very well worth observing that, as it often happens in the world (what the wise ends in God's providence are, in such a disposition of things, I cannot say), the two honest fellows had the two worst wives; and the three reprobates, that were scarce worth hanging, that were fit for nothing, and neither seemed born to do themselves good nor any one else, had three clever, careful, and ingenious wives; not that the first two were bad wives as to their temper or humour, for all the five were most willing, quiet, passive, and subjected creatures, rather like slaves than wives; but my meaning is, they were not alike capable, ingenious, or industrious, or alike cleanly and neat. Another observation I must make, to the honour of a diligent application on one hand, and to the disgrace of a slothful, negligent, idle temper on the other, that when I came to the place, and viewed the several improvements, plantings, and management of the several little colonies, the two men had so far out-gone the three, that there was no comparison. They had, indeed, both of them as much ground laid out for corn as they wanted, and the reason was, because, according to my rule, nature dictated that it was to no purpose to sow more corn than they wanted; but the difference of the cultivation, of the planting, of the fences, and indeed, of everything else, was easy to be seen at first view.

The two men had innumerable young trees planted about their huts, so that, when you came to the place, nothing was to be seen but a wood; and though they had twice had their plantation demolished, once by their own countrymen, and once by the enemy, as shall be shown in its place, yet they had restored all again, and everything was thriving and flourishing about them; they had grapes planted in order, and managed like a vineyard, though they had themselves never seen anything of that kind; and by their good ordering their vines, their grapes were as good again as any of the others. They had also found themselves out a retreat in the thickest part of the woods, where, though there was not a natural cave, as I had found, yet they made one with incessant labour of their hands, and where, when the mischief which followed happened, they secured their wives and children so as they could never be found; they having, by sticking innumerable stakes and poles of the wood which, as I said, grew so readily, made the grove impassable, except in some places, when they climbed up to get over the outside part, and then went on by ways of their own leaving.

As to the three reprobates, as I justly call them, though they were much civilized by their settlement compared to what they were before, and were not so quarrelsome, having not the same opportunity; yet one of the certain companions of a profligate mind never left them, and that was their idleness. It is true, they planted corn and made fences; but Solomon's words were never better verified than in them, "I went by the vineyard of the slothful, and it was all overgrown with thorns": for when the Spaniards came to view their crop they could not see it in some places for weeds, the hedge had several gaps in it, where the wild goats had got in and eaten up the corn; perhaps here and there a dead bush was crammed in, to stop them out for the present, but it was only shutting the stable-door after the steed was stolen. Whereas, when they looked on the colony of the other two, there was the very face of industry and success upon all they did; there was not a weed to be seen in all their corn, or a gap in any of their hedges; and they, on the other hand, verified Solomon's words in another place, "that the diligent hand maketh rich"; for everything grew and thrived, and they had plenty within and without; they had more tame cattle than the others, more utensils and necessaries within doors, and yet more pleasure and diversion too.

It is true, the wives of the three were very handy and cleanly within doors; and having learned the English ways of dressing, and cooking from one of the other Englishmen, who, as I said, was a cook's mate on board the ship, they dressed their husbands' victuals very nicely and well; whereas the others could not be brought to understand it; but then the husband, who, as I say, had been cook's mate, did it himself. But as for the husbands of the three wives, they loitered about, fetched turtles' eggs, and caught fish and birds: in a word, anything but labour; and they fared accordingly. The diligent lived well and comfortably, and the slothful hard and beggarly; and so, I believe, generally speaking, it is all over the world.

But I now come to a scene different from all that had happened before, either to them or to me; and the origin of the story was this: Early one morning there came on shore five or six canoes of Indians or savages, call them which you please, and there is no room to doubt they came upon the old errand of feeding upon their slaves; but that part was now so familiar to the Spaniards, and to our men too, that they did not concern themselves about it, as I did: but having been made sensible, by their experience, that their only business was to lie concealed, and that if they were not seen by any of the savages they would go off again quietly, when their business was done, having as yet not the least notion of there being any inhabitants in the island; I say, having been made sensible of this, they had nothing to do but to give notice to all the three plantations to keep within doors, and not show themselves, only placing a scout in a proper place, to give notice when the boats went to sea again.

This was, without doubt, very right; but a disaster spoiled all these measures, and made it known among the savages that there were inhabitants there; which was, in the end, the desolation of almost the whole colony. After the canoes with the savages were gone off, the Spaniards peeped abroad again; and some of them had the curiosity to go to the place where they had been, to see what they had been doing. Here, to their great surprise, they found three savages left behind, and lying fast asleep upon the ground. It was supposed they had either been so gorged with their inhuman feast, that, like beasts, they were fallen asleep, and would not stir when the others went, or they had wandered into the woods, and did not come back in time to be taken in.

The Spaniards were greatly surprised at this sight and perfectly at a loss what to do. The Spaniard governor, as it happened, was with them, and his advice was asked, but he professed he knew not what to do. As for slaves, they had enough already; and as to killing them, there were none of them inclined to do that: the Spaniard governor told me they could not think of shedding innocent blood; for as to them, the poor creatures had done them no wrong, invaded none of their property, and they thought they had no just quarrel against them, to take away their lives. And here I must, in justice to these Spaniards, observe that, let the accounts of Spanish cruelty in Mexico and Peru be what they will, I never met with seventeen men of any nation whatsoever, in any foreign country, who were so universally modest, temperate, virtuous, so very good-humoured, and so courteous, as these Spaniards: and as to cruelty, they had nothing of it in their very nature; no inhumanity, no barbarity, no outrageous passions; and yet all of them men of great courage and spirit. Their temper and calmness had appeared in their bearing the insufferable usage of the three Englishmen; and their justice and humanity appeared now in the case of the savages above. After some consultation they resolved upon this; that they would lie still a while longer, till, if possible, these three men might be gone. But then the governor recollected that the three savages had no boat; and if they were left to rove about the island, they would certainly discover that there were inhabitants in it; and so they should be undone that way. Upon this, they went back again, and there lay the fellows fast asleep still, and so they resolved to awaken them, and take them prisoners; and they did so. The poor fellows were strangely frightened when they were seized upon and bound; and afraid, like the women, that they should be murdered and eaten: for it seems those people think all the world does as they do, in eating men's flesh; but they were soon made easy as to that, and away they carried them.

It was very happy for them that they did not carry them home to the castle, I mean to my palace under the hill; but they carried them first to the bower, where was the chief of their country work, such as the keeping the goats, the planting the corn, &c.; and afterward they carried them to the habitation of the two Englishmen. Here they were set to work, though it was not much they had for them to do; and whether it was by negligence in guarding them, or that they thought the fellows could not mend themselves, I know not, but one of them ran away, and, taking to the woods, they could never hear of him any more. They had good reason to believe he got home again soon after in some other boats or canoes of savages who came on shore three or four weeks afterwards, and who, carrying on their revels as usual, went off in two days' time. This thought terrified them exceedingly; for they concluded, and that not without good cause indeed, that if this fellow came home safe among his comrades, he would certainly give them an account that there were people in the island, and also how few and weak they were; for this savage, as observed before, had never been told, and it was very happy he had not, how many there were or where they lived; nor had he ever seen or heard the fire of any of their guns, much less had they shown him any of their other retired places; such as the cave in the valley, or the new retreat which the two Englishmen had made, and the like.

The first testimony they had that this fellow had given intelligence of them was, that about two mouths after this six canoes of savages, with about seven, eight, or ten men in a canoe, came rowing along the north side of the island, where they never used to come before, and landed, about an hour after sunrise, at a convenient place, about a mile from the habitation of the two Englishmen, where this escaped man had been kept. As the chief Spaniard said, had they been all there the damage would not have been so much, for not a man of them would have escaped; but the case differed now very much, for two men to fifty was too much odds. The two men had the happiness to discover them about a league off, so that it was above an hour before they landed; and as they landed a mile from their huts, it was some time before they could come at them. Now, having great reason to believe that they were betrayed, the first thing they did was to bind the two slaves which were left, and cause two of the three men whom they brought with the women (who, it seems, proved very faithful to them) to lead them, with their two wives, and whatever they could carry away with them, to their retired places in the woods, which I have spoken of above, and there to bind the two fellows hand and foot, till they heard farther. In the next place, seeing the savages were all come on shore, and that they had bent their course directly that way, they opened the fences where the milch cows were kept, and drove them all out; leaving their goats to straggle in the woods, whither they pleased, that the savages might think they were all bred wild; but the rogue who came with them was too cunning for that, and gave them an account of it all, for they went directly to the place.

When the two poor frightened men had secured their wives and goods, they sent the other slave they had of the three who came with the women, and who was at their place by accident, away to the Spaniards with all speed, to give them the alarm, and desire speedy help, and, in the meantime, they took their arms and what ammunition they had, and retreated towards the place in the wood where their wives were sent; keeping at a distance, yet so that they might see, if possible, which way the savages took. They had not gone far but that from a rising ground they could see the little army of their enemies come on directly to their habitation, and, in a moment more, could see all their huts and household stuff flaming up together, to their great grief and mortification; for this was a great loss to them, irretrievable, indeed, for some time. They kept their station for a while, till they found the savages, like wild beasts, spread themselves all over the place, rummaging every way, and every place they could think of, in search of prey; and in particular for the people, of whom now it plainly appeared they had intelligence.

The two Englishmen seeing this, thinking themselves not secure where they stood, because it was likely some of the wild people might come that way, and they might come too many together, thought it proper to make another retreat about half a mile farther; believing, as it afterwards happened, that the further they strolled, the fewer would be together. Their next halt was at the entrance into a very thick-grown part of the woods, and where an old trunk of a tree stood, which was hollow and very large; and in this tree they both took their standing, resolving to see there what might offer. They had not stood there long before two of the savages appeared running directly that way, as if they had already had notice where they stood, and were coming up to attack them; and a little way farther they espied three more coming after them, and five more beyond them, all coming the same way; besides which, they saw seven or eight more at a distance, running another way; for in a word, they ran every way, like sportsmen beating for their game.

The poor men were now in great perplexity whether they should stand and keep their posture or fly; but after a very short debate with themselves, they considered that if the savages ranged the country thus before help came, they might perhaps find their retreat in the woods, and then all would be lost; so they resolved to stand them there, and if they were too many to deal with, then they would get up to the top of the tree, from whence they doubted not to defend themselves, fire excepted, as long as their ammunition lasted, though all the savages that were landed, which was near fifty, were to attack them.

Having resolved upon this, they next considered whether they should fire at the first two, or wait for the three, and so take the middle party, by which the two and the five that followed would be separated; at length they resolved to let the first two pass by, unless they should spy them the tree, and come to attack them. The first two savages confirmed them also in this resolution, by turning a little from them towards another part of the wood; but the three, and the five after them, came forward directly to the tree, as if they had known the Englishmen were there. Seeing them come so straight towards them, they resolved to take them in a line as they came: and as they resolved to fire but one at a time, perhaps the first shot might hit them all three; for which purpose the man who was to fire put three or four small bullets into his piece; and having a fair loophole, as it were, from a broken hole in the tree, he took a sure aim, without being seen, waiting till they were within about thirty yards of the tree, so that he could not miss.

While they were thus waiting, and the savages came on, they plainly saw that one of the three was the runaway savage that had escaped from them; and they both knew him distinctly, and resolved that, if possible, he should not escape, though they should both fire; so the other stood ready with his piece, that if he did not drop at the first shot, he should be sure to have a second. But the first was too good a marksman to miss his aim; for as the savages kept near one another, a little behind in a line, he fired, and hit two of them directly; the foremost was killed outright, being shot in the head; the second, which was the runaway Indian, was shot through the body, and fell, but was not quite dead; and the third had a little scratch in the shoulder, perhaps by the same ball that went through the body of the second; and being dreadfully frightened, though not so much hurt, sat down upon the ground, screaming and yelling in a hideous manner.

The five that were behind, more frightened with the noise than sensible of the danger, stood still at first; for the woods made the sound a thousand times bigger than it really was, the echoes rattling from one side to another, and the fowls rising from all parts, screaming, and every sort making a different noise, according to their kind; just as it was when I fired the first gun that perhaps was ever shot off in the island.

However, all being silent again, and they not knowing what the matter was, came on unconcerned, till they came to the place where their companions lay in a condition miserable enough. Here the poor ignorant creatures, not sensible that they were within reach of the same mischief, stood all together over the wounded man, talking, and, as may be supposed, inquiring of him how he came to be hurt; and who, it is very rational to believe, told them that a flash of fire first, and immediately after that thunder from their gods, had killed those two and wounded him. This, I say, is rational; for nothing is more certain than that, as they saw no man near them, so they had never heard a gun in all their lives, nor so much as heard of a gun; neither knew they anything of killing and wounding at a distance with fire and bullets: if they had, one might reasonably believe they would not have stood so unconcerned to view the fate of their fellows, without some apprehensions of their own.

Our two men, as they confessed to me, were grieved to be obliged to kill so many poor creatures, who had no notion of their danger; yet, having them all thus in their power, and the first having loaded his piece again, resolved to let fly both together among them; and singling out, by agreement, which to aim at, they shot together, and killed, or very much wounded, four of them; the fifth, frightened even to death, though not hurt, fell with the rest; so that our men, seeing them all fall together, thought they had killed them all.

The belief that the savages were all killed made our two men come boldly out from the tree before they had charged their guns, which was a wrong step; and they were under some surprise when they came to the place, and found no less than four of them alive, and of them two very little hurt, and one not at all. This obliged them to fall upon them with the stocks of their muskets; and first they made sure of the runaway savage, that had been the cause of all the mischief, and of another that was hurt in the knee, and put them out of their pain; then the man that was not hurt at all came and kneeled down to them, with his two hands held up, and made piteous moans to them, by gestures and signs, for his life, but could not say one word to them that they could understand. However, they made signs to him to sit down at the foot of a tree hard by; and one of the Englishmen, with a piece of rope-yarn, which he had by great chance in his pocket, tied his two hands behind him, and there they left him; and with what speed they could made after the other two, which were gone before, fearing they, or any more of them, should find way to their covered place in the woods, where their wives, and the few goods they had left, lay. They came once in sight of the two men, but it was at a great distance; however, they had the satisfaction to see them cross over a valley towards the sea, quite the contrary way from that which led to their retreat, which they were afraid of; and being satisfied with that, they went back to the tree where they left their prisoner, who, as they supposed, was delivered by his comrades, for he was gone, and the two pieces of rope-yarn with which they had bound him lay just at the foot of the tree.

They were now in as great concern as before, not knowing what course to take, or how near the enemy might be, or in what number; so they resolved to go away to the place where their wives were, to see if all was well there, and to make them easy. These were in fright enough, to be sure; for though the savages were their own countrymen, yet they were most terribly afraid of them, and perhaps the more for the knowledge they had of them. When they came there, they found the savages had been in the wood, and very near that place, but had not found it; for it was indeed inaccessible, from the trees standing so thick, unless the persons seeking it had been directed by those that knew it, which these did not: they found, therefore, everything very safe, only the women in a terrible fright. While they were here they had the comfort to have seven of the Spaniards come to their assistance; the other ten, with their servants, and Friday's father, were gone in a body to defend their bower, and the corn and cattle that were kept there, in case the savages should have roved over to that side of the country, but they did not spread so far. With the seven Spaniards came one of the three savages, who, as I said, were their prisoners formerly; and with them also came the savage whom the Englishmen had left bound hand and foot at the tree; for it seems they came that way, saw the slaughter of the seven men, and unbound the eighth, and brought him along with them; where, however, they were obliged to bind again, as they had the two others who were left when the third ran away.

The prisoners now began to be a burden to them; and they were so afraid of their escaping, that they were once resolving to kill them all, believing they were under an absolute necessity to do so for their own preservation. However, the chief of the Spaniards would not consent to it, but ordered, for the present, that they should be sent out of the way to my old cave in the valley, and be kept there, with two Spaniards to guard them, and have food for their subsistence, which was done; and they were bound there hand and foot for that night.

When the Spaniards came, the two Englishmen were so encouraged, that they could not satisfy themselves to stay any longer there; but taking five of the Spaniards, and themselves, with four muskets and a pistol among them, and two stout quarter-staves, away they went in quest of the savages. And first they came to the tree where the men lay that had been killed; but it was easy to see that some more of the savages had been there, for they had attempted to carry their dead men away, and had dragged two of them a good way, but had given it over. From thence they advanced to the first rising ground, where they had stood and seen their camp destroyed, and where they had the mortification still to see some of the smoke; but neither could they here see any of the savages. They then resolved, though with all possible caution, to go forward towards their ruined plantation; but, a little before they came thither, coming in sight of the sea-shore, they saw plainly the savages all embarked again in their canoes, in order to be gone. They seemed sorry at first that there was no way to come at them, to give them a parting blow; but, upon the whole, they were very well satisfied to be rid of them.

The poor Englishmen being now twice ruined, and all their improvements destroyed, the rest all agreed to come and help them to rebuild, and assist them with needful supplies. Their three countrymen, who were not yet noted for having the least inclination to do any good, yet as soon as they heard of it (for they, living remote eastward, knew nothing of the matter till all was over), came and offered their help and assistance, and did, very friendly, work for several days to restore their habitation and make necessaries for them. And thus in a little time they were set upon their legs again.

About two days after this they had the farther satisfaction of seeing three of the savages' canoes come driving on shore, and, at some distance from them, two drowned men, by which they had reason to believe that they had met with a storm at sea, which had overset some of them; for it had blown very hard the night after they went off. However, as some might miscarry, so, on the other hand, enough of them escaped to inform the rest, as well of what they had done as of what had happened to them; and to whet them on to another enterprise of the same nature, which they, it seems, resolved to attempt, with sufficient force to carry all before them; for except what the first man had told them of inhabitants, they could say little of it of their own knowledge, for they never saw one man; and the fellow being killed that had affirmed it, they had no other witness to confirm it to, them.

CHAPTER V. A GREAT VICTORY

It was five or six months after this before they heard any more of the savages, in which time our men were in hopes they had either forgot their former bad luck, or given over hopes of better; when, on a sudden, they were invaded with a most formidable fleet of no less than eight-and-twenty canoes, full of savages, armed with bows and arrows, great clubs, wooden swords, and such like engines of war; and they brought such numbers with them, that, in short, it put all our people into the utmost consternation.

As they came on shore in the evening, and at the easternmost side of the island, our men had that night to consult and consider what to do. In the first place, knowing that their being entirely concealed was their only safety before and would be much more so now, while the number of their enemies would be so great, they resolved, first of all, to take down the huts which were built for the two Englishmen, and drive away their goats to the old cave; because they supposed the savages would go directly thither, as soon as it was day, to play the old game over again, though they did not now land within two leagues of it. In the next place, they drove away all the flocks of goats they had at the old bower, as I called it, which belonged to the Spaniards; and, in short, left as little appearance of inhabitants anywhere as was possible; and the next morning early they posted themselves, with all their force, at the plantation of the two men, to wait for their coming. As they guessed, so it happened: these new invaders, leaving their canoes at the east end of the island, came ranging along the shore, directly towards the place, to the number of two hundred and fifty, as near as our men could judge. Our army was but small indeed; but, that which was worse, they had not arms for all their number. The whole account, it seems, stood thus: first, as to men, seventeen Spaniards, five Englishmen, old Friday, the three slaves taken with the women, who proved very faithful, and three other slaves, who lived with the Spaniards. To arm these, they had eleven muskets, five pistols, three fowling-pieces, five muskets or fowling-pieces which were taken by me from the mutinous seamen whom I reduced, two swords, and three old halberds.

To their slaves they did not give either musket or fusée; but they had each a halberd, or a long staff, like a quarter-staff, with a great spike of iron fastened into each end of it, and by his side a hatchet; also every one of our men had a hatchet. Two of the women could not be prevailed upon but they would come into the fight, and they had bows and arrows, which the Spaniards had taken from the savages when the first action happened, which I have spoken of, where the Indians fought with one another; and the women had hatchets too.

The chief Spaniard, whom I described so often, commanded the whole; and Will Atkins, who, though a dreadful fellow for wickedness, was a most daring, bold fellow, commanded under him. The savages came forward like lions; and our men, which was the worst of their fate, had no advantage in their situation; only that Will Atkins, who now proved a most useful fellow, with six men, was planted just behind a small thicket of bushes as an advanced guard, with orders to let the first of them pass by and then fire into the middle of them, and as soon as he had fired, to make his retreat as nimbly as he could round a part of the wood, and so come in behind the Spaniards, where they stood, having a thicket of trees before them.

When the savages came on, they ran straggling about every way in heaps, out of all manner of order, and Will Atkins let about fifty of them pass by him; then seeing the rest come in a very thick throng, he orders three of his men to fire, having loaded their muskets with six or seven bullets apiece, about as big as large pistol-bullets. How many they killed or wounded they knew not, but the consternation and surprise was inexpressible among the savages; they were frightened to the last degree to hear such a dreadful noise, and see their men killed, and others hurt, but see nobody that did it; when, in the middle of their fright, Will Atkins and his other three let fly again among the thickest of them; and in less than a minute the first three, being loaded again, gave them a third volley.

Had Will Atkins and his men retired immediately, as soon as they had fired, as they were ordered to do, or had the rest of the body been at hand to have poured in their shot continually, the savages had been effectually routed; for the terror that was among them came principally from this, that they were killed by the gods with thunder and lightning, and could see nobody that hurt them. But Will Atkins, staying to load again, discovered the cheat: some of the savages who were at a distance spying them, came upon them behind; and though Atkins and his men fired at them also, two or three times, and killed above twenty, retiring as fast as they could, yet they wounded Atkins himself, and killed one of his fellow-Englishmen with their arrows, as they did afterwards one Spaniard, and one of the Indian slaves who came with the women. This slave was a most gallant fellow, and fought most desperately, killing five of them with his own hand, having no weapon but one of the armed staves and a hatchet.

Our men being thus hard laid at, Atkins wounded, and two other men killed, retreated to a rising ground in the wood; and the Spaniards, after firing three volleys upon them, retreated also; for their number was so great, and they were so desperate, that though above fifty of them were killed, and more than as many wounded, yet they came on in the teeth of our men, fearless of danger, and shot their arrows like a cloud; and it was observed that their wounded men, who were not quite disabled, were made outrageous by their wounds, and fought like madmen.

When our men retreated, they left the Spaniard and the Englishman that were killed behind them: and the savages, when they came up to them, killed them over again in a wretched manner, breaking their arms, legs, and heads, with their clubs and wooden swords, like true savages; but finding our men were gone, they did not seem inclined to pursue them, but drew themselves up in a ring, which is, it seems, their custom, and shouted twice, in token of their victory; after which, they had the mortification to see several of their wounded men fall, dying with the mere loss of blood.

The Spaniard governor having drawn his little body up together upon a rising ground, Atkins, though he was wounded, would have had them march and charge again all together at once: but the Spaniard replied, "Seignior Atkins, you see how their wounded men fight; let them alone till morning; all the wounded men will be stiff and sore with their wounds, and faint with the loss of blood; and so we shall have the fewer to engage." This advice was good: but Will Atkins replied merrily, "That is true, seignior, and so shall I too; and that is the reason I would go on while I am warm." "Well, Seignior Atkins," says the Spaniard, "you have behaved gallantly, and done your part; we will fight for you if you cannot come on; but I think it best to stay till morning:" so they waited.

But as it was a clear moonlight night, and they found the savages in great disorder about their dead and wounded men, and a great noise and hurry among them where they lay, they afterwards resolved to fall upon them in the night, especially if they could come to give them but one volley before they were discovered, which they had a fair opportunity to do; for one of the Englishmen in whose quarter it was where the fight began, led them round between the woods and the seaside westward, and then turning short south, they came so near where the thickest of them lay, that before they were seen or heard eight of them fired in among them, and did dreadful execution upon them; in half a minute more eight others fired after them, pouring in their small shot in such a quantity that abundance were killed and wounded; and all this while they were not able to see who hurt them, or which way to fly.

The Spaniards charged again with the utmost expedition, and then divided themselves into three bodies, and resolved to fall in among them all together. They had in each body eight persons, that is to say, twenty-two men and the two women, who, by the way, fought desperately. They divided the firearms equally in each party, as well as the halberds and staves. They would have had the women kept back, but they said they were resolved to die with their husbands. Having thus formed their little army, they marched out from among the trees, and came up to the teeth of the enemy, shouting and hallooing as loud as they could; the savages stood all together, but were in the utmost confusion, hearing the noise of our men shouting from three quarters together. They would have fought if they had seen us; for as soon as we came near enough to be seen, some arrows were shot, and poor old Friday was wounded, though not dangerously. But our men gave them no time, but running up to them, fired among them three ways, and then fell in with the butt-ends of their muskets, their swords, armed staves, and hatchets, and laid about them so well that, in a word, they set up a dismal screaming and howling, flying to save their lives which way so ever they could.

Our men were tired with the execution, and killed or mortally wounded in the two fights about one hundred and eighty of them; the rest, being frightened out of their wits, scoured through the woods and over the hills, with all the speed that fear and nimble feet could help them to; and as we did not trouble ourselves much to pursue them, they got all together to the seaside, where they landed, and where their canoes lay. But their disaster was not at an end yet; for it blew a terrible storm of wind that evening from the sea, so that it was impossible for them to go off; nay, the storm continuing all night, when the tide came up their canoes were most of them driven by the surge of the sea so high upon the shore that it required infinite toil to get them off; and some of them were even dashed to pieces against the beach. Our men, though glad of their victory, yet got little rest that night; but having refreshed themselves as well as they could, they resolved to march to that part of the island where the savages were fled, and see what posture they were in. This necessarily led them over the place where the fight had been, and where they found several of the poor creatures not quite dead, and yet past recovering life; a sight disagreeable enough to generous minds, for a truly great man though obliged by the law of battle to destroy his enemy, takes no delight in his misery. However, there was no need to give any orders in this case; for their own savages, who were their servants, dispatched these poor creatures with their hatchets.

At length they came in view of the place where the more miserable remains of the savages' army lay, where there appeared about a hundred still; their posture was generally sitting upon the ground, with their knees up towards their mouth, and the head put between the two hands, leaning down upon the knees. When our men came within two musket-shots of them, the Spaniard governor ordered two muskets to be fired without ball, to alarm them; this he did, that by their countenance he might know what to expect, whether they were still in heart to fight, or were so heartily beaten as to be discouraged, and so he might manage accordingly. This stratagem took: for as soon as the savages heard the first gun, and saw the flash of the second, they started up upon their feet in the greatest consternation imaginable; and as our men advanced swiftly towards them, they all ran screaming and yelling away, with a kind of howling noise, which our men did not understand, and had never heard before; and thus they ran up the hills into the country.

At first our men had much rather the weather had been calm, and they had all gone away to sea: but they did not then consider that this might probably have been the occasion of their coming again in such multitudes as not to be resisted, or, at least, to come so many and so often as would quite desolate the island, and starve them. Will Atkins, therefore, who notwithstanding his wound kept always with them, proved the best counselor in this case: his advice was, to take the advantage that offered, and step in between them and their boats, and so deprive them of the capacity of ever returning any more to plague the island. They consulted long about this; and some were against it for fear of making the wretches fly to the woods and live there desperate, and so they should have them to hunt like wild beasts, be afraid to stir out about their business, and have their plantations continually rifled, all their tame goats destroyed, and, in short, be reduced to a life of continual distress.

Will Atkins told them they had better have to do with a hundred men than with a hundred nations; that, as they must destroy their boats, so they must destroy the men, or be all of them destroyed themselves. In a word, he showed them the necessity of it so plainly that they all came into it; so they went to work immediately with the boats, and getting some dry wood together from a dead tree, they tried to set some of them on fire, but they were so wet that they would not burn; however, the fire so burned the upper part that it soon made them unfit for use at sea.

When the Indians saw what they were about, some of them came running out of the woods, and coming as near as they could to our men, kneeled down and cried, "Oa, Oa, Waramokoa," and some other words of their language, which none of the others understood anything of; but as they made pitiful gestures and strange noises, it was easy to understand they begged to have their boats spared, and that they would be gone, and never come there again. But our men were now satisfied that they had no way to preserve themselves, or to save their colony, but effectually to prevent any of these people from ever going home again; depending upon this, that if even so much as one of them got back into their country to tell the story, the colony was undone; so that, letting them know that they should not have any mercy, they fell to work with their canoes, and destroyed every one that the storm had not destroyed before; at the sight of which, the savages raised a hideous cry in the woods, which our people heard plain enough, after which they ran about the island like distracted men, so that, in a word, our men did not really know what at first to do with them. Nor did the Spaniards, with all their prudence, consider that while they made those people thus desperate, they ought to have kept a good guard at the same time upon their plantations; for though it is true they had driven away their cattle, and the Indians did not find out their main retreat, I mean my old castle at the hill, nor the cave in the valley, yet they found out my plantation at the bower, and pulled it all to pieces, and all the fences and planting about it; trod all the corn under foot, tore up the vines and grapes, being just then almost ripe, and did our men inestimable damage, though to themselves not one farthing's worth of service.

Though our men were able to fight them upon all occasions, yet they were in no condition to pursue them, or hunt them up and down; for as they were too nimble of foot for our people when they found them single, so our men durst not go abroad single, for fear of being surrounded with their numbers. The best was they had no weapons; for though they had bows, they had no arrows left, nor any materials to make any; nor had they any edge-tool among them. The extremity and distress they were reduced to was great, and indeed deplorable; but, at the same time, our men were also brought to very bad circumstances by them, for though their retreats were preserved, yet their provision was destroyed, and their harvest spoiled, and what to do, or which way to turn themselves, they knew not. The only refuge they had now was the stock of cattle they had in the valley by the cave, and some little corn which grew there, and the plantation of the three Englishmen. Will Atkins and his comrades were now reduced to two; one of them being killed by an arrow, which struck him on the side of his head, just under the temple, so that he never spoke more; and it was very remarkable that this was the same barbarous fellow that cut the poor savage slave with his hatchet, and who afterwards intended to have murdered the Spaniards.

I looked upon their case to have been worse at this time than mine was at any time, after I first discovered the grains of barley and rice, and got into the manner of planting and raising my corn, and my tame cattle; for now they had, as I may say, a hundred wolves upon the island, which would devour everything they could come at, yet could be hardly come at themselves.

When they saw what their circumstances were, the first thing they concluded was, that they would, if possible, drive the savages up to the farther part of the island, south-west, that if any more came on shore they might not find one another; then, that they would daily hunt and harass them, and kill as many of them as they could come at, till they had reduced their number; and if they could at last tame them, and bring them to anything, they would give them corn, and teach them how to plant, and live upon their daily labour. In order to do this, they so followed them, and so terrified them with their guns, that in a few days, if any of them fired a gun at an Indian, if he did not hit him, yet he would fall down for fear. So dreadfully frightened were they that they kept out of sight farther and farther; till at last our men followed them, and almost every day killing or wounding some of them, they kept up in the woods or hollow places so much, that it reduced them to the utmost misery for want of food; and many were afterwards found dead in the woods, without any hurt, absolutely starved to death.

When our men found this, it made their hearts relent, and pity moved them, especially the generous-minded Spaniard governor; and he proposed, if possible, to take one of them alive and bring him to understand what they meant, so far as to be able to act as interpreter, and go among them and see if they might be brought to some conditions that might be depended upon, to save their lives and do us no harm.

It was some while before any of them could be taken; but being weak and half-starved, one of them was at last surprised and made a prisoner. He was sullen at first, and would neither eat nor drink; but finding himself kindly used, and victuals given to him, and no violence offered him, he at last grew tractable, and came to himself. They often brought old Friday to talk to him, who always told him how kind the others would be to them all; that they would not only save their lives, but give them part of the island to live in, provided they would give satisfaction that they would keep in their own bounds, and not come beyond it to injure or prejudice others; and that they should have corn given them to plant and make it grow for their bread, and some bread given them for their present subsistence; and old Friday bade the fellow go and talk with the rest of his countrymen, and see what they said to it; assuring them that, if they did not agree immediately, they should be all destroyed.

The poor wretches, thoroughly humbled, and reduced in number to about thirty-seven, closed with the proposal at the first offer, and begged to have some food given them; upon which twelve Spaniards and two Englishmen, well armed, with three Indian slaves and old Friday, marched to the place where they were. The three Indian slaves carried them a large quantity of bread, some rice boiled up to cakes and dried in the sun, and three live goats; and they were ordered to go to the side of a hill, where they sat down, ate their provisions very thankfully, and were the most faithful fellows to their words that could be thought of; for, except when they came to beg victuals and directions, they never came out of their bounds; and there they lived when I came to the island and I went to see them. They had taught them both to plant corn, make bread, breed tame goats, and milk them: they wanted nothing but wives in order for them soon to become a nation. They were confined to a neck of land, surrounded with high rocks behind them, and lying plain towards the sea before them, on the south-east corner of the island. They had land enough, and it was very good and fruitful; about a mile and a half broad, and three or four miles in length. Our men taught them to make wooden spades, such as I made for myself, and gave among them twelve hatchets and three or four knives;

and there they lived, the most subjected, innocent creatures that ever were heard of.

After this the colony enjoyed a perfect tranquility with respect to the savages, till I came to revisit them, which was about two years after; not but that, now and then, some canoes of savages came on shore for their triumphal, unnatural feasts; but as they were of several nations, and perhaps had never heard of those that came before, or the reason of it, they did not make any search or inquiry after their countrymen; and if they had, it would have been very hard to have found them out.

Thus, I think, I have given a full account of all that happened to them till my return, at least that was worth notice. The Indians were wonderfully civilized by them, and they frequently went among them; but they forbid, on pain of death, any one of the Indians coming to them, because they would not have their settlement betrayed again. One thing was very remarkable, viz. that they taught the savages to make wicker-work, or baskets, but they soon outdid their masters: for they made abundance of ingenious things in wicker-work, particularly baskets, sieves, bird-cages, cupboards, &c.; as also chairs, stools, beds, couches, being very ingenious at such work when they were once put in the way of it.

My coming was a particular relief to these people, because we furnished them with knives, scissors, spades, shovels, pick-axes, and all things of that kind which they could want. With the help of those tools they were so very handy that they came at last to build up their huts or houses very handsomely, raddling or working it up like basket-work all the way round. This piece of ingenuity, although it looked very odd, was an exceeding good fence, as well against heat as against all sorts of vermin; and our men were so taken with it that they got the Indians to come and do the like for them; so that when I came to see the two Englishmen's colonies, they looked at a distance as if they all lived like bees in a hive.

As for Will Atkins, who was now become a very industrious, useful, and sober fellow, he had made himself such a tent of basket-work as I believe was never seen; it was one hundred and twenty paces round on the outside, as I measured by my steps; the walls were as close worked as a basket, in panels or squares of thirty-two in number, and very strong, standing about seven feet high; in the middle was another not above twenty-two paces round, but built stronger, being octagon in its form, and in the eight corners stood eight very strong posts; round the top of which he laid strong pieces, knit together with wooden pins, from which he raised a pyramid for a handsome roof of eight rafters, joined together very well, though he had no nails, and only a few iron spikes, which he made himself, too, out of the old iron that I had left there. Indeed, this fellow showed abundance of ingenuity in several things which he had no knowledge of: he made him a forge, with a pair of wooden bellows to blow the fire; he made himself charcoal for his work; and he formed out of the iron crows a middling good anvil to hammer upon: in this manner he made many things, but especially hooks, staples, and spikes, bolts and hinges. But to return to the house: after he had pitched the roof of his innermost tent, he worked it up between the rafters with basket-work, so firm, and thatched that over again so ingeniously with rice-straw, and over that a large leaf of a tree, which covered the top, that his house was as dry as if it had been tiled or slated. He owned, indeed, that the savages had made the basket-work for him. The outer circuit was covered as a lean-to all round this inner apartment, and long rafters lay from the thirty-two angles to the top posts of the inner house, being about twenty feet distant, so that there was a space like a walk within the outer wicker-wall, and without the inner, near twenty feet wide.

The inner place he partitioned off with the same wickerwork, but much fairer, and divided into six apartments, so that he had six rooms on a floor, and out of every one of these there was a door: first into the entry, or coming into the main tent, another door into the main tent, and another door into the space or walk that was round it; so that walk was also divided into six equal parts, which served not only for a retreat, but to store up any necessaries which the family had occasion for. These six spaces not taking up the whole circumference, what other apartments the outer circle had were thus ordered: As soon as you were in at the door of the outer circle you had a short passage straight before you to the door of the inner house; but on either side was a wicker partition and a door in it, by which you went first into a large room or storehouse, twenty feet wide and about thirty feet long, and through that into another not quite so long; so that in the outer circle were ten handsome rooms, six of which were only to be come at through the apartments of the inner tent, and served as closets or retiring rooms to the respective chambers of the inner circle; and four large warehouses, or barns, or what you please to call them, which went through one another, two on either hand of the passage, that led through the outer door to the inner tent. Such a piece of basket-work, I believe, was never seen in the world, nor a house or tent so neatly contrived, much less so

322

built. In this great bee-hive lived the three families, that is to say, Will Atkins and his companion; the third was killed, but his wife remained with three children, and the other two were not at all backward to give the widow her full share of everything, I mean as to their corn, milk, grapes, &c., and when they killed a kid, or found a turtle on the shore; so that they all lived well enough; though it was true they were not so industrious as the other two, as has been observed already.

One thing, however, cannot be omitted, viz. that as for religion, I do not know that there was anything of that kind among them; they often, indeed, put one another in mind that there was a God, by the very common method of seamen, swearing by His name: nor were their poor ignorant savage wives much better for having been married to Christians, as we must call them; for as they knew very little of God themselves, so they were utterly incapable of entering into any discourse with their wives about a God, or to talk anything to them concerning religion.

The utmost of all the improvement which I can say the wives had made from them was, that they had taught them to speak English pretty well; and most of their children, who were near twenty in all, were taught to speak English too, from their first learning to speak, though they at first spoke it in a very broken manner, like their mothers. None of these children were above six years old when I came thither, for it was not much above seven years since they had fetched these five savage ladies over; they had all children, more or less: the mothers were all a good sort of well-governed, quiet, laborious women, modest and decent, helpful to one another, mighty observant, and subject to their masters (I cannot call them husbands), and lacked nothing but to be well instructed in the Christian religion, and to be legally married; both of which were happily brought about afterwards by my means, or at least in consequence of my coming among them.

CHAPTER VI. THE FRENCH CLERGYMAN'S COUNSEL

Having thus given an account of the colony in general, and pretty much of my runagate Englishmen, I must say something of the Spaniards, who were the main body of the family, and in whose story there are some incidents also remarkable enough.

I had a great many discourses with them about their circumstances when they were among the savages. They told me readily that they had no instances to give of their application or ingenuity in that country; that they were a poor, miserable, dejected handful of people; that even if means had been put into their hands, yet they had so abandoned themselves to despair, and were so sunk under the weight of their misfortune, that they thought of nothing but starving. One of them, a grave and sensible man, told me he was convinced they were in the wrong; that it was not the part of wise men to give themselves up to their misery, but always to take hold of the helps which reason offered, as well for present support as for future deliverance: he told me that grief was the most senseless, insignificant passion in the world, for that it regarded only things past, which were generally impossible to be recalled or to be remedied, but had no views of things to come, and had no share in anything that looked like deliverance, but rather added to the affliction than proposed a remedy; and upon this he repeated a Spanish proverb, which, though I cannot repeat in the same words that he spoke it in, yet I remember I made it into an English proverb of my own, thus: —

"In trouble to be troubled,   Is to have your trouble doubled."

He then ran on in remarks upon all the little improvements I had made in my solitude: my unwearied application, as he called it; and how I had made a condition, which in its circumstances was at first much worse than theirs, a thousand times more happy than theirs was, even now when they were all together. He told me it was remarkable that Englishmen had a greater presence of mind in their distress than any people that ever he met with; that their unhappy nation and the Portuguese were the worst men in the world to struggle with misfortunes; for that their first step in dangers, after the common efforts were over, was to despair, lie down under it, and die, without rousing their thoughts up to proper remedies for escape.

I told him their case and mine differed exceedingly; that they were cast upon the shore without necessaries, without supply of food, or present sustenance till they could provide for it; that, it was true, I had

324

this further disadvantage and discomfort, that I was alone; but then the supplies I had providentially thrown into my hands, by the unexpected driving of the ship on the shore, was such a help as would have encouraged any creature in the world to have applied himself as I had done. "Seignior," says the Spaniard, "had we poor Spaniards been in your case, we should never have got half those things out of the ship, as you did: nay," says he, "we should never have found means to have got a raft to carry them, or to have got the raft on shore without boat or sail: and how much less should we have done if any of us had been alone!" Well, I desired him to abate his compliments, and go on with the history of their coming on shore, where they landed. He told me they unhappily landed at a place where there were people without provisions; whereas, had they had the common sense to put off to sea again, and gone to another island a little further, they had found provisions, though without people: there being an island that way, as they had been told, where there were provisions, though no people — that is to say, that the Spaniards of Trinidad had frequently been there, and had filled the island with goats and hogs at several times, where they had bred in such multitudes, and where turtle and sea-fowls were in such plenty, that they could have been in no want of flesh, though they had found no bread; whereas, here they were only sustained with a few roots and herbs, which they understood not, and which had no substance in them, and which the inhabitants gave them sparingly enough; and they could treat them no better, unless they would turn cannibals and eat men's flesh.

They gave me an account how many ways they strove to civilize the savages they were with, and to teach them rational customs in the ordinary way of living, but in vain; and how they retorted upon them as unjust that they who came there for assistance and support should attempt to set up for instructors to those that gave them food; intimating, it seems, that none should set up for the instructors of others but those who could live without them. They gave me dismal accounts of the extremities they were driven to; how sometimes they were many days without any food at all, the island they were upon being inhabited by a sort of savages that lived more indolent, and for that reason were less supplied with the necessaries of life, than they had reason to believe others were in the same part of the world; and yet they found that these savages were less ravenous and voracious than those who had better supplies of food. Also, they added, they could not but see with what demonstrations of wisdom and goodness the governing providence of God directs the events of things in this world, which, they said, appeared in their circumstances: for if, pressed by the hardships they were under, and the barrenness of the country where they were, they had searched after a better to live in, they had then been out of the way of the relief that happened to them by my means.

They then gave me an account how the savages whom they lived amongst expected them to go out with them into their wars; and, it was true, that as they had firearms with them, had they not had the disaster to lose their ammunition, they could have been serviceable not only to their friends, but have made themselves terrible both to friends and enemies; but being without powder and shot, and yet in a condition that they could not in reason decline to go out with their landlords to their wars; so when they came into the field of battle they were in a worse condition than the savages themselves, for they had neither bows nor arrows, nor could they use those the savages gave them. So they could do nothing but stand still and be wounded with arrows, till they came up to the teeth of the enemy; and then, indeed, the three halberds they had were of use to them; and they would often drive a whole little army before them with those halberds, and sharpened sticks put into the muzzles of their muskets. But for all this they were sometimes surrounded with multitudes, and in great danger from their arrows, till at last they found the way to make themselves large targets of wood, which they covered with skins of wild beasts, whose names they knew not, and these covered them from the arrows of the savages: that, notwithstanding these, they were sometimes in great danger; and five of them were once knocked down together with the clubs of the savages, which was the time when one of them was taken prisoner — that is to say, the Spaniard whom I relieved. At first they thought he had been killed; but when they afterwards heard he was taken prisoner, they were under the greatest grief imaginable, and would willingly have all ventured their lives to have rescued him.

They told me that when they were so knocked down, the rest of their company rescued them, and stood over them fighting till they were come to themselves, all but him whom they thought had been dead; and then they made their way with their halberds and pieces, standing close together in a line, through a body of above a thousand savages, beating down all that came in their way, got the victory over their enemies, but to their great sorrow, because it was with the loss of their friend, whom the other party finding alive, carried off with some others, as I gave an account before. They described, most affectionately, how they were surprised with joy at the return of their friend and companion in misery, who they thought had been devoured by wild beasts of the worst kind — wild men; and yet, how more and more they were surprised with the account he gave them of his errand, and that there was a Christian in any place near, much more one that was able, and had humanity enough, to contribute to their deliverance.

They described how they were astonished at the sight of the relief I sent them, and at the appearance of loaves of bread — things they had not seen since their coming to that miserable place; how often they crossed it and blessed it as bread sent from heaven; and what a reviving cordial it was to their spirits to taste it, as also the other things I had sent for their supply; and, after all, they would have told me something of the joy they were in at the sight of a boat and pilots, to carry them away to the person and place from whence all these new comforts came. But it was impossible to express it by words, for their excessive joy naturally driving them to unbecoming extravagances, they had no way to describe them but by telling me they bordered upon lunacy, having no way to give vent to their passions suitable to the sense that was upon them; that in some it worked one way and in some another; and that some of them, through a surprise of joy, would burst into tears, others be stark mad, and others immediately faint. This discourse extremely affected me, and called to my mind Friday's ecstasy when he met his father, and the poor people's ecstasy when I took them up at sea after their ship was on fire; the joy of the mate of the ship when he found himself delivered in the place where he expected to perish; and my own joy, when, after twenty-eight years' captivity, I found a good ship ready to carry me to my own country. All these things made me more sensible of the relation of these poor men, and more affected with it.

Having thus given a view of the state of things as I found them, I must relate the heads of what I did for these people, and the condition in which I left them. It was their opinion, and mine too, that they would be troubled no more with the savages, or if they were, they would be able to cut them off, if they were twice as many as before; so they had no concern about that. Then I entered into a serious discourse with the Spaniard, whom I call governor, about their stay in the island; for as I was not come to carry any of them off, so it would not be just to carry off some and leave others, who, perhaps, would be unwilling to stay if their strength was diminished. On the other hand, I told them I came to establish them there, not to remove them; and then I let them know that I had brought with me relief of sundry kinds for them; that I had been at a great charge to supply them with all things necessary, as well for their convenience as their defence; and that I had such and such particular persons with me, as well to increase and recruit their number, as by the particular necessary employments which they were bred to, being artificers, to assist them in those things in which at present they were in want.

They were all together when I talked thus to them; and before I delivered to them the stores I had brought, I asked them, one by one, if they had entirely forgot and buried the first animosities that had been among them, and would shake hands with one another, and engage in a strict friendship and union of interest, that so there might be no more misunderstandings and jealousies.

Will Atkins, with abundance of frankness and good humour, said they had met with affliction enough to make them all sober, and enemies enough to make them all friends; that, for his part, he would live and die with them, and was so far from designing anything against the Spaniards, that he owned they had done nothing to him but what his own mad humour made necessary, and what he would have done, and perhaps worse, in their case; and that he would ask them pardon, if I desired it, for the foolish and brutish things he had done to them, and was very willing and desirous of living in terms of entire friendship and union with them, and would do anything that lay in his power to convince them of it; and as for going to England, he cared not if he did not go thither these twenty years.

The Spaniards said they had, indeed, at first disarmed and excluded Will Atkins and his two countrymen for their ill conduct, as they had let me know, and they appealed to me for the necessity they were under to do so; but that Will Atkins had behaved himself so bravely in the great fight they had with the savages, and on several occasions since, and had showed himself so faithful to, and concerned for, the general interest of them all, that they had forgotten all that was past, and thought he merited as much to be trusted with arms and supplied with necessaries as any of them; that they had testified their satisfaction in him by committing the command to him next to the governor himself; and as they had entire confidence in him and all his countrymen, so they acknowledged they had merited that confidence by all the methods that honest men could merit to be valued and trusted; and they most heartily embraced the occasion of giving me this assurance, that they would never have any interest separate from one another.

Upon these frank and open declarations of friendship, we appointed the next day to dine all together; and, indeed, we made a splendid feast. I caused the ship's cook and his mate to come on shore and dress our dinner, and the old cook's mate we had on shore assisted. We brought on shore six pieces of good beef and four pieces of pork, out of the ship's provisions, with our punch-bowl and materials to fill it; and in particular I gave them ten bottles of French claret, and ten bottles of English beer; things that neither the Spaniards nor the English had tasted for many years, and which it may be supposed they were very glad of. The Spaniards added to our feast five whole kids, which the cooks roasted; and three of them were sent, covered up close, on board the ship to the seamen, that they might feast on fresh meat from on shore, as we did with their salt meat from on board.

After this feast, at which we were very innocently merry, I brought my cargo of goods; wherein, that there might be no dispute about dividing, I showed them that there was a sufficiency for them all, desiring that they might all take an equal quantity, when made up, of the goods that were for wearing. As, first, I distributed linen sufficient to make every one of them four shirts, and, at the Spaniard's request, afterwards made them up six; these were exceeding comfortable to them, having been what they had long since forgot the use of, or what it was to wear them. I allotted the thin English stuffs, which I mentioned before, to make every one a light coat, like a frock, which I judged fittest for the heat of the season, cool and loose; and ordered that whenever they decayed, they should make more, as they thought fit; the like for pumps, shoes, stockings, hats, &c. I cannot express what pleasure sat upon the countenances of all these poor men when they saw the care I had taken of them, and how well I had furnished them. They told me I was a father to them; and that having such a correspondent as I was in so remote a part of the world, it would make them forget that they were left in a desolate place; and they all voluntarily engaged to me not to leave the place without my consent.

Then I presented to them the people I had brought with me, particularly the tailor, the smith, and the two carpenters, all of them most necessary people; but, above all, my general artificer, than whom they could not name anything that was more useful to them; and the tailor, to show his concern for them, went to work immediately, and, with my leave, made them every one a shirt, the first thing he did; and, what was still more, he taught the women not only how to sew and stitch, and use the needle, but made them assist to make the shirts for their husbands, and for all the rest. As to the carpenters, I scarce need mention how useful they were; for they took to pieces all my clumsy, unhandy things, and made clever convenient tables, stools, bedsteads, cupboards, lockers, shelves, and everything they wanted of that kind. But to let them see how nature made artificers at first, I carried the carpenters to see Will Atkins' basket-house, as I called it; and they both owned they never saw an instance of such natural ingenuity before, nor anything so regular and so handily built, at least of its kind; and one of them, when he saw it, after musing a good while, turning about to me, "I am sure," says he, "that man has no need of us; you need do nothing but give him tools."

Then I brought them out all my store of tools, and gave every man a digging-spade, a shovel, and a rake, for we had no barrows or ploughs; and to every separate place a pickaxe, a crow, a broad axe, and a saw; always appointing, that as often as any were broken or worn out, they should be supplied without grudging out of the general stores that I left behind. Nails, staples, hinges, hammers, chisels, knives, scissors, and all sorts of ironwork, they had without reserve, as they required; for no man would take more than he wanted, and he must be a fool that would waste or spoil them on any account whatever; and for the use of the smith I left two tons of unwrought iron for a supply.

My magazine of powder and arms which I brought them was such, even to profusion, that they could not but rejoice at them; for now they could march as I used to do, with a musket upon each shoulder, if there was occasion; and were able to fight a thousand savages, if they had but some little advantages of situation, which also they could not miss, if they had occasion.

I carried on shore with me the young man whose mother was starved to death, and the maid also; she was a sober, well-educated, religious young woman, and behaved so inoffensively that every one gave her a good word; she had, indeed, an unhappy life with us, there being no woman in the ship but herself, but she bore it with patience. After a while, seeing things so well ordered, and in so fine a way of thriving upon my island, and considering that they had neither business nor acquaintance in the East Indies, or reason for taking so long a voyage, both of them came to me and desired I would give them leave to remain on the island, and be entered among my family, as they called it. I agreed to this readily; and they had a little plot of ground allotted to them, where they had three tents or houses set up, surrounded with a basket-work, palisadoed like Atkins's, adjoining to his plantation.

Their tents were contrived so that they had each of them a room apart to lodge in, and a middle tent like a great storehouse to lay their goods in, and to eat and to drink in. And now the other two Englishmen removed their habitation to the same place; and so the island was divided into three colonies, and no more — viz. the Spaniards, with old Friday and the first servants, at my habitation under the hill, which was, in a word, the capital city, and where they had so enlarged and extended their works, as well under as on the outside of the hill, that they lived, though perfectly concealed, yet full at large. Never was there such a little city in a wood, and so hid, in any part of the world; for I verify believe that a thousand men might have ranged the island a month, and, if they had not known there was such a thing, and looked on purpose for it, they would not have found it. Indeed the trees stood so thick and so close, and grew so fast woven one into another, that nothing but cutting them down first could discover the place, except the only two narrow entrances where they went in and out could be found, which was not very easy; one of them was close down at the water's edge, on the side of the creek, and it was afterwards above two hundred yards to the place; and the other was up a ladder at twice, as I have already described it; and they had also a large wood, thickly planted, on the top of the hill, containing above an acre, which grew apace, and concealed the place from all discovery there, with only one narrow place between two trees, not easily to be discovered, to enter on that side.

The other colony was that of Will Atkins, where there were four families of Englishmen, I mean those I had left there, with their wives and children; three savages that were slaves, the widow and children of the Englishman that was killed, the young man and the maid, and, by the way, we made a wife of her before we went away. There were besides the two carpenters and the tailor, whom I brought with me for them: also the smith, who was a very necessary man to them, especially as a gunsmith, to take care of their arms; and my other man, whom I called Jack-of-all-trades, who was in himself as good almost as twenty men; for he was not only a very ingenious fellow, but a very merry fellow, and before I went away we married him to the honest maid that came with the youth in the ship I mentioned before.

And now I speak of marrying, it brings me naturally to say something of the French ecclesiastic that I had brought with me out of the ship's crew whom I took up at sea. It is true this man was a Roman, and perhaps it may give offence to some hereafter if I leave anything extraordinary upon record of a man whom, before I begin, I must (to set him out in just colours) represent in terms very much to his disadvantage, in the account of Protestants; as, first, that he was a Papist; secondly, a Popish priest; and thirdly, a French Popish priest. But justice demands of me to give him a due character; and I must say, he was a grave, sober, pious, and most religious person; exact in his life, extensive in his charity, and exemplary in almost everything he did. What then can any one say against being very sensible of the value of such a man, notwithstanding his profession? though it may be my opinion perhaps, as well as the opinion of others who shall read this, that he was mistaken.

The first hour that I began to converse with him after he had agreed to go with me to the East Indies, I found reason to delight exceedingly in his conversation; and he first began with me about religion in the most obliging manner imaginable. "Sir," says he, "you have not only under God" (and at that he crossed his breast) "saved my life, but you have admitted me to go this voyage in your ship, and by your obliging civility have taken me into your family, giving me an opportunity of free conversation. Now, sir, you see by my habit what my profession is, and I guess by your nation what yours is; I may think it is my duty, and doubtless it is so, to use my utmost endeavours, on all occasions, to bring all the souls I can to the knowledge of the truth, and to embrace the Catholic doctrine; but as I am here under your permission, and in your family, I am bound, in justice to your kindness as well as in decency and good manners, to be under your government; and therefore I shall not, without your leave, enter into any debate on the points of religion in which we may not agree, further than you shall give me leave."

I told him his carriage was so modest that I could not but acknowledge it; that it was true we were such people as they call heretics, but that he was not the first Catholic I had conversed with without falling into inconveniences, or carrying the questions to any height in debate; that he should not find himself the worse used for being of a different opinion from us, and if we did not converse without any dislike on either side, it should be his fault, not ours.

He replied that he thought all our conversation might be easily separated from disputes; that it was not his business to cap principles with every man he conversed with; and that he rather desired me to converse with him as a gentleman than as a religionist; and that, if I would give him leave at any time to discourse upon religious subjects, he would readily comply with it, and that he did not doubt but I would

332

allow him also to defend his own opinions as well as he could; but that without my leave he would not break in upon me with any such thing. He told me further, that he would not cease to do all that became him, in his office as a priest, as well as a private Christian, to procure the good of the ship, and the safety of all that was in her; and though, perhaps, we would not join with him, and he could not pray with us, he hoped he might pray for us, which he would do upon all occasions. In this manner we conversed; and as he was of the most obliging, gentlemanlike behaviour, so he was, if I may be allowed to say so, a man of good sense, and, as I believe, of great learning.

He gave me a most diverting account of his life, and of the many extraordinary events of it; of many adventures which had befallen him in the few years that he had been abroad in the world; and particularly, it was very remarkable, that in the voyage he was now engaged in he had had the misfortune to be five times shipped and unshipped, and never to go to the place whither any of the ships he was in were at first designed. That his first intent was to have gone to Martinico, and that he went on board a ship bound thither at St. Malo; but being forced into Lisbon by bad weather, the ship received some damage by running aground in the mouth of the river Tagus, and was obliged to unload her cargo there; but finding a Portuguese ship there bound for the Madeiras, and ready to sail, and supposing he should meet with a ship there bound to Martinico, he went on board, in order to sail to the Madeiras; but the master of the Portuguese ship being but an indifferent mariner, had been out of his reckoning, and they drove to Fayal; where, however, he happened to find a very good market for his cargo, which was corn, and therefore resolved not to go to the Madeiras, but to load salt at the Isle of May, and to go away to Newfoundland. He had no remedy in this exigency but to go with the ship, and had a pretty good voyage as far as the Banks (so they call the place where they catch the fish), where, meeting with a French ship bound from France to Quebec, and from thence to Martinico, to carry provisions, he thought he should have an opportunity to complete his first design, but when he came to Quebec, the master of the ship died, and the vessel proceeded no further; so the next voyage he shipped himself for France, in the ship that was burned when we took them up at sea, and then shipped with us for the East Indies, as I have already said. Thus he had been disappointed in five voyages; all, as I may call it, in one voyage, besides what I shall have occasion to mention further of him.

But I shall not make digression into other men's stories which have no relation to my own; so I return to what concerns our affair in the island. He came to me one morning (for he lodged among us all the while we were upon the island), and it happened to be just when I was going to visit the Englishmen's colony, at the furthest part of the island; I say, he came to me, and told me, with a very grave countenance, that he had for two or three days desired an opportunity of some discourse with me, which he hoped would not be displeasing to me, because he thought it might in some measure correspond with my general design, which was the prosperity of my new colony, and perhaps might put it, at least more than he yet thought it was, in the way of God's blessing.

I looked a little surprised at the last of his discourse, and turning a little short, "How, sir," said I, "can it be said that we are not in the way of God's blessing, after such visible assistances and deliverances as we have seen here, and of which I have given you a large account?" "If you had pleased, sir," said he, with a world of modesty, and yet great readiness, "to have heard me, you would have found no room to have been displeased, much less to think so hard of me, that I should suggest that you have not had wonderful assistances and deliverances; and I hope, on your behalf, that you are in the way of God's blessing, and your design is exceeding good, and will prosper. But, sir, though it were more so than is even possible to you, yet there may be some among you that are not equally right in their actions: and you know that in the story of the children of Israel, one Achan in the camp removed God's blessing from them, and turned His hand so against them, that six-and-thirty of them, though not concerned in the crime, were the objects of divine vengeance, and bore the weight of that punishment."

I was sensibly touched with this discourse, and told him his inference was so just, and the whole design seemed so sincere, and was really so religious in its own nature, that I was very sorry I had interrupted him, and begged him to go on; and, in the meantime, because it seemed that what we had both to say might take up some time, I told him I was going to the Englishmen's plantations, and asked him to go with me, and we might discourse of it by the way. He told me he would the more willingly wait on me thither, because there partly the thing was acted which he desired to speak to me about; so we walked on, and I pressed him to be free and plain with me in what he had to say.

"Why, then, sir," said he, "be pleased to give me leave to lay down a few propositions, as the foundation of what I have to say, that we may not differ in the general principles, though we may be of some differing opinions in the practice of particulars. First, sir, though we differ in some of the doctrinal articles of religion (and it is very unhappy it is so, especially in the case before us, as I shall show afterwards), yet there are some general principles in which we both agree — that there is a God; and that this God having given us some stated general rules for our service and obedience, we ought not willingly and knowingly to offend Him, either by neglecting to do what He has commanded, or by doing what He has expressly forbidden. And let our different religions be what they will, this general principle is readily owned by us all, that the blessing of God does not ordinarily follow presumptuous sinning against His command; and every good Christian will be affectionately concerned to prevent any that are under his care living in a total neglect of God and His commands. It is not your men being Protestants, whatever my opinion may be of such, that discharges me from being concerned for their souls, and from endeavouring, if it lies before me, that they should live in as little distance from enmity with their Maker as possible, especially if you give me leave to meddle so far in your circuit."

I could not yet imagine what he aimed at, and told him I granted all he had said, and thanked him that he would so far concern himself for us: and begged he would explain the particulars of what he had observed, that like Joshua, to take his own parable, I might put away the accursed thing from us.

"Why, then, sir," says he, "I will take the liberty you give me; and there are three things, which, if I am right, must stand in the way of God's blessing upon your endeavours here, and which I should rejoice, for your sake and their own, to see removed. And, sir, I promise myself that you will fully agree with me in them all, as soon as I name them; especially because I shall convince you, that every one of them may, with great ease, and very much to your satisfaction, be remedied. First, sir," says he, "you have here four Englishmen, who have fetched women from among the savages, and have taken them as their wives, and have had many children by them all, and yet are not married to them after any stated legal manner, as the laws of God and man require. To this, sir, I know, you will object that there was no clergyman or priest of any kind to perform the ceremony; nor any pen and ink, or paper, to write down a contract of marriage, and have it signed between them. And I know also, sir, what the Spaniard governor has told you, I mean of the agreement that he obliged them to make when they took those women, viz. that they should choose them out by consent, and keep separately to them; which, by the way, is nothing of a marriage, no agreement with the women as wives, but only an agreement among themselves, to keep them from quarrelling. But, sir, the essence of the sacrament of matrimony" (so he called it, being a Roman) "consists not only in the mutual consent of the parties to take one another as man and wife, but in the formal and legal obligation that there is in the contract to compel the man and woman, at all times, to own and acknowledge each other; obliging the man to abstain from all other women, to engage in no other contract while these subsist; and, on all occasions, as ability allows, to provide honestly for them and their children; and to oblige the women to the same or like conditions, on their side. Now, sir," says he, "these men may, when they please, or when occasion presents, abandon these women, disown their children, leave them to perish, and take other women, and marry them while these are living;" and here he added, with some warmth, "How, sir, is God honoured in this unlawful liberty? And how shall a blessing succeed your endeavours in this place, however good in themselves, and however sincere in your design, while these men, who at present are your subjects, under your absolute government and dominion, are allowed by you to live in open adultery?"

I confess I was struck with the thing itself, but much more with the convincing arguments he supported it with; but I thought to have got off my young priest by telling him that all that part was done when I was not there: and that they had lived so many years with them now, that if it was adultery, it was past remedy; nothing could be done in it now.

"Sir," says he, "asking your pardon for such freedom, you are right in this, that, it being done in your absence, you could not be charged with that part of the crime; but, I beseech you, flatter not yourself that you are not, therefore, under an obligation to do your utmost now to put an end to it. You should legally and effectually marry them; and as, sir, my way of marrying may not be easy to reconcile them to, though it will be effectual, even by your own laws, so your way may be as well before God, and as valid among men. I mean by a written contract signed by both man and woman, and by all the witnesses present, which all the laws of Europe would decree to be valid."

336

I was amazed to see so much true piety, and so much sincerity of zeal, besides the unusual impartiality in his discourse as to his own party or church, and such true warmth for preserving people that he had no knowledge of or relation to from transgressing the laws of God. But recollecting what he had said of marrying them by a written contract, which I knew he would stand to, I returned it back upon him, and told him I granted all that he had said to be just, and on his part very kind; that I would discourse with the men upon the point now, when I came to them; and I knew no reason why they should scruple to let him marry them all, which I knew well enough would be granted to be as authentic and valid in England as if they were married by one of our own clergymen.

I then pressed him to tell me what was the second complaint which he had to make, acknowledging that I was very much his debtor for the first, and thanking him heartily for it. He told me he would use the same freedom and plainness in the second, and hoped I would take it as well; and this was, that notwithstanding these English subjects of mine, as he called them, had lived with these women almost seven years, had taught them to speak English, and even to read it, and that they were, as he perceived, women of tolerable understanding, and capable of instruction, yet they had not, to this hour, taught them anything of the Christian religion — no, not so much as to know there was a God, or a worship, or in what manner God was to be served, or that their own idolatry, and worshipping they knew not whom, was false and absurd. This he said was an unaccountable neglect, and what God would certainly call them to account for, and perhaps at last take the work out of their hands. He spoke this very affectionately and warmly.

"I am persuaded," says he, "had those men lived in the savage country whence their wives came, the savages would have taken more pains to have brought them to be idolaters, and to worship the devil, than any of these men, so far as I can see, have taken with them to teach the knowledge of the true God. Now, sir," said he, "though I do not acknowledge your religion, or you mine, yet we would be glad to see the devil's servants and the subjects of his kingdom taught to know religion; and that they might, at least, hear of God and a Redeemer, and the resurrection, and of a future state — things which we all believe; that they might, at least, be so much nearer coming into the bosom of the true Church than they are now in the public profession of idolatry and devil-worship."

I could hold no longer: I took him in my arms and embraced him eagerly. "How far," said I to him, "have I been from understanding the most essential part of a Christian, viz. to love the interest of the Christian Church, and the good of other men's souls! I scarce have known what belongs to the being a Christian." — "Oh, sir! do not say so," replied he; "this thing is not your fault." — "No," said I; "but why did I never lay it to heart as well as you?" — "It is not too late yet," said he; "be not too forward to condemn yourself." — "But what can be done now?" said I: "you see I am going away." — "Will you give me leave to talk with these poor men about it?" — "Yes, with all my heart," said I: "and oblige them to give heed to what you say too." — "As to that," said he, "we must leave them to the mercy of Christ; but it is your business to assist them, encourage them, and instruct them; and if you give me leave, and God His blessing, I do not doubt but the poor ignorant souls shall be brought home to the great circle of Christianity, if not into the particular faith we all embrace, and that even while you stay here." Upon this I said, "I shall not only give you leave, but give you a thousand thanks for it."

I now pressed him for the third article in which we were to blame. "Why, really," says he, "it is of the same nature. It is about your poor savages, who are, as I may say, your conquered subjects. It is a maxim, sir, that is or ought to be received among all Christians, of what church or pretended church so ever, that the Christian knowledge ought to be propagated by all possible means and on all possible occasions. It is on this principle that our Church sends missionaries into Persia, India, and China; and that our clergy, even of the superior sort, willingly engage in the most hazardous voyages, and the most dangerous residence amongst murderers and barbarians, to teach them the knowledge of the true God, and to bring them over to embrace the Christian faith. Now, sir, you have such an opportunity here to have six or seven and thirty poor savages brought over from a state of idolatry to the knowledge of God, their Maker and Redeemer, that I wonder how you can pass such an occasion of doing good, which is really worth the expense of a man's whole life."

I was now struck dumb indeed, and had not one word to say. I had here the spirit of true Christian zeal for God and religion before me. As for me, I had not so much as entertained a thought of this in my heart before, and I believe I should not have thought of it; for I looked upon these savages as slaves, and people whom, had we not had any work for them to do, we would have used as such, or would have been glad to have transported them to any part of the world; for our business was to get rid of them, and we would all have been satisfied if they had been sent to any country, so they had never seen their own. I was confounded at his discourse, and knew not what answer to make him.

He looked earnestly at me, seeing my confusion. "Sir," says he, "I shall be very sorry if what I have said gives you any offence." — "No, no," said I, "I am offended with nobody but myself; but I am perfectly confounded, not only to think that I should never take any notice of this before, but with reflecting what notice I am able to take of it now. You know, sir," said I, "what circumstances I am in; I am bound to the East Indies in a ship freighted by merchants, and to whom it would be an insufferable piece of injustice to detain their ship here, the men lying all this while at victuals and wages on the owners' account. It is true, I agreed to be allowed twelve days here, and if I stay more, I must pay three pounds sterling *per diem* demurrage; nor can I stay upon demurrage above eight days more, and I have been here thirteen already; so that I am perfectly unable to engage in this work unless I would suffer myself to be left behind here again; in which case, if this single ship should miscarry in any part of her voyage, I should be just in the same condition that I was left in here at first, and from which I have been so wonderfully delivered." He owned the case was very hard upon me as to my voyage; but laid it home upon my conscience whether the blessing of saving thirty-seven souls was not worth venturing all I had in the world for. I was not so sensible of that as he was. I replied to him thus: "Why, sir, it is a valuable thing, indeed, to be an instrument in God's hand to convert thirty-seven heathens to the knowledge of Christ: but as you are an ecclesiastic, and are given over to the work, so it seems so naturally to fall in the way of your profession; how is it, then, that you do not rather offer yourself to undertake it than to press me to do it?"

Upon this he faced about just before me, as he walked along, and putting me to a full stop, made me a very low bow. "I most heartily thank God and you, sir," said he, "for giving me so evident a call to so blessed a work; and if you think yourself discharged from it, and desire me to undertake it, I will most readily do it, and think it a happy reward for all the hazards and difficulties of such a broken, disappointed voyage as I have met with, that I am dropped at last into so glorious a work."

I discovered a kind of rapture in his face while he spoke this to me; his eyes sparkled like fire; his face glowed, and his colour came and went; in a word, he was fired with the joy of being embarked in such a work. I paused a considerable while before I could tell what to say to him; for I was really surprised to find a man of such sincerity, and who seemed possessed of a zeal beyond the ordinary rate of men. But after I had considered it a while, I asked him seriously if he was in earnest, and that he would venture, on the single consideration of an attempt to convert those poor people, to be locked up in an unplanted island for perhaps his life, and at last might not know whether he should be able to do them good or not? He turned short upon me, and asked me what I called a venture? "Pray, sir," said he, "what do you think I consented to go in your ship to the East Indies for?" — "ay," said I, "that I know not, unless it was to preach to the Indians." — "Doubtless it was," said he; "and do you think, if I can convert these thirty-seven men to the faith of Jesus Christ, it is not worth my time, though I should never be fetched off the island again? — nay, is it not infinitely of more worth to save so many souls than my life is, or the life of twenty more of the same profession? Yes, sir," says he, "I would give God thanks all my days if I could be made the happy instrument of saving the souls of those poor men, though I were never to get my foot off this island or see my native country any more. But since you will honour me with putting me into this work, for which I will pray for you all the days of my life, I have one humble petition to you besides." — "What is that?" said I. — "Why," says he, "it is, that you will leave your man Friday with me, to be my interpreter to them, and to assist me; for without some help I cannot speak to them, or they to me."

I was sensibly touched at his requesting Friday, because I could not think of parting with him, and that for many reasons: he had been the companion of my travels; he was not only faithful to me, but sincerely affectionate to the last degree; and I had resolved to do something considerable for him if he out-lived me, as it was probable he would. Then I knew that, as I had bred Friday up to be a Protestant, it would quite confound him to bring him to embrace another religion; and he would never, while his eyes were open, believe that his old master was a heretic, and would be damned; and this might in the end ruin the poor fellow's principles, and so turn him back again to his first idolatry. However, a sudden thought relieved me in this strait, and it was this: I told him I could not say that I was willing to part with Friday on any account whatever, though a work that to him was of

340

more value than his life ought to be of much more value than the keeping or parting with a servant. On the other hand, I was persuaded that Friday would by no means agree to part with me; and I could not force him to it without his consent, without manifest injustice; because I had promised I would never send him away, and he had promised and engaged that he would never leave me, unless I sent him away.

He seemed very much concerned at it, for he had no rational access to these poor people, seeing he did not understand one word of their language, nor they one of his. To remove this difficulty, I told him Friday's father had learned Spanish, which I found he also understood, and he should serve him as an interpreter. So he was much better satisfied, and nothing could persuade him but he would stay and endeavour to convert them; but Providence gave another very happy turn to all this.

I come back now to the first part of his objections. When we came to the Englishmen, I sent for them all together, and after some account given them of what I had done for them, viz. what necessary things I had provided for them, and how they were distributed, which they were very sensible of, and very thankful for, I began to talk to them of the scandalous life they led, and gave them a full account of the notice the clergyman had taken of it; and arguing how unchristian and irreligious a life it was, I first asked them if they were married men or bachelors? They soon explained their condition to me, and showed that two of them were widowers, and the other three were single men, or bachelors. I asked them with what conscience they could take these women, and call them their wives, and have so many children by them, and not be lawfully married to them? They all gave me the answer I expected, viz. that there was nobody to marry them; that they agreed before the governor to keep them as their wives, and to maintain them and own them as their wives; and they thought, as things stood with them, they were as legally married as if they had been married by a parson and with all the formalities in the world.

I told them that no doubt they were married in the sight of God, and were bound in conscience to keep them as their wives; but that the laws of men being otherwise, they might desert the poor women and children hereafter; and that their wives, being poor desolate women, friendless and moneyless, would have no way to help themselves. I therefore told them that unless I was assured of their honest intent, I could do nothing for them, but would take care that what I did should be for the women and children without them; and that, unless they would give me some assurances that they would marry the women, I could not think it was convenient they should continue together as man and wife; for that it was both scandalous to men and offensive to God, who they could not think would bless them if they went on thus.

All this went on as I expected; and they told me, especially Will Atkins, who now seemed to speak for the rest, that they loved their wives as well as if they had been born in their own native country, and would not leave them on any account whatever; and they did verily believe that their wives were as virtuous and as modest, and did, to the utmost of their skill, as much for them and for their children, as any woman could possibly do: and they would not part with them on any account. Will Atkins, for his own particular, added that if any man would take him away, and offer to carry him home to England, and make him captain of the best man-of-war in the navy, he would not go with him if he might not carry his wife and children with him; and if there was a clergyman in the ship, he would be married to her now with all his heart.

This was just as I would have it. The priest was not with me at that moment, but he was not far off; so to try him further, I told him I had a clergyman with me, and, if he was sincere, I would have him married next morning, and bade him consider of it, and talk with the rest. He said, as for himself, he need not consider of it at all, for he was very ready to do it, and was glad I had a minister with me, and he believed they would be all willing also. I then told him that my friend, the minister, was a Frenchman, and could not speak English, but I would act the clerk between them. He never so much as asked me whether he was a Papist or Protestant, which was, indeed, what I was afraid of. We then parted, and I went back to my clergyman, and Will Atkins went in to talk with his companions. I desired the French gentleman not to say anything to them till the business was thoroughly ripe; and I told him what answer the men had given me.

Before I went from their quarter they all came to me and told me they had been considering what I had said; that they were glad to hear I had a clergyman in my company, and they were very willing to give me the satisfaction I desired, and to be formally married as soon as I pleased; for they were far from desiring to part with their wives, and that they meant nothing but what was very honest when they chose them. So I appointed them to meet me the next morning; and, in the meantime, they should let their wives know the meaning of the marriage law; and that it was not only to prevent any scandal, but also to oblige them that they should not forsake them, whatever might happen.

The women were easily made sensible of the meaning of the thing, and were very well satisfied with it, as, indeed, they had reason to be: so they failed not to attend all together at my apartment next morning, where I brought out my clergyman; and though he had not on a minister's gown, after the manner of England, or the habit of a priest, after the manner of France, yet having a black vest something like a cassock, with a sash round it, he did not look very unlike a minister; and as for his language, I was his interpreter. But the seriousness of his behaviour to them, and the scruples he made of marrying the women, because they were not baptized and professed Christians, gave them an exceeding reverence for his person; and there was no need, after that, to inquire whether he was a clergyman or not. Indeed, I was afraid his scruples would have been carried so far as that he would not have married them at all; nay, notwithstanding all I was able to say to him, he resisted me, though modestly, yet very steadily, and at last refused absolutely to marry them, unless he had first talked with the men and the women too; and though at first I was a little backward to it, yet at last I agreed to it with a good will, perceiving the sincerity of his design.

When he came to them he let them know that I had acquainted him with their circumstances, and with the present design; that he was very willing to perform that part of his function, and marry them, as I had desired; but that before he could do it, he must take the liberty to talk with them. He told them that in the sight of all indifferent men, and in the sense of the laws of society, they had lived all this while in a state of sin; and that it was true that nothing but the consenting to marry, or effectually separating them from one another, could now put an end to it; but there was a difficulty in it, too, with respect to the laws of Christian matrimony, which he was not fully satisfied about, that of marrying one that is a professed Christian to a savage, an idolater, and a heathen — one that is not baptized; and yet that he did not see that there was time left to endeavour to persuade the women to be baptized, or to profess the name of Christ, whom they had, he doubted, heard nothing of, and without which they could not be baptized. He told them he doubted they were but indifferent Christians themselves; that they had but little knowledge of God or of His ways, and, therefore, he could not expect that they had said much to their wives on that head yet; but that unless they would promise him to use their endeavours with their wives to persuade them to become Christians, and would, as

343

well as they could, instruct them in the knowledge and belief of God that made them, and to worship Jesus Christ that redeemed them, he could not marry them; for he would have no hand in joining Christians with savages, nor was it consistent with the principles of the Christian religion, and was, indeed, expressly forbidden in God's law.

They heard all this very attentively, and I delivered it very faithfully to them from his mouth, as near his own words as I could; only sometimes adding something of my own, to convince them how just it was, and that I was of his mind; and I always very carefully distinguished between what I said from myself and what were the clergyman's words. They told me it was very true what the gentleman said, that they were very indifferent Christians themselves, and that they had never talked to their wives about religion. "Lord, sir," says Will Atkins, "how should we teach them religion? Why, we know nothing ourselves; and besides, sir," said he, "should we talk to them of God and Jesus Christ, and heaven and hell, it would make them laugh at us, and ask us what we believe ourselves. And if we should tell them that we believe all the things we speak of to them, such as of good people going to heaven, and wicked people to the devil, they would ask us where we intend to go ourselves, that believe all this, and are such wicked fellows as we indeed are? Why, sir; 'tis enough to give them a surfeit of religion at first hearing; folks must have some religion themselves before they begin to teach other people." — "Will Atkins," said I to him, "though I am afraid that what you say has too much truth in it, yet can you not tell your wife she is in the wrong; that there is a God and a religion better than her own; that her gods are idols; that they can neither hear nor speak; that there is a great Being that made all things, and that can destroy all that He has made; that He rewards the good and punishes the bad; and that we are to be judged by Him at last for all we do here? You are not so ignorant but even nature itself will teach you that all this is true; and I am satisfied you know it all to be true, and believe it yourself." — "That is true, sir," said Atkins; "but with what face can I say anything to my wife of all this, when she will tell me immediately it cannot be true?" — "Not true!" said I; "what do you mean by that?" — "Why, sir," said he, "she will tell me it cannot be true that this God I shall tell her of can be just, or can punish or reward, since I am not punished and sent to the devil, that have been such a wicked creature as she knows I have been, even to her, and to everybody else; and that I should be suffered to live, that have been always acting so contrary to what I must tell her is good, and to what I

344

ought to have done." — "Why, truly, Atkins," said I, "I am afraid thou speakest too much truth;" and with that I informed the clergyman of what Atkins had said, for he was impatient to know. "Oh," said the priest, "tell him there is one thing will make him the best minister in the world to his wife, and that is repentance; for none teach repentance like true penitents. He wants nothing but to repent, and then he will be so much the better qualified to instruct his wife; he will then be able to tell her that there is not only a God, and that He is the just rewarder of good and evil, but that He is a merciful Being, and with infinite goodness and long-suffering forbears to punish those that offend; waiting to be gracious, and willing not the death of a sinner, but rather that he should return and live; and even reserves damnation to the general day of retribution; that it is a clear evidence of God and of a future state that righteous men receive not their reward, or wicked men their punishment, till they come into another world; and this will lead him to teach his wife the doctrine of the resurrection and of the last judgment. Let him but repent himself, he will be an excellent preacher of repentance to his wife."

I repeated all this to Atkins, who looked very serious all the while, and, as we could easily perceive, was more than ordinarily affected with it; when being eager, and hardly suffering me to make an end, "I know all this, master," says he, "and a great deal more; but I have not the impudence to talk thus to my wife, when God and my conscience know, and my wife will be an undeniable evidence against me, that I have lived as if I had never heard of a God or future state, or anything about it; and to talk of my repenting, alas!" (and with that he fetched a deep sigh, and I could see that the tears stood in his eyes) "'tis past all that with me." — "Past it, Atkins?" said I: "what dost thou mean by that?" — "I know well enough what I mean," says he; "I mean 'tis too late, and that is too true."

I told the clergyman, word for word, what he said, and this affectionate man could not refrain from tears; but, recovering himself, said to me, "Ask him but one question. Is he easy that it is too late; or is he troubled, and wishes it were not so?" I put the question fairly to Atkins; and he answered with a great deal of passion, "How could any man be easy in a condition that must certainly end in eternal destruction? that he was far from being easy; but that, on the contrary, he believed it would one time or other ruin him." — "What do you mean by that?" said I. — "Why," he said, "he believed he should one time or other cut his throat, to put an end to the terror of it."

345

The clergyman shook his head, with great concern in his face, when I told him all this; but turning quick to me upon it, says, "If that be his case, we may assure him it is not too late; Christ will give him repentance. But pray," says he, "explain this to him: that as no man is saved but by Christ, and the merit of His passion procuring divine mercy for him, how can it be too late for any man to receive mercy? Does he think he is able to sin beyond the power or reach of divine mercy? Pray tell him there may be a time when provoked mercy will no longer strive, and when God may refuse to hear, but that it is never too late for men to ask mercy; and we, that are Christ's servants, are commanded to preach mercy at all times, in the name of Jesus Christ, to all those that sincerely repent: so that it is never too late to repent."

I told Atkins all this, and he heard me with great earnestness; but it seemed as if he turned off the discourse to the rest, for he said to me he would go and have some talk with his wife; so he went out a while, and we talked to the rest. I perceived they were all stupidly ignorant as to matters of religion, as much as I was when I went rambling away from my father; yet there were none of them backward to hear what had been said; and all of them seriously promised that they would talk with their wives about it, and do their endeavours to persuade them to turn Christians.

The clergyman smiled upon me when I reported what answer they gave, but said nothing a good while; but at last, shaking his head, "We that are Christ's servants," says he, "can go no further than to exhort and instruct: and when men comply, submit to the reproof, and promise what we ask, 'tis all we can do; we are bound to accept their good words; but believe me, sir," said he, "whatever you may have known of the life of that man you call Will Atkin's, I believe he is the only sincere convert among them: I will not despair of the rest; but that man is apparently struck with the sense of his past life, and I doubt not, when he comes to talk of religion to his wife, he will talk himself effectually into it: for attempting to teach others is sometimes the best way of teaching ourselves. If that poor Atkins begins but once to talk seriously of Jesus Christ to his wife, he will assuredly talk himself into a thorough convert, make himself a penitent, and who knows what may follow."

Upon this discourse, however, and their promising, as above, to endeavour to persuade their wives to embrace Christianity, he married the two other couple; but Will Atkins and his wife were not yet come in. After this, my clergyman, waiting a while, was curious to know

346

where Atkins was gone, and turning to me, said, "I entreat you, sir, let us walk out of your labyrinth here and look; I daresay we shall find this poor man somewhere or other talking seriously to his wife, and teaching her already something of religion." I began to be of the same mind; so we went out together, and I carried him a way which none knew but myself, and where the trees were so very thick that it was not easy to see through the thicket of leaves, and far harder to see in than to see out: when, coming to the edge of the wood, I saw Atkins and his tawny wife sitting under the shade of a bush, very eager in discourse: I stopped short till my clergyman came up to me, and then having showed him where they were, we stood and looked very steadily at them a good while. We observed him very earnest with her, pointing up to the sun, and to every quarter of the heavens, and then down to the earth, then out to the sea, then to himself, then to her, to the woods, to the trees. "Now," says the clergyman, "you see my words are made good, the man preaches to her; mark him now, he is telling her that our God has made him, her, and the heavens, the earth, the sea, the woods, the trees, &c." — "I believe he is," said I. Immediately we perceived Will Atkins start upon his feet, fall down on his knees, and lift up both his hands. We supposed he said something, but we could not hear him; it was too far for that. He did not continue kneeling half a minute, but comes and sits down again by his wife, and talks to her again; we perceived then the woman very attentive, but whether she said anything to him we could not tell. While the poor fellow was upon his knees I could see the tears run plentifully down my clergyman's cheeks, and I could hardly forbear myself; but it was a great affliction to us both that we were not near enough to hear anything that passed between them. Well, however, we could come no nearer for fear of disturbing them: so we resolved to see an end of this piece of still conversation, and it spoke loud enough to us without the help of voice. He sat down again, as I have said, close by her, and talked again earnestly to her, and two or three times we could see him embrace her most passionately; another time we saw him take out his handkerchief and wipe her eyes, and then kiss her again with a kind of transport very unusual; and after several of these things, we saw him on a sudden jump up again, and lend her his hand to help her up, when immediately leading her by the hand a step or two, they both kneeled down together, and continued so about two minutes.

My friend could bear it no longer, but cries out aloud, "St. Paul! St. Paul! behold he prayeth." I was afraid Atkins would hear him, therefore I entreated him to withhold himself a while, that we might see an end of the scene, which to me, I must confess, was the most affecting that ever I saw in my life. Well, he strove with himself for a while, but was in such raptures to think that the poor heathen woman was become a Christian, that he was not able to contain himself; he wept several times, then throwing up his hands and crossing his breast, said over several things ejaculatory, and by the way of giving God thanks for so miraculous a testimony of the success of our endeavours. Some he spoke softly, and I could not well hear others; some things he said in Latin, some in French; then two or three times the tears would interrupt him, that he could not speak at all; but I begged that he would contain himself, and let us more narrowly and fully observe what was before us, which he did for a time, the scene not being near ended yet; for after the poor man and his wife were risen again from their knees, we observed he stood talking still eagerly to her, and we observed her motion, that she was greatly affected with what he said, by her frequently lifting up her hands, laying her hand to her breast, and such other postures as express the greatest seriousness and attention; this continued about half a quarter of an hour, and then they walked away, so we could see no more of them in that situation.

I took this interval to say to the clergyman, first, that I was glad to see the particulars we had both been witnesses to; that, though I was hard enough of belief in such cases, yet that I began to think it was all very sincere here, both in the man and his wife, however ignorant they might both be, and I hoped such a beginning would yet have a more happy end. "But, my friend," added I, "will you give me leave to start one difficulty here? I cannot tell how to object the least thing against that affectionate concern which you show for the turning of the poor people from their paganism to the Christian religion; but how does this comfort you, while these people are, in your account, out of the pale of the Catholic Church, without which you believe there is no salvation? so that you esteem these but heretics, as effectually lost as the pagans themselves."

To this he answered, with abundance of candour, thus: "Sir, I am a Catholic of the Roman Church, and a priest of the order of St. Benedict, and I embrace all the principles of the Roman faith; but yet, if you will believe me, and that I do not speak in compliment to you, or in respect to my circumstances and your civilities; I say nevertheless, I do not look upon you, who call yourselves reformed, without some charity. I dare not say (though I know it is our opinion in general) that you cannot be saved; I will by no means limit the mercy of Christ so far as think that He cannot receive you into the bosom of His Church, in a manner to us unperceivable; and I hope you have the same charity for us: I pray daily for you being all restored to Christ's Church, by whatsoever method He, who is all-wise, is pleased to direct. In the meantime, surely you will allow it consists with me as a Roman to distinguish far between a Protestant and a pagan; between one that calls on Jesus Christ, though in a way which I do not think is according to the true faith, and a savage or a barbarian, that knows no God, no Christ, no Redeemer; and if you are not within the pale of the Catholic Church, we hope you are nearer being restored to it than those who know nothing of God or of His Church: and I rejoice, therefore, when I see this poor man, who you say has been a profligate, and almost a murderer kneel down and pray to Jesus Christ, as we suppose he did, though not fully enlightened; believing that God, from whom every such work proceeds, will sensibly touch his heart, and bring him to the further knowledge of that truth in His own time; and if God shall influence this poor man to convert and instruct the ignorant savage, his wife, I can never believe that he shall be cast away himself. And have I not reason, then, to rejoice, the nearer any are brought to the knowledge of Christ, though they may not be brought quite home into the bosom of the Catholic Church just at the time when I desire it, leaving it to the goodness of Christ to perfect His work in His own time, and in his own way? Certainly, I would rejoice if all the savages in America were brought, like this poor woman, to pray to God, though they were all to be Protestants at first, rather than they should continue pagans or heathens; firmly believing, that He that had bestowed the first light on them would farther illuminate them with a beam of His heavenly grace, and bring them into the pale of His Church when He should see good."

CHAPTER VII. CONVERSATION BETWIXT WILL ATKINS AND HIS WIFE

I was astonished at the sincerity and temper of this pious Papist, as much as I was oppressed by the power of his reasoning; and it presently occurred to my thoughts, that if such a temper was universal, we might be all Catholic Christians, whatever Church or particular profession we joined in; that a spirit of charity would soon work us all up into right principles; and as he thought that the like charity would make us all Catholics, so I told him I believed, had all the members of his Church the like moderation, they would soon all be Protestants. And there we left that part; for we never disputed at all. However, I talked to him another way, and taking him by the hand, "My friend," says I, "I wish all the clergy of the Romish Church were blessed with such moderation, and had an equal share of your charity. I am entirely of your opinion; but I must tell you that if you should preach such doctrine in Spain or Italy, they would put you into the Inquisition." — "It may be so," said he; "I know not what they would do in Spain or Italy; but I will not say they would be the better Christians for that severity; for I am sure there is no heresy in abounding with charity."

Well, as Will Atkins and his wife were gone, our business there was over, so we went back our own way; and when we came back, we found them waiting to be called in. Observing this, I asked my clergyman if we should discover to him that we had seen him under the bush or not; and it was his opinion we should not, but that we should talk to him first, and hear what he would say to us; so we called him in alone, nobody being in the place but ourselves, and I began by asking him some particulars about his parentage and education. He told me frankly enough that his father was a clergyman who would have taught him well, but that he, Will Atkins, despised all instruction and correction; and by his brutish conduct cut the thread of all his father's comforts and shortened his days, for that he broke his heart by the most ungrateful, unnatural return for the most affectionate treatment a father ever gave.

In what he said there seemed so much sincerity of repentance, that it painfully affected me. I could not but reflect that I, too, had shortened the life of a good, tender father by my bad conduct and obstinate self-will. I was, indeed, so surprised with what he had told me, that I thought, instead of my going about to teach and instruct him, the man was made a teacher and instructor to me in a most unexpected manner.

I laid all this before the young clergyman, who was greatly affected with it, and said to me, "Did I not say, sir, that when this man was converted he would preach to us all? I tell you, sir, if this one man be made a true penitent, there will be no need of me; he will make Christians of all in the island." — But having a little composed myself, I renewed my discourse with Will Atkins. "But, Will," said I, "how comes the sense of this matter to touch you just now?"

W.A. — Sir, you have set me about a work that has struck a dart though my very soul; I have been talking about God and religion to my wife, in order, as you directed me, to make a Christian of her, and she has preached such a sermon to me as I shall never forget while I live.

R.C. — No, no, it is not your wife has preached to you; but when you were moving religious arguments to her, conscience has flung them back upon you.

W.A. — Ay, sir, with such force as is not to be resisted.

R.C. — Pray, Will, let us know what passed between you and your wife; for I know something of it already.

W.A. — Sir, it is impossible to give you a full account of it; I am too full to hold it, and yet have no tongue to express it; but let her have said what she will, though I cannot give you an account of it, this I can tell you, that I have resolved to amend and reform my life.

R.C. — But tell us some of it: how did you begin, Will? For this has been an extraordinary case, that is certain. She has preached a sermon, indeed, if she has wrought this upon you.

W.A. — Why, I first told her the nature of our laws about marriage, and what the reasons were that men and women were obliged to enter into such compacts as it was neither in the power of one nor other to break; that otherwise, order and justice could not be maintained, and men would run from their wives, and abandon their children, mix confusedly with one another, and neither families be kept entire, nor inheritances be settled by legal descent.

R.C. — You talk like a civilian, Will. Could you make her understand what you meant by inheritance and families? They know no such things among the savages, but marry anyhow, without regard to relation, consanguinity, or family; brother and sister, nay, as I have been told, even the father and the daughter, and the son and the mother.

W.A. — I believe, sir, you are misinformed, and my wife assures me of the contrary, and that they abhor it; perhaps, for any further

351

relations, they may not be so exact as we are; but she tells me never in the near relationship you speak of.

R.C. — Well, what did she say to what you told her?

W.A. — She said she liked it very well, as it was much better than in her country.

R.C. — But did you tell her what marriage was?

W.A. — Ay, ay, there began our dialogue. I asked her if she would be married to me our way. She asked me what way that was; I told her marriage was appointed by God; and here we had a strange talk together, indeed, as ever man and wife had, I believe.

N.B. — This dialogue between Will Atkins and his wife, which I took down in writing just after he told it me, was as follows: —

Wife. — Appointed by your God! — Why, have you a God in your country?

W.A. — Yes, my dear, God is in every country.

Wife. — No your God in my country; my country have the great old Benamuckee God.

W.A. — Child, I am very unfit to show you who God is; God is in heaven and made the heaven and the earth, the sea, and all that in them is.

Wife. — No makee de earth; no you God makee all earth; no makee my country.

(Will Atkins laughed a little at her expression of God not making her country.)

Wife. — No laugh; why laugh me? This no ting to laugh.

(He was justly reproved by his wife, for she was more serious than he at first.)

W.A. — That's true, indeed; I will not laugh any more, my dear.

Wife. — Why you say you God makee all?

W.A. — Yes, child, our God made the whole world, and you, and me, and all things; for He is the only true God, and there is no God but Him. He lives for ever in heaven.

Wife. — Why you no tell me long ago?

W.A. — That's true, indeed; but I have been a wicked wretch, and have not only forgotten to acquaint thee with anything before, but have lived without God in the world myself.

Wife. — What, have you a great God in your country, you no know Him? No say O to Him? No do good ting for Him? That no possible.

W.A. — It is true; though, for all that, we live as if there was no God in heaven, or that He had no power on earth.

Wife. — But why God let you do so? Why He no makee you good live?

W.A. — It is all our own fault.

Wife. — But you say me He is great, much great, have much great power; can makee kill when He will: why He no makee kill when you no serve Him? no say O to Him? no be good mans?

W.A. — That is true, He might strike me dead; and I ought to expect it, for I have been a wicked wretch, that is true; but God is merciful, and does not deal with us as we deserve.

Wife. — But then do you not tell God thankee for that too?

W. A. — No, indeed, I have not thanked God for His mercy, any more than I have feared God from His power.

Wife. — Then you God no God; me no think, believe He be such one, great much power, strong: no makee kill you, though you make Him much angry.

W.A. — What, will my wicked life hinder you from believing in God? What a dreadful creature am I! and what a sad truth is it, that the horrid lives of Christians hinder the conversion of heathens!

Wife. — How me tink you have great much God up there (she points up to heaven), and yet no do well, no do good ting? Can He tell? Sure He no tell what you do?

W.A. — Yes, yes, He knows and sees all things; He hears us speak, sees what we do, knows what we think though we do not speak.

Wife. — What! He no hear you curse, swear, speak de great damn?

W.A. — Yes, yes, He hears it all.

Wife. — Where be then the much great power strong?

W.A. — He is merciful, that is all we can say for it; and this proves Him to be the true God; He is God, and not man, and therefore we are not consumed.

(Here Will Atkins told us he was struck with horror to think how he could tell his wife so clearly that God sees, and hears, and knows the secret thoughts of the heart, and all that we do, and yet that he had dared to do all the vile things he had done.)

Wife. — Merciful! What you call dat?

W.A. — He is our Father and Maker, and He pities and spares us.

353

Wife. — So then He never makee kill, never angry when you do wicked; then He no good Himself, or no great able.

W.A. — Yes, yes, my dear, He is infinitely good and infinitely great, and able to punish too; and sometimes, to show His justice and vengeance, He lets fly His anger to destroy sinners and make examples; many are cut off in their sins.

Wife. — But no makee kill you yet; then He tell you, maybe, that He no makee you kill: so you makee the bargain with Him, you do bad thing, He no be angry at you when He be angry at other mans.

W.A. — No, indeed, my sins are all presumptions upon His goodness; and He would be infinitely just if He destroyed me, as He has done other men.

Wife. — Well, and yet no kill, no makee you dead: what you say to Him for that? You no tell Him thankee for all that too?

W.A. — I am an unthankful, ungrateful dog, that is true.

Wife. — Why He no makee you much good better? you say He makee you.

W.A. — He made me as He made all the world: it is I have deformed myself and abused His goodness, and made myself an abominable wretch.

Wife. — I wish you makee God know me. I no makee Him angry — I no do bad wicked thing.

(Here Will Atkins said his heart sunk within him to hear a poor untaught creature desire to be taught to know God, and he such a wicked wretch, that he could not say one word to her about God, but what the reproach of his own carriage would make most irrational to her to believe; nay, that already she had told him that she could not believe in God, because he, that was so wicked, was not destroyed.)

W.A. — My dear, you mean, you wish I could teach you to know God, not God to know you; for He knows you already, and every thought in your heart.

Wife. — Why, then, He know what I say to you now: He know me wish to know Him. How shall me know who makee me?

W.A. — Poor creature, He must teach thee: I cannot teach thee. I will pray to Him to teach thee to know Him, and forgive me, that am unworthy to teach thee.

(The poor fellow was in such an agony at her desiring him to make her know God, and her wishing to know Him, that he said he fell down on his knees before her, and prayed to God to enlighten her mind with the saving knowledge of Jesus Christ, and to pardon his sins, and

354

accept of his being the unworthy instrument of instructing her in the principles of religion: after which he sat down by her again, and their dialogue went on. This was the time when we saw him kneel down and hold up his hands.)

Wife. — What you put down the knee for? What you hold up the hand for? What you say? Who you speak to? What is all that?

W.A. — My dear, I bow my knees in token of my submission to Him that made me: I said O to Him, as you call it, and as your old men do to their idol Benamuckee; that is, I prayed to Him.

Wife. — What say you O to Him for?

W.A. — I prayed to Him to open your eyes and your understanding, that you may know Him, and be accepted by Him.

Wife. — Can He do that too?

W.A. — Yes, He can: He can do all things.

Wife. — But now He hear what you say?

W.A. — Yes, He has bid us pray to Him, and promised to hear us.

Wife. — Bid you pray? When He bid you? How He bid you? What you hear Him speak?

W.A. — No, we do not hear Him speak; but He has revealed Himself many ways to us.

(Here he was at a great loss to make her understand that God has revealed Himself to us by His word, and what His word was; but at last he told it to her thus.)

W.A. — God has spoken to some good men in former days, even from heaven, by plain words; and God has inspired good men by His Spirit; and they have written all His laws down in a book.

Wife. — Me no understand that; where is book?

W.A. — Alas! my poor creature, I have not this book; but I hope I shall one time or other get it for you, and help you to read it.

(Here he embraced her with great affection, but with inexpressible grief that he had not a Bible.)

Wife. — But how you makee me know that God teachee them to write that book?

W.A. — By the same rule that we know Him to be God.

Wife. — What rule? What way you know Him?

W.A. — Because He teaches and commands nothing but what is good, righteous, and holy, and tends to make us perfectly good, as well as perfectly happy; and because He forbids and commands us to avoid all that is wicked, that is evil in itself, or evil in its consequence.

Wife. — That me would understand, that me fain see; if He teachee all good thing, He makee all good thing, He give all thing, He hear me when I say O to Him, as you do just now; He makee me good if I wish to be good; He spare me, no makee kill me, when I no be good: all this you say He do, yet He be great God; me take, think, believe Him to be great God; me say O to Him with you, my dear.

Here the poor man could forbear no longer, but raised her up, made her kneel by him, and he prayed to God aloud to instruct her in the knowledge of Himself, by His Spirit; and that by some good providence, if possible, she might, some time or other, come to have a Bible, that she might read the word of God, and be taught by it to know Him. This was the time that we saw him lift her up by the hand, and saw him kneel down by her, as above.

They had several other discourses, it seems, after this; and particularly she made him promise that, since he confessed his own life had been a wicked, abominable course of provocations against God, that he would reform it, and not make God angry any more, lest He should make him dead, as she called it, and then she would be left alone, and never be taught to know this God better; and lest he should be miserable, as he had told her wicked men would be after death.

This was a strange account, and very affecting to us both, but particularly to the young clergyman; he was, indeed, wonderfully surprised with it, but under the greatest affliction imaginable that he could not talk to her, that he could not speak English to make her understand him; and as she spoke but very broken English, he could not understand her; however, he turned himself to me, and told me that he believed that there must be more to do with this woman than to marry her. I did not understand him at first; but at length he explained himself, viz. that she ought to be baptized. I agreed with him in that part readily, and wished it to be done presently. "No, no; hold, sir," says he; "though I would have her be baptized, by all means, for I must observe that Will Atkins, her husband, has indeed brought her, in a wonderful manner, to be willing to embrace a religious life, and has given her just ideas of the being of a God; of His power, justice, and mercy: yet I desire to know of him if he has said anything to her of Jesus Christ, and of the salvation of sinners; of the nature of faith in Him, and redemption by Him; of the Holy Spirit, the resurrection, the last judgment, and the future state."

I called Will Atkins again, and asked him; but the poor fellow fell immediately into tears, and told us he had said something to her of all

356

those things, but that he was himself so wicked a creature, and his own conscience so reproached him with his horrid, ungodly life, that he trembled at the apprehensions that her knowledge of him should lessen the attention she should give to those things, and make her rather contemn religion than receive it; but he was assured, he said, that her mind was so disposed to receive due impressions of all those things, and that if I would but discourse with her, she would make it appear to my satisfaction that my labour would not be lost upon her.

Accordingly I called her in, and placing myself as interpreter between my religious priest and the woman, I entreated him to begin with her; but sure such a sermon was never preached by a Popish priest in these latter ages of the world; and as I told him, I thought he had all the zeal, all the knowledge, all the sincerity of a Christian, without the error of a Roman Catholic; and that I took him to be such a clergyman as the Roman bishops were before the Church of Rome assumed spiritual sovereignty over the consciences of men. In a word, he brought the poor woman to embrace the knowledge of Christ, and of redemption by Him, not with wonder and astonishment only, as she did the first notions of a God, but with joy and faith; with an affection, and a surprising degree of understanding, scarce to be imagined, much less to be expressed; and, at her own request, she was baptized.

When he was preparing to baptize her, I entreated him that he would perform that office with some caution, that the man might not perceive he was of the Roman Church, if possible, because of other ill consequences which might attend a difference among us in that very religion which we were instructing the other in. He told me that as he had no consecrated chapel, nor proper things for the office, I should see he would do it in a manner that I should not know by it that he was a Roman Catholic myself, if I had not known it before; and so he did; for saying only some words over to himself in Latin, which I could not understand, he poured a whole dishful of water upon the woman's head, pronouncing in French, very loud, "Mary" (which was the name her husband desired me to give her, for I was her godfather), "I baptize thee in the name of the Father, and of the Son, and of the Holy Ghost;" so that none could know anything by it what religion he was of. He gave the benediction afterwards in Latin, but either Will Atkins did not know but it was French, or else did not take notice of it at that time.

As soon as this was over we married them; and after the marriage was over, he turned to Will Atkins, and in a very affectionate manner exhorted him, not only to persevere in that good disposition he was in, but to support the convictions that were upon him by a resolution to reform his life: told him it was in vain to say he repented if he did not forsake his crimes; represented to him how God had honoured him with being the instrument of bringing his wife to the knowledge of the Christian religion, and that he should be careful he did not dishonour the grace of God; and that if he did, he would see the heathen a better Christian than himself; the savage converted, and the instrument cast away. He said a great many good things to them both; and then, recommending them to God's goodness, gave them the benediction again, I repeating everything to them in English; and thus ended the ceremony. I think it was the most pleasant and agreeable day to me that ever I passed in my whole life. But my clergyman had not done yet: his thoughts hung continually upon the conversion of the thirty-seven savages, and fain be would have stayed upon the island to have undertaken it; but I convinced him, first, that his undertaking was impracticable in itself; and, secondly, that perhaps I would put it into a way of being done in his absence to his satisfaction.

Having thus brought the affairs of the island to a narrow compass, I was preparing to go on board the ship, when the young man I had taken out of the famished ship's company came to me, and told me he understood I had a clergyman with me, and that I had caused the Englishmen to be married to the savages; that he had a match too, which he desired might be finished before I went, between two Christians, which he hoped would not be disagreeable to me.

I knew this must be the young woman who was his mother's servant, for there was no other Christian woman on the island: so I began to persuade him not to do anything of that kind rashly, or because be found himself in this solitary circumstance. I represented to him that he had some considerable substance in the world, and good friends, as I understood by himself, and the maid also; that the maid was not only poor, and a servant, but was unequal to him, she being six or seven and twenty years old, and he not above seventeen or eighteen; that he might very probably, with my assistance, make a remove from this wilderness, and come into his own country again; and that then it would be a thousand to one but he would repent his choice, and the dislike of that circumstance might be disadvantageous to both. I was going to say more, but he interrupted me, smiling, and told me, with a great deal of modesty, that I mistook in my guesses — that he had nothing of that kind in his thoughts; and he was very glad to hear that I had an intent of putting them in a way to see their own country again;

358

and nothing should have made him think of staying there, but that the voyage I was going was so exceeding long and hazardous, and would carry him quite out of the reach of all his friends; that he had nothing to desire of me but that I would settle him in some little property in the island where he was, give him a servant or two, and some few necessaries, and he would live here like a planter, waiting the good time when, if ever I returned to England, I would redeem him. He hoped I would not be unmindful of him when I came to England: that he would give me some letters to his friends in London, to let them know how good I had been to him, and in what part of the world and what circumstances I had left him in: and he promised me that whenever I redeemed him, the plantation, and all the improvements he had made upon it, let the value be what it would, should be wholly mine.

His discourse was very prettily delivered, considering his youth, and was the more agreeable to me, because he told me positively the match was not for himself. I gave him all possible assurances that if I lived to come safe to England, I would deliver his letters, and do his business effectually; and that he might depend I should never forget the circumstances I had left him in. But still I was impatient to know who was the person to be married; upon which he told me it was my Jack-of-all-trades and his maid Susan. I was most agreeably surprised when he named the match; for, indeed, I thought it very suitable. The character of that man I have given already; and as for the maid, she was a very honest, modest, sober, and religious young woman: had a very good share of sense, was agreeable enough in her person, spoke very handsomely and to the purpose, always with decency and good manners, and was neither too backward to speak when requisite, nor impertinently forward when it was not her business; very handy and housewifely, and an excellent manager; fit, indeed, to have been governess to the whole island; and she knew very well how to behave in every respect.

The match being proposed in this manner, we married them the same day; and as I was father at the altar, and gave her away, so I gave her a portion; for I appointed her and her husband a handsome large space of ground for their plantation; and indeed this match, and the proposal the young gentleman made to give him a small property in the island, put me upon parceling it out amongst them, that they might not quarrel afterwards about their situation.

This sharing out the land to them I left to Will Atkins, who was now grown a sober, grave, managing fellow, perfectly reformed, exceedingly pious and religious; and, as far as I may be allowed to speak positively in such a case, I verily believe he was a true penitent. He divided things so justly, and so much to every one's satisfaction, that they only desired one general writing under my hand for the whole, which I caused to be drawn up, and signed and sealed, setting out the bounds and situation of every man's plantation, and testifying that I gave them thereby severally a right to the whole possession and inheritance of the respective plantations or farms, with their improvements, to them and their heirs, reserving all the rest of the island as my own property, and a certain rent for every particular plantation after eleven years, if I, or any one from me, or in my name, came to demand it, producing an attested copy of the same writing. As to the government and laws among them, I told them I was not capable of giving them better rules than they were able to give themselves; only I made them promise me to live in love and good neighbourhood with one another; and so I prepared to leave them.

One thing I must not omit, and that is, that being now settled in a kind of commonwealth among themselves, and having much business in hand, it was odd to have seven-and-thirty Indians live in a nook of the island, independent, and, indeed, unemployed; for except the providing themselves food, which they had difficulty enough to do sometimes, they had no manner of business or property to manage. I proposed, therefore, to the governor Spaniard that he should go to them, with Friday's father, and propose to them to remove, and either plant for themselves, or be taken into their several families as servants to be maintained for their labour, but without being absolute slaves; for I would not permit them to make them slaves by force, by any means; because they had their liberty given them by capitulation, as it were articles of surrender, which they ought not to break.

They most willingly embraced the proposal, and came all very cheerfully along with him: so we allotted them land and plantations, which three or four accepted of, but all the rest chose to be employed as servants in the several families we had settled. Thus my colony was in a manner settled as follows: The Spaniards possessed my original habitation, which was the capital city, and extended their plantations all along the side of the brook, which made the creek that I have so often described, as far as my bower; and as they increased their culture, it went always eastward. The English lived in the north-east part, where Will Atkins and his comrades began, and came on southward and south-west, towards the back part of the Spaniards; and every plantation had a great addition of land to take in, if they found occasion, so that they need not jostle one another for want of room. All the east end of the island was left uninhabited, that if any of the savages should come on shore there only for their customary barbarities, they might come and go; if they disturbed nobody, nobody would disturb them: and no doubt but they were often ashore, and went away again; for I never heard that the planters were ever attacked or disturbed any more.

CHAPTER VIII.

SAILS FROM THE ISLAND FOR THE BRAZILS

It now came into my thoughts that I had hinted to my friend the clergyman that the work of converting the savages might perhaps be set on foot in his absence to his satisfaction, and I told him that now I thought that it was put in a fair way; for the savages, being thus divided among the Christians, if they would but every one of them do their part with those which came under their hands, I hoped it might have a very good effect.

He agreed presently in that, if they did their part. "But how," says he, "shall we obtain that of them?" I told him we would call them all together, and leave it in charge with them, or go to them, one by one, which he thought best; so we divided it — he to speak to the Spaniards, who were all Papists, and I to speak to the English, who were all Protestants; and we recommended it earnestly to them, and made them promise that they would never make any distinction of Papist or Protestant in their exhorting the savages to turn Christians, but teach them the general knowledge of the true God, and of their Saviour Jesus Christ; and they likewise promised us that they would never have any differences or disputes one with another about religion.

When I came to Will Atkins's house, I found that the young woman I have mentioned above, and Will Atkins's wife, were become intimates; and this prudent, religious young woman had perfected the work Will Atkins had begun; and though it was not above four days after what I have related, yet the new-baptized savage woman was made such a Christian as I have seldom heard of in all my observation or conversation in the world. It came next into my mind, in the morning before I went to them, that amongst all the needful things I had to leave with them I had not left them a Bible, in which I showed myself less considering for them than my good friend the widow was for me when she sent me the cargo of a hundred pounds from Lisbon, where she packed up three Bibles and a Prayer-book. However, the good woman's charity had a greater extent than ever she imagined, for they were reserved for the comfort and instruction of those that made much better use of them than I had done.

I took one of the Bibles in my pocket, and when I came to Will Atkins's tent, or house, and found the young woman and Atkins's baptized wife had been discoursing of religion together — for Will

Atkins told it me with a great deal of joy — I asked if they were together now, and he said, "Yes"; so I went into the house, and he with me, and we found them together very earnest in discourse. "Oh, sir," says Will Atkins, "when God has sinners to reconcile to Himself, and aliens to bring home, He never wants a messenger; my wife has got a new instructor: I knew I was unworthy, as I was incapable of that work; that young woman has been sent hither from heaven — she is enough to convert a whole island of savages." The young woman blushed, and rose up to go away, but I desired her to sit-still; I told her she had a good work upon her hands, and I hoped God would bless her in it.

We talked a little, and I did not perceive that they had any book among them, though I did not ask; but I put my hand into my pocket, and pulled out my Bible. "Here," said I to Atkins, "I have brought you an assistant that perhaps you had not before." The man was so confounded that he was not able to speak for some time; but, recovering himself, he takes it with both his hands, and turning to his wife, "Here, my dear," says he, "did not I tell you our God, though He lives above, could hear what we have said? Here's the book I prayed for when you and I kneeled down under the bush; now God has heard us and sent it." When he had said so, the man fell into such passionate transports, that between the joy of having it, and giving God thanks for it, the tears ran down his face like a child that was crying.

The woman was surprised, and was like to have run into a mistake that none of us were aware of; for she firmly believed God had sent the book upon her husband's petition. It is true that providentially it was so, and might be taken so in a consequent sense; but I believe it would have been no difficult matter at that time to have persuaded the poor woman to have believed that an express messenger came from heaven on purpose to bring that individual book. But it was too serious a matter to suffer any delusion to take place, so I turned to the young woman, and told her we did not desire to impose upon the new convert in her first and more ignorant understanding of things, and begged her to explain to her that God may be very properly said to answer our petitions, when, in the course of His providence, such things are in a particular manner brought to pass as we petitioned for; but we did not expect returns from heaven in a miraculous and particular manner, and it is a mercy that it is not so.

This the young woman did afterwards effectually, so that there was no priestcraft used here; and I should have thought it one of the most unjustifiable frauds in the world to have had it so. But the effect upon Will Atkins is really not to be expressed; and there, we may be sure, was no delusion. Sure no man was ever more thankful in the world for anything of its kind than he was for the Bible, nor, I believe, never any man was glad of a Bible from a better principle; and though he had been a most profligate creature, headstrong, furious, and desperately wicked, yet this man is a standing rule to us all for the well instructing children, viz. that parents should never give over to teach and instruct, nor ever despair of the success of their endeavours, let the children be ever so refractory, or to appearance insensible to instruction; for if ever God in His providence touches the conscience of such, the force of their education turns upon them, and the early instruction of parents is not lost, though it may have been many years laid asleep, but some time or other they may find the benefit of it. Thus it was with this poor man: however ignorant he was of religion and Christian knowledge, he found he had some to do with now more ignorant than himself, and that the least part of the instruction of his good father that now came to his mind was of use to him.

Among the rest, it occurred to him, he said, how his father used to insist so much on the inexpressible value of the Bible, and the privilege and blessing of it to nations, families, and persons; but he never entertained the least notion of the worth of it till now, when, being to talk to heathens, savages, and barbarians, he wanted the help of the written oracle for his assistance. The young woman was glad of it also for the present occasion, though she had one, and so had the youth, on board our ship among their goods, which were not yet brought on shore. And now, having said so many things of this young woman, I cannot omit telling one story more of her and myself, which has something in it very instructive and remarkable.

I have related to what extremity the poor young woman was reduced; how her mistress was starved to death, and died on board that unhappy ship we met at sea, and how the whole ship's company was reduced to the last extremity. The gentlewoman, and her son, and this maid, were first hardly used as to provisions, and at last totally neglected and starved — that is to say, brought to the last extremity of hunger. One day, being discoursing with her on the extremities they suffered, I asked her if she could describe, by what she had felt, what it was to starve, and how it appeared? She said she believed she could, and told her tale very distinctly thus: —

"First, we had for some days fared exceedingly hard, and suffered very great hunger; but at last we were wholly without food of any kind except sugar, and a little wine and water. The first day after I had received no food at all, I found myself towards evening, empty and sick at the stomach, and nearer night much inclined to yawning and sleep. I lay down on the couch in the great cabin to sleep, and slept about three hours, and awaked a little refreshed, having taken a glass of wine when I lay down; after being about three hours awake, it being about five o'clock in the morning, I found myself empty, and my stomach sickish, and lay down again, but could not sleep at all, being very faint and ill; and thus I continued all the second day with a strange variety — first hungry, then sick again, with retchings to vomit. The second night, being obliged to go to bed again without any food more than a draught of fresh water, and being asleep, I dreamed I was at Barbados, and that the market was mightily stocked with provisions; that I bought some for my mistress, and went and dined very heartily. I thought my stomach was full after this, as it would have been after a good dinner; but when I awaked I was exceedingly sunk in my spirits to find myself in the extremity of family. The last glass of wine we had I drank, and put sugar in it, because of its having some spirit to supply nourishment; but there being no substance in the stomach for the digesting office to work upon, I found the only effect of the wine was to raise disagreeable fumes from the stomach into the head; and I lay, as they told me, stupid and senseless, as one drunk, for some time. The third day, in the morning, after a night of strange, confused, and inconsistent dreams, and rather dozing than sleeping, I awaked ravenous and furious with hunger; and I question, had not my understanding returned and conquered it, whether if I had been a mother, and had had a little child with me, its life would have been safe or not. This lasted about three hours, during which time I was twice raging mad as any creature in Bedlam, as my young master told me, and as he can now inform you.

"In one of these fits of lunacy or distraction I fell down and struck my face against the corner of a pallet-bed, in which my mistress lay, and with the blow the blood gushed out of my nose; and the cabin-boy bringing me a little basin, I sat down and bled into it a great deal; and as the blood came from me I came to myself, and the violence of the flame or fever I was in abated, and so did the ravenous part of the hunger. Then I grew sick, and retched to vomit, but could not, for I had nothing in my stomach to bring up. After I had bled some time I swooned, and they all believed I was dead; but I came to myself soon after, and then had a most dreadful pain in my stomach not to be described — not like the colic, but a gnawing, eager pain for food; and towards night it went off with a kind of earnest wishing or longing for food. I took another draught of water with sugar in it; but my stomach loathed the sugar and brought it all up again; then I took a draught of water without sugar, and that stayed with me; and I laid me down upon the bed, praying most heartily that it would please God to take me away; and composing my mind in hopes of it, I slumbered a while, and then waking, thought myself dying, being light with vapours from an empty stomach. I recommended my soul then to God, and then earnestly wished that somebody would throw me into the into the sea.

"All this while my mistress lay by me, just, as I thought, expiring, but she bore it with much more patience than I, and gave the last bit of bread she had left to her child, my young master, who would not have taken it, but she obliged him to eat it; and I believe it saved his life. Towards the morning I slept again, and when I awoke I fell into a violent passion of crying, and after that had a second fit of violent hunger. I got up ravenous, and in a most dreadful condition; and once or twice I was going to bite my own arm. At last I saw the basin in which was the blood I had bled at my nose the day before: I ran to it, and swallowed it with such haste, and such a greedy appetite, as if I wondered nobody had taken it before, and afraid it should be taken from me now. After it was down, though the thoughts of it filled me with horror, yet it checked the fit of hunger, and I took another draught of water, and was composed and refreshed for some hours after. This was the fourth day; and this I kept up till towards night, when, within the compass of three hours, I had all the several circumstances over again, one after another, viz. sick, sleepy, eagerly hungry, pain in the stomach, then ravenous again, then sick, then lunatic, then crying, then ravenous again, and so every quarter of an hour, and my strength wasted exceedingly; at night I lay me down, having no comfort but in the hope that I should die before morning.

"All this night I had no sleep; but the hunger was now turned into a disease; and I had a terrible colic and griping, by wind instead of food having found its way into the bowels; and in this condition I lay till morning, when I was surprised by the cries and lamentations of my young master, who called out to me that his mother was dead. I lifted myself up a little, for I had not strength to rise, but found she was not dead, though she was able to give very little signs of life. I had then such convulsions in my stomach, for want of some sustenance, as I cannot describe; with such frequent throes and pangs of appetite as nothing but the tortures of death can imitate; and in this condition I was when I heard the seamen above cry out, 'A sail! a sail!' and halloo and jump about as if they were distracted. I was not able to get off from the bed, and my mistress much less; and my young master was so sick that I thought he had been expiring; so we could not open the cabin door, or get any account what it was that occasioned such confusion; nor had we had any conversation with the ship's company for twelve days, they having told us that they had not a mouthful of anything to eat in the ship; and this they told us afterwards — they thought we had been dead. It was this dreadful condition we were in when you were sent to save our lives; and how you found us, sir, you know as well as I, and better too."

This was her own relation, and is such a distinct account of starving to death, as, I confess, I never met with, and was exceeding instructive to me. I am the rather apt to believe it to be a true account, because the youth gave me an account of a good part of it; though I must own, not so distinct and so feeling as the maid; and the rather, because it seems his mother fed him at the price of her own life: but the poor maid, whose constitution was stronger than that of her mistress, who was in years, and a weakly woman too, might struggle harder with it; nevertheless she might be supposed to feel the extremity something sooner than her mistress, who might be allowed to keep the last bit something longer than she parted with any to relieve her maid. No question, as the case is here related, if our ship or some other had not so providentially met them, but a few days more would have ended all their lives. I now return to my disposition of things among the people. And, first, it is to be observed here, that for many reasons I did not think fit to let them know anything of the sloop I had framed, and which I thought of setting up among them; for I found, at least at my first coming, such seeds of division among them, that I saw plainly, had I set up the sloop, and left it among them, they would, upon every light disgust, have separated, and gone away from one another; or perhaps have turned pirates, and so made the island a den of thieves, instead of a plantation of sober and religious people, as I intended it; nor did I leave the two pieces of brass cannon that I had on board, or the extra two quarter-deck guns that my nephew had provided, for the same reason. I thought it was enough to qualify them for a defensive war against any that should invade them, but not to set them up for an offensive war, or to go abroad to attack others; which, in the end, would only bring ruin and destruction upon them. I reserved the sloop, therefore, and the guns, for their service another way, as I shall observe in its place.

Having now done with the island, I left them all in good circumstances and in a flourishing condition, and went on board my ship again on the 6th of May, having been about twenty-five days among them: and as they were all resolved to stay upon the island till I came to remove them, I promised to send them further relief from the Brazils, if I could possibly find an opportunity. I particularly promised to send them some cattle, such as sheep, hogs, and cows: as to the two cows and calves which I brought from England, we had been obliged, by the length of our voyage, to kill them at sea, for want of hay to feed them.

The next day, giving them a salute of five guns at parting, we set sail, and arrived at the bay of All Saints in the Brazils in about twenty-two days, meeting nothing remarkable in our passage but this: that about three days after we had sailed, being becalmed, and the current setting strong to the ENE., running, as it were, into a bay or gulf on the land side, we were driven something out of our course, and once or twice our men cried out, "Land to the eastward!" but whether it was the continent or islands we could not tell by any means. But the third day, towards evening, the sea smooth, and the weather calm, we saw the sea as it were covered towards the land with something very black; not being able to discover what it was till after some time, our chief mate, going up the main shrouds a little way, and looking at them with a perspective, cried out it was an army. I could not imagine what he meant by an army, and thwarted him a little hastily. "Nay, sir," says he, "don't be angry, for 'tis an army, and a fleet too: for I believe there are a thousand canoes, and you may see them paddle along, for they are coming towards us apace."

I was a little surprised then, indeed, and so was my nephew the captain; for he had heard such terrible stories of them in the island, and having never been in those seas before, that he could not tell what to think of it, but said, two or three times, we should all be devoured. I must confess, considering we were becalmed, and the current set strong towards the shore, I liked it the worse; however, I bade them not be afraid, but bring the ship to an anchor as soon as we came so near as to know that we must engage them. The weather continued calm, and they came on apace towards us, so I gave orders to come to an anchor, and furl all our sails; as for the savages, I told them they had nothing to fear but fire, and therefore they should get their boats out, and fasten them, one close by the head and the other by the stern, and man them both well, and wait the issue in that posture: this I did, that the men in the boats might be ready with sheets and buckets to put out any fire these savages might endeavour to fix to the outside of the ship.

In this posture we lay by for them, and in a little while they came up with us; but never was such a horrid sight seen by Christians; though my mate was much mistaken in his calculation of their number, yet when they came up we reckoned about a hundred and twenty-six canoes; some of them had sixteen or seventeen men in them, and some more, and the least six or seven. When they came nearer to us, they seemed to be struck with wonder and astonishment, as at a sight which doubtless they had never seen before; nor could they at first, as we afterwards understood, know what to make of us; they came boldly up, however, very near to us, and seemed to go about to row round us; but we called to our men in the boats not to let them come too near them. This very order brought us to an engagement with them, without our designing it; for five or six of the large canoes came so near our long-boat, that our men beckoned with their hands to keep them back, which they understood very well, and went back: but at their retreat about fifty arrows came on board us from those boats, and one of our men in the long-boat was very much wounded. However, I called to them not to fire by any means; but we handed down some deal boards into the boat, and the carpenter presently set up a kind of fence, like waste boards, to cover them from the arrows of the savages, if they should shoot again.

About half-an-hour afterwards they all came up in a body astern of us, and so near that we could easily discern what they were, though we could not tell their design; and I easily found they were some of my old friends, the same sort of savages that I had been used to engage with. In a short time more they rowed a little farther out to sea, till they came directly broadside with us, and then rowed down straight upon us, till they came so near that they could hear us speak; upon this, I ordered all my men to keep close, lest they should shoot any more arrows, and made all our guns ready; but being so near as to be within hearing, I made Friday go out upon the deck, and call out aloud to them in his language, to know what they meant. Whether they understood him or not, that I knew not; but as soon as he had called to them, six of them, who were in the foremost or nighest boat to us, turned their canoes from us, and stooping down, showed us their naked backs; whether this was a defiance or challenge we knew not, or whether it was done in mere contempt, or as a signal to the rest; but immediately Friday cried out they were going to shoot, and, unhappily for him, poor fellow, they let fly about three hundred of their arrows, and to my inexpressible grief, killed poor Friday, no other man being in their sight. The poor fellow was shot with no less than three arrows, and about three more fell very near him; such unlucky marksmen they were!

I was so annoyed at the loss of my old trusty servant and companion, that I immediately ordered five guns to be loaded with small shot, and four with great, and gave them such a broadside as they had never heard in their lives before. They were not above half a cable's length off when we fired; and our gunners took their aim so well, that three or four of their canoes were overset, as we had reason to believe, by one shot only. The ill manners of turning up their bare backs to us gave us no great offence; neither did I know for certain whether that which would pass for the greatest contempt among us might be understood so by them or not; therefore, in return, I had only resolved to have fired four or five guns at them with powder only, which I knew would frighten them sufficiently: but when they shot at us directly with all the fury they were capable of, and especially as they had killed my poor Friday, whom I so entirely loved and valued, and who, indeed, so well deserved it, I thought myself not only justifiable before God and man, but would have been very glad if I could have overset every canoe there, and drowned every one of them.

I can neither tell how many we killed nor how many we wounded at this broadside, but sure such a fright and hurry never were seen among such a multitude; there were thirteen or fourteen of their canoes split and overset in all, and the men all set a-swimming: the rest, frightened out of their wits, scoured away as fast as they could, taking but little care to save those whose boats were split or spoiled with our shot; so I suppose that many of them were lost; and our men took up one poor fellow swimming for his life, above an hour after they were all gone. The small shot from our cannon must needs kill and wound a great many; but, in short, we never knew how it went with them, for they fled so fast, that in three hours or thereabouts we could not see above three or four straggling canoes, nor did we ever see the rest any more; for a breeze of wind springing up the same evening, we weighed and set sail for the Brazils.

We had a prisoner, indeed, but the creature was so sullen that he would neither eat nor speak, and we all fancied he would starve himself to death. But I took a way to cure him: for I had made them take him and turn him into the long-boat, and make him believe they would toss him into the sea again, and so leave him where they found him, if he would not speak; nor would that do, but they really did throw him into the sea, and came away from him. Then he followed them, for he swam like a cork, and called to them in his tongue, though they knew not one word of what he said; however at last they took him in again., and then he began to be more tractable: nor did I ever design they should drown him.

We were now under sail again, but I was the most disconsolate creature alive for want of my man Friday, and would have been very glad to have gone back to the island, to have taken one of the rest from thence for my occasion, but it could not be: so we went on. We had one prisoner, as I have said, and it was a long time before we could make him understand anything; but in time our men taught him some English, and he began to be a little tractable. Afterwards, we inquired what country he came from; but could make nothing of what he said; for his speech was so odd, all gutturals, and he spoke in the throat in such a hollow, odd manner, that we could never form a word after him; and we were all of opinion that they might speak that language as well if they were gagged as otherwise; nor could we perceive that they had any occasion either for teeth, tongue, lips, or palate, but formed their words just as a hunting-horn forms a tune with an open throat. He told us, however, some time after, when we had taught him to speak a little English, that they were going with their kings to fight a great battle. When he said kings, we asked him how many kings? He said they were five nation (we could not make him understand the plural 's), and that they all joined to go against two nation. We asked him what made them come up to us? He said, "To makee te great wonder look." Here it is to be observed that all those natives, as also those of Africa when they learn English, always add two e's at the end of the words where we use one; and they place the accent upon them, as makee, takee, and the like; nay, I could hardly make Friday leave it off, though at last he did.

And now I name the poor fellow once more, I must take my last leave of him. Poor honest Friday! We buried him with all the decency and solemnity possible, by putting him into a coffin, and throwing him into the sea; and I caused them to fire eleven guns for him. So ended the life of the most grateful, faithful, honest, and most affectionate servant that ever man had.

We went now away with a fair wind for Brazil; and in about twelve days' time we made land, in the latitude of five degrees south of the line, being the north-easternmost land of all that part of America. We kept on S. by E., in sight of the shore four days, when we made

Cape St. Augustine, and in three days came to an anchor off the bay of All Saints, the old place of my deliverance, from whence came both my good and evil fate. Never ship came to this port that had less business than I had, and yet it was with great difficulty that we were admitted to hold the least correspondence on shore: not my partner himself, who was alive, and made a great figure among them, not my two merchant-trustees, not the fame of my wonderful preservation in the island, could obtain me that favour. My partner, however, remembering that I had given five hundred moidores to the prior of the monastery of the Augustines, and two hundred and seventy-two to the poor, went to the monastery, and obliged the prior that then was to go to the governor, and get leave for me personally, with the captain and one more, besides eight seamen, to come on shore, and no more; and this upon condition, absolutely capitulated for, that we should not offer to land any goods out of the ship, or to carry any person away without licence. They were so strict with us as to landing any goods, that it was with extreme difficulty that I got on shore three bales of English goods, such as fine broadcloths, stuffs, and some linen, which I had brought for a present to my partner.

He was a very generous, open-hearted man, although he began, like me, with little at first. Though he knew not that I had the least design of giving him anything, he sent me on board a present of fresh provisions, wine, and sweetmeats, worth about thirty moidores, including some tobacco, and three or four fine medals of gold: but I was even with him in my present, which, as I have said, consisted of fine broadcloth, English stuffs, lace, and fine holland; also, I delivered him about the value of one hundred pounds sterling in the same goods, for other uses; and I obliged him to set up the sloop, which I had brought with me from England, as I have said, for the use of my colony, in order to send the refreshments I intended to my plantation.

Accordingly, he got hands, and finished the sloop in a very few days, for she was already framed; and I gave the master of her such instructions that he could not miss the place; nor did he, as I had an account from my partner afterwards. I got him soon loaded with the small cargo I sent them; and one of our seamen, that had been on shore with me there, offered to go with the sloop and settle there, upon my letter to the governor Spaniard to allot him a sufficient quantity of land for a plantation, and on my giving him some clothes and tools for his planting work, which he said he understood, having been an old planter at Maryland, and a buccaneer into the bargain. I encouraged the fellow by granting all he desired; and, as an addition, I gave him the savage whom we had taken prisoner of war to be his slave, and ordered the governor Spaniard to give him his share of everything he wanted with the rest.

When we came to fit this man out, my old partner told me there was a certain very honest fellow, a Brazil planter of his acquaintance, who had fallen into the displeasure of the Church. "I know not what the matter is with him," says he, "but, on my conscience, I think he is a heretic in his heart, and he has been obliged to conceal himself for fear of the Inquisition." He then told me that he would be very glad of such an opportunity to make his escape, with his wife and two daughters; and if I would let them go to my island, and allot them a plantation, he would give them a small stock to begin with — for the officers of the Inquisition had seized all his effects and estate, and he had nothing left but a little household stuff and two slaves; "and," adds he, "though I hate his principles, yet I would not have him fall into their hands, for he will be assuredly burned alive if he does." I granted this presently, and joined my Englishman with them: and we concealed the man, and his wife and daughters, on board our ship, till the sloop put out to go to sea; and then having put all their goods on board some time before, we put them on board the sloop after she was got out of the bay. Our seaman was mightily pleased with this new partner; and their stocks, indeed, were much alike, rich in tools, in preparations, and a farm — but nothing to begin with, except as above: however, they carried over with them what was worth all the rest, some materials for planting sugar-canes, with some plants of canes, which he, I mean the Brazil planter, understood very well.

Among the rest of the supplies sent to my tenants in the island, I sent them by the sloop three milch cows and five calves; about twenty-two hogs, among them three sows; two mares, and a stone-horse. For my Spaniards, according to my promise, I engaged three Brazil women to go, and recommended it to them to marry them, and use them kindly. I could have procured more women, but I remembered that the poor persecuted man had two daughters, and that there were but five of the Spaniards that wanted partners; the rest had wives of their own, though in another country. All this cargo arrived safe, and, as you may easily suppose, was very welcome to my old inhabitants, who were now, with this addition, between sixty and seventy people, besides little children, of which there were a great many. I found letters at London from them all, by way of Lisbon, when I came back to England.

I have now done with the island, and all manner of discourse about it: and whoever reads the rest of my memorandums would do well to turn his thoughts entirely from it, and expect to read of the follies of an old man, not warned by his own harms, much less by those of other men, to beware; not cooled by almost forty years' miseries and disappointments — not satisfied with prosperity beyond expectation, nor made cautious by afflictions and distress beyond example.

CHAPTER IX.

DREADFUL OCCURRENCES IN MADAGASCAR

I had no more business to go to the East Indies than a man at full liberty has to go to the turnkey at Newgate, and desire him to lock him up among the prisoners there, and starve him. Had I taken a small vessel from England and gone directly to the island; had I loaded her, as I did the other vessel, with all the necessaries for the plantation and for my people; taken a patent from the government here to have secured my property, in subjection only to that of England; had I carried over cannon and ammunition, servants and people to plant, and taken possession of the place, fortified and strengthened it in the name of England, and increased it with people, as I might easily have done; had I then settled myself there, and sent the ship back laden with good rice, as I might also have done in six months' time, and ordered my friends to have fitted her out again for our supply — had I done this, and stayed there myself, I had at least acted like a man of common sense. But I was possessed of a wandering spirit, and scorned all advantages: I pleased myself with being the patron of the people I placed there, and doing for them in a kind of haughty, majestic way, like an old patriarchal monarch, providing for them as if I had been father of the whole family, as well as of the plantation. But I never so much as pretended to plant in the name of any government or nation, or to acknowledge any prince, or to call my people subjects to any one nation more than another; nay, I never so much as gave the place a name, but left it as I found it, belonging to nobody, and the people under no discipline or government but my own, who, though I had influence over them as a father and benefactor, had no authority or power to act or command one way or other, further than voluntary consent moved them to comply. Yet even this, had I stayed there, would have done well enough; but as I rambled from them, and came there no more, the last letters I had from any of them were by my partner's means, who afterwards sent another sloop to the place, and who sent me word, though I had not the letter till I got to London, several years after it was written, that they went on but poorly; were discontented with their long stay there; that Will Atkins was dead; that five of the Spaniards were come away; and though they had not been much molested by the savages, yet they had had some skirmishes with them; and that they begged of him to write to me to think of the promise I had made to fetch them away, that they might see their country again before they died.

But I was gone a wild goose chase indeed, and they that will have any more of me must be content to follow me into a new variety of follies, hardships, and wild adventures, wherein the justice of Providence may be duly observed; and we may see how easily Heaven can gorge us with our own desires, make the strongest of our wishes be our affliction, and punish us most severely with those very things which we think it would be our utmost happiness to be allowed to possess. Whether I had business or no business, away I went: it is no time now to enlarge upon the reason or absurdity of my own conduct, but to come to the history — I was embarked for the voyage, and the voyage I went.

I shall only add a word or two concerning my honest Popish clergyman, for let their opinion of us, and all other heretics in general, as they call us, be as uncharitable as it may, I verily believe this man was very sincere, and wished the good of all men: yet I believe he used reserve in many of his expressions, to prevent giving me offence; for I scarce heard him once call on the Blessed Virgin, or mention St. Jago, or his guardian angel, though so common with the rest of them. However, I say I had not the least doubt of his sincerity and pious intentions; and I am firmly of opinion, if the rest of the Popish missionaries were like him, they would strive to visit even the poor Tartars and Laplanders, where they have nothing to give them, as well as covet to flock to India, Persia, China, &c., the most wealthy of the heathen countries; for if they expected to bring no gains to their Church by it, it may well be admired how they came to admit the Chinese Confucius into the calendar of the Christian saints.

A ship being ready to sail for Lisbon, my pious priest asked me leave to go thither; being still, as he observed, bound never to finish any voyage he began. How happy it had been for me if I had gone with him. But it was too late now; all things Heaven appoints for the best: had I gone with him I had never had so many things to be thankful for, and the reader had never heard of the second part of the travels and adventures of Robinson Crusoe: so I must here leave exclaiming at myself, and go on with my voyage. From the Brazils we made directly over the Atlantic Sea to the Cape of Good Hope, and had a tolerably good voyage, our course generally south-east, now and then a storm, and some contrary winds; but my disasters at sea were at an end — my future rubs and cross events were to befall me on shore, that it might appear the land was as well prepared to be our scourge as the sea.

Our ship was on a trading voyage, and had a supercargo on board, who was to direct all her motions after she arrived at the Cape, only being limited to a certain number of days for stay, by charter-party, at the several ports she was to go to. This was none of my business, neither did I meddle with it; my nephew, the captain, and the supercargo adjusting all those things between them as they thought fit. We stayed at the Cape no longer than was needful to take in-fresh water, but made the best of our way for the coast of Coromandel. We were, indeed, informed that a French man-of-war, of fifty guns, and two large merchant ships, were gone for the Indies; and as I knew we were at war with France, I had some apprehensions of them; but they went their own way, and we heard no more of them.

I shall not pester the reader with a tedious description of places, journals of our voyage, variations of the compass, latitudes, trade-winds, &c.; it is enough to name the ports and places which we touched at, and what occurred to us upon our passages from one to another. We touched first at the island of Madagascar, where, though the people are fierce and treacherous, and very well armed with lances and bows, which they use with inconceivable dexterity, yet we fared very well with them a while. They treated us very civilly; and for some trifles which we gave them, such as knives, scissors, &c., they brought us eleven good fat bullocks, of a middling size, which we took in, partly for fresh provisions for our present spending, and the rest to salt for the ship's use.

We were obliged to stay here some time after we had furnished ourselves with provisions; and I, who was always too curious to look into every nook of the world wherever I came, went on shore as often as I could. It was on the east side of the island that we went on shore one evening: and the people, who, by the way, are very numerous, came thronging about us, and stood gazing at us at a distance. As we had traded freely with them, and had been kindly used, we thought ourselves in no danger; but when we saw the people, we cut three boughs out of a tree, and stuck them up at a distance from us; which, it seems, is a mark in that country not only of a truce and friendship, but when it is accepted the other side set up three poles or boughs, which is a signal that they accept the truce too; but then this is a known condition of the truce, that you are not to pass beyond their three poles towards them, nor they to come past your three poles or boughs towards you; so that you are perfectly secure within the three poles, and all the space between your poles and theirs is allowed like a market for free converse, traffic, and commerce. When you go there you must not carry your weapons with you; and if they come into that space they stick up their javelins and lances all at the first poles, and come on unarmed; but if any violence is offered them, and the truce thereby broken, away they run to the poles, and lay hold of their weapons, and the truce is at an end.

It happened one evening, when we went on shore, that a greater number of their people came down than usual, but all very friendly and civil; and they brought several kinds of provisions, for which we satisfied them with such toys as we had; the women also brought us milk and roots, and several things very acceptable to us, and all was quiet; and we made us a little tent or hut of some boughs or trees, and lay on shore all night. I know not what was the occasion, but I was not so well satisfied to lie on shore as the rest; and the boat riding at an anchor at about a stone's cast from the land, with two men in her to take care of her, I made one of them come on shore; and getting some boughs of trees to cover us also in the boat, I spread the sail on the bottom of the boat, and lay under the cover of the branches of the trees all night in the boat.

About two o'clock in the morning we heard one of our men making a terrible noise on the shore, calling out, for God's sake, to bring the boat in and come and help them, for they were all like to be murdered; and at the same time I heard the fire of five muskets, which was the number of guns they had, and that three times over; for it seems the natives here were not so easily frightened with guns as the savages were in America, where I had to do with them. All this while, I knew not what was the matter, but rousing immediately from sleep with the noise, I caused the boat to be thrust in, and resolved with three fusées we had on board to land and assist our men. We got the boat soon to the shore, but our men were in too much haste; for being come to the shore, they plunged into the water, to get to the boat with all the expedition they could, being pursued by between three and four hundred men. Our men were but nine in all, and only five of them had fusées with them; the rest had pistols and swords, indeed, but they were of small use to them.

We took up seven of our men, and with difficulty enough too, three of them being very ill wounded; and that which was still worse was, that while we stood in the boat to take our men in, we were in as much danger as they were in on shore; for they poured their arrows in upon us so thick that we were glad to barricade the side of the boat up with the benches, and two or three loose boards which, to our great satisfaction, we had by mere accident in the boat. And yet, had it been daylight, they are, it seems, such exact marksmen, that if they could have seen but the least part of any of us, they would have been sure of us. We had, by the light of the moon, a little sight of them, as they stood pelting us from the shore with darts and arrows; and having got ready our firearms, we gave them a volley that we could hear, by the cries of some of them, had wounded several; however, they stood thus in battle array on the shore till break of day, which we supposed was that they might see the better to take their aim at us.

In this condition we lay, and could not tell how to weigh our anchor, or set up our sail, because we must needs stand up in the boat, and they were as sure to hit us as we were to hit a bird in a tree with small shot. We made signals of distress to the ship, and though she rode a league off, yet my nephew, the captain, hearing our firing, and by glasses perceiving the posture we lay in, and that we fired towards the shore, pretty well understood us; and weighing anchor with all speed, he stood as near the shore as he durst with the ship, and then sent another boat with ten hands in her, to assist us. We called to them not to come too near, telling them what condition we were in; however, they stood in near to us, and one of the men taking the end of a tow-line in his hand, and keeping our boat between him and the enemy, so that they could not perfectly see him, swam on board us, and made fast the line to the boat: upon which we slipped out a little cable, and leaving our anchor behind, they towed us out of reach of the arrows; we all the while lying close behind the barricade we had made. As soon as we were got from between the ship and the shore, that we could lay her side to the shore, she ran along just by them, and poured in a broadside among them, loaded with pieces of iron and lead, small bullets, and such stuff, besides the great shot, which made a terrible havoc among them.

When we were got on board and out of danger, we had time to examine into the occasion of this fray; and indeed our supercargo, who had been often in those parts, put me upon it; for he said he was sure the inhabitants would not have touched us after we had made a truce, if we had not done something to provoke them to it. At length it came out that an old woman, who had come to sell us some milk, had brought it within our poles, and a young woman with her, who also brought us some roots or herbs; and while the old woman (whether she was mother to the young woman or no they could not tell) was selling us the milk, one of our men offered some rudeness to the girl that was with her, at which the old woman made a great noise: however, the seaman would not quit his prize, but carried her out of the old woman's sight among the trees, it being almost dark; the old woman went away without her, and, as we may suppose, made an outcry among the people she came from; who, upon notice, raised that great army upon us in three or four hours, and it was great odds but we had all been destroyed.

One of our men was killed with a lance thrown at him just at the beginning of the attack, as he sallied out of the tent they had made; the rest came off free, all but the fellow who was the occasion of all the mischief, who paid dear enough for his brutality, for we could not hear what became of him for a great while. We lay upon the shore two days after, though the wind presented, and made signals for him, and made our boat sail up shore and down shore several leagues, but in vain; so we were obliged to give him over; and if he alone had suffered for it, the loss had been less. I could not satisfy myself, however, without venturing on shore once more, to try if I could learn anything of him or them; it was the third night after the action that I had a great mind to learn, if I could by any means, what mischief we had done, and how the game stood on the Indians' side. I was careful to do it in the dark, lest we should be attacked again: but I ought indeed to have been sure that the men I went with had been under my command, before I engaged in a thing so hazardous and mischievous as I was brought into by it, without design.

We took twenty as stout fellows with us as any in the ship, besides the supercargo and myself, and we landed two hours before midnight, at the same place where the Indians stood drawn up in the evening before. I landed here, because my design, as I have said, was chiefly to see if they had quitted the field, and if they had left any marks behind them of the mischief we had done them, and I thought if we could surprise one or two of them, perhaps we might get our man again, by way of exchange.

We landed without any noise, and divided our men into two bodies, whereof the boatswain commanded one and I the other. We neither saw nor heard anybody stir when we landed: and we marched up, one body at a distance from another, to the place. At first we could see nothing, it being very dark; till by-and-by our boatswain, who led the first party, stumbled and fell over a dead body. This made them halt a while; for knowing by the circumstances that they were at the place where the Indians had stood, they waited for my coming up there. We concluded to halt till the moon began to rise, which we knew would be in less than an hour, when we could easily discern the havoc we had made among them. We told thirty-two bodies upon the ground, whereof two were not quite dead; some had an arm and some a leg shot off, and one his head; those that were wounded, we supposed, they had carried away. When we had made, as I thought, a full discovery of all we could come to the knowledge of, I resolved on going on board; but the boatswain and his party sent me word that they were resolved to make a visit to the Indian town, where these dogs, as they called them, dwelt, and asked me to go along with them; and if they could find them, as they still fancied they should, they did not doubt of getting a good booty; and it might be they might find Tom Jeffry there: that was the man's name we had lost.

Had they sent to ask my leave to go, I knew well enough what answer to have given them; for I should have commanded them instantly on board, knowing it was not a hazard fit for us to run, who had a ship and ship-loading in our charge, and a voyage to make which depended very much upon the lives of the men; but as they sent me word they were resolved to go, and only asked me and my company to go along with them, I positively refused it, and rose up, for I was sitting on the ground, in order to go to the boat. One or two of the men began to importune me to go; and when I refused, began to grumble, and say they were not under my command, and they would go. "Come, Jack," says one of the men, "will you go with me? I'll go for one." Jack said he would — and then another — and, in a word, they all left me but one, whom I persuaded to stay, and a boy left in the boat. So the supercargo and I, with the third man, went back to the boat, where we told them we would stay for them, and take care to take in as many of them as should be left; for I told them it was a mad thing they were going about, and supposed most of them would have the fate of Tom Jeffry.

They told me, like seamen, they would warrant it they would come off again, and they would take care, &c.; so away they went. I entreated them to consider the ship and the voyage, that their lives were not their own, and that they were entrusted with the voyage, in some measure; that if they miscarried, the ship might be lost for want of their help, and that they could not answer for it to God or man. But I might as well have talked to the mainmast of the ship: they were mad upon their journey; only they gave me good words, and begged I would not be angry; that they did not doubt but they would be back again in about an hour at furthest; for the Indian town, they said, was not above half-a mile off, though they found it above two miles before they got to it.

Well, they all went away, and though the attempt was desperate, and such as none but madmen would have gone about, yet, to give them their due, they went about it as warily as boldly; they were gallantly armed, for they had every man a fusée or musket, a bayonet, and a pistol; some of them had broad cutlasses, some of them had hangers, and the boatswain and two more had poleaxes; besides all which they had among them thirteen hand grenadoes. Bolder fellows, and better provided, never went about any wicked work in the world. When they went out their chief design was plunder, and they were in mighty hopes of finding gold there; but a circumstance which none of them were aware of set them on fire with revenge, and made devils of them all.

When they came to the few Indian houses which they thought had been the town, which was not above half a mile off, they were under great disappointment, for there were not above twelve or thirteen houses, and where the town was, or how big, they knew not. They consulted, therefore, what to do, and were some time before they could resolve; for if they fell upon these, they must cut all their throats; and it was ten to one but some of them might escape, it being in the night, though the moon was up; and if one escaped, he would run and raise all the town, so they should have a whole army upon them; on the other hand, if they went away and left those untouched, for the people were all asleep, they could not tell which way to look for the town; however, the last was the best advice, so they resolved to leave them, and look for the town as well as they could. They went on a little way, and found a cow tied to a tree; this, they presently concluded, would be a good guide to them; for, they said, the cow certainly belonged to the town before them, or the town behind them, and if they untied her, they should see which way she went: if she went back, they had nothing to say to her; but if she went forward, they would follow her. So they cut the cord, which was made of twisted flags, and the cow went on before them, directly to the town; which, as they reported, consisted of above two hundred houses or huts, and in some of these they found several families living together.

Here they found all in silence, as profoundly secure as sleep could make them: and first, they called another council, to consider what they

382

had to do; and presently resolved to divide themselves into three bodies, and so set three houses on fire in three parts of the town; and as the men came out, to seize them and bind them (if any resisted, they need not be asked what to do then), and so to search the rest of the houses for plunder: but they resolved to march silently first through the town, and see what dimensions it was of, and if they might venture upon it or no.

They did so, and desperately resolved that they would venture upon them: but while they were animating one another to the work, three of them, who were a little before the rest, called out aloud to them, and told them that they had found — Tom Jeffry: they all ran up to the place, where they found the poor fellow hanging up naked by one arm, and his throat cut. There was an Indian house just by the tree, where they found sixteen or seventeen of the principal Indians, who had been concerned in the fray with us before, and two or three of them wounded with our shot; and our men found they were awake, and talking one to another in that house, but knew not their number.

The sight of their poor mangled comrade so enraged them, as before, that they swore to one another that they would be revenged, and that not an Indian that came into their hands should have any quarter; and to work they went immediately, and yet not so madly as might be expected from the rage and fury they were in. Their first care was to get something that would soon take fire, but, after a little search, they found that would be to no purpose; for most of the houses were low, and thatched with flags and rushes, of which the country is full; so they presently made some wildfire, as we call it, by wetting a little powder in the palm of their hands, and in a quarter of an hour they set the town on fire in four or five places, and particularly that house where the Indians were not gone to bed.

As soon as the fire begun to blaze, the poor frightened creatures began to rush out to save their lives, but met with their fate in the attempt; and especially at the door, where they drove them back, the boatswain himself killing one or two with his poleaxe. The house being large, and many in it, he did not care to go in, but called for a hand grenado, and threw it among them, which at first frightened them, but, when it burst, made such havoc among them that they cried out in a hideous manner. In short, most of the Indians who were in the open part of the house were killed or hurt with the grenado, except two or three more who pressed to the door, which the boatswain and two more kept, with their bayonets on the muzzles of their pieces, and dispatched all that came in their way; but there was another apartment in the house, where the prince or king, or whatever he was, and several others were; and these were kept in till the house, which was by this time all in a light flame, fell in upon them, and they were smothered together.

All this while they fired not a gun, because they would not waken the people faster than they could master them; but the fire began to waken them fast enough, and our fellows were glad to keep a little together in bodies; for the fire grew so raging, all the houses being made of light combustible stuff, that they could hardly bear the street between them. Their business was to follow the fire, for the surer execution: as fast as the fire either forced the people out of those houses which were burning, or frightened them out of others, our people were ready at their doors to knock them on the head, still calling and hallooing one to another to remember Tom Jeffry.

While this was doing, I must confess I was very uneasy, and especially when I saw the flames of the town, which, it being night, seemed to be close by me. My nephew, the captain, who was roused by his men seeing such a fire, was very uneasy, not knowing what the matter was, or what danger I was in, especially hearing the guns too, for by this time they began to use their firearms; a thousand thoughts oppressed his mind concerning me and the supercargo, what would become of us; and at last, though he could ill spare any more men, yet not knowing what exigency we might be in, he took another boat, and with thirteen men and himself came ashore to me.

He was surprised to see me and the supercargo in the boat with no more than two men; and though he was glad that we were well, yet he was in the same impatience with us to know what was doing; for the noise continued, and the flame increased; in short, it was next to an impossibility for any men in the world to restrain their curiosity to know what had happened, or their concern for the safety of the men: in a word, the captain told me he would go and help his men, let what would come. I argued with him, as I did before with the men, the safety of the ship, the danger of the voyage, the interests of the owners and merchants, &c., and told him I and the two men would go, and only see if we could at a distance learn what was likely to be the event, and come back and tell him. It was in vain to talk to my nephew, as it was to talk to the rest before; he would go, he said; and he only wished he had left but ten men in the ship, for he could not think of having his men lost for want of help: he had rather lose the ship, the voyage, and his life, and all; and away he went.

I was no more able to stay behind now than I was to persuade them not to go; so the captain ordered two men to row back the pinnace, and fetch twelve men more, leaving the long-boat at an anchor; and that, when they came back, six men should keep the two boats, and six more come after us; so that he left only sixteen men in the ship: for the whole ship's company consisted of sixty-five men, whereof two were lost in the late quarrel which brought this mischief on.

Being now on the march, we felt little of the ground we trod on; and being guided by the fire, we kept no path, but went directly to the place of the flame. If the noise of the guns was surprising to us before, the cries of the poor people were now quite of another nature, and filled us with horror. I must confess I was never at the sacking a city, or at the taking a town by storm. I had heard of Oliver Cromwell taking Drogheda, in Ireland, and killing man, woman, and child; and I had read of Count Tilly sacking the city of Magdeburg and cutting the throats of twenty-two thousand of all sexes; but I never had an idea of the thing itself before, nor is it possible to describe it, or the horror that was upon our minds at hearing it. However, we went on, and at length came to the town, though there was no entering the streets of it for the fire. The first object we met with was the ruins of a hut or house, or rather the ashes of it, for the house was consumed; and just before it, plainly now to be seen by the light of the fire, lay four men and three women, killed, and, as we thought, one or two more lay in the heap among the fire; in short, there were such instances of rage, altogether barbarous, and of a fury something beyond what was human, that we thought it impossible our men could be guilty of it; or, if they were the authors of it, we thought they ought to be every one of them put to the worst of deaths. But this was not all: we saw the fire increase forward, and the cry went on just as the fire went on; so that we were in the utmost confusion. We advanced a little way farther, and behold, to our astonishment, three naked women, and crying in a most dreadful manner, came flying as if they had wings, and after them sixteen or seventeen men, natives, in the same terror and consternation, with three of our English butchers in the rear, who, when they could not overtake them, fired in among them, and one that was killed by their shot fell down in our sight. When the rest saw us, believing us to be their enemies, and that we would murder them as well as those that pursued them, they set up a most dreadful shriek, especially the women; and two of them fell down, as if already dead, with the fright.

My very soul shrunk within me, and my blood ran chill in my veins, when I saw this; and, I believe, had the three English sailors that pursued them come on, I had made our men kill them all; however, we took some means to let the poor flying creatures know that we would not hurt them; and immediately they came up to us, and kneeling down, with their hands lifted up, made piteous lamentation to us to save them, which we let them know we would: whereupon they crept all together in a huddle close behind us, as for protection. I left my men drawn up together, and, charging them to hurt nobody, but, if possible, to get at some of our people, and see what devil it was possessed them, and what they intended to do, and to command them off; assuring them that if they stayed till daylight they would have a hundred thousand men about their ears: I say I left them, and went among those flying people, taking only two of our men with me; and there was, indeed, a piteous spectacle among them. Some of them had their feet terribly burned with trampling and running through the fire; others their hands burned; one of the women had fallen down in the fire, and was very much burned before she could get out again; and two or three of the men had cuts in their backs and thighs, from our men pursuing; and another was shot through the body and died while I was there.

I would fain have learned what the occasion of all this was; but I could not understand one word they said; though, by signs, I perceived some of them knew not what was the occasion themselves. I was so terrified in my thoughts at this outrageous attempt that I could not stay there, but went back to my own men, and resolved to go into the middle of the town, through the fire, or whatever might be in the way, and put an end to it, cost what it would; accordingly, as I came back to my men, I told them my resolution, and commanded them to follow me, when, at the very moment, came four of our men, with the boatswain at their head, roving over heaps of bodies they had killed, all covered with blood and dust, as if they wanted more people to massacre, when our men hallooed to them as loud as they could halloo; and with much ado one of them made them hear, so that they knew who we were, and came up to us.

As soon as the boatswain saw us, he set up a halloo like a shout of triumph, for having, as he thought, more help come; and without waiting to hear me, "Captain," says he, "noble captain! I am glad you are come; we have not half done yet. Villainous hell-hound dogs! I'll kill as many of them as poor Tom has hairs upon his head: we have sworn to spare none of them; we'll root out the very nation of them from the earth;" and thus he ran on, out of breath, too, with action, and would not give us leave to speak a word. At last, raising my voice that I might silence him a little, "Barbarous dog!" said I, "what are you doing! I won't have one creature touched more, upon pain of death; I charge you, upon your life, to stop your hands, and stand still here, or you are a dead man this minute." — "Why, sir," says he, "do you know what you do, or what they have done? If you want a reason for what we have done, come hither;" and with that he showed me the poor fellow hanging, with his throat cut.

I confess I was urged then myself, and at another time would have been forward enough; but I thought they had carried their rage too far, and remembered Jacob's words to his sons Simeon and Levi: "Cursed be their anger, for it was fierce; and their wrath, for it was cruel." But I had now a new task upon my hands; for when the men I had carried with me saw the sight, as I had done, I had as much to do to restrain them as I should have had with the others; nay, my nephew himself fell in with them, and told me, in their hearing, that he was only concerned for fear of the men being overpowered; and as to the people, he thought not one of them ought to live; for they had all glutted themselves with the murder of the poor man, and that they ought to be used like murderers. Upon these words, away ran eight of my men, with the boatswain and his crew, to complete their bloody work; and I, seeing it quite out of my power to restrain them, came away pensive and sad; for I could not bear the sight, much less the horrible noise and cries of the poor wretches that fell into their hands.

I got nobody to come back with me but the supercargo and two men, and with these walked back to the boat. It was a very great piece of folly in me, I confess, to venture back, as it were, alone; for as it began now to be almost day, and the alarm had run over the country, there stood about forty men armed with lances and boughs at the little place where the twelve or thirteen houses stood, mentioned before: but by accident I missed the place, and came directly to the seaside, and by the time I got to the seaside it was broad day: immediately I took the pinnace and went on board, and sent her back to assist the men in what might happen. I observed, about the time that I came to the boat-side, that the fire was pretty well out, and the noise abated; but in about half-an-hour after I got on board, I heard a volley of our men's firearms, and saw a great smoke. This, as I understood afterwards, was our men falling upon the men, who, as I said, stood at the few houses on the way, of whom they killed sixteen or seventeen, and set all the houses on fire, but did not meddle with the women or children.

By the time the men got to the shore again with the pinnace our men began to appear; they came dropping in, not in two bodies as they went, but straggling here and there in such a manner, that a small force of resolute men might have cut them all off. But the dread of them was upon the whole country; and the men were surprised, and so frightened, that I believe a hundred of them would have fled at the sight of but five of our men. Nor in all this terrible action was there a man that made any considerable defence: they were so surprised between the terror of the fire and the sudden attack of our men in the dark, that they knew not which way to turn themselves; for if they fled one way they were met by one party, if back again by another, so that they were everywhere knocked down; nor did any of our men receive the least hurt, except one that sprained his foot, and another that had one of his hands burned.

CHAPTER X.

HE IS LEFT ON SHORE

I was very angry with my nephew, the captain, and indeed with all the men, but with him in particular, as well for his acting so out of his duty as a commander of the ship, and having the charge of the voyage upon him, as in his prompting, rather than cooling, the rage of his blind men in so bloody and cruel an enterprise. My nephew answered me very respectfully, but told me that when he saw the body of the poor seaman whom they had murdered in so cruel and barbarous a manner, he was not master of himself, neither could he govern his passion; he owned he should not have done so, as he was commander of the ship; but as he was a man, and nature moved him, he could not bear it. As for the rest of the men, they were not subject to me at all, and they knew it well enough; so they took no notice of my dislike. The next day we set sail, so we never heard any more of it. Our men differed in the account of the number they had killed; but according to the best of their accounts, put all together, they killed or destroyed about one hundred and fifty people, men, women, and children, and left not a house standing in the town. As for the poor fellow Tom Jeffry, as he was quite dead (for his throat was so cut that his head was half off), it would do him no service to bring him away; so they only took him down from the tree, where he was hanging by one hand.

However just our men thought this action, I was against them in it, and I always, after that time, told them God would blast the voyage; for I looked upon all the blood they shed that night to be murder in them. For though it is true that they had killed Tom Jeffry, yet Jeffry was the aggressor, had broken the truce, and had ill-used a young woman of theirs, who came down to them innocently, and on the faith of the public capitulation.

The boatswain defended this quarrel when we were afterwards on board. He said it was true that we seemed to break the truce, but really had not; and that the war was begun the night before by the natives themselves, who had shot at us, and killed one of our men without any just provocation; so that as we were in a capacity to fight them now, we might also be in a capacity to do ourselves justice upon them in an extraordinary manner; that though the poor man had taken a little liberty with the girl, he ought not to have been murdered, and that in such a villainous manner: and that they did nothing but what was just and what the laws of God allowed to be done to murderers. One would think this should have been enough to have warned us against going on shore amongst the heathens and barbarians; but it is impossible to make mankind wise but at their own expense, and their experience seems to be always of most use to them when it is dearest bought.

We were now bound to the Gulf of Persia, and from thence to the coast of Coromandel, only to touch at Surat; but the chief of the supercargo's design lay at the Bay of Bengal, where, if he missed his business outward-bound, he was to go out to China, and return to the coast as he came home. The first disaster that befell us was in the Gulf of Persia, where five of our men, venturing on shore on the Arabian side of the gulf, were surrounded by the Arabians, and either all killed or carried away into slavery; the rest of the boat's crew were not able to rescue them, and had but just time to get off their boat. I began to upbraid them with the just retribution of Heaven in this case; but the boatswain very warmly told me, he thought I went further in my censures than I could show any warrant for in Scripture; and referred to Luke xiii. 4, where our Saviour intimates that those men on whom the Tower of Siloam fell were not sinners above all the Galileans; but that which put me to silence in the case was, that not one of these five men who were now lost were of those who went on shore to the massacre of Madagascar, so I always called it, though our men could not bear to hear the word *massacre* with any patience.

But my frequent preaching to them on this subject had worse consequences than I expected; and the boatswain, who had been the head of the attempt, came up boldly to me one time, and told me he found that I brought that affair continually upon the stage; that I made unjust reflections upon it, and had used the men very ill on that account, and himself in particular; that as I was but a passenger, and had no command in the ship, or concern in the voyage, they were not obliged to bear it; that they did not know but I might have some ill-design in my head, and perhaps to call them to an account for it when they came to England; and that, therefore, unless I would resolve to have done with it, and also not to concern myself any further with him, or any of his affairs, he would leave the ship; for he did not think it safe to sail with me among them.

I heard him patiently enough till he had done, and then told him that I confessed I had all along opposed the massacre of Madagascar, and that I had, on all occasions, spoken my mind freely about it, though not more upon him than any of the rest; that as to having no command in the ship, that was true; nor did I exercise any authority, only took the liberty of speaking my mind in things which publicly concerned us all; and what concern I had in the voyage was none of his business; that I was a considerable owner in the ship. In that claim I conceived I had a right to speak even further than I had done, and would not be accountable to him or any one else, and began to be a little warm with him. He made but little reply to me at that time, and I thought the affair had been over. We were at this time in the road at Bengal; and being willing to see the place, I went on shore with the supercargo in the ship's boat to divert myself; and towards evening was preparing to go on board, when one of the men came to me, and told me he would not have me trouble myself to come down to the boat, for they had orders not to carry me on board any more. Any one may guess what a surprise I was in at so insolent a message; and I asked the man who bade him deliver that message to me? He told me the coxswain.

I immediately found out the supercargo, and told him the story, adding that I foresaw there would be a mutiny in the ship; and entreated him to go immediately on board and acquaint the captain of it. But I might have spared this intelligence, for before I had spoken to him on shore the matter was effected on board. The boatswain, the gunner, the carpenter, and all the inferior officers, as soon as I was gone off in the boat, came up, and desired to speak with the captain; and then the boatswain, making a long harangue, and repeating all he had said to me, told the captain that as I was now gone peaceably on shore, they were loath to use any violence with me, which, if I had not gone on shore, they would otherwise have done, to oblige me to have gone. They therefore thought fit to tell him that as they shipped themselves to serve in the ship under his command, they would perform it well and faithfully; but if I would not quit the ship, or the captain oblige me to quit it, they would all leave the ship, and sail no further with him; and at that word *all* he turned his face towards the main-mast, which was, it seems, a signal agreed on, when the seamen, being got together there, cried out, "*One and all! one and all!*"

My nephew, the captain, was a man of spirit, and of great presence of mind; and though he was surprised, yet he told them calmly that he would consider of the matter, but that he could do nothing in it till he had spoken to me about it. He used some arguments with them, to show them the unreasonableness and injustice of the thing, but it was all in vain; they swore, and shook hands round before his face, that they would all go on shore unless he would engage to them not to suffer me to come any more on board the ship.

This was a hard article upon him, who knew his obligation to me, and did not know how I might take it. So he began to talk smartly to them; told them that I was a very considerable owner of the ship, and that if ever they came to England again it would cost them very dear; that the ship was mine, and that he could not put me out of it; and that he would rather lose the ship, and the voyage too, than disoblige me so much: so they might do as they pleased. However, he would go on shore and talk with me, and invited the boatswain to go with him, and perhaps they might accommodate the matter with me. But they all rejected the proposal, and said they would have nothing to do with me any more; and if I came on board they would all go on shore. "Well," said the captain, "if you are all of this mind, let me go on shore and talk with him." So away he came to me with this account, a little after the message had been brought to me from the coxswain.

I was very glad to see my nephew, I must confess; for I was not without apprehensions that they would confine him by violence, set sail, and run away with the ship; and then I had been stripped naked in a remote country, having nothing to help myself; in short, I had been in a worse case than when I was alone in the island. But they had not come to that length, it seems, to my satisfaction; and when my nephew told me what they had said to him, and how they had sworn and shook hands that they would, one and all, leave the ship if I was suffered to come on board, I told him he should not be concerned at it at all, for I would stay on shore. I only desired he would take care and send me all my necessary things on shore, and leave me a sufficient sum of money, and I would find my way to England as well as I could. This was a heavy piece of news to my nephew, but there was no way to help it but to comply; so, in short, he went on board the ship again, and satisfied the men that his uncle had yielded to their importunity, and had sent for his goods from on board the ship; so that the matter was over in a few hours, the men returned to their duty, and I began to consider what course I should steer.

I was now alone in a most remote part of the world, for I was near three thousand leagues by sea farther off from England than I was at my island; only, it is true, I might travel here by land over the Great Mogul's country to Surat, might go from thence to Bassora by sea, up the Gulf of Persia, and take the way of the caravans, over the desert of Arabia, to Aleppo and Scanderoon; from thence by sea again to Italy, and so overland into France. I had another way before me, which was to wait for some English ships, which were coming to Bengal from Achin, on the island of Sumatra, and get passage on board them from England. But as I came hither without any concern with the East Indian Company, so it would be difficult to go from hence without their licence, unless with great favour of the captains of the ships, or the company's factors: and to both I was an utter stranger.

Here I had the mortification to see the ship set sail without me; however, my nephew left me two servants, or rather one companion and one servant; the first was clerk to the purser, whom he engaged to go with me, and the other was his own servant. I then took a good lodging in the house of an Englishwoman, where several merchants lodged, some French, two Italians, or rather Jews, and one Englishman. Here I stayed above nine months, considering what course to take. I had some English goods with me of value, and a considerable sum of money; my nephew furnishing me with a thousand pieces of eight, and a letter of credit for more if I had occasion, that I might not be straitened, whatever might happen. I quickly disposed of my goods to advantage; and, as I originally intended, I bought here some very good diamonds, which, of all other things, were the most proper for me in my present circumstances, because I could always carry my whole estate about me.

During my stay here many proposals were made for my return to England, but none falling out to my mind, the English merchant who lodged with me, and whom I had contracted an intimate acquaintance with, came to me one morning, saying: "Countryman, I have a project to communicate, which, as it suits with my thoughts, may, for aught I know, suit with yours also, when you shall have thoroughly considered it. Here we are posted, you by accident and I by my own choice, in a part of the world very remote from our own country; but it is in a country where, by us who understand trade and business, a great deal of money is to be got. If you will put one thousand pounds to my one thousand pounds, we will hire a ship here, the first we can get to our minds. You shall be captain, I'll be merchant, and we'll go a trading voyage to China; for what should we stand still for? The whole world is in motion; why should we be idle?"

I liked this proposal very well; and the more so because it seemed to be expressed with so much goodwill. In my loose, unhinged circumstances, I was the fitter to embrace a proposal for trade, or indeed anything else. I might perhaps say with some truth, that if trade was not my element, rambling was; and no proposal for seeing any part of the world which I had never seen before could possibly come amiss to me. It was, however, some time before we could get a ship to our minds, and when we had got a vessel, it was not easy to get English sailors — that is to say, so many as were necessary to govern the voyage and manage the sailors which we should pick up there. After some time we got a mate, a boatswain, and a gunner, English; a Dutch carpenter, and three foremast men. With these we found we could do well enough, having Indian seamen, such as they were, to make up.

When all was ready we set sail for Achin, in the island of Sumatra, and from thence to Siam, where we exchanged some of our wares for opium and some arrack; the first a commodity which bears a great price among the Chinese, and which at that time was much wanted there. Then we went up to Saskan, were eight months out, and on our return to Bengal I was very well satisfied with my adventure. Our people in England often admire how officers, which the company send into India, and the merchants which generally stay there, get such very great estates as they do, and sometimes come home worth sixty or seventy thousand pounds at a time; but it is little matter for wonder, when we consider the innumerable ports and places where they have a free commerce; indeed, at the ports where the English ships come there is such great and constant demands for the growth of all other countries, that there is a certain vent for the returns, as well as a market abroad for the goods carried out.

I got so much money by my first adventure, and such an insight into the method of getting more, that had I been twenty years younger, I should have been tempted to have stayed here, and sought no farther for making my fortune; but what was all this to a man upwards of threescore, that was rich enough, and came abroad more in obedience to a restless desire of seeing the world than a covetous desire of gaining by it? A restless desire it really was, for when I was at home I was restless to go abroad; and when I was abroad I was restless to be at home. I say, what was this gain to me? I was rich enough already, nor had I any uneasy desires about getting more money; therefore the profit of the voyage to me was of no great force for the prompting me forward to further undertakings. Hence, I thought that by this voyage I had made no progress at all, because I was come back, as I might call it, to the place from whence I came, as to a home: whereas, my eye, like that which Solomon speaks of, was never satisfied with seeing. I was come into a part of the world which I was never in before, and that part, in particular, which I heard much of, and was resolved to see as much of it as I could: and then I thought I might say I had seen all the world that was worth seeing.

But my fellow-traveler and I had different notions: I acknowledge his were the more suited to the end of a merchant's life: who, when he is abroad upon adventures, is wise to stick to that, as the best thing for him, which he is likely to get the most money by. On the other hand, mine was the notion of a mad, rambling boy, that never cares to see a thing twice over. But this was not all: I had a kind of impatience upon me to be nearer home, and yet an unsettled resolution which way to go. In the interval of these consultations, my friend, who was always upon the search for business, proposed another voyage among the Spice Islands, to bring home a loading of cloves from the Manillas, or thereabouts.

We were not long in preparing for this voyage; the chief difficulty was in bringing me to come into it. However, at last, nothing else offering, and as sitting still, to me especially, was the unhappiest part of life, I resolved on this voyage too, which we made very successfully, touching at Borneo and several other islands, and came home in about five months, when we sold our spices, with very great profit, to the Persian merchants, who carried them away to the Gulf. My friend, when we made up this account, smiled at me: "Well, now," said he, with a sort of friendly rebuke on my indolent temper, "is not this better than walking about here, like a man with nothing to do, and spending our time in staring at the nonsense and ignorance of the Pagans?" — "Why, truly," said I, "my friend, I think it is, and I begin to be a convert to the principles of merchandising; but I must tell you, by the way, you do not know what I am doing; for if I once conquer my backwardness, and embark heartily, old as I am, I shall harass you up and down the world till I tire you; for I shall pursue it so eagerly, I shall never let you lie still."

CHAPTER XI.

WARNED OF DANGER BY A COUNTRYMAN

A little while after this there came in a Dutch ship from Batavia; she was a coaster, not an European trader, of about two hundred tons burden; the men, as they pretended, having been so sickly that the captain had not hands enough to go to sea with, so he lay by at Bengal; and having, it seems, got money enough, or being willing, for other reasons, to go for Europe, he gave public notice he would sell his ship. This came to my ears before my new partner heard of it, and I had a great mind to buy it; so I went to him and told him of it. He considered a while, for he was no rash man neither; and at last replied, "She is a little too big — however, we will have her." Accordingly, we bought the ship, and agreeing with the master, we paid for her, and took possession. When we had done so we resolved to engage the men, if we could, to join with those we had, for the pursuing our business; but, on a sudden, they having received not their wages, but their share of the money, as we afterwards learned, not one of them was to be found; we inquired much about them, and at length were told that they were all gone together by land to Agra, the great city of the Mogul's residence, to proceed from thence to Surat, and then go by sea to the Gulf of Persia.

Nothing had so much troubled me a good while as that I should miss the opportunity of going with them; for such a ramble, I thought, and in such company as would both have guarded and diverted me, would have suited mightily with my great design; and I should have both seen the world and gone homeward too. But I was much better satisfied a few days after, when I came to know what sort of fellows they were; for, in short, their history was, that this man they called captain was the gunner only, not the commander; that they had been a trading voyage, in which they had been attacked on shore by some of the Malays, who had killed the captain and three of his men; and that after the captain was killed, these men, eleven in number, having resolved to run away with the ship, brought her to Bengal, leaving the mate and five men more on shore.

Well, let them get the ship how they would, we came honestly by her, as we thought, though we did not, I confess, examine into things so exactly as we ought; for we never inquired anything of the seamen, who would certainly have faltered in their account, and contradicted one another. Somehow or other we should have had reason to have suspected, them; but the man showed us a bill of sale for the ship, to one Emanuel Clostershoven, or some such name, for I suppose it was all a forgery, and called himself by that name, and we could not contradict him: and withal, having no suspicion of the thing, we went through with our bargain. We picked up some more English sailors here after this, and some Dutch, and now we resolved on a second voyage to the south-east for cloves, &c. — that is to say, among the Philippine and Malacca isles. In short, not to fill up this part of my story with trifles when what is to come is so remarkable, I spent, from first to last, six years in this country, trading from port to port, backward and forward, and with very good success, and was now the last year with my new partner, going in the ship above mentioned, on a voyage to China, but designing first to go to Siam to buy rice.

In this voyage, being by contrary winds obliged to beat up and down a great while in the Straits of Malacca and among the islands, we were no sooner got clear of those difficult seas than we found our ship had sprung a leak, but could not discover where it was. This forced us to make some port; and my partner, who knew the country better than I did, directed the captain to put into the river of Cambodia; for I had made the English mate, one Mr. Thompson, captain, not being willing to take the charge of the ship upon myself. This river lies on the north side of the great bay or gulf which goes up to Siam. While we were here, and going often on shore for refreshment, there comes to me one day an Englishman, a gunner's mate on board an English East India ship, then riding in the same river. "Sir," says he, addressing me, "you are a stranger to me, and I to you; but I have something to tell you that very nearly concerns you. I am moved by the imminent danger you are in, and, for aught I see, you have no knowledge of it." — "I know no danger I am in," said I, "but that my ship is leaky, and I cannot find it out; but I intend to lay her aground to-morrow, to see if I can find it." — "But, sir," says he, "leaky or not leaky, you will be wiser than to lay your ship on shore to-morrow when you hear what I have to say to you. Do you know, sir," said he, "the town of Cambodia lies about fifteen leagues up the river; and there are two large English ships about five leagues on this side, and three Dutch?" — "Well," said I, "and what is that to me?" — "Why, sir," said be, "is it for a man that is upon such adventures as you are to come into a port, and not examine first what ships there are there, and whether he is able to deal with them? I suppose you do not think you are a match for them?" I could not

397

conceive what he meant; and I turned short upon him, and said: "I wish you would explain yourself; I cannot imagine what reason I have to be afraid of any of the company's ships, or Dutch ships. I am no interloper. What can they have to say to me?" — "Well, sir," says he, with a smile, "if you think yourself secure you must take your chance; but take my advice, if you do not put to sea immediately, you will the very next tide be attacked by five longboats full of men, and perhaps if you are taken you will be hanged for a pirate, and the particulars be examined afterwards. I thought, sir," added he, "I should have met with a better reception than this for doing you a piece of service of such importance." — "I can never be ungrateful," said I, "for any service, or to any man that offers me any kindness; but it is past my comprehension what they should have such a design upon me for: however, since you say there is no time to be lost, and that there is some villainous design on hand against me, I will go on board this minute, and put to sea immediately, if my men can stop the leak; but, sir," said I, "shall I go away ignorant of the cause of all this? Can you give me no further light into it?"

"I can tell you but part of the story, sir," says he; "but I have a Dutch seaman here with me, and I believe I could persuade him to tell you the rest; but there is scarce time for it. But the short of the story is this — the first part of which I suppose you know well enough — that you were with this ship at Sumatra; that there your captain was murdered by the Malays, with three of his men; and that you, or some of those that were on board with you, ran away with the ship, and are since turned pirates. This is the sum of the story, and you will all be seized as pirates, I can assure you, and executed with very little ceremony; for you know merchant ships show but little law to pirates if they get them into their power." — "Now you speak plain English," said I, "and I thank you; and though I know nothing that we have done like what you talk of, for I am sure we came honestly and fairly by the ship; yet seeing such a work is doing, as you say, and that you seem to mean honestly, I will be upon my guard." — "Nay, sir," says he, "do not talk of being upon your guard; the best defence is to be out of danger. If you have any regard for your life and the lives of all your men, put to sea without fail at high-water; and as you have a whole tide before you, you will be gone too far out before they can come down; for they will come away at high-water, and as they have twenty miles to come, you will get near two hours of them by the difference of the tide, not reckoning the length of the way: besides, as they are only boats, and not ships, they will not venture to follow you far out to sea, especially if it blows." — "Well," said I, "you have been very kind in this: what shall I do to make you amends?" — "Sir," says he, "you may not be willing to make me any amends, because you may not be convinced of the truth of it. I will make an offer to you: I have nineteen months' pay due to me on board the ship — -, which I came out of England in; and the Dutchman that is with me has seven months' pay due to him. If you will make good our pay to us we will go along with you; if you find nothing more in it we will desire no more; but if we do convince you that we have saved your lives, and the ship, and the lives of all the men in her, we will leave the rest to you."

I consented to this readily, and went immediately on board, and the two men with me. As soon as I came to the ship's side, my partner, who was on board, came out on the quarter-deck, and called to me, with a great deal of joy, "We have stopped the leak — we have stopped the leak!" — "Say you so?" said I; "thank God; but weigh anchor, then, immediately." — "Weigh!" says he; "what do you mean by that? What is the matter?" — "Ask no questions," said I; "but set all hands to work, and weigh without losing a minute." He was surprised; however, he called the captain, and he immediately ordered the anchor to be got up; and though the tide was not quite down, yet a little land-breeze blowing, we stood out to sea. Then I called him into the cabin, and told him the story; and we called in the men, and they told us the rest of it; but as it took up a great deal of time, before we had done a seaman comes to the cabin door, and called out to us that the captain bade him tell us we were chased by five sloops, or boats, full of men. "Very well," said I, "then it is apparent there is something in it." I then ordered all our men to be called up, and told them there was a design to seize the ship, and take us for pirates, and asked them if they would stand by us, and by one another; the men answered cheerfully, one and all, that they would live and die with us. Then I asked the captain what way he thought best for us to manage a fight with them; for resist them I was resolved we would, and that to the last drop. He said readily, that the way was to keep them off with our great shot as long as we could, and then to use our small arms, to keep them from boarding us; but when neither of these would do any longer, we would retire to our close quarters, for perhaps they had not materials to break open our bulkheads, or get in upon us.

The gunner had in the meantime orders to bring two guns, to bear fore and aft, out of the steerage, to clear the deck, and load them with musket-bullets, and small pieces of old iron, and what came next to hand. Thus we made ready for fight; but all this while we kept out to sea, with wind enough, and could see the boats at a distance, being five large longboats, following us with all the sail they could make.

Two of those boats (which by our glasses we could see were English) outsailed the rest, were near two leagues ahead of them, and gained upon us considerably, so that we found they would come up with us; upon which we fired a gun without ball, to intimate that they should bring to: and we put out a flag of truce, as a signal for parley: but they came crowding after us till within shot, when we took in our white flag, they having made no answer to it, and hung out a red flag, and fired at them with a shot. Notwithstanding this, they came on till they were near enough to call to them with a speaking-trumpet, bidding them keep off at their peril.

It was all one; they crowded after us, and endeavoured to come under our stern, so as to board us on our quarter; upon which, seeing they were resolute for mischief, and depended upon the strength that followed them, I ordered to bring the ship to, so that they lay upon our broadside; when immediately we fired five guns at them, one of which had been leveled so true as to carry away the stern of the hindermost boat, and we then forced them to take down their sail, and to run all to the head of the boat, to keep her from sinking; so she lay by, and had enough of it; but seeing the foremost boat crowd on after us, we made ready to fire at her in particular. While this was doing one of the three boats that followed made up to the boat which we had disabled, to relieve her, and we could see her take out the men. We then called again to the foremost boat, and offered a truce, to parley again, and to know what her business was with us; but had no answer, only she crowded close under our stern. Upon this, our gunner who was a very dexterous fellow ran out his two case-guns, and fired again at her, but the shot missing, the men in the boat shouted, waved their caps, and came on. The gunner, getting quickly ready again, fired among them a second time, one shot of which, though it missed the boat itself, yet fell in among the men, and we could easily see did a great deal of mischief among them. We now wore the ship again, and brought our quarter to bear upon them, and firing three guns more, we found the boat was almost split to pieces; in particular, her rudder and a piece of her stern were shot quite away; so they handed her sail immediately, and were in great disorder. To complete their misfortune, our gunner let fly two guns at them again; where he hit them we could not tell, but we found the boat was sinking, and some of the men already in the water: upon this, I immediately manned out our pinnace, with orders to pick up some of the men if they could, and save them from drowning, and immediately come on board ship with them, because we saw the rest of the boats began to come up. Our men in the pinnace followed their orders, and took up three men, one of whom was just drowning, and it was a good while before we could recover him. As soon as they were on board we crowded all the sail we could make, and stood farther out to the sea; and we found that when the other boats came up to the first, they gave over their chase.

Being thus delivered from a danger which, though I knew not the reason of it, yet seemed to be much greater than I apprehended, I resolved that we should change our course, and not let any one know whither we were going; so we stood out to sea eastward, quite out of the course of all European ships, whether they were bound to China or anywhere else, within the commerce of the European nations. When we were at sea we began to consult with the two seamen, and inquire what the meaning of all this should be; and the Dutchman confirmed the gunner's story about the false sale of the ship and of the murder of the captain, and also how that he, this Dutchman, and four more got into the woods, where they wandered about a great while, till at length he made his escape, and swam off to a Dutch ship, which was sailing near the shore in its way from China.

He then told us that he went to Batavia, where two of the seamen belonging to the ship arrived, having deserted the rest in their travels, and gave an account that the fellow who had run away with the ship, sold her at Bengal to a set of pirates, who were gone a-cruising in her, and that they had already taken an English ship and two Dutch ships very richly laden. This latter part we found to concern us directly, though we knew it to be false; yet, as my partner said, very justly, if we had fallen into their hands, and they had had such a prepossession against us beforehand, it had been in vain for us to have defended ourselves, or to hope for any good quarter at their hands; especially considering that our accusers had been our judges, and that we could have expected nothing from them but what rage would have dictated, and an ungoverned passion have executed. Therefore it was his opinion we should go directly back to Bengal, from whence we came, without putting in at any port whatever — because where we could give a good account of ourselves, could prove where we were when the ship put in, of whom we bought her, and the like; and what was more than all the rest, if we were put upon the necessity of bringing it before the proper judges, we should be sure to have some justice, and not to be hanged first and judged afterwards.

I was some time of my partner's opinion; but after a little more serious thinking, I told him I thought it was a very great hazard for us to attempt returning to Bengal, for that we were on the wrong side of the Straits of Malacca, and that if the alarm was given, we should be sure to be waylaid on every side — that if we should be taken, as it were, running away, we should even condemn ourselves, and there would want no more evidence to destroy us. I also asked the English sailor's opinion, who said he was of my mind, and that we certainly should be taken. This danger a little startled my partner and all the ship's company, and we immediately resolved to go away to the coast of Tonquin, and so on to the coast of China — and pursuing the first design as to trade, find some way or other to dispose of the ship, and come back in some of the vessels of the country such as we could get. This was approved of as the best method for our security, and accordingly we steered away NNE., keeping above fifty leagues off from the usual course to the eastward. This, however, put us to some inconvenience: for, first, the winds, when we came that distance from the shore, seemed to be more steadily against us, blowing almost trade, as we call it, from the E. and ENE., so that we were a long while upon our voyage, and we were but ill provided with victuals for so long a run; and what was still worse, there was some danger that those English and Dutch ships whose boats pursued us, whereof some were bound that way, might have got in before us, and if not, some other ship bound to China might have information of us from them, and pursue us with the same vigour.

I must confess I was now very uneasy, and thought myself, including the late escape from the longboats, to have been in the most dangerous condition that ever I was in through my past life; for whatever ill circumstances I had been in, I was never pursued for a thief before; nor had I ever done anything that merited the name of dishonest or fraudulent, much less thievish. I had chiefly been my own enemy, or, as I may rightly say, I had been nobody's enemy but my own; but now I was woefully embarrassed: for though I was perfectly innocent, I was in no condition to make that innocence appear; and if I had been taken, it had been under a supposed guilt of the worst kind. This made me very anxious to make an escape, though which way to do it I knew not, or what port or place we could go to. My partner endeavoured to encourage me by describing the several ports of that coast, and told me he would put in on the coast of Cochin China, or the bay of Tonquin, intending afterwards to go to Macao, where a great many European families resided, and particularly the missionary priests, who usually went thither in order to their going forward to China.

Hither then we resolved to go; and, accordingly, though after a tedious course, and very much straitened for provisions, we came within sight of the coast very early in the morning; and upon reflection on the past circumstances of danger we were in, we resolved to put into a small river, which, however, had depth enough of water for us, and to see if we could, either overland or by the ship's pinnace, come to know what ships were in any port thereabouts. This happy step was, indeed, our deliverance: for though we did not immediately see any European ships in the bay of Tonquin, yet the next morning there came into the bay two Dutch ships; and a third without any colours spread out, but which we believed to be a Dutchman, passed by at about two leagues' distance, steering for the coast of China; and in the afternoon went by two English ships steering the same course; and thus we thought we saw ourselves beset with enemies both one way and the other. The place we were in was wild and barbarous, the people thieves by occupation; and though it is true we had not much to seek of them, and, except getting a few provisions, cared not how little we had to do with them, yet it was with much difficulty that we kept ourselves from being insulted by them several ways. We were in a small river of this country, within a few leagues of its utmost limits northward; and by our boat we coasted north-east to the point of land which opens the great bay of Tonquin; and it was in this beating up along the shore that we discovered we were surrounded with enemies. The people we were among were the most barbarous of all the inhabitants of the coast; and among other customs they have this one: that if any vessel has the misfortune to be shipwrecked upon their coast, they make the men all prisoners or slaves; and it was not long before we found a spice of their kindness this way, on the occasion following.

I have observed above that our ship sprung a leak at sea, and that we could not find it out; and it happened that, as I have said, it was stopped unexpectedly, on the eve of our being pursued by the Dutch and English ships in the bay of Siam; yet, as we did not find the ship so perfectly tight and sound as we desired, we resolved while we were at this place to lay her on shore, and clean her bottom, and, if possible, to find out where the leaks were. Accordingly, having lightened the ship, and brought all our guns and other movables to one side, we tried to bring her down, that we might come at her bottom; but, on second thoughts, we did not care to lay her on dry ground, neither could we find out a proper place for it.

CHAPTER XII.

THE CARPENTER'S WHIMSICAL CONTRIVANCE

The inhabitants came wondering down the shore to look at us; and seeing the ship lie down on one side in such a manner, and heeling in towards the shore, and not seeing our men, who were at work on her bottom with stages, and with their boats on the off-side, they presently concluded that the ship was cast away, and lay fast on the ground. On this supposition they came about us in two or three hours' time with ten or twelve large boats, having some of them eight, some ten men in a boat, intending, no doubt, to have come on board and plundered the ship, and if they found us there, to have carried us away for slaves.

When they came up to the ship, and began to row round her, they discovered us all hard at work on the outside of the ship's bottom and side, washing, and graving, and stopping, as every seafaring man knows how. They stood for a while gazing at us, and we, who were a little surprised, could not imagine what their design was; but being willing to be sure, we took this opportunity to get some of us into the ship, and others to hand down arms and ammunition to those that were at work, to defend themselves with if there should be occasion. And it was no more than need: for in less than a quarter of an hour's consultation, they agreed, it seems, that the ship was really a wreck, and that we were all at work endeavouring to save her, or to save our lives by the help of our boats; and when we handed our arms into the boat, they concluded, by that act, that we were endeavouring to save some of our goods. Upon this, they took it for granted we all belonged to them, and away they came directly upon our men, as if it had been in a line-of-battle.

Our men, seeing so many of them, began to be frightened, for we lay but in an ill posture to fight, and cried out to us to know what they should do. I immediately called to the men that worked upon the stages to slip them down, and get up the side into the ship, and bade those in the boat to row round and come on board. The few who were on board worked with all the strength and hands we had to bring the ship to rights; however, neither the men upon the stages nor those in the boats could do as they were ordered before the Cochin Chinese were upon them, when two of their boats boarded our longboat, and began to lay hold of the men as their prisoners.

The first man they laid hold of was an English seaman, a stout, strong fellow, who having a musket in his hand, never offered to fire it, but laid it down in the boat, like a fool, as I thought; but he understood his business better than I could teach him, for he grappled the Pagan, and dragged him by main force out of their boat into ours, where, taking him by the ears, he beat his head so against the boat's gunnel that the fellow died in his hands. In the meantime, a Dutchman, who stood next, took up the musket, and with the butt-end of it so laid about him, that he knocked down five of them who attempted to enter the boat. But this was doing little towards resisting thirty or forty men, who, fearless because ignorant of their danger, began to throw themselves into the longboat, where we had but five men in all to defend it; but the following accident, which deserved our laughter, gave our men a complete victory.

Our carpenter being prepared to grave the outside of the ship, as well as to pay the seams where he had caulked her to stop the leaks, had got two kettles just let down into the boat, one filled with boiling pitch, and the other with rosin, tallow, and oil, and such stuff as the shipwrights use for that work; and the man that attended the carpenter had a great iron ladle in his hand, with which he supplied the men that were at work with the hot stuff. Two of the enemy's men entered the boat just where this fellow stood in the foresheets; he immediately saluted them with a ladle full of the stuff, boiling hot which so burned and scalded them, being half-naked that they roared out like bulls, and, enraged with the fire, leaped both into the sea. The carpenter saw it, and cried out, "Well done, Jack! give them some more of it!" and stepping forward himself, takes one of the mops, and dipping it in the pitch-pot, he and his man threw it among them so plentifully that, in short, of all the men in the three boats, there was not one that escaped being scalded in a most frightful manner, and made such a howling and crying that I never heard a worse noise.

I was never better pleased with a victory in my life; not only as it was a perfect surprise to me, and that our danger was imminent before, but as we got this victory without any bloodshed, except of that man the seaman killed with his naked hands, and which I was very much concerned at. Although it maybe a just thing, because necessary (for there is no necessary wickedness in nature), yet I thought it was a sad sort of life, when we must be always obliged to be killing our fellow-creatures to preserve ourselves; and, indeed, I think so still; and I would even now suffer a great deal rather than I would take away the life even of the worst person injuring me; and I believe all considering people, who know the value of life, would be of my opinion, if they entered seriously into the consideration of it.

All the while this was doing, my partner and I, who managed the rest of the men on board, had with great dexterity brought the ship almost to rights, and having got the guns into their places again, the gunner called to me to bid our boat get out of the way, for he would let fly among them. I called back again to him, and bid him not offer to fire, for the carpenter would do the work without him; but bid him heat another pitch-kettle, which our cook, who was on broad, took care of. However, the enemy was so terrified with what they had met with in their first attack, that they would not come on again; and some of them who were farthest off, seeing the ship swim, as it were, upright, began, as we suppose, to see their mistake, and gave over the enterprise, finding it was not as they expected. Thus we got clear of this merry fight; and having got some rice and some roots and bread, with about sixteen hogs, on board two days before, we resolved to stay here no longer, but go forward, whatever came of it; for we made no doubt but we should be surrounded the next day with rogues enough, perhaps more than our pitch-kettle would dispose of for us. We therefore got all our things on board the same evening, and the next morning were ready to sail: in the meantime, lying at anchor at some distance from the shore, we were not so much concerned, being now in a fighting posture, as well as in a sailing posture, if any enemy had presented. The next day, having finished our work within board, and finding our ship was perfectly healed of all her leaks, we set sail. We would have gone into the bay of Tonquin, for we wanted to inform ourselves of what was to be known concerning the Dutch ships that had been there; but we durst not stand in there, because we had seen several ships go in, as we supposed, but a little before; so we kept on NE. towards the island of Formosa, as much afraid of being seen by a Dutch or English merchant ship as a Dutch or English merchant ship in the Mediterranean is of an Algerine man-of-war.

When we were thus got to sea, we kept on NE., as if we would go to the Manillas or the Philippine Islands; and this we did that we might not fall into the way of any of the European ships; and then we steered north, till we came to the latitude of 22 degrees 30 seconds, by which means we made the island of Formosa directly, where we came to an anchor, in order to get water and fresh provisions, which the people there, who are very courteous in their manners, supplied us with willingly, and dealt very fairly and punctually with us in all their agreements and bargains. This is what we did not find among other people, and may be owing to the remains of Christianity which was once planted here by a Dutch missionary of Protestants, and it is a testimony of what I have often observed, viz. that the Christian religion always civilizes the people, and reforms their manners, where it is received, whether it works saving effects upon them or no.

From thence we sailed still north, keeping the coast of China at an equal distance, till we knew we were beyond all the ports of China where our European ships usually come; being resolved, if possible, not to fall into any of their hands, especially in this country, where, as our circumstances were, we could not fail of being entirely ruined. Being now come to the latitude of 30 degrees, we resolved to put into the first trading port we should come at; and standing in for the shore, a boat came of two leagues to us with an old Portuguese pilot on board, who, knowing us to be an European ship, came to offer his service, which, indeed, we were glad of and took him on board; upon which, without asking us whither we would go, he dismissed the boat he came in, and sent it back. I thought it was now so much in our choice to make the old man carry us whither we would, that I began to talk to him about carrying us to the Gulf of Nankin, which is the most northern part of the coast of China. The old man said he knew the Gulf of Nankin very well; but smiling, asked us what we would do there? I told him we would sell our cargo and purchase China wares, calicoes, raw silks, tea, wrought silks, &c.; and so we would return by the same course we came. He told us our best port would have been to put in at Macao, where we could not have failed of a market for our opium to our satisfaction, and might for our money have purchased all sorts of China goods as cheap as we could at Nankin.

Not being able to put the old man out of his talk, of which he was very opinionated or conceited, I told him we were gentlemen as well as merchants, and that we had a mind to go and see the great city of Pekin, and the famous court of the monarch of China. "Why, then," says the old man, "you should go to Ningpo, where, by the river which runs into the sea there, you may go up within five leagues of the great canal. This canal is a navigable stream, which goes through the heart of that vast empire of China, crosses all the rivers, passes some considerable hills by the help of sluices and gates, and goes up to the city of Pekin, being in length near two hundred and seventy leagues." — "Well," said I, "Seignior Portuguese, but that is not our business now; the great question is, if you can carry us up to the city of Nankin, from whence we can travel to Pekin afterwards?" He said he could do so very well, and that there was a great Dutch ship gone up that way just before. This gave me a little shock, for a Dutch ship was now our terror, and we had much rather have met the devil, at least if he had not come in too frightful a figure; and we depended upon it that a Dutch ship would be our destruction, for we were in no condition to fight them; all the ships they trade with into those parts being of great burden, and of much greater force than we were.

The old man found me a little confused, and under some concern when he named a Dutch ship, and said to me, "Sir, you need be under no apprehensions of the Dutch; I suppose they are not now at war with your nation?" — "No," said I, "that's true; but I know not what liberties men may take when they are out of the reach of the laws of their own country." — "Why," says he, "you are no pirates; what need you fear? They will not meddle with peaceable merchants, sure." These words put me into the greatest disorder and confusion imaginable; nor was it possible for me to conceal it so, but the old man easily perceived it.

"Sir," says he, "I find you are in some disorder in your thoughts at my talk: pray be pleased to go which way you think fit, and depend upon it, I'll do you all the service I can." Upon this we fell into further discourse, in which, to my alarm and amazement, he spoke of the villainous doings of a certain pirate ship that had long been the talk of mariners in those seas; no other, in a word, than the very ship he was now on board of, and which we had so unluckily purchased. I presently saw there was no help for it but to tell him the plain truth, and explain all the danger and trouble we had suffered through this misadventure, and, in particular, our earnest wish to be speedily quit of the ship altogether; for which reason we had resolved to carry her up to Nankin.

The old man was amazed at this relation, and told us we were in the right to go away to the north; and that, if he might advise us, it should be to sell the ship in China, which we might well do, and buy, or build another in the country; adding that I should meet with customers enough for the ship at Nankin, that a Chinese junk would serve me very well to go back again, and that he would procure me people both to buy one and sell the other. "Well, but, seignior," said I, "as you say they know the ship so well, I may, perhaps, if I follow your measures, be instrumental to bring some honest, innocent men into a terrible broil; for wherever they find the ship they will prove the guilt upon the men, by proving this was the ship." — "Why," says the old man, "I'll find out a way to prevent that; for as I know all those commanders you speak of very well, and shall see them all as they pass by, I will be sure to set them to rights in the thing, and let them know that they had been so much in the wrong; that though the people who were on board at first might run away with the ship, yet it was not true that they had turned pirates; and that, in particular, these were not the men that first went off with the ship, but innocently bought her for their trade; and I am persuaded they will so far believe me as at least to act more cautiously for the time to come."

In about thirteen days' sail we came to an anchor, at the south-west point of the great Gulf of Nankin; where I learned by accident that two Dutch ships were gone the length before me, and that I should certainly fall into their hands. I consulted my partner again in this exigency, and he was as much at a loss as I was. I then asked the old pilot if there was no creek or harbour which I might put into and pursue my business with the Chinese privately, and be in no danger of the enemy. He told me if I would sail to the southward about forty-two leagues, there was a little port called Quinchang, where the fathers of the mission usually landed from Macao, on their progress to teach the Christian religion to the Chinese, and where no European ships ever put in; and if I thought to put in there, I might consider what further course to take when I was on shore. He confessed, he said, it was not a place for merchants, except that at some certain times they had a kind of a fair there, when the merchants from Japan came over thither to buy Chinese merchandises. The name of the port I may perhaps spell wrong, having lost this, together with the names of many other places set down in a little pocket-book, which was spoiled by the water by an accident; but this I remember, that the Chinese merchants we corresponded with called it by a different name from that which our Portuguese pilot gave it, who pronounced it Quinchang. As we were unanimous in our resolution to go to this place, we weighed the next day, having only gone twice on shore where we were, to get fresh water; on both which occasions the people of the country were very civil, and brought abundance of provisions to sell to us; but nothing without money.

We did not come to the other port (the wind being contrary) for five days; but it was very much to our satisfaction, and I was thankful when I set my foot on shore, resolving, and my partner too, that if it was possible to dispose of ourselves and effects any other way, though not profitably, we would never more set foot on board that unhappy vessel. Indeed, I must acknowledge, that of all the circumstances of life that ever I had any experience of, nothing makes mankind so completely miserable as that of being in constant fear. Well does the Scripture say, "The fear of man brings a snare"; it is a life of death, and the mind is so entirely oppressed by it, that it is capable of no relief.

Nor did it fail of its usual operations upon the fancy, by heightening every danger; representing the English and Dutch captains to be men incapable of hearing reason, or of distinguishing between honest men and rogues; or between a story calculated for our own turn, made out of nothing, on purpose to deceive, and a true, genuine account of our whole voyage, progress, and design; for we might many ways have convinced any reasonable creatures that we were not pirates; the goods we had on board, the course we steered, our frankly showing ourselves, and entering into such and such ports; and even our very manner, the force we had, the number of men, the few arms, the little ammunition, short provisions; all these would have served to convince any men that we were no pirates. The opium and other goods we had on board would make it appear the ship had been at Bengal. The Dutchmen, who, it was said, had the names of all the men that were in the ship, might easily see that we were a mixture of English, Portuguese, and Indians, and but two Dutchmen on board. These, and many other particular circumstances, might have made it evident to the understanding of any commander, whose hands we might fall into, that we were no pirates.

But fear, that blind, useless passion, worked another way, and threw us into the vapours; it bewildered our understandings, and set the imagination at work to form a thousand terrible things that perhaps might never happen. We first supposed, as indeed everybody had related to us, that the seamen on board the English and Dutch ships, but especially the Dutch, were so enraged at the name of a pirate, and especially at our beating off their boats and escaping, that they would not give themselves leave to inquire whether we were pirates or no, but would execute us off-hand, without giving us any room for a defence. We reflected that there really was so much apparent evidence before them, that they would scarce inquire after any more; as, first, that the ship was certainly the same, and that some of the seamen among them knew her, and had been on board her; and, secondly, that when we had intelligence at the river of Cambodia that they were coming down to examine us, we fought their boats and fled. Therefore we made no doubt but they were as fully satisfied of our being pirates as we were satisfied of the contrary; and, as I often said, I know not but I should have been apt to have taken those circumstances for evidence, if the tables were turned, and my case was theirs; and have made no scruple of cutting all the crew to pieces, without believing, or perhaps considering, what they might have to offer in their defence.

But let that be how it will, these were our apprehensions; and both my partner and I scarce slept a night without dreaming of halters and yard-arms; of fighting, and being taken; of killing, and being killed: and one night I was in such a fury in my dream, fancying the Dutchmen had boarded us, and I was knocking one of their seamen down, that I struck my doubled fist against the side of the cabin I lay in with such a force as wounded my hand grievously, broke my knuckles, and cut and bruised the flesh, so that it awaked me out of my sleep. Another apprehension I had was, the cruel usage we might meet with from them if we fell into their hands; then the story of Amboyna came into my head, and how the Dutch might perhaps torture us, as they did our countrymen there, and make some of our men, by extremity of torture, confess to crimes they never were guilty of, or own themselves and all of us to be pirates, and so they would put us to death with a formal appearance of justice; and that they might be tempted to do this for the gain of our ship and cargo, worth altogether four or five thousand pounds. We did not consider that the captains of ships have no authority to act thus; and if we had surrendered prisoners to them, they could not answer the destroying us, or torturing us, but would be accountable for it when they came to their country. However, if they were to act thus with us, what advantage would it be to us that they should be called to an account for it? — or if we were first to be murdered, what satisfaction would it be to us to have them punished when they came home?

I cannot refrain taking notice here what reflections I now had upon the vast variety of my particular circumstances; how hard I thought it that I, who had spent forty years in a life of continual difficulties, and was at last come, as it were, to the port or haven which all men drive at, viz. to have rest and plenty, should be a volunteer in new sorrows by my own unhappy choice, and that I, who had escaped so many dangers in my youth, should now come to be hanged in my old age, and in so remote a place, for a crime which I was not in the least inclined to, much less guilty of. After these thoughts something of religion would come in; and I would be considering that this seemed to me to be a disposition of immediate Providence, and I ought to look

412

upon it and submit to it as such. For, although I was innocent as to men, I was far from being innocent as to my Maker; and I ought to look in and examine what other crimes in my life were most obvious to me, and for which Providence might justly inflict this punishment as a retribution; and thus I ought to submit to this, just as I would to a shipwreck, if it had pleased God to have brought such a disaster upon me.

In its turn natural courage would sometimes take its place, and then I would be talking myself up to vigorous resolutions; that I would not be taken to be barbarously used by a parcel of merciless wretches in cold blood; that it were much better to have fallen into the hands of the savages, though I were sure they would feast upon me when they had taken me, than those who would perhaps glut their rage upon me by inhuman tortures and barbarities; that in the case of the savages, I always resolved to die fighting to the last gasp, and why should I not do so now? Whenever these thoughts prevailed, I was sure to put myself into a kind of fever with the agitation of a supposed fight; my blood would boil, and my eyes sparkle, as if I was engaged, and I always resolved to take no quarter at their hands; but even at last, if I could resist no longer, I would blow up the ship and all that was in her, and leave them but little booty to boast of.

CHAPTER XIII.

ARRIVAL IN CHINA

The greater weight the anxieties and perplexities of these things were to our thoughts while we were at sea, the greater was our satisfaction when we saw ourselves on shore; and my partner told me he dreamed that he had a very heavy load upon his back, which he was to carry up a hill, and found that he was not able to stand longer under it; but that the Portuguese pilot came and took it off his back, and the hill disappeared, the ground before him appearing all smooth and plain: and truly it was so; they were all like men who had a load taken off their backs. For my part I had a weight taken off from my heart that it was not able any longer to bear; and as I said above we resolved to go no more to sea in that ship. When we came on shore, the old pilot, who was now our friend, got us a lodging, together with a warehouse for our goods; it was a little hut, with a larger house adjoining to it, built and also palisadoed round with canes, to keep out pilferers, of which there were not a few in that country: however, the magistrates allowed us a little guard, and we had a soldier with a kind of half-pike, who stood sentinel at our door, to whom we allowed a pint of rice and a piece of money about the value of three-pence per day, so that our goods were kept very safe.

The fair or mart usually kept at this place had been over some time; however, we found that there were three or four junks in the river, and two ships from Japan, with goods which they had bought in China, and were not gone away, having some Japanese merchants on shore.

The first thing our old Portuguese pilot did for us was to get us acquainted with three missionary Romish priests who were in the town, and who had been there some time converting the people to Christianity; but we thought they made but poor work of it, and made them but sorry Christians when they had done. One of these was a Frenchman, whom they called Father Simon; another was a Portuguese; and a third a Genoese. Father Simon was courteous, and very agreeable company; but the other two were more reserved, seemed rigid and austere, and applied seriously to the work they came about, viz. to talk with and insinuate themselves among the inhabitants wherever they had opportunity. We often ate and drank with those men; and though I must confess the conversion, as they call it, of the Chinese to Christianity is so far from the true conversion required to bring heathen

414

people to the faith of Christ, that it seems to amount to little more than letting them know the name of Christ, and say some prayers to the Virgin Mary and her Son, in a tongue which they understood not, and to cross themselves, and the like; yet it must be confessed that the religionists, whom we call missionaries, have a firm belief that these people will be saved, and that they are the instruments of it; and on this account they undergo not only the fatigue of the voyage, and the hazards of living in such places, but oftentimes death itself, and the most violent tortures, for the sake of this work.

Father Simon was appointed, it seems, by order of the chief of the mission, to go up to Pekin, and waited only for another priest, who was ordered to come to him from Macao, to go along with him. We scarce ever met together but he was inviting me to go that journey; telling me how he would show me all the glorious things of that mighty empire, and, among the rest, Pekin, the greatest city in the world: "A city," said he, "that your London and our Paris put together cannot be equal to." But as I looked on those things with different eyes from other men, so I shall give my opinion of them in a few words, when I come in the course of my travels to speak more particularly of them.

Dining with Father Simon one day, and being very merry together, I showed some little inclination to go with him; and he pressed me and my partner very hard to consent. "Why, father," says my partner, "should you desire our company so much? you know we are heretics, and you do not love us, nor cannot keep us company with any pleasure." — "Oh," says he, "you may perhaps be good Catholics in time; my business here is to convert heathens, and who knows but I may convert you too?" — "Very well, father," said I, "so you will preach to us all the way?" — "I will not be troublesome to you," says he; "our religion does not divest us of good manners; besides, we are here like countrymen; and so we are, compared to the place we are in; and if you are Huguenots, and I a Catholic, we may all be Christians at last; at least, we are all gentlemen, and we may converse so, without being uneasy to one another." I liked this part of his discourse very well, and it began to put me in mind of my priest that I had left in the Brazils; but Father Simon did not come up to his character by a great deal; for though this friar had no appearance of a criminal levity in him, yet he had not that fund of Christian zeal, strict piety, and sincere affection to religion that my other good ecclesiastic had.

But to leave him a little, though he never left us, nor solicited us to go with him; we had something else before us at first, for we had all this while our ship and our merchandise to dispose of, and we began to be very doubtful what we should do, for we were now in a place of very little business. Once I was about to venture to sail for the river of Kilam, and the city of Nankin; but Providence seemed now more visibly, as I thought, than ever to concern itself in our affairs; and I was encouraged, from this very time, to think I should, one way or other, get out of this entangled circumstance, and be brought home to my own country again, though I had not the least view of the manner. Providence, I say, began here to clear up our way a little; and the first thing that offered was, that our old Portuguese pilot brought a Japan merchant to us, who inquired what goods we had: and, in the first place, he bought all our opium, and gave us a very good price for it, paying us in gold by weight, some in small pieces of their own coin, and some in small wedges, of about ten or twelve ounces each. While we were dealing with him for our opium, it came into my head that he might perhaps deal for the ship too, and I ordered the interpreter to propose it to him. He shrunk up his shoulders at it when it was first proposed to him; but in a few days after he came to me, with one of the missionary priests for his interpreter, and told me he had a proposal to make to me, which was this: he had bought a great quantity of our goods, when he had no thoughts of proposals made to him of buying the ship; and that, therefore, he had not money to pay for the ship: but if I would let the same men who were in the ship navigate her, he would hire the ship to go to Japan; and would send them from thence to the Philippine Islands with another loading, which he would pay the freight of before they went from Japan: and that at their return he would buy the ship. I began to listen to his proposal, and so eager did my head still run upon rambling, that I could not but begin to entertain a notion of going myself with him, and so to set sail from the Philippine Islands away to the South Seas; accordingly, I asked the Japanese merchant if he would not hire us to the Philippine Islands and discharge us there. He said No, he could not do that, for then he could not have the return of his cargo; but he would discharge us in Japan, at the ship's return. Well, still I was for taking him at that proposal, and going myself; but my partner, wiser than myself, persuaded me from it, representing the dangers, as well of the seas as of the Japanese, who are a false, cruel, and treacherous people; likewise those of the Spaniards at the Philippines, more false, cruel, and treacherous than they.

But to bring this long turn of our affairs to a conclusion; the first thing we had to do was to consult with the captain of the ship, and with his men, and know if they were willing to go to Japan. While I was doing this, the young man whom my nephew had left with me as my companion came up, and told me that he thought that voyage promised very fair, and that there was a great prospect of advantage, and he would be very glad if I undertook it; but that if I would not, and would give him leave, he would go as a merchant, or as I pleased to order him; that if ever he came to England, and I was there and alive, he would render me a faithful account of his success, which should be as much mine as I pleased. I was loath to part with him; but considering the prospect of advantage, which really was considerable, and that he was a young fellow likely to do well in it, I inclined to let him go; but I told him I would consult my partner, and give him an answer the next day. I discoursed about it with my partner, who thereupon made a most generous offer: "You know it has been an unlucky ship," said he, "and we both resolve not to go to sea in it again; if your steward" (so he called my man) "will venture the voyage, I will leave my share of the vessel to him, and let him make the best of it; and if we live to meet in England, and he meets with success abroad, he shall account for one half of the profits of the ship's freight to us; the other shall be his own."

If my partner, who was no way concerned with my young man, made him such an offer, I could not do less than offer him the same; and all the ship's company being willing to go with him, we made over half the ship to him in property, and took a writing from him, obliging him to account for the other, and away he went to Japan. The Japan merchant proved a very punctual, honest man to him: protected him at Japan, and got him a licence to come on shore, which the Europeans in general have not lately obtained. He paid him his freight very punctually; sent him to the Philippines loaded with Japan and China wares, and a supercargo of their own, who, trafficking with the Spaniards, brought back European goods again, and a great quantity of spices; and there he was not only paid his freight very well, and at a very good price, but not being willing to sell the ship, then the merchant furnished him goods on his own account; and with some money, and some spices of his own which he brought with him, he went back to the Manillas, where he sold his cargo very well. Here, having made a good acquaintance at Manilla, he got his ship made a free ship, and the governor of Manilla hired him to go to Acapulco, on the coast of America, and gave him a licence to land there, and to travel to Mexico, and to pass in any Spanish ship to Europe with all his men. He made the voyage to Acapulco very happily, and there he sold his ship: and having there also obtained allowance to travel by land to Porto Bello, he found means to get to Jamaica, with all his treasure, and about eight years after came to England exceeding rich.

But to return to our particular affairs, being now to part with the ship and ship's company, it came before us, of course, to consider what recompense we should give to the two men that gave us such timely notice of the design against us in the river Cambodia. The truth was, they had done us a very considerable service, and deserved well at our hands; though, by the way, they were a couple of rogues, too; for, as they believed the story of our being pirates, and that we had really run away with the ship, they came down to us, not only to betray the design that was formed against us, but to go to sea with us as pirates. One of them confessed afterwards that nothing else but the hopes of going a-roguing brought him to do it: however, the service they did us was not the less, and therefore, as I had promised to be grateful to them, I first ordered the money to be paid them which they said was due to them on board their respective ships: over and above that, I gave each of them a small sum of money in gold, which contented them very well. I then made the Englishman gunner in the ship, the gunner being now made second mate and purser; the Dutchman I made boatswain; so they were both very well pleased, and proved very serviceable, being both able seamen, and very stout fellows.

We were now on shore in China; if I thought myself banished, and remote from my own country at Bengal, where I had many ways to get home for my money, what could I think of myself now, when I was about a thousand leagues farther off from home, and destitute of all manner of prospect of return? All we had for it was this: that in about four months' time there was to be another fair at the place where we were, and then we might be able to purchase various manufactures of the country, and withal might possibly find some Chinese junks from Tonquin for sail, that would carry us and our goods whither we pleased. This I liked very well, and resolved to wait; besides, as our particular persons were not obnoxious, so if any English or Dutch ships came thither, perhaps we might have an opportunity to load our goods, and get passage to some other place in India nearer home. Upon these hopes we resolved to continue here; but, to divert ourselves, we took two or three journeys into the country.

First, we went ten days' journey to Nankin, a city well worth seeing; they say it has a million of people in it: it is regularly built, and the streets are all straight, and cross one another in direct lines. But when I come to compare the miserable people of these countries with ours, their fabrics, their manner of living, their government, their religion, their wealth, and their glory, as some call it, I must confess that I scarcely think it worth my while to mention them here. We wonder at the grandeur, the riches, the pomp, the ceremonies, the government, the manufactures, the commerce, and conduct of these people; not that there is really any matter for wonder, but because, having a true notion of the barbarity of those countries, the rudeness and the ignorance that prevail there, we do not expect to find any such thing so far off. Otherwise, what are their buildings to the palaces and royal buildings of Europe? What their trade to the universal commerce of England, Holland, France, and Spain? What are their cities to ours, for wealth, strength, gaiety of apparel, rich furniture, and infinite variety? What are their ports, supplied with a few junks and barks, to our navigation, our merchant fleets, our large and powerful navies? Our city of London has more trade than half their mighty empire: one English, Dutch, or French man-of-war of eighty guns would be able to fight almost all the shipping belonging to China: but the greatness of their wealth, their trade, the power of their government, and the strength of their armies, may be a little surprising to us, because, as I have said, considering them as a barbarous nation of pagans, little better than savages, we did not expect such things among them. But all the forces of their empire, though they were to bring two millions of men into the field together, would be able to do nothing but ruin the country and starve themselves; a million of their foot could not stand before one embattled body of our infantry, posted so as not to be surrounded, though they were not to be one to twenty in number; nay, I do not boast if I say that thirty thousand German or English foot, and ten thousand horse, well managed, could defeat all the forces of China. Nor is there a fortified town in China that could hold out one month against the batteries and attacks of an European army. They have firearms, it is true, but they are awkward and uncertain in their going off; and their powder has but little strength. Their armies are badly disciplined, and want skill to attack, or temper to retreat; and therefore, I must confess, it seemed strange to me, when I came home, and heard our people say such fine things of the power, glory, magnificence, and trade of the Chinese; because, as far as I saw, they appeared to be a contemptible herd or crowd of ignorant, sordid slaves, subjected to a government qualified only to rule such a people; and were not its distance inconceivably, great from Muscovy, and that empire in a manner as rude, impotent, and ill governed as they, the Czar of Muscovy might with ease drive them all out of their country, and conquer them in one campaign; and had the Czar (who is now a growing prince) fallen this way, instead of attacking the warlike Swedes, and equally improved himself in the art of war, as they say he has done; and if none of the powers of Europe had envied or interrupted him, he might by this time have been Emperor of China, instead of being beaten by the King of Sweden at Narva, when the latter was not one to six in number.

As their strength and their grandeur, so their navigation, commerce, and husbandry are very imperfect, compared to the same things in Europe; also, in their knowledge, their learning, and in their skill in the sciences, they are either very awkward or defective, though they have globes or spheres, and a smattering of the mathematics, and think they know more than all the world besides. But they know little of the motions of the heavenly bodies; and so grossly and absurdly ignorant are their common people, that when the sun is eclipsed, they think a great dragon has assaulted it, and is going to run away with it; and they fall a clattering with all the drums and kettles in the country, to fright the monster away, just as we do to hive a swarm of bees!

As this is the only excursion of the kind which I have made in all the accounts I have given of my travels, so I shall make no more such. It is none of my business, nor any part of my design; but to give an account of my own adventures through a life of inimitable wanderings, and a long variety of changes, which, perhaps, few that come after me will have heard the like of: I shall, therefore, say very little of all the mighty places, desert countries, and numerous people I have yet to pass through, more than relates to my own story, and which my concern among them will make necessary.

I was now, as near as I can compute, in the heart of China, about thirty degrees north of the line, for we were returned from Nankin. I had indeed a mind to see the city of Pekin, which I had heard so much of, and Father Simon importuned me daily to do it. At length his time of going away being set, and the other missionary who was to go with him being arrived from Macao, it was necessary that we should resolve either to go or not; so I referred it to my partner, and left it wholly to his choice, who at length resolved it in the affirmative, and we prepared for our journey. We set out with very good advantage as to finding the way; for we got leave to travel in the retinue of one of their mandarins, a kind of viceroy or principal magistrate in the province where they reside, and who take great state upon them, traveling with great attendance, and great homage from the people, who are sometimes greatly impoverished by them, being obliged to furnish provisions for them and all their attendants in their journeys. I particularly observed in our traveling with his baggage, that though we received sufficient provisions both for ourselves and our horses from the country, as belonging to the mandarin, yet we were obliged to pay for everything we had, after the market price of the country, and the mandarin's steward collected it duly from us. Thus our traveling in the retinue of the mandarin, though it was a great act of kindness, was not such a mighty favour to us, but was a great advantage to him, considering there were above thirty other people traveled in the same manner besides us, under the protection of his retinue; for the country furnished all the provisions for nothing to him, and yet he took our money for them.

We were twenty-five days traveling to Pekin, through a country exceeding populous, but I think badly cultivated; the husbandry, the economy, and the way of living miserable, though they boast so much of the industry of the people: I say miserable, if compared with our own, but not so to these poor wretches, who know no other. The pride of the poor people is infinitely great, and exceeded by nothing but their poverty, in some parts, which adds to that which I call their misery; and I must needs think the savages of America live much more happy than the poorer sort of these, because as they have nothing, so they desire nothing; whereas these are proud and insolent and in the main are in many parts mere beggars and drudges. Their ostentation is inexpressible; and, if they can, they love to keep multitudes of servants or slaves, which is to the last degree ridiculous, as well as their contempt of all the world but themselves.

I must confess I traveled more pleasantly afterwards in the deserts and vast wildernesses of Grand Tartary than here, and yet the roads here are well paved and well kept, and very convenient for travelers; but nothing was more awkward to me than to see such a haughty, imperious, insolent people, in the midst of the grossest simplicity and ignorance; and my friend Father Simon and I used to be very merry upon these occasions, to see their beggarly pride. For example, coming by the house of a country gentleman, as Father Simon called him, about ten leagues off the city of Nankin, we had first of all the honour to ride with the master of the house about two miles; the state he rode in was a perfect Don Quixotism, being a mixture of pomp and poverty. His habit was very proper for a merry-andrew, being a dirty calico, with hanging sleeves, tassels, and cuts and slashes almost on every side: it covered a taffeta vest, so greasy as to testify that his honour must be a most exquisite sloven. His horse was a poor, starved, hobbling creature, and two slaves followed him on foot to drive the poor creature along; he had a whip in his hand, and he belaboured the beast as fast about the head as his slaves did about the tail; and thus he rode by us, with about ten or twelve servants, going from the city to his country seat, about half a league before us. We traveled on gently, but this figure of a gentleman rode away before us; and as we stopped at a village about an hour to refresh us, when we came by the country seat of this great man, we saw him in a little place before his door, eating a repast. It was a kind of garden, but he was easy to be seen; and we were given to understand that the more we looked at him the better he would be pleased. He sat under a tree, something like the palmetto, which effectually shaded him over the head, and on the south side; but under the tree was placed a large umbrella, which made that part look well enough. He sat lolling back in a great elbow-chair, being a heavy corpulent man, and had his meat brought him by two women slaves. He had two more, one of whom fed the squire with a spoon, and the other held the dish with one hand, and scraped off what he let fall upon his worship's beard and taffeta vest.

Leaving the poor wretch to please himself with our looking at him, as if we admired his idle pomp, we pursued our journey. Father Simon had the curiosity to stay to inform himself what dainties the country justice had to feed on in all his state, which he had the honour to taste of, and which was, I think, a mess of boiled rice, with a great piece of garlic in it, and a little bag filled with green pepper, and another plant which they have there, something like our ginger, but smelling like musk, and tasting like mustard; all this was put together, and a small piece of lean mutton boiled in it, and this was his worship's repast. Four or five servants more attended at a distance, who we supposed were to eat of the same after their master. As for our mandarin with whom we traveled, he was respected as a king, surrounded always with his gentlemen, and attended in all his appearances with such pomp, that I saw little of him but at a distance. I observed that there was not a horse in his retinue but that our carrier's packhorses in England seemed to me to look much better; though it was hard to judge rightly, for they were so covered with equipage, mantles, trappings, &c., that we could scarce see anything but their feet and their heads as they went along.

I was now light-hearted, and all my late trouble and perplexity being over, I had no anxious thoughts about me, which made this journey the pleasanter to me; in which no ill accident attended me, only in passing or fording a small river, my horse fell and made me free of the country, as they call it — that is to say, threw me in. The place was not deep, but it wetted me all over. I mention it because it spoiled my pocket-book, wherein I had set down the names of several people and places which I had occasion to remember, and which not taking due care of, the leaves rotted, and the words were never after to be read.

At length we arrived at Pekin. I had nobody with me but the youth whom my nephew had given me to attend me as a servant and who proved very trusty and diligent; and my partner had nobody with him but one servant, who was a kinsman. As for the Portuguese pilot, he being desirous to see the court, we bore his charges for his company, and for our use of him as an interpreter, for he understood the language of the country, and spoke good French and a little English. Indeed, this old man was most useful to us everywhere; for we had not been above a week at Pekin, when he came laughing. "Ah, Seignior Inglese," says he, "I have something to tell will make your heart glad." — "My heart glad," says I; "what can that be? I don't know anything in this country can either give me joy or grief to any great degree." — "Yes, yes," said the old man, in broken English, "make you glad, me sorry." — "Why," said I, "will it make you sorry?" — "Because," said he, "you have brought me here twenty-five days' journey, and will leave me to go back alone; and which way shall I get to my port afterwards, without a ship, without a horse, without *pecune?*" so he called money, being his broken Latin, of which he had abundance to make us merry with. In short, he told us there was a great caravan of Muscovite and Polish merchants in the city, preparing to set out on their journey by land to Muscovy, within four or five weeks; and he was sure we would take the opportunity to go with them, and leave him behind, to go back alone.

I confess I was greatly surprised with this good news, and had scarce power to speak to him for some time; but at last I said to him, "How do you know this? are you sure it is true?" — "Yes," says he; "I met this morning in the street an old acquaintance of mine, an Armenian, who is among them. He came last from Astrakhan, and was designed to go to Tonquin, where I formerly knew him, but has altered his mind, and is now resolved to go with the caravan to Moscow, and so down the river Volga to Astrakhan." — "Well, Seignior," says I, "do not be uneasy about being left to go back alone; if this be a method for my return to England, it shall be your fault if you go back to Macao at all." We then went to consult together what was to be done; and I asked my partner what he thought of the pilot's news, and whether it would suit with his affairs? He told me he would do just as I would; for he had settled all his affairs so well at Bengal, and left his effects in such good hands, that as we had made a good voyage, if he could invest it in China silks, wrought and raw, he would be content to go to England, and then make a voyage back to Bengal by the Company's ships.

Having resolved upon this, we agreed that if our Portuguese pilot would go with us, we would bear his charges to Moscow, or to England, if he pleased; nor, indeed, were we to be esteemed over-generous in that either, if we had not rewarded him further, the service he had done us being really worth more than that; for he had not only been a pilot to us at sea, but he had been like a broker for us on shore; and his procuring for us a Japan merchant was some hundreds of pounds in our pockets. So, being willing to gratify him, which was but doing him justice, and very willing also to have him with us besides, for he was a most necessary man on all occasions, we agreed to give him a quantity of coined gold, which, as I computed it, was worth one hundred and seventy-five pounds sterling, between us, and to bear all his charges, both for himself and horse, except only a horse to carry his goods. Having settled this between ourselves, we called him to let him know what we had resolved. I told him he had complained of our being willing to let him go back alone, and I was now about to tell him we designed he should not go back at all. That as we had resolved to go to Europe with the caravan, we were very willing he should go with us; and that we called him to know his mind. He shook his head and said it was a long journey, and that he had no *pecune* to carry him thither, or to subsist himself when he came there. We told him we believed it was so, and therefore we had resolved to do something for him that should let him see how sensible we were of the service he had done us, and also how agreeable he was to us: and then I told him what we had resolved to give him here, which he might lay out as we would do our own; and that as for his charges, if he would go with us we would set him safe on shore (life and casualties excepted), either in Muscovy or England, as he would choose, at our own charge, except only the carriage of his goods. He received the proposal like a man transported, and told us he would go with us over all the whole world; and so we all prepared for our journey. However, as it was with us, so it was with the other merchants:

they had many things to do, and instead of being ready in five weeks, it was four months and some days before all things were got together.

CHAPTER XIV.

ATTACKED BY TARTARS

It was the beginning of February, new style, when we set out from Pekin. My partner and the old pilot had gone express back to the port where we had first put in, to dispose of some goods which we had left there; and I, with a Chinese merchant whom I had some knowledge of at Nankin, and who came to Pekin on his own affairs, went to Nankin, where I bought ninety pieces of fine damasks, with about two hundred pieces of other very fine silk of several sorts, some mixed with gold, and had all these brought to Pekin against my partner's return. Besides this, we bought a large quantity of raw silk, and some other goods, our cargo amounting, in these goods only, to about three thousand five hundred pounds sterling; which, together with tea and some fine calicoes, and three camels' loads of nutmegs and cloves, loaded in all eighteen camels for our share, besides those we rode upon; these, with two or three spare horses, and two horses loaded with provisions, made together twenty-six camels and horses in our retinue.

The company was very great, and, as near as I can remember, made between three and four hundred horses, and upwards of one hundred and twenty men, very well armed and provided for all events; for as the Eastern caravans are subject to be attacked by the Arabs, so are these by the Tartars. The company consisted of people of several nations, but there were above sixty of them merchants or inhabitants of Moscow, though of them some were Livonians; and to our particular satisfaction, five of them were Scots, who appeared also to be men of great experience in business, and of very good substance.

When we had traveled one day's journey, the guides, who were five in number, called all the passengers, except the servants, to a great council, as they called it. At this council every one deposited a certain quantity of money to a common stock, for the necessary expense of buying forage on the way, where it was not otherwise to be had, and for satisfying the guides, getting horses, and the like. Here, too, they constituted the journey, as they call it, viz. they named captains and officers to draw us all up, and give the word of command, in case of an attack, and give every one their turn of command; nor was this forming us into order any more than what we afterwards found needful on the way.

The road all on this side of the country is very populous, and is full of potters and earth-makers — that is to say, people, that temper the earth for the China ware. As I was coming along, our Portuguese pilot, who had always something or other to say to make us merry, told me he would show me the greatest rarity in all the country, and that I should have this to say of China, after all the ill-humoured things that I had said of it, that I had seen one thing which was not to be seen in all the world beside. I was very importunate to know what it was; at last he told me it was a gentleman's house built with China ware. "Well," says I, "are not the materials of their buildings the products of their own country, and so it is all China ware, is it not?" — "No, no," says he, "I mean it is a house all made of China ware, such as you call it in England, or as it is called in our country, porcelain." — "Well," says I, "such a thing may be; how big is it? Can we carry it in a box upon a camel? If we can we will buy it." — "Upon a camel!" says the old pilot, holding up both his hands; "why, there is a family of thirty people lives in it."

I was then curious, indeed, to see it; and when I came to it, it was nothing but this: it was a timber house, or a house built, as we call it in England, with lath and plaster, but all this plastering was really China ware — that is to say, it was plastered with the earth that makes China ware. The outside, which the sun shone hot upon, was glazed, and looked very well, perfectly white, and painted with blue figures, as the large China ware in England is painted, and hard as if it had been burnt. As to the inside, all the walls, instead of wainscot, were lined with hardened and painted tiles, like the little square tiles we call galley-tiles in England, all made of the finest china, and the figures exceeding fine indeed, with extraordinary variety of colours, mixed with gold, many tiles making but one figure, but joined so artificially, the mortar being made of the same earth, that it was very hard to see where the tiles met. The floors of the rooms were of the same composition, and as hard as the earthen floors we have in use in several parts of England; as hard as stone, and smooth, but not burnt and painted, except some smaller rooms, like closets, which were all, as it were, paved with the same tile; the ceiling and all the plastering work in the whole house were of the same earth; and, after all, the roof was covered with tiles of the same, but of a deep shining black. This was a China warehouse indeed, truly and literally to be called so, and had I not been upon the journey, I could have stayed some days to see and examine the particulars of it. They told me there were fountains and fishponds in the garden, all paved on the bottom and sides with the same; and fine statues set up in rows on the walks, entirely formed of the porcelain earth, burnt whole.

As this is one of the singularities of China, so they may be allowed to excel in it; but I am very sure they excel in their accounts of it; for they told me such incredible things of their performance in crockery-ware, for such it is, that I care not to relate, as knowing it could not be true. They told me, in particular, of one workman that made a ship with all its tackle and masts and sails in earthenware, big enough to carry fifty men. If they had told me he launched it, and made a voyage to Japan in it, I might have said something to it indeed; but as it was, I knew the whole of the story, which was, in short, that the fellow lied: so I smiled, and said nothing to it. This odd sight kept me two hours behind the caravan, for which the leader of it for the day fined me about the value of three shillings; and told me if it had been three days' journey without the wall, as it was three days' within, he must have fined me four times as much, and made me ask pardon the next council-day. I promised to be more orderly; and, indeed, I found afterwards the orders made for keeping all together were absolutely necessary for our common safety.

In two days more we passed the great China wall, made for a fortification against the Tartars: and a very great work it is, going over hills and mountains in an endless track, where the rocks are impassable, and the precipices such as no enemy could possibly enter, or indeed climb up, or where, if they did, no wall could hinder them. They tell us its length is near a thousand English miles, but that the country is five hundred in a straight measured line, which the wall bounds without measuring the windings and turnings it takes; it is about four fathoms high, and as many thick in some places.

I stood still an hour or thereabouts without trespassing on our orders (for so long the caravan was in passing the gate), to look at it on every side, near and far off; I mean what was within my view: and the guide, who had been extolling it for the wonder of the world, was mighty eager to hear my opinion of it. I told him it was a most excellent thing to keep out the Tartars; which he happened not to understand as I meant it and so took it for a compliment; but the old pilot laughed! "Oh, Seignior Inglese," says he, "you speak in colours." — "In colours!" said I; "what do you mean by that?" — "Why, you speak what looks white this way and black that way — gay one way and dull another. You tell him it is a good wall to keep out Tartars; you tell me by that it is good for nothing but to keep out Tartars. I understand you, Seignior Inglese, I understand you; but Seignior Chinese understood you his own way." — "Well," says I, "do you think it would stand out an army of our country people, with a good train of artillery; or our engineers, with two companies of miners? Would not they batter it down in ten days, that an army might enter in battalia; or blow it up in the air, foundation and all, that there should be no sign of it left?" — "Ay, ay," says he, "I know that." The Chinese wanted mightily to know what I said to the pilot, and I gave him leave to tell him a few days after, for we were then almost out of their country, and he was to leave us a little time after this; but when he knew what I said, he was dumb all the rest of the way, and we heard no more of his fine story of the Chinese power and greatness while he stayed.

After we passed this mighty nothing, called a wall, something like the Picts' walls so famous in Northumberland, built by the Romans, we began to find the country thinly inhabited, and the people rather confined to live in fortified towns, as being subject to the inroads and depredations of the Tartars, who rob in great armies, and therefore are not to be resisted by the naked inhabitants of an open country. And here I began to find the necessity of keeping together in a caravan as we traveled, for we saw several troops of Tartars roving about; but when I came to see them distinctly, I wondered more that the Chinese empire could be conquered by such contemptible fellows; for they are a mere horde of wild fellows, keeping no order and understanding no discipline or manner of it. Their horses are poor lean creatures, taught nothing, and fit for nothing; and this we found the first day we saw them, which was after we entered the wilder part of the country. Our leader for the day gave leave for about sixteen of us to go a hunting as they call it; and what was this but a hunting of sheep! — however, it may be called hunting too, for these creatures are the wildest and swiftest of foot that ever I saw of their kind! only they will not run a great way, and you are sure of sport when you begin the chase, for they appear generally thirty or forty in a flock, and, like true sheep, always keep together when they fly.

In pursuit of this odd sort of game it was our hap to meet with about forty Tartars: whether they were hunting mutton, as we were, or whether they looked for another kind of prey, we know not; but as soon as they saw us, one of them blew a hideous blast on a kind of horn. This was to call their friends about them, and in less than ten minutes a troop of forty or fifty more appeared, at about a mile distance; but our work was over first, as it happened.

One of the Scots merchants of Moscow happened to be amongst us; and as soon as he heard the horn, he told us that we had nothing to do but to charge them without loss of time; and drawing us up in a line, he asked if we were resolved. We told him we were ready to follow him; so he rode directly towards them. They stood gazing at us like a mere crowd, drawn up in no sort of order at all; but as soon as they saw us advance, they let fly their arrows, which missed us, very happily. Not that they mistook their aim, but their distance; for their arrows all fell a little short of us, but with so true an aim, that had we been about twenty yards nearer we must have had several men wounded, if not killed.

Immediately we halted, and though it was at a great distance, we fired, and sent them leaden bullets for wooden arrows, following our shot full gallop, to fall in among them sword in hand — for so our bold Scot that led us directed. He was, indeed, but a merchant, but he behaved with such vigour and bravery on this occasion, and yet with such cool courage too, that I never saw any man in action fitter for command. As soon as we came up to them we fired our pistols in their faces and then drew; but they fled in the greatest confusion imaginable. The only stand any of them made was on our right, where three of them stood, and, by signs, called the rest to come back to them, having a kind of scimitar in their hands, and their bows hanging to their backs. Our brave commander, without asking anybody to follow him, gallops up close to them, and with his fusée knocks one of them off his horse, killed the second with his pistol, and the third ran away. Thus ended our fight; but we had this misfortune attending it, that all our mutton we had in chase got away. We had not a man killed or hurt; as for the Tartars, there were about five of them killed — how many were wounded we knew not; but this we knew, that the other party were so frightened with the noise of our guns that they fled, and never made any attempt upon us.

We were all this while in the Chinese dominions, and therefore the Tartars were not so bold as afterwards; but in about five days we entered a vast wild desert, which held us three days' and nights' march; and we were obliged to carry our water with us in great leathern bottles, and to encamp all night, just as I have heard they do in the desert of Arabia. I asked our guides whose dominion this was in, and they told me this was a kind of border that might be called no man's land, being a part of Great Karakathy, or Grand Tartary: that, however, it was all reckoned as belonging to China, but that there was no care taken here to preserve it from the inroads of thieves, and therefore it was reckoned the worst desert in the whole march, though we were to go over some much larger.

In passing this frightful wilderness we saw, two or three times, little parties of the Tartars, but they seemed to be upon their own affairs, and to have no design upon us; and so, like the man who met the devil, if they had nothing to say to us, we had nothing to say to them: we let them go. Once, however, a party of them came so near as to stand and gaze at us. Whether it was to consider if they should attack us or not, we knew not; but when we had passed at some distance by them, we made a rear-guard of forty men, and stood ready for them, letting the caravan pass half a mile or thereabouts before us. After a while they marched off, but they saluted us with five arrows at their parting, which wounded a horse so that it disabled him, and we left him the next day, poor creature, in great need of a good farrier. We saw no more arrows or Tartars that time.

We traveled near a month after this, the ways not being so good as at first, though still in the dominions of the Emperor of China, but lay for the most part in the villages, some of which were fortified, because of the incursions of the Tartars. When we were come to one of these towns (about two days and a half's journey before we came to the city of Naum), I wanted to buy a camel, of which there are plenty to be sold all the way upon that road, and horses also, such as they are, because, so many caravans coming that way, they are often wanted. The person that I spoke to to get me a camel would have gone and fetched one for me; but I, like a fool, must be officious, and go myself along with him; the place was about two miles out of the village, where it seems they kept the camels and horses feeding under a guard.

I walked it on foot, with my old pilot and a Chinese, being very desirous of a little variety. When we came to the place it was a low, marshy ground, walled round with stones, piled up dry, without mortar or earth among them, like a park, with a little guard of Chinese soldiers at the door. Having bought a camel, and agreed for the price, I came away, and the Chinese that went with me led the camel, when on a sudden came up five Tartars on horseback. Two of them seized the fellow and took the camel from him, while the other three stepped up to me and my old pilot, seeing us, as it were, unarmed, for I had no weapon about me but my sword, which could but ill defend me against three horsemen. The first that came up stopped short upon my drawing my sword, for they are arrant cowards; but a second, coming upon my left, gave me a blow on the head, which I never felt till afterwards, and wondered, when I came to myself, what was the matter, and where I was, for he laid me flat on the ground; but my never-failing old pilot, the Portuguese, had a pistol in his pocket, which I knew nothing of, nor the Tartars either: if they had, I suppose they would not have attacked us, for cowards are always boldest when there is no danger. The old man seeing me down, with a bold heart stepped up to the fellow that had struck me, and laying hold of his arm with one hand, and pulling him down by main force a little towards him, with the other shot him into the head, and laid him dead upon the spot. He then immediately stepped up to him who had stopped us, as I said, and before he could come forward again, made a blow at him with a scimitar, which he always wore, but missing the man, struck his horse in the side of his head, cut one of the ears off by the root, and a great slice down by the side of his face. The poor beast, enraged with the wound, was no more to be governed by his rider, though the fellow sat well enough too, but away he flew, and carried him quite out of the pilot's reach; and at some distance, rising upon his hind legs, threw down the Tartar, and fell upon him.

In this interval the poor Chinese came in who had lost the camel, but he had no weapon; however, seeing the Tartar down, and his horse fallen upon him, away he runs to him, and seizing upon an ugly weapon he had by his side, something like a pole-axe, he wrenched it from him, and made shift to knock his Tartarian brains out with it. But my old man had the third Tartar to deal with still; and seeing he did not fly, as he expected, nor come on to fight him, as he apprehended, but stood stock still, the old man stood still too, and fell to work with his tackle to charge his pistol again: but as soon as the Tartar saw the pistol away he scoured, and left my pilot, my champion I called him afterwards, a complete victory.

By this time I was a little recovered. I thought, when I first began to wake, that I had been in a sweet sleep; but, as I said above, I wondered where I was, how I came upon the ground, and what was the matter. A few moments after, as sense returned, I felt pain, though I did not know where; so I clapped my hand to my head, and took it away bloody; then I felt my head ache: and in a moment memory returned, and everything was present to me again. I jumped upon my feet instantly, and got hold of my sword, but no enemies were in view: I found a Tartar lying dead, and his horse standing very quietly by him; and, looking further, I saw my deliverer, who had been to see what the

Chinese had done, coming back with his hanger in his hand. The old man, seeing me on my feet, came running to me, and joyfully embraced me, being afraid before that I had been killed. Seeing me bloody, he would see how I was hurt; but it was not much, only what we call a broken head; neither did I afterwards find any great inconvenience from the blow, for it was well again in two or three days.

We made no great gain, however, by this victory, for we lost a camel and gained a horse. I paid for the lost camel, and sent for another; but I did not go to fetch it myself: I had had enough of that.

The city of Naum, which we were approaching, is a frontier of the Chinese empire, and is fortified in their fashion. We wanted, as I have said, above two days' journey of this city when messengers were sent express to every part of the road to tell all travelers and caravans to halt till they had a guard sent for them; for that an unusual body of Tartars, making ten thousand in all, had appeared in the way, about thirty miles beyond the city.

This was very bad news to travelers: however, it was carefully done of the governor, and we were very glad to hear we should have a guard. Accordingly, two days after, we had two hundred soldiers sent us from a garrison of the Chinese on our left, and three hundred more from the city of Naum, and with these we advanced boldly. The three hundred soldiers from Naum marched in our front, the two hundred in our rear, and our men on each side of our camels, with our baggage and the whole caravan in the centre; in this order, and well prepared for battle, we thought ourselves a match for the whole ten thousand Mogul Tartars, if they had appeared; but the next day, when they did appear, it was quite another thing.

CHAPTER XV.

DESCRIPTION OF AN IDOL, WHICH THEY DESTROY

Early in the morning, when marching from a little town called Changu, we had a river to pass, which we were obliged to ferry; and, had the Tartars had any intelligence, then had been the time to have attacked us, when the caravan being over, the rear-guard was behind; but they did not appear there. About three hours after, when we were entered upon a desert of about fifteen or sixteen miles over, we knew by a cloud of dust they raised, that the enemy was at hand, and presently they came on upon the spur.

Our Chinese guards in the front, who had talked so big the day before, began to stagger; and the soldiers frequently looked behind them, a certain sign in a soldier that he is just ready to run away. My old pilot was of my mind; and being near me, called out, "Seignior Inglese, these fellows must be encouraged, or they will ruin us all; for if the Tartars come on they will never stand it." — "If am of your mind," said I; "but what must be done?" — "Done?" says he, "let fifty of our men advance, and flank them on each wing, and encourage them. They will fight like brave fellows in brave company; but without this they will every man turn his back." Immediately I rode up to our leader and told him, who was exactly of our mind; accordingly, fifty of us marched to the right wing, and fifty to the left, and the rest made a line of rescue; and so we marched, leaving the last two hundred men to make a body of themselves, and to guard the camels; only that, if need were, they should send a hundred men to assist the last fifty.

At last the Tartars came on, and an innumerable company they were; how many we could not tell, but ten thousand, we thought, at the least. A party of them came on first, and viewed our posture, traversing the ground in the front of our line; and, as we found them within gunshot, our leader ordered the two wings to advance swiftly, and give them a salvo on each wing with their shot, which was done. They then went off, I suppose to give an account of the reception they were like to meet with; indeed, that salute cloyed their stomachs, for they immediately halted, stood a while to consider of it, and wheeling off to the left, they gave over their design for that time, which was very agreeable to our circumstances.

Two days after we came to the city of Naun, or Naum; we thanked the governor for his care of us, and collected to the value of a

434

hundred crowns, or thereabouts, which we gave to the soldiers sent to guard us; and here we rested one day. This is a garrison indeed, and there were nine hundred soldiers kept here; but the reason of it was, that formerly the Muscovite frontiers lay nearer to them than they now do, the Muscovites having abandoned that part of the country, which lies from this city west for about two hundred miles, as desolate and unfit for use; and more especially being so very remote, and so difficult to send troops thither for its defence; for we were yet above two thousand miles from Muscovy properly so called. After this we passed several great rivers, and two dreadful deserts; one of which we were sixteen days passing over; and on the 13th of April we came to the frontiers of the Muscovite dominions. I think the first town or fortress, whichever it may he called, that belonged to the Czar, was called Arguna, being on the west side of the river Arguna.

I could not but feel great satisfaction that I was arrived in a country governed by Christians; for though the Muscovites do, in my opinion, but just deserve the name of Christians, yet such they pretend to be, and are very devout in their way. It would certainly occur to any reflecting man who travels the world as I have done, what a blessing it is to be brought into the world where the name of God and a Redeemer is known, adored, and worshipped; and not where the people, given up to strong delusions, worship the devil, and prostrate themselves to monsters, elements, horrid-shaped animals, and monstrous images. Not a town or city we passed through but had their pagodas, their idols, and their temples, and ignorant people worshipping even the works of their own hands. Now we came where, at least, a face of the Christian worship appeared; where the knee was bowed to Jesus: and whether ignorantly or not, yet the Christian religion was owned, and the name of the true God was called upon and adored; and it made my soul rejoice to see it. I saluted the brave Scots merchant with my first acknowledgment of this; and taking him by the hand, I said to him, "Blessed be God, we are once again amongst Christians." He smiled, and answered, "Do not rejoice too soon, countryman; these Muscovites are but an odd sort of Christians; and but for the name of it you may see very little of the substance for some months further of our journey." — "Well," says I, "but still it is better than paganism, and worshipping of devils." — "Why, I will tell you," says he; "except the Russian soldiers in the garrisons, and a few of the inhabitants of the cities upon the road, all the rest of this country, for above a thousand miles farther,

435

is inhabited by the worst and most ignorant of pagans." And so, indeed, we found it.

We now launched into the greatest piece of solid earth that is to be found in any part of the world; we had, at least, twelve thousand miles to the sea eastward; two thousand to the bottom of the Baltic Sea westward; and above three thousand, if we left that sea, and went on west, to the British and French channels: we had full five thousand miles to the Indian or Persian Sea south; and about eight hundred to the Frozen Sea north.

We advanced from the river Arguna by easy and moderate journeys, and were very visibly obliged to the care the Czar has taken to have cities and towns built in as many places as it is possible to place them, where his soldiers keep garrison, something like the stationary soldiers placed by the Romans in the remotest countries of their empire; some of which I had read of were placed in Britain, for the security of commerce, and for the lodging of travelers. Thus it was here; for wherever we came, though at these towns and stations the garrisons and governors were Russians, and professed Christians, yet the inhabitants were mere pagans, sacrificing to idols, and worshipping the sun, moon, and stars, or all the host of heaven; and not only so, but were, of all the heathens and pagans that ever I met with, the most barbarous, except only that they did not eat men's flesh.

Some instances of this we met with in the country between Arguna, where we enter the Muscovite dominions, and a city of Tartars and Russians together, called Nortziousky, in which is a continued desert or forest, which cost us twenty days to travel over. In a village near the last of these places I had the curiosity to go and see their way of living, which is most brutish and insufferable. They had, I suppose, a great sacrifice that day; for there stood out, upon an old stump of a tree, a diabolical kind of idol made of wood; it was dressed up, too, in the most filthy manner; its upper garment was of sheepskins, with the wool outward; a great Tartar bonnet on the head, with two horns growing through it; it was about eight feet high, yet had no feet or legs, nor any other proportion of parts.

This scarecrow was set up at the outer side of the village; and when I came near to it there were sixteen or seventeen creatures all lying flat upon the ground round this hideous block of wood; I saw no motion among them, any more than if they had been all logs, like the idol, and at first I really thought they had been so; but, when I came a little nearer, they started up upon their feet, and raised a howl, as if it had been so many deep-mouthed hounds, and walked away, as if they were displeased at our disturbing them. A little way off from the idol, and at the door of a hut, made of sheep and cow skins dried, stood three men with long knives in their hands; and in the middle of the tent appeared three sheep killed, and one young bullock. These, it seems, were sacrifices to that senseless log of an idol; the three men were priests belonging to it, and the seventeen prostrated wretches were the people who brought the offering, and were offering their prayers to that stock.

I confess I was more moved at their stupidity and brutish worship of a hobgoblin than ever I was at anything in my life, and, overcome with rage, I rode up to the hideous idol, and with my sword made a stroke at the bonnet that was on its head, and cut it in two; and one of our men that was with me, taking hold of the sheepskin that covered it, pulled at it, when, behold, a most hideous outcry ran through the village, and two or three hundred people came about my ears, so that I was glad to scour for it, for some had bows and arrows; but I resolved from that moment to visit them again. Our caravan rested three nights at the town, which was about four miles off, in order to provide some horses which they wanted, several of the horses having been lamed and jaded with the long march over the last desert; so we had some leisure here to put my design in execution. I communicated it to the Scots merchant, of whose courage I had sufficient testimony; I told him what I had seen, and with what indignation I had since thought that human nature could be so degenerate; I told him if I could get but four or five men well armed to go with me, I was resolved to go and destroy that vile, abominable idol, and let them see that it had no power to help itself, and consequently could not be an object of worship, or to be prayed to, much less help them that offered sacrifices to it.

He at first objected to my plan as useless, seeing that, owing to the gross ignorance of the people, they could not be brought to profit by the lesson I meant to teach them; and added that, from his knowledge of the country and its customs, he feared we should fall into great peril by giving offence to these brutal idol worshippers. This somewhat stayed my purpose, but I was still uneasy all that day to put my project in execution; and that evening, meeting the Scots merchant in our walk about the town, I again called upon him to aid me in it. When he found me resolute he said that, on further thoughts, he could not but applaud the design, and told me I should not go alone, but he would go with me; but he would go first and bring a stout fellow, one of his countrymen, to go also with us; "and one," said he, "as famous for his zeal as you can desire any one to be against such devilish things as these." So we agreed to go, only we three and my man-servant, and resolved to put it in execution the following night about midnight, with all possible secrecy.

We thought it better to delay it till the next night, because the caravan being to set forward in the morning, we suppose the governor could not pretend to give them any satisfaction upon us when we were out of his power. The Scots merchant, as steady in his resolution for the enterprise as bold in executing, brought me a Tartar's robe or gown of sheepskins, and a bonnet, with a bow and arrows, and had provided the same for himself and his countryman, that the people, if they saw us, should not determine who we were. All the first night we spent in mixing up some combustible matter, with aqua vitae, gunpowder, and such other materials as we could get; and having a good quantity of tar in a little pot, about an hour after night we set out upon our expedition.

We came to the place about eleven o'clock at night, and found that the people had not the least suspicion of danger attending their idol. The night was cloudy: yet the moon gave us light enough to see that the idol stood just in the same posture and place that it did before. The people seemed to be all at their rest; only that in the great hut, where we saw the three priests, we saw a light, and going up close to the door, we heard people talking as if there were five or six of them; we concluded, therefore, that if we set wildfire to the idol, those men would come out immediately, and run up to the place to rescue it from destruction; and what to do with them we knew not. Once we thought of carrying it away, and setting fire to it at a distance; but when we came to handle it, we found it too bulky for our carriage, so we were at a loss again. The second Scotsman was for setting fire to the hut, and knocking the creatures that were there on the head when they came out; but I could not join with that; I was against killing them, if it were possible to avoid it. "Well, then," said the Scots merchant, "I will tell you what we will do: we will try to make them prisoners, tie their hands, and make them stand and see their idol destroyed."

As it happened, we had twine or packthread enough about us, which we used to tie our firelocks together with; so we resolved to attack these people first, and with as little noise as we could. The first thing we did, we knocked at the door, when one of the priests coming to it, we immediately seized upon him, stopped his mouth, and tied his hands behind him, and led him to the idol, where we gagged him that

438

he might not make a noise, tied his feet also together, and left him on the ground.

Two of us then waited at the door, expecting that another would come out to see what the matter was; but we waited so long till the third man came back to us; and then nobody coming out, we knocked again gently, and immediately out came two more, and we served them just in the same manner, but were obliged to go all with them, and lay them down by the idol some distance from one another; when, going back, we found two more were come out of the door, and a third stood behind them within the door. We seized the two, and immediately tied them, when the third, stepping back and crying out, my Scots merchant went in after them, and taking out a composition we had made that would only smoke and stink, he set fire to it, and threw it in among them. By that time the other Scotsman and my man, taking charge of the two men already bound, and tied together also by the arm, led them away to the idol, and left them there, to see if their idol would relieve them, making haste back to us.

When the fuse we had thrown in had filled the hut with so much smoke that they were almost suffocated, we threw in a small leather bag of another kind, which flamed like a candle, and, following it in, we found there were but four people, who, as we supposed, had been about some of their diabolical sacrifices. They appeared, in short, frightened to death, at least so as to sit trembling and stupid, and not able to speak either, for the smoke.

We quickly took them from the hut, where the smoke soon drove us out, bound them as we had done the other, and all without any noise. Then we carried them all together to the idol; when we came there, we fell to work with him. First, we daubed him all over, and his robes also, with tar, and tallow mixed with brimstone; then we stopped his eyes and ears and mouth full of gunpowder, and wrapped up a great piece of wildfire in his bonnet; then sticking all the combustibles we had brought with us upon him, we looked about to see if we could find anything else to help to burn him; when my Scotsman remembered that by the hut, where the men were, there lay a heap of dry forage; away he and the other Scotsman ran and fetched their arms full of that. When we had done this, we took all our prisoners, and brought them, having untied their feet and ungagged their mouths, and made them stand up, and set them before their monstrous idol, and then set fire to the whole.

We stayed by it a quarter of an hour or thereabouts, till the powder in the eyes and mouth and ears of the idol blew up, and, as we could perceive, had split altogether; and in a word, till we saw it burned so that it would soon be quite consumed. We then began to think of going away; but the Scotsman said, "No, we must not go, for these poor deluded wretches will all throw themselves into the fire, and burn themselves with the idol." So we resolved to stay till the forage has burned down too, and then came away and left them. After the feat was performed, we appeared in the morning among our fellow-travelers, exceedingly busy in getting ready for our journey; nor could any man suppose that we had been anywhere but in our beds.

But the affair did not end so; the next day came a great number of the country people to the town gates, and in a most outrageous manner demanded satisfaction of the Russian governor for the insulting their priests and burning their great Cham Chi-Thaungu. The people of Nertsinkay were at first in a great consternation, for they said the Tartars were already no less than thirty thousand strong. The Russian governor sent out messengers to appease them, assuring them that he knew nothing of it, and that there had not a soul in his garrison been abroad, so that it could not be from anybody there: but if they could let him know who did it, they should be exemplarily punished. They returned haughtily, that all the country reverenced the great Cham Chi-Thaungu, who dwelt in the sun, and no mortal would have dared to offer violence to his image but some Christian miscreant; and they therefore resolved to denounce war against him and all the Russians, who, they said, were miscreants and Christians.

The governor, unwilling to make a breach, or to have any cause of war alleged to be given by him, the Czar having strictly charged him to treat the conquered country with gentleness, gave them all the good words he could. At last he told them there was a caravan gone towards Russia that morning, and perhaps it was some of them who had done them this injury; and that if they would be satisfied with that, he would send after them to inquire into it. This seemed to appease them a little; and accordingly the governor sent after us, and gave us a particular account how the thing was; intimating withal, that if any in our caravan had done it they should make their escape; but that whether we had done it or no, we should make all the haste forward that was possible: and that, in the meantime, he would keep them in play as long as he could.

This was very friendly in the governor; however, when it came to the caravan, there was nobody knew anything of the matter; and as for us that were guilty, we were least of all suspected. However, the captain

440

of the caravan for the time took the hint that the governor gave us, and we traveled two days and two nights without any considerable stop, and then we lay at a village called Plothus: nor did we make any long stop here, but hastened on towards Jarawena, another Muscovite colony, and where we expected we should be safe. But upon the second day's march from Plothus, by the clouds of dust behind us at a great distance, it was plain we were pursued. We had entered a vast desert, and had passed by a great lake called Schanks Oser, when we perceived a large body of horse appear on the other side of the lake, to the north, we traveling west. We observed they went away west, as we did, but had supposed we would have taken that side of the lake, whereas we very happily took the south side; and in two days more they disappeared again: for they, believing we were still before them, pushed on till they came to the Udda, a very great river when it passes farther north, but when we came to it we found it narrow and fordable.

The third day they had either found their mistake, or had intelligence of us, and came pouring in upon us towards dusk. We had, to our great satisfaction, just pitched upon a convenient place for our camp; for as we had just entered upon a desert above five hundred miles over, where we had no towns to lodge at, and, indeed, expected none but the city Jarawena, which we had yet two days' march to; the desert, however, had some few woods in it on this side, and little rivers, which ran all into the great river Udda; it was in a narrow strait, between little but very thick woods, that we pitched our camp that night, expecting to be attacked before morning. As it was usual for the Mogul Tartars to go about in troops in that desert, so the caravans always fortify themselves every night against them, as against armies of robbers; and it was, therefore, no new thing to be pursued. But we had this night a most advantageous camp: for as we lay between two woods, with a little rivulet running just before our front, we could not be surrounded, or attacked any way but in our front or rear. We took care also to make our front as strong as we could, by placing our packs, with the camels and horses, all in a line, on the inside of the river, and felling some trees in our rear.

In this posture we encamped for the night; but the enemy was upon us before we had finished. They did not come on like thieves, as we expected, but sent three messengers to us, to demand the men to be delivered to them that had abused their priests and burned their idol, that they might burn them with fire; and upon this, they said, they would go away, and do us no further harm, otherwise they would destroy us all. Our men looked very blank at this message, and began to stare at one another to see who looked with the most guilt in their faces; but nobody was the word — nobody did it. The leader of the caravan sent word he was well assured that it was not done by any of our camp; that we were peaceful merchants, traveling on our business; that we had done no harm to them or to any one else; and that, therefore, they must look further for the enemies who had injured them, for we were not the people; so they desired them not to disturb us, for if they did we should defend ourselves.

They were far from being satisfied with this for an answer: and a great crowd of them came running down in the morning, by break of day, to our camp; but seeing us so well posted, they durst come no farther than the brook in our front, where they stood in such number as to terrify us very much; indeed, some spoke of ten thousand. Here they stood and looked at us a while, and then, setting up a great howl, let fly a crowd of arrows among us; but we were well enough sheltered under our baggage, and I do not remember that one of us was hurt.

Some time after this we saw them move a little to our right, and expected them on the rear: when a cunning fellow, a Cossack of Jarawena, calling to the leader of the caravan, said to him, "I will send all these people away to Sibeilka." This was a city four or five days' journey at least to the right, and rather behind us. So he takes his bow and arrows, and getting on horseback, he rides away from our rear directly, as it were back to Nertsinskay; after this he takes a great circuit about, and comes directly on the army of the Tartars as if he had been sent express to tell them a long story that the people who had burned the Cham Chi-Thaungu were gone to Sibeilka, with a caravan of miscreants, as he called them — that is to say, Christians; and that they had resolved to burn the god Scal-Isar, belonging to the Tonguses. As this fellow was himself a Tartar, and perfectly spoke their language, he counterfeited so well that they all believed him, and away they drove in a violent hurry to Sibeilka. In less than three hours they were entirely out of our sight, and we never heard any more of them, nor whether they went to Sibeilka or no. So we passed away safely on to Jarawena, where there was a Russian garrison, and there we rested five days.

From this city we had a frightful desert, which held us twenty-three days' march. We furnished ourselves with some tents here, for the better accommodating ourselves in the night; and the leader of the caravan procured sixteen wagons of the country, for carrying our water or provisions, and these carriages were our defence every night round our little camp; so that had the Tartars appeared, unless they had been very numerous indeed, they would not have been able to hurt us. We may well be supposed to have wanted rest again after this long journey; for in this desert we neither saw house nor tree, and scarce a bush; though we saw abundance of the sable-hunters, who are all Tartars of Mogul Tartary; of which this country is a part; and they frequently attack small caravans, but we saw no numbers of them together.

After we had passed this desert we came into a country pretty well inhabited — that is to say, we found towns and castles, settled by the Czar with garrisons of stationary soldiers, to protect the caravans and defend the country against the Tartars, who would otherwise make it very dangerous traveling; and his czarish majesty has given such strict orders for the well guarding the caravans, that, if there are any Tartars heard of in the country, detachments of the garrison are always sent to see the travelers safe from station to station. Thus the governor of Adinskoy, whom I had an opportunity to make a visit to, by means of the Scots merchant, who was acquainted with him, offered us a guard of fifty men, if we thought there was any danger, to the next station.

I thought, long before this, that as we came nearer to Europe we should find the country better inhabited, and the people more civilized; but I found myself mistaken in both: for we had yet the nation of the Tonguses to pass through, where we saw the same tokens of paganism and barbarity as before; only, as they were conquered by the Muscovites, they were not so dangerous, but for rudeness of manners and idolatry no people in the world ever went beyond them. They are all clothed in skins of beasts, and their houses are built of the same; you know not a man from a woman, neither by the ruggedness of their countenances nor their clothes; and in the winter, when the ground is covered with snow, they live underground in vaults, which have cavities going from one to another. If the Tartars had their Cham Chi-Thaungu for a whole village or country, these had idols in every hut and every cave. This country, I reckon, was, from the desert I spoke of last, at least four hundred miles, half of it being another desert, which took us up twelve days' severe traveling, without house or tree; and we were obliged again to carry our own provisions, as well water as bread. After we were out of this desert and had traveled two days, we came to Janezay, a Muscovite city or station, on the great river Janezay, which, they told us there, parted Europe from Asia.

All the country between the river Oby and the river Janezay is as entirely pagan, and the people as barbarous, as the remotest of the

Tartars. I also found, which I observed to the Muscovite governors whom I had an opportunity to converse with, that the poor pagans are not much wiser, or nearer Christianity, for being under the Muscovite government, which they acknowledged was true enough — but that, as they said, was none of their business; that if the Czar expected to convert his Siberian, Tonguse, or Tartar subjects, it should be done by sending clergymen among them, not soldiers; and they added, with more sincerity than I expected, that it was not so much the concern of their monarch to make the people Christians as to make them subjects.

From this river to the Oby we crossed a wild uncultivated country, barren of people and good management, otherwise it is in itself a pleasant, fruitful, and agreeable country. What inhabitants we found in it are all pagans, except such as are sent among them from Russia; for this is the country — I mean on both sides the river Oby — whither the Muscovite criminals that are not put to death are banished, and from whence it is next to impossible they should ever get away. I have nothing material to say of my particular affairs till I came to Tobolski, the capital city of Siberia, where I continued some time on the following account.

We had now been almost seven months on our journey, and winter began to come on apace; whereupon my partner and I called a council about our particular affairs, in which we found it proper, as we were bound for England, to consider how to dispose of ourselves. They told us of sledges and reindeer to carry us over the snow in the winter time, by which means, indeed, the Russians travel more in winter than they can in summer, as in these sledges they are able to run night and day: the snow, being frozen, is one universal covering to nature, by which the hills, vales, rivers, and lakes are all smooth and hard is a stone, and they run upon the surface, without any regard to what is underneath.

But I had no occasion to urge a winter journey of this kind. I was bound to England, not to Moscow, and my route lay two ways: either I must go on as the caravan went, till I came to Jarislaw, and then go off west for Narva and the Gulf of Finland, and so on to Dantzic, where I might possibly sell my China cargo to good advantage; or I must leave the caravan at a little town on the Dwina, from whence I had but six days by water to Archangel, and from thence might be sure of shipping either to England, Holland, or Hamburg.

Now, to go any one of these journeys in the winter would have been preposterous; for as to Dantzic, the Baltic would have been frozen up and I could not get passage; and to go by land in those countries was far less safe than among the Mogul Tartars; likewise, as to Archangel in October, all the ships would be gone from thence, and even the merchants who dwell there in summer retire south to Moscow in the winter, when the ships are gone; so that I could have nothing but extremity of cold to encounter, with a scarcity of provisions, and must lie in an empty town all the winter. Therefore, upon the whole, I thought it much my better way to let the caravan go, and make provision to winter where I was, at Tobolski, in Siberia, in the latitude of about sixty degrees, where I was sure of three things to wear out a cold winter with, viz. plenty of provisions, such as the country afforded, a warm house, with fuel enough, and excellent company.

I was now in quite a different climate from my beloved island, where I never felt cold, except when I had my ague; on the contrary, I had much to do to bear any clothes on my back, and never made any fire but without doors, which was necessary for dressing my food, &c. Now I had three good vests, with large robes or gowns over them, to hang down to the feet, and button close to the wrists; and all these lined with furs, to make them sufficiently warm. As to a warm house, I must confess I greatly dislike our way in England of making fires in every room of the house in open chimneys, which, when the fire is out, always keeps the air in the room cold as the climate. So I took an apartment in a good house in the town, and ordered a chimney to be built like a furnace, in the centre of six several rooms, like a stove; the funnel to carry the smoke went up one way, the door to come at the fire went in another, and all the rooms were kept equally warm, but no fire seen, just as they heat baths in England. By this means we had always the same climate in all the rooms, and an equal heat was preserved, and yet we saw no fire, nor were ever incommoded with smoke.

The most wonderful thing of all was, that it should be possible to meet with good company here, in a country so barbarous as this — one of the most northerly parts of Europe. But this being the country where the state criminals of Muscovy, as I observed before, are all banished, the city was full of Russian noblemen, gentlemen, soldiers, and courtiers. Here was the famous Prince Galitzin, the old German Robostiski, and several other persons of note, and some ladies. By means of my Scotch merchant, whom, nevertheless, I parted with here, I made an acquaintance with several of these gentlemen; and from these, in the long winter nights in which I stayed here, I received several very agreeable visits.

445

CHAPTER XVI.

SAFE ARRIVAL IN ENGLAND

It was talking one night with a certain prince, one of the banished ministers of state belonging to the Czar, that the discourse of my particular case began. He had been telling me abundance of fine things of the greatness, the magnificence, the dominions, and the absolute power of the Emperor of the Russians: I interrupted him, and told him I was a greater and more powerful prince than ever the Czar was, though my dominion were not so large, or my people so many. The Russian grandee looked a little surprised, and, fixing his eyes steadily upon me, began to wonder what I meant. I said his wonder would cease when I had explained myself, and told him the story at large of my living in the island; and then how I managed both myself and the people that were under me, just as I have since minuted it down. They were exceedingly taken with the story, and especially the prince, who told me, with a sigh, that the true greatness of life was to be masters of ourselves; that he would not have exchanged such a state of life as mine to be Czar of Muscovy; and that he found more felicity in the retirement he seemed to be banished to there, than ever he found in the highest authority he enjoyed in the court of his master the Czar; that the height of human wisdom was to bring our tempers down to our circumstances, and to make a calm within, under the weight of the greatest storms without. When he came first hither, he said, he used to tear the hair from his head, and the clothes from his back, as others had done before him; but a little time and consideration had made him look into himself, as well as round him to things without; that he found the mind of man, if it was but once brought to reflect upon the state of universal life, and how little this world was concerned in its true felicity, was perfectly capable of making a felicity for itself, fully satisfying to itself, and suitable to its own best ends and desires, with but very little assistance from the world. That being now deprived of all the fancied felicity which he enjoyed in the full exercise of worldly pleasures, he said he was at leisure to look upon the dark side of them, where he found all manner of deformity; and was now convinced that virtue only makes a man truly wise, rich, and great, and preserves him in the way to a superior happiness in a future state; and in this, he said, they were more happy in their banishment than all their enemies were, who had the full possession of all the wealth and power they had left behind them. "Nor, sir," says he, "do I bring my mind to this politically, from the necessity of my circumstances, which some call miserable; but, if I know anything of myself, I would not now go back, though the Czar my master should call me, and reinstate me in all my former grandeur."

He spoke this with so much warmth in his temper, so much earnestness and motion of his spirits, that it was evident it was the true sense of his soul; there was no room to doubt his sincerity. I told him I once thought myself a kind of monarch in my old station, of which I had given him an account; but that I thought he was not only a monarch, but a great conqueror; for he that had got a victory over his own exorbitant desires, and the absolute dominion over himself, he whose reason entirely governs his will, is certainly greater than he that conquers a city.

I had been here eight months, and a dark, dreadful winter I thought it; the cold so intense that I could not so much as look abroad without being wrapped in furs, and a kind of mask of fur before my face, with only a hole for breath, and two for sight: the little daylight we had was for three months not above five hours a day, and six at most; only that the snow lying on the ground continually, and the weather being clear, it was never quite dark. Our horses were kept, or rather starved, underground; and as for our servants, whom we hired here to look after ourselves and horses, we had, every now and then, their fingers and toes to thaw and take care of, lest they should mortify and fall off.

It is true, within doors we were warm, the houses being close, the walls thick, the windows small, and the glass all double. Our food was chiefly the flesh of deer, dried and cured in the season; bread good enough, but baked as biscuits; dried fish of several sorts, and some flesh of mutton, and of buffaloes, which is pretty good meat. All the stores of provisions for the winter are laid up in the summer, and well cured: our drink was water, mixed with aqua vitae instead of brandy; and for a treat, mead instead of wine, which, however, they have very good. The hunters, who venture abroad all weathers, frequently brought us in fine venison, and sometimes bear's flesh, but we did not much care for the last. We had a good stock of tea, with which we treated our friends, and we lived cheerfully and well, all things considered.

It was now March, the days grown considerably longer, and the weather at least tolerable; so the other travelers began to prepare sledges to carry them over the snow, and to get things ready to be going; but my measures being fixed, as I have said, for Archangel, and not for

Muscovy or the Baltic, I made no motion; knowing very well that the ships from the south do not set out for that part of the world till May or June, and that if I was there by the beginning of August, it would be as soon as any ships would be ready to sail. Therefore I made no haste to be gone, as others did: in a word, I saw a great many people, nay, all the travelers, go away before me. It seems every year they go from thence to Muscovy, for trade, to carry furs, and buy necessaries, which they bring back with them to furnish their shops: also others went on the same errand to Archangel.

In the month of May I began to make all ready to pack up; and, as I was doing this, it occurred to me that, seeing all these people were banished by the Czar to Siberia, and yet, when they came there, were left at liberty to go whither they would, why they did not then go away to any part of the world, wherever they thought fit: and I began to examine what should hinder them from making such an attempt. But my wonder was over when I entered upon that subject with the person I have mentioned, who answered me thus: "Consider, first, sir," said he, "the place where we are; and, secondly, the condition we are in; especially the generality of the people who are banished thither. We are surrounded with stronger things than bars or bolts; on the north side, an unnavigable ocean, where ship never sailed, and boat never swam; every other way we have above a thousand miles to pass through the Czar's own dominion, and by ways utterly impassable, except by the roads made by the government, and through the towns garrisoned by his troops; in short, we could neither pass undiscovered by the road, nor subsist any other way, so that it is in vain to attempt it."

I was silenced at once, and found that they were in a prison every jot as secure as if they had been locked up in the castle at Moscow: however, it came into my thoughts that I might certainly be made an instrument to procure the escape of this excellent person; and that, whatever hazard I ran, I would certainly try if I could carry him off. Upon this, I took an occasion one evening to tell him my thoughts. I represented to him that it was very easy for me to carry him away, there being no guard over him in the country; and as I was not going to Moscow, but to Archangel, and that I went in the retinue of a caravan, by which I was not obliged to lie in the stationary towns in the desert, but could encamp every night where I would, we might easily pass uninterrupted to Archangel, where I would immediately secure him on board an English ship, and carry him safe along with me; and as to his subsistence and other particulars, it should be my care till he could better supply himself.

He heard me very attentively, and looked earnestly on me all the while I spoke; nay, I could see in his very face that what I said put his spirits into an exceeding ferment; his colour frequently changed, his eyes looked red, and his heart fluttered, till it might be even perceived in his countenance; nor could he immediately answer me when I had done, and, as it were, hesitated what he would say to it; but after he had paused a little, he embraced me, and said, "How unhappy are we, unguarded creatures as we are, that even our greatest acts of friendship are made snares unto us, and we are made tempters of one another!" He then heartily thanked me for my offers of service, but withstood resolutely the arguments I used to urge him to set himself free. He declared, in earnest terms, that he was fully bent on remaining where he was rather than seek to return to his former miserable greatness, as he called it: where the seeds of pride, ambition, avarice, and luxury might revive, take root, and again overwhelm him. "Let me remain, dear sir," he said, in conclusion — "let me remain in this blessed confinement, banished from the crimes of life, rather than purchase a show of freedom at the expense of the liberty of my reason, and at the future happiness which I now have in my view, but should then, I fear, quickly lose sight of; for I am but flesh; a man, a mere man; and have passions and affections as likely to possess and overthrow me as any man: Oh, be not my friend and tempter both together!"

If I was surprised before, I was quite dumb now, and stood silent, looking at him, and, indeed, admiring what I saw. The struggle in his soul was so great that, though the weather was extremely cold, it put him into a most violent heat; so I said a word or two, that I would leave him to consider of it, and wait on him again, and then I withdrew to my own apartment.

About two hours after I heard somebody at or near the door of my room, and I was going to open the door, but he had opened it and come in. "My dear friend," says he, "you had almost overset me, but I am recovered. Do not take it ill that I do not close with your offer. I assure you it is not for want of sense of the kindness of it in you; and I came to make the most sincere acknowledgment of it to you; but I hope I have got the victory over myself." — "My lord," said I, "I hope you are fully satisfied that you do not resist the call of Heaven." — "Sir," said he, "if it had been from Heaven, the same power would have influenced me to have accepted it; but I hope, and am fully satisfied, that it is from Heaven that I decline it, and I have infinite satisfaction in the parting, that you shall leave me an honest man still, though not a free man."

I had nothing to do but to acquiesce, and make professions to him of my having no end in it but a sincere desire to serve him. He embraced me very passionately, and assured me he was sensible of that, and should always acknowledge it; and with that he offered me a very fine present of sables — too much, indeed, for me to accept from a man in his circumstances, and I would have avoided them, but he would not be refused. The next morning I sent my servant to his lordship with a small present of tea, and two pieces of China damask, and four little wedges of Japan gold, which did not all weigh above six ounces or thereabouts, but were far short of the value of his sables, which, when I came to England, I found worth near two hundred pounds. He accepted the tea, and one piece of the damask, and one of the pieces of gold, which had a fine stamp upon it, of the Japan coinage, which I found he took for the rarity of it, but would not take any more: and he sent word by my servant that he desired to speak with me.

When I came to him he told me I knew what had passed between us, and hoped I would not move him any more in that affair; but that, since I had made such a generous offer to him, he asked me if I had kindness enough to offer the same to another person that he would name to me, in whom he had a great share of concern. In a word, he told me it was his only son; who, though I had not seen him, was in the same condition with himself, and above two hundred miles from him, on the other side of the Oby; but that, if I consented, he would send for him.

I made no hesitation, but told him I would do it. I made some ceremony in letting him understand that it was wholly on his account; and that, seeing I could not prevail on him, I would show my respect to him by my concern for his son. He sent the next day for his son; and in about twenty days he came back with the messenger, bringing six or seven horses, loaded with very rich furs, which, in the whole, amounted to a very great value. His servants brought the horses into the town, but left the young lord at a distance till night, when he came incognito into our apartment, and his father presented him to me; and, in short, we concerted the manner of our traveling, and everything proper for the journey.

I had bought a considerable quantity of sables, black fox-skins, fine ermines, and such other furs as are very rich in that city, in exchange for some of the goods I had brought from China; in particular for the cloves and nutmegs, of which I sold the greatest part here, and the rest afterwards at Archangel, for a much better price than I could have got at London; and my partner, who was sensible of the profit, and whose business, more particularly than mine, was merchandise, was mightily pleased with our stay, on account of the traffic we made here.

It was the beginning of June when I left this remote place. We were now reduced to a very small caravan, having only thirty-two horses and camels in all, which passed for mine, though my new guest was proprietor of eleven of them. It was natural also that I should take more servants with me than I had before; and the young lord passed for my steward; what great man I passed for myself I know not, neither did it concern me to inquire. We had here the worst and the largest desert to pass over that we met with in our whole journey; I call it the worst, because the way was very deep in some places, and very uneven in others; the best we had to say for it was, that we thought we had no troops of Tartars or robbers to fear, as they never came on this side of the river Oby, or at least very seldom; but we found it otherwise.

My young lord had a faithful Siberian servant, who was perfectly acquainted with the country, and led us by private roads, so that we avoided coming into the principal towns and cities upon the great road, such as Tumen, Soloy Kamaskoy, and several others; because the Muscovite garrisons which are kept there are very curious and strict in their observation upon travelers, and searching lest any of the banished persons of note should make their escape that way into Muscovy; but, by this means, as we were kept out of the cities, so our whole journey was a desert, and we were obliged to encamp and lie in our tents, when we might have had very good accommodation in the cities on the way; this the young lord was so sensible of, that he would not allow us to lie abroad when we came to several cities on the way, but lay abroad himself, with his servant, in the woods, and met us always at the appointed places.

We had just entered Europe, having passed the river Kama, which in these parts is the boundary between Europe and Asia, and the first city on the European side was called Soloy Kamaskoy, that is, the great city on the river Kama. And here we thought to see some evident alteration in the people; but we were mistaken, for as we had a vast desert to pass, which is near seven hundred miles long in some places, but not above two hundred miles over where we passed it, so, till we came past that horrible place, we found very little difference between

451

that country and Mogul Tartary. The people are mostly pagans; their houses and towns full of idols; and their way of living wholly barbarous, except in the cities and villages near them, where they are Christians, as they call themselves, of the Greek Church: but have their religion mingled with so many relics of superstition, that it is scarce to be known in some places from mere sorcery and witchcraft.

In passing this forest (after all our dangers were, to our imagination, escaped), I thought, indeed, we must have been plundered and robbed, and perhaps murdered, by a troop of thieves: of what country they were I am yet at a loss to know; but they were all on horseback, carried bows and arrows, and were at first about forty-five in number. They came so near to us as to be within two musket-shot, and, asking no questions, surrounded us with their horses, and looked very earnestly upon us twice; at length, they placed themselves just in our way; upon which we drew up in a little line, before our camels, being not above sixteen men in all. Thus drawn up, we halted, and sent out the Siberian servant, who attended his lord, to see who they were; his master was the more willing to let him go, because he was not a little apprehensive that they were a Siberian troop sent out after him. The man came up near them with a flag of truce, and called to them; but though he spoke several of their languages, or dialects of languages rather, he could not understand a word they said; however, after some signs to him not to come near them at his peril, the fellow came back no wiser than he went; only that by their dress, he said, he believed them to be some Tartars of Kalmuck, or of the Circassian hordes, and that there must be more of them upon the great desert, though he never heard that any of them were seen so far north before.

This was small comfort to us; however, we had no remedy: there was on our left hand, at about a quarter of a mile distance, a little grove, and very near the road. I immediately resolved we should advance to those trees, and fortify ourselves as well as we could there; for, first, I considered that the trees would in a great measure cover us from their arrows; and, in the next place, they could not come to charge us in a body: it was, indeed, my old Portuguese pilot who proposed it, and who had this excellency attending him, that he was always readiest and most apt to direct and encourage us in cases of the most danger. We advanced immediately, with what speed we could, and gained that little wood; the Tartars, or thieves, for we knew not what to call them, keeping their stand, and not attempting to hinder us. When we came thither, we found, to our great satisfaction, that it was a swampy piece of ground, and on the one side a very great spring of water, which, running out in a little brook, was a little farther joined by another of the like size; and was, in short, the source of a considerable river, called afterwards the Wirtska; the trees which grew about this spring were not above two hundred, but very large, and stood pretty thick, so that as soon as we got in, we saw ourselves perfectly safe from the enemy unless they attacked us on foot.

While we stayed here waiting the motion of the enemy some hours, without perceiving that they made any movement, our Portuguese, with some help, cut several arms of trees half off, and laid them hanging across from one tree to another, and in a manner fenced us in. About two hours before night they came down directly upon us; and though we had not perceived it, we found they had been joined by some more, so that they were near fourscore horse; whereof, however, we fancied some were women. They came on till they were within half-shot of our little wood, when we fired one musket without ball, and called to them in the Russian tongue to know what they wanted, and bade them keep off; but they came on with a double fury up to the wood-side, not imagining we were so barricaded that they could not easily break in. Our old pilot was our captain as well as our engineer, and desired us not to fire upon them till they came within pistol-shot, that we might be sure to kill, and that when we did fire we should be sure to take good aim; we bade him give the word of command, which he delayed so long that they were some of them within two pikes' length of us when we let fly. We aimed so true that we killed fourteen of them, and wounded several others, as also several of their horses; for we had all of us loaded our pieces with two or three bullets apiece at least.

They were terribly surprised with our fire, and retreated immediately about one hundred rods from us; in which time we loaded our pieces again, and seeing them keep that distance, we sallied out, and caught four or five of their horses, whose riders we supposed were killed; and coming up to the dead, we judged they were Tartars, but knew not how they came to make an excursion such an unusual length.

About an hour after they again made a motion to attack us, and rode round our little wood to see where they might break in; but finding us always ready to face them, they went off again; and we resolved not to stir for that night.

We slept little, but spent the most part of the night in strengthening our situation, and barricading the entrances into the wood, and keeping a strict watch. We waited for daylight, and when it came, it gave us a very unwelcome discovery indeed; for the enemy, who we thought were discouraged with the reception they met with, were now greatly increased, and had set up eleven or twelve huts or tents, as if they were resolved to besiege us; and this little camp they had pitched upon the open plain, about three-quarters of a mile from us. I confess I now gave myself over for lost, and all that I had; the loss of my effects did not lie so near me, though very considerable, as the thoughts of falling into the hands of such barbarians at the latter end of my journey, after so many difficulties and hazards as I had gone through, and even in sight of our port, where we expected safety and deliverance. As to my partner, he was raging, and declared that to lose his goods would be his ruin, and that he would rather die than be starved, and he was for fighting to the last drop.

The young lord, a most gallant youth, was for fighting to the last also; and my old pilot was of opinion that we were able to resist them all in the situation we were then in. Thus we spent the day in debates of what we should do; but towards evening we found that the number of our enemies still increased, and we did not know but by the morning they might still be a greater number: so I began to inquire of those people we had brought from Tobolski if there were no private ways by which we might avoid them in the night, and perhaps retreat to some town, or get help to guard us over the desert. The young lord's Siberian servant told us, if we designed to avoid them, and not fight, he would engage to carry us off in the night, to a way that went north, towards the river Petruz, by which he made no question but we might get away, and the Tartars never discover it; but, he said, his lord had told him he would not retreat, but would rather choose to fight. I told him he mistook his lord: for that he was too wise a man to love fighting for the sake of it; that I knew he was brave enough by what he had showed already; but that he knew better than to desire seventeen or eighteen men to fight five hundred, unless an unavoidable necessity forced them to it; and that if he thought it possible for us to escape in the night, we had nothing else to do but to attempt it. He answered, if his lordship gave him such orders, he would lose his life if he did not perform it; we soon brought his lord to give that order, though privately, and we immediately prepared for putting it in practice.

And first, as soon as it began to be dark, we kindled a fire in our little camp, which we kept burning, and prepared so as to make it burn all night, that the Tartars might conclude we were still there; but as

454

soon as it was dark, and we could see the stars (for our guide would not stir before), having all our horses and camels ready loaded, we followed our new guide, who I soon found steered himself by the north star, the country being level for a long way.

After we had traveled two hours very hard, it began to be lighter still; not that it was dark all night, but the moon began to rise, so that, in short, it was rather lighter than we wished it to be; but by six o'clock the next morning we had got above thirty miles, having almost spoiled our horses. Here we found a Russian village, named Kermazinskoy, where we rested, and heard nothing of the Kalmuck Tartars that day. About two hours before night we set out again, and traveled till eight the next morning, though not quite so hard as before; and about seven o'clock we passed a little river, called Kirtza, and came to a good large town inhabited by Russians, called Ozomys; there we heard that several troops of Kalmucks had been abroad upon the desert, but that we were now completely out of danger of them, which was to our great satisfaction. Here we were obliged to get some fresh horses, and having need enough of rest, we stayed five days; and my partner and I agreed to give the honest Siberian who conducted us thither the value of ten pistoles.

In five days more we came to Veussima, upon the river Witzogda, and running into the Dwina: we were there, very happily, near the end of our travels by land, that river being navigable, in seven days' passage, to Archangel. From hence we came to Lawremskoy, the 3rd of July; and providing ourselves with two luggage boats, and a barge for our own convenience, we embarked the 7th, and arrived all safe at Archangel the 18th; having been a year, five months, and three days on the journey, including our stay of about eight months at Tobolski.

We were obliged to stay at this place six weeks for the arrival of the ships, and must have tarried longer, had not a Hamburger come in above a month sooner than any of the English ships; when, after some consideration that the city of Hamburg might happen to be as good a market for our goods as London, we all took freight with him; and, having put our goods on board, it was most natural for me to put my steward on board to take care of them; by which means my young lord had a sufficient opportunity to conceal himself, never coming on shore again all the time we stayed there; and this he did that he might not be seen in the city, where some of the Moscow merchants would certainly have seen and discovered him.

We then set sail from Archangel the 20th of August, the same year; and, after no extraordinary bad voyage, arrived safe in the Elbe the 18th of September. Here my partner and I found a very good sale for our goods, as well those of China as the sables, &c., of Siberia: and, dividing the produce, my share amounted to 3475 pounds, 17s 3d., including about six hundred pounds' worth of diamonds, which I purchased at Bengal.

Here the young lord took his leave of us, and went up the Elbe, in order to go to the court of Vienna, where he resolved to seek protection and could correspond with those of his father's friends who were left alive. He did not part without testimonials of gratitude for the service I had done him, and for my kindness to the prince, his father.

To conclude: having stayed near four months in Hamburg, I came from thence by land to the Hague, where I embarked in the packet, and arrived in London the 10th of January 1705, having been absent from England ten years and nine months. And here, resolving to harass myself no more, I am preparing for a longer journey than all these, having lived seventy-two years a life of infinite variety, and learned sufficiently to know the value of retirement, and the blessing of ending our days in peace.

THE CONSOLIDATOR,

OR MEMOIRS OF SUNDRY TRANSACTIONS FROM THE WORLD IN THE MOON

Translated from the Lunar Language by the Author of *The True-born English Man*

It cannot be unknown to any that have traveled into the Dominions of the Czar of Muscovy, that this famous rising Monarch, having studied all Methods for the Increase of his Power, and the Enriching as well as Polishing his Subjects, has traveled through most part of Europe, and visited the Courts of the greatest Princes; from whence, by his own Observation, as well as by carrying with him Artists in most useful Knowledge, he has transmitted most of our General Practice, especially in War and Trade, to his own Unpolite People; and the Effects of this Curiosity of his are exceeding visible in his present Proceedings; for by the Improvements he obtained in his European Travels, he has Modeled his Armies, formed new Fleets, settled Foreign Negoce in several remote Parts of the World; and we now see his Forces besieging strong Towns, with regular Approaches; and his Engineers raising Batteries, throwing Bombs, &c. like other Nations; whereas before, they had nothing of Order among them, but carried all by Onslaught and Scalado, wherein they either prevailed by the Force of Irresistible Multitude, or were Slaughtered by heaps, and left the Ditches of their Enemies filled with their Dead Bodies.

We see their Armies now formed into regular Battalions; and their Strelitz Musqueteers, a People equivalent to the Turks Janizaries, cloathed like our Guards, firing in Platoons, and behaving themselves with extraordinary Bravery and Order.

We see their Ships now completely fitted, built and furnished, by the English and Dutch Artists, and their Men of War Cruise in the Baltick. Their New City of Petersburg built by the present Czar, begins now to look like our Portsmouth, fitted with Wet and Dry Docks, Storehouses, and Magazines of Naval Preparations, vast and Incredible; which may serve to remind us, how we once taught the French to build Ships, till they are grown able to teach us how to use them.

As to Trade, our large Fleets to Arch-Angel may speak for it, where we now send 100 Sail yearly, instead of 8 or 9, which were the greatest number we ever sent before; and the Importation of Tobaccos from England into his Dominions, would still increase the Trade thither, was not the Covetousness of our own Merchants the Obstruction of their Advantages. But all this by the by.

As this great Monarch has Improved his Country, by introducing the Manners and Customs of the Politer Nations of Europe; so, with Indefatigable Industry, he has settled a new, but constant Trade, between his Country and China, by Land; where his Caravans go twice or thrice a Year, as Numerous almost, and as strong, as those from Egypt to Persia: Nor is the Way shorter, or the Deserts they pass over less wild and uninhabitable, only that they are not so subject to Floods of Sand, if that Term be proper, or to Troops of Arabs, to destroy them by the way; for this powerful Prince, to make this terrible Journey feasible to his Subjects, has built Forts, planted Colonies and Garrisons at proper Distances; where, though they are seated in Countries entirely Barren, and among uninhabited Rocks and Sands; yet, by his continual furnishing them from his own Stores, the Merchants traveling are relieved on good Terms, and meet both with Convoy and Refreshment.

More might be said of the admirable Decorations of this Journey, and how so prodigious an Attempt is made easy; so that now they have an exact Correspondence, and drive a prodigious Trade between Muscow and Tonquin; but having a longer Voyage in Hand, I shall not detain the Reader, nor keep him till he grows too big with Expectation.

Now, as all Men know the Chineses are an Ancient, Wise, Polite, and most Ingenious People; so the Muscovites begun to reap the Benefit of this open Trade; and not only to grow exceeding Rich by the bartering for all the Wealth of those Eastern Countries; but to polish and refine their Customs and Manners, as much on that side as they have from their European Improvements on this.

And as the Chineses have many sorts of Learning which these Parts of the World never heard of, so all those useful Inventions which we admire ourselves so much for, are vulgar and common with them, and were in use long before our Parts of the World were Inhabited. Thus Gun-powder, Printing, and the use of the Magnet and Compass, which we call Modern Inventions, are not only far from being Inventions, but fall so far short of the Perfection of Art they have attained to, that it is hardly Credible, what wonderful things we are told of from thence, and all the Voyages the Author has made thither being

458

employed another way, have not yet furnished him with the Particulars fully enough to transmit them to view; not but that he is preparing a Scheme of all those excellent Arts those Nations are Masters of, for public View, by way of Detection of the monstrous Ignorance and Deficiencies of European Science; which may serve as a Lexicon Technicum for this present Age, with useful Diagrams for that purpose; wherein I shall not fail to acquaint the World, I. With the Art of Gunnery, as Practiced in China long before the War of the Giants, and by which those Presumptuous Animals fired Red-hot Bullets right up into Heaven, and made a Breach sufficient to encourage them to a General Storm; but being Repulsed with great Slaughter, they gave over the Siege for that time. This memorable part of History shall be a faithful Abridgement of Ibra chizra-le-peglizar, Historiographer-Royal to the Emperor of China, who wrote Anno Mundi 114. his Volumes extant, in the Public Library at Tonquin, Printed in Leaves of Vitrified Diamond, by an admirable Dexterity, struck all at an oblique Motion, the Engine remaining entire, and still fit for use, in the Chamber of the Emperor's Rarities.

And here I shall give you a Draft of the Engine it self, and a Plan of its Operation, and the wonderful Dexterity of its Performance.

If these Labours of mine shall prove successful, I may in my next Journey that way, take an Abstract of their most admirable Tracts in Navigation, and the Mysteries of Chinese Mathematics; which out-do all Modern Invention at that Rate, that 'tis Inconceivable: In this Elaborate Work I must run thro' the 365 Volumes of Augro-machi-lanquaro-zi, the most ancient Mathematician in all China: From thence I shall give a Description of a Fleet of Ships of 100000 Sail, built at the Expense of the Emperor Tangro the 15th; who having Notice of the General Deluge, prepared these Vessels, to every City and Town in his Dominions One, and in Bulk proportioned to the number of its Inhabitants; into which Vessel all the People, with such Movables as they thought fit to save, and with 120 Days Provisions, were received at the time of the Flood; and the rest of their Goods being put into great Vessels made of China Ware, and fast luted down on the top, were preserved unhurt by the Water: These Ships they furnished with 600 Fathom of Chain instead of Cables; which being fastened by wonderful Arts to the Earth, every Vessel rid out the Deluge just at the Town's end; so that when the Waters abated, the People had nothing to do, but to open the Doors made in the Ship-sides, and come out, repair their

Houses, open the great China Pots their Goods were in, and so put themselves in Statu Quo.

The Draft of one of these Ships I may perhaps obtain by my Interest in the present Emperor's Court, as it has been preserved ever since, and constantly repaired, riding at Anchor in a great Lake, about 100 Miles from Tonquin; in which all the People of that City were perfervid, amounting by their Computation to about a Million and half.

And as these things must be very useful in these Parts, to abate the Pride and Arrogance of our Modern Undertakers of great Enterprises, Authors of strange Foreign Accounts, Philosophical Transactions, and the like; if Time and Opportunity permit, I may let them know, how Infinitely we are out-done by those refined Nations, in all manner of Mechanic Improvements and Arts; and in discoursing of this, it will necessarily come in my way to speak of a most Noble Invention, being an Engine I would recommend to all People to whom 'tis necessary to have a good Memory; and which I design, if possible, to obtain a Draft of, that it may be Erected in our Royal Societies Laboratory: It has the wonderfulest Operations in the World: One part of it furnishes a Man of Business to dispatch his Affairs strangely; for if he be a Merchant, he shall write his Letters with one Hand, and Copy them with the other; if he is posting his Books, he shall post the Debtor side with one Hand, and the Creditor with the other; if he be a Lawyer, he draws his Drafts with one Hand, and Engrosses them with the other.

Another part of it furnishes him with such an Expeditious way of Writing, or Transcribing, that a Man cannot speak so fast, but he that hears shall have it down in Writing before 'tis spoken; and a Preacher shall deliver himself to his Auditory, and having this Engine before him, shall put down every thing he says in Writing at the same time; and so exactly is this Engine squared by Lines and Rules, that it does not require him that Writes to keep his Eye upon it.

I am told, in some Parts of China, they had arrived to such a Perfection of Knowledge, as to understand one another's Thoughts; and that it was found to be an excellent Preservative to humane Society, against all sorts of Frauds, Cheats, Sharping, and many Thousand European Inventions of that Nature, at which only we can be said to out-do those Nations.

I confess, I have not yet had leisure to travel those Parts, having been diverted by an accidental Opportunity of a new Voyage I had occasion to make for farther Discoveries, and which the Pleasure and Usefulness thereof having been very great, I have omitted the other for the present, but shall not fail to make a Visit to those Parts the first Opportunity, and shall give my Country-men the best Account I can of those things; for I doubt not in Time to bring our Nation, so famed for improving other People's Discoveries, to be as wise as any of those Heathen Nations; I wish I had the same Prospect of making them half so honest.

I had spent but a few Months in this Country, but my search after the Prodigy of humane Knowledge the People abounds with, led me into Acquaintance with some of their principal Artists, Engineers, and Men of Letters; and I was astonished at every Day's Discovery of new and of unheard-of Worlds of Learning; but I Improved in the Superficial Knowledge of their General, by no body so much as by my Conversation with the Library-keeper of Tonquin, by whom I had Admission into the vast Collection of Books, which the Emperors of that Country have treasured up.

It would be endless to give you a Catalogue, and they admit of no Strangers to write any thing down, but what the Memory can retain, you are welcome to carry away with you; and amongst the wonderful Volumes of Ancient and Modern Learning, I could not but take Notice of a few; which, besides those I mentioned before, I saw, when I looked over this vast Collection; and a larger Account may be given in our next.

It would be needless to Transcribe the Chinese Character, or to put their Alphabet into our Letters, because the Words would be both Unintelligible, and very hard to Pronounce; and therefore, to avoid hard Words, and Hieroglyphics, I'll translate them as well as I can.

The first Class I came to of Books, was the Constitutions of the Empire; these are vast great Volumes, and have a sort of Engine like our Magna Charta, to remove 'em, and with placing them in a Frame, by turning a Screw, opened the Leaves, and folded them this way, or that, as the Reader desires. It was present Death for the Library-keeper to refuse the meanest Chinese Subject to come in and read them; for 'tis their Maxim, That all People ought to know the Laws by which they are to be governed; and as above all People, we find no Fools in this Country, so the Emperors, though they seem to be Arbitrary, enjoy the greatest Authority in the World, by always observing, with the greatest Exactness, the Pacta Conventa of their Government: From these Principles it is impossible we should ever hear, either of the Tyranny of Princes, or Rebellion of Subjects, in all their Histories.

At the Entrance into this Class, you find some Ancient Comments, upon the Constitution of the Empire, written many Ages before we pretend the World began; but above all, One I took particular notice of, which might bear this Title, Natural Right proved Superior to Temporal Power; wherein the old Author proves, the Chinese Emperors were Originally made so, by Nature's directing the People, to place the Power of Government in the most worthy Person they could find; and the Author giving a most exact History of 2000 Emperors, brings them into about 35 or 36 Periods of Lines when the Race ended; and when a Collective Assembly of the Nobles, Cities, and People, Nominated a new Family to the Government.

This being an heretical Book as to European Politics, and our Learned Authors having long since exploded this Doctrine, and proved that Kings and Emperors came down from Heaven with Crowns on their Heads, and all their Subjects were born with Saddles on their Backs; I thought fit to leave it where I found it, least our excellent Tracts of Sir Robert Filmer, Dr. Hammond L...y, S....l, and Others, who have so learnedly treated of the more useful Doctrine of Passive Obedience, Divine Right, &c. should be blasphemed by the Mob, grow into Contempt of the People; and they should take upon them to question their Superiors for the Blood of Algernon Sidney, and Argyle.

For I take the Doctrines of Passive Obedience, &c. among the States-men, to be like the Copernican System of the Earths Motion among Philosophers; which, though it be contrary to all ancient Knowledge, and not capable of Demonstration, yet is adhered to in general, because by this they can better solve, and give a more rational Account of several dark Phenomena in Nature, than they could before.

Thus our Modern States-men approve of this Scheme of Government; not that it admits of any rational Defence, much less of Demonstration, but because by this Method they can the better explain, as well as defend, all Coercion in Cases invasive of Natural Right, than they could before.

Here I found two famous Volumes in Chirurgery, being an exact Description of the Circulation of the Blood, discovered long before King Solomon's Allegory of the Bucket's going to the Well; with several curious Methods by which the Demonstration was to be made so plain, as would make even the worthy Doctor B — — — himself become a Convert to his own Eye-sight, make him damn his own Elaborate Book, and think it worse Nonsense than ever the Town had the Freedom to imagine.

All our Philosophers are Fools, and their Transactions a parcel of empty Stuff, to the Experiments of the Royal Societies in this Country.

Here I came to a Learned Tract of Winds, which outdoes even the Sacred Text, and would make us believe it was not wrote to those People; for they tell Folks whence it comes, and whither it goes. There you have an Account how to make Glasses of Hogs Eyes, that can see the Wind; and they give strange Accounts both of its regular and irregular Motions, its Compositions and Quantities; from whence, by a sort of Algebra, they can cast up its Duration, Violence, and Extent: In these Calculations, some say, those Authors have been so exact, that they can, as our Philosophers say of Comets, state their Revolutions, and tell us how many Storms there shall happen to any Period of time, and when; and perhaps this may be with much about the same Truth.

It was a certain Sign Aristotle had never been at China; for, had he seen the 216th Volume of the Chinese Navigation, in the Library I am speaking of, a large Book in Double Folio, wrote by the Famous Mira-cho-cho-lasmo, Vice-Admiral of China, and said to be printed there about 2000 Years before the Deluge, in the Chapter of Tides he would have seen the Reason of all the certain and uncertain Fluxes and Refluxes of that Element, how the exact Pace is kept between the Moon and the Tides, with a most elaborate Discourse there, of the Power of Sympathy, and the manner how the heavenly Bodies Influence the Earthly: Had he seen this, the Stagyrite would never have Drowned himself, because he could not comprehend this Mystery.

'Tis farther related of this Famous Author, that he was no Native of this World, but was Born in the Moon, and coming hither to make Discoveries, by a strange Invention arrived to by the Virtuosos of that habitable World, the Emperor of China prevailed with him to stay and improve his Subjects, in the most exquisite Accomplishments of those Lunar Regions; and no wonder the Chinese are such exquisite Artists, and Masters of such sublime Knowledge, when this Famous Author has blest them with such unaccountable Methods of Improvement.

There was abundance of vast Classes full of the Works of this wonderful Philosopher: He gave the how, the modus of all the secret Operations of Nature; and told us, how Sensation is conveyed to and from the Brain; why Respiration preserves Life; and how Locomotion is directed to, as well as performed by the Parts. There are some Anatomical Dissections of Thought, and a Mathematical Description of Nature's strong Box, the Memory, with all its Locks and Keys.

There you have that part of the Head turned in-side outward, in which Nature has placed the Materials of reflecting; and like a Glass Bee-hive, represents to you all the several Cells in which are lodged things past, even back to Infancy and Conception. There you have the Repository, with all its Cells, Classically, Annually, Numerically, and Alphabetically Disposed. There you may see how, when the perplexed Animal, on the loss of a Thought or Word, scratches his Pole: Every Attack of his Invading Fingers knocks at Nature's Door, alarms all the Register-keepers, and away they run, unlock all the Classes, search diligently for what he calls for, and immediately deliver it up to the Brain; if it cannot be found, they entreat a little Patience, till they step into the Revolvery, where they run over little Catalogues of the minutest Passages of Life, and so in time never fail to hand on the thing; if not just when he calls for it, yet at some other time.

And thus, when a thing lies very Abstruse, and all the rummaging of the whole House cannot find it; nay, when all the People in the House have given it over, they very often find one thing when they are looking for another.

Next you have the Retentive in the remotest part of the Place, which, like the Records in the Tower, takes Possession of all Matters, as they are removed from the Classes in the Repository, for want of room. These are carefully Locked, and kept safe, never to be opened but upon solemn Occasions, and have swinging great Bars and Bolts upon them; so that what is kept here, is seldom lost. Here Conscience has one large Ware-house, and the Devil another; the first is very seldom opened, but has a Chink or Till, where all the Follies and Crimes of Life being minuted are dropt in; but as the Man seldom cares to look in, the Locks are very Rusty, and not opened but with great Difficulty, and on extraordinary Occasions, as Sickness, Afflictions, Jails, Casualties, and Death; and then the Bars all give way at once; and being pressed from within with a more than ordinary Weight, burst as a Cask of Wine upon the Fret, which for want of Vent, makes all the Hoops fly.

As for the Devil's Ware-house, he has two constant Warehouse-keepers, Pride and Conceit, and these are always at the Door, showing their Wares, and exposing the pretended Virtues and Accomplishments of the Man, by way of Ostentation.

In the middle of this curious part of Nature, there is a clear Thorough-fare, representing the World, through which so many Thousand People pass so easily, and do so little worth taking notice of, that 'tis for no manner of Signification to leave Word they have been here. Thro' this Opening pass Millions of things not worth remembering, and which the Register-Keepers, who stand at the Doors of the Classes, as they go by, take no notice of; such as Friendships, helps in Distress, Kindnesses in Affliction, Voluntary Services, and all sorts of Importunate Merit; things which being but Trifles in their own Nature, are made to be forgotten.

In another Angle is to be seen the Memory's Garden, in which her most pleasant things are not only Deposited, but Planted, Transplanted, Grafted, Inoculated, and obtain all possible Propagation and Increase; these are the most pleasant, delightful, and agreeable things, called Envy, Slander, Revenge, Strife and Malice, with the Additions of Ill-turns, Reproaches, and all manner of Wrong; these are caressed in the Cabinet of the Memory, with a World of Pleasure never let pass, and carefully Cultivated with all imaginable Art.

There are multitudes of Weeds, Toys, Chat, Story, Fiction, and Lying, which in the great throng of passant Affairs, stop by the way, and crowding up the Place, leave no room for their Betters that come behind, which makes many a good Guess be put by, and left to go clear thro' for want of Entertainment.

There are a multitude of things very curious and observable, concerning this little, but very accurate thing, called Memory; but above all, I see nothing so very curious, as the wonderful Art of Willful Forgetfulness; and as 'tis a thing, indeed, I never could find any Person completely Master of, it pleased me very much, to find this Author has made a large Essay, to prove there is really no such Power in Nature; and that the Pretenders to it are all Impostors, and put a Banter upon the World; for that it is impossible for any Man to oblige himself to forget a thing, since he that can remember to forget, and at the same time forget to remember, has an Art above the Devil.

In his Laboratory you see a Fancy preserved a la Mummy, several Thousand Years old; by examining which you may perfectly discern, how Nature makes a Poet: Another you have taken from a mere Natural, which discovers the Reasons of Nature's Negative in the Case of humane Understanding; what Deprivation of Parts She suffers, in the Composition of a Coxcomb; and with what wonderful Art She prepares a Man to be a Fool.

Here being the product of this Author's wonderful Skill, you have the Skeleton of a Wit, with all the Readings of Philosophy and Chirurgery upon the Parts: Here you see all the Lines Nature has drawn to form a Genius, how it performs, and from what Principles.

Also you are Instructed to know the true reason of the Affinity between Poetry and Poverty; and that it is equally derived from what's

465

Natural and Intrinsic, as from Accident and Circumstance; how the World being always full of Fools and Knaves, Wit is sure to miss of a good Market; especially, if Wit and Truth happen to come in Company; for the Fools don't understand it, and the Knaves can't bear it.

But still 'tis owned, and is most apparent, there is something also Natural in the Case too, since there are some particular Vessels Nature thinks necessary, to the more exact Composition of this nice thing called a Wit, which as they are, or are not Interrupted in the peculiar Offices for which they are appointed, are subject to various Distempers, and more particularly to Effluxions and Vapour, Deliriums Giddiness of the Brain, and Lapsa, or Looseness of the Tongue; and as these Distempers, occasioned by the exceeding quantity of Volatiles, Nature is obliged to make use of in the Composition, are hardly to be avoided, the Disasters which generally they push the Animal into, are as necessarily consequent to them as Night is to the Setting of the Sun; and these are very many, as disobliging Parents, who have frequently in this Country whipped their Sons for making Verses; and here I could not but reflect how useful a Discipline early Correction must be to a Poet; and how easy the Town had been had N — t, E — w, T. B — P — s, D — S — D — fy, and an Hundred more of the jingling Train of our modern Rhymers, been Whipped young, very young, for Poetasting, they had never perhaps sucked in that Venom of Ribaldry, which all the Satyr of the Age has never been able to scourge out of them to this Day.

The further fatal Consequences of these unhappy Defects in Nature, where she has damned a Man to Wit and Rhyme, has been loss of Inheritance, Parents being aggravated by the obstinate young Beaus, resolving to be Wits in spite of Nature, the wiser Head has been obliged to Confederate with Nature, and with-hold the Birth-right of Brains, which otherwise the young Gentleman might have enjoyed, to the great support of his Family and Posterity. Thus the famous Waller, Denham, Dryden, and sundry Others, were obliged to condemn their Race to Lunacy and Blockheadism, only to prevent the fatal Destruction of their Families, and entailing the Plague of Wit and Weathercocks upon their Posterity.

The yet farther Extravagancies which naturally attend the Mischief of Wit, are Beau-ism, Dogmaticality, Whimsification, Impudensity, and various kinds of Fopperosities (according to Mr. Boyl,) which issuing out of the Brain, descend into all the Faculties, and branch themselves by infinite Variety, into all the Actions of Life.

These by Consequence, Beggar the Head, the Tail, the Purse, and the whole Man, till he becomes as poor and despicable as Negative Nature can leave him, abandoned of his Sense, his Manners, his Modesty, and what's worse, his Money, having nothing left but his Poetry, dies in a Ditch, or a Garret, A-la-mode de Tom Brown, uttering Rhymes and Nonsense to the last Moment.

In Pity to all my unhappy Brethren, who suffer under these Inconveniencies, I cannot but leave it on Record, that they may not be reproached with being Agents of their own Misfortunes, since I assure them, Nature has formed them with the very Necessity of acting like Coxcombs, fixed upon them by the force of Organic Consequences, and placed down at the very Original Effusion of that fatal thing called Wit.

Nor is the Discovery less wonderful than edifying, and no humane Art on our side the World ever found out such a Sympathetic Influence, between the Extremes of Wit and Folly, till this great Lunarian Naturalist furnished us with such unheard-of Demonstrations.

Nor is this all I learnt from him, tho' I cannot part with this, till I have published a Memento Mori, and told 'em what I had discovered of Nature in these remote Parts of the World, from whence I take the Freedom to tell these Gentlemen, That if they please to Travel to these distant Parts, and examine this great Master of Nature's Secrets, they may every Man see what cross Strokes Nature has struck, to finish and form every extravagant Species of that Heterogeneous Kind we call Wit.

There C — S — may be informed how he comes to be very Witty, and a Mad-man all at once; and P — r may see, That with less Brains and more P — x he is more a Wit and more a Mad-man than the Coll. Ad — son may tell his Master my Lord — — the reason from Nature, why he would not take the Court's Word, nor write the Poem called, The Campaign, till he had 200 l. per Annum secured to him; since 'tis known they have but one Author in the Nation that writes for 'em for nothing, and he is labouring very hard to obtain the Title of Blockhead, and not be paid for it: Here D. might understand, how he came to be able to banter all Mankind, and yet all Mankind be able to banter him; at the fame time our numerous throng of Parnassians may see Reasons for the variety of the Negative and Positive Blessings they enjoy; some for having Wit and no Verse, some Verse and no Wit, some Mirth without Jest, some Jest without Fore-cast, some Rhyme and no Jingle, some all Jingle and no Rhyme, some

467

Language without measure; some all Quantity and no Cadence, some all Wit and no Sense, some all Sense and no Flame, some Preach in Rhyme, some sing when they Preach, some all Song and no Tune, some all Tune and no Song; all these Unaccountables have their Originals, and can be answered for in unerring Nature, tho' in our out-side Guesses we can say little to it. Here is to be seen, why some are all Nature, some all Art; some beat Verse out of the Twenty-four rough Letters, with Ten Hammers and Anvils to every Line, and maul the Language as a Swede beats Stock-Fish; Others buff Nature, and bully her out of whole Stanza's of ready-made Lines at a time, carry all before them, and rumble like distant Thunder in a black Cloud: Thus Degrees and Capacities are fitted by Nature, according to Organic Efficacy; and the Reason and Nature of Things are found in themselves: Had D — y seen his own Draft by this Light of Chinese Knowledge, he might have known he should be a Coxcomb without writing Twenty-two Plays, to stand as so many Records against him. Dryden might have told his Fate, that having his extraordinary Genius flung and pitched upon a Swivel, it would certainly turn round as fast as the Times, and instruct him how to write Elegies to O. C. and King C. the Second, with all the Coherence imaginable; how to write Religio Laicy, and the Hind and Panther, and yet be the same Man, every Day to change his Principle, change his Religion, change his Coat, change his Master, and yet never change his Nature.

There are abundance of other Secrets in Nature discovered in relation to these things, too many to repeat, and yet too useful to omit, as the reason why Physicians are generally Atheists; and why Atheists are universally Fools, and generally live to know it themselves, the real Obstructions, which prevent fools being mad, all the Natural Causes of Love, abundance of Demonstrations of the Synonymous Nature of Love and Lechery, especially considered a la Modern, with an absolute Specific for the Frenzy of Love, found out in the Constitution, Anglice, a Halter.

It would be endless to reckon up the numerous Improvements, and wonderful Discoveries this extraordinary Person has brought down, and which are to be seen in his curious Chamber of Rarities.

Particularly, a Map of Parnassus, with an exact Delineation of all the Cells, Apartments, Palaces and Dungeons, of that most famous Mountain; with a Description of its Height, and a learned Dissertation, proving it to be the properest Place next to the P — e House to take a Rise at, for a flight to the World in the Moon.

Also some Enquiries, whether Noah's Ark did not first rest upon it; and this might be one of the Summits of Ararat, with some Confutations of the gross and palpable Errors, which place this extraordinary Skill among the Mountains of the Moon in Africa.

Also you have here a Muse calcined, a little of the Powder of which given to a Woman big with Child, if it be a Boy it will be a Poet, if a Girl she'll be a Whore, if an Hermaphrodite it will be Lunatic.

Strange things, they tell us, have been done with this calcined Womb of Imagination; if the Body it came from was a Lyric Poet, the Child will be a Beau, or a Beauty; if an Heroic Poet, he will be a Bully; if his Talent was Satyr, he'll be a Philosopher.

Another Muse they tell us, they have dissolved into a Liquid, and kept with wondrous Art, the Virtues of which are Sovereign against Idiotism, Dullness, and all sorts of Lethargic Diseases; but if given in too great a quantity, creates Poesy, Poverty, Lunacy, and the Devil in the Head ever after.

I confess, I always thought these Muses strange intoxicating things, and have heard much talk of their Original, but never was acquainted with their Virtue a la Simple before; however, I would always advise People against too large a Dose of Wit, and think the Physician must be a Mad-man that will venture to prescribe it.

As all these noble Acquirements came down with this wonderful Man from the World in the Moon, it furnished me with these useful Observations.

1. That Country must needs be a Place of strange Perfection, in all parts of extraordinary Knowledge.

2. How useful a thing it would be for most sorts of our People, especially Statesmen, P — — t-men, Convocation-men, Philosophers, Physicians, Quacks, Mountebanks, Stock-jobbers, and all the Mob of the Nation's Civil or Ecclesiastical Bone-setters, together with some Men of the Law, some of the Sword, and all of the Pen: I say, how useful and improving a thing it must be to them, to take a Journey up to the World in the Moon; but above all, how much more beneficial it would be to them that stayed behind.

3. That it is not to be wondered at, why the Chinese excel so much all these Parts of the World, since but for that Knowledge which comes down to them from the World in the Moon, they would be like other People.

4. No Man need to Wonder at my exceeding desire to go up to the World in the Moon, having heard of such extraordinary Knowledge

to be obtained there, since in the search of Knowledge and Truth, wiser Men than I have taken as unwarrantable Flights, and gone a great deal higher than the Moon, into a strange Abyss of dark Phenomena, which they neither could make other People understand, nor ever rightly understood themselves, witness Malbranch, Mr. Lock, Hobbs, the Honourable Boyle and a great many others, besides Messieurs Norris, Asgil, Coward, and the Tale of a Tub.

This great Searcher into Nature has, besides all this, left wonderful Discoveries and Experiments behind him; but I was with nothing more exceedingly diverted, than with his various Engines, and curious Contrivances, to go to and from his own Native Country the Moon. All our Mechanic Motions of Bishop Wilkins, or the artificial Wings of the Learned Spaniard, who could have taught God Almighty how to have mended the Creation, are Fools to this Gentleman; and because no Man in China has made more Voyages up into the Moon than my self, I cannot but give you some Account of the easiness of the Passage, as well as of the Country.

Nor are his wonderful Telescopes of a mean Quality, by which such plain Discoveries are made, of the Lands and Seas in the Moon, and in all the habitable Planets, that one may as plainly fee what a Clock it is by one of the Dials in the Moon, as if it were no farther off than Windsor-Castle; and had he lived to finish the Speaking-trumpet which he had contrived to convey Sound thither, Harlequin's Mock-Trumpet had been a Fool to it; and it had no doubt been an admirable Experiment, to have given us a general Advantage from all their acquired Knowledge in those Regions, where no doubt several useful Discoveries are daily made by the Men of Thought for the Improvement of all sorts of humane Understanding, and to have discoursed with them on those things, must have been very pleasant, besides, its being very much to our particular Advantage.

I confess, I have thought it might have been very useful to this Nation, to have brought so wonderful an Invention hither, and I was once very desirous to have set up my rest here, and for the Benefit of my Native Country, have made my self Master of these Engines, that I might in due time have conveyed them to our Royal Society, that once in 40 Years they might have been said to do something for Public Good; and that the Reputation and Usefulness of the so so's might be recovered in England; but being told that in the Moon there were many of these Glasses to be had very cheap, and I having declared my Resolution of undertaking a Voyage thither, I deferred my Design, and shall defer my treating of them, till I give some Account of my Arrival there.

But above all his Inventions for making this Voyage, I saw none more pleasant or profitable, than a certain Engine formed in the shape of a Chariot, on the Backs of two vast Bodies with extended Wings, which spread about 50 Yards in Breadth, composed of Feathers so nicely put together, that no Air could pass; and as the Bodies were made of Lunar Earth which would bear the Fire, the Cavities were filled with an Ambient Flame, which fed on a certain Spirit deposited in a proper quantity, to last out the Voyage; and this Fire so ordered as to move about such Springs and Wheels as kept the Wings in a most exact and regular Motion, always ascendant; thus the Person being placed in this airy Chariot, drinks a certain dozing Draught, that throws him into a gentle Slumber, and Dreaming all the way, never wakes till he comes to his Journey's end.

Of the Consolidator.

These Engines are called in their Country Language, Dupekasses; and according to the Ancient Chinese, or Tartarian, Apezolanthukanistes; in English, a Consolidator.

The Composition of this Engine is very admirable; for, as is before noted, 'tis all made up of Feathers, and the quality of the Feathers, is no less wonderful than their Composition; and therefore, I hope the Reader will bear with the Description for the sake of the Novelty, since I assure him such things as these are not to be seen in every Country.

The number of Feathers are just 513, they are all of a length and breadth exactly, which is absolutely necessary to the floating Figure, or else one side or any one part being wider or longer than the rest, it would interrupt the motion of the whole Engine; only there is one extraordinary Feather which, as there is an odd one in the number, is placed in the Center, and is the Handle, or rather Rudder to the whole Machine: This Feather is every way larger than its Fellows, 'tis almost as long and broad again; but above all, its Quill or Head is much larger, and it has as it were several small bushing Feathers round the bottom of it, which all make but one presiding or superintendent Feather, to guide, regulate, and pilot the whole Body.

Nor are these common Feathers, but they are picked and culled out of all parts of the Lunar Country, by the Command of the Prince; and every Province sends up the best they can find, or ought to do so at least, or else they are very much to blame; for the Employment they are put to being of so great use to the Public, and the Voyage or Flight so exceeding high, it would be very ill done if, when the King sends his Letters about the Nation, to pick him up the best Feathers they can lay their Hands on, they should send weak, decayed, or half-grown Feathers, and yet sometimes it happens so; and once there was such rotten Feathers collected, whether it was a bad Year for Feathers, or whether the People that gathered them had a mind to abuse their King; but the Feathers were so bad, the Engine was good for nothing, but broke before it was got half way; and by a double Misfortune, this happened to be at an unlucky time, when the King himself had resolved on a Voyage, or Flight to the Moon; but being deceived, by the unhappy Miscarriage of the deficient Feathers, he fell down from so great a height, that he struck himself against his own Palace, and beat his Head off.

Nor had the Sons of this Prince much better Success, tho' the first of them was a Prince mightily beloved by his Subjects; but his Misfortunes chiefly proceeded from his having made use of one of the Engines so very long, that the Feathers were quite worn out, and good for nothing: He used to make a great many Voyages and Flights into the Moon, and then would make his Subjects give him great Sums of Money to come down to them again; and yet they were so fond of him, That they always complied with him, and would give him every thing he asked, rather than to be without him: But they grew wiser since.

At last, this Prince used his Engine so long, it could hold together no longer; and being obliged to write to his Subjects to pick him out some new Feathers, they did so; but withal sent him such strong Feathers, and so stiff, that when he had placed 'em in their proper places, and made a very beautiful Engine, it was too heavy for him to manage: He made a great many Essays at it, and had it placed on the top of an old Idol Chapel, dedicated to an old Bramyn Saint of those Countries, called, Phantosteinaschap; in Latin, chap. de Saint Stephano; or in English, St. Stephen's: Here the Prince tried all possible Contrivances, and a vast deal of Money it cost him; but the Feathers were so stiff they would not work, and the Fire within was so choked and smothered with its own Smoke, for want of due Vent and Circulation, that it would not burn; so he was obliged to take it down again; and from thence he carried it to his College of Bramyn Priests, and set it up in one of their Public Buildings: There he drew Circles of Ethics and Politics, and fell to casting of Figures and Conjuring, but all would not do, the Feathers could not be brought to move; and, indeed,

I have observed, That these Engines are seldom helped by Art and Contrivance; there is no way with them, but to have the People spoke to, to get good Feathers; and they are easily placed, and perform all the several Motions with the greatest Ease and Accuracy imaginable; but it must be all Nature; any thing of Force distorts and dislocates them, and the whole Order is spoiled; and if there be but one Feather out of place, or pinched, or stands wrong, the D — l would not ride in the Chariot.

The Prince thus finding his Labour in vain, broke the Engine to pieces, and sent his Subjects Word what bad Feathers they had sent him: But the People, who knew it was his own want of Management, and that the Feathers were good enough, only a little stiff at first, and with good Usage would have been brought to be fit for use, took it ill, and never would send him any other as long as he lived: However, it had this good effect upon him, That he never made any more Voyages to the Moon as long as he reigned.

His Brother succeeded him; and truly he was resolved upon a Voyage to the Moon, as soon as ever he came to the Crown. He had met with some unkind Usage from the Religious Lunesses of his own Country; and he turned Abogratziarian, a zealous fiery Sect something like our Anti-every-body-arians in England. 'Tis confessed, some of the Bramyns of his Country were very false to him, put him upon several Ways of extending his Power over his Subjects, contrary to the Customs of the People, and contrary to his own Interest; and when the People expressed their Dislike of it, he thought to have been supported by those Clergy-men; but they failed him, and made good, that Old English Verse;

That Priests of all Religions are the same.

He took this so heinously, that he conceived a just Hatred against those that had deceived him; and as Resentments seldom keep Rules, unhappily entertained Prejudices against all the rest; and not finding it easy to bring all his Designs to pass better, he resolved upon a Voyage to the Moon.

Accordingly, he sends a Summons to all his People according to Custom, to collect the usual quantity of Feathers for that purpose; and because he would be sure not be used as his Brother and Father had been, he took care to send certain Cunning-men Express, all over the Country, to bespeak the People's Care, in collecting, picking and culling them out, these were called in their Language, Tsopablesdetoo; which being Translated may signify in English, Men of Zeal, or Booted Apostles: Nor was this the only Caution this Prince used; for he took

473

care, as the Feathers were sent up to him, to search and examine them one by one in his own Closet, to see if they were fit for his purpose; but, alas! he found himself in his Brother's Case exactly; and perceived, That his Subjects were generally disgusted at his former Conduct, about Abrogratzianism, and such things, and particularly set in a Flame by some of their Priests, called, Dullobardians, or Passive-Obedience-men, who had lately turned their Tale, and their Tail too upon their own Princes; and upon this, he laid aside any more Thoughts of the Engine, but took up a desperate and implacable Resolution, viz. to fly up to the Moon without it; in order to this, abundance of his Cunning-men were summoned together to assist him, strange Engines contrived, and Methods proposed; and a great many came from all Parts, to furnish him with Inventions and equivalent for their Journey; but all were so preposterous and ridiculous, that his Subjects seeing him going on to ruin himself, and by Consequence them too, unanimously took Arms; and if their Prince had not made his Escape into a foreign Country, 'tis thought they would have secured him for a Mad-man.

And here 'tis observable, That as it is in most such Cases, the mad Counselors of this Prince, when the People begun to gather about him, fled; and every one shifted for themselves; nay, and some of them plundered him first of his Jewels and Treasure, and never were heard of since.

From this Prince none of the Kings or Government of that Country have ever seemed to incline to the hazardous Attempt of the Voyage to the Moon, at least not in such a hair-brained manner.

However, the Engine has been very accurately Re-built and finished; and the People are now obliged by a Law, to send up new Feathers every three Years, to prevent the Mischiefs which happened by that Prince aforesaid, keeping one Set so long that it was dangerous to venture with them; and thus the Engine is preserved fit for use.

And yet has not this Engine been without its continual Disasters, and often out of repair; for though the Kings of the Country, as has been Noted, have done riding on the back of it, yet the restless Courtiers and Ministers of State have frequently obtained the Management of it, from the too easy Goodness of their Masters, or the Evils of the Times.

To Cure this, the Princes frequently changed Hands, turned one Set of Men out and put another in: But this made things still worse; for it divided the People into Parties and Factions in the State, and still the Strife was, who should ride in this Engine; and no sooner were these

Skate-Riders got into it, but they were for driving all the Nation up to the Moon: But of this by it self.

Authors differ concerning the Original of these Feathers, and by what most exact Hand they were first appointed to this particular use; and as their Original is hard to be found, so it seems a Difficulty to resolve from what sort of Bird these Feathers are obtained: Some have named one, some another; but the most Learned in those Climates call it by a hard Word, which the Printer having no Letters to express, and being in that place Hieroglyphical, I can translate no better, than by the Name of a Collective: This must be a Strange Bird without doubt; it has Heads, Claws, Eyes and Teeth innumerable; and if I should go about to describe it to you, the History would be so Romantic, it would spoil the Credit of these more Authentic Relations which are yet behind.

'Tis sufficient, therefore, for the present, only to leave you this short Abridgement of the Story, as follows: This great Monstrous Bird, called the Collective, is very seldom seen, and indeed never, but upon Great Revolutions, and portending terrible Desolations and Destructions to a Country.

But he frequently sheds his Feathers; and they are carefully picked up, by the Proprietors of those Lands where they fall; for none but those Proprietors may meddle with them; and they no sooner pick them up but they are sent to Court, where they obtain a new Name, and are called in a Word equally difficult to pronounce as the other, but Very like our English Word, Representative; and being placed in their proper Rows, with the Great Feather in the Center, and fitted for use, they lately obtained the Venerable Title of, The Consolidators; and the Machine it self, the Consolidator; and by that Name the Reader is desired for the future to let it be dignified and distinguished.

I cannot, however, forbear to descant a little here, on the Dignity and Beauty of these Feathers, being such as are hardly to be seen in any part of the World, but just in these remote Climates.

And First, Every Feather has various Colours, and according to the Variety of the Weather, are apt to look brighter and clearer, or paler and fainter, as the Sun happens to look on them with a stronger or weaker Aspect. The Quill or Head of every Feather is or ought to be full of a vigorous Substance, which gives Spirit, and supports the brightness and colour of the Feather; and as this is more or less in quantity, the bright Colour of the Feather is increased, or turns languid and pale.

Tis true, some of those Quills are exceeding empty and dry; and the Humid being totally exhaled, those Feathers grow very useless and insignificant in a short time.

Some again are so full of Wind, and puffed up with the Vapour of the Climate, that there's not Humid enough to Condense the Steam; and these are so fleet, so light, and so continually fluttering and troublesome, that they greatly serve to disturb and keep the Motion unsteady.

Others either placed too near the inward concealed Fire, or the Head of the Quill being thin, the Fire causes too great a Fermentation; and the Consequence of this is so fatal, that sometimes it mounts the Engine up too fast, and endangers Precipitation: But 'tis happily observed, That these ill Feathers are but a very few, compared to the whole number; at the most, I never heard they were above 134 of the whole number: As for the empty ones, they are not very dangerous, but a sort of Good-for-nothing Feathers, that will fly when the greatest number of the rest fly, or stand still when they stand still. The fluttering hot-headed Feathers are the most dangerous, and frequently struggle hard to mount the Engine to extravagant heights; but still the greater number of the Feathers being stanch, and well fixed, as well as well furnished, they always prevail, and check the Disorders the other would bring upon the Motion; so that upon the whole Matter, tho' there has sometimes been oblique Motions, Variations, and sometimes great Wanderings out of the way, which may make the Passage tedious, yet it has always been a certain and safe Voyage; and no Engine was ever known to miscarry or overthrow, but that one mentioned before, and that was very much owing to the precipitate Methods the Prince took in guiding it; and tho' all the fault was laid in the Feathers, and they were to blame enough, yet I never heard any Wise Man, but what blamed his Discretion, and particularly, a certain great Man has wrote three large Tracts of those Affairs, and called them, The History of the Opposition of the Feathers; wherein, tho' it was expected he would have curst the Engine it self and all the Feathers to the Devil, on the contrary, he lays equal blame on the Prince, who guided the Chariot with so unsteady a hand, now as much too slack, as then too hard, turning them this way and that so hastily, that the Feathers could not move in their proper order; and this at last put the Fire in the Center quite out, and so the Engine over-set at once. This Impartiality has done great Justice to the Feathers, and set things in a clearer light: But of this I shall say more, when I come to treat of the Works of the Learned in this Lunar World.

This is hinted here only to inform the Reader, That this Engine is the safest Passage that ever was found out; and that saving that one time, it never miscarried; nor if the common Order of things be observed, cannot Miscarry; for the good Feathers are always Negatives, when any precipitant Motion is felt, and immediately suppress it by their number; and these Negative Feathers are indeed the Travelers safety; the other are always upon the flutter, and upon every occasion hey for the Moon, up in the Clouds presently; but these Negative Feathers are never for going up, but when there is occasion for it; and from hence these fluttering fermented Feathers were called by the Ancients High-flying Feathers, and the blustering things seemed proud of the Name.

But to come to their general Character, the Feathers, speaking of them all together, are generally very Comely, Strong, Large, Beautiful things, their Quills or Heads well fixed, and the Cavities filled with a solid substantial Matter, which tho' it is full of Spirit, has a great deal of Temperament, and full of suitable well-disposed Powers, to the Operation for which they are designed.

These placed, as I Noted before, in an extended Form like two great Wings, and operated by that sublime Flame; which being concealed in proper Receptacles, obtains its vent at the Cavities appointed, are supplied from thence with Life and Motion; and as Fire it fell, in the Opinion of some Learned Men, is nothing but Motion, and Motion tends to Fire: It can no more be a Wonder, if exalted in the Center of this famous Engine, a whole Nation should be carried up to the World in the Moon.

'Tis true, this Engine is frequently assaulted with fierce Winds, and furious Storms, which sometimes drive it a great way out of its way; and indeed, considering the length of the Passage, and the various Regions it goes through, it would be strange if it should meet with no Obstructions: These are oblique Gales, and cannot be said to blow from any of the Thirty-two Points, but Retrograde and Thwart: Some of these are called in their Language, Pensionazima, which is as much as to say, being Interpreted, a Court-breeze; another sort of Wind, which generally blows directly contrary to the Pensionazima, is the Clamorio, or in English, a Country Gale; this is generally Tempestuous, full of Gusts and Disgusts, Squauls and sudden Blasts, not without claps of Thunder, and not a little flashing of Heat and Party-fires.

There are a great many other Internal Blasts, which proceed from the Fire within, which sometimes not circulating right, breaks out in little Gusts of Wind and Heat, and is apt to endanger setting Fire to the Feathers, and this is more or less dangerous, according as among which of the Feathers it happens; for some of the Feathers are more apt to take Fire than others, as their Quills or Heads are more or less full of that solid Matter mentioned before.

The Engine suffers frequent Convulsions and Disorders from these several Winds; and which if they chance to overblow very much, hinder the Passage; but the Negative Feathers always apply Temper and Moderation; and this brings all to rights again.

For a Body like this, what can it not do? what cannot such an Extension perform in the Air? And when one thing is tacked to another, and properly Consolidated into one mighty Consolidator, no question but whoever shall go up to the Moon, will find himself so improved in this wonderful Experiment, that not a Man ever performed that wonderful Flight, but he certainly came back again as wise as he went.

Well, Gentlemen, and what if we are called High-flyers now, and an Hundred Names of Contempt and Distinction, what is this to the purpose? who would not be a High-flyer, to be Tacked and Consolidated in an Engine of such sublime Elevation, and which lifts Men, Monarchs, Members, yea, and whole Nations, up into the Clouds; and performs with such wondrous Art, the long expected Experiment of a Voyage to the Moon? And thus much for the Description of the Consolidator.

The first Voyage I ever made to this Country, was in one of these Engines; and I can safely affirm, I never waked all the way; and now having been as often there as most that have used that Trade, it may be expected I should give some Account of the Country; for it appears, I can give but little of the Road.

Only this I understand, That when this Engine, by help of these Artificial Wings, has raised it self up to a certain height, the Wings are as useful to keep it from falling into the Moon, as they were before to raise it, and keep it from falling back into this Region again.

This may happen from an Alteration of Centers, and Gravity having past a certain Line, the Equipoise changes its Tendency, the Magnetic Quality being beyond it, it inclines of Course, and pursues a Center, which it finds in the Lunar World, and lands us safe upon the Surface.

I was told, I need take no Bills of Exchange with me, nor Letters of Credit; for that upon my first Arrival, the Inhabitants would be very civil to me: That they never suffered any of Our World to want any thing when they came there: That they were very free to show them any thing, and inform them in all needful Cases; and that whatever Rarities the Country afforded, should be exposed immediately.

I shall not enter into the Customs, Geography, or History of the Place, only acquaint the Reader, That I found no manner of Difference in any thing Natural, except as hereafter excepted, but all was exactly as is here, an Elementary World, peopled with Folks, as like us as if they were only Inhabitants of the same Continent, but in a remote Climate.

The Inhabitants were Men, Women, Beasts, Birds, Fishes, and Insects, of the same individual Species as Ours, the latter excepted: The Men no wiser, better, nor bigger than here; the Women no handsomer or honester than Ours: There were Knaves and honest Men, honest Women and Whores of all Sorts, Countries, Nations and Kindreds, as on this side the Skies.

They had the same Sun to shine, the Planets were equally visible as to us, and their Astrologers were as busily Impertinent as Ours, only that those wonderful Glasses hinted before made strange Discoveries that we were unacquainted with; by them they could plainly discover, That this World was their Moon, and their World our Moon; and when I came first among them, the People that flocked about me, distinguished me by the Name of, the Man that came out of the Moon.

I cannot, however, but acquaint the Reader, with some Remarks I made in this new World, before I come to any thing Historical.

I have heard, that among the Generality of our People, who being not much addicted to Revelation, have much concerned themselves about Demonstrations, a Generation have risen up, who to solve the Difficulties of Supernatural Systems, imagine a mighty vast Something, who has no Form but what represents him to them as one Great Eye: This infinite Optic they imagine to be Natura Naturans, or Power-forming; and that as we pretend the Soul of Man has a Similitude in quality to its Original, according to a Notion some People have, who read that so much ridiculed Old Legend, called Bible, That Man was made in the Image of his Maker: The Soul of Man, therefore, in the Opinion of these Naturalists, is one vast Optic Power diffused through him into all his Parts, but seated principally in his Head.

From hence they resolve all Beings to Eyes, some more capable of Sight and receptive of Objects than others; and as to things Invisible, they reckon nothing so, only so far as our Sight is deficient, contracted or darkened by Accidents from without, as Distance of Place, Interposition of Vapours, Clouds, liquid Air, Exhalations, &c. or from within, as wandering Errors, wild Notions, cloudy Understandings, and empty Fancies, with a Thousand other interposing Obstacles to the Sight, which darken it, and prevent its Operation; and particularly obstruct the perceptive Faculties, weaken the Head, and bring Mankind in General to stand in need of the Spectacles of Education as soon as ever they are born: Nay, and as soon as they have made use of these Artificial Eyes, all they can do is but to clear the Sight so far as to see that they can't see; the utmost Wisdom of Mankind, and the highest Improvement a Man ought to wish for, being but to be able to see that he was Born blind; this pushes him upon search after Mediums for the Recovery of his Sight, and away he runs to School to Art and Science, and there he is furnished with Horoscopes, Microscopes, Telescopes, Caliscopes, Money-scopes, and the D — l and all of Glasses, to help and assist his Moon-blind Understanding; these with wonderful Skill and Ages of Application, after wandering thro' Bogs and Wildernesses of Guess, Conjectures, Supposes, Calculations, and he knows not what, which he meets with in Physics, Politics, Ethics, Astronomy, Mathematics, and such sort of bewildering Things, bring him with vast Difficulty to a little Minute-spot, called Demonstration; and as not one in Ten Thousand ever finds the way thither, but are lost in the tiresome uncouth Journey, so they that do, 'tis so long before they come there, that they are grown Old and good for little in the Journey; and no sooner have they obtained a glimmering of this Universal Eye-sight, this Eclaricissment General, but they Die, and have hardly time to show the way to those that come after.

Now, as the earnest search after this thing called Demonstration filled me with Desires of seeing every thing, so my Observations of the strange multitude of Mysteries I met with in all Men's Actions here, spurred my Curiosity to examine, if the Great Eye of the World had no People to whom he had given a clearer Eye-sight, or at least, that made a better use of it than we had here.

If pursuing this search I was much delighted at my Arrival into China, it cannot be thought strange, since there we find Knowledge as much advanced beyond our common Pitch, as it was pretended to be derived from a more Ancient Original.

We are told, that in the early Age of the World, the Strength of Invention exceeded all that ever has been arrived to since: That we in these latter Ages, having lost all that pristine Strength of Reason and Invention, which died with the Ancients in the Flood, and receiving no helps from that Age, have by long Search arrived at several remote Parts of Knowledge, by the helps of reading Conversation and Experience; but that all amounts to no more than faint Imitations, Apings, and Resemblances of what was known in those masterly Ages.

Now, if it be true as is hinted before, That the Chinese Empire was Peopled long before the Flood; and that they were not destroyed in the General Deluge in the Days of Noah; 'tis no such strange thing, that they should so much out-do us in this sort of Eye-sight we call General Knowledge, since the Perfections bestowed on Nature, when in her Youth and Prime met with no General Suffocation by that Calamity.

But if I was extremely delighted with the extraordinary things I saw in those Countries, you cannot but imagine I was exceedingly moved, when I heard of a Lunar World; and that the way was passable from these Parts.

I had heard of a World in the Moon among some of our Learned Philosophers, and Moor, as I have been told, had a Moon in his Head; but none of the fine Pretenders, no not Bishop Wilkins, ever found Mechanic Engines, whose Motion was sufficient to attempt the Passage. A late happy Author indeed, among his Mechanic Operations of the Spirit, had found out an Enthusiasm, which if he could have pursued to its proper Extreme, without doubt might, either in the Body or out of the Body, have Landed him somewhere hereabout; but that he formed his System wholly upon the mistaken Notion of Wind, which Learned Hypothesis being directly contrary to the Nature of things in this Climate, where the Elasticity of the Air is quite different and where the pressure of the Atmosphere has for want of Vapour no Force, all his Notion dissolved in its Native Vapour called Wind, and flew upward in blew Strakes of a livid Flame called Blasphemy, which burnt up all the Wit and Fancy of the Author, and left a strange stench behind it, that has this unhappy quality in it, that every Body that Reads the Book, smells the Author, tho' he be never so far off; nay, tho' he took Shipping to Dublin, to secure his Friends from the least danger of a Conjecture.

But to return, to the happy Regions of the Lunar Continent, I was no sooner Landed there, and had looked about me, but I was surprised with the strange Alteration of the Climate and Country; and particularly a strange Salubrity and Fragrancy in the Air, which I felt so Nourishing, so Pleasant and Delightful, that tho' I could perceive some small

Respiration, it was hardly discernable, and the least requisite for Life, supplied so long that the Bellows of Nature were hardly employed.

But as I shall take occasion to consider this in a Critical Examination into the Nature, Uses and Advantages of Good Lungs, of which by it self, so I think fit to confine my present Observations to things more particularly concerning the Eye-sight.

I was, you may be sure, not a little surprised, when being upon an Eminence I found my self capable by common Observation, to see and distinguish things at the distance of 100 Miles and more, and seeking some Information on this point, I was acquainted by the People, that there was a certain grave Philosopher hard by, that could give me a very good Account of things.

It is not worth while to tell you this Man's Lunar Name, of whether he had a Name, or no; 'tis plain, 'twas a Man in the Moon; but all the Conference I had with him was very strange: At my first coming to him, he asked me if I came from the World in the Moon? I told him, no: At which he began to be angry, told me I Lied, he knew whence I came as well as I did; for he saw me all the way. I told him, I came to the World in the Moon, and began to be as surly as he. It was a long time before we could agree about it, he would have it, that I came down from the Moon; and I, that I came up to the Moon: From this, we came to Explications, Demonstrations, Spheres, Globes, Regions, Atmospheres, and a Thousand odd Diagrams, to make the thing out to one another. I insisted on my part, as that my Experiment qualified me to know, and challenged him to go back with me to prove it. He, like a true Philosopher, raised a Thousand Scruples, Conjectures, and Spherical Problems, to Confront me; and as for Demonstrations, he called 'em Fancies of my own. Thus we differed a great many ways; both of us were certain, and both uncertain; both right, and yet both directly contrary; how to reconcile this Jangle was very hard, till at last this Demonstration happened, the Moon as he called it, turning her blind-side upon us three Days after the Change, by which, with the help of his extraordinary Glasses, I that knew the Country, perceived that side the Sun looked upon was all Moon, and the other was all world; and either I fancied I saw or else really saw all the lofty Towers of the Immense Cities of China: Upon this, and a little more Debate, we came to this Conclusion, and there the Old Man and I agreed, That they were both Moons and both Worlds, this a Moon to that, and that a Moon to this, like the Sun between two Looking-Glasses, and shone upon one another by Reflection, according to the oblique or direct Position of each other.

This afforded us a great deal of Pleasure; for all the World covet to be found in the right, and are pleased when their Notions are acknowledged by their Antagonists: It also afforded us many very useful Speculations, such as these;

1. How easy it is for Men to fall out, and yet all sides to be in the right?

2. How Natural it is for Opinion to despise Demonstration?

3. How proper mutual Enquiry is to mutual Satisfaction?

From the Observation of these Glasses, we also drew some Puns, Crotchets and Conclusions.

1st, That the whole World has a Blind-side, a Dark-side, and a Bright-side, and consequently so has every Body in it.

2dly, That the Dark-side of Affairs to Day, may be the Bright-side to Morrow; from whence abundance of useful Morals were also raised; such as,

1. No Man's Fate is so dark, but when the Sun shines upon it, it will return its Rays, and shine for it self.

2. All things turn like the Moon, up to Day, down to Morrow, Full and Change, Flux and Reflux.

3. Humane Understanding is like the Moon at the First Quarter, half dark.

3dly, The Changing-sides ought not to be thought so strange, or so much Condemned by Mankind, having its Original from the Lunar Influence, and governed by the Powerful Operation of Heavenly Motion.

4thly, If there be any such thing as Destiny in the World, I know nothing Man is so predestinated to, as to be eternally turning round; and but that I purpose to entertain the Reader with at least a whole Chapter or Section of the Philosophy of Humane Motion, Spherically and Hypocritically Examined and Calculated, I should enlarge upon that Thought in this place.

Having thus jumped in our Opinions, and perfectly satisfied our selves with Demonstration, That these Worlds were Sisters, both in Form, Function, and all their Capacities; in short, a pair of Moons, and a pair of Worlds, equally Magnetical, Sympathetical, and Influential, we set up our rest as to that Affair, and went forward.

I desired no better Acquaintance in my new Travels, than this new Sociate; never was there such a Couple of People met; he was the Man in the Moon to me, and I the Man in the Moon to him; he wrote down all I said, and made a Book of it, and called it, News from the World in the Moon; and all the Town is like to see my Minutes under the same Title; nay, and I have been told, he published some such bold Truths there, from the Allegorical Relations he had of me from our World: That he was called before the Public Authority, who could not bear the just Reflections of his damned Satirical way of Writing; and there they punished the Poor Man, put him in Prison, ruined his Family; and not only Fined him Ultra tenementum, but exposed him in the high Places of their Capital City, for the Mob to laugh at him for a Fool: This is a Punishment not unlike our Pillory, and was appointed for mean Criminals, Fellows that Cheat and Cozen People, Forge Writings, Forswear themselves, and the like; and the People, that it was expected would have treated this Man very ill, on the contrary Pitied him, wished those that set him there placed in his room, and expressed their Affections, by loud Shouts and Acclamations, when he was taken down.

But as this happened before my first Visit to that World, when I came there all was over with him, his particular Enemies were disgraced and turned out, and the Man was not at all the worse received by his Country-folks than he was before; and so much for the Man in the Moon.

After we had settled the Debate between us, about the Nature and Quality, I desired him to show me some Plan or Draft of this new World of his; upon which, he brought me out a pair of very beautiful Globes, and there I had an immediate Geographical Description of the Place.

I found it less by Degrees than Our Terrestrial Globe, but more Land and less Water; and as I was particularly concerned to see something in or near the same Climate with Our selves, I observed a large extended Country to the North, about the Latitude of 50 to 56 Northern Distance; and enquiring of that Country, he told me it was one of the best Countries in all their World: That it was his Native Climate, and he was just a going to it, and would take me with him.

He told me in General, the Country was Good, Wholesome, Fruitful, rarely Situate for Trade, extraordinarily Accommodated with Harbours, Rivers and Bays for Shipping; full of Inhabitants; for it had been Peopled from all Parts, and had in it some of the Blood of all the Nations in the Moon.

He told me, as the Inhabitants were the most Numerous, so they were the strangest People that lived; both their Natures, Tempers,

Qualities, Actions, and way of Living, was made up of innumerable Contradictions: That they were the Wisest Fools, and the Foolishest Wise Men in the World; the Weakest Strongest, Richest Poorest, most Generous Covetous, Bold Cowardly, False Faithful, Sober Dissolute, Surly Civil, Slothful Diligent, Peaceable Quarrelling, Loyal Seditious Nation that ever was known.

Besides my Observations which I made my self, and which could only furnish me with what was present, and which I shall take time to inform my Reader with as much Care and Conciseness as possible; I was beholding to this Old Lunarian, for every thing that was Historical or Particular.

And First, He informed me, That in this new Country they had very seldom any Clouds at all, and consequently no extraordinary Storms, but a constant Serenity, moderate Breezes cooled the Air, and constant Evening Exhalations kept the Earth moist and fruitful; and as the Winds they had were various and strong enough to assist their Navigation, so they were without the Terrors, Dangers, Ship-wrecks and Destructions, which he knew we were troubled with in this our Lunar World, as he called it.

The first just Observation I made of this was, That I supposed from hence the wonderful Clearness of the Air, and the Advantage of so vast Optic Capacities they enjoyed, was obtained: Alas! says the Old Fellow, You see nothing to what some of our Great Eyes see in some Parts of this World, nor do you see any thing compared to what you may see by the help of some new Invented Glasses, of which I may in time let you see the Experiment; and perhaps you may find this to be the reason why we do not so abound in Books as in your Lunar World; and that except it be some extraordinary Translations out of your Country, you will find but little in our Libraries, worth giving you a great deal of Trouble.

We immediately quitted the Philosophical Discourse of Winds, and I began to be mighty Inquisitive after these Glasses and Translations, and

Ist, I understood here was a strange sort of Glass that did not so much bring to the Eye, as by I know not what wonderful Operation carried out the Eye to the Object, and quite varies from all our Doctrine of Optics, by forming several strange Phenomena in Sight, which we are utterly unacquainted with; nor could Vision, Rarification, or any of our School-mens fine Terms, stand me in any stead in this case; but here was such Additions of piercing Organs, Particles of Transparence,

Emission, Transmission, Mediums, Contraction of Rays, and a Thousand Applications of things prepared for the wondrous Operation, that you may be sure are requisite for the bringing to pass something yet unheard of on this side the Moon.

First we were informed, by the help of these Glasses, strange things, which pass in our World for Non-Entities, is to be seen, and very perceptible; for Example:

State Polity, in all its Meanders, Shifts, Turns, Tricks, and Contraries, are so exactly Delineated and Described, That they are in hopes in time to draw a pair of Globes out, to bring all those things to a certainty.

Not but that it made some Puzzle, even among these Clear-sighted Nations, to determine what Figure the Plans and Drafts of this undiscovered World of Mysteries ought to be described in: Some were of Opinion, it ought, to be an Irregular Centagon, a Figure with an Hundred Cones or Angles: Since the Unaccountables of this State-Science, are hid in a Million of undiscovered Corners; as the Craft, Subtlety and Hypocrisy of Knaves and Courtiers have concealed them, never to be found out, but by this wonderful D — l-scope, which seemed to threaten a perfect Discovery of all those Nudities, which have lain hid in the Embryo, and false Conceptions of Abortive Policy, ever since the Foundation of the World.

Some were of Opinion, this Plan ought to be Circular, and in a Globular Form, since it was on all sides alike, full of dark Spots, untrod Mazes, waking Mischiefs, and sleeping Mysteries; and being delineated like the Globes displayed, would discover all the Lines of Wickedness to the Eye at one view: Besides, they fancied some sort of Analogy in the Rotundity of the Figure, with the continued Circular Motion of all Court-Policies, in the stated Round of Universal Knavery.

Others would have had it Hieroglyphical as by a Hand in Hand, the Form representing the Affinity between State Policy here, and State Policy in the Infernal Regions, with some unkind Similes between the Economy of Satan's Kingdom, and those of most of the Temporal Powers on Earth; but this was thought too unkind. At last it was determined, That neither of these Schemes were capable of the vast Description; and that, therefore, the Drafts must be made single, tho' not dividing the Governments, yet dividing the Arts of Governing into proper distinct Schemes, viz.

I. A particular Plan of Public Faith; and here we had the Experiment immediately made: The Representation is qualified for the

486

Meridian of any Country, as well in our World as theirs; and turning it to'ards our own World, there I saw plainly an Exchequer shut up, and 20000 Mourning Families selling their Coaches, Horses, Whores, Equipages, &c. for Bread, the Government standing by laughing, and looking on: Hard by I saw the Chamber of a great City shut up, and Forty Thousand Orphans turned adrift in the World; some had no Clothes, some no Shoes, some no Money; and still the City Magistrates calling upon other Orphans, to pay their money in. These things put me in mind of the Prophet Ezekiel, and methoughts I heard the same Voice that spoke to him, calling me, and telling me, Come hither, and I'll show thee greater Abominations than these: So looking still on that vast Map, by the help of these Magnifying Glasses, I saw huge Fleets hired for Transport-Service, but never paid; vast Taxes Anticipated, that were never Collected; others Collected and Appropriated, but Misapplied: Millions of Talleys struck to be Discounted, and the Poor paying 40 per Cent, to receive their Money. I saw huge Quantities of Money drawn in, and little or none issued out; vast Prizes taken from the Enemy, and then taken away again at home by Friends; Ships saved on the Sea, and sunk in the Prize Offices; Merchants escaping from Enemies at Sea, and be Pirated by Sham Embargoes, Counterfeit Claims, Confiscations, &c a-shore: There we saw Turkey-Fleets taken into Convoys, and Guarded to the very Mouth of the Enemy, and then abandoned for their better Security: Here we saw Mons. Pouchartrain shutting up the Town-house of Paris, and plundering the Bank of Lyons.

2. Here we law the State of the War among Nations; Here was the French giving Sham-thanks for Victories they never got, and some body else addressing and congratulating the sublime Glory of running away: Here was Te Deum for Sham-Victories by Land; and there was Thanksgiving for Ditto by Sea: Here we might see two Armies fight, both run away, and both come and thank GOD for nothing: Here we saw a Plan of a late War like that in Ireland; there was all the Officers cursing a Dutch General, because the damned Rogue would fight, and spoil a good War, that with decent Management and good Husbandry, might have been eked out this Twenty Years; there was whole Armies hunting two Cows to one Irishman, and driving of black Cattle declared the Noble End of the War: Here we saw a Country full of Stone Walls and strong Towns, where every Campaign, the Trade of War was carried on by the Soldiers, with the same Intriguing as it was carried on in the Council Chambers; there was Millions of Contributions raised,

487

and vast Sums Collected, but no Taxes lessened; whole Plate Fleets surprised, but no Treasure found; vaffed Sums lost by Enemies, and yet never found by Friends, Ships loaded with Volatile Silver, that came away full, and gat home empty; whole Voyages made to beat No body, and plunder Every body; two Millions robbed from the honest Merchants, and not a Groat saved for the honest Subjects: There we saw Captains Lifting Men with the Governments Money, and letting them go again for their own; Ships fitted out at the Rates of Two Millions a Year, to fight but once in Three Years, and then run away for want of Powder and Shot.

There we saw Partition Treaties damned, and the whole given away, Confederations without Allies, Allies without Quota's, Princes without Armies, Armies without Men, and Men without Money, Crowns without Kings, Kings without Subjects, more Kings than Countries, and more Countries than were worth fighting for.

Here we could see the King of France upbraiding his Neighbours with dishonourably assisting his Rebels, though the Mischief was, they did it not neither; and in the same Breath, assisting the Hungarian Rebels against the Emperor; M. Ld N. refusing so dishonourable an Action, as to aid the Rebellious Commissars, but Leaguing with the Admirant de Castile, to Invade the Dominions of his Master to whom he swore Allegiance: Here we saw Protestants fight against Protestants, to help Papists, Papists against Papists to help Protestants, Protestants call in Turks, to keep Faith against Christians that break it: Here we could see Swedes fighting for Revenge, and call it Religion; Cardinals deposing their Catholic Prince, to introduce the Tyranny of a Lutheran and call it Liberty; Armies Electing Kings, and call it Free Choice; French conquering Savoy, to secure the Liberty of Italy.

3. The Map of State Policy contains abundance of Civil Transactions, no where to be discovered but in this wonderful Country, and by this prodigious Invention: As first, it shows an Eminent Prelate running in every body's Debt to relieve the Poor, and bring to God Robbery for Burnt-Offering: It opens a Door to the Fate of Nations; and there we might see the Duke of S — y bought three times, and his subjects sold every time; Portugal bought twice, and neither time worth the Earnest; Spain bought once, but loth to go with the Bidder; Venice willing to be Bought, if there had been any Buyers; Bavaria Bought, and run away with the Money; the Emperor Bought and Sold, but Bilked the Chapman; the French buying Kingdoms he can't keep, the Dutch

keep Kingdoms they never Bought; and the English paying their Money without Purchase.

In Matters of Civil Concerns, here was to be seen Religion with no out-side, and much Out-side with no Religion, much Strife about Peace, and no Peace in the Design: Here was Plunder without Violence, Violence without Persecution, Conscience without Good Works, and Good Works without Charity; Parties cutting one another's Throats for God's Sake, pulling down Churches de propaganda fide, and making Divisions by way of Association.

Here we have Peace and Union brought to pass The Shortest Way, Extirpation and Destruction proved to be the Road to Plenty and Pleasure: Here all the Wise Nations, a Learned Author would have Quoted, if he could have found them, are to be seen, who carry on Exclusive Laws to the general Safety and Satisfaction of their Subjects.

Occasional Bills may have here a particular Historical, Categorical Description: But of them by themselves.

Here you might have the Rise, Original, Lawfulness, Usefulness, and Necessity of Passive Obedience, as fairly represented as a System of Divinity, and as clearly demonstrated as by a Geographical Description; and which exceeds our mean Understanding here, 'tis by the wonderful Assistance of these Glasses, plainly discerned to be Coherent with Resistance, taking Arms, calling in Foreign Powers, and the like. — Here you have a plain Discovery of C. of E. Politics, and a Map of Loyalty: Here 'tis as plainly demonstrated as the Nose in a Man's Face, provided he has one, that a Man may Abdicate, drive away, and Dethrone his Prince, and yet be absolutely and entirely free from, and innocent of the least Fracture, Breach, Encroachment, or Entrenchment, upon the Doctrine of Non-Resistance: Can shoot at his Prince without any Design to kill him, fight against him without raising Rebellion, and take up Arms, without leaving War against his Prince.

Here they can persecute Dissenters, without desiring they should Conform, conform to the Church they would overthrow; Pray for the Prince they dare not Name, and Name the Prince they do not pray for.

By the help of these Glasses strange Insights are made, into the vast mysterious dark World of State Policy; but that which is yet more strange, and requires vast Volumes to descend to the Particulars of, and huge Diagrams, Spheres, Charts, and a Thousand nice things to display is, That in this vast Intelligent Discovery it is not only made plain, that those things are so, but all the vast Contradictions are made Rational, reconciled to Practice, and brought down to Demonstration.

German Clock-Work, the perpetual Motions, the Prim Mobilies of Our short-sighted World, are Trifles to these Nicer Disquisitions.

Here it would be plain and rational, why a Parliament-Man will spend 5000 l. to be Chosen, that cannot get a Groat Honestly by setting there: It would be easily made out to be rational, why he that rails most at a Court is soonest received into it: Here it would be very plain, how great Estates are got in little Places, and Double in none at all. 'Tis easy to be proved honest and faithful to Victual the French Fleet out of English Stores, and let our own Navy want them; a long Sight, or a large Lunar Perspective, will make all these things not only plain in Fact, but Rational and Justifiable to all the World.

'Tis a strange thing to any body without doubt, that has not been in that clear-sighted Region, to comprehend, That those we call High-flyers in England are the only Friends to the Dissenters, and have been the most Diligent and Faithful in their Interest, of any People in the Nation; and yet so it is, Gentlemen, and they ought to have the Thanks of the whole Body for it.

In this advanced Station, we see it plainly by Reflection, That the Dissenters, like a parcel of Knaves, have retained all the High-Church-men in their Pay; they are certainly all in their Pension-Roll: Indeed, I could not see the Money paid them there, it was too remote; but I could plainly see the thing; all the deep Lines of the Project are laid as true, they are so Tacked and Consolidated together, that if any one will give themselves leave to consider, they will be most effectually convinced, That the High-Church and the Dissenters here, are all in a Cabal, a mere Knot, a piece of Clock-work; the Dissenters are the Dial-Plate, and the High-Church the Movement, the Wheel within the Wheels, the Spring and the Screw to bring all things to Motion, and make the Hand on the Dial-plate point which way the Dissenters please.

For what else have been all the Shams they have put upon the Governments, Kings, States, and People they have been concerned with? What Schemes have they laid on purpose to be broken? What vast Contrivances, on purpose to be ridiculed and exposed? The Men are not Fools, they had never V — d to Consolidate a B — but that they were willing to save the Dissenters, and put it into a posture, in which they were sure it would miscarry. I defy all the Wise Men of the Moon to show another good reason for it.

Methinks I begin to pity my Brethren, the moderate Men of the Church, that they cannot see into this New Plot, and to wish they would but get up into our Consolidator, and take a Journey to the Moon, and there, by the help of these Glasses, they would see the Allegorical, Symbolical, Heterodoxicallity of all this Matter; it would make immediate Converts of them; they would see plainly, that to Tack and Consolidate, to make Exclusive Laws, to persecute for Conscience, disturb, and distress Parties; these are all Fanatic Plots, mere Combinations against the Church, to bring her into Contempt, and to fix and establish the Dissenters to the end of the Chapter: But of this I shall find occasion to speak Occasionally, when an Occasion presents it self, to examine a certain Occasional Bill, transacting in these Lunar Regions, some time before I had the Happiness to arrive there.

In examining the Multitude and Variety of these most admirable Glasses for the assisting the Optics, or indeed the Formation of a new perceptive Faculty; it was you may be sure most surprising to find there, that Art had exceeded Nature; and the Power of Vision was assisted to that prodigious Degree, as even to distinguish Non-Entity it self; and in these strange Engines of Light it could not but be very pleasing, to distinguish plainly betwixt Being and Matter, and to come to a Determination, in the so long Canvassed Dispute of Substance, vel Materialis, vel Spiritualis; and I can solidly affirm, That in all our Contention between Entity and Non-Entity, there is so little worth meddling with, that had we had these Glasses some Ages ago, we should have left troubling our heads with it.

I take upon me, therefore, to assure my Reader, That whoever pleases to take a Journey, or Voyage, or Flight up to these Lunar Regions, as soon as ever he comes ashore there, will presently be convinced, of the Reasonableness of Immaterial Substance, and the Immortality, as well as Immateriality of the Soul: He will no sooner look into these Explicating Glasses, but he will be-able to know the separate meaning of Body, Soul, Spirit, Life, Motion, Death, and a Thousand things that Wise-men puzzle themselves about here, because they are not Fools enough to understand.

Here too I find Glasses for the Second Sight, as our Old Women call it. This Second Sight has been often pretended to in Our Regions, and some Famous Old Wives have told us, they can see Death, the Soul, Futurity, and the Neighbourhood of them, in the Countenance: By this wonderful Art, these good People unfold strange Mysteries, as under some Irrecoverable Disease, to foretell Death; under Hypochondriac Melancholy, to presage Trouble of Mind; in pining Youth, to predict Contagious Love; and an Hundred other

Infallibilities, which never fail to be true as soon as ever they come to pass, and are all grounded upon the same Infallibility, by which a Shepherd may always know when any one of his Sheep is Rotten, viz. when he shakes himself to pieces.

But all this Guess and Uncertainty is a Trifle, to the vast Discoveries of these Explicatory Glasses-Glasses; for here are seen the Nature and Consequences of Secret Mysteries: Here are read strange Mysteries relating to Predestination, Eternal Decrees, and the like: Here 'tis plainly proved, That Predestination is, in spite of all Enthusiastic Pretences, so entirely committed into Man's Power, that whoever pleases to hang himself to Day, won't Live till to Morrow: no, though Forty Predestination Prophets were to tell him, His time was not yet come. There abstruse Points are commonly and solemnly Discussed here; and these People are such Heretics, that they say God's Decrees are all subservient to the means of his Providence; That what we call Providence is a subjecting all things to the great Chain of Causes and Consequences, by which that one Grand Decree, That all Effects shall Obey, without reserve to their proper moving Causes, supercedes all subsequent Doctrines, or pretended Decrees, or Predestination in the World: That by this Rule, he that will kill himself, GOD, Nature, Providence, or Decree, will not be concerned to hinder him, but he shall Die; any Decrees, Predestination, or Fore-Knowledge of Infinite Power, to the contrary in any wise, notwithstanding that it is in a Man's Power to throw himself into the Water, and be Drowned; and to kill another Man, and he shall Die, and to say, God appointed it, is to make him the Author of Murder, and to injure the Murderer in putting him to Death for what he could not help doing.

All these things are received Truths here, and no doubt would be so every where else, if the Eyes of Reason were opened to the Testimony of Nature, or if they had the helps of these most Incomparable Glasses.

Some pretended, by the help of these Second-sight Glasses, to see the common Periods of Life; and Others said, they could see a great way beyond the leap in the Dark: I confess, all I could see of the first was, that holding up the Glass against the Sea, I plainly saw, as it were on the edge of the Horizon, these Words,

The Verge of Life and Death is here. 'Tis best to know where 'tis, but not how far.

As to seeing beyond Death, all the Glasses I looked into for that purpose, made but little of it; and these were the only Tubes that I found Defective; for here I could discern nothing but Clouds, Mists, and thick dark hazy Weather; but revolving in my Mind, that I had read a certain Book in our own Country, called, Nature; it presently occurred, That the Conclusion of it, to all such as gave themselves the trouble of making out those foolish things called Inferences, was always Look up; upon which, turning one of their Glasses Up, and erecting the Point of it towards the Zenith, I saw these Words in the Air, REVELATION, in large Capital Letters.

I had like to have raised the Mob upon me for looking upright with this Glass; for this, they said, was prying into the Mysteries of the Great Eye of the World; That we ought to enquire no farther than he has informed us, and to believe what he had left us more Obscure: Upon this, I laid down the Glasses, and concluded, that we had Moses and the Prophets, and should be never the likelier to be taught by One come from the Moon.

In short, I found, indeed, they had a great deal more Knowledge of things than we in this World; and that Nature, Science, and Reason, had obtained great Improvements in the Lunar World; but as to Religion, it was the same equally resigned to and concluded in Faith and Redemption; so I shall give the World no great Information of these things.

I come next to some other strange Acquirements obtained by the helps of these Glasses; and particularly for the discerning the Imperceptibles of Nature; such as, the Soul, Thought, Honesty, Religion, Virginity, and an Hundred other nice things, too small for humane Discerning.

The Discoveries made by these Glasses, as to the Soul, are of a very diverting Variety; some Hieroglyphical, and Emblematical, and some Demonstrative.

The Hieroglyphical Discoveries of the Soul make it appear in the Image of its Maker; and the Analogy is remarkable, even in the very Simile; for as they represent the Original of Nature as One Great Eye, illuminating as well as discerning all things; so the Soul, in its Allegorical, or Hieroglyphical Resemblance, appears as a Great Eye, embracing the Man, enveloping, operating, and informing every Part; from whence those sort of People who we falsely call Politicians, acting so much to put out this Great Eye, by acting against their common Understandings, are very aptly represented by a great Eye, with Six or Seven pair of Spectacles on; not but that the Eye of their Souls may be clear enough of it self, as to the common Understanding; but that they happen to have occasion to look sometimes so many ways at once, and to judge, conclude, and understand so many contrary ways upon one and the same thing; that they are fain to put double Glasses upon their Understanding, as we look at the Solar Eclipses, to represent 'em in different Lights, least their Judgments should not be wheedled into a Compliance with the Hellish Resolutions of their Wills; and this is what I call the Emblematic Representation of the Soul.

As for the Demonstrations of the Soul's Existence, 'tis a plain case, by these Explicative Glasses, that it is, some have pretended to give us the Parts; and we have heard of Chirurgeons, that could read an Anatomical Lecture on the Parts Of the Soul; and these pretend it to be a Creature in form, whether Camelion or Salamander, Authors have not determined; nor is it completely discovered when it comes into the Body, or how it goes out, or where its Locality or Habitation is, while 'tis a Resident.

But they very aptly show it, like a Prince, in his Seat, in the middle of his Palace the Brain, issuing out his incessant Orders to innumerable Troops of Nerves, Sinews, Muscles, Tendons, Veins, Arteries, Fibres, Capilaris, and useful Officers, called Organici, who faithfully execute all the Parts of Sensation, Locomotion, Concoction, &c. and in the Hundred Thousandth part of a Moment, return with particular Messages for Information, and demand New Instructions. If any part of his Kingdom, the Body, suffers a Depredation, or an Invasion of the Enemy, the Expresses fly to the Seat of the Soul, the Brain, and immediately are ordered back to smart, that the Body may of course send more Messengers to complain; immediately other Expresses are dispatched to the Tongue, with Orders to cry out, that the Neighbours may come in and help, or Friends send for the Chirurgeon: Upon the Application, and a Cure, all is quiet, and the same Expresses are dispatched to the Tongue to be hush, and say no more of it till farther Orders: All this is as plain to be seen in these Engines, as the Moon of Our World from the World in the Moon.

As the Being, Nature, and Situation of humane Soul is thus Spherically and Mathematically discovered, I could not find any Second Thoughts about it in all their Books, whether of their own Composition or by Translation; for it was a General received Notion, That there could not be a greater Absurdity in humane Knowledge, than to employ the Thoughts in Questioning, what is as plainly known by its Consequences, as if seen with the Eye; and that to doubt the Being or Extent of the Soul's Operation, is to employ her against her self; and therefore, when I began to argue with my Old Philosopher, against the Materiality and Immortality of this Mystery we call Soul, he laughed at me, and told me, he found we had none of their Glasses in our World; and bid me send all our Skeptics, Soul-Sleepers, our Cowards, Bakers, Kings and Bakewells, up to him into the Moon, if they wanted Demonstrations; where, by the help of their Engines, they would make it plain to them, that the Great Eye being one vast Intellect, Infinite and Eternal, all Inferior Life is a Degree of himself, and as exactly represents him as one little Flame the whole Mass of Fire; That it is therefore uncapable of Dissolution, being like its Original in Duration, as well as in its Powers and Faculties, but that it goes and returns by Emission, Regression, as the Great Eye governs and determines; and this was plainly made out, by the Figure I had seen it in, viz. an Eye, the exact Image of its Maker: 'Tis true, it was darkened by Ignorance, Folly and Crime, and therefore obliged to wear Spectacles; but tho' these were Defects or Interruptions in its Operation, they were none in its Nature; which as it had its immediate Efflux from the Great Eye, and its return to him must partake of himself, and could not but be of a Quality uncomatable, by Casualty or Death.

From this Discourse we the more willingly adjourned our present Thoughts, I being clearly convinced of the Matter; and as for our Learned Doctors, with their Second and Third Thoughts, I told him I would recommend them to the Man in the Moon for their farther Illumination, which if they refuse to accept, it was but just they should remain in a Wood, where they are, and are like to be, puzzling themselves about Demonstrations, squaring of Circles, and converting oblique into right Angles, to bring out a Mathematical Clock-Work Soul, that will go till the Weight is down, and then stand still till they know not who must wind it up again.

However, I cannot pass over a very strange and extraordinary piece of Art which this Old Gentleman informed me of, and that was an Engine to screw a Man into himself: Perhaps our Country-men may be at some Difficulty to comprehend these things by my dull Description; and to such I cannot but recommend, a Journey in my Engine to the Moon.

This Machine that I am speaking of, contains a multitude of strange Springs and Screws, and a Man that puts himself into it, is very insensibly carried into vast Speculations, Reflections, and regular Debates with himself: They have a very hard Name for it in those Parts;

but if I were to give it an English Name, it should be called, The Cogitator, or the Chair of Reflection.

And First, The Person that is seated here feels some pain in passing some Negative Springs, that are wound up, effectually to shut out all Injecting, Disturbing Thoughts; and the better to prepare him for the Operation that is to follow, and this is without doubt a very rational way; for when a Man can absolutely shut out all manner of thinking, but what he is upon, he shall think the more Intensely upon the one object before him.

This Operation past, here are certain Screws that draw direct Lines from every Angle of the Engine to the Brain of the Man, and at the same time, other direct Lines to his Eyes; at the other end of which Lines, there are Glasses which convey or reflect the Objects the Person is desirous to think upon.

Then the main Wheels are turned, which wind up according to their several Offices; this the Memory, that the Understanding; a third the Will, a fourth the thinking Faculty; and these being put all into regular Motions, pointed by direct Lines to their proper Objects, and perfectly uninterrupted by the Intervention of Whimsy, Chimera, and a Thousand fluttering Demons that Gender in the Fancy, but are effectually Locked out as before, assist one another to receive right Notions, and form just Ideas of the things they are directed to, and from thence the Man is empowered to make right Conclusions, to think and act like himself, suitable to the sublime Qualities his Soul was originally blest with.

There never was a Man went into one of these thinking Engines, but he came wiser out than he was before; and I am persuaded, it would be a more effectual Cure to our Deism, Atheism, Skepticism, and all other Schisms, than ever the Italian's Engine, for Curing the Gout by cutting off the Toe.

This is a most wonderful Engine, and performs admirably, and my Author gave me extraordinary Accounts of the good Effects of it; and I cannot but tell my Reader, That our Sublunar World suffers Millions of Inconveniencies, for want of this thinking Engine: I have had a great many Projects in my Head, how to bring our People to regular thinking, but 'tis in vain without this Engine; and how to get the Model of it I know not; how to screw up the Will, the Understanding, and the rest of the Powers; how to bring the Eye, the Thought, the Fancy, and the Memory, into Mathematical Order, and obedient to Mechanic Operation; help Boyl, Norris, Newton, Manton, Hammond, Tillotson, and all the Learned Race, help Philosophy, Divinity, Physics, Economics, all's in vain, a Mechanic Chair of Reflection is the only Remedy that ever I found in my Life for this Work.

As to the Effects of Mathematical thinking, what Volumes might be writ of it will more easily appear, if we consider the wondrous Usefulness of this Engine in all humane Affairs; as of War, Peace, Justice, Injuries, Passion, Love, Marriage, Trade, Policy, and Religion.

When a Man has been screwed into himself, and brought by this Art to a Regularity of Thought, he never commits any Absurdity after it; his Actions are squared by the same Lines, for Action is but the Consequence of Thinking; and he that acts before he thinks, sets humane Nature with the bottom upward.

M. would never have made his Speech, nor the famous B — — ly wrote a Book, if ever they had been in this thinking Engine: One would have never told us of Nations he never saw, nor the other told us, he had seen a great many, and was never the Wiser.

H. had never ruined his Family to Marry Whore, Thief and Beggar-Woman, in one Salient Lady, after having been told so honestly, and so often of it by the very Woman her self.

Our late unhappy Monarch had never trusted the English Clergy, when they preached up that Non-Resistance, which he must needs see they could never Practice; had his Majesty been screwed up into this Cogitator, he had presently reflected, that it was against Nature to expect they should stand still, and let him tread upon them: That they should, whatever they had preached or pretended to, hold open their Throats to have them be cut, and tie their own Hands from resisting the Lord's Anointed.

Had some of our Clergy been screwed in this Engine, they had never turned Martyrs for their Allegiance to the Late King, only for the Lechery of having Dr. S — — — in their Company.

Had our Merchants been managed in this Engine, they had never trusted their Turkey Fleet with a famous Squadron, that took a great deal of care to Convoy them safe into the Enemies Hands.

Had some People been in this Engine, when they had made a certain League in the World, in order to make amends for a better made before, they would certainly have considered farther, before they had embarked with a Nation, that are neither fit to go abroad nor stay at Home.

As for the Thinking practiced in Noble Speeches, Occasional Bills, Addressings about Prerogative, Convocation Disputes, Turnings in and Turnings out at Ours, and all the Courts of Christendom, I have nothing to say to it.

Had the Duke of Bavaria been in our Engine, he would never have begun a Quarrel, which he knew all the Powers of Europe were concerned to suppress, and lay all other Business down till it was done.

Had the Elector of Saxony past the Operation of this Engine, he would never have beggared a Rich Electorate, to ruin a beggared Crown, nor sold himself for a Kingdom hardly worth any Man's taking: He would never have made himself less than he was, in hopes of being really no greater; and stepped down from a Protestant Duke, and Imperial Elector, to be a Nominal Mock King with a shadow of Power, and a Name without honour, Dignity or Strength.

Had Mons. Tallard been in our Engine, he would not only not have attacked the Confederates when they past the Morass and Rivulet in his Front, but not have attacked them at all, nor have suffered them to have attacked him, it being his Business not to have fought at all, but have lingered out the War, till the Duke of Savoy having been reduced, the Confederate Army must have been forced to have divided themselves of course, in order to defend their own.

Some that have been very forward to have us proceed The Shortest Way with the Scots, may be said to stand in great need of this Chair of Reflection, to find out a just Cause for such a War, and to make a Neighbour-Nation making themselves secure, a sufficient Reason for another Neighbour-Nation to fall upon them: Our Engine would presently show it them in a clear sight, by way of Parallel, that 'tis just with the fame Right as a Man may break open a House, because the People bar and bolt the Windows.

If some-body has changed Hands there from bad to worse, and opened instead of closing Differences in those Cases, the Cogitator might have brought them, by more regular Thinking, to have known that was not at all the Method of bringing the S — s to Reason.

Our Cogitator would be a very necessary thing to show some People, That Poverty and Weakness is not a sufficient Ground to oppress a Nation, and their having but little Trade, cannot be a sufficient Ground to equip Fleets to take away what they have.

I cannot deny, that I have often thought they have had something of this Engine in our Neighbouring Ancient Kingdom, since no Man, however we pretend to be angry, but will own they are in the right of it, as to themselves, to Vote and procure Bills for their own Security, and not to do as others demand without Conditions fit to be accepted: But of that by it self.

There are abundance of People in Our World, of all sorts and Conditions, that stand in need of our thinking Engines, and to be screwed into themselves a little, that they might think as directly as they speak absurdly: But of these also in a Class by it self.

This Engine has a great deal of Philosophy in it; and particularly, 'tis a wonderful Remedy against Poring; and as it was said of Mons. Jurieu at Amsterdam, that he used to lose himself in himself; by the Assistance of this piece of Regularity, a Man is most effectually secured against bewildering Thoughts, and by direct thinking, he prevents all manner of dangerous wandering, since nothing can come to more speedy Conclusions, than that which in right Lines, points to the proper Subject of Debate.

All sorts of Confusion of Thoughts are perfectly avoided and prevented in this case, and a Man is never troubled with Spleen, Hyppo, or Mute Madness, when once he has been thus under the Operation of the Screw: It prevents abundance of Capital Disasters in Men, in private Affairs; it prevents hasty Marriages, rash Vows, Duels, Quarrels, Suits at Law, and most sorts of Repentance. In the State, it saves a Government from many Inconveniences; it checks immoderate Ambition, stops Wars, Navies and Expeditions; especially it prevents Members making long Speeches when they have nothing to say; it keeps back Rebellions, Insurrections, Clashings of Houses, Occasional Bills, Tacking, &c.

It has a wonderful Property in our Affairs at Sea, and has prevented many a Bloody Fight, in which a great many honest Men might have lost their Lives that are now useful Fellows, and help to Man and manage Her Majesty's Navy.

What if some People are apt to charge Cowardice upon some People in those Cases? 'Tis plain that cannot be it, for he that dare incur the Resentment of the English Mob, shows more Courage than would be able to carry him through Forty Sea-fights.

'Tis therefore for want of being in this Engine, that we censure People, because they don't be knocking one another on the Head, like the People at the Bear-Garden; where, if they do not see the Blood run about, they always cry out, A Cheat; and the poor Fellows are fain to cut one another, that they may not be pulled a pieces; where the Case is plain, they are bold for fear, and pull up Courage enough to Fight, because they are afraid of the People.

This Engine prevents all sorts of Lunacies, Love-Frenzies, and Melancholy-Madness, for preserving the Thought in right Lines to direct Objects, it is impossible any Deliriums, Whimsies, or fluttering Air of Ideas, can interrupt the Man, he can never be Mad; for which reason I cannot but recommend it to my Lord S — , my Lord N — , and my Lord H — — , as absolutely necessary to defend them from the State-Madness, which for some Ages has possessed their Families, and which runs too much in the Blood.

It is also an excellent Introduction to Thought, and therefore very well adapted to those People whose peculiar Talent and Praise is, That they never think at all. Of these, if his Grace of B — d would please to accept Advice from the Man in the Moon, it should be to put himself into this Engine, as a Sovereign Cure to the known Disease called the Thoughtless Evil.

But above all, it is an excellent Remedy, and very useful to a sort of People, who are always Traveling in Thought, but never Delivered into Action; who are so exceeding busy at Thinking, they have no leisure for Action; of whom the late Poet sung well to the purpose;

— — Some modern Coxcombs, who Retire to Think, 'cause they have naught to do; For Thoughts were given for Actions Government, Where Action ceases, Thought Impertinent: The Sphere of Action is Life's Happiness, And he that Thinks beyond, Thinks like an Ass. Rochest. Poems, p. 9.

These Gentlemen would make excellent use of this Engine, for it would teach 'em to dispatch one thing before they begin another; and therefore is of singular use to honest S — — , whose peculiar it was, to be always beginning Projects, but never finish any.

The Variety of this Engine, its Uses, and Improvements, are Innumerable, and the Reader must not expect I can give any thing like a perfect Description of it.

There are yet another sort of Machine, which I never obtained a sight of, till the last Voyage I made to this Lunar Orb, and these are called Elevators: The Mechanic Operations of these are wonderful, and helped by Fire; by which the Senses are raised to all the strange Extremes we can imagine, and whereby the Intelligent Soul is made to converse with its own Species, whether embodied or not.

Those that are raised to a due pitch in this wondrous Frame, have a clear Prospect into the World of Spirits, and converse with Visions, Guardian-Angels, Spirits departed, and what not: And as this is a wonderful Knowledge, and not to be obtained, but by the help of this

Fire; so those that have tried the Experiment, give strange Accounts of Sympathy, Preexistence of Souls, Dreams, and the like.

I confess, I always believed a converse of Spirits, and have heard of some who have experienced so much of it, as they could obtain upon no Body else to believe.

I never saw any reason to doubt the Existent State of the Spirit before embodied, any more than I did of its Immortality after it shall be uncased, and the Scriptures saying, the Spirit returns to God that gave it, implies a coming from, or how could it be called a return.

Nor can I see a reason why Embodying a Spirit should altogether Interrupt its Converse with the World of Spirits, from whence it was taken; and to what else shall we ascribe Guardian Angels, in which the Scripture is also plain; and from whence come Secret Notices, Impulse of Thought, pressing Urgencies of Inclination, to or from this or that altogether Involuntary; but from some waking kind Assistant wandering Spirit, which gives secret hints to its Fellow-Creature, of some approaching Evil or Good, which it was not able to foresee.

For Spirits without the helps of Voice converse.

I know we have supplied much of this with Enthusiasm and conceited Revelation; but the People of this World convince us, that it may be all Natural, by obtaining it in a Mechanic way, viz. by forming something suitable to the sublime Nature, which working by Art, shall only rectify the more vigorous Particles of the Soul, and work it up to a suitable Elevation. This Engine is wholly applied to the Head, and Works by Injection; the chief Influence being on what we call Fancy, or Imagination, which by the heat of strong Ideas, is fermented to a strange height, and is thus brought to see backward and forward every way, beyond it self: By this a Man fancies himself in the Moon, and realizes things there as distinctly, as if he was actually talking to my Old Philosopher.

This indeed is an admirable Engine, 'tis composed of an Hundred Thousand rational Consequences, Five times the number of Conjectures, Supposes, and Probabilities, besides an innumerable Company of fluttering Suggestions, and Injections, which hover round the Imagination, and are all taken in as fast as they can be Concocted and Digested there: These are formed into Ideas, and some of those so well put together, so exactly shaped, so well dressed and set out by the Additional Fire of Fancy, that it is no uncommon thing for the Person to be entirely deceived by himself, not knowing the brat of his own Begetting, nor be able to distinguish between Reality and

Representation: From hence we have some People talking to Images of their own forming, and seeing more Devils and Spectres than ever appeared: From hence we have weaker Heads not able to bear the Operation, seeing imperfect Visions, as of Horses and Men without Heads or Arms, Light without Fire, hearing Voices without Sound, and Noises without Shapes, as their own Fears or Fancies broke the Phenomena before the entire Formation.

But the more Genuine and perfect Use of these vast Elevations of the Fancy, which are performed, as I said, by the Mechanic Operation of Innate Fire, is to guide Mankind to as much Fore-sight of things, as either by Nature, or by the Aid of any thing Extranatural, may be obtained; and by this exceeding Knowledge, a Man shall forebode to himself approaching Evil or Good, so as to avoid this, or be in the way of that; and what if I should say, That the Notices of these things are not only frequent, but constant, and require nothing of us, but to make use of this Elevator, to keep our Eyes, our Ears, and our Fancies open to the hints; and observe them;

You may suppose me, if you please, come by this time into those Northern Kingdoms I mentioned before, where my Old Philosopher was a Native, and not to trouble you with any of the needful Observations, Learned Inscriptions, &c. on the way, according to the laudable practices of the Famous Mr. Br — mly, 'tis sufficient to tell you I found there an Opulent, Populous, Potent and Terrible People.

I found them at War with one of the greatest Monarchs of the Lunar World, and at the same time miserably rent and torn, mangled and disordered among themselves.

As soon as I observed the Political posture of their Affairs, (for here a Man sees things mighty soon by the helps of such a Masterly Eye-sight as I have mentioned) and remembering what is said for our Instruction, That a Kingdom divided against its self cannot stand; I asked the Old Gentleman if he had any Estate in that Country? He told me, no great matter; but asked me why I put that Question to him? Because, said I, if this People go on fighting and snarling at all the World, and one among another in this manner, they will certainly be Ruined and Undone, either subdued by some more powerful Neighbour; whilst one Party will stand still and see the t'others Throat cut, tho' their own Turn immediately follows, or else they will destroy and devour one another. Therefore I told him I would have him Turn his Estate into Money, and go some where else; or go back to the other World with me.

502

No, no, replied the Old Man, I am in no such Fear at this Time, the Scale of Affairs is very lately changed here, says he, in but a very few Years.

I know nothing of that, said I, but I am sure there never was but one spot of Ground in that World which I came from, that was divided like them, and that's that very Country I lived in. Here are three Kingdoms of you in one spot, said I, One has already been Conquered and Subdued, the t'other suppressed its Native inhabitants, and planted it with her own, and now carries it with so high a Hand over them of her own Breed, that she limits their Trade, stops their Ports, when the Inhabitants have made their Manufactures, these wont give them leave to send them abroad, impose Laws upon them, refuse to alter and amend those they would make for themselves, make them pay Customs, Excises, and Taxes, and yet pay the Garrisons and Guards that defend them, themselves; Press their Inhabitants to their Fleets, and carry away their Old Veteran Troops that should defend them, and leave them to raise more to be served in the same manner, will let none of their Money be carried over thither, nor let them Coin any of their own; and a great many such hardships they suffer under the Hand of this Nation as mere Slaves and Conquered People, tho' the greatest part of the Traders are the People of the very Nation that treats 'em thus.

On the other hand, this creates Eternal Murmurs, Heart-burnings and Regret, both in the Natives and the Transplanted Inhabitants; the first have shown their Uneasiness by frequent Insurrections and Rebellions, for Nature prompts the meanest Animal to struggle for Liberty; and these struggles have often been attended with great Cruelty, Ravages, Death, Massacres, and Ruin both of Families and the Country it self: As to the Transplanted Inhabitants, they run into Clandestine Trade, into corresponding with their Masters Enemies, Victualing their Navies, Colonies and the like, receiving and importing their Goods in spite of all the Orders and Directions to the contrary.

These are the effects of Divisions, and Feuds on that side; on the other hand there is a Kingdom Entire Unconquered and Independent, and for the present, under the same Monarch with the rest. —— But here their Feuds are greater than with the other, and more dangerous by far because National: This Kingdom joins to the North part of the first Kingdom, and Terrible Divisions lie among the two Nations.

The People of these two Kingdoms are called if you please for distinction sake, for I cannot well make you understand their hard Names, Solunarians and Nolunarians, these to the South and those to the North, the Solunarians were divided in their Articles of Religion; the Governing Party, or the Established Church, I shall call the Solunarian Church; but the whole Kingdom was full of a sort of Religious People called Crolians, who like our Dissenters in England profess divers sub-divided Opinions by themselves, and cooed not, or wooed not, let it go which way it will, join with the Established Church.

On the other hand, the Established Church in the Northern Kingdom was all Crolians, but full of Solunarians in Opinions, who were Dissenters there, as the Crolians were Dissenters in the South, and this unhappy mixture occasioned endless Feuds, Divisions, Sub-divisions and Animosities without Number, of which hereafter.

The Northern Men are Bold, Terrible Numerous and Brave, to the last Degree, but Poor, and by the Encroachments of their Neighbours, growing poorer every Day.

The Southern are equally Brave, more Numerous and Terrible, but Wealthy and care not for Wars, had rather stay at Home and Quarrel with one another, than go Abroad to Fight, making good an Old Maxim, Too Poor t'Agree, and yet too Rich to Fight.

Between these the Feud is great, and every Day growing greater; and those People who pretend to have been in the Cogitator or thinking Engine tell us, all the lines of Consequences in that Affair point at a fatal period between the Kingdoms.

The Complaints also are great, and backed with fiery Arguments on both sides; the Northern Men say, the Solunarians have dealt unjustly and unkindly by them in several Articles; but the Southern Men reply with a most powerful Argument, viz. they are Poor, and therefore ought to be Oppressed, Suppressed, or any thing.

But the main Debate is like to lye upon the Article of Choosing a King; both the Nations being under one Government at present, but the Settlement ending in the Reigning Line, the Northern Men refuse to join in Government again, unless they have a rectification of some Conditions in which, they say, they have the worst of it.

In this case, even the Southern Men themselves, say, they believe the Nolunarians have been in the Chair of Reflection, the thinking Engine, and that having screwed their Understandings into a Direct Position to that Matter before them, they have made a right Judgment of their own Affairs, and with all their Poverty stand on the best Foot as to Right.

But as the matter of this Northern Quarrel comes under a Second Head, and is more properly the Subject of a Second Voyage to the

Moon; the Reader may have it more at large considered in another Class, and some farther Enlightenings in that Affair than perhaps can be reasonably expected of me here.

But of all the Feuds and Brangles that ever poor Nation was embroiled in, of all the Quarrels, the Factions and Parties that ever the People of any Nation thought worth while to fall out for, none were ever in reality so light, in effect so heavy, in appearance so great, in substance so small, in name so terrible, in nature so trifling, as those for which this Southern Country was altogether by the Ears among themselves.

And this was one Reason why I so earnestly enquired of my Lunarian Philosopher, whether he had an Estate in that Country or no. But having told him the Cause of that enquiry, he replied, there was one thing in the Nature of his Country-men which secured them from the ruin which usually attended divided Nations, viz. that if any Foreign Nation thinking to take the advantage of their Intestine Divisions fell upon them in the highest of all their Feuds, they lay aside their Parties and Quarrels and presently fall in together to beat out the common Enemy; and then no sooner had they obtained Peace abroad, by their Conduct and Bravery, but they would fall to cutting one another's Throats again at home as naturally as if it had been their proper Calling, and that for Trifles too, mere Trifles.

Very well, said I to my learned Self, pretty like my own Country still, that whatever Peace they have abroad, are sure to have none at home.

To come at the historical Account of these Lunarian Dissentions, it will be absolutely necessary to enter a little into the Story of the Place, at least as far as relates to the present Constitution, both of the People, the Government, and the Subject of their present Quarrels.

And first we are to understand, that there has for some Ages been carried on in these Countries, a private feud or quarrel among the People, about a thing called by them Upogyla, with us very vulgarly called Religion.

This Difference, as in its Original it was not great, nor indeed upon Points accounted among themselves Essential, so it had never been a Difference of any height, if there had not always been some one thing, or other, happening in the State which made the Court-Politicians think it necessary to keep the People busy and embroiled, to prevent their more narrow Inspection into Depredations and

505

Encroachments on their Liberties, which was always making on them by the Court.

'Tis not denied but there might be a Native want of Charity in the Inhabitant, adapting them to Feud, and particularly qualifying them to be always Piquing one another; and some of their own Nation, who by the help of the famous Perspectives before-mentioned, pretend to have seen farther into the Insides of Nature and Constitution than other People, tell us the cross Lines of Nature which appear in the make of those particular People, signify a direct Negative as to the Article of Charity and good Neighbour-hood.

'Twas particularly unhappy to this wrangling People, that Reasons of State should always fall in, to make that uncharitableness and continual quarrelling Humour necessary to carry on the Public Affairs of the Nation, and may pass for a certain Proof, that the State was under some Diseases and Convulsions, which, like a Body that digests nothing so well as what is hurtful to its Constitution, makes use of those things for its Support, which are in their very Nature, fatal to its being, and must at last tend to its Destruction.

But as this however inclined them to be continually Snarling at one another, so as in all Quarrels it generally appears one Side must go down.

The prevailing Party therefore always kept the Power in their Hands, and as the under were always Subject to the lash they soon took care to hook their Quarrel into the Affairs of State, and so join Religious Differences, and Civil Differences together.

These things had long embroiled the Nation, and frequently involved them in bitter Enmities, Feuds, and Quarrels, and once in a tedious, ruinous, and bloody War in their own Bowels, in which, contrary to all expectation, this lesser Party prevailed.

And since the allegoric Relation may bear great Similitude with our European Affairs on this side the Moon: I shall for the ease of Expression, and the better Understanding of the Reader, frequently call them by the same Names our unhappy Parties are called by in England, as Solunnarian Churchmen, and Crolian Dissenters, at the same time desiring my Reader to observe, that he is always to remember who it is we are talking of, and that he is by no means to understand me of any Person, Party, People, Nation, or Place on this side the Moon, any Expression, Circumstance, Similitude, or Appearance to the contrary in any wise notwithstanding.

This premised, I am to tell the Reader that the last Civil War in this Lunar Country ended in the Victors confounding their own Conquests by their intestine Broils, they being as is already noted a most Eternally Quarrelling Nation; upon this new Breach, they that first began the War, turned about, and pleading that they took up Arms to regulate the Government, not to overthrow it, fell in with the Family of their Kings, who had been banished, and one of them destroyed, and restored the Crown to the Family, and the Nation to the Crown, just for all the World as the Presbyterians in England did, in the Case of King Charles the Second.

The Party that was thus restored, accepted the return the others made to their Duty, and their Assistance in restoring the Family of their Monarch, but abated not a Tittle of the old Rancour against them as a Party which they entertained at their first taking Arms, not allowing the return they had made to be any atonement at all for the Crimes they had been guilty of before. 'Tis true they passed an Act or Grant of General Pardon, and Oblivion, as in all such Cases is usual, and as without which the other would never ha' come in, or have joined Powers to form the Restoration they were bringing to pass, but the old Feud of Religion continued with this addition, that the Dissenters were Rebels, Murderers, King-killers, Enemies to Monarchy and Civil Government, lovers of Confusion, popular, anarchial Governments, and movers of Sedition; that this was in their very Nature and Principles, and the like.

In this Condition, and under these Mortifications this Party of People lived just an Egyptian Servitude, viz. of 40 Years, in which time they were frequently vexed with Persecution, Harassed, Plundered, Fined, Imprisoned, and very hardly Treated, insomuch that they pretend to be able to give an account of vast Sums of their Country-Money, levied upon them on these Occasions, amounting as I take it to 2 Millions of Lunatians, a Coin they keep their Accounts by there, and much about the value of our Pound Sterling; besides this they were hooked into a great many Sham Plots, and Sworn out of their Lives and Estates in such a manner, that in the very next Reign the Government was so sensible of their hard treatment, that they reversed several Sentences by the same Authority that had Executed them; a most undeniable Proof they were ashamed of what had been done; at last, the Prince who was restored as above said, died, and his Brother mounted the Throne; and now began a third Scene of Affairs, for this Prince was neither Church-man, nor Dissenter, but of a different Religion from them all, known in that Country by the Name of Abrogratzianism, and this Religion of his had this one absolutely necessary Consequence in it, that a Man could not be sincerely and heartily of this, but he must be an Implacable hater of both the other. As this is laid down as a previous Supposition, we are with the same Reason to imagine this Prince to be entirely bent upon the Suppression and Destruction of both the other, if not absolutely as to Life and Estate, yet entirely as to Religion.

To bring this the more readily to pass like a true Politician, had his Methods and Particulars been equally Politic with his Generals, he began at the right End, viz. to make the Breach between the Solunnarian Church, and the Crolian Dissenters as wide as possible, and to do this it was resolved to shift Sides, and as the Crown had always took part with the Church, crushed, humbled, persecuted, and by all means possible mortified the Dissenters, as is noted in the Reign of his Predecessor. This Prince resolved to caress, cherish, and encourage the Crolians by all possible Arts and outward Endearments, not so much that they purposed them any real Favour, for the destruction of both was equally determined, nor so much that they expected to draw them over to Abrogratzianism, but Two Reasons may be supposed to give Rise to this Project.

I. The Lunarian Church Party had all along Preached up for a part of their Religion, that Absolute undisputed Obedience, was due from every Subject to their Prince without any Reserve, Reluctance or Repining; that as to Resistance, it was Fatal to Body, Soul, Religion, Justice and Government; and tho' the Doctrine was Repugnant to Nature, and to the very Supreme Command it self, yet he that resisted, received to himself Damnation, just for all the World like our Doctrine of Passive Obedience. Now tho' these Solunarian Church-Men did not absolutely believe all they said themselves to be true, yet they found it necessary to push these things to the uttermost Extremities, because they might the better fix upon the Crolian Dissenters, the Charge of professing less Loyal Principles than they. For as to the Crolians, they professed openly they would pay Obedience to the Prince, as far as the Laws directed, but no farther.

These things were run up to strange heights, and the People were always falling out about what they would do, or wooed not do, if things were so or so, as they were not, and were never likely to be; and the hot Men on both sides were every now and then going together by the Ears about Chimeras, Shadows, May-be's and Supposes.

The hot Men of the Solunarian Church were for knocking the Crolians in the Head, because as they said they were Rebels, their Fathers were Rebels, and they would certainly turn Rebels again upon occasion.

The Crolians insisted upon it, that they had nothing to do with what was done before they were Born, that if they were Criminal, because their Fathers were so, then a great many who were now of the Solunarian Church were as Guilty as they, several of the best Members of that Church having been Born of Crolian Parents.

In the matter of Loyalty they insisted upon it, they were as Loyal as the Solunarians, for that they were as Loyal as Nature, Reason and the Laws both of God and Man required, and what the Other talked of more, was but a mere pretence, and so it would be found if ever their Prince should have occasion to put them to the Trial, that he that pretended to go beyond the Power of Nature and Reason, must indeed go beyond them, and they never desired to be brought into the extreme, but they were ready at any time to show such Proofs, and give such Demonstrations of their Loyalty, as would satisfy any reasonable Prince, and for more they had nothing to say.

In this posture of Affairs, this new Prince found his Subjects when he came to the Crown, the Solunarian Church Caressed him, and notwithstanding his being Devoted to the Abrogratzian Faith, they Crowned him with extraordinary Acclamations.

They were the rather inclined to push this forward by how much they thought it would singularly mortify the Crolians, and all the sorts of Dissenters, for they had all along declared their abhorrence of the Abrogratzians to such a Degree that they publicly endeavoured to have got a general Concurrence of the whole Nation in the Public Cortez, or Diet of the Kingdom, to have joined with them in Excluding this very Prince by Name, and all other Princes that should ever embrace the Abrogratzian Faith.

And it wanted but a very little of bringing it to pass, for almost all the Great Men of the Nation, tho' Solunarians, yet that were Men of Temper, Moderation, and Fore-sight, were for this exclusive Law. But the High Priests and Patriarchs of the Solunarian Church prevented it, and upon pretence of this Passive Obedience Principle, made their Interest and gave their Voices for Crowning, or Entailing the Crown and Government on the Head of one of the most Implacable Enemies both to their Religion and Civil Right that ever the Nation saw; but they lived to Repent it too late.

This Conquest over the Crolians and the Moderate Solunarians, if it did not suppress them entirely, it yet gave the other Part such an ascendant over them, that they made no Doubt when that Prince came to the Crown, they had done so much to oblige him, that he could deny them nothing, and therefore in expectation they swallowed up the whole Body of the Crolians at once, and began to talk of nothing less than Banishing them to the Northern part of the Country, or to certain Islands, and Countries a vast way off, where formerly great numbers of them had fled for shelter in like Cases.

And this was the more probable by an unhappy Stroke these Crolians attempted to strike, but miscarried in at the very beginning of this Prince's Reign: for as they had always professed an aversion to this Prince on account of his Religion, as soon as their other King was dead, they set up one of his Natural Sons against this King, which the Solunarians had so joyfully Crowned. This young Prince invaded his Dominions, and great Numbers of the most zealous Crolians joined him — — But to cut the Story short, he was entirely routed by the Forces of the new Prince, for all the Solunarian Church joined with him against the Crolians without any respect to the Interest of Religion, so they overthrew their Brethren: The young invaded Prince was taken and put to Death openly, and Great Cruelties were exercised in cold Blood upon the poor unhappy People that were taken in the Defeat!

Thus a second time these Loyal Solunarian Church-men Established their Enemy, and built up what they were glad afterwards to pull down again, and to beg the assistance of those Crolians whom they had so rudely handled, to help them demolish the Power they had erected themselves, and which now began to set its foot upon the Throat of those that nourished and supported it.

Upon this exceeding Loyalty and blind Assistance given to their Prince, the Solunarians made no question but they had so Eternally bound him to them, that it would be in their Power to pull down the very Name of Crolianism, and utterly destroy it from the Nation.

But the time came on to Undeceive them, for this Prince, whose Principle as an Abrogratzian, was to destroy them both, as it happened, was furnished with Counselors and Ecclesiastics of his own Profession, ten thousand Times more bent for their general Ruin, than himself.

For abstracted from the Venom and Rancour of his Profession as an Abrogratzian, and from the furious Zeal of his Brahmin, Priests, and Religious People, that continually hung about him, and that prompted him to act against his Temper and Inclination, by which he ruined all, he was else a forward and generous Prince, and likely to have made his People Great and Flourishing.

But his furious Church-Men ruined all his good Designs, and turned all his Projects to compass the Introduction of his own Religion into his Dominions.

Nay, and had he not fatally been pushed on by such as really designed his Ruin, to drive this deep Design on too hastily and turn the Scale of his Management from a close and concealed, to an open and professed Design, he might have gone a great way with it. — — — — Had he been content to have let that have been twenty Year a doing, which he impatiently as well as preposterously attempted all at once. — — — Wise Men have thought he might in time have suppressed the Solunarian Religion, and have set up his own.

To give a short Scheme of his Proceedings, and with them of the reason of his Miscarriage.

I. Having defeated the Rebellious Crolians, as is before noted, and reflecting on the Danger he was in upon the sudden Progress of that Rebellion, for indeed he was within a trifle of Ruin in that Affair; and had not the Crolians been deceived by the darkness of the Night and led to a large Ditch of Water, which they could not pass over, they had certainly surprised and overthrown his Army, and cut them in pieces, before they had known who had hurt them. Upon the Sense of this Danger, he takes up a pretence of necessity for the being always ready to resist the Factious Crolians, as he called them, and by that Insinuation hooks himself into a standing Army in time of Peace; — — nay, and so easy were the Solunarian Church to yield up any point, which they did but imagine would help to crush their Brethren the Crolians, that they not only consented to this unusual Invasion of their ancient Liberties, but sent up several Testimonials of their free Consent, nay, and of their Joy of having arrived to so great a Happiness, as to have a Prince that setting aside the formality of Laws would vouchsafe to Govern them by the glorious Method of a Standing Army. — — —

These Testimonials were things not much unlike our Addresses in England, and which when I heard I could not but remember our Case, in the time of the late King James, when the City of Carlisle in their Address, Thanked his Majesty for the Establishing a Standing Army in England in time of Peace, calling it the Strength, and Glory of the Kingdom.

So strong is the Ambition and Envy of Parties, these Solunarian Gentlemen not grudging to put out one of their own eyes, so they might at the same time put out both the Eyes of their Enemies; the Crolians rather consented to this badge of their own Slavery, and brought themselves who were a free People before, under the Power and Slavery of the Sword.

The ease with which this Prince got over so considerable a Point as this, made him begin to be too credulous and to persuade himself that the Solunarian Church-Men were really in earnest, as to their Pageant-Doctrine of Non-Resistance, and that as he had seen them bear with strange extravagancies on the Crolian Part, they were real and in earnest when they Preached that Men ought to obey for Conscience's sake, whatever hardship were imposed upon them, and however unjust, or contrary to the Laws of God, Nature, Reason, or their Country; what Principle in the World could more readily prompt a Prince to attempt what he so earnestly coveted, as this zealous Prince did the restoring the Abrogratzian Faith, for since he had but two sorts of People to do with; one he had crushed by force, and had brought the other to profess it their Religion, their Duty, and their Resolution to bear every thing he thought fit to Impose upon them, and that they should be Damned if they resisted, the Work seemed half done to his Hand.

And indeed when I reflected on the Coherence of things, I could not so much blame this Prince for his venturing upon the probability, for whoever was but to go up to this Lunar World and read the Stories of that Time, with what Fury the hot Men of the Solunarian Church acted against the Dissenting Crolians, and with what warmth they assisted their Prince against them, and how Cruelly they insulted them after they were defeated in their attempt of Dethroning him, how zealously they Preached up the Doctrine of absolute undisputed Resignation to his Will, how frequently they obeyed several of his encroachments upon their Liberties, and what solemn Protestations they made to submit to him in any thing, and to stand by and assist him in whatever he Commanded them to the last Drop, much with the same Zeal and Forwardness, as our Life-and-Fortune Men did here in England. I say, when all this was considered, I could not so much condemn his Credulity, nor blame him for believing them, for no Man could have doubted their Sincerity, but he that at the same time must have Taxed them with most unexampled Hypocrisy.

For the Solunarians now began to discern their Prince was not really on their side, that neither in State Matters any more than Religion, he had any affection for them, and the first absolute Shock he gave them, was in Publishing a general Liberty to the Crolians. 'Tis true this was not out of respect to the Crolian Religion any more than the Solunarian, but purely because by that means he made way for an Introduction of the Abrogratzian Religion which now began to appear publicly in the Country.

But however, as this was directly contrary to the expectation of the Solunarians, it gave them such a disgust against their Prince, that from that very time being disappointed in the Sovereign Authority they expected, they entered into the deepest and blackest Conspiracy against their Prince and his Government that ever was heard of.

Many of the Crolians were deluded by the new Favour and Liberty they received from the Prince to believe him real, and were glad of the Mortification of their Brethren; but the more Judicious seeing plainly the Prince's Design, declared against their own Liberty, because given them by an illegal Authority, without the assent of the whole Body legally assembled.

When the Solunarians saw this they easily reconciled themselves to the Crolians, at least from the Outside of the Face, for the carrying on their Design, and so here was a Nation full of Plots, here was the Prince and his Abrogratzians plotting to introduce their Religion, here was a parcel of blind short-sighted Crolians plotting to ruin the Solunarian Establishment, and weakly joining with the Abrogratzians to satisfy their private Resentments; and here was the wiser Crolians joining heartily with the Solunarians of all sorts, laying aside private Resentments, and forgetting old Grudges about Religion, in order to ruin the invading Projects of the Prince and his Party.

There was indeed some verbal Conditions past between them, and the Solunarians willing to bring them into their Party promised them upon the Faith of their Nation, and the Honour of the Solunarian Religion, that there should be no more Hatred, Disturbance or Persecution for the sake of Religion between them, but that they would come to a Temper with them, and always be Brethren for the future. They declared that Persecution ran contrary to their Religion in general, and to their Doctrine in particular; and backed their Allegations with some Truths they have not since thought fit to like, nor much to regard.

However by this Artifice, and on these Conditions, they brought the Crolians to join with them in their Resolutions to countermine their designing Prince; these indeed were for doing it by the old way down-right, and to oppose Oppression with Force, a Doctrine they acknowledged, and professed to join with all the Lunar part of

Mankind in the practice, and began to tell their Brethren how they had imposed upon themselves and the World, in pretending to absolute Submission against Nature and universal Lunarian Practice.

But a cunning Fellow personating a Solunarian, and who was in the Plot, gravely answered them thus,

'Look ye, Gentlemen, we own with you that Nature, Reason, Law, Justice, and Custom of Nations is on your side, and that all Power Derives from, Centers in, and on all Recesses or Demises of Power returns to its Great Original the Party Governed: Nay we own our Great Eye from whom all the habitable Parts of this Globe are enlightened, has always directed us to practice what Nature thus dictates, always approved and generally succeeded the attempt of Dethroning Tyrants. But our Case differs, we have always pretended to this absolute undisputed Obedience, which we did indeed to gain the Power of your Party; and if we should turn round at once to your Opinion, tho' never so right, we should so fly in the Face of our own Doctrine, Sermons, innumerable Pamphlets and Pretensions, as would give all our Enemies too great a Power over us in Argument, and we should never be able to look Mankind in the Face: But we have laid our Measures so that by prompting the King to run upon us in all sorts of bare-faced Extremes and Violences, we shall bring him to exasperate the whole Nation; then we may underhand foment the breach on this side, raise the Mob upon him, and by acting on both sides seem to suffer a Force in falling in with the People, and preserve our Reputation.

'Thus we shall bring the thing to pass, betray our Prince, take Arms against his Power, call in Foreign Force to do the Work, and even then keep our Hands seemingly out of the Broil, by being pretended Sticklers for our former Prince; so save our Reputation, and bring all to pass with Ease and Calmness; while the eager Party of the Abrogratzians will do their own Work by expecting we will do it for them.

The Crolians astonished both at the Policy, the Depth, the Knavery and the Hypocrisy of the Design, left them to carry it on, owning it was a Masterpiece of Craft, and so stood still to observe the Issue, which every way answered the exactness of its Contrivance.

When I saw into the bottom of all this Deceit, I began to take up new Resolutions of returning back into our Old World again, and going home to England, where tho' I had conceived great Indignation at the Treatment our Passive Obedience Men gave their Prince here, and was in hopes in these my remote Travels to have found out some

Nations of Honour and Principles. I was filled with Amazement to see our Moderate Knaves so much out-done, and I was informed that all these things were mere Amusements, Visors, and Shams, to bring an Innocent Prince into the Snare.

Would any Mortal imagine who has read this short Part of the Story, that all this was a Solunarian Church Plot, a mere Conspiracy between these Gentlemen and the Crolian Dissenters, only to wheedle in the unhappy Prince to his own Destruction, and bring the popular Advantage of the Mob, to a greater Ascendant on the Crown.

Of all the Richelieus, Mazarines, Gondamours, Oliver Cromwells, and the whole Train of Politicians that our World has produced, the greatest of their Arts are Follies to the unfathomable depth of these Lunarian Policies; and for Wheedle, Lying, Swearing, Preaching, Printing, &c. what is said in our World by Priests and Politicians, we thank God may be believed; but if ever I believe a Solunarian Priest Preaching Non-Resistance of Monarchs, or a Solunarian Politician turning Abrogratzian, I ought to be marked down for a Fool; nor will ever any Prince in that Country take their Word again, if ever they have their Senses about 'em, but as this is a most extraordinary Scene, so I cannot omit a more particular and sufficient Relation of some Parts of it, than I used to give.

The Solunarian Clergy had carried on their Non-Resistance Doctrine to such Extremities, and had given this new Prince such unusual demonstrations of it, that he fell absolutely into the Snare, and entirely believed them; he had tried them with such Impositions as they would never have born from any Prince in the World, nor from him neither, had they not had a deep Design, and consequently stood in need of the deepest Disguise imaginable; they had yielded to a Standing Army, and applauded it as a thing they had desired; they had submitted to levying Taxes upon them by New Methods, and illegal Practices; they had yielded to the abrogation or suspension at least of their Laws, when the King's absolute Will required it; not that they were blind, and did not see what their Prince was doing, but that the black Design was so deeply laid, they found it was the only way to ruin him, to push him upon the highest Extremes, and then they should have their turn served. — — Thus if he desired one illegal Thing of them, they would immediately grant two; one would have thought they had read our Bible, and the Command, when a Man takes away the Cloak, to give him the Coat also.

Nor was this enough, but they seemed willing to admit of the public Exercise of the Abrogratzian Religion in all Parts; and when the Prince set it up in his own Chapel, they suffered it to be set up in their Cities, and Towns, and the Abrogratzian Clergy began to be seen up and down in their very Habits; a thing which had never been permitted before in that Country, and which the Common People began to be very uneasy at. But still the Solunarian Clergy, and all such of the Gentry, especially as were in the Plot, by their Sermons, printed Books, and public Discourses, carried on this high topping Notion of absolute Submission, so that the People were kept under, and began to submit to all the impositions of the Prince.

These things were so acted to the Life, that not only the Prince, but none of his Abrogratzian Counselors could see the Snare, the Hook was so finely covered by the Church-Artificers, and the Bait so delicious, that they all swallowed it with eagerness and delight.

But the Conspirators willing to make a sure game of it, and not thinking the King, or all his Counselors would drive on so fast as they would have them, tho' they had already made a fair progress for the Time, resolved to play home, and accordingly they persuade their Prince, that they will not only submit to his Arbitrary Will, in Matters of State, and Government, but in Matters of Religion; and in order to carry this Jest on, one of the heads of their Politics, and a Person of great Esteem for his Abilities in Matters of State, being without question one of the ablest Heads of all the Solunarian Nobility, pretended to be converted, and turned Abrogratzian. This immediately took as they desired, for the Prince caressed him, and entertained him with all possible endearments, proffered him to several Posts of Honour and Advantage, always kept him near him, consulted him in all Emergencies, took him with him to the Abrogian Sacrifices, and he made no Scruple publicly to appear there, and by these degrees and a super-achitophalian Hypocrisy, so insinuated himself into the credulous Prince's favour, that he became his only Confident, and absolute Master of all his Designs.

Now the Plot had its desired effect, for he pushed the King upon all manner of Precipitations; and if even the Abrogratzians themselves who were about the King, interposed for more temperate Proceedings, he would call them Cowards, Strangers, ignorant of the Temper of the Lunarians, who when they were a going, might be driven, but if they were suffered to cool and consider, would face about and fall off.

Indeed the Men of Prudence and Estates among his own Party, I mean the Abrogratzians in the Country, frequently warned him to take more moderate Measures, and to proceed with more Caution; told him he would certainly ruin them all, and himself, and that there must be some Body about his Majesty that pushed him upon these Extremes, on purpose to set all the Nation in a Flame, and to overthrow all the good Designs, which with Temper and good Conduct, might be brought to perfection.

Had these wary Councils been observed, and a Prudence and Policy agreeable to the mighty consequence of Things been practiced, the Solunarian Church had run a great risk of being over thrown, and to have sunk gradually in the Abrogian Errors, the People began to be drawn off gradually, and the familiarity of the thing made it appear less frightful to unthinking People, who had entertained strange Notions of the monstrous things that were to be seen in it, so that common Vogue had filled the Peoples Minds with ignorant Aversions, that 'tis no absurdity to say, I believe there was 200000 People who would have spent the last drop of their Blood against Abrogratzianism, that did not know whether it was a Man or a Horse.

This thing considered well, would of it self have been sufficient to have made the Prince and his Friends wary, and to have taught them to suit their Measures to the Nature and Circumstances of Things before them; but Success in their beginnings blinded their Eyes, and they fell into this Church Snare with the most unpitied willingness that could be imagined.

The first thing therefore this new Counselor put his Master upon, in order to the beginning his more certain Ruin, was to introduce several of his Abrograzians into Places of all kinds, both in the Army, Navy, Treasure, and Civil Affairs, tho' contrary to some of the general Constitutions of Government; he had done it into the Army before, tho' it had disgusted several of his Military Men, but now he pushed him upon making it Universal, and still the Passive Solunarians bore it with patience.

From this tameness and submission, his next Step was to argue that he might depend upon it the Solunarian Church had so sincerely embraced the Doctrine of Non-Resistance, that they were now ripened not only to sit still, and see their Brethren the Crolians suppressed, but to stand still and be oppressed themselves, and he might assure himself the Matter was now ripe, he might do just what he wooed himself with them, they were prepared to bare any thing.

This was the fatal Stroke, for having possessed the Prince with the belief of this, he let loose the Reins to all his long concealed Desires. Down went their Laws, their Liberties, their Corporations, their Churches, their Colleges, all went to wreck, and the eager Abrograzians thought the Day their own. The Solunarians made no opposition, but what was contained within the narrow circumference of Petitions, Addresses, Prayers, and Tears; and these the Prince was prepared to reject, and upon all occasions to let them know he was resolved to be obeyed.

Thus he drove on by the treacherous Advice of his new Counsels, till he ripened all the Nation for the general Defection which afterward followed.

For as the Encroachments of the Prince pushed especially at their Church Liberties, and threatened the overthrow of all their Ecclesiastical Privileges, the Clergy no sooner began to feel that they were like to be the first Sacrifice, but they immediately threw off the Visor, and beat the Concionazimir; this is a certain Ecclesiastic Engine which is usual in cases of general Alarm, as the Churches Signal of Universal Tumult.

This is truly a strange Engine, and when a Clergy-Man gets into the Inside of it, and beats it, it Roars, and makes such a terrible Noise from the several Cavities, that 'tis heard a long way; and there are always a competent number of them placed in all Parts so conveniently, that the Alarm is heard all over the Kingdom in one Day.

I had some Thoughts to have given the Reader a Diagram of this piece of Art, but as I am but a bad Drafts Man, I have not yet been able so exactly to describe it, as that a Scheme can be drawn, but to the best of my Skill, take it as follows. 'Tis a hollow Vessel, large enough to hold the biggest Clergy-Man in the Nation; it is generally an Octagon in Figure, open before, from the Waist upward, but whole at the Back, with a Flat extended over it for Reverberation, or doubling the Sound; doubling and redoubling, being frequently thought necessary to be made use of on these occasions; 'tis very Mathematically contrived, erected on a Pedestal of Wood like a Windmill, and has a pair of winding Stairs up to it, like those at the great Tun at Hiedlebergh.

I could make some Hieroglyphical Discourses upon it, from these References, thus. I. That as it is erected on a Pedestal like a Wind-Mill, so it is no new thing for the Clergy, who are the only Persons permitted to make use of it, to make it turn round with the Wind, and serve to all the Points of the Compass. 2. As the Flat over it assists to increase the

Sound, by forming a kind of hollow, or cavity proper to that purpose, so there is a certain natural hollowness, or emptiness, made use of sometimes in it, by the Gentlemen of the Gown, which serves exceedingly to the propagation of all sorts of Clamour, Noise, Railing, and Disturbance. 3. As the Stairs to it go winding up like those by which one mounts to the vast Tun of Wine at Hiedleburgh, which has no equal in our World, so the use made of these ascending Steps, is not altogether different, being frequently employed to raise People up to all sorts of Enthusiasms, spiritual Intoxications, mad and extravagant Action, high exalted Flights, Precipitations, and all kinds of Ecclesiastic Drunkenness and Excesses.

The sound of this Emblem of emptiness, the Concionazimir, was no sooner heard over the Nation, but all the People discovered their readiness to join in with the Summons, and as the thing had been concerted before, they send over their Messengers to demand Assistance from a powerful Prince beyond the Sea, one of their own Religion, and who was allied by Marriage to the Crown.

They made their Story out so plain, and their King had by the contrivance of their Achitophel rendered himself so suspected to all his Neighbours, that this Prince, without any hesitation, resolved to join with them, and accordingly makes vast Preparations to invade their King.

During this interval their Behaviour was quite altered at home, the Doctrine of absolute Submission and Non-Resistance was heard no more among them, the Concionazimir beat daily to tell all the People they should stand up to Defend the Rights of the Church, and that it was time to look about them for the Abrograzians were upon them. The eager Clergy made this Ecclesiastic Engine sound as loud and make all the Noise they could, and no Men in the Nation were so forward as they to acknowledge that it was a State-Trick, and they were drawn in to make such a stir about the pretended Doctrines of absolute Submission, that they did not see the Snare which lay under it, that now their Eyes were opened, and they had learnt to see the Power and Superiority of Natural Right, and would be deceived no longer. Others were so honest to tell the Truth, that they knew the emptiness and weakness of the pretence all along, and knew what they did when they Preached it up, viz. to suppress and pull down the Crolians: But they thought their Prince who they always served in crying up that Doctrine, and whose Exclusion was prevented by it, would ha' had more Gratitude, or at least more Sense, than to try the Experiment upon them, since whatever to serve his Designs and their own, which they always thought well united, they were willing to pretend, he could not but see they always knew better than to suffer the practice of it in their own Case. That since he had turned the Tables upon them, 'tis true he had them at an advantage and might pretend they were Knaves, and perhaps had an opportunity to call them so with some reason; but they were resolved, since he had drove them to the necessity of being one or t'other, tho' he might call them Knaves, they would take care he should have no reason to call them Fools too.

Thus the Vapour of absolute Subjection was lost on a sudden, and as if it had been preparatory to what was coming after, the Experiment was quickly made; for the King pursuing his Encroachments upon the Church, and being possessed with a Belief that pursuant to their open Professions they would submit to any thing, he made a beginning with them, in sending his positive Command to one of his Superintendent Priests, or Patriarchs, to forbid a certain Ecclesiastic to officiate any more till his Royal Pleasure was known.

Now it happened very unluckily that this Patriarch, tho' none of the most Learned of his Fraternity, yet had always been a mighty zealous Promoter of this blind Doctrine of Non-Resistance, and had not a little triumphed over and insulted the Crolian Dissenters upon the Notion of Rebellion, antimonarchical Principles and Obedience, with a reserve for the Laws, and the like, as a scandalous practice, and comprehensive of Faction, Sedition, dangerous to the Church and State, and the like.

This Reverend Father was singled out as the first Mark of the King's Design; the deluded Prince believed he could not but comply, having so publicly professed his being all Submission and absolute Subjection; but as this was all Conceit, he was pushed on to make the Assault where he was most certain to meet a repulse; and this Gentleman had long since thrown off the Mask, so his first Order was disobeyed.

The Patriarch pretended to make humble Remonstrances, and to offer his Reasons why he could not in Conscience, as he called it, comply. The King, who was now made but a mere Engine, or Machine, screwed up or down by this false Counselor to act his approaching Destruction with his own Hand, was prompted to resent this Repulse with the utmost Indignation, to reject all manner of Submissions, Excuses or Arguments, or any thing but an immediate, absolute compliance, according to the Doctrine so often inculcated; and this he run on so high, as to put the Patriarch in Prison for Contumacy.

The Patriarch as absolutely refused to submit, and offered himself to the Decision of the Law.

Now it was always a sacred Rule in these Lunar Countries, that both King and People are bound to stand by the arbitrement of the Law in all Cases of Right or Claim, whether public or private; and this has been the reason that all the Princes have endeavoured to cover their Actions with pretences of Law, whatever really has been in their Design; for this reason the King could not refuse to bring the Patriarch to a Trial, where the Humour of the People first discovered it self, for here Passive Obedience was Tried and Cast, the Law proved to be superior to the King, the Patriarch was acquitted, his Disobedience to the King justified, and the King's Command proved unjust.

The Applause of the Patriarch, the Acclamations of the People, and the general Rejoicings of the whole Nation at this Transaction, gave a black prospect to the Abrograzians; and a great many of them came very honestly and humbly to the King and told him, if he continued to go on by these Measures he would ruin them all; they told him what general Alarm had been over the whole Nation by the Clamours of the Clergy; and the beating of the Concionazimir in all Parts, informed him how the Doctrine of absolute Obedience was ridiculed in all Places, and how the Clergy began to preach it back again like a Witches Prayer, and that it would infallibly raise the Devil of Rebellion in all the Nation, they besought him to content himself with the liberty of their Religion, and the freedom they enjoyed of being let into Places and Offices of Trust and Honour, and to wait all reasonable Occasions to increase their Advantages, and gradually to gain Ground; they entreated him to consider the impossibility of reducing so mighty, so obstinate, and so resolute a Nation all at once. They pleaded how rational a thing it was to expect that by Degrees and good Management, which by precipitate Measures would be endangered and overthrown.

Had these wholesome Counsels taken place in the King's Mind he had been King to his last hour, and the Solunarians and Crolians too had been all undone, for he had certainly encroached upon them gradually, and brought that to pass in time which by precipitant Measures he was not likely to effect.

It was therefore a master-piece of Policy in the Solunarian Church-men to place a feigned Convert near their Prince, who showed always bias him with contrary Advices, puff him up with vast prospect of Success, prompt him to all Extremes, and always Fool him with the certainty of bringing Things to pass his own way.

These Arts made him set light by the repulse he met with in the Matter of the Patriarch, and now he proceeds to make two Attacks more upon the Church; one was by putting some of his Abrograzian Priests into a College among some of the Solunarian Clergy; and the other was to oblige all the Solunarian Clergy to read a certain Act of his Council, in which his Majesty admitted all the Abrograzians, Crolians, and all sorts of Dissenters, to a freedom of their Religious Exercises, Sacrifices, Exorcisms, Dippings, Preachings, &c. and to prohibit the Solunarians to Molest or Disturb them.

Now as this last was a bitter reproach to the Solunarian Church for all the ill Treatment the Dissenting Crolians had received from them, and as it was expressed in the Act that all such Treatment was Unjust and Unchristian, so for them to read it in their Temples, was to acknowledge that they had been guilty of most unjust and irreligious Dealings to the Crolians, and that their Prince had taken care to do them Justice.

The matter of introducing the Abrograzians into the Colleges or Seminaries of the Solunarian Priests, was actually against the Sacred Constitutions and Foundation Laws of those Seminaries.

Wherefore in both these Articles they not only disobeyed their Prince, but they opposed him with those trifling Things called Laws, which they had before declared had no Defensive Force against their Prince; these they had recourse to now, insisted upon the Justice and Right devolved upon them by the Laws, and absolutely refused their compliance with his Commands.

The Prince, pushed upon the Tenters before, received their Denial with exceeding Resentment, and was heard with deep regret, to break out in Exclamations at their unexpected faithless Proceedings, and sometimes to express himself thus: Horrid Hypocrisy! Surprising Treachery! Is this the absolute Subjection which in such numerous Testimonials or Addresses you professed, and for which you so often and so constantly branded the poor Crolians, and told me that your Church was wholly made up of Principles of Loyalty and Obedience! But I'll be fully satisfied for this Treatment.

In the minute of one of those Excursions of his Passion, came into his Presence the seemingly revolted Lunarian Noble Man, and falling in with his present Passions, prompts him to a speedy revenge; and proposed his erecting a Court of Searches, something like the Spanish

Inquisition, giving them plenipotentiary Authority to hear and determine all Ecclesiastical Causes absolutely, and without Appeal.

He empowered these Judges to place by his absolute Will, all the Abrograzian Students in the Solunarian College, and tho' they might make a formal Hearing for the sake of the Form, yet that by Force it should be done.

He gave them Power to displace all those Solunarian Clergy-Men that had refused to read his Act of Demission to the Abrograzian, and Crolian Dissenters, and 'twas thought he designed to keep their Revenues in Petto, till he might in time fill them up to some of his own Religion.

The Commission accordingly began to act, and discovering a full Resolution to fulfill his Command, they by Force proceeded with the Students of the Solunarian College; and it was very remarkable, that even some of the Solunarian Patriarchs were of this number, who turned out their Brethren the Solunarian Students, to place Abrograzians in their room.

This indeed they are said to have repented of since, but however, these it seems were not of the Plot, and therefore did not foresee what was at hand.

The rest of the Patriarchs who were all in the Grand Design, and saw things ripening for its Execution, upon the apprehension of this Court of Searches beginning with them, make an humble Address to their Prince, containing the Reasons why they could not comply with his Royal Command. — — —

The incensed King upbraided them with his having been told by them of their absolute and unreserved Obedience, and refusing their Submissions or their Reasons, sent them all to Jail, and resolved to have brought them before his new High Court of Searches, in order, as was believed, to have them all displaced.

And now all began to be in a Flame, the Solicitations of the Solunarian Party, having obtained powerful Relief Abroad, they began to make suitable preparations at Home. The Gentry and Nobility who the Clergy had brought to join with them, furnished themselves with Horses and Arms, and prepared with their Tenants and Dependants to join the Succours as soon as they should Arrive.

In short, the Foreign Troops they had procured, Arrived, Landed, and published a long Declaration of all the Grievances which they came to redress.

No sooner was this Foreign Army arrived with the Prince at the head of them, but the face of Affairs altered on a sudden. The King indeed, like a brave Prince, drew all his Forces together, and marching out of his Capital City, advanced above 500 Stages, things they measure Land with in those Countries, and much about our Furlong, to meet his Enemy.

He had a gallant Army well appointed and furnished, and all things much superior to his Adversary, but alas the Poison of Disobedience was gotten in there, and upon the first March he offered to make towards the Enemy one of his great Captains with a strong Party of his Men went over and revolted.

This Example was applauded all over the Nation, and by this time one of the Patriarchs, even the same mentioned before that had so often preached Non-Resistance of Princes, lays by his Sacred Vestments, Mitre, and Staff, and exchanging his Robes for a Soldier's Coat, mounts on Horseback, and in short, appears in Arms against his Lord. — — Nor was this all, but the Treacherous Prelate takes along with him several Solunarian Lords, and Persons of the highest Figure, and of the Household, and Family of the King, and with him went the King's own Daughter, his principle Favourites and Friends.

At the News of this, the poor deserted Prince lost all Courage, and abandoning himself to Despair, he causes his Army to retreat without fighting a Stroke, quits them and the Kingdom at once, and takes Sanctuary with such as could escape with him, in the Court of a Neighbouring Prince.

I have heard this Prince exceedingly blamed, for giving himself up to Despair so soon. — — That he thereby abandoned the best and faithfulest of his Friends, and Servants, and left them to the Mercy of the Solunarians; that when all these that would have forsaken him were gone, he had Forces equal to his Enemies; that his Men were in Heart, fresh and forward; that he should have stood to the last; retreated to a strong Town, where his Ships rod, and which was over against the Territories of his great Allie, to whom he might have delivered up the Ships which were there, and have thereby made him Superior at Sea to his Enemies, and he was already much Superior at Land; that there he might have been relieved with Forces too strong for them to match, and at least might have put it to the issue of a fair Battle. — — — Others, that he might have retreated to his own Court, and capital City, and taking possession of the Citadel, which was his own, might so have awed the Citizens who were infinitely Rich, and Numerous, with the apprehensions of having their Houses burnt, they would not have dared to have declared for his Enemies, for fear of being reduced to heaps and ruins; and that at last he might have set the City on Fire in 500 Places, and left the Solunarian Church-Men a Token to remember their Non-Resisting Doctrine by, and yet have made an easy Retreat down the Harbour, to other Forts he had below, and might with ease have destroyed all the Shipping, as he went.

'Tis confessed had he done either, or both these things, he had left them a dear bought Victory, but he was deprived of his Counselor, for as soon as things came to this height, the Achitophel we have so often mentioned, left him also, and went away; all his Abrograzian Priests too forsook him, and he was so bereft of Counsel that he fell into the Hands of his Enemies as he was making his escape, but he got away again, not without the connivance of the Enemy, who were willing enough he should go; so he got a Vessel to carry him over to the Neighbouring Kingdom, and all his Armies, Ships, Forts, Castles, Magazines, and Treasure, fell into his Enemies Hands.

The Neighbouring Prince entertained him very kindly, Cherished him, Succoured him, and furnished him with Armies and Fleets for the recovery of his Dominions, which has occasioned a tedious War with that Prince, which continues to this Day.

Thus far Passive Doctrines, and Absolute Submission served a Turn, bubbled the Prince, wheedled him in to take their Word who professed it, 'till he laid his Finger upon the Men themselves, and that unraveled all the Cheat; they were the first that called in Foreign Power, and took up Arms against their Prince.

Nor did they end here, but all this Scene being over, and the Foreign Prince having thus delivered them, and their own King being thus chased away, the People call themselves together, and as Reason good, having been delivered by him from the Miseries, Brangles, Oppressions, and Divisions of the former Reign, they thought they could do no less than to Crown their Deliverer; and having Summoned a general Assembly of all their Capital Men, they gave the Crown to this Prince who had so generously saved them.

And here again I heard the first King exceedingly blamed for quitting his Dominions, for had he staid here, tho' he had actually been in their Hands, unless they wooed have Murdered him, they could never have proceeded to the Extremities they did reach to, nor cowed they ever have Crowned the other Prince, he being yet alive and in his own Dominions.

But by quitting the Country, they fixed a legal Period to their Obedience, he having deserted their Protection, and Defence, and openly laid down the Administration.

But as these sort of Politics cannot be decided by us, unless we know the Constitutions of those Lunar Regions, so we cannot pretend to make a Decision of what might, or might not have happened.

It remains to examine how those Solunarians behaved themselves, who had so earnedly cried up the Principles of Obedience, and absolute Submission.

Nothing was so Ridiculous, now they saw what they had done, they began to repent, and upon recollection of Thoughts some were so ashamed of themselves, that having broken their Doctrine, and being now called upon to transpose their Allegiance, truly they stopped in the mid-way, and so became Martyrs on both sides.

I can liken these to nothing so well as to those Gentlemen of our English Church, who tho' they broke into the Principles of Passive Obedience by joining, and calling over the P. of O. yet suffered deprivations of Benefices, and loss of their Livings, for not taking the Oath; as if they had not as effectually perjured themselves by taking up Arms against their King, and joining a Foreign Power, as they could possibly do afterward, by Swearing to live quietly under the next King.

But these nice Gentlemen are infinitely outdone in these Countries, for these Solunarians by a true Church turn, not only refuse to transpose their Allegiance, but pretend to wipe their Mouths as to former taking Arms, and return to their old Doctrines of absolute Submission, boast of Martyrdom, and boldly reconcile the contraries of taking up Arms, and Non-Resistance, charging all their Brethren with Schism, Rebellion, Perjury, and the damnable Sin of Resistance.

Nor is this all, for as a great many of these Solunarian Church-Men had no affection to this new Prince, but were not equally furnished, or qualified for Martyrdom with their Brethren; they went to certain Wise Men, who being cunning at splitting Hairs, and making distinctions, might perhaps furnish them with some mediums between Loyalty and Disloyalty; they applied themselves with great diligence to these Men, and they by deep Study, and long Search, either found or made the quaintest Device for them that ever was heard of.

By this unheard of Discovery, to their great Joy and Satisfaction, they have arrived at a Power, which all the Wise Men in our World could never pretend to, and which 'tis thought, could the description of it be regularly made, and brought down hither, would serve for the

Satisfaction and Repose of a great many tender Consciences, who are very uneasy at Swearing to save their Benefices.

These great Makers of Distinction, have learned to distinguish between active Swearing, and passive Swearing, between de facto Loyalty, and de jure Loyalty, and by this decent acquirement they obtained the Art of reconciling Swearing Allegiance without Loyalty, and Loyalty without Swearing, so that native and original Loyalty may be preserved pure and uninterrupted, in spite of all subsequent Oaths, to prevailing Usurpations.

Many are the Mysteries, and vast the Advantages of this new invented Method, Mental Reservations, Innuendoes, and Double Meanings are Toys to this, for they may be provided for in the literal terms of an Oath, but no Provision can be made against this; for these Men after they have taken the Oath, make no Scruple to declare, they only Swear to be quiet, as long as they can make no Disturbance; that they are left liberty still to espouse the Interest and Cause of their former Prince, they nicely distinguish between Obedience and Submission, and tell you a Slave taken into Captivity, tho' he Swears to live peaceably, does not thereby renounce his Allegiance to his natural Prince, nor abridge himself of a Right to attempt his own Liberty if ever opportunity present.

Had these neat Distinctions been found out before, none of our Solunarian Clergy, no not the Patriarchs themselves surely would have stood out, and suffered such Depredations on their Fortunes and Characters as they did; they wooed never have been such Fools to have been turned out of their Livings for not Swearing, when they might have learnt here that they might have swore to one Prince, and yet have retained their Allegiance to another; might have taken an Oath to the new, without impeachment of their old Oaths to the absent Prince. — — — It is great pity these Gentlemen had not gone up to the Moon for Instruction in this difficult Case.

There they might have met with excellent Logicians, Men of most sublime Reasons, Dr. Overall, Dr. Sherlock, and all our nice Examiners of these things wooed appear to be no Body to them; for as the People in these Regions have an extraordinary Eye-sight, and the clearness of the Air contributes much to the help of their Optics, so they have without doubt a proportioned clearness of discerning, by which they see as far into Mill-stones, and all sorts of Solids, as the nature of things will permit, but above all, their Faculties are blest with two exceeding Advantages.

I. With an extraordinary distinguishing Power, by which they can distinguish even Indivisibles, part Unity it self, divide Principles, and distinguish Truth into such and so many minute Particles, till they dwindle it away into a very Nose of Wax, and mould it into any Form they have occasion for, by which means they can distinguish themselves into or out of any Opinion, either in Religion, Politics or Civil Right, that their present Emergencies may call for.

2. Their reasoning Faculties have this further advantage, that upon occasion they can see clearly for themselves, and prevent others from the same discovery, so that when they have occasion to see any thing which presents for their own Advantage, they can search into the Particulars, make it clear to themselves, and yet let it remain dark and mysterious to all the World besides. Whether this is performed by their exceeding Penetration, or by casting an artificial Veil over the Understandings of the Vulgar, Authors have not yet determined; but that the Fact is true, admits of no Dispute.

And the wonderful Benefit of these Things in point of Dispute is extraordinary, for they can see clearly they have the better of an Argument, when all the rest of the World think they have not a Word to say for themselves: 'Tis plain to them that this or that proves a thing, when Nature, by common Reasoning, knows no such Consequences.

I confess I have seen some weak Attempts at this extraordinary Talent, particularly in the Disputes in England between the Church and the Dissenter, and between the High and Low Church, wherein People have tolerably well convinced themselves when no Body else could see any thing of the Matter, as particularly the famous Mr. W — ly about the Antimonarchical Principles taught in the Dissenters Academies; ditto in L — — sly, about the Dissenters burning the City, and setting Fire to their own Houses to destroy their Neighbours; and another famous Author, who proved that Christopher Love lost his Head for attempting to pull down Monarchy by restoring King Charles the Second.

These indeed are some faint Resemblances of what I am upon; but alas! these are tender sort of People, that have not obtained a complete Victory over their Consciences, but suffer that Trifle to reproach them all the while they are doing it, to rebel against their resolved Wills, and check them in the middle of the Design; from which Interruptions arise Palpitations of the Heart, Sickness and squeamishness of Stomach; and these have proceeded to Castings and Vomit, whereby they have been forced sometimes to throw up some such unhappy Truths as have confounded all the rest, and flown in their own Faces so violently, as in spite of Custom has made them blush and look downward; and tho' in kindness to one another they have carefully licked up one another's Filth, yet this unhappy squeamishness of Stomach has spoiled all the Design, and turned the Appetites of their Party, to the no small prejudice of a Cause that stood in need of more Art and more Face to carry it on as it showed be with a thoro'-paced Case-hardened Policy, such as I have been relating, is completely obtained in these Regions, where the Arts and Excellencies of sublime Reasonings are carried up to all the extraordinaries of banishing Scruples, reconciling Contradictions, uniting Opposites, and all the necessary Circumstances required in a complete Casuist.

'Tis not easily conceivable to what extraordinary Flights they have carried this strength of Reasoning, for besides the distinguishing nicely between Truth and Error, they obtain a most refined Method of distinguishing Truth it self into Seasons and Circumstances, and so can bring any thing to be Truth, when it serves the turn that happens just then to be needful, and make the same thing to be false at another time.

And this method of circumstantiating Matters of Fact into Truth or Falsehood, suited to occasion, is found admirably useful to the solving the most difficult Phenomena of State, for by this Art the Solunarian Church made Persecution be against their Principles at one time, and reducible to Practice at another. They made taking up Arms, and calling in Foreign Power to depose their Prince, consistent with Non-Resistance, and Passive Obedience; nay they went farther, they distinguished between a Crolian's taking Arms, and a Solunarians, and fairly proved this to be Rebellion and that to be Non-Resistance.

Nay, and which exceeded all the Power of human Art in the highest degrees of Attainment that ever it arrived to on our side the Moon; they turned the Tables so dexterously, as to argument upon one sort of Crolians, called Prestarians; that tho' they repented of the War they had raised in former Times, and protested against the violence offered their Prince; and after another Party had in spite of them Beheaded him, took Arms against the other Party, and never left contriving their Ruin, till they had brought in his Son, and set him upon the Throne again.

Yet by this most dexterous way of Twisting, Extending, Contracting, and Distinguishing of Phrases and Reasoning, they presently made it as plain as the Sun at Noon Day; that these Prestarians were King-killers, Common-wealths Men, Rebels, Traitors, and Enemies to Monarchy; that they restored the Monarchy only in order to Destroy it, and that they Preached up Sedition, Rebellion and the like: This was proved so plain by these sublime Distinctions, that they convinced themselves and their Posterity of it, by a rare and newly acquired Art, found out by extraordinary Study, which proves the wonderful power of Custom, insomuch, that let any Man by this method, tell a Lye over a certain number of times, he shall arrive to a Satisfaction of its certainty, tho' he knew it to be a Fiction before, and shall freely tell it for a Truth all his life after.

Thus the Prestarians were called the Murderers of the Father, tho' they restored the Son, and all the Testimonials of their Sufferings, Protests and Insurrections to prevent his Death, signified nothing, for this method of Distinguishing has that powerful Charm in it, that all those Trifles we call Proofs and Demonstration were of no use in that Case. Custom brought the Story up to a Truth, and in an instant all the Crolians were hooked in under the general Name of Prestarians, at the same time to hook all Parties in the Crime.

Now as it happened at last that these Solunarian Gentlemen found it necessary to do the same thing themselves, viz. To lay aside their Loyalty, Depose, Fight against, shoot Bullets at, and throw Bombs at their King till they frighted him away, and sent him abroad to beg his Bread. The Crolians began to take Heart and tell them, now they ought to be Friends with them, and tell them no more of Rebellion and Disloyalty; nay, they carried it so far as to challenge them to bring their Loyalty to the Test, and compare Crolian Loyalty and Solunarian Loyalty together, and see who had raised more Wars, taken up Arms oftenest, or appeared in most Rebellions against their Kings; nay, who had killed most Kings, the Crolians or the Solunarians, for there having been then newly fought a great Battle between the Solunarian Church-Men under their new Prince, and the Armies of Foreign Succours under their old King, in which their old King was beaten and forced to fly a second time, the Crolians told them that every Bullet they shot at the Battle was as much a murdering their King, as cutting off the Head with a Hatchet was a killing his Father.

These Arguments in our World would have been unanswerable, but when they came to be brought to the Test of Lunar Reasoning, alas they signified nothing; they distinguished and distinguished till they brought the Prestarian War to be mere Rebellion, King-killing, Bloody and Unnatural; and the Solunarian fighting against their King, and turning him adrift to seek his Fortune, no prejudice at all to their

530

Loyalty, no, nor to the famous Doctrine of Passive Obedience and Absolute Subjection.

When I saw this, I really bewailed the unhappiness of some of our Gentlemen in England, who standing exceedingly in need of such a wonderful Dexterity of Argument to defend their share in our late Revolution, and to reconcile it to their antecedent and subsequent Conduct, should not be furnished from this more accurate World with the suitable Powers, in order the better to defend them against the Banter and just Raillery of their ill-natured Enemies the Whigs.

By this they might have attained suitable reserves of Argument to distinguish themselves out of their Loyalty, and into their Loyalty, as occasion presented to dismiss this Prince, and entertain that, as they found it to their purpose; but above all, they might have learnt a way how to justify Swearing to one King and Praying for another, Eating one Prince's Bread and doing another Prince's Work, Serving one King they don't Love and Loving another they don't Serve; they might easily reconcile the Schisms of the Church, and prove they are still Loyal Subjects to King James, while they are only forced Bonds-Men to the Act of Settlement, for the sake of that comfortable Importance, called Food and Raiment; and thus their Reputation might have been saved, which is most unhappily tarnished and blurred, with the malicious Attacks of the Whigs on one Hand, and the Non-Jurants on the other.

These Tax them as above with Rebellion by their own Principles, and contradicting the Doctrine of Passive Submission and Non-Resistance, by taking up Arms against their Prince, calling in a Foreign Power, and deposing him: They charge them with killing the Lord's Anointed, by Shooting at him at the Boyn, where if he was not killed it was his own fault, at least 'tis plain 'twas none of theirs.

On the other Hand, the Non Jurant Clergy charge them with Schism, declare the whole Church of England Schismatics, and breakers off from the general Union of the Church, in renouncing their Allegiance, and Swearing to another Power, their former Prince being yet alive.

'Tis confessed all the Answers they have been able to make to these things, are very weak and mean, unworthy Men of their Rank and Capacities, and 'tis pity they should not be assisted by some kind Communication of these Lunar Arguments and Distinctions, without which, and till they can obtain which, a Conforming Jacobite must be the absurdest Contradiction in Nature; a thing that admits of no manner of Defence, no, not by the People themselves, and which they

531

would willingly abandon, but that they can find no side to join with them.

The Dissenting Jacobites have some Plea for themselves, for let their Opinion be never so repugnant to their own Interest, or general Vogue, they are faithful to some thing, and they wont join with these People, because they have Perjured their Faith, and yet pretend to adhere to it at the same time. The Conforming Whigs won't receive them, because they pretend to rail at the Government they have Sworn to, and espouse the Interest they have Sworn against; so that these poor Creatures have but one way left them, which is to go along with me, next time I Travel to the Moon, and that will most certainly do their Business, for when they come down again, they will be quite another sort of Men, the Distinctions, the Power of Argument, the way of Reasoning, they will be then furnished with will quite change the Scene of the World with them, they'll certainly be able to prove they are the only People, both in Justice, in Politics and in Prudence; that the extremities of every side are in the Wrong, they'll prove their Loyalty preserved, untainted, thro' all the Swearings, Fightings, Shootings and the like, and no Body will be able to come to the Test with them; so that upon the whole, they are all distracted if they don't go up to the Moon for Illumination, and that they may easily do in the next Consolidator.

But as this is a very long Digression, and for which I am to beg my Reader's Pardon, being an Error I slipped into from my abundant respect to these Gentlemen, and for their particular Instruction, I shall endeavour to make my Reader amends, by keeping more close to my Subject.

To return therefore to the Historical part of the Solunarian Church-Men, in the World in the Moon.

Having as is related Deposed their King, and placed the Crown upon the Head of the Prince that came to their assistance, a new Scene began all over the Kingdom.

I. A terrible and bloody War began thro' all the parts of the Lunar World, where their banished Prince and his new Allie had any Interest; and the new King having a universal Character over all the Northern Kingdoms of the Moon, he brought in a great many Potent Kings, Princes, Emperors and States, to take part with him, and so it became the most general War that had happened in those Ages.

I did not trouble my self to enquire into the particular Successes of this War, but at what had a more particular regard to the Country from whence I came, and for whose Instruction I have designed these Sheets, the Strife of Parties, the Internal Feuds at home, and their Analogy to ours; and whatever is instructively to be deduced from them, was the Subject of immediate Inquiry.

No sooner was this Prince placed on the Throne, but according to his Promises to them that invited him over, he convened the Estates of the Realm, and giving them free Liberty to make, alter, add or repeal, all such Laws as they thought fit, it must be their own fault if they did not Establish themselves upon such Foundation of Liberty, and Right, as they desired; for he gave them their full Swing, never interposed one Negative upon them for several Years, and let them do almost every thing they pleased.

This full Liberty had like to have spoiled all, for as is before noted, this Nation had one unhappy Quality they could never be broke of, always to be falling out one among another.

The Crolians, according to Capitulation, demanded the full Liberty and Toleration of Religion, which the Solunarians had conditioned with them for, when they drew them off from joining with the old King, and when they promised to come to a Temper, and to be Brethren in Peace and Love ever after.

Nor were the Solunarian Church-Men backward, either to remember, or perform the Conditions but by the consent of the King, who had been by agreement made Guarantee of their former Stipulations, an Act was drawn up in full Form, and as complete, as both satisfied the desires of the Crolians, and testified the Honesty and Probity of the Solunarians, as they were abstractedly and moderately considered.

During the whole Reign of this King, this Union of Parties continued without any considerable Interruption, there was indeed brooding Mischiefs which hovered over every accident, in order to generate Strife, but the Candor of the Prince, and the Prudence of his Ministers, kept it under for a long time.

At last an occasion offered it self, which gave an unhappy Stroke to the Nation's Peace. The King thro' innumerable Hazards, terrible Battles and a twelve Years War, had reduced his powerful Adversary to such a necessity of Peace, that he became content to abandon the fugitive King, and to own the Title of this Warlike Prince; and upon these, among various other Conditions, very Honourable for him, and his Allies, and by which vast Conquests were surrendered, and disgorged to the Losers, a Peace was made to the Universal Satisfaction of all those Parts of the Moon that had been involved in a tiresome and expensive War.

This Peace was no sooner made, but the Inhabitants of this unhappy Country, according to the constant Practice of the Place, fell out in the most horrid manner among themselves, and with the very Prince that had done all these great things for them; and I cannot forget how the Old Gentleman I had these Relations from, being once deeply engaged in Discourse with some Senators of that Country, and hearing them reproach the Memory of that Prince from whom they received so much, and on the foot of whose Gallantry and Merit the Constitution then subsisted, it put him into some heat, and he told them to their Faces that they were guilty both of Murder and Ingratitude.

I thought the Charge was very high, but as they returned upon him, and challenged him to make it out, he answered he was ready to do it, and went on thus.

His Majesty, said he, left a quiet, retired, completely happy Condition, full of Honour, beloved of his Country, Valued and Esteemed, as well as Feared by his Enemies, to come over hither at your own Request, to deliver you from the Encroachments and Tyranny as you called it, of your Prince.

Ever since he came hither, he has been your mere Journey-Man, your Servant, your Soldier of Fortune, he has Fought for you, Fatigued and Harassed his Person, and robed himself of all his Peace for you; he has been in a constant Hurry, and run thro' a Million of Hazards for you; he has conversed with Fire and Blood, Storms at Sea, Camps and Trenches ashore, and given himself no rest for twelve Years, and all for your Use, Safety and Repose: In requital of which, he has been always treated with Jealousies, and Suspicions, with Reproaches, and Abuses of all Sorts, and on all Occasions, till the ungrateful Treatment of the Solunarians eat into his very Soul, tired it with serving an unthankful Nation, and absolutely broke his Heart; for which reason I think him as much Murdered as his Predecessor was, whose Head was cut off by his Subjects.

I could not when this was over, but ask the Old Gentlemen, what was the reason of his Exclamation, and how it was the People treated their Prince upon this occasion?

He told me it was a grievous Subject, and a long one, and too long to rehearse, but he would give me a short Abridgment of it; and not to look back into his Wars, in which he was abominably ill served, his subjects constantly ill treated him in giving him Supplies too late, that he cowed not get into the Field, nor forward his Preparations in time to be ready for his Enemies, who frequently were ready to insult him in his Quarters.

By giving him sham Taxes and Funds, that raised little or no Money, by which he having borrowed Money of his People by Anticipation, the Funds not answering, he contracted such vast Debts as the Nation could never Pay which brought the War into disrepute, sunk the Credit of his Exchequer, and filled the Nation with Murmurs and Complaint.

By betraying his Counsel and well laid Designs to his Enemies, selling their Native Country to Foreigners, retarding their Navies and Expeditions, till the Enemies were provided to receive them, betraying their Merchants and Trade, spending vast Sums to fit out Fleets, just time enough to go Abroad, and do nothing, and then get Home again.

But as these were too numerous Evils, and too long to repeat, the particular things he related to in his Discourse, were these that follow.

There had been a hasty Peace concluded with a furious and powerful Enemy, the King foresaw it would be of no continuance, and that the demise of a neighbouring King, who by all appearance could not live long, would certainly embroil them again. —— He saw that Prince keep up numerous Legions of Forces, in order to be in a posture to break the Peace with advantage. This the King fairly represented to them, and told them the necessity of keeping up such a Force, and for such a Time, at least as might be necessary to awe the Enemy from putting any affront upon them in case of the Death of that Prince, which they daily expected.

The Party who had all along maligned the Prosperity of this Prince, took fire at the Offer, and here began another State Plot, which tho' it hooked in two or three sets of Men for different Ends, yet altogether joined in affronting and ill treating their Prince, upon this Article of the Army.

The Nation had been in danger enough from the designs of former Princes invading their Privileges, and putting themselves in a Posture to Tyrannize by the help of standing Forces, and the Party that first took Fire at this Proposal tho' the very same Men who in the time of an Abrogratzian Prince, were for caressing him, and giving him Thanks for his Standing Army, as has been noted before, were the very People that began the outcry against this Demand, and so specious were the Pretences they made, that they drew in the very Crolians themselves upon the pretence of Liberty, and Exemption from Arbitrary Methods of Government to oppose their King.

It grieved this good Prince to be suspected of Tyrannic Designs, and that by a Nation who he had done so much, and ventured so far to save from Tyranny, and Standing Armies; 'twas in vain he represented to them the pressing occasion; in vain he gave them a Description of approaching Dangers, and the threatening posture of the Enemies Armies; in vain he told them of the probabilities of renewing the War, and how keeping but a needful Force might be a means of preventing it; in vain he proposed the subjecting what Force should be necessary to the Absolute Power, both as to Time and Number of their own Cortez or National Assembly.

It was all one, the Design being formed in the Breasts of those who were neither Friends to the Nation, nor the King, those Reasons which would have been of Force in another Case, made them the more eager; bitter Reflections were made on the King, and scurrilous Lampoons published upon the Subject of Tyrants, and Governing by Armies.

Nothing could be more ungrateful to a generous Prince, nor could any thing more deeply affect this King, than whom none ever had a more genuine, single-hearted Design for the Peoples good, but above all, like Caesar in the Case of Brutus, it heartily moved him to find himself pushed at by those very People whom he had all along seen, pretending to adhere to his Interest, and the Public Benefit, which he had always taken care should never be parted, and to find these People join against this Proposal, as a Design against their Liberties, and as a Foundation of Tyranny heartily and sensibly afflicted him.

It was a strange Mystery, and not easily unriddled, that those Men who had always a known aversion to the Interest of the deposed King should fall in with this Party, and those that were Friends to the general Good, never forgave it them.

All that could be said to excuse them, was the Plot I am speaking of, that by carrying this Point for that Party, they hooked in those forward People to join in a popular Cry of Liberty and Property, things they were never fond of before, and to make some Settlement of the Peoples Claims which they always had opposed, and which they would since have been very glad to have repealed.

So great an Ascendant had the Personal Spleen of this Party over their other Principles, that they were content to let the Liberties of the People be declared in their highest Claims, rather than not obtain this one Article, which they knew would so exceedingly mortify their Prince, and strengthen the Nations Enemies. They freely joined in Acts of Succession, Abjuration, Declaration of the Power and Claims of the People, and the Superiority of their Right to the Princes Prerogative, and abundance of such things, which they could never be otherwise brought to.

'Tis true these were great things, but 'twas thought all this might have been obtained in Conjunction with their Prince, rather than by putting Affronts and Mortifications upon the Man that had next to the Influence of Heaven been the only Agent of restoring them to a Power and Capacity of enjoying, as well as procuring, such things as National Privileges.

'Twas vigourously alleged that Standing Armies in times of Peace, were inconsistent with the Public Safety, the Laws and Constitutions of all the Nations in the Moon.

But these Allegations were strenuously answered, that it was true without the consent of the great National Council, it was so, but that being obtained, it was not illegal, and public Necessities might make that consent, not only legal, but convenient.

'Twas all to no purpose, the whole was carried with a Torrent of Clamour and Reflection against the good Prince, who consented, because he would in nothing oppose the Current of the People; but withal, told them plainly what would be the consequences of their Heat, which they have effectually found true since to their Cost, and to the loss of some Millions of Treasure.

For no sooner was this Army broke, which was the best ever that Nation saw, and was justly the Terror of the Enemy, but the great Monarch we mentioned before, broke all Measures with this Prince and the Confederate Nations, a Proof what just apprehensions they had of his Conduct, at the head of such an Army. For they broke with contempt, a Treaty which the Prince upon a prospect of this unkindness of his People had entered into with the Enemy, and which he engaged in, if possible, to prevent a new War, which he foresaw he should be very unfit to begin, or carry on, and which they would never have dared to break had not this Feud happened.

It was but a little before I came into this Country, when such repeated Accounts came, of the Encroachments, Insults and Preparations of their great powerful Neighbour, that all the World saw the necessity of a War, and the very People who were to feel it most applied to the Prince to begin it.

He was forward enough to begin it, and in compliance with his People, resolved on it; but the Grief of the usage he had received, the unkind Treatment he had met with from those very People that brought him thither, had sunk so deep upon his Spirits, that he could never recover it; but being very weak in Body and Mind, and joined to a slight hurt he received by a fall from his Horse, he died, to the unspeakable grief of all his Subjects that wished well to their Native Country.

This was the melancholy Account of this great Prince's end, and I have been told that at once every Year, there is a kind of Fast, or solemn Commemoration kept up for the Murder of that former Prince, who, as I noted, was Beheaded by his Subjects; So it seems some of the People, who are of Opinion this Prince was Murdered by the ill Treatment of his Friends, a way which I must own, is the cruelest of Deaths, keep the same Day, to commemorate his Death, and this is a Day, in which it seems both Parties are very free with one another, as to Raillery and ill Language.

But the Friends of this last Prince have a double advantage, for they also commemorate the Birth Day of this Prince, and are generally very merry on that Day; and the custom is at their Feast on that Day, just like our drinking Healths, they pledge one another to the immortal Memory of their Deliverer; as the Historical part of this Matter was absolutely necessary to introduce the following Remarks, and to instruct the Ignorant in those things, I hope it shall not be thought a barren Digression, especially when I shall tell you that it is a most exact Representation of what is yet to come in a Scene of Affairs, of which I must make a short Abstract, by way of Introduction.

The deceased Prince we have heard of, was succeeded by his Sister in-Law, the second Daughter of the banished Prince, a Lady of an extraordinary Character, of the Old Race of their Kings, a Native by Birth, a Solunarian by Profession; exceeding Pious, Just and Good, of an Honesty peculiar to her self, and for which she was justly beloved of all sorts and degrees of her Subjects.

This Princess having the Experience of her Father and Grandfather before her, joined to her own Prudence and Honesty of Design; it was no wonder if she prudently shunned all manner of rash Counsels, and endeavoured to carry it with a steady Hand between her contending Parties.

At her first coming to the Crown, she made a solemn Declaration of her resolutions for Peace and just Government; she gave the Crolians her Royal Word, that she would inviolably preserve the Toleration of their Religion and Worship, and always afford them her Protection, and by this she hoped they would be easy.

But to the Solunarians, as those among whom she had been Educated, and whose Religion she had always professed, been trained up in, and Piously pursued; she expressed her self with an uncommon Tenderness, told them they should be the Men of her Favour, and those that were most zealous for that Church should have most of her Countenance; and she backed this soon after with an unparalleled Act of Royal Bounty to them, freely parting with a considerable Branch of her Royal Revenue, for the poor Priests of that Religion, of which there were many in the remote Parts of her Kingdom.

What vast Consequences, and prodigiously differing from the Design, may Words have when mistaken and misapplied by the Hearers. Never were significant Expressions spoken from a sincere, honest and generous Principle, with a single Design to engage all the Subjects in the Moon, to Peace and Union, so perverted, misapplied and turned by a Party, to a meaning directly contrary to the Royal Thoughts of the Queen: For from this very Expression, most Zealous, grew all the Divisions and Subdivisions in the Solunarian Church, to the Ruin of their own Cause, and the vast advantage of the Crolian Interest. The eager Men of the Church, especially those we have been talking of, hastily catched at this Expression of the Queen, Most Zealous, and Millions of fatal Constructions, and unhappy Consequences they made of it, some of which are as follows.

I. They took it to imply that the Queen whatever she had said to the Crolians, really designed their Destruction, and that those that were of that Opinion, must be meant by the Most Zealous Members of the Solunarian Church, and they could understand Zeal no otherwise than their own way.

2. From this Speech, and their mistaking the Words Most Zealous, arose an unhappy Distinction among the Solunarians themselves, some Zealous, some More Zealous, which afterwards divided them into two most opposite Parties, being fomented by an accident of a Book published on an Occasion, of which presently.

The Consequences of this mistake, appeared presently in the Most Zealous, in their offering all possible Insults to the Crolian Dissenters, Preaching them down, Printing them down, and Talking them down, as a People not fit to be suffered in the Nation, and now they thought they had the Game sure.

Down with the Crolians began to be all the Cry, and truly the Crolians themselves began to be uneasy, and had nothing to rely upon but the Queens Promise, which however her Majesty always made good to them.

The other Party proceeded so far, that they begun to Insult the very Queen her self, upon the Matter of her Word, and one of her College-Priests told her plainly in Print, she could not be a true Friend to the Solunarian Church, if she did not declare War against, and root out all the Crolians in her Dominions.

But these Proceedings met with a Check, by a very odd accident: A certain Author of those Countries, a very mean, obscure and despicable Fellow, of no great share of Wit, but that had a very unlucky way of telling his Story, seeing which way things were a going, writes a Book, and Personating this high Solunarian Zeal, musters up all their Arguments, as if they were his own, and strenuously pretends to prove that all the Crolians ought to be Destroyed, Hanged, Banished, and the D — — l and all. As this Book was a perfect Surprise to all the Country, so the Proceedings about it on all sides were as extraordinary.

The Crolians themselves were surprised at it, and so closely had the Author couched his Design, that they never saw the irony of the Stile, but began to look about them, to see which way they should fly to save themselves.

The Men of Zeal we talked of, were so blinded with the Notion which suited so exactly with their real Design, that they hugged the Book, applauded the unknown Author, and placed the Book next their Oracular Writings, or Laws of Religion.

The Author was all this while concealed, and the Paper had all the effect he wished for.

For as it caused these first Gentlemen to caress, applaud and approve it, and thereby discovered their real Intention, so it met with Abhorrence and Detestation in all the Men of Principles, Prudence and Moderation in the Kingdom, who tho' they were Solunarians in Religion, yet were not for Blood, Desolation and Persecution of their Brethren, but with the Queen were willing they should enjoy their Liberties and Estates, they behaving themselves quietly and peaceably to the Government.

At last it came out that it was writ by a Crolian; but good God! what a Clamour was raised at the poor Man, the Crolians flew at him like Lightning, ignorantly and blindly, not seeing that he had sacrificed himself and his Fortunes in their behalf; they rummaged his Character for Reproaches, tho' they could find little that way to hurt him; they plentifully loaded him with ill Language and Railing, and took a great deal of pains to let the World see their own Ignorance and Ingratitude.

The Ministers of State, tho' at that time of the fiery Party, yet seeing the general Detestation of such a Proposal, and how ill it would go down with the Nation, tho' they approved the thing, yet began to scent the Design, and were also obliged to declare against it, for fear of being thought of the same Mind.

Thus the Author was Proscribed by Proclamation, and a Reward of 50000 Hecato's, a small imaginary Coin in those Parts, put upon his Head.

The Cortez of the Nation being at the same time assembled joined in Censuring the Book, and thus the Party blindly damned their own Principles for mere shame of the practice, not daring to own the thing in public which they had underhand professed, and the fury of all Parties fell upon the poor Author.

The Man fled the first popular Fury, but at last being betrayed fell into the Hands of the public Ministry.

When they had him they hardly knew what to do with him; they could not proceed against him as Author of a Proposal for the Destruction of the Crolians because it appeared he was a Crolian himself; they were loth to charge him with suggesting that the Solunarian Church-men were guilty of such a Design, least he should bring their own Writings to prove it true; so they fell to wheedling him with good Words to throw himself into their Hands and submit, giving him that Geu-gau the Public Faith for a Civil and Gentleman-like Treatment; the Man, believing like a Coxcomb that they spoke as they meant, quitted his own Defence, and threw himself on the Mercy of the Queen as he thought; but they abusing their Queen with false Representations, Perjured all their Promises with him, and treated him in a most barbarous manner, on pretence that there were no such Promises made, tho' he proved it upon them by the Oath of the Persons to whom they were made.

Thus they laid him under a heavy Sentence, Fined him more than they thought him able to pay, and ordered him to be exposed to the Mob in the Streets.

Having him at this Advantage they set upon him with their Emissaries to discover to them his Adherents, as they called them, and promised him great Things on one Hand, threatening him with his utter Ruin on the other; and the Great Scribe of the Country, with another of their great Courtiers, took such a low Step as to go to him to the Dungeon where they had put him, to see if they could tempt him to betray his Friends. The Comical Dialogue between them there the Author of this has seen in Manuscript, exceeding diverting, but having not time to Translate it 'tis omitted for the present; tho' he promises to publish it in its proper Season for public Instruction.

However for the present it may suffice to tell the World, that neither by promises of Reward or fear of Punishment they could prevail upon him to discover any thing, and so it remains a Secret to this day.

The Title of this unhappy Book was The shortest way with the Crolians. The Effects of it were various, as will be seen in our ensuing Discourse: As to the Author nothing was more unaccountable than the Circumstances of his Treatment; for he met with all that Fate which they must expect who attempt to open the Eyes of a Nation willfully blind.

The hot Men of the Solunarian Church damned him without Bell, Book, or Candle; the more Moderate pitied him, but looked on as unconcerned: But the Crolians, for whom he had run this Venture, used him worst of all; for they not only abandoned him, but reproached him as an Enemy that would ha' them destroyed: So one side railed at him because they did understand him, and the other because they did not.

Thus the Man sunk under the general Neglect, was ruined and undone, and left a Monument of what every Man must expect that serves a good Cause, professed by an unthankful People.

And here it was I found out that my Lunar Philosopher was only so in Disguise, and that he was no Philosopher, but the very Man I have been talking of.

From this Book, and the Treatment its Author received, for they used him with all possible Rigour, a new Scene of Parties came upon the Stage, and this Queen's Reign began to be filled with more Divisions and Feuds than any before her.

These Parties began to be so numerous and violent that it endangered the Public Good, and gave great Disadvantages to the general Affairs abroad.

The Queen invited them all to Peace and Union, but 'twas in vain; nay, one had the Impudence to publish that to procure Peace and Union it was necessary to suppress all the Crolians, and have no Party but one, and then all must be of a Mind.

From this heat of Parties all the moderate Men fell in with their Queen, and were heartily for Peace and Union: The other, who were now distinguished by the Title of High Solunarians, called these all Crolians and Low Solunarians, and began to Treat them with more Inveteracy than they used to do the Crolians themselves, calling them Traitors to their Country, Betrayers of their Mother, Serpents harboured in the Bosom, who bite, sting and hiss at the Hand that succoured them; and in short the Enmity grew so violent, that from hence proceeded one of the subtlest, foolishest, deep, shallow Contrivances and Plots that ever was hatched or set on foot by any Party of Men in the whole Moon, at least who pretended to any Brains, or to half a degree of common Understanding.

There had always been Dislikes and Distastes between even the most moderate Solunarians and the Crolians, as I have noted in the beginning of this Relation, and these were derived from Dissenting in Opinions of Religion, ancient Feuds, private Interest, Education, and the like; and the Solunarians had frequently, on pretence of securing the Government, made Laws to exclude the Crolians from any part of the Administration, unless they submitted to some Religious Tests and Ceremonies which were prescribed them.

Now as the keeping them out of Offices was more the Design than the Conversion of the Crolians to the Solunarian Church, the Crolians, at least many of them, submitted to the Test, and frequently Conformed to qualify themselves for public Employments.

The most moderate of the Solunarians were in their Opinion against this practice, and the High Men taking advantage of them, drew them in to Concur in making a Law with yet more Severity against them, effectually to keep them out of Employment.

The low Solunarians were easy to be drawn into this Project, as it was only a Confirming former Laws of their own making, and all Things run fair for the Design; but as the High Men had further Ends in it than barely reducing the Crolians to Conformity, they couched so many gross Clauses into their Law, that even the Grandees of the Solunarians themselves could not comply with; nay even the Patriarchs of the Solunarian Church declared against it, as tending to Persecution and Confusion.

This Disappointment enraged the Party, and that very Rage entirely ruined their Project; for now the Nobility, the Patriarchs, and all the wise Men of the Nation, joining together against these Men of Heat and Fury, the Queen began to see into their Designs, and as she was of a most pious and peaceable Temper, she conceived a just Hatred of so wicked and barbarous a Design, and immediately dismissed from her Council and Favour the Great Scribe, and several others who were Leaders in the Design, to the great mortification of the whole Party, and utter Ruin of the intended Law against the Crolians.

Here I could not but observe, as I have done before in the Case of the banished King, how impolitic these high Solunarian Church-men acted in all their Proceedings, for had they contented themselves by little and little to ha' done their Work, they had done it effectually; but pushing at Extremities they overshot themselves, and ruined all.

For the Grandees and Patriarchs made but a few trifling Objections at first, nay and came off, and yielded some of them too; and if these would ha' consented to ha' parted with some Clauses which they have willingly left out since, they had had it passed; but these were as hot Men always are, too eager and sure of their Game, they thought all was their own, and so they lost themselves.

If they railed at the low Solunarian Church-men before, they doubled their Clamors at them now, all the Patriarchs, and all the Nobility and Grandees, nay even the Queen her self came under their Censure, and every Body who was not of their Mind were Prestarians and Crolians.

As this Rage of theirs was implacable, so, as I hinted before, it drove them into another Subdivision of Parties, and now began the Mysterious Plot to be laid which I mentioned before; for the Cortez being summoned, and the Law being proposed, some of these high Solunarians appeared in Confederacy with the Crolians, in perfect Confederacy with them, a thing no Body would have imagined could ever ha' been brought to pass.

Now as these sorts of Plots must always be carried very nicely, so these high Gentlemen who Confederated with the Crolians, having, to spite the other, resolved effectually to prevent the passing the Law against the Qualification of the Crolians, it was not their Business immediately to declare themselves against it as a Law, but by still loading it with some Extravagance or other, and pushing it on to some intolerable Extreme, secure its miscarriage.

In the managing this Plot, one of their Authors was specially employed, and that all that was really true of the Crolian Dissenters might be ridiculed, his Work was to draw monstrous Pictures of them, which no Body could believe; this took immediately, for now People began to look at their Shoes to see if they were not Cloven Footed as they went a long Streets; and at last finding they were really shaped like the rest of the Lunar Inhabitants, they went back to the Author, who was a Learned Member of a certain Seminary, or Brother-hood of the Solunarian Clergy, and enquired if he were not Mad, Distracted and Raving, or Moon-blind, and in want of the thinking Engine; but finding all things right there, and that he was in his Senses, especially in a Morning when he was a little free from, &c. that he was a Good, Honest, Jolly, Solunarian Priest, and no room could be found for an Objection there. Upon all these Searches it presently appeared, and all Men concluded it was a mere Fanatic Crolian Plot; that this High Party of all were but Pretenders, and mere Traitors to the True High Solunarian Church-Men, that wearing the same Cloth had herded among them in Disguise, only to wheedle them into such wild Extravagancies as must of necessity confuse their Councils, expose their Persons, and ruin their Cause. — — According to the like Practice, put upon their Abrograzian Prince, and of which I have spoken before.

And since I am upon the detection of this most refined Practice, I crave leave to descend to some particular Instances, which will the better evince the Truth of this Matter, and make it appear that either this was really a Crolian Plot, or else all these People were perfectly Distracted; and as their Wits in that Lunar World, are much higher strained than ours, so their Lunacy, where it happens, must according to the Rules of Mathematical Nature, bear an extreme Equal in proportion.

This College Fury of a Man was the first on whom this useful Discovery was made, and having writ several Learned Tracts wherein he invited the People to Murder and Destroy all the Crolians, Branded all the Solunarian Patriarchs, Clergy and Gentry that would not come into his Proposal, with the name of Cowards, Traitors and Betrayers of Lunar Religion; having beat the Concionazimir at a great Assembly of the Cadirs, or Judges, and told them all the Crolians were Devils, and they were all Perjured that did not use them as such: He carried on Matters so dexterously, and with such surprising Success, that he filled even the Solunarians themselves with Horror at his Proposals. — — And as I happened to be in one of their public Halls where all such Writings as are new are laid a certain time to be read by every Comer, I saw a little knot of Men round a Table, where one was reading this Book.

There were two Solunarian High Priests in their proper Vestments, one Privy Counselor of the State, one other Noble Man, and one who had in his Hat a Token, to signify that he possessed one of the fine Feathers of the Consolidator, of which I have given the Description already.

The Book being read by one of the habited Priests, he starts up with some warmth, by the Moon, says he, I have found this Fellow out, he is certainly a Crolian, a mere Prestarian Crolian, and is crept into our Church only in Disguise, for 'tis certain all this is but mere Banter and Irony to expose us, and to ridicule the Solunarian Interest.

The Privy Counselor took it presently, whether he is a Crolian or no, says he, I cannot tell, but he has certainly done the Crolians so much Service, that if they had hired him to act for them, they could not have desired he should serve them better.

Truly, says the Man of the Feather, I was always for pulling down the Crolians, for I thought them dangerous to the State; but this Man has brought the Matter nearer to my View, and shown me what destroying them is, for he put me upon examining the Consequences, and now I find it would be lopping off the Limbs of the Government, and laying it at the Mercy of the Enemy that they might lop off its Head; I assure you he has done the Crolians great Service, for whereas abundance of our Men of the Feather were for routing the Crolians, they lately fell down to 134 or thereabouts.

All this confirmed the first Man's Opinion that he was a Crolian in Disguise, or an Emissary employed by them to ruin the Project of their Enemies; for these Crolians are damned cunning People in their way, and they have Money enough to engage Hirelings to their side.

Another Party concerned in this Plot was an old cast-out Solunarian Priest, who, tho' professing himself a Solunarian, was turned out for adhering to the Abrograzian King, a mighty Stickler for the Doctrine of absolute Subjection.

This Man draws the most monstrous Picture of a Crolian that could be invented, he put him in a Wolf's Skin with long Asses Ears, and hung him all over full of Associations, Massacres, Persecutions, Rebellions, and Blood. Here the People began to stare again, and a Crolian cowed not go along the Street but they were always looking for the long Ears, the Wolf's Claws, and the like; 'till at last nothing of these Things appearing, but the Crolians looking and acting like other Folks, they begun to examine the Matter, and found this was a mere Crolian Plot too, and this Man was hired to run these extravagant lengths to point out the right meaning.

The Discovery being made, People ever since understand him that when he talks of the Dissenters Associations, Murders, Persecutions, and the like, he means that his Readers should look back to the Murders, Oppressions and Persecutions they had suffered for several past years, and the Associations that were now forming to bring them into the same Condition again.

From this famous Author I could not but proceed to observe the farther Progress of this most refined piece of Cunning, among the very great Ones, Grandees, Feathers, and Consolidators of the Country. For these Cunning Crolians managed their Intrigues so nicely, that they brought about a Famous Division even among the High Solunarian Party themselves; and whereas the Law of Qualification was revived again, and in great Danger of being completed; these subtle Crolians brought over One Hundred and Thirty Four of the Feathers in the Famous Consolidator to be of their side, and to Contrive the utter Destruction of it; and thus fell the Design which the High Solunarian Church Men had laid for the Ruin of the Crolians Interest, by their own Friends first joining in all the Extremes they had proposed, and then pushing it so much farther, and to such mad Periods that the very highest of them stood amazed at the Design, startled, flew back and made a full stop; they were willing to Ruin the Crolians, but they were not willing to Ruin the whole Nation. The more these Men began to consider, the more furiously these Plotters carried on their Extravagances; at last they made a General push at a thing in which they knew if the other High Men joined, they must throw all into Confusion, bring a Foreign Enemy on their Backs, unravel all the Thread of the War, fight all their Victories back again, and involve the whole Nation in Blood and Confusion.

They knew well enough that most of the High Men would hesitate at this, they knew if they did not the Grandees and Patriarchs would reject it, and so they plaid the surest Game to blast and overthrow this Law, that could possibly be plaid.

If any Man, in the whole World in the Moon, will pretend this was not a Plot, a Crolian Design, a mere Conspiracy to destroy the Law, let him tell me for what other end could these Men offer such extremes as they needs must know would meet with immediate opposition, things that they knew all the Honest Men, all the Grandees, all the Patriarchs, and almost all the Feathers would oppose.

From hence all the Men of any fore-sight brought it to this pass, as is before Noted, that either these One Hundred and Thirty Four were Fools or Mad-Men, or that it was a Fanatic Crolian Plot and

Conspiracy to Ruin the making this Law, which the rest of the Solunarian Church Men were very forward to carry on.

I heard indeed some Men Argue that this could not be, the breach was too wide between the Crolians and these Gentlemen ever to come to such an Agreement; but the Wiser Heads who argued the other way, always brought them, as is noted above, to this pinch of Argument; that either it must be so, be a Fanatic Crolian Plot, or else the Men of Fury were all Fools, Madmen, and fitter for an Hospital, than a State-House, or a Pulpit.

It must be allowed, these Crolians were Cunning People, thus to wheedle in these High Flying Solunarians to break the Neck of their dear Project.

But upon the whole, for ought I cowed see, whether it went one way or t'other, all the Nation esteemed the other People Fools — — — Fools of the most extraordinary Size in all the Moon, for either way they pulled down what they had been many Years a Building.

I cannot say that this was in kindness to the Crolians, but in mere Malice to the Low Solunarian Party, who had the Government in their Hands, for Malice always carries Men on to monstrous Extremes.

Some indeed have thought it hard to call this a Plot, and a Confederacy with the Crolians. — — — But I cannot but think it the kindest thing that can be said of them, and that 'tis impossible those People who pushed at some imaginary Things in that Law could but be in a Plot as aforesaid, or be perfectly Lunatic, down right Mad-Men, or Traitors to their Country, and let them choose which Character they like.

I cannot in Charity but spare them their Honesty, and their Senses, and attribute it all to their Policy.

When I had understood all things at large, and found the exceeding depth of the Design; I must confess the Discovery of these things was very diverting, and the more so, when I made the proper Reflections upon the Analogy there seemed to be between these Solunarian High Church-Men in the Moon, and ours here in England; our High Church-Men are no more to compare to these, than the Hundred and Thirty Four, are to the Consolidators.

Ours can Plot now and then a little among themselves, but then 'tis all Gross and plain Sailing, down right taking Arms, calling in Foreign Forces, Assassinations and the like; but these are nothing to the more Exquisite Heads in the Moon. For they have the subtlest Ways with them, that ever were heard of. They can make War with a Prince, on purpose to bring him to the Crown; fit out vast Navies against him, that he may have the more leisure to take their Merchant Men; make Descents upon him, on purpose to come Home and do nothing; if they have a mind to a Sea Fight, they carefully send out Admirals that care not to come within half a Mile of the Enemy, that coming off safe they may have the boasting Part of the Victory, and the beaten Part both together.

'Twould be endless to call over the Roll of their sublime Politics. They damn Moderation in order to Peace and Union, set the House on Fire to save it from Desolation, Plunder to avoid Persecution, and consolidate Things in order to their more immediate Dissolution.

Had our High Church-Men been Masters of these excellent Arts, they had long ago brought their Designs to pass.

The exquisite Plot of these High Solunarians answered the Crolians End, for it broke all their Enemies Measures, the Law vanished, the Grandees could hardly be persuaded to read it, and when it was proposed to be read again, they hissed at it, and threw it by with Contempt.

Nor was this all; for it not only lost them their Design as to this Law, but it also absolutely broke the Party, and just as it was with Adam and Eve, as soon as they Sinned they Quarreled, and fell out with one another; so, as soon as things came to this height, the Party fell out one among another, and even the High Men themselves were divided, some were for Consolidating, and some not for Consolidating, some were for Tacking, and some not for Tacking, as they were, or were not let into the Secret.

If this Confusion of Languages, or Interest, lost them the real Design, it cannot be a wonder; have we not always seen it in our World, that dividing an Interest, weakens and exposes it? Has not a great many both good and bad Designs been rendered Abortive in this our Lower World, for want of the Harmony of Parties, and the Unanimity of those concerned in the Design?

How had the knot of Rebellion been dissolved in England, if it had not been untied by the very Hands of those that knit it? All the contrary Force had been entirely broken and subdued, and the Restoration of Monarchy had never happened in England, if Union and Agreement had been found among the managers of that Age.

The Enemies of the present Establishment have shown sufficiently that they perfectly understand the shortest way to our infallible

Destruction, when they bend their principle Force at dividing us into Parties, and keeping those parties at the utmost variance.

But this is not all, the Author of this cannot but observe here that as England is unhappily divided among Parties, so it has this one Felicity even to be found in the very matter of her Misfortunes, that those Parties are all again subdivided among themselves.

How easily might the Church have crushed and subdued the Dissenters if they had been all as mad as one Party, if they had not been some High and some Low Church-men. And what Mischief might not that one Party ha' done in this Nation, had not they been divided again into Jurant Jacobites and Non-Jurant, into Consolidators and Non-Consolidators? From whence 'tis plain to me, that just as it is in the Moon these Consolidating Church-men are mere Confederates with the Whigs; and it must be so, unless we should suppose them mere mad Men that don't know what they are a doing, and who are the Drudges of their Enemies, and kno' nothing of the Matter.

And from this Lunar Observation it presently occurred to my Understanding, that my Masters the Dissenters may come in for a share among the Moon-blind Men of this Generation, since had they done for their own Interest what the Laws fairly admits to be done, had they been united among themselves, had they formed themselves into a Politic Body to have acted in a public, united Capacity by general Concert, and as Persons that had but one Interest and understood it, they had never been so often Insulted by every rising Party, they had never had so many Machines and Intrigues to ruin and suppress them, they had never been so often Tacked and Consolidated to Oppression and Persecution, and yet never have rebelled or broke the Peace, incurred the Displeasure of their Princes, or have been upbraided with Plots, Insurrections and Antimonarchical Principles; when they had made Treaties and Capitulations with the Church for Temper and Toleration, the Articles would have been kept, and these would have demanded Justice with an Authority that would upon all Occasions be respected.

Were they united in Civil Polity in Trade and Interest, would they Buy and Sell with one another, abstract their Stocks, erect Banks and Companies in Trade of their own, lend their Cash to the Government in a Body, and as a Body.

If I were to tell them what Advantages the Crolians in the Moon make of this sort of management, how the Government finds it their Interest to treat them civilly, and use them like Subjects of

Consideration; how upon all Occasions some of the Grandees and Nobility appear as Protectors of the Crolians, and treat with their Princes in their Names, present their Petitions, and make Demands from the Prince of such Loans and Sums of Money as the public Occasions require; and what abundance of Advantages are reaped from such a Union, both to their own Body as a Party, and to the Government also they would be convinced; wherefore I cannot but very earnestly desire of the Dissenters and Whigs in my own Country that they would take a Journey in my Consolidator up to the Moon, they would certainly see there what vast Advantages they lose for want of a Spirit of Union, and a concert of Measures among themselves.

The Crolians in the Moon are Men of large Souls, and Generously stand by one another on all Occasions; it was never known that they deserted any Body that suffered for them, my Old Philosopher excepted, and that was a surprise upon them.

The Reason of the Difference is plain, our Dissenters here have not the Advantage of a Cogitator, or thinking Engine, as they have in the Moon. — — We have the Elevator here and are lifted up pretty much, but in the Moon they always go into the Thinking Engine upon every Emergency, and in this they out-do us of this World on every Occasion.

In general therefore I must note that the wisest Men I found in the Moon, when they understood the Notes I had made as above, of the sub-divisions of our Parties, told me that it was the greatest Happiness that could ha' been obtained to our Country, for that if our Parties had not been thus divided, the Nation had been undone. They owned that had not their Solunarian Party been divided among themselves, the Crolians had been undone, and all the Moon had been involved in Persecution, and been very probably subjected to the Gallunarian Monarch.

Thus the fatal Errors of Men have their advantages, the separate ends they serve are not foreseen by their Authors and they do good against the very Design of the People, and the nature of the Evil it self.

And now that I may encourage our People to that Peace and good Understanding among themselves, which can alone produce their Safety and Deliverance; I shall give a brief Account how the Crolians in the Moon came to open their Eyes to their own Interest, how they came to Unite; and how the Fruits of that Union secured them from ever being insulted again by the Solunarian Party, who in time gave over the vain and fruitless Attempt, and so a universal Lunar Calm has spread the whole Moon ever since.

If our People will not listen to their own Advantages, nor do their own Business, let them take the consequences to themselves, they cannot blame the Man in the Moon.

To endeavour to bring this to pass, as these Memoirs have run thro' the general History of the Feuds and unhappy Breaches between the Solunarian Church and the Crolian Dissenters in the World of the Moon, it would seem an imperfect and abrupt Relation, if I should not tell you how, and by what Method, tho' long hid from their Eyes, the Crolians came to understand their own Interest and know their own Strength.

'Tis true, it seemed a Wonder to me when I considered the Excellence and Variety of those perspective Glasses I have mentioned, the clearness of the Air, and consequently of the Head, in this Lunar World. I say it was very strange the Crolians should ha' been Moon Blind so long as they were, that they could not see it was always in their Power if they had but pursued their own Interest, and made use of those, legal Opportunities which lay before them, to put themselves in a Posture, as that the Government it self should think them a Body too big to be insulted, and find it their Interest to keep Measures with them.

It was indeed a long time before they opened their Eyes to these advantages, but bore the Insults of the hair-brained Party, with a weakness and negligence that was as unjustifiable in them, as unaccountable to all the Nations of the Moon.

But at last, as all violent Extremes rouse their contrary Extremities, the folly and extravagance of the High Solunarians drove the Crolians into their Senses, and roused them to their own Interest, the occasion was among a great many others as follows.

The eager Solunarian could not on all occasions forbear to show their deep Regret at the Dissenting Crolians enjoying the Toleration of their Religion, by a Law — .

And when all their legal Attempts to lessen that Liberty had proved Abortive, her Solunarian Majesty on all Occasions repeating her assurances of the continuance of her Protection, and particularly the maintaining this Toleration Inviolable. They proceeded then to show the remains of their Malice, in little Insults, mean and illegal Methods, and continual private Disturbances upon particular Persons, in which, however the Crolians having recourse to the Law, always found Justice on their side, and had redress with Advantage, of which the following Instance is more than ordinarily Remarkable.

There had been a Law made by the Men of the Feather, that all the meaner Idle sort of People, who had no settled way of living should go to the Wars, and the Lazognians, a sort of Magistrates there, in the nature of our Justices of the Peace, were to send them away by Force.

Now it happened in a certain Solunarian Island, that for want of a better, one of their High Priests was put into the Civil Administration, and made a Lazognian. — — In the Neighbourhood of this Man's Jurisdiction, one of their own Solunarian Priests had turned Crolian, and whether he had a better Talent at performance, or rather was more diligent in his Office is not material, but he set up a kind of a Crolian Temple in an old Barn, or some such Mechanic Building, and all the People flocked after him.

This so provoked his Neighbours of the black Girdle, an Order of Priests, of which he had been one, that they resolved to suppress him let it cost what it would.

They run strange lengths to bring this to pass.

They forged strange Stories of him, defamed him, run him into Jail upon frivolous and groundless Occasions, represented him as a Monster of a Man, told their Story so plain, and made it so specious, that even the Crolians themselves to their Shame, believed it, and took up Prejudices against the Poor Man, which had like to ha' been his Ruin.

They proscribed him in Print for Crimes they could never prove, they branded him with Forgery, Adultery, Drunkenness, Swearing, breaking Jail, and abundance of Crimes; but when Matters were examined and things came to the Test, they could never prove the least thing upon him. — — In this manner however they continually worried the poor Man, till they ruined his Family and reduced him to Beggary; and tho' he came out of the Prison they cast him into by the mere force of Innocence, yet they never left pursuing him with all sorts of violence. — — — At last they made use of their Brother of the Girdle who was in Commission as above, and this Man being High Priest and Lazonian too, by the first was a Party, and by the last had a Power to act the Tragedy they had plotted against the poor Man.

In short, they seized him without any Crime alleged, took violently from him his Licence, as a Crolian Priest, by which the Law justified what he had done, pretending it was forged, and after very ill

Treating him, condemned him to the Wars, delivers him up for a Soldier, and accordingly carried him away.

But it happened, to their great Mortification, that this Man found more Mercy from the Men of the Sword, than from those of the Word, and so found means to get out of their Hands, and afterwards to undeceive all the Moon, both as to his own Character, and as to what he had Suffered.

For some of the Crolians, who began to be made sensible of the Injury done the poor Man, advised him to have recourse to the Law, and to bring his Adversaries before the Criminal Bar.

But as soon as this was done, good God! what a Scene of Villainy was here opened: The poor Man brought up such a Cloud of Witnesses to confront every Article of their Charge, and to vindicate his own Character, that when the very Judges heard it, tho' they were all Solunarians themselves, they held up their Hands, and declared in open Court it was the deepest Track of Villainy that ever came before them, and that the Actors ought to be made Examples to all the Moon.

The Persons concerned, used all possible Arts to avoid, or at least to delay the Shame, and adjourn the Punishment, thinking still to weary the poor Man out. — — — But now his Brethren the Crolians began to see themselves wounded thro' his Sides, and above all, finding his Innocence cleared up beyond all manner of dispute, they espoused his Cause, and assisted him to prosecute his Enemies, which he did, till he brought them all to Justice, exposed them to the last Degree, obtained the reparation of all his Losses, and a public Decree of the Judges of his Justification and future Repose.

Indeed when I saw the Proceedings against this poor Man run to a height so extravagant and monstrous, when I found Malice, Forgery, Subornation, Perjury, and a thousand unjustifiable Things which their own Sense, if they had any, might ha' been their Protection against, and which any Child in the Moon might ha' told them must one time or other come upon the Stage and expose them; I began to think these People were all in the Crolian Plot too.

For really such Proceedings as these were the greatest pieces of Service to the Crolians as could possibly be done; for as it generally proves in other Places as well as in the Moon, that Mischief unjustly contrived falls upon the Head of the Authors, and redounds to their treble Dishonour, so it was here; the barbarity and inhumane Treatment of this Man, made the sober and honest Part even of the Solanarians themselves blush for their Brethren, and own that the Punishment awarded on them was just.

Thus the Crolians got ground by the Folly and Madness of their Enemies, and the very Engines and Plots laid to injure them, served to bring their Enemies on the Stage, and expose both them and their Cause.

But this was not all, by these incessant Attacks on them as a Party, they began to come to their Senses out of a 50 Year slumber, they found the Law on their side, and the Government Moderate and Just; they found they might oppose Violence with Law, and that when they did fly to the Refuge of Justice, they always had the better of their Enemy; flushed with this Success, it put them upon considering what Fools they had been all along to bear the Insolence of a few hot-headed Men, who contrary to the true Intent and Meaning of the Queen, or of the Government, had resolved their Destruction.

It put them upon revolving the State of their own Case, and comparing it with their Enemies; upon Examining on what foot they stood, and tho' Established upon a firm Law, yet a violent Party pushing at the overthrow of that Establishment, and dissolving the legal Right they had to their Liberty and Religion; it put them upon duly weighing the nearness of their approaching Ruin and Destruction, and finding things run so hard against them, reflecting upon the Extremity of their Affairs, and how if they had not drawn in the High Church-Champions to damn the Projects of their own Party, by running at such desperate Extremes as all Men of any Temper must of course abhor, they had been undone; truly now they began to consider, and to consult with one another what was to be done.

Abundance of Projects were laid before them, some too Dangerous, some too Foolish to be put in practice; at last they resolved to consult with my Philosopher.

He had been but scurvily treated by them in his Troubles, and so Universally abandoned by the Crolians, that even the Solunarians themselves insulted them on that Head, and laughed at them for expecting any Body should venture for them again. — — But he forgetting their unkindness, asked them what it was they desired of him?

They told him, they had heard that he had reported he could put the Crolians in a way to secure themselves from any possibility of being insulted again by the Solunarians, and yet not disturb the public Tranquility, nor break the Laws; and they desired him, if he knew such a Secret, he would communicate it to them, and they would be sure to remember to forget him for it as long as he lived.

He frankly told them he had said so, and it was true, he could put them in a way to do all this if they would follow his Directions. What's that, says one of the most earnest Enquirers? —— 'Tis included in one Word, says he, UNITE.

This most significant Word, deeply and solidly reflected upon, put them upon strange and various Conjectures, and many long Debates they had with themselves about it; at last they came again to him, and asked him what he meant by it?

He told them he knew they were Strangers to the meaning of the thing, and therefore if they would meet him the next Day he would come prepared to explain himself; accordingly they meet, when instead of a long Speech they expected from him what sort of Union he meant, and with who, he brings them a Thinking Press, or Cogitator, and setting it down, goes away without speaking one Word.

This Hyeroglphical Admonition was too plain not to let them all into his meaning; but still as they are an obstinate People, and not a little valuing themselves upon their own Knowledge and Penetration, they slighted the Engine and fell to off-hand-Surmises, Guesses and Supposes.

1. Some concluded he meant Unite with the Solunarian Church, and they reflected upon his Understanding, that not being the Question in Hand, and something remote from their Intention, or the High Solunarians Desire.

2. Some meant Unite to the moderate Party of the Solunarians, and this they said they had done already.

At last some being very Cunning, found it out, that it must be his meaning Unite one among another; and even there again they misunderstood him too; and some imagined he meant down right Rebellion, Uniting Power, and Mobbing the whole Moon, but he soon convinced them of that too.

At last they took the Hint, that his Advice directed them to Unite their subdivided Parties into one general Interest, and to act in Concert upon one bottom, to lay aside the Selfish, Narrow, Suspicious Spirit; three Qualifications the Crolians were but too justly charged with, and begin to act with Courage, Unanimity and Largeness of Soul, to open their Eyes to their own Interest, maintain a regular and constant Correspondence with one another in all parts of the Kingdom, and to bring their civil Interest into a Form.

The Author of this Advice having thus brought them to understand, and approve his Proposal, they demanded his assistance for making the Essay, and 'tis a most wonderful thing to consider what a strange effect the alteration of their Measures had upon the whole Solunarian Nation.

As soon as ever they had settled the Methods they resolved to act in, they formed a general Council of the Heads of their Party, to be always sitting, to reconcile Differences, to unite Parties, to suppress Feuds in their beginning.

They appointed 3 general Meetings in 3 of the most remote Parts of the Kingdom, to be half yearly, and one universal Meeting of Persons deputed to concert matters among them in General.

By that time these Meetings had sat but once, and the Conduct of the Council of 12 began to appear, 'twas a wonder to see the prodigious alteration it made all over the Country.

Immediately a Crolian would never buy any thing but of a Crolian; would hire no Servants, employ neither Porter nor Carman, but what were Crolians.

The Crolians in the Country that wrought and managed the Manufactures, would employ no body but Crolian Spinners, Crolian Weavers, and the like.

In their capital City the Merchandizing Crolians would freight no Ships but of which the Owners and Commanders were Crolians.

They called all their Cash out of the Solunarian Bank; and as the Act of the Cortez confirming the Bank then in being seemed to be their Support, they made it plain that Cash and Credit will make a Bank without a public Settlement of Law; and without these all the Laws in the Moon will never be able to support it.

They brought all their running Cash into one Bank, and settled a sub-Cash depending upon the Grand-Bank in every Province of the Kingdom; in which, by a strict Correspondence and crediting their Bills, they might be able to settle a Paper Credit over the whole Nation.

They went on to settle themselves in all sorts of Trade in open Companies, and sold off their Interests in the public Stocks then in Trade.

If the Government wanted a Million of Money upon any Emergency, they were ready to lend it as a Body, not by different Sums and private Hands blended together with their Enemies, but as will appear at large presently, it was only Crolian Money, and passed as such.

Nor were the Consequences of this New Model less considerable than the Proposer expected, for the Crolians being generally of the Trading Manufacturing part of the World, and very Rich; the influence this method had upon the common People, upon Trade, and upon the Public was very considerable every way.

I. All the Solunarian Trades-Men and Shop-keepers were at their Wits end, they sat in their Shops and had little or nothing to do, while the Shops of the Crolians were full of Customers, and their People over Head and Ears in Business; this turned many of the Solunarian Trades-Men quite off of the hooks, and they began to break and decay strangely, till at last a great many of them to prevent their utter Ruin, turned Crolians on purpose to get a Trade; and what forwarded that part of it was, that when a Solunarian, who had little or no Trade before, came but over to the Crolians, immediately every Body come to Trade with him, and his Shop would be full of Customers, so that this presently increased the number of the Crolians.

2. The poor People in the Countries, Carders, Spinners, Weavers, Knitters, and all sorts of Manufacturers, run in Crowds to the Crolian Temples for fear of being starved, for the Crolians were two thirds of the Masters or Employers in the Manufactures all over the Country, and the Poor would ha' been starved and undone if they had cast them out of Work. Thus insensibly the Crolians increased their number.

3. The Crolians being Men of vast Cash, they no sooner withdrew their Money from the General Bank but the Bank languished, Credit sunk, and in a short time they had little to do, but dissolved of Course.

One thing remained which People expected would ha' put a Check to this Undertaking, and that was a way of Trading in Classes, or Societies, much like our East-India Companies in England; and these depending upon public Privileges granted by the Queen of the Country, or her Predecessors, no Body could Trade to those Parts but the Persons who had those privileges: The cunning Crolians, who had great Stocks in those Trades, and foresaw they could not Trade by themselves without the public Grant or Charter, contrived a way to get almost all that Capital Trade into their Hands as follows.

They concerted Matters, and all at once fell to selling off their Stock, giving out daily Reports that they would be no longer concerned, that it was a losing Trade, that the Fund at bottom was good for nothing, and that of two Societies the Old one had not 20 per Cent. to divide, all their Debts being paid; that the New Society had Traded several Years, but if they were dissolved could not say that they had got any thing; and that this must be a Cheat at last, and so they resolved to sell.

By this Artifice, they daily offering to Sale, and yet in all their Discourse discouraging the thing they were to sell no Body could be found to buy.

The offering a thing to Sale and no Bidders, is a certain never-failing prospect of a lowering the Price; from this Method therefore the value of all the Banks, Companies, Societies and Stocks in the Country fell to be little or nothing worth; and that was to be bought for 40 or 45 Lunarians that was formerly sold at 150, and so in proportion of all the rest.

All this while the Crolians employed their Emissaries to buy up privately all the Interest or Shares in these Things that any of the Solunarian Party would sell.

This Plot took readily, for these Gentlemen exposing the weakness of these Societies, and running down the value of their Stocks, and at the same time warily buying at the lowest Prices, not only in time got Possession of the whole Trade, with their Grants, Privileges and Stocks, but got into them at a prodigiously low and despicable Price.

They had no sooner thus wormed them out of the Trade, and got the greatest part of the Effects in their own Hands, and consequently the whole Management, but they run up the Price of the Funds again as high as ever, and laughed at the folly of those that sold out.

Nor could the other People make any Reflections upon the honesty of the practice, for it was no Original, but had its birth among the Solunarians themselves, of whom 3 or 4 had frequently made a Trade of raising and lowering the Funds of the Societies by all the Clandestine Contrivances in the World, and had ruined abundance of Families to raise their own Fortunes and Estates.

One of the greatest Merchants in the Moon raised himself by this Method to such a height of Wealth, that he left all his Children married to Grandees, Dukes, and Great Folks; and from a Mechanic Original, they are now ranked among the Lunarian Nobility, while multitudes of ruined Families helped to build his Fortune, by sinking under the Knavery of his Contrivance.

His Brother in the same Iniquity, being at this time a Man of the Feather, has carried on the same intriguing Trade with all the Face and Front imaginable; it has been nothing with him to persuade his most intimate Friends to Sell, or Buy, just as he had occasion for his own Interest to have it rise, or fall, and so to make his own Market of their

Misfortune. Thus he has twice raised his Fortunes, for the House of Feathers demolished him once, and yet he has by the same clandestine Management worked himself up again.

This civil way of Robbing Houses, for I can esteem it no better, was carried on by a middle sort of People, called in the Moon BLOUTEGONDEGOURS, which signifies Men with two Tongues, or in English, Stock-Jobbing Brokers.

These had formerly such an unlimited Power and were so numerous, that indeed they governed the whole Trade of the Country; no Man knew when he Bought or Sold, for tho' they pretended to Buy and Sell, and Manage for other Men whose Stocks they had very much at Command, yet nothing was more frequent than when they bought a thing cheap, to buy it for themselves; if dear, for their Employer; if they were to Sell, if the Price rise, it was Sold, if it Fell, it was Unsold; and by this Art no body got any Money but themselves, that at last, excepting the two capital Men we spoke of before, these governed the Prizes of all things, and nothing could be Bought or Sold to Advantage but thro' their hands; and as the Profit was prodigious, their number increased accordingly, so that Business seemed engrossed by these Men, and they governed the main Articles of Trade.

This Success, and the Imprudence of their Conduct, brought great Complaints against them to the Government, and a Law was made to restrain them, both in Practice and Number.

This Law has in some measure had its Effect, the number is not only lessened, but by chance some honester Men than usual are got in among them, but they are so very, very, very Few, hardly enough to save a Man's Credit that shall vouch for them.

Nay, some People that pretend to understand their Business better than I do, having been of their Number, have affirmed, it is impossible to be honest in the employment.

I confess when I began to search into the Conduct of these Men, at least of some of them, I found there were abundance of black Stories to be told of them, a great deal known, and a great deal more unknown; for they were from the beginning continually Encroaching into all sorts of People and Societies, and in Conjunction with some that were not qualified by Law, but merely Voluntarily, called in the Moon by a hard long Word, in English signifying PROJECTORS these erected Stocks in Shadows, Societies in Nubibus, and Bought and Sold mere Vapour, Wind, Emptiness and Bluster for Money, till they drew People in to lay out their Cash, and then laughed at them.

Thus they erected Paper Societies, Linen Societies, Sulfur Societies, Copper Societies, Glass Societies, Sham Banks, and a thousand mock Whimsies to hook unwary People in; at last sold themselves out, left the Bubble to float a little in the Air, and then vanish of it self.

The other sort of People go on after all this; and tho' these Projectors began to be out of Fashion, they always found one thing or other to amuse and deceive the Ignorant, and went Jobbing on into all manner of things, Public as well as Private, whether the Revenue, the Public Funds, Loans, Annuities, Bear-Skins, or any thing.

Nay they were once grown to that extravagant height, that they began to Stock-Job the very Feathers of the Consolidator, and in time the King's employing those People might have had what Feathers they had occasion for, without concerning the Proprietors of the Lands much about them.

'Tis true this began to be notorious, and received some check in a former meeting of the Feathers; but even now, when I came away, the three Years expiring, and by Course a new Consolidator being to be built, they were as busy as ever. Bidding, Offering, Procuring, Buying, Selling, and Jobbing of Feathers to who bid most; and notwithstanding several late wholesome and strict Laws against all manner of Collusion, Bribery and clandestine Methods, in the Countries procuring these Feathers; never was the Moon in such an uproar about picking and culling the Feathers, such Bribery, such Drunkenness, such Caballing, especially among the High Solunarian Clergy and the Lazognians, such Feasting, Fighting and Distraction, as the like has never been known.

And that which is very Remarkable, all this not only before the Old Consolidator was broke up, but even while it was actually whole and in use.

Had this hurry been to send up good Feathers, there had been the less to say, but that which made it very strange to me was, that where the very worst of all the Feathers were to be found, there was the most of this wicked Work; and tho' it was bad enough every where, yet the greatest bustle and contrivance was in order to send up the worst Feathers they could get.

And indeed some Places such Sorry, Scoundrel, Empty, Husky, Withered, Decayed Feathers were offered to the Proprietors, that I have sometimes wondered any one could have the Impudence to send up such ridiculous Feathers to make a Consolidator, which, as is before observed, is an Engine of such Beauty, Usefulness and Necessity.

And still in all my Observation, this Note came in my way, there was always the most bustle and disturbance about the worst Feathers.

It was really a melancholy Thing to consider, and had this Lunar World been my Native Country, I should ha' been full of concern to see that one thing, on which the welfare of the whole Nation so much depended, put in so ill a Method, and gotten into the management of such Men, who for Money would certainly ha' set up such Feathers, that wherever the Consolidator should be formed, it would certainly over-set the first Voyage; and if the whole Nation should happen to be Embarked in it, on the dangerous Voyage to the Moon, the fall would certainly give them such a Shock, as would put them all into Confusion, and open the Door to the Gallunarian, or any Foreign Enemy to destroy them.

It was really strange that this should be the Case, after so many Laws, and so lately made, against it; but in this, those People are too like our People in England, who have the best Laws the worst executed of any Nation under Heaven.

For in the Moon this hurry about choosing of Feathers was grown to the greatest height imaginable, as if it increased by the very Laws that were made to suppress it; for now at a certain public Place where the Bloutegondegours used to meet every Day, any Body that had but Money enough might buy a Feather at a reasonable Rate, and never go down into the Country to fetch it; nay, the Trade grew so hot, that of a sudden as if no other Business was in Hand, all people were upon it, and the whole Market was changed from Selling of Bear-Skins, to Buying of Feathers.

Some gave this for a Reason why all the Stocks of the Societies fell so fast, but there were other Reasons to be given for that, such as Clubs, Cabals, Stock-Jobbers, Knights, Merchants and Thie — s. I mean a private Sort, not such as are frequently Hanged there, but of a worse Sort, by how much they merit that Punishment more, but are out of the reach of the Law, can Rob and Pickpockets in the Face of the Sun, and laugh at the Families they Ruin, bidding Defiance to all legal Resentment.

To this height things were come under the growing Evil of this sort of People.

And yet in the very Moon where, as I have noted, the People are so exceeding clear Sighted, and have such vast helps to their perceptive Faculties, such Mists are sometimes cast before the public Understanding, that they cannot see the general Interest.

562

This was manifest, in that just as I came away from that Country, the great Council of their Wise Men, the Men of the Feather, were a going to repeal the old Law of Restraining the Number of these People; and tho' as it was, there was not Employment for half of them, there being 100 in all, and not above 5 honest ones; yet when I came away they were going to increase their Number. I have nothing to say to this here, only that all Wise Men that understand Trade were very much concerned at it, and looked upon it as a most destructive Thing to the Public, and foreboding the same mischiefs that Trade suffered before.

It was the particular Misfortune to these Lunar People that this Country had a better Stock of Governors in all Articles of their Well-fare, than in their Trade; their Law Affairs had good Judges, their Church good Patriarchs, except, as might be excepted; their State good Ministers, their Army good Generals, and their Consolidator good Feathers; but in Matters relating to Trade, they had this particular Misfortune, that those Cases always came before People that did not understand them.

Even the Judges themselves were often found at a Loss to determine Causes of Negoce, such as Protests, Charter-Parties, Averages, Barratry, Demurrage of Ships, Right of detaining Vessels on Demurrage, and the like; nay, the very Laws themselves are fain to be silent and yield in many things a Superiority to the Custom of Merchants.

And here I began to Congratulate my Native Country, where the Prudence of the Government has provided for these things, by Establishing in a Commission of Trade some of the most experienced Gentlemen in the Nation, to Regulate, Settle, Improve, and revive Trade in General, by their unwearied Labours, and most consummate Understanding; and this made me pity these Countries, and think it would be an Action worthy of this Nation, and be spoken of for Ages to come to their Glory, if in mere Charity they would appoint or depute these Gentlemen to go a Voyage to those Countries of the Moon, and bless those Regions with the Schemes of their sublime Undertakings, and discoveries in Trade.

But when I was expressing my self thus, my Philosopher interrupted me, and told me I should see they were already furnished for that purpose, when I came to examine the public Libraries, of which by it self.

But I was farther confirmed in my Observation of the weakness of the public Heads of that Country, as to Trade, when I saw another most preposterous Law going forward among them, the Title of which was specious, and contained something relating to employing the Poor, but the substance of it absolutely destructive to the very Nature of their Trade, tending to Transposing, Confounding and Destroying their Manufactures, and to the Ruin of all their Home-Commerce; never was Nation so blind to their own Interest as these Lunarian Law Makers, and the People who were the Contrivers of this Law were so vainly Conceited, so fond of the gilded Title, and so positively Dogmatic, that they would not hear the frequent Applications of Persons better acquainted with those things than themselves, but pushed it on merely by the strength of their Party, for the Vanity of being Authors of such a Contrivance.

But to return to the new Model of the Crolians. The advice of the Lunarian Philosopher run now thro' all their Affairs, UNITE was the Word thro' all the Nation, in Trade, in Cash, in Stocks, as I noted before.

If a Solunarian Ship was bound to any Out Port, no Crolian would load any Goods aboard; if any Ship came to seek Freight abroad, none of the Crolians Correspondents would Ship any thing unless they knew the Owners were Crolians; the Crolian Merchants turned out all their Solunarian Masters, Sailors and Captains from their Ships; and thus, as the Solunarians would have them be separated in respect of the Government, Profits, Honours and Offices, they resolved to separate in every thing else too, and to stand by themselves.

At last, upon some public Occasion, the public Treasurers of the Land sent to the capital City, to borrow 500000 Lunarians upon very good Security of established Funds; truly no Body would lend any Money, or at least they could not raise above a 5th part of that Sum, enquiring at the Bank, at their general Societies Cash, and other Places, all was languid and dull, and no Money to be had; but being informed that the Crolians had erected a Bank of their own, they sent thither, and were answered readily, that whatever Sum the Government wanted, was at their Service, only it was to be lent not by particular Persons, but such a Grandee being one of the prime Nobility, and who the Crolians now called their Protector, was to be Treated with about it.

The Government saw no harm in all this; here was no Law broken, here was nothing but Oppression answered with Policy, and Mischief fenced against with Reason.

The Government therefore took no Notice of it, nor made any Scruple when they wanted any Money to Treat with this Nobleman, and borrow any Sum of the Crolians, as Crolians; on the contrary in the Name of the Crolians; their Head or Protector presented their Addresses and Petitions, procured Favours on one Hand, and Assistance on the other; and thus by degrees and insensibly the Crolians became a Politic Body, settled and established by Orders and Rules among themselves; and while a Spirit of Unanimity thus run thro' all their Proceedings, their Enemies could never hurt them, their Princes always saw it was their Interest to keep Measures with them, and they were sure to have Justice upon any Complaint whatsoever.

When I saw this, it forced me to reflect upon Affairs in our own Country; Well, said I, 'tis happy for England that our Dissenters have not this Spirit of Union and Largeness of Heart among them; for if they were not a Narrow, mean-Spirited, short-Sighted, self-Preserving, friend-Betraying, poor-Neglecting People, they might ha' been every way as Safe, as Considerable, as Regarded and as Numerous as the Crolians in the Moon; but it is not in their Souls to do themselves Good, nor to Espouse, or Stand by those that would do it for them; and 'tis well for the Church-Men that it is so, for many Attempts have been made to save them, but their own narrowness of Soul, and dividedness in Interest has always prevented its being effectual, and discouraged all the Instruments that ever attempted to serve them.

'Tis confessed the Case was thus at first among the Crolians, they were full of Divisions among themselves, as I have noted already of the Solunarians, and the unhappy Feuds among them, had always not only exposed them to the Censure, Reproach and Banter of their Solunarian Enemies, but it had served to keep them under, prevent their being valued in the Government, and given the other Party vast Advantages against.

But the Solunarians driving thus furiously at their Destruction and entire Ruin, opened their Eyes to the following Measures for their preservation: And here again the high Solunarians may see, and doubtless whenever they made use of the Lunar-Glasses they must see it, that nothing could ha' driven the Crolians to make use of such Methods for their Defence, but the rash Proceedings of their own warm Men, in order to suppressing the whole Crolian Interest. And this might inform our Country-men of the Church of England, that it cannot but be their Interest to Treat their Brethren with Moderation and Temper, least their Extravagances should one time or other drive the other as it were by Force into their Senses, and open their Eyes to do only all those

Things which by Law they may do, and which they are laughed at by all the World for not doing.

This was the very Case in the Moon: The Philosopher, or pretended-such as before, had often published, that it was their Interest to UNITE; but their Eyes not being open to the true Causes and Necessity of it, their Ears were shut against the Council, till Oppression and Necessities drove them to it.

Accordingly they entered into a serious Debate, of the State of their own Affairs, and finding the Advice given, very reasonable; they set about it, and the Author gave them a Model, Entitled An enquiry into what the Crolians may lawfully do, to prevent the certain Ruin of their Interest, and bring their Enemies to Peace.

I will not pretend to examine the Contents of this sublime Tract; but from this very Day, we found the Crolians in the Moon, acting quite on a different Foot from all their former Conduct, putting on a new Temper, and a new Face, as you have heard.

All this while the hot Solunarians cried out Plots, Associations, Confederacies, and Rebellions, when indeed here was nothing done but what the Laws justified, what Reason directed, and what had the Crolians but made use of the Cogitator, they would ha' done 40 Year before.

The Truth is, the other People had no Remedy, but to cry Murder, and make a Noise; for the Crolians went on with their Affairs, and Established themselves so, that when I came away, they were become a most Solid, and well United Body, made a considerable Figure in the Nation, and yet the Government was easy; for the Solunarians found when they had attained the utmost end of their Wishes, her Solunarian Majesty was as safe as before, and the Crolians Property being secured, they were as Loyal Subjects as the Solunarians, as consistent with Monarchy, as useful to it, and as pleased with it.

I cannot but Remark here, that this Union of the Crolians among themselves had another Consequence, which made it appear it was not only to their own Advantage, but to the general Good of all the Nation.

For, by little, and little, the Feuds of the Parties cooled, and the Solunarians began to be better reconciled to them; the Government was easy and safe, and the private Quarrels, as I have been told since, begin to be quite forgot.

What Blindness, said I to my self, has possessed the Dissenters in our unhappy Country of England, where by eternal Discords, Feuds, Distrusts and Disgusts among themselves, they always fill their Enemies

566

with Hopes, that by pushing at them, they may one time or other complete their Ruin; which Expectation has always served as a means to keep open the Quarrel; whereas had the Dissenters been United in Interest, Affection and Management among themselves, all this Heat had long ago been over, and the Nation, tho' there had been two Opinions had retained but one Interest, been joined in Affection, and Peace at Home been raised up to that Degree that all Wise Men wish, as it is now among the Inhabitants of the World in the Moon.

Tis true, in all the Observations I made in this Lunar Country, the vast deference paid to the Persons of Princes began to lessen, and whatever Respect they had for the Office, they found it necessary frequently to tell the World that on occasion, they could Treat them with less Respect than they pretended to owe them.

For about this time, the Divine Right of Kings, and the Inheritances of Princes in the Moon, met with a terrible Shock, and that by the Solunarian Party themselves; and insomuch that even my Philosopher, and he was none of the Jure Divino Men, neither declared, against it.

They made Crowns perfect Foot-balls, set up what Kings they would, and pulled down such as they did not like, Ratitione Voluntas, right or wrong, as they thought best, of which some Examples shall be given by and by.

After I had thus enquired into the Historical Affairs of this Lunar Nation, which for its Similitude to my Native Country, I could not but be inquisitive in; I waved a great many material Things, which at least I cannot enter upon the Relation of here, and began to enquire into their Affairs abroad.

I think I took notice in the beginning of my Account of these parts, that I found them engaged in a tedious and bloody War, with one of the most mighty Monarchs of all the Moon.

I must therefore hint, that among the multitude of things, which for brevity sake I omit, the Reader may observe these were some.

1. That this was the same Monarch who harboured and entertained the Abrogratzian Prince, who was fled as before, and who we are to call the King of Gallunaria.

2. I have omitted the Account of a long and bloody War, which lasted a great many Years, and which the present Queens Predecessor, managed with a great deal of Bravery and Conduct, and finished very much to his own Glory, and the Nations Advantage.

3. I have too much omitted to Note, how Barbarously the High Solunarian Church Men treated him for all his Services, upbraided him with the Expense of the War; and tho' he saved them all from Ruin and Abrogratzianism, yet had not one good Word for him, and indeed 'tis with some difficulty that I pass this over, because it might be necessary to observe, besides what is said before, that Ingratitude is a Vice in Nature, and practiced every where, as well as in England. So that we need not upbraid the Party among us with their ill Treatment of the late King, for these People used their good King every Jot as bad, till their unkindness perfectly broke his Heart.

Here also I am obliged to omit the Historical Part of the War, and of the Peace that followed; only I must observe that this Peace was very Precarious, Short and Unhappy, and in a few Months the War broke out again, with as much Fury as ever.

In this War happened one of the strangest, unaccountable and most preposterous Actions, that ever a People in their National Capacity could be guilty of.

Certainly if our People in England, who pretend that Kingship is Jure Divino, did but know the Story of which I speak, they would be quite of another Mind; wherefore I crave leave to relate part of the History, or Original of this last War, as a necessary Introduction to the proper Observations I shall make upon it.

There was a King of a certain Country in the Moon, called in their Language, Ebronia, who was formerly a Confederate with the Solunarians. This Prince dying without Issue, the great Monarch we speak of, seized upon all his Dominions as his Right. — — Tho' if I remember right, he had formerly Sworn never to lay Claim to it, and after that by a subsequent Treaty had agreed with the Solunarian Prince, that another Monarch who claimed a Right as well as he, should divide it between them.

The breach of this Agreement, and seizing this Kingdom, put almost all the Lunar World into a Flame, and War hung over the Heads of all the Northern Nations of the Moon, for several Claims were made to the Succession by other Princes, and particularly by a certain Potent Prince called the Eagle, of an Ancient Family, whose Lunar Name I cannot well express, but in English it signifies the Men of the great Lip; whether it was Originally a sort of a Nickname, or whether they had any such thing as a great Lip Hereditary to the Family, by which they were distinguished, is not worth my while to Examine.

'Tis without question that the successive Right, if their Lunar Successions, are Governed as ours are in this world, devolved upon this Man with the Lip and his Families; but the Gallunarian Monarch brought things so to pass, by his extraordinary Conduct, that the Ebronian King was drawn in by some of his Nobility, who this Prince had Bought and Bribed to betray their Country to his Interest, and particularly a certain High Priest of that Country, to make an Assignment, or deed of Gift of all his Dominions to the Grandson of this Gallunarian Monarch.

By Virtue of this Gift, or Legacy, as soon as the King died, who was then languishing, and as the other Parry alleged, not in a very good capacity to make a Will; the Gallunarian King sent his Grandson to seize upon the Crown, and backing him with suitable Forces, took Possession of all his strong Fortifications and Frontiers.

Nor was this all, the Man with the Lip indeed talked big, and threatened War immediately, but the Solunarians were so unsettled at Home, so unprepared for War, having but just dismissed their Auxiliary Troops, and disbanded their own, and the Prince was so ill served by his Subjects, that both he and a Powerful Neighbour, Nations in the same Interest, were merely Bullied by this Gallunarian; and as he threatened immediately to Invade them, which they were then in no Condition to prevent, he forced them both to submit to his Demand, tacitly allow what he had done in breaking the Treaty with him, and at last openly acknowledge his new King.

This was indeed a most unaccountable Step, but there was a necessity to plead, for he was at their very Doors with his Forces; and this Neighbouring People, who they call Mogenites, could not resist him without help from the Solunarians, which they were very backward in, notwithstanding the earnest Solicitations of their Prince, and notwithstanding they were obliged to do it by a solemn Treaty.

These delays obliged them to this strange Step of acknowledging the Invasion of their Enemy, and pulling off the Hat to the New King he had set up.

'Tis true, the Policy of these Lunar Nations was very Remarkable in this Case, and they out-witted the Gallunarian Monarch in it; for by the owning this Prince, whom they immediately after Declared a Usurper, and made War against; they stopped the Mouth of the Gallunarian his Grandfather, took from him all pretence of Invading them, and making him believe they were Sincere, Wheedled him to restore several Thousands of their Men who he had taken Prisoners in the Frontier Towns of the Ebronians.

Had the Gallunarian Prince had but the forecast to ha' seen, that this was but a forced pretence to gain Time, and that as soon as they had their Troops clear and Time to raise more, they would certainly turn upon him again, he would never ha' been put by with so weak a Trifle as the Ceremony of Congratulation; whereas had he immediately pushed at them with all his Forces, they must ha' been Ruined, and he had carried his Point without much Interruption.

But here he lost his Opportunity, which he never retrieved; for 'tis in the Moon, just as 'tis here, when an Occasion is lost, it is not easy to be recovered, for both the Solunarians and the Mogenites quickly threw off the Mask, and declaring this new Prince an Usurper, and his Grandfather an Unjust breaker of Treaties, they prepared for War against them both.

As to the Honesty of this matter, my Philosopher and I differed extremely, he exclaimed against the Honour of acknowledging a King, with a design to Depose him, and pretending Peace when War is designed; tho' 'tis true, they are too customary in our World; but however, as to him I insisted upon the lawfulness of it, from the universal Custom of Nations, who generally do things ten times more Preposterous and Inconsistent, when they suit their Occasions. Yet I hope no Body will think I am recommending them by this Relation to the Practice of our own Nations, but rather exposing them as unaccountable things never to be put in Practice, without quitting all pretences to Justice and national Honesty.

The Case was this.

As upon the Progress of Matters before related, the Solunarians and Mogenites had made a formal acknowledgment of this new Monarch, the Grandson of the Gallunarian King, so as I have hinted already, they had no other design than to Depose him, and pull him down.

Accordingly, as soon as by the aforesaid Wile they had gained Breath, and furnished themselves with Forces, they declared War against both the Gallunarian King, and his Grandson, and entered into strict Confederacy with the Man of the great Lip, who was the Monarch of the Eagle, and who by right of Succession, had the true Claim to the Ebronian Crowns.

In these Declarations they allege that Crowns do not descend by Gift, nor are Kingdoms given away by Legacy, like a Gold Ring at a

Funeral, and therefore this young Prince could have no Right, the former deceased King having no Right to dispose it by Gift.

I must allow, that judging by our Reason, and the Practice in our Countries here, on this side the Moon; this seemed plain, and I saw no difference in matters of Truth there, or here, but Right and Liberty both of Princes and People seems to be the same in that World, as it is in this, and upon this account I thought the Reasons of this War very Just, and that the Claim of Right to the Succession of the Ebronian Crown, was undoubtedly in the Man with the Lip, and his Heirs, and so far the War was most Just, and the Design reasonable.

And thus far my Lunar Companion agreed with me, and had they gone on so, says he, they had my good Wishes, and my Judgment had been Witness to my Pretences, that they were in the right.

But in the prosecution of this War, says he, they went on to one of the most Impolitic, Ridiculous, Dishonest, and Inconsistent Actions, that ever any Nation in the Moon was guilty of; the Fact was thus.

Having agreed among themselves that the Ebronian Crown should not be possessed by the Gallunarian King's Grandson, they in the next Place began to consider who should have it.

The Man with the Lip had the Title, but he had a great Government of his own, Powerful, Happy and Remote, being as is noted, the Lord of the great Eagle, and he told them he could not pretend to come to Ebronia to be a King there; his eldest Son truly was not only declared Heir apparent to his Father, but had another Lunarian Kingdom of his own still more remote than that, and he would not quit all this for the Crown of Ebronia, so it was concerted by all the Confederated Parties, that the second Son of this Prince, the Man with the Lip, should be declared King, and here lay the Injustice of all the Case.

I confess at my first examining this Matter, I did not see far into it, nor could I reach the Dishonesty of it, and perhaps the Reader of these Sheets may be in the same Case; but my old Lunarian Friend being continually exclaiming against the Matter, and blaming his Country-men the Solunarians for the Dishonesty of it, but especially the Mogenites, he began to be something peevish with me that I should be so dull as not to reach it, and asked me if he should screw me into the Thinking-Press for the Clearing up my Understanding.

At last he told me he would write his particular Sentiments of this whole Affair in a Letter to me, which he would so order as it should effectually open mine Eyes; which indeed it did, and so I believe it will the Eyes of all that read it; to which purpose I have obtained of the Author to assist me in the Translation of it, he having some Knowledge also in our Sublunar Languages.

The Substance of a Letter, wrote to the Author of these Sheets, while he was in the Regions of the Moon.

'Friend from the Moon,

'According to my promise, I hereby give you a Scheme of Solunarian Honesty, joined with Mogenite Policy, and my Opinion of the Action of my Country-men and their Confederates, in declaring their new made Ebronian King.

'The Mogenites and Solunarians are looked upon here to be the Original Contrivers of this ridiculous piece of Pageantry, and tho' some of their Neighbours are supposed to have a Hand in it, yet we all lay it at the door of their Politics, and for the Honesty of it let them answer it if they can.

"Tis observed here, that as soon as the King of Gallunaria had declared that he accepted the Will and Disposition of the Crown of Ebronia, in favour of his Grandson, and that according to the said Disposition, he had owned him for King; and in order to make it effectual, had put him into immediate Possession of the Kingdom. The Mogenites and their Confederates made wonderful Clamours at the Injustice of his Proceedings, and particularly on account of his breaking the Treaty then lately entered into with the King of the Solunarians and the Mogenites, for the settling the Matter of Right and Possession, in case of the Demise of the Ebronian King.

'However, the King of Gallunaria had no sooner placed his Grandson on the Throne, but the Mogenites and other Nations, and to all our Wonder, the King of Solunaria himself acknowledged him, owned him, sent their Ministers, and Compliments of Congratulation, and the like, giving him the Title of King of Ebronia.

'Tho' this proceeding had something of Surprise in it, and all Men expected to see something more than ordinary Politic in the effect of it, yet it did not give half the astonishment to the Lunar World, as this unaccountable Monster of Politics begins to do.

'We have here two unlucky Fellows, called Pasquin and Marforio, these had a long Dialogue about this very Matter, and Pasquin as he always loved Mischief, told a very unlucky Story to his Comrade, of a high Mogenite Skipper, as follows.

'A Mogenite Ship coming from a far Country, the Custom House Officers found some Goods on Board, which were Contraband, and for which they pretended the Ship and Goods were all Confiscated; the Skipper, or Captain in a great Fright, comes up to the Custom-House, and being told he must Swear to something relating to his taking in those Goods, replied in his Country Jargon, Ya, dat sall Ick doen Myn Heer; or in English, Ay, Ay, I'll Swear. —— But finding they did not assure him that it would clear his Ship he scruples the Oath again, at which they told him it would clear his Ship immediately. Hael, well Myn Heer, says the Mogen Man, vat mot Ick sagen, Ick sall all Swear myn Skip to salvare, i.e. I shall Swear any thing to save my Skip.

'We apply this Story thus.

'If the Mogenites did acknowledge the King of Ebronia, we did believe it was done to save the Skip; and when they reproached the Gallunarian King, with breaking the Treaty of Division, we used to say we would all break thro' twice as many Engagements for half as much Advantage.

'This setting up a new King, against a King on the Throne, Acknowledged and Congratulated by them, is not only looked on in the Lunar World, as a thing Ridiculous, but particularly Infamous, that they should first acknowledge a King, and then set up the Title of another. If the Title of the first Ebronian King be good, this must be an Impostor, an Usurper of another Man's Right; if it was not good, why did they acknowledge him, and give him the full Title of all the Ebronian Dominions? Caress and Congratulate him, and make a public Action of it to his Ambassador.

'Will they tell us they were Bullied, and Frighted into it? that is to own they may be huffed into an ill Action; for owing a Man in the Possession of what is none of his own, is an ill thing, and he that may be huffed into one ill Action, may by Consequence be huffed into another, and so into any thing.

'What will they say for doing it? we have heard there has been in the World you came from, a way found out to own Kings de Facto, but not de Jure; if they will fly to that ridiculous Shift, let them tell the World so, that we may know what they mean, for those foolish things are not known here.

'If they owned the King of Ebronia voluntarily, and acknowledged his Right as we thought they had; how then can this young Gentleman have a Title, unless they have found out a new Division, and so will have two Kings of Ebronia, make them Partners, and have a Gallunarian King of Ebronia, and a Mogenite King of Ebronia, both together?

'Our Lunar Nations, Princes and States, whatever they may do in your World, always seek for some Pretences at least to make their Actions seem Honest, whither they are so or no; and therefore they generally publish Memorials, Manifesto's and Declarations, of their Reasons why, and on what account they do so, or so; that those who have any Grounds to charge them with Unjustice, may be answered, and silenced; 'tis for the People in your Country, to fall upon their Neighbours, only because they will do it, and make probability of Conquest, a sufficient Reason of Conquest; the Lunarian Nations are seldom so destitute of Modesty, but that they will make a show of Justice, and make out the Reasons of their Proceedings; and tho' sometimes we find even the Reasons given for some Actions are weak enough; yet it is a bad Cause indeed, that can neither have a true Reason, nor a pretended one. The custom of the Moon has obliged us to show so much respect to Honesty, that when our Actions have the least colour of Honesty, yet we will make Reasons to look like a Defence, whether it be so or no.

'But here is an Action that has neither reality, nor pretence, here is not Face enough upon it to bear an Apology. First, they acknowledge one King, and then set up another King against him; either they first acknowledged a wrong King, and thereby became Parties to a Usurper, or they act now against all the Rules of common Justice in the World, to set up a sham King, to pull down a true one, only because 'tis their Interest to have it so.

'This makes the very Name of a Solunarian scandalous to all the Moon, and Mankind look upon them with the utmost Prejudice, as if they were a Nation who had sold all their Honesty to their Interest; and who could act this way to Day, and that way to Morrow, without any regard to Truth, or the Rule of Honour, Equity or Conscience; This is Swearing any thing to save the Skip; and never let any Man Reproach the Gallunarian King with breaking the Treaty of Division, and disregarding the Faith and Stipulations of Leagues; for this is an Action so inconsistent with it self, so incongruous to common Justice, to the Reason and Nature of things, that no History of any of these latter Times can parallel it, and 'tis past the Power of Art to make any reasonable Defence for it.

'Indeed some lame Reasons are given for it by our Politicians. First, they say the Prince with the great Lip was extremely pressed by the Gallunarians at Home in his own Country, and not without apprehensions of seeing them e'er long, under the Walls of his capital City.

'From this circumstance of the Man with the Lip, 'twas not irrational to expect that he might be induced to make a separate Peace with the Gallunarians, and serve them as he did once the Prince of Berlindia at the Treaty of Peace in a former War, where he deserted him after the solemnest Engagements never to make Peace without him; but his pressing Occasions requiring it, concluded a Peace without him, and left him to come out of the War, as well as he could, tho' he had come into it only for his Assistance. Now finding him in danger of being ruined by the Gallunarian Power, and judging from former Practice in like Cases, that he might be hurried into a Peace, and leave them in the Lurch; they have drawn him into this Labrinth, as into a Step, which can never be receded from without the utmost Affront and Disgrace, either to the Family of the Gallunarian, or of the Lip; an Action which in its own Nature, is a Defiance of the whole Gallunarian Power, and without any other Manifesto, may be taken as a Declaration from the House of the Lip, to the Gallunarian, that this War shall never end, till one of those two Families are ruined and reduced.

'What Condition the Prince with the Lip's Power is in, to make such a huff at this Time, shall come under Examination by and by; in the mean time the Solunarians have clenched the Nail, and secured the War to last as long as they think convenient.

'If the Gallunarians should get the better, and reduce the Man with the Lip to Terms never so disadvantageous, he cannot now make a Peace without leave from the Solunarians and the Mogenites, least his Son should be ruined also. —— Or if he should make Articles for himself, it must be with ten times the Dishonour that he might have done before.

'Politicians say, 'tis never good for a Prince to put himself into a case of Desperation. This is drawing the Sword, and throwing away the Scabbard; if a Disaster should befall him, his Retreat is impossible, and this must have been done only to secure the Man with the Lip from being huffed, or frighted into a separate Peace.

'The second Reason People here give, why the Solunarians are concerning themselves in this Matter, is drawn from Trade.

'The continuing of Ebronia in the Hands of the Gallunarians, will most certainly be the Destruction of the Solunarian and Mogenites Trade, both to that Kingdom, and the whole Seas on that side of the Moon; as this Article includes a fifth Part of all the Trade of the Moon, and would in Conjunction with the Gallunarians at last bring the Mastership of the Sea, out of the Hands of the other, so it would in effect be more detriment to those two Nations, than ten Kingdoms lost, if they had them to part with.

'This the Solunarians foreseeing, and being extremely sensible of the entire Ruin of their Trade, have left no Stone unturned to bring this piece of Pageantry on the Stage, by which they have hooked in the Old Black Eagle to plunge himself over Head and Ears in the Quarrel, in such a manner, as he can never go back with any tolerable Honour; he can never quit his Son and the Crown of Ebronia, without the greatest Reproach and Disgrace of all the World in the Moon.

'Now whether one, or both of these Reasons are true in this Case, as most believe both of them to be true; the Policy of my Country-men, the Solunarians is visible indeed, but as for their Honesty, it is past finding out.

'But it is objected here, this Son of the Lip has an undoubted Right to the Crown of Ebronia. We do not Fight now to set up an Usurper, but to pull down an Usurper, and it has been made plain by the Manifesto, that the giving a Kingdom by Will, is no conveyance of Right; the Prince of the Eagle has an undoubted Right, and they Fight to maintain it.

'If this be true, then we must ask these High and Mighty Gentlemen how came they to recognize and acknowledge the present King on the Throne? why did they own an Usurper if he be such? either one or other must be an act of Cowardice and Injustice, and all the Politics of the Moon cannot clear them of one of these two Charges; either they were Cowardly Knaves before, or else they must be Cunning Knaves now.

'If the Young Eagle has an undoubted Title now, so he had before, and they knew it as well before, as they do now; what can they say for themselves, why they should own a King, who they knew had no Title, or what can they say for going to pull down one that has a Title?

'I must be allowed to distinguish between Fighting with a Nation, and Fighting with the King. For Example. Our Quarrel with the Gallunarians is with the whole Nation, as they are grown too strong for their Neighbours. But our Quarrel with Ebronia is not with the Nation, but with their King, and this Quarrel seems to be unjust in this particular, at least in them who owned him to be King, for that put an end to the Controversy.

"Tis true, the Justice of public Actions, either in Princes, or in States, is no such nice Thing, that any Body should be surprised, to see the Government forfeit their Faith, and it seems the Solunarians are no more careful this way, than their Neighbours. But then those People should in especial manner forbear to reproach Other Nations and Princes, with the breaches which they themselves are subject too.

'As to the Eagle, we have nothing to say to the Honesty of his declaring his Son King of Ebronia, for as is hinted before, he never acknowledged the Title of the Usurper, but always declared, and insisted on his own undoubted Right, and that he would recover it if he could.

'Without doubt the Eagle has a Title by Proximity of Blood, founded on the renunciation of the King of Gallunaria formerly mentioned, and if the Will of the late King be Invalid, or he had no Right to give the Sovereignty of his Kingdoms away, then the Eagle is next Heir.

'But as we quit his Morals, and justify the Honesty of his Proceedings in the War, against the present King of Ebronia, so in this Action of declaring his second Son. We must begin to question his Understanding, and saying a respect of decency, it looks as if his Musical Head was out of Tune, to Illus tratellus. I crave leave to tell you a Story out of your own Country, which we have heard of hither. A French Man that could speak but broken English, was at the Court of England, when on some occasion he happened to hear the Title of the King of England read thus, Charles the II. King of England, Scotland France and Ireland.

'Vat is dat you say? says Monsieur, being a little affronted, the Man reads it again, as before. Charles the Second, King of England, Scotland, France and Ireland. — — — Charles the Second, King of France! Ma Foy, says the French Man, you can no read, Charles the Second, King of France, ha! ha! ha! Charles the Second, King of France, when he can catch. Any one may apply the Story, whether it was a true one or no.

'All the Lunar World looks on it, therefore, as a most Ridiculous, Senseless Thing, to make a Man a King of a Country he has not one Foot of Land in, nor can have a Foot there, but what he must Fight for. As to the probability of gaining it, I have nothing to say to it, but if we may guess at his Success there, by what has been done in other Parts of the Moon, we find he has Fought three Campaigns, to lose every Foot he had got.

'It had been much more to the Honour of the Eagle's Conduct, and of the young Hero himself, first to ha' let him ha' faced his Enemy in the Field, and as soon as he had beaten him, the Ebronians would have acknowledged him fast enough; or his own Victorious Troops might have Proclaimed him at the Gate of their Capital City; and if after all, the Success of the War had denied him the Crown he had fought for, he had the Honour to have shown his Bravery, and he had been where he was, a Prince of the Great Lip. A Son of the Eagle is a Title much more Honourable than a King Without a Crown, without Subjects, without a Kingdom, and another Man upon his Throne; but by this declaring him King, the old Eagle has put him under a necessity of gaining the Kingdom of Ebronia, which at best is a great hazard, or if he fails to be miserably despicable, and to bear all his Life the constant Chagrin of a great Title and no Possession.

'How ridiculous will this poor Young Gentleman look, if at last he should be forced to come Home again without his Kingdom? what a King of Clouts will he pass for, and what will this King-making old Gentlemen, his Father say, when the young Hero shall tell him, your Majesty has made me Mock King for all the World to laugh at.

"Twas certainly the weakest Thing that could be, for the Eagle thus to make him a King of that, which, were the probability greater than it is, he may easily, without the help of a Miracle, be disappointed of.

"Tis true, the Confederates talk big, and have lately had a great Victory, and if Talk will beat the King of Ebronia out of his Kingdom, he is certainly undone, but we do not find the Gallunarians part with any thing they can keep, nor that they quit any thing without Blows; It must cost a great deal of Blood and Treasure before this War can be ended; if absolute Conquest on one side must be the Matter, and if the Design on Ebronia should miscarry, as one Voyage thither has done already, where are we then? Let any Man but look back, and consider what a sorry Figure your Confederate Fleet in your World had made, after their Andalusian Expedition, if they had not more by Fate than Conduct, chopped upon a Booty at Vigo as they came back.

'In the like condition, will this new King come back, if he should go for a Kingdom and should not Catch, as the French Man called it. 'Tis in the Sense of the probability of this miscarriage, that most Men wonder at these unaccountable Measures, and think the Eagles Councils look a little Wildish, as if some of his great Men were grown Delirious and Whimsical, that fancied Crowns and Kingdoms were to come and

578

go, just as the great Divan at their Court should direct. This confusion of Circumstances has occasioned a certain Copy of Verses to appear about the Moon, which in our Characters may be read as follows.

Wondelis Idulasin na Perixola Metartos, Strigunia Crolias Xerin Hytale fylos; Farnicos Galvare Orpto sonamel Egonsberch, Sih lona Sipos Gullia Ropta Tylos.

'Which may be Englished thus.

Caesar you Trifle with the World in vain, Think rather now of Germany than Spain; He's hardly fit to fill th' Eagle's Throne, Who gives new Crowns, and can't protect his own.

'But after all to come closer to the Point, if I can now make it out that whatever it was before, this very Practice of declaring a second Son to be King of Ebronia, has publicly owned the Proceedings of the King of Gallunaria to be Just, and the Title of his Grandson to be much better than the Title of the now declared King, what shall we call it then?

'In order to this, 'tis first necessary to examine the Title of the present King, and to enter into the history of his coming to the Crown, in which I shall be very Brief.

'The last King of Ebronia dying without Issue, and a former Renunciation taking place, the Succession devolves on the House of the Eagle as before, of whom the present Eagle is the eldest Branch.

'But the late King of Ebronia, to prevent the Succession of the Eagle's Line, makes a Will, and supplies the Proviso of Renunciation by Devising, Giving or Bequeathing the Crown to the Grandson of his Sister.

'The King of Gallunaria insists that this is a lawful Title to the Crown, and seizes it accordingly, inflating his Grandson in the Possession.

'The Eagle alleges the Renunciation to confirm his Title as Heir; and as to the Will of the late King, he says Crowns cannot descend by Gift, and tho' the late King had an undoubted Right to enjoy it himself, he had none to give it away.

'To make the application of this History as short as may be, I demand then what Right has the Eagle to give it to his second Son? if Crowns are not to descend by Gift, he may have a Right to enjoy it, but can have none to give it away, but if he has a Right to give it away; so had the former King, and then the present King has a better Title to it than the new one, because his Gift was Prior to this of the Eagle.

'I would be glad to see this answered; and if it can't, then I Query whether the Eagle's Senses ought not to be questioned, for setting up a Title very Foundation for which he quarrels at him that is in Possession, and so confirm the honesty of the Possessor's Title by his own Practice.?

'From the whole, I make no Scruple to say that either the Eagle's second Son has no Title to the Kingdom of Ebronia, or else giving of Crowns is a legal Practice; and if Crowns may descend by Gift, then has the other King a better Title than he, because it was given him first, and the Eagle has only given away what he had no Right to, because 'twas given away before he had any Title to it himself.

'Further, the Posterity of the Eagle's eldest Son are manifestly injured in this Action, for Kings can no more give away their Crowns from their Posterity, than from themselves; if the Right be in the Eagle, 'tis his, as he's the eldest Male Branch of the House of the great Lip, not as he is Eagle, and from him the Crown of Ebronia by the same Right of Devolution descends to his Posterity, and rests on the Male Line of every eldest Branch. If so, no Act of Renunciation can alter this Succession, for that is a Gift, and the Gift is exploded, or else the whole House of the great Lip is excluded; so that let the Argument be turned and twisted never so many ways, it all Centers in this, that the present Person can have no Title to the Crown of Ebronia.

'If he has any Title, 'tis from the Gift of his Father and elder Brother; if the Gift of a Crown is no good Title, then his Title cannot be good; If the Gift of a Crown is a good Title, then the Crown was given away before, and so neither he nor his Father has any Title.

'Let him that can answer these Paradoxes defend his Title if he can; and what shall we now say to the War in Ebronia, only this, that they are going to fight for the Crown of Ebronia? and to take it away from one that has no Right to it, to give it to one that has a less Right than he, and 'tis to be feared that if Heaven be Righteous, 'twill succeed accordingly.

'The Gentlemen of Letters who have wrote of this in our Lunar World, on the Subject of the Gallunarians Title, have took a great deal of Liberty in the Eagle's behalf, to Banter and Ridicule the Gallunarian sham of a Title, as if it were a pretence too weak for any Prince to make use of, to talk of Kings giving their Crowns by Will.

Kingdoms and Governments, says a Learned Lunar author, are not things of such indifferent Value to be given away, like a Token left for a Legacy. If any Prince has ever given or transferred his Government, it has been done by solemn Act, and the People have been called to assent and confirm such Concessions.

'Then the same Author goes on, to Treat the King of Gallunaria with a great deal of Severity, and exposes his Politics, that he should think to put upon the Moon with so empty, so weak, so ridiculous a Pretence, as the Will of a weak Headed Prince, who neither had a Right to give his Crown, nor a Brain to know what he was doing, and he laughs to think what the King of Gallunaria would have said to have such a dull Trick as that, put upon him in any such Case.

'Now when we have been so Witty upon this very Article, of giving away the Crown to the King of Gallunaria's Grandson, as an incongruous and ridiculous Thing, shall we come to make the same Incongruity be the Foundation of a War?

'With what Justice can we make a War for a Prince who has only a good Title, by Virtue of the self same Action which makes the Grandson of his Enemy have a bad Title.

'I always thought we had a Just Ground to make War on Ebronia, as we were bound by former Alliances to assist the Eagle in the recovery of it in case of the death of the late King of that Country.

'But now the Eagle has refused the Succession, and his Eldest Son has refused it, I would be glad to see it proved how the second Son can have a Title, and yet the other King have no Title.

'What a strange sort of a Thing is the Crown of Ebronia, that two of the greatest Princes of the Lunar World should Fight, not who shall have it, for neither of them will accept of it, but who shall have the Power of giving it away.

'Here are four Princes refuse it; the King of Gallunaria's Sons had a Title in Right of their Mother, and 'twas not the former Renunciations that would have barred them, if this softer way had not been found out; for time was it has been pleaded on behalf of the eldest Son of the Gallunarian King, that his Mother could not give away his Right before he was born.

'Then the Eagle has a Right, and under him his eldest Son; and none of all these four will accept of the Crown; I believe all the Moon can't find four more that would refuse it.

'Now, tho' none of these think it worth accepting themselves, yet they fall out about the Right of giving it away. The King of Gallunaria will not accept of it himself, but he gets a Gift from the last Incumbent. This, says the Eagle, can't be a good Title, for the late King had no Right to make a Deed of Gift of the Crown, since a King is only

581

Tennant for Life, and Succession of Crowns either must descend by a Lineal Progression in the Right of Primogeniture, or else they lose the Tenure, and devolve on the People.

'Now as this Argument holds good the Eagle has an undoubted Title to the Crown of Ebronia: But then, says his English Majesty, I cannot accept of the Crown my self for I am the Eagle, and my eldest Son has two Kingdoms already, and is in a fair way to be Eagle after me, and 'tis not worth while for him, but I have a second Son, and we will give it him.

'Now may the King of Gallunaria say, if one Gift is good, another is good, and ours is the first Gift, and therefore we will keep it; and tho' I solemnly declare I should be very sorry to see the Crown of Ebronia rest in the House of the Gallunarian, because our Trade will suffer exceedingly; yet if never so much damage were to come of it, we ought to do Justice in the World; if neither the Eagle nor his eldest Son will be King of Ebronia, but a Deed of Gift shall be made, the first Gift has the Right, for nothing can be given away to two People at once, and 'tis apparent that the late King had as much Right to give it away as any Body.

'The poor Ebronians are in a fine Condition all this while, that no Body concerns them in the Matter; neither Party has so much as thought it worth while to ask them who they would have to Reign over them, here has been no Assembly, no Cortez, no Meeting of the People of Ebronia, neither Collectively or Representatively, no general Convention of the Nobility, no House of Feathers, but Ebronia lies as the spoil of the Victor wholly passive, and her People and Princes, as if they were wholly unconcerned, lie by and look on, whoever is like to be King, they are like to suffer deeply by the Strife, and yet neither side has thought fit to consult them about it.

'The conclusion of the whole Matter is in short this, here is certainly a false Step taken, how it shall be rectified is not the present Business, nor am I Wise enough to Prescribe. One Man may do in a Moment what all the Lunar World cannot undo in an Age. 'Tis not be thought the Eagle will be prevailed on to undo it, nay he has Sworn not to alter it.

'I am not concerned to prove the Title of the present King of Ebronia, no, nor of the Eagles neither; but I think I can never be answered in this, that this Gift of the Eagles to his second Son is preposterous, inconsistent with all his Claim to the Crown, and the greatest confirmation of the Title of his Enemy that it was possible to give, and no doubt the Gallunarians will lay hold of the Argument.

'If this Prince was the Eagle's eldest Son, he might have a Just Right from the concession of his Father, because the Right being inherent, he only received from him an Investiture of Time, but as this young Gentleman is a second Son he has no more Right, his elder Brother being alive, than your Grand Seignior, or Czar of Muscovy in your World.

'Let them Fight then for such a Cause, who valuing only the Pay, make War a Trade, and Fight for any thing they are bid to Fight for, and as such value not the Justice of the War, nor trouble their Heads about Causes and Consequences, so they have their Pay, 'tis well enough for them.

'But were the Justice of the War examined, I can see none, this Declaring a new King who has no Right but by a Gift, and pulling down one that had it by a Gift before, has so much Contradiction in it, that I am afraid no Wise Man, or Honest Man will embark in it.

Your Humble Servant, The Man in the Moon.

I wooed have no Body now pretend to scandalize the Writer of this Letter, which being for the Gallunarians, for no Man in the Moon had more Aversion for them than he, but he would have had the War carried on upon a right Bottom, Justice and Honesty regarded in it, and as he said often, they had no need to go out of the Road of Justice, for had they made War in the great Eagle's Name all had been well.

Nor was he a false Prophet, for as this was ill grounded, so it was as ill carried on, met with Shocks, Rubs and Disappointments every way. The very first Voyage the new King made, he had like to ha' been drowned by a very violent Tempest, things not very usual in those Countries; and all the Progress that had been made in his behalf when I came away from that Lunar World, had not brought him so much as to be able to set his Foot upon his new Kingdom of Ebronia, but his Adversary by wonderful Dexterity, and the Assistance of his old Grandfather the Gallunarian Monarch, beat his Troops upon all Occasions, invaded his Ally that pretended to assist him, and kept a quiet Possession of all the vast Ebronian Monarchy; and but at last by the powerful Diversion of the Solunarian Fleet, a Shock was given them on another Side, which if it had not happened, it was thought the new King had been sent home again Re Infecta.

Being very much Shocked in my Judgment of this Affair, by these unanswerable Reasons; I enquired of my Author who were the

583

Directors of this Matter? he told me plainly it was done by those great States Men, which the Solunarian Queen had lately very Justly turned out, whose Politics were very unaccountable in a great many other things, as well as in that.

'Tis true, the War was carried on under the new Ministry, and no War in the World can be Juster, on account of the Injustice and Encroachment of the Gallunarian Monarch.

The Queen therefore and her present Ministers, go on with the War on Principles of Confederacy; 'tis the business of the Solunarians to beat the Invader out, and then let the People come and make a fair Decision who they will have to Reign over them.

This indeed justifies the War in Ebronia to be Right, but for the Personal Procedure as before, 'tis all Contradiction and can never be answered.

I hope no Man will be so malicious, as to say I am hereby reflecting on our War with Spain. I am very forward to say, it is a most Just and Reasonable War, as to parallels between the Case of the Princes, in defending the Matter of Personal Right, Hic labor, Hoc opus.

Thus however you see Humanum est Errare, whether in this World or in the Moon, 'tis all one, Infallibility of Councils any more than of Doctrine, is not in Man.

The Reader may observe, I have formerly noted there was a new Consolidator to be Built, and observed what struggle there was in the Moon about choosing the Feathers.

I cannot omit some further Remarks here, as

I. It is to be observed, that this last Consolidator was in a manner quite worn out. —— It had indeed continued but 3 Year, which was the stated Time by Law, but it had been so Hurried, so Party Rid, so often had been up in the Moon, and made so many such extravagant Flights, and unnecessary Voyages thither, that it began to be exceedingly worn and defective.

2. This occasioned that the light fluttering Feathers, and the fermented Feathers made strange Work of it; nay, sometimes they were so hot, they were like to ha' ruined the whole Fabric, and had it not been for the great Feather in the Center, and a few Negative Feathers who were Wiser than the rest, all the Machines had been broke to pieces, and the whole Nation put into a most strange Confusion.

Sometimes their Motion was so violent an precipitant, that there was great apprehensions of its being set on Fire by its own Velocity, for

584

swiftness of Motion is allowed by the Sages and so so's to produce Fire as in Wheels, Mills and several sorts of Mechanic Engines which are frequently Fired, and so in Thoughts, Brains, Assemblies, Consolidators, and all such combustible Things.

Indeed these things were of great Consequence, and therefore require some more nice Examination than ordinary, and the following Story will in part explain it.

Among the rest of the Broils they had with the Grandees, one happened on this occasion.

One of the Tacking Feathers being accidentally met by a Grandee's Footman, whom it seems wanted some Manners, the Slave began to halloo him in the Street, with a Tacker, a Tacker, a Feather-Fool, a Tacker, &c. and so brought the Mob about him, and had not the Grandee himself come in the very interim, and rescued the Feather, the Mob had demolished him, they were so enraged.

As this Gentleman-Feather was rescued with great Courtesy by the Grandee, taken into his Coach and carried home to his House, he desired to speak with the Footman.

The Fellow being called in, was asked by him who employed him, or set him on to offer him this Insult? the Footman being a ready bold Fellow, told him no Body Sir, but you are all grown so ridiculous to the whole Nation, that if the 134 of you were left but to us Footmen, and it was not in more respect to our Masters, than you, we should Cure you of ever coming into the Consolidator again, and all the People in the Moon are of our Mind.

But says the Feather, why do you call me Fool too? why Sir, says he, because no Body could ever tell us what it was you drove at, and we ha' been told you never knew your selves; now if one of you Tacking Feathers would but tell the World what your real Design was, they would be satisfied, but to be leaders in the Consolidator, and to Act without Meaning, without Thought or Design, must argue your' Fools, or worse, and you will find all the Moon of my Mind.

But what if we had a meaning, says the Feather-Man? why then, says the Footman, we shall leave calling you Fools, and call you Knaves, for it could never be an Honest one, so that you had better stand as you do: and I make it out thus.

You knew, that upon your Tacking the Crolians to the Tribute Bill, the Grandees must reject both, they having declared against reading any Bills Tacked together, as being against their Privileges. Now if you had any Design, it must be to have the Bill of Tribute lost, and that must be to disappoint all the public Affairs, expose the Queen, break all Measures, discourage the Confederates, and putting all things backward, bring the Gallunarian Forces upon them, and put all Solunaria into Confusion. Now Sir, says he, we cannot have such course Thoughts of you, as to believe you could design such dark, mischievous things as these, and therefore we chose to believe you all Fools, and not fit to be put into a Consolidator again; than Knaves and Traitors to your Country, and consequently fit for a worse Place.

The plainness of the Footman was such, and so unanswerable, that his Master was fain to check him, and so the Discourse broke off, and we shall leave it there, and proceed to the Story.

The Men of the Feather as I have noted, who are represented here by the Consolidator, fell all together by the Ears, and all the Moon was in a combustion. The Case was as follows.

They had three times lost their qualifying Law, and particularly they observed the Grandees were the Men that threw it out, and notwithstanding the Plot of the Tackers, as they called them, who were as I noted, observed to be in Conjunction with the Crolians, yet the Law always past the Feathers, but still the Grandees quashed it.

To show their Resentment at the Grandees, they had often made attempts to mortify them, sometimes Arraigning them in general, sometimes Impeaching private Members of their House, but still all wooed not do, the Grandees had the better of them, and going on with Regularity and Temper, the Consolidators or Feather-Men always had the worst, the Grandees had the applause of all the Moon, had the last Blow on every Occasion, and the other sunk in their Reputation exceedingly.

It is necessary to understand here, that the Men of the Feather serve in several Capacities, and under several Denominations, and act by themselves, singly considered, they are called the Consolidator, and the Feathers we mentioned abstracted from their Persons, make the glorious Engine we speak of, and in which, when any sudden Motion takes them, they can all shut themselves up, and away for the Moon.

But when these are joined with the Grandees, and the Queen, so United, they make a great Cortez, or general Collection of all the Governing Authority of the Nation.

When this last Fraction happened, the Men of the Feather were under an exceeding Ferment, they had in some Passion taken into their Custody, some good Honest Lunar Country-Men, for an Offence, which indeed few but themselves ever imagined was a Crime, for the poor Men did nothing but pursue their own Right by the Law.

'Tis thought the Men of the Feather soon saw they were in the Wrong, but acted like some Men in our World, that when they make a mistake, being too Proud to own themselves in the wrong, run themselves into worse Errors to mend it.

So these Lunar Gentlemen disdaining to have it said they could be mistaken, committed two Errors to conceal one, 'till at last they came to be laughed at by all the Moon.

These poor Men having lain a long while in Prison, for little or no Crime, at last were advised to apply themselves to the Law for Discharge; the Law would fairly have Discharged them; for in that Country, no Man may be Imprisoned, but he must in a certain Time be Tried, or let go upon pledges of his Friends, much like our giving Bail on a Writ of Habeas Corpus; but the Judges, whether over-awed by the Feathers, or what was the Cause, Authors have not determined, did not care to venture Discharging them.

The poor Men thus remanded, applied themselves to the Grandees who were then Sitting, and who are the Sovereign Judicature of the Country, and before whom Appeals lie from all Courts of Justice. The Grandees as in Duty bound, appeared ready to do them Justice, but the Queen was to be applied to, first to grant a Writ, or a Warrant for a Writ, called in their Country a Writ of Follies, which is as much as to say Mistakes.

The Consolidators foreseeing the Consequence, immediately applied themselves to the Queen with an Address, the Terms of which were so Undu — — l and Unman — ly, that had she not been a Queen of unusual Candor and Goodness, she would have Treated them as they deserved, for they upbraided her with their Freedom and Readiness in granting her Supplies, and therefore as good as told her they expected she should do as they desired.

These People that knew the Supplies given, were from necessity, Legal, and for their own Defence, while the granting their Request, must have been Illegal, Arbitrary, a Dispensing with the Laws, and denying Justice to her Subjects, the very thing they ruined her Father for, were justly provoked to see their good Queen so barbarously Treated.

The Queen full of Goodness and Calmness, gave them a gentle kind Answer, but told them she must be careful to Act with due Regard to the Laws, and could not interrupt the course of Judicial Proceedings;

and at the same time granted the Writ, having first consulted with her Council, and received the Opinion of all the Judges, that it was not only Safe, but Just and Reasonable, and a Right to her People which she could not deny.

This Proceeding galled the Feathers to the quick, and finding the Grandees resolved to proceed Judicially upon the said Writ of Follies, which if they did, the Prisoners would be delivered and the Follies fixed upon the Feathers, they sent their Poursuivants took them out of the Common Prison, and conveyed them separately and privately into Prisons of their own.

This rash and unprecedented Proceedings, pushed them farther into a Labyrinth, from whence it was impossible they could ever find their way out, but with infinite Loss to their Reputation, like a Sheep in a thick Wood, that at every Briar pulls some of the Wool from her Back, till she comes out in a most scandalous Pickle of Nakedness and Scratches.

The Grandees immediately published six Articles in Vindication of the Peoples Right, against the assumed Privileges of the Feathers, the Abstract of which is as follows.

I. That the Feathers had no Right to Claim, or make any new Privileges for themselves, other than they had before.

2. That every Freeman of the Moon had a Right to repel Injury with Law.

3. That Imprisoning the 5 Countrymen by the Feathers, was assuming a new Privilege they had no Right to, and a subjecting the Subjects Right to their Arbitrary Votes.

4. That a Writ of Deliverance, or removing the Body, is the legal Right of every Subject in the Moon, in order to his Liberty, in case of Imprisonment.

5. That to punish any Person for assisting the Subjects, in procuring or prosecuting the said Writ of Deliverance, is a breach of the Laws, and a thing of dangerous Consequence.

6. That a Writ of Follies is not a Grace, but a Right, and ought not to be denied to the Subject.

These Resolves struck the languishing Reputation of the Feathers with the dead Palsy, and they began to stink in the Nostrils of all the Nations in the Moon.

But besides this, they had one strange effect, which was a prodigious disappointment to the Men of the Feather.

I had observed before, that there was to be a new Set of Feathers, provided in order to Building another Consolidator, according to a late Law for a new Engine every three Years. Now several of these Men of the Feather, who thought their Feathers capable of serving again, had made great Interest, and been at great Cost to have their old Feathers chosen again, but the People had entertained such scoundrel Opinions of these Proceedings, such as Tacking, Consolidating, Imprisoning Electors, Impeaching without Trial, Writs of Follies and the like, that if any one was known to be concerned in any of these things, no Body would Vote for him.

The Gentlemen were so mortified at this, that even the hottest High-Church Solunarian of them all, if he put in any where to be re-chosen, the first thing he had to do, was to assure the People he was no Tacker, none of the 134, and a vast deal of difficulty they had to Purge themselves of this blessed Action, which they used to value themselves on before, as their Glory and Merit.

Thus they grew ashamed of it as a Crime, got Men to go about to vouch for them to the Country People, that they were no Tackers, nay, one of them to clear himself loudly forswore it, and taking a Glass of Wine wished it might never pass thro' him, if he was a Tacker, tho' all Men suspected him to be of that Number too, he having been one of the forwardest that way on all Occasions, of any Person among the South Folk of the Moon.

In like manner, one of the Feathers for the middle Province of the Country, who used to think it his Honour to be for the qualifying Law, seeing which way the humour of the Country ran, took as much Pains now to tell the People he was no Tacker, as he did before, to promise them that he would do his utmost to have the Crolians reduced, and that Bill to pass, the Reason of which was plain, that he saw if it should be known he was a Tacker, he should never have his Feather returned to be put into the Consolidator.

The Heats and Feuds that the Feathers and the Grandees were now run into, began to make the latter very uneasy, and they sent to the Grandees to hasten them, and put them in mind of passing some Laws they had sent up to them for raising Money, and which lay before them, knowing that as soon as those Laws were past, the Queen would break 'em up, and they being very willing to be gone, before these things came too far upon the Stage, urged them to dispatch.

But the Grandees resolving to go thoro' with the Matter, sent to them to come to a Treaty on the foot of the six Articles, and to bring any Reasons they could, to prove the Power they had to Act as they had done with the Country-men, and with the Lawyers they had put in Prison for assisting them.

The Feathers were very backward and stiff about this Conference, or Treaty, 'till at last the Grandees having sufficiently exposed them to all the Nation, the Bills were past, the Grandees caused the particulars to be Printed, and a Representation of their Proceedings, and the Feathers foul Dealings to the Queen of the Country, and so her Majesty sent them Home.

But if they were ashamed of being called Tackers before, they were doubly mortified at this now, nay the Country resented it so exceedingly, that some of them began to consider whether they should venture to go Home or no; Printed Lists of their Names were Published, tho' we do not say they were true Lists, for it was a hard thing to know which were true Lists, and which were not, nor indeed could a true List be made, no Man being able to retain the exact Account of who were the Men in his Memory.

For as there were 134 Tackers, so there were 141 of these, who by a Name of Distinction, were called Lebusyraneim, in English Ailesbury-men.

The People were so exasperated against these, that they expressed their Resentment upon all Occasions, and least the Queen should think that the Nation approved the Proceedings, they drew up a Representation or Complaint, full of most dutiful Expressions to their Queen, and full of Resentment against the Feathers, the Copy of which being handed about the Moon the last time I was there, I shall take the Pains to put it into English in the best manner I can, keeping as near the Original as possible.

If any Man shall now wickedly suggest, that this Relation has any retrospect to the Affairs of England, the Author declares them malicious Misconstruers of his honest Relation of Matters from this remote Country, and offers his positive Oath for their Satisfaction, that the very last Journey he made into those Lunar Regions, this Matter was upon the Stage, of which, if this Treatise was not so near its conclusion, the Reader might expect a more particular Account.

If there is any Analogy or similitude between the Transactions of either World, he cannot account for that, 'tis application makes the Ass.

And yet sometimes he has thought, as some People Fable of the Platonic Year, that after such a certain Revolution of Time, all Things are Transacted over again, and the same People live again, are the fame

590

Fools, Knaves, Philosophers and Mad-men they were before, tho'
without any Knowledge of, or Retrospect to what they acted before; so
why should it be impossible, that as the Moon and this World are
noted before to be Twins and Sisters, equal in Motion and in Influence,
and perhaps in Qualities, the same secret Power should so act them, as
that like Actions and Circumstances should happen in all Parts of both
Worlds at the same time.

I leave this Thought to the improvement of our Royal Learned
Societies of the Anticacofanums, Opposotians, Periodicarians,
Antepredestinarians, Universal Soulians, and such like unfathomable
People, who, without question, upon mature Enquiry will find out the
Truth of this Matter.

But if any one shall scruple the Matter of Fact as I have here
related it, I freely give him leave to do as I did, and go up to the Moon
for a Demonstration; and if upon his return he does not give ample
Testimony to the Case in every part of it, as here related, I am content
to pass for the Contriver of it my self, and be punished as the Law shall
say I deserve.

Nor was this all the public Matters, in which this Nation of
Solunarians took wrong Measures, for about this time, the
Misunderstandings between the Southern and Northern Men began
again, and the Solunarians made several Laws, as they called them, to
secure themselves against the Dangers they pretended might accrue from
the new Measures the Nolunarians had taken; but so unhappily were
they blinded by the strife among themselves, and by-set by Opinion and
Interest, that every Law they made, or so much as attempted to make,
was really to the Advantage, and to the Interest of the Northern-Men,
and to their own loss; so Ignorantly and Weak-headed was these High
Solunarian Church-Men in the true Interest of their Country, led by
their implacable Malice at Crolianism, which as is before noted, was the
Established Religion of that Country.

But as this Matter was but Transacting when I took the other
Remarks, and that I did not obtain a full Understanding of it, 'till my
second Voyage, I refer it to a more full Relation of my farther Travels
that way, when I shall not fail to give a clear State of the Debate of the
two Kingdoms, in which the Southern Men had the least Reason, and
the worst Success that ever they had in any Affair of that Nature for
many Years before.

It was always my Opinion in Affairs on this side the Moon, that
tho' sometimes a foolish Bolt may hit the Point, and a random Shot kill

the Enemy, yet that generally Discretion and Prudence of Management, had the Advantage, and met with a proportioned Success, find things were, or were not happy, in their Conclusion as they were, more or less wisely Contrived and Directed.

And tho' it may not be allowed to be so here, yet I found it more constantly so there, Effects were true to their Causes, and confusion of Councils never failed in the Moon to be followed by distracted and destructive Consequences.

This appeared more eminently in the Dispute between these two Lunar Nations we are speaking of; never were People in the Moon, whatever they might be in other Places, so divided in their Opinions about a matter of such Consequence. Some were for declaring War immediately upon the Northern Men, tho' they could show no Reason at all why, only because they would not do as they would have 'em; a parcel of poor Scoundrel, Scabby Rogues, they ought to be made submit, what! won't they declare the same King as we do! hang them Rogues! a pack of Crolian Prestarian Devils, we must make them do it, down with them the shortest Way, declare War immediately, and down with them. — — — Nay some were for falling on them directly, without the formality of declaring War.

Others, more afraid than hurt, cried out Invasions, Depredation, Fire and Sword, the Northern Men would be upon them immediately, and proposed to Fortify their Frontiers, and file off their Forces to the Borders; nay, so apprehensive did those Men of Prudence pretend to be, that they ordered Towns to be Fortified 100 Mile off of the Place, when all this while the poor Northern Men did nothing but tell them, that unless they would come to Terms, they would not have the same King as they, and they took some Measures to let them see they did not purpose to be forced to it.

Another sort of Wiser Men than these, proposed to Unite with them, hear their Reasons, and do them Right. These indeed were the only Men that were in the right Method of concluding this unhappy Broil, and for that Reason, were the most unlikely to succeed.

But the Wildest Notion of all, was, when some of the Grandees made a grave Address to the Queen of the Country, to desire the Northern Men to settle Matters first, and to tell them, that when that was done, they should see what these would do for them. This was a home Stroke, if it had but hit, and the Misfortune only lay in this, That the Northern Men were not Fools enough; the clearness of the Air in those cold Climates generally clearing the Head so early, that those

592

People see much farther into a Mill-stone than any Blind Man in all the Southern Nations of the Moon.

There was an another unhappiness in this Case, which made the Matter yet more confused, and that was, that the Soldiers had generally no gust to this War. — This was an odd Case; for those sort of Gentlemen, especially in the World in the Moon, don't use to enquire into the Justice of the Case they Fight for, but they reckon 'tis their Business to go where they are sent, and kill any Body they are ordered to kill, leaving their Governors to answer for the Justice of it; but there was another Reason to be given why the Men of the Sword were so averse, and always talked coldly of the fighting Part, and tho' the Northern Men called it fear, yet I cannot join with them in that, for to fear requires Thinking; and some of our Solunarians are absolutely protected from the first, because they never meddle with the last, except when they come to the Engine, and therefore 'tis plain it could not proceed from Fear.

It has puzzled the most discerning Heads of the Age, to give a Reason from whence this Aversion proceeded, and various Judgments have been given of it.

The Nolunarians jested with them, and when they talked of Fighting, bad them look back into History, and examine what they ever made of a Nolunarian War, and whether they had not been often well beaten, and sent short home, bid them have a care of catching a Tartar, as we call it, and always made themselves merry with it.

They bantered the Solunarians too, about the Fears and Terrors they were under, from their Arming themselves, and putting themselves in a posture of Defence, — — When it was easy to see by the nature of the thing, that their Design was not a War, but a Union upon just Conditions, that it was a plain Token that they designed either to put some affront upon the Nolunarians, to deny them some just Claims, or to impose something very Provoking upon them more than they had yet done, that they were so exceeding fearful of an Invasion from them.

Tho' these were sufficient to pass for Reasons in other Cases, yet it could not be so here, but I saw there must be something else in it. As I was thus wondering at this unusual backwardness of the Soldiers, I enquired a little farther into the meaning of it, and quickly found the Reason was plain, there was nothing to be got by it, that People were Brave, Desperate and Poor, the Country Barren, Mountainous and Empty, so that in short there would be nothing but Blows, and Soldiers

Fellows to be had, and I always observed that Soldiers never care to be knocked on the Head, and get nothing by the Bargain.

In short, I saw plainly the Reasons that prompted the Solunarians to Insult their Neighbours of the North, were more derived from the regret at their Establishing Crolianism, than at any real Causes they had given, or indeed were in a condition to give them.

These, and abundance more particular Observations I made, but as I left the thing still in agitation, and undetermined, I shall refer it to another Voyage which I purpose to make thither, and at my return, may perhaps set that Case in a clearer Light than our Sight can yet bear to look at it in.

If in my second Vovage I should undeceive People in the Notions they entertained of those Northern People, and convince them that the Solunarians were really the Aggressors, and had put great hardships upon them, I might possibly do a Work, that if it met with Encouragement, might bring the Solunarians to do them Justice, and that would set all to Rights, the two Nations might easily become one, and Unite for ever, or at least become Friends, and give mutual Assistance to each other; and I cannot but own such an Agreement would make them both very formidable, but this I refer to another time.

— —

At the same time I cannot leave it without a Remark that this Jealousy between the two Nations, may perhaps in future Ages be necessary to be maintained, in order to find some better Reasons for Fortifications, Standing Armies, Guards and Garrisons than could be given in the Reign of the great Prince I speak of, the Queen's Predecessor, tho' his was against Foreign insulting Enemy.

But the Temper of the Solunarian High Party was always such, that they would with much more case give thanks for a Standing Army against the Nolunarians and Crolians, than agree to one Legion against the Abrogratzians and Gallunarians.

But of these Things I am also promised a more particular Account upon my Journey into that Country.

I cannot however conclude this Matter, without giving some Account of my private Observations, upon what was farther to be seen in this Country.

And had not my Remarks on their State Matters taken up more of my Thoughts than I expected, I might have entered a little upon their other Affairs, such as their Companies, their Commerce, their Public Offices, their Stock-Jobbers, their Temper, their Conversation, their

Women, their Stages, Universities, their Courtiers, their Clergy, and the Characters of the severals under all these Denominations, but these must be referred to time, and my more perfect Observations.

But I cannot omit, that tho' I have very little Knowledge of Books, and had obtained less upon their Language, yet I could not but be very inquisitive after their Libraries and Men of Letters.

Among their Libraries I found not abundance of their own Books, their Learning having so much of Demonstration, and being very Hieroglyphical, but I found to my great Admiration vast quantities of Translated Books out of all Languages of our World.

As I thought my self one of the first, at least of our Nation, that ever came thus far; it was, you may be sure no small surprise to me to find all the most valuable parts of Modern Learning, especially of Politics, Translated from our Tongue, into the Lunar Dialect, and stored up in their Libraries with the Remarks, Notes and Observations of the Learned Men of that Climate upon the Subject.

Here, among a vast crowd of French Authors condemned in this polite World for trifling, came a huge Volume containing, Les Oeuvres de sçavans, which has 19 small Bells painted upon the Book of several disproportioned sizes.

I enquired the meaning of that Hieroglyphic, which the Master of the Books told me, was to signify that the substance was all Jingle and Noise, and that of 30 Volumes which that one Book contains, 29 of them have neither Substance, Music, Harmony nor value in them.

The History of the Fulsoms, or a Collection of 300 fine Speeches made in the French Academy at Paris, and 1500 gay Flourishes out of Monsieur Boileau, all in Praise of the invincible Monarch of France.

The Duke of Bavaria's Manifesto, showing the Right of making War against our Sovereigns, from whence the People of that Lunar World have noted that the same Reasons which made it lawful to him to attempt the Imperial Power, entitle him to lose his own, viz. Conquest, and the longest Sword.

Jack a both Sides, or a Dialogue between Pasquin and Marforio, upon the Subject Matter of the Pope's sincerity in Case of the War in Italy. Written by a Citizen of Ferrara. One side arguing upon the occasion of the Pope's General wheedling the Imperialists to quit that Country. The other bantering Imperial Policy, or the Germans pretending they were Tricked out of Italy, when they could stay there no longer.

Lewis the Invincible, by Monsieur Boileau. A Poem, on the Glory of his most Christian Majesties Arms at Hochstedt, and Verue.

All these Translations have innumerable Hyeroglyphical Notes, and Emblems painted on them, which pass as Comments, and are readily understood in that Climate. For Example, on the Vol. of Dialogues are two Cardinals washing the Pope's Hands under a Cloud that often bespatters them with Blood, signifying that in spite of all his Pretensions he has a Hand in the Broils of Italy. And before him the Sun setting in a Cloud, and a Blind Ballad-Singer making Sonnets upon the brightness of its Lustre.

The three Kings of Brentford, being some Historical Observations on three mighty Monarchs in our World, whose Heroic Actions may be the Subject of future Ages, being like to do little in this, the King of England, King of Poland, and King of Spain. These are described by a Figure, representing a Castle in the Air, and three Knights pointing at it, but they could not catch.

I omit abundance of very excellent pieces, because remote, as three great Volumes of European Mysteries, among the vast varieties of which, and very entertaining, I observed but a few, such as these:

1. Why Prince Ragotski will make no Peace with the Emperor. — But more particularly why the Emperor won't make Peace with him.

2. Where the Policy of the King of Sweden lies, to pursue the King of Poland, and let the Muscovites ravage and destroy his own Subjects.

3. What the Duke of Bavaria proposed to himself in declaring for France.

4. Why the Protestants of the Confederacy never relieved the Commissars.

5. Why there are no Cowards found in the English Service, but among their Sea Captains.

6. Why the King of Portugal did not take Madrid, why the English did not take Cadiz, and why the Spaniards did not take Gibraltar, viz. because the first were Fools, the second Knaves, and the last Spaniards.

7. What became of all the Silver taken at Vigo.

8. Who will be the next King of Scotland.

9. If England should ever want a King, who would think it worth while to accept of it.

10. What specific difference can be produced between a Knave, a Coward, and a Traitor.

596

Abundance of these Mysteries are Hieroglyphically described in this ample Collection, and without doubt our great Collection of Annals, and Historical Observations, particularly the Learned Mr. Walker, would make great Improvements there.

But to come nearer home, There, to my great Amazement, I found several new Tracts out of our own Language, which I could hardly have imagined it possible should have reached so far.

As first, sundry Transactions of our Royal Society about Winds, and a valuable Dissertation of Dr. B.....'s about Wind in the Brain.

A Discourse of Poisons, by the Learned Dr. M..... with Lunar Notes upon it, wherein it appears that Dr. C....d had more Poison in his Tongue, than all the Adders the Moon have in their Teeth.

Nec Non, or Lawyers Latin turned into Lunar Burlesque. The Hieroglyphic was the Queen's Money tossed in a Blanket, Dedicated to the Attorney General, and five false Latin Counselors.

Mandamus, as it was Acted at Abb...ton Assizes, by Mr. So....r General, where the Qu..n had her own So...r against her for a bad Cause, and never a Counsel for her in a good one.

Lunar Reflections, being a List of about 2000 ridiculous Errors in History, palpable Falsities, and scandalous Omissions in Mr. Collier's Geographical Dictionary; with a subsequent Enquiry by way of Appendix, into which are his own, and which he has ignorantly deduced from ancient Authors.

Assassination and Killing of Kings, proved to be a Church of England Doctrine; humbly Dedicated to the Prince of Wales, by Mr. Collier and Mr. Snat; wherein their Absolving Sir John Friend and Sir William Parkins without Repentance, and while they both owned and justified the Fact, is Vindicated and Defended.

Les Bagatelles, or Brom..ys Travels into Italy, a choice Book, and by great Accident preserved from the malicious Design of the Author, who diligently Bought up the whole Impression, for fear they should be seen, as a thing of which this ungrateful Age was not worthy.

Killing no Murder, being an Account of the severe Justice designed to be inflicted on the barbarous Murderers of the honest Constable at Bow, but unhappily prevented by my Lord N.....m being turned out of his Office.

De modo Belli, or an Account of the best Method of making Conquests and Invasion a la Mode de Port St. Mary, 3 Volumes in 80. Dedicated to Sir Hen. Bell...s.

King Charles the first proved a T...t. By Edward Earl of Clarendon, 3 Vol. in Fol. Dedicated to the University of Oxford.

The Bawdy Poets, or new and accurate Editions of Catullus, Propertius, and Tibullus, being the Maiden-head of the new Printing Press at Cambridge, Dedicated by the Editor Mr. Ann...y to the University, and in consideration of which, and some Disorders near Casterton, the University thought him fit to represent them in P......t.

Alms no Charity, or the Skeleton of Sir Humphry Mackworth's Bill for relief of the Poor: Being an excellent new Contrivance to find Employment for all the Poor in the Nation, viz. By setting them at Work, to make all the rest of the People as Poor as themselves.

Synodicum Superlativum, being sixteen large Volumes of the vigorous Proceedings of the English Convocation, digested into Years, one Volume to every Year. — Wherein are several large Lists of the Heretical, Atheistical, Deistical and other pernicious Errors which have been Condemned in that Venerable Assembly, the various Services done, and weighty Matters dispatched, for the Honour of the English Church, for sixteen Years last past, with their formal Proceedings against Asgil, Coward, Toland and others, for reviving old Antiquated Errors in Doctrine, and Publishing them to the World as their own.

New Worlds in Trade, being a vast Collection out of the Journals of the Proceedings of the Right Honourable the Commissioners of Trade, with several Eminent Improvements in general Negoce, vast Schemes of Business, and new Discoveries of Settlements and Correspondences in Foreign Parts, for the Honour and Advantage of the English Merchants, being 12 Volumes in Fol. and very scarce and valuable Books.

Legal Rebellion, or an Argument proving that all sorts of Insurrections of Subjects against their Princes, are lawful, and to be supported whenever they suit with our Occasions, made good from the Practice of France with the Hungarians, the English with the Commissars, the Swede with the Poles, the Emperor with the Subjects of Naples, and all the Princes of the World as they find occasion, a large Volume in Folio, with a Poem upon the Sacred Right of Kingly Power.

Ignis Fatuus or the Occasional Bill in Miniature, a Farce, as it was acted by his Excellency the Lord Gr...il's Servants in Carolina.

Running away the shortest way to Victory, being a large Dissertation, showing to save the Queens Ships, is the best way to beat the French.

The Tookites, a Poem upon the 134.

A new Tract upon Trade, being a Demonstration that to be always putting the People upon customary Mourning, and wearing Black upon every State Occasion, is an excellent Encouragement to Trade, and a means to employ the Poor.

City Gratitude, being a Poem on the Statue erected by the Court of Aldermen at the upper end of Cheapside, to the Immortal Memory of King William.

There were many more Tracts to be found in this place; but these may suffice for a Specimen, and to excite all Men that would increase their Understandings in humane Mysteries, to take a Voyage to this enlightened Country. Where their Memories, thinking Faculties and Penetration, will no question be so Tacked and Consolidated, that when they return, they all Write Memoirs of the Place, and communicate to their Country the Advantages they have reaped by their Voyage, according to the laudable Example of their

Most humble Servant, The Man in the Moon.

THE LIFE ADVENTURES AND PIRACIES OF THE FAMOUS CAPTAIN SINGLETON

As it is usual for great persons, whose lives have been remarkable, and whose actions deserve recording to posterity, to insist much upon their originals, give full accounts of their families, and the histories of their ancestors, so, that I may be methodical, I shall do the same, though I can look but a very little way into my pedigree, as you will see presently.

If I may believe the woman whom I was taught to call mother, I was a little boy, of about two years old, very well dressed, had a nursery-maid to attend me, who took me out on a fine summer's evening into the fields towards Islington, as she pretended, to give the child some air; a little girl being with her, of twelve or fourteen years old, that lived in the neighbourhood. The maid, whether by appointment or otherwise, meets with a fellow, her sweetheart, as I suppose; he carries her into a public-house, to give her a pot and a cake; and while they were toying in the house the girl plays about, with me in her hand, in the garden and at the door, sometimes in sight, sometimes out of sight, thinking no harm.

At this juncture comes by one of those sort of people who, it seems, made it their business to spirit away little children. This was a hellish trade in those days, and chiefly practiced where they found little children very well dressed, or for bigger children, to sell them to the plantations.

The woman, pretending to take me up in her arms and kiss me, and play with me, draws the girl a good way from the house, till at last she makes a fine story to the girl, and bids her go back to the maid, and tell her where she was with the child; that a gentlewoman had taken a fancy to the child, and was kissing of it, but she should not be frighted, or to that purpose; for they were but just there; and so, while the girl went, she carries me quite away.

From this time, it seems, I was disposed of to a beggar woman that wanted a pretty little child to set out her case; and after that, to a gipsy, under whose government I continued till I was about six years old. And this woman, though I was continually dragged about with her from one part of the country to another, yet never let me want for anything; and I called her mother; though she told me at last she was not my mother, but that she bought me for twelve shillings of another woman, who told her how she came by me, and told her that my name was Bob Singleton, not Robert, but plain Bob; for it seems they never knew by what name I was christened.

It is in vain to reflect here, what a terrible fright the careless hussy was in that lost me; what treatment she received from my justly enraged father and mother, and the horror these must be in at the thoughts of their child being thus carried away; for as I never knew anything of the matter, but just what I have related, nor who my father and mother were, so it would make but a needless digression to talk of it here.

My good gipsy mother, for some of her worthy actions no doubt, happened in process of time to be hanged; and as this fell out something too soon for me to be perfected in the strolling trade, the parish where I was left, which for my life I can't remember, took some care of me, to be sure; for the first thing I can remember of myself afterwards, was, that I went to a parish school, and the minister of the parish used to talk to me to be a good boy; and that, though I was but a poor boy, if I minded my book, and served God, I might make a good man.

I believe I was frequently removed from one town to another, perhaps as the parishes disputed my supposed mother's last settlement. Whether I was so shifted by passes, or otherwise, I know not; but the town where I last was kept, whatever its name was, must be not far off from the seaside; for a master of a ship who took a fancy to me, was the first that brought me to a place not far from Southampton, which I afterwards knew to be Bussleton; and there I attended the carpenters, and such people as were employed in building a ship for him; and when it was done, though I was not above twelve years old, he carried me to sea with him on a voyage to Newfoundland.

I lived well enough, and pleased my master so well that he called me his own boy; and I would have called him father, but he would not allow it, for he had children of his own. I went three or four voyages with him, and grew a great sturdy boy, when, coming home again from the banks of Newfoundland, we were taken by an Algerine rover, or man-of-war; which, if my account stands right, was about the year 1695, for you may be sure I kept no journal.

I was not much concerned at the disaster, though I saw my master, after having been wounded by a splinter in the head during the engagement, very barbarously used by the Turks; I say, I was not much concerned, till, upon some unlucky thing I said, which, as I remember, was about abusing my master, they took me and beat me most unmercifully with a flat stick on the soles of my feet, so that I could neither go or stand for several days together.

But my good fortune was my friend upon this occasion; for, as they were sailing away with our ship in tow as a prize, steering for the Straits, and in sight of the bay of Cadiz, the Turkish rover was attacked by two great Portuguese men-of-war, and taken and carried into Lisbon.

As I was not much concerned at my captivity, not indeed understanding the consequences of it, if it had continued, so I was not suitably sensible of my deliverance; nor, indeed, was it so much a deliverance to me as it would otherwise have been, for my master, who was the only friend I had in the world, died at Lisbon of his wounds; and I being then almost reduced to my primitive state, viz., of starving, had this addition to it, that it was in a foreign country too, where I knew nobody and could not speak a word of their language. However, I fared better here than I had reason to expect; for when all the rest of our men had their liberty to go where they would, I, that knew not whither to go, stayed in the ship for several days, till at length one of the lieutenants seeing me, inquired what that young English dog did there, and why they did not turn him on shore.

I heard him, and partly understood what he meant, though not what he said, and began then to be in a terrible fright; for I knew not where to get a bit of bread; when the pilot of the ship, an old seaman, seeing me look very dull, came to me, and speaking broken English to me, told me I must be gone. "Whither must I go?" said I. "Where you will," said he, "home to your own country, if you will." "How must I go thither?" said I. "Why, have you no friend?" said he. "No," said I, "not in the world, but that dog," pointing to the ship's dog (who, having stolen a piece of meat just before, had brought it close by me, and I had taken it from him, and ate it), "for he has been a good friend, and brought me my dinner."

"Well, well," says he, "you must have your dinner. Will you go with me?" "Yes," says I, "with all my heart." In short, the old pilot took me home with him, and used me tolerably well, though I fared hard enough; and I lived with him about two years, during which time he was soliciting his business, and at length got to be master or pilot under Don Garcia de Pimentesia de Carravallas, captain of a Portuguese galleon or carrack, which was bound to Goa, in the East Indies; and immediately having gotten his commission, put me on board to look after his cabin, in which he had stored himself with abundance of liquors, saccades, sugar, spices, and other things, for his accommodation in the voyage, and laid in afterwards a considerable quantity of European goods, fine lace and linen; and also baize, woolen cloth, stuffs, &c., under the pretence of his clothes.

I was too young in the trade to keep any journal of this voyage, though my master, who was, for a Portuguese, a pretty good artist, prompted me to it; but my not understanding the language was one hindrance; at least it served me for an excuse. However, after some time, I began to look into his charts and books; and, as I could write a tolerable hand, understood some Latin, and began to have a little smattering of the Portuguese tongue, so I began to get a superficial knowledge of navigation, but not such as was likely to be sufficient to carry me through a life of adventure, as mine was to be. In short, I learned several material things in this voyage among the Portuguese; I learned particularly to be an arrant thief and a bad sailor; and I think I may say they are the best masters for teaching both these of any nation in the world.

We made our way for the East Indies, by the coast of Brazil; not that it is in the course of sailing the way thither, but our captain, either on his own account, or by the direction of the merchants, went thither first, where at All Saints' Bay, or, as they call it in Portugal, the Rio de Todos los Santos, we delivered near a hundred tons of goods, and took in a considerable quantity of gold, with some chests of sugar, and seventy or eighty great rolls of tobacco, every roll weighing at least a hundredweight.

Here, being lodged on shore by my master's order, I had the charge of the captain's business, he having seen me very diligent for my own master; and in requital for his mistaken confidence, I found means to secure, that is to say, to steal, about twenty moidores out of the gold that was shipped on board by the merchants, and this was my first adventure.

We had a tolerable voyage from hence to the Cape de Bona Speranza; and I was reputed as a mighty diligent servant to my master, and very faithful. I was diligent indeed, but I was very far from honest; however, they thought me honest, which, by the way, was their very great mistake. Upon this very mistake the captain took a particular liking to me, and employed me frequently on his own occasion; and, on the other hand, in recompense for my officious diligence, I received several particular favours from him; particularly, I was, by the captain's command, made a kind of a steward under the ship's steward, for such provisions as the captain demanded for his own table. He had another steward for his private stores besides, but my office concerned only what the captain called for of the ship's stores for his private use.

However, by this means I had opportunity particularly to take care of my master's man, and to furnish myself with sufficient provisions to make me live much better than the other people in the ship; for the captain seldom ordered anything out of the ship's stores, as above, but I snipped some of it for my own share. We arrived at Goa, in the East Indies, in about seven months from Lisbon, and remained there eight more; during which time I had indeed nothing to do, my master being generally on shore, but to learn everything that is wicked among the Portuguese, a nation the most perfidious and the most debauched, the most insolent and cruel, of any that pretend to call themselves Christians, in the world.

Thieving, lying, swearing, forswearing, joined to the most abominable lewdness, was the stated practice of the ship's crew; adding to it, that, with the most insufferable boasts of their own courage, they were, generally speaking, the most complete cowards that I ever met with; and the consequence of their cowardice was evident upon many occasions. However, there was here and there one among them that was not so bad as the rest; and, as my lot fell among them, it made me have the most contemptible thoughts of the rest, as indeed they deserved.

I was exactly fitted for their society indeed; for I had no sense of virtue or religion upon me. I had never heard much of either, except what a good old parson had said to me when I was a child of about eight or nine years old; nay, I was preparing and growing up apace to be as wicked as anybody could be, or perhaps ever was. Fate certainly thus directed my beginning, knowing that I had work which I had to do in the world, which nothing but one hardened against all sense of honesty or religion could go through; and yet, even in this state of original wickedness, I entertained such a settled abhorrence of the abandoned vileness of the Portuguese, that I could not but hate them most heartily from the beginning, and all my life afterwards. They were so brutishly wicked, so base and perfidious, not only to strangers but to one another, so meanly submissive when subjected, so insolent, or barbarous and tyrannical, when superior, that I thought there was something in them that shocked my very nature. Add to this that it is natural to an Englishman to hate a coward, it all joined together to make the devil and a Portuguese equally my aversion.

However, according to the English proverb, he that is shipped with the devil must sail with the devil; I was among them, and I managed myself as well as I could. My master had consented that I should assist the captain in the office, as above; but, as I understood afterwards that the captain allowed my master half a moidore a month for my service, and that he had my name upon the ship's books also, I expected that when the ship came to be paid four months' wages at the Indies, as they, it seems, always do, my master would let me have something for myself.

But I was wrong in my man, for he was none of that kind; he had taken me up as in distress, and his business was to keep me so, and make his market of me as well as he could, which I began to think of after a different manner than I did at first, for at first I thought he had entertained me in mere charity, upon seeing my distressed circumstances, but did not doubt but when he put me on board the ship, I should have some wages for my service.

But he thought, it seems, quite otherwise; and when I procured one to speak to him about it, when the ship was paid at Goa, he flew into the greatest rage imaginable, and called me English dog, young heretic, and threatened to put me into the Inquisition. Indeed, of all the names the four-and-twenty letters could make up, he should not have called me heretic; for as I knew nothing about religion, neither Protestant from Papist, or either of them from a Mahometan, I could never be a heretic. However, it passed but a little, but, as young as I was, I had been carried into the Inquisition, and there, if they had asked me if I was a Protestant or a Catholic, I should have said yes to that which came first. If it had been the Protestant they had asked first, it had certainly made a martyr of me for I did not know what.

But the very priest they carried with them, or chaplain of the ship, as we called him, saved me; for seeing me a boy entirely ignorant of religion, and ready to do or say anything they bid me, he asked me some questions about it, which he found I answered so very simply, that he took it upon him to tell them he would answer for my being a good Catholic, and he hoped he should be the means of saving my soul, and he pleased himself that it was to be a work of merit to him; so he made me as good a Papist as any of them in about a week's time.

I then told him my case about my master; how, it is true, he had taken me up in a miserable case on board a man-of-war at Lisbon; and I was indebted to him for bringing me on board this ship; that if I had been left at Lisbon, I might have starved, and the like; and therefore I was willing to serve him, but that I hoped he would give me some little consideration for my service, or let me know how long he expected I should serve him for nothing.

It was all one; neither the priest nor any one else could prevail with him, but that I was not his servant but his slave, that he took me in the Algerine, and that I was a Turk, only pretended to be an English boy to get my liberty, and he would carry me to the Inquisition as a Turk.

This frighted me out of my wits, for I had nobody to vouch for me what I was, or from whence I came; but the good Padre Antonio, for that was his name, cleared me of that part by a way I did not understand; for he came to me one morning with two sailors, and told me they must search me, to bear witness that I was not a Turk. I was amazed at them, and frighted, and did not understand them, nor could I imagine what they intended to do to me. However, stripping me, they were soon satisfied, and Father Antony bade me be easy, for they could all witness that I was no Turk. So I escaped that part of my master's cruelty.

And now I resolved from that time to run away from him if I could, but there was no doing of it there, for there were not ships of any nation in the world in that port, except two or three Persian vessels from Ormus, so that if I had offered to go away from him, he would have had me seized on shore, and brought on board by force; so that I had no remedy but patience. And this he brought to an end too as soon as he could, for after this he began to use me ill, and not only to straiten my provisions, but to beat and torture me in a barbarous manner for every trifle, so that, in a word, my life began to be very miserable.

The violence of this usage of me, and the impossibility of my escape from his hands, set my head a-working upon all sorts of mischief, and in particular I resolved, after studying all other ways to deliver myself, and finding all ineffectual, I say, I resolved to murder him. With this hellish resolution in my head, I spent whole nights and days contriving how to put it in execution, the devil prompting me very warmly to the fact. I was indeed entirely at a loss for the means, for I had neither gun or sword, nor any weapon to assault him with; poison I had my thoughts much upon, but knew not where to get any; or, if I might have got it, I did not know the country word for it, or by what name to ask for it.

In this manner I quitted the fact, intentionally, a hundred and a hundred times; but Providence, either for his sake or for mine, always frustrated my designs, and I could never bring it to pass; so I was obliged to continue in his chains till the ship, having taken in her loading, set sail for Portugal.

I can say nothing here to the manner of our voyage, for, as I said, I kept no journal; but this I can give an account of, that having been once as high as the Cape of Good Hope, as we call it, or Cabo de Bona Speranza, as they call it, we were driven back again by a violent storm from the W.S.W., which held us six days and nights a great way to the eastward, and after that, standing afore the wind for several days more, we at last came to an anchor on the coast of Madagascar.

The storm had been so violent that the ship had received a great deal of damage, and it required some time to repair her; so, standing in nearer the shore, the pilot, my master, brought the ship into a very good harbour, where we rid in twenty-six fathoms water, about half a mile from the shore.

While the ship rode here there happened a most desperate mutiny among the men, upon account of some deficiency in their allowance, which came to that height that they threatened the captain to set him on shore, and go back with the ship to Goa. I wished they would with all my heart, for I was full of mischief in my head, and ready enough to do any. So, though I was but a boy, as they called me, yet I prompted the mischief all I could, and embarked in it so openly, that I escaped very little being hanged in the first and most early part of my life; for the captain had some notice that there was a design laid by some of the company to murder him; and having, partly by money and promises, and partly by threatening and torture, brought two fellows to confess the particulars, and the names of the persons concerned, they were presently apprehended, till, one accusing another, no less than sixteen men were seized and put into irons, whereof I was one.

The captain, who was made desperate by his danger, resolving to clear the ship of his enemies, tried us all, and we were all condemned to die. The manner of his process I was too young to take notice of; but the purser and one of the gunners were hanged immediately, and I expected it with the rest. I do not remember any great concern I was under about it, only that I cried very much, for I knew little then of this world, and nothing at all of the next.

However, the captain contented himself with executing these two, and some of the rest, upon their humble submission and promise of future good behaviour, were pardoned; but five were ordered to be set on shore on the island and left there, of which I was one. My master used all his interest with the captain to have me excused, but could not obtain it; for somebody having told him that I was one of them who was singled out to have killed him, when my master desired I might not be set on shore, the captain told him I should stay on board if he desired it, but then I should be hanged, so he might choose for me which he thought best. The captain, it seems, was particularly provoked at my being concerned in the treachery, because of his having been so kind to me, and of his having singled me out to serve him, as I have said above; and this, perhaps, obliged him to give my master such a rough choice, either to set me on shore or to have me hanged on board. And had my master, indeed, known what good-will I had for him, he would not have been long in choosing for me; for I had certainly determined to do him a mischief the first opportunity I had for it. This was, therefore, a good providence for me to keep me from dipping my hands in blood, and it made me more tender afterwards in matters of blood than I believe I should otherwise have been. But as to my being one of them that was to kill the captain, that I was wronged in, for I was not the person, but it was really one of them that were pardoned, he having the good luck not to have that part discovered.

I was now to enter upon a part of independent life, a thing I was indeed very ill prepared to manage, for I was perfectly loose and dissolute in my behaviour, bold and wicked while I was under government, and now perfectly unfit to be trusted with liberty, for I was as ripe for any villainy as a young fellow that had no solid thought ever placed in his mind could be supposed to be. Education, as you have heard, I had none; and all the little scenes of life I had passed through had been full of dangers and desperate circumstances; but I was either so young or so stupid, that I escaped the grief and anxiety of them, for want of having a sense of their tendency and consequences.

This thoughtless, unconcerned temper had one felicity indeed in it, that it made me daring and ready for doing any mischief, and kept off the sorrow which otherwise ought to have attended me when I fell into any mischief; that this stupidity was instead of a happiness to me, for it left my thoughts free to act upon means of escape and deliverance in my distress, however great it might be; whereas my companions in the misery were so sunk by their fear and grief, that they abandoned themselves to the misery of their condition, and gave over all thought but of their perishing and starving, being devoured by wild beasts, murdered, and perhaps eaten by cannibals, and the like.

I was but a young fellow, about seventeen or eighteen; but hearing what was to be my fate, I received it with no appearance of discouragement; but I asked what my master said to it, and being told that he had used his utmost interest to save me, but the captain had answered I should either go on shore or be hanged on board, which he pleased, I then gave over all hope of being received again. I was not very thankful in my thoughts to my master for his soliciting the captain for me, because I knew that what he did was not in kindness to me so much as in kindness to himself; I mean, to preserve the wages which he got for me, which amounted to above six dollars a month, including what the captain allowed him for my particular service to him.

When I understood that my master was so apparently kind, I asked if I might not be admitted to speak with him, and they told me I might, if my master would come down to me, but I could not be allowed to come up to him; so then I desired my master might be spoke to to come to me, and he accordingly came to me. I fell on my knees to him, and begged he would forgive me what I had done to displease him; and indeed the resolution I had taken to murder him lay with some horror upon my mind just at that time, so that I was once just a-going to confess it, and beg him to forgive me, but I kept it in. He told me he had done all he could to obtain my pardon of the captain, but could not and he knew no way for me but to have patience, and submit to my fate; and if they came to speak with any ship of their nation at the Cape, he would endeavour to have them stand in, and fetch us off again, if we might be found.

Then I begged I might have my clothes on shore with me. He told me he was afraid I should have little need of clothes, for he did not see how we could long subsist on the island, and that he had been told that the inhabitants were cannibals or men-eaters (though he had no reason for that suggestion), and we should not be able to live among them. I told him I was not so afraid of that as I was of starving for want of victuals; and as for the inhabitants being cannibals, I believed we should be more likely to eat them than they us, if we could but get at them. But I was mightily concerned, I said, we should have no weapons with us to defend ourselves, and I begged nothing now, but that he would give me a gun and a sword, with a little powder and shot.

He smiled, and said they would signify nothing to us, for it was impossible for us to pretend to preserve our lives among such a populous and desperate nation as the people of this island were. I told him that, however, it would do us this good, for we should not be devoured or destroyed immediately; so I begged hard for the gun. At last he told me he did not know whether the captain would give him leave to give me a gun, and if not, he durst not do it; but he promised to use his interest to obtain it for me, which he did, and the next day he sent me a gun, with some ammunition, but told me the captain would not suffer the ammunition to be given us till we were set all on shore, and till he was just going to set sail. He also sent me the few clothes I had in the ship, which indeed were not many.

Two days after this, we were all carried on shore together; the rest of my fellow-criminals hearing I had a gun, and some powder and shot, solicited for liberty to carry the like with them, which was also granted them; and thus we were set on shore to shift for ourselves.

At our first coming into the island we were terrified exceedingly with the sight of the barbarous people, whose figure was made more terrible to us than it really was by the report we had of them from the seamen; but when we came to converse with them awhile, we found they were not cannibals, as was reported, or such as would fall immediately upon us and eat us up; but they came and sat down by us, and wondered much at our clothes and arms, and made signs to give us some victuals, such as they had, which was only roots and plants dug out of the ground for the present, but they brought us fowls and flesh afterwards in good plenty.

This encouraged the other four men that were with me very much, for they were quite dejected before; but now they began to be very familiar with them, and made signs, that if they would use us kindly, we would stay and live with them; which they seemed glad of, though they knew little of the necessity we were under to do so, or how much we were afraid of them.

However, upon second thoughts we resolved that we would only stay in that part so long as the ship rid in the bay, and then making them believe we were gone with the ship, we would go and place ourselves, if possible, where there were no inhabitants to be seen, and so live as we could, or perhaps watch for a ship that might be driven upon the coast as we were.

The ship continued a fortnight in the roads, repairing some damage which had been done her in the late storm, and taking in wood and water; and during this time, the boat coming often on shore, the men brought us several refreshments, and the natives believing we only belonged to the ship, were civil enough. We lived in a kind of a tent on the shore, or rather a hut, which we made with the boughs of trees, and sometimes in the night retired to a wood a little out of their way, to let them think we were gone on board the ship. However, we found them barbarous, treacherous, and villainous enough in their nature, only civil from fear, and therefore concluded we should soon fall into their hands when the ship was gone.

The sense of this wrought upon my fellow-sufferers even to distraction; and one of them, being a carpenter, in his mad fit, swam off to the ship in the night, though she lay then a league to sea, and made such pitiful moan to be taken in, that the captain was prevailed with at last to take him in, though they let him lie swimming three hours in the water before he consented to it.

Upon this, and his humble submission, the captain received him, and, in a word, the importunity of this man (who for some time petitioned to be taken in, though they hanged him as soon as they had him) was such as could not be resisted; for, after he had swam so long about the ship, he was not able to reach the shore again; and the captain saw evidently that the man must be taken on board or suffered to drown, and the whole ship's company offering to be bound for him for his good behaviour, the captain at last yielded, and he was taken up, but almost dead with his being so long in the water.

When this man was got in, he never left importuning the captain, and all the rest of the officers, in behalf of us that were behind, but to the very last day the captain was inexorable; when, at the time their preparations were making to sail, and orders given to hoist the boats into the ship, all the seamen in a body came up to the rail of the quarter-deck, where the captain was walking with some of his officers, and appointing the boatswain to speak for them, he went up, and falling on his knees to the captain, begged of him, in the humblest manner possible, to receive the four men on board again, offering to answer for their fidelity, or to have them kept in chains till they came to Lisbon, and there to be delivered up to justice, rather than, as they said, to have them left to be murdered by savages, or devoured by wild beasts. It was a great while ere the captain took any notice of them, but when he did, he ordered the boatswain to be seized, and threatened to bring him to the capstan for speaking for them.

Upon this severity, one of the seamen, bolder than the rest, but still with all possible respect to the captain, besought his honour, as he called him, that he would give leave to some more of them to go on shore, and die with their companions, or, if possible, to assist them to resist the barbarians. The captain, rather provoked than cowed with this, came to the barricade of the quarter-deck, and speaking very prudently to the men (for had he spoken roughly, two-thirds of them would have left the ship, if not all of them), he told them, it was for their safety as well as his own that he had been obliged to that severity; that mutiny on board a ship was the same thing as treason in a king's palace, and he could not answer it to his owners and employers to trust the ship and goods committed to his charge with men who had entertained thoughts of the worst and blackest nature; that he wished heartily that it had been anywhere else that they had been set on shore, where they might have been in less hazard from the savages; that, if he had designed they should be destroyed, he could as well have executed them on board as the other two; that he wished it had been in some other part of the world, where he might have delivered them up to the civil justice, or might have left them among Christians; but it was better their lives were put in hazard than his life, and the safety of the ship; and that though he did not know that he had deserved so ill of any of them as that they should leave the ship rather than do their duty, yet if any of them were resolved to do so unless he would consent to take a gang of traitors on board, who, as he had proved before them all, had conspired to murder him, he would not hinder them, nor for the present would he resent their importunity; but, if there was nobody left in the ship but himself, he would never consent to take them on board.

This discourse was delivered so well, was in itself so reasonable, was managed with so much temper, yet so boldly concluded with a negative, that the greatest part of the men were satisfied for the present. However, as it put the men into juntos and cabals, they were not composed for some hours; the wind also slackening towards night, the captain ordered not to weigh till next morning.

The same night twenty-three of the men, among whom was the gunner's mate, the surgeon's assistant, and two carpenters, applying to the chief mate told him, that as the captain had given them leave to go on shore to their comrades, they begged that he would speak to the captain not to take it ill that they were desirous to go and die with their companions; and that they thought they could do no less in such an extremity than go to them; because, if there was any way to save their lives, it was by adding to their numbers, and making them strong enough to assist one another in defending themselves against the savages, till perhaps they might one time or other find means to make their escape, and get to their own country again.

The mate told them, in so many words, that he durst not speak to the captain upon any such design, and was very sorry they had no more respect for him than to desire him to go upon such an errand; but, if they were resolved upon such an enterprise, he would advise them to take the long-boat in the morning betimes, and go off, seeing the captain had given them leave, and leave a civil letter behind them to the captain, and to desire him to send his men on shore for the boat, which should be delivered very honestly, and he promised to keep their counsel so long.

Accordingly, an hour before day, those twenty-three men, with every man a firelock and a cutlass, with some pistols, three halberds or half-pikes, and good store of powder and ball, without any provision but about half a hundred of bread, but with all their chests and clothes, tools, instruments, books, &c., embarked themselves so silently, that the captain got no notice of it till they were gotten half the way on shore.

As soon as the captain heard of it he called for the gunner's mate, the chief gunner being at the time sick in his cabin, and ordered to fire at them; but, to his great mortification, the gunner's mate was one of the number, and was gone with them; and indeed it was by this means they got so many arms and so much ammunition. When the captain found how it was, and that there was no help for it, he began to be a little appeased, and made light of it, and called up the men, and spoke kindly to them, and told them he was very well satisfied in the fidelity and ability of those that were now left, and that he would give to them, for their encouragement, to be divided among them, the wages which were due to the men that were gone, and that it was a great satisfaction to him that the ship was free from such a mutinous rabble, who had not the least reason for their discontent.

The men seemed very well satisfied, and particularly the promise of the wages of those who were gone went a great way with them. After this, the letter which was left by the men was given to the captain by his boy, with whom, it seems, the men had left it. The letter was much to the same purpose of what they had said to the mate, and which he declined to say for them, only that at the end of their letter they told the captain that, as they had no dishonest design, so they had taken nothing away with them which was not their own, except some arms and ammunition, such as were absolutely necessary to them, as well for their defence against the savages as to kill fowls or beasts for their food, that they might not perish; and as there were considerable sums due to them for wages, they hoped he would allow the arms and ammunition upon their accounts. They told him that, as to the ship's longboat, which they had taken to bring them on shore, they knew it was necessary to him, and they were very willing to restore it to him, and if he pleased to send for it, it should be very honestly delivered to his men, and not the least injury offered to any of those who came for it, nor the least persuasion or invitation made use of to any of them to stay with them; and, at the bottom of the letter, they very humbly besought him that, for their defence, and for the safety of their lives, he would be pleased to send them a barrel of powder and some ammunition, and give them leave to keep the mast and sail of the boat, that if it was possible for them to make themselves a boat of any kind, they might shift off to sea, to save themselves in such part of the world as their fate should direct them to.

Upon this the captain, who had won much upon the rest of his men by what he had said to them, and was very easy as to the general peace (for it was very true that the most mutinous of the men were gone), came out to the quarter-deck, and, calling the men together, let them know the substance of the letter, and told the men that, however they had not deserved such civility from him, yet he was not willing to expose them more than they were willing to expose themselves; he was inclined to send them some ammunition, and as they had desired but one barrel of powder, he would send them two barrels, and shot, or lead and moulds to make shot, in proportion; and, to let them see that he was civiler to them than they deserved, he ordered a cask of arrack and a great bag of bread to be sent them for subsistence till they should be able to furnish themselves.

The rest of the men applauded the captain's generosity, and every one of them sent us something or other, and about three in the afternoon the pinnace came on shore, and brought us all these things, which we were very glad of, and returned the long-boat accordingly; and as to the men that came with the pinnace, as the captain had singled out such men as he knew would not come over to us, so they had positive orders not to bring any one of us on board again, upon pain of death; and indeed both were so true to our points, that we neither asked them to stay, nor they us to go.

We were now a good troop, being in all twenty-seven men, very well armed, and provided with everything but victuals; we had two carpenters among us, a gunner, and, which was worth all the rest, a surgeon or doctor; that is to say, he was an assistant to a surgeon at Goa, and was entertained as a supernumerary with us. The carpenters had brought all their tools, the doctor all his instruments and medicines, and indeed we had a great deal of baggage, that is to say, on the whole, for some of us had little more than the clothes on our backs, of whom I was one; but I had one thing which none of them had, viz., I had the twenty-two moidores of gold which I had stole at the Brazils, and two pieces of eight. The two pieces of eight I showed, and one moidore, and none of them ever suspected that I had any more money in the world, having been known to be only a poor boy taken up in charity, as you have heard, and used like a slave, and in the worst manner of a slave, by my cruel master the pilot.

It will be easy to imagine we four that were left at first were joyful, nay, even surprised with joy at the coming of the rest, though at first we were frighted, and thought they came to fetch us back to hang us; but they took ways quickly to satisfy us that they were in the same condition with us, only with this additional circumstance, theirs was voluntary, and ours by force.

The first piece of news they told us after the short history of their coming away was, that our companion was on board, but how he got thither we could not imagine, for he had given us the slip, and we never imagined he could swim so well as to venture off to the ship, which lay at so great a distance; nay, we did not so much as know that he could swim at all, and not thinking anything of what really happened, we thought he must have wandered into the woods and was devoured, or was fallen into the hands of the natives, and was murdered; and these thoughts filled us with fears enough, and of several kinds, about its being some time or other our lot to fall into their hands also. But hearing how he had with much difficulty been received on board the ship again and pardoned, we were much better satisfied than before.

Being now, as I have said, a considerable number of us, and in condition to defend ourselves, the first thing we did was to give every one his hand that we would not separate from one another upon any occasion whatsoever, but that we would live and die together; that we would kill no food, but that we would distribute it in public; and that we would be in all things guided by the majority, and not insist upon our own resolutions in anything if the majority were against it; that we would appoint a captain among us to be our governor or leader during pleasure; that while he was in office we would obey him without reserve, on pain of death; and that every one should take turn, but the captain was not to act in any particular thing without advice of the rest, and by the majority.

Having established these rules, we resolved to enter into some measures for our food, and for conversing with the inhabitants or natives of the island for our supply. As for food, they were at first very useful to us, but we soon grew weary of them, being an ignorant, ravenous, brutish sort of people, even worse than the natives of any other country that we had seen; and we soon found that the principal part of our subsistence was to be had by our guns, shooting of deer and other creatures, and fowls of all other sorts, of which there is abundance.

We found the natives did not disturb or concern themselves much about us; nor did they inquire, or perhaps know, whether we stayed among them or not, much less that our ship was gone quite away, and had cast us off, as was our case; for the next morning, after we had sent back the long-boat, the ship stood away to the south-east, and in four hours' time was out of our sight.

The next day two of us went out into the country one way, and two another, to see what kind of a land we were in; and we soon found the country was very pleasant and fruitful, and a convenient place enough to live in; but, as before, inhabited by a parcel of creatures scarce human, or capable of being made social on any account whatsoever.

We found the place full of cattle and provisions; but whether we might venture to take them where we could find them or not, we did not know; and though we were under a necessity to get provisions, yet we were loth to bring down a whole nation of devils upon us at once, and therefore some of our company agreed to try to speak with some of the country, if we could, that we might see what course was to be taken with them. Eleven of our men went on this errand, well armed and furnished for defence. They brought word that they had seen some of the natives, who appeared very civil to them, but very shy and afraid, seeing their guns, for it was easy to perceive that the natives knew what their guns were, and what use they were of.

They made signs to the natives for some food, and they went and fetched several herbs and roots, and some milk; but it was evident they did not design to give it away, but to sell it, making signs to know what our men would give them.

Our men were perplexed at this, for they had nothing to barter; however, one of the men pulled out a knife and showed them, and they were so fond of it that they were ready to go together by the ears for the knife. The seaman seeing that, was willing to make a good market of his knife, and keeping them chaffering about it a good while, some offered him roots, and others milk; at last one offered him a goat for it, which he took. Then another of our men showed them another knife, but they had nothing good enough for that, whereupon one of them made signs that he would go and fetch something; so our men stayed three hours for their return, when they came back and brought him a small-sized, thick, short cow, very fat and good meat, and gave him for his knife.

This was a good market, but our misfortune was we had no merchandise; for our knives were as needful to us as to them, and but that we were in distress for food, and must of necessity have some, these men would not have parted with their knives.

However, in a little time more we found that the woods were full of living creatures, which we might kill for our food, and that without giving offence to them; so that our men went daily out a-hunting, and never failed in killing something or other; for, as to the natives, we had no goods to barter; and for money, all the stock among us would not have subsisted us long. However, we called a general council to see what money we had, and to bring it all together, that it might go as far as possible; and when it came to my turn, I pulled out a moidore and the two dollars I spoke of before.

This moidore I ventured to show, that they might not despise me too much for adding too little to the store, and that they might not pretend to search me; and they were very civil to me, upon the presumption that I had been so faithful to them as not to conceal anything from them.

But our money did us little service, for the people neither knew the value or the use of it, nor could they justly rate the gold in proportion with the silver; so that all our money, which was not much when it was all put together, would go but a little way with us, that is to say, to buy us provisions.

Our next consideration was to get away from this cursed place, and whither to go. When my opinion came to be asked, I told them I would leave that all to them, and I told them I had rather they would let me go into the woods to get them some provisions, than consult with me, for I would agree to whatever they did; but they would not agree to that, for they would not consent that any of us should go into the woods alone; for though we had yet seen no lions or tigers in the woods, we were assured there were many in the island, besides other creatures as dangerous, and perhaps worse, as we afterwards found by our own experience.

We had many adventures in the woods, for our provisions, and often met with wild and terrible beasts, which we could not call by their names; but as they were, like us, seeking their prey, but were themselves good for nothing, so we disturbed them as little as possible.

Our consultations concerning our escape from this place, which, as I have said, we were now upon, ended in this only, that as we had two carpenters among us, and that they had tools almost of all sorts with them, we should try to build us a boat to go off to sea with, and that then, perhaps, we might find our way back to Goa, or land on some more proper place to make our escape. The counsels of this assembly were not of great moment, yet as they seem to be introductory of many more remarkable adventures which happened under my conduct hereabouts many years after, I think this miniature of my future enterprises may not be unpleasant to relate.

To the building of a boat I made no objection, and away they went to work immediately; but as they went on, great difficulties occurred, such as the want of saws to cut our plank; nails, bolts, and spikes, to fasten the timbers; hemp, pitch, and tar, to caulk and pay her seams, and the like. At length, one of the company proposed that, instead of building a bark or sloop, or shallop, or whatever they would call it, which they found was so difficult, they would rather make a large periagua, or canoe, which might be done with great ease.

It was presently objected, that we could never make a canoe large enough to pass the great ocean, which we were to go over to get to the coast of Malabar; that it not only would not bear the sea, but it would never bear the burden, for we were not only twenty-seven men of us, but had a great deal of luggage with us, and must, for our provision, take in a great deal more.

I never proposed to speak in their general consultations before, but finding they were at some loss about what kind of vessel they should make, and how to make it, and what would be fit for our use, and what not, I told them I found they were at a full stop in their counsels of every kind; that it was true we could never pretend to go over to Goa on the coast of Malabar in a canoe, which though we could all get into it, and that it would bear the sea well enough, yet would not hold our provisions, and especially we could not put fresh water enough into it for the voyage; and to make such an adventure would be nothing but mere running into certain destruction, and yet that nevertheless I was for making a canoe.

They answered, that they understood all I had said before well enough, but what I meant by telling them first how dangerous and impossible it was to make our escape in a canoe, and yet then to advise making a canoe, that they could not understand.

To this I answered, that I conceived our business was not to attempt our escape in a canoe, but that, as there were other vessels at sea besides our ship, and that there were few nations that lived on the sea-shore that were so barbarous, but that they went to sea in some boats or other, our business was to cruise along the coast of the island, which was very long, and to seize upon the first we could get that was better than our own, and so from that to another, till perhaps we might at last get a good ship to carry us wherever we pleased to go.

"Excellent advice," says one of them. "Admirable advice," says another. "Yes, yes," says the third (which was the gunner), "the English dog has given excellent advice; but it is just the way to bring us all to the gallows. The rogue has given us devilish advice, indeed, to go a-thieving, till from a little vessel we came to a great ship, and so we shall turn downright pirates, the end of which is to be hanged."

"You may call us pirates," says another, "if you will, and if we fall into bad hands, we may be used like pirates; but I care not for that, I'll be a pirate, or anything, nay, I'll be hanged for a pirate rather than starve here, therefore I think the advice is very good." And so they cried all, "Let us have a canoe." The gunner, over-ruled by the rest, submitted; but as we broke up the council, he came to me, takes me by the hand, and, looking into the palm of my hand, and into my face too, very gravely, "My lad," says he, "thou art born to do a world of mischief; thou hast commenced pirate very young; but have a care of the gallows, young man; have a care, I say, for thou wilt be an eminent thief."

I laughed at him, and told him I did not know what I might come to hereafter, but as our case was now, I should make no scruple to take the first ship I came at to get our liberty; I only wished we could see one, and come at her. Just while we were talking, one of our men that was at the door of our hut, told us that the carpenter, who it seems was upon a hill at a distance, cried out, "A sail! a sail!"

We all turned out immediately; but, though it was very clear weather, we could see nothing; but the carpenter continuing to halloo to us, "A sail! a sail!" away we run up the hill, and there we saw a ship plainly; but it was at a very great distance, too far for us to make any signal to her. However, we made a fire upon the hill, with all the wood we could get together, and made as much smoke as possible. The wind was down, and it was almost calm; but as we thought, by a perspective glass which the gunner had in his pocket, her sails were full, and she stood away large with the wind at E.N.E., taking no notice of our signal, but making for the Cape de Bona Speranza; so we had no comfort from her.

We went, therefore, immediately to work about our intended canoe; and, having singled out a very large tree to our minds, we fell to work with her; and having three good axes among us, we got it down, but it was four days' time first, though we worked very hard too. I do not remember what wood it was, or exactly what dimensions, but I remember that it was a very large one, and we were as much encouraged when we launched it, and found it swam upright and steady, as we would have been at another time if we had had a good man-of-war at our command.

She was so very large, that she carried us all very, very easily, and would have carried two or three tons of baggage with us; so that we began to consult about going to sea directly to Goa; but many other considerations checked that thought, especially when we came to look nearer into it; such as want of provisions, and no casks for fresh water; no compass to steer by; no shelter from the breach of the high sea, which would certainly founder us; no defence from the heat of the weather, and the like; so that they all came readily into my project, to cruise about where we were, and see what might offer.

Accordingly, to gratify our fancy, we went one day all out to sea in her together, and we were in a very fair way to have had enough of it; for when she had us all on board, and that we were gotten about half a league to sea, there happening to be a pretty high swell of the sea, though little or no wind, yet she wallowed so in the sea, that we all of us thought she would at last wallow herself bottom up; so we set all to work to get her in nearer the shore, and giving her fresh way in the sea, she swam more steady, and with some hard work we got her under the land again.

We were now at a great loss; the natives were civil enough to us, and came often to discourse with us; one time they brought one whom they showed respect to as a king with them, and they set up a long pole between them and us, with a great tassel of hair hanging, not on the top, but something above the middle of it, adorned with little chains, shells, bits of brass, and the like; and this, we understood afterwards, was a token of amity and friendship; and they brought down to us victuals in abundance, cattle, fowls, herbs, and roots; but we were in the utmost confusion on our side; for we had nothing to buy with, or exchange for;

and as to giving us things for nothing they had no notion of that again. As to our money, it was mere trash to them, they had no value for it; so that we were in a fair way to be starved. Had we had but some toys and trinkets, brass chains, baubles, glass beads, or, in a word, the veriest trifles that a shipload of would not have been worth the freight, we might have bought cattle and provisions enough for an army, or to victual a fleet of men-of-war; but for gold or silver we could get nothing.

Upon this we were in a strange consternation. I was but a young fellow, but I was for falling upon them with our firearms, and taking all the cattle from them, and send them to the devil to stop their hunger, rather than be starved ourselves; but I did not consider that this might have brought ten thousand of them down upon us the next day; and though we might have killed a vast number of them, and perhaps have frighted the rest, yet their own desperation, and our small number, would have animated them so that, one time or other, they would have destroyed us all.

In the middle of our consultation, one of our men who had been a kind of a cutler, or worker in iron, started up and asked the carpenter if, among all his tools, he could not help him to a file. "Yes," says the carpenter, "I can, but it is a small one." "The smaller the better," says the other. Upon this he goes to work, and first by heating a piece of an old broken chisel in the fire, and then with the help of his file, he made himself several kinds of tools for his work. Then he takes three or four pieces of eight, and beats them out with a hammer upon a stone, till they were very broad and thin; then he cuts them out into the shape of birds and beasts; he made little chains of them for bracelets and necklaces, and turned them into so many devices of his own head, that it is hardly to be expressed.

When he had for about a fortnight exercised his head and hands at this work, we tried the effect of his ingenuity; and, having another meeting with the natives, were surprised to see the folly of the poor people. For a little bit of silver cut in the shape of a bird, we had two cows, and, which was our loss, if it had been in brass, it had been still of more value. For one of the bracelets made of chain-work, we had as much provision of several sorts, as would fairly have been worth, in England, fifteen or sixteen pounds; and so of all the rest. Thus, that which when it was in coin was not worth sixpence to us, when thus converted into toys and trifles, was worth a hundred times its real value, and purchased for us anything we had occasion for.

In this condition we lived upwards of a year, but all of us began to be very much tired of it, and, whatever came of it, resolved to attempt an escape. We had furnished ourselves with no less than three very good canoes; and as the monsoons, or trade-winds, generally affect that country, blowing in most parts of this island one six months of a year one way, and the other six months another way, we concluded we might be able to bear the sea well enough. But always, when we came to look into it, the want of fresh water was the thing that put us off from such an adventure, for it is a prodigious length, and what no man on earth could be able to perform without water to drink.

Being thus prevailed upon by our own reason to set the thoughts of that voyage aside, we had then but two things before us; one was, to put to sea the other way; viz., west, and go away for the Cape of Good Hope, where, first or last, we should meet with some of our own country ships, or else to put for the mainland of Africa, and either travel by land, or sail along the coast towards the Red Sea, where we should, first or last, find a ship of some nation or other, that would take us up; or perhaps we might take them up, which, by-the-bye, was the thing that always ran in my head.

It was our ingenious cutler, whom ever after we called silversmith, that proposed this; but the gunner told him, that he had been in the Red Sea in a Malabar sloop, and he knew this, that if we went into the Red Sea, we should either be killed by the wild Arabs, or taken and made slaves of by the Turks; and therefore he was not for going that way.

Upon this I took occasion to put in my vote again. "Why," said I, "do we talk of being killed by the Arabs, or made slaves of by the Turks? Are we not able to board almost any vessel we shall meet with in those seas; and, instead of their taking us, we to take them?" "Well done, pirate," said the gunner (he that had looked in my hand, and told me I should come to the gallows), "I'll say that for him," says he, "he always looks the same way. But I think, of my conscience, it is our only way now." "Don't tell me," says I, "of being a pirate; we must be pirates, or anything, to get fairly out of this cursed place."

In a word, they concluded all, by my advice, that our business was to cruise for anything we could see. "Why then," said I to them, "our first business is to see if the people upon this island have no navigation, and what boats they use; and, if they have any better or bigger than ours, let us take one of them." First, indeed, all our aim was to get, if possible, a boat with a deck and a sail; for then we might have saved our provisions, which otherwise we could not.

We had, to our great good fortune, one sailor among us, who had been assistant to the cook; he told us, that he would find a way how to preserve our beef without cask or pickle; and this he did effectually by curing it in the sun, with the help of saltpeter, of which there was great plenty in the island; so that, before we found any method for our escape, we had dried the flesh of six or seven cows and bullocks, and ten or twelve goats, and it relished so well, that we never gave ourselves the trouble to boil it when we ate it, but either broiled it or ate it dry. But our main difficulty about fresh water still remained; for we had no vessel to put any into, much less to keep any for our going to sea.

But our first voyage being only to coast the island, we resolved to venture, whatever the hazard or consequence of it might be, and in order to preserve as much fresh water as we could, our carpenter made a well athwart the middle of one of our canoes, which he separated from the other parts of the canoe, so as to make it tight to hold the water and covered so as we might step upon it; and this was so large that it held near a hogshead of water very well. I cannot better describe this well than by the same kind which the small fishing-boats in England have to preserve their fish alive in; only that this, instead of having holes to let the salt water in, was made sound every way to keep it out; and it was the first invention, I believe, of its kind for such an use; but necessity is a spur to ingenuity and the mother of invention.

It wanted but a little consultation to resolve now upon our voyage. The first design was only to coast it round the island, as well to see if we could seize upon any vessel fit to embark ourselves in, as also to take hold of any opportunity which might present for our passing over to the main; and therefore our resolution was to go on the inside or west shore of the island, where, at least at one point, the land stretching a great way to the north-west, the distance is not extraordinary great from the island to the coast of Africa.

Such a voyage, and with such a desperate crew, I believe was never made, for it is certain we took the worst side of the island to look for any shipping, especially for shipping of other nations, this being quite out of the way; however, we put to sea, after taking all our provisions and ammunition, bag and baggage, on board; we had made both mast and sail for our two large periaguas, and the other we paddled along as well as we could; but when a gale sprung up, we took her in tow.

We sailed merrily forward for several days, meeting with nothing to interrupt us. We saw several of the natives in small canoes catching fish, and sometimes we endeavoured to come near enough to speak with them, but they were always shy and afraid of us, making in for the shore as soon as we attempted it; till one of our company remembered the signal of friendship which the natives made us from the south part of the island, viz., of setting up a long pole, and put us in mind that perhaps it was the same thing to them as a flag of truce to us. So we resolved to try it; and accordingly the next time we saw any of their fishing-boats at sea we put up a pole in our canoe that had no sail, and rowed towards them. As soon as they saw the pole they stayed for us, and as we came nearer paddled towards us; when they came to us they showed themselves very much pleased, and gave us some large fish, of which we did not know the names, but they were very good. It was our misfortune still that we had nothing to give them in return; but our artist, of whom I spoke before, gave them two little thin plates of silver, beaten, as I said before, out of a piece of eight; they were cut in a diamond square, longer one way than the other, and a hole punched at one of the longest corners. This they were so fond of that they made us stay till they had cast their lines and nets again, and gave us as many fish as we cared to have.

All this while we had our eyes upon their boats, viewed them very narrowly, and examined whether any of them were fit for our turn, but they were poor, sorry things; their sail was made of a large mat, only one that was of a piece of cotton stuff fit for little, and their ropes were twisted flags of no strength; so we concluded we were better as we were, and let them alone. We went forward to the north, keeping the coast close on board for twelve days together, and having the wind at east and E.S.E., we made very fresh way. We saw no towns on the shore, but often saw some huts by the water-side upon the rocks, and always abundance of people about them, who we could perceive run together to stare at us.

It was as odd a voyage as ever man went; we were a little fleet of three ships, and an army of between twenty and thirty as dangerous fellows as ever they had amongst them; and had they known what we were, they would have compounded to give us everything we desired to be rid of us.

On the other hand, we were as miserable as nature could well make us to be, for we were upon a voyage and no voyage, we were bound somewhere and nowhere; for though we knew what we intended

625

to do, we did really not know what we were doing. We went forward and forward by a northerly course, and as we advanced the heat increased, which began to be intolerable to us, who were on the water, without any covering from heat or wet; besides, we were now in the month of October, or thereabouts, in a southern latitude; and as we went every day nearer the sun, the sun came also every day nearer to us, till at last we found ourselves in the latitude of 20 degrees; and having passed the tropic about five or six days before that, in a few days more the sun would be in the zenith, just over our heads.

Upon these considerations we resolved to seek for a good place to go on shore again, and pitch our tents, till the heat of the weather abated. We had by this time measured half the length of the island, and were come to that part where the shore tending away to the north-west, promised fair to make our passage over to the mainland of Africa much shorter than we expected. But, notwithstanding that, we had good reason to believe it was about 120 leagues.

So, the heats considered, we resolved to take harbour; besides, our provisions were exhausted, and we had not many days' store left. Accordingly, putting in for the shore early in the morning, as we usually did once in three or four days for fresh water, we sat down and considered whether we would go on or take up our standing there; but upon several considerations, too long to repeat here, we did not like the place, so we resolved to go on a few days longer.

After sailing on N.W. by N. with a fresh gale at S.E., about six days, we found, at a great distance, a large promontory or cape of land, pushing out a long way into the sea, and as we were exceeding fond of seeing what was beyond the cape, we resolved to double it before we took into harbour, so we kept on our way, the gale continuing, and yet it was four days more before we reached the cape. But it is not possible to express the discouragement and melancholy that seized us all when we came thither; for when we made the headland of the cape, we were surprised to see the shore fall away on the other side as much as it had advanced on this side, and a great deal more; and that, in short, if we would venture over to the shore of Africa, it must be from hence, for that if we went further, the breadth of the sea still increased, and to what breadth it might increase we knew not.

While we mused upon this discovery, we were surprised with very bad weather, and especially violent rains, with thunder and lightning, most unusually terrible to us. In this pickle we run for the shore, and getting under the lee of the cape, run our frigates into a little creek, where we saw the land overgrown with trees, and made all the haste possible to get on shore, being exceeding wet, and fatigued with the heat, the thunder, lightning, and rain.

Here we thought our case was very deplorable indeed, and therefore our artist, of whom I have spoken so often, set up a great cross of wood on the hill which was within a mile of the headland, with these words, but in the Portuguese language: —

"Point Desperation. Jesus have mercy."

We set to work immediately to build us some huts, and to get our clothes dried; and though I was young and had no skill in such things, yet I shall never forget the little city we built, for it was no less, and we fortified it accordingly; and the idea is so fresh in my thought, that I cannot but give a short description of it.

Our camp was on the south side of a little creek on the sea, and under the shelter of a steep hill, which lay, though on the other side of the creek, yet within a quarter of a mile of us, N.W. by N., and very happily intercepted the heat of the sun all the after part of the day. The spot we pitched on had a little fresh water brook, or a stream running into the creek by us; and we saw cattle feeding in the plains and low ground east and to the south of us a great way.

Here we set up twelve little huts like soldiers' tents, but made of the boughs of trees stuck in the ground, and bound together on the top with withies, and such other things as we could get; the creek was our defence on the north, a little brook on the west, and the south and east sides were fortified with a bank, which entirely covered our huts; and being drawn oblique from the north-west to the south-east, made our city a triangle. Behind the bank or line our huts stood, having three other huts behind them at a good distance. In one of these, which was a little one, and stood further off, we put our gunpowder, and nothing else, for fear of danger; in the other, which was bigger, we dressed our victuals, and put all our necessaries; and in the third, which was biggest of all, we ate our dinners, called our councils, and sat and diverted ourselves with such conversation as we had one with another, which was but indifferent truly at that time.

Our correspondence with the natives was absolutely necessary, and our artist the cutler having made abundance of those little diamond-cut squares of silver, with these we made shift to traffic with the black people for what we wanted; for indeed they were pleased wonderfully with them, and thus we got plenty of provisions. At first, and in particular, we got about fifty head of black cattle and goats, and our cook's mate took care to cure them and dry them, salt and preserve them for our grand supply; nor was this hard to do, the salt and saltpeter being very good, and the sun excessively hot; and here we lived about four months.

The southern solstice was over, and the sun gone back towards the equinoctial, when we considered of our next adventure, which was to go over the sea of Zanguebar, as the Portuguese call it, and to land, if possible, upon the continent of Africa.

We talked with many of the natives about it, such as we could make ourselves intelligible to, but all that we could learn from them was, that there was a great land of lions beyond the sea, but that it was a great way off. We knew as well as they that it was a long way, but our people differed mightily about it; some said it was 150 leagues, others not above 100. One of our men, that had a map of the world, showed us by his scale that it was not above eighty leagues. Some said there were islands all the way to touch at, some that there were no islands at all. For my own part, I knew nothing of this matter one way or another, but heard it all without concern, whether it was near or far off; however, this we learned from an old man who was blind and led about by a boy, that if we stayed till the end of August, we should be sure of the wind to be fair and the sea smooth all the voyage.

This was some encouragement; but staying again was very unwelcome news to us, because that then the sun would be returning again to the south, which was what our men were very unwilling to. At last we called a council of our whole body; their debates were too tedious to take notice of, only to note, that when it came to Captain Bob (for so they called me ever since I had taken state upon me before one of their great princes), truly I was on no side; it was not one farthing matter to me, I told them, whether we went or stayed; I had no home, and all the world was alike to me; so I left it entirely to them to determine.

In a word, they saw plainly there was nothing to be done where we were without shipping; that if our business indeed was only to eat and drink, we could not find a better place in the world; but if our business was to get away, and get home into our country, we could not find a worse.

I confess I liked the country wonderfully, and even then had strange notions of coming again to live there; and I used to say to them very often that if I had but a ship of twenty guns, and a sloop, and both well manned, I would not desire a better place in the world to make myself as rich as a king.

But to return to the consultations they were in about going. Upon the whole, it was resolved to venture over for the main; and venture we did, madly enough, indeed, for it was the wrong time of the year to undertake such a voyage in that country; for, as the winds hang easterly all the months from September to March, so they generally hang westerly all the rest of the year, and blew right in our teeth; so that, as soon as we had, with a kind of a land-breeze, stretched over about fifteen or twenty leagues, and, as I may say, just enough to lose ourselves, we found the wind set in a steady fresh gale or breeze from the sea, at west, W.S.W., or S.W. by W., and never further from the west; so that, in a word, we could make nothing of it.

On the other hand, the vessel, such as we had, would not lie close upon a wind; if so, we might have stretched away N.N.W., and have met with a great many islands in our way, as we found afterwards; but we could make nothing of it, though we tried, and by the trying had almost undone us all; for, stretching away to the north, as near the wind as we could, we had forgotten the shape and position of the island of Madagascar itself; how that we came off at the head of a promontory or point of land, that lies about the middle of the island, and that stretches out west a great way into the sea; and that now, being run a matter of forty leagues to the north, the shore of the island fell off again above 200 miles to the east, so that we were by this time in the wide ocean, between the island and the main, and almost 100 leagues from both.

Indeed, as the winds blew fresh at west, as before, we had a smooth sea, and we found it pretty good going before it, and so, taking our smallest canoe in tow, we stood in for the shore with all the sail we could make. This was a terrible adventure, for, if the least gust of wind had come, we had been all lost, our canoes being deep and in no condition to make way in a high sea.

This voyage, however, held us eleven days in all; and at length, having spent most of our provisions, and every drop of water we had, we spied land, to our great joy, though at the distance of ten or eleven leagues; and as, under the land, the wind came off like a land-breeze, and blew hard against us, we were two days more before we reached the shore, having all that while excessive hot weather, and not a drop of water or any other liquor, except some cordial waters, which one of our company had a little of left in a case of bottles.

This gave us a taste of what we should have done if we had ventured forward with a scant wind and uncertain weather, and gave us a surfeit of our design for the main, at least until we might have some better vessels under us; so we went on shore again, and pitched our camp as before, in as convenient manner as we could, fortifying ourselves against any surprise; but the natives here were exceeding courteous, and much more civil than on the south part of the island; and though we could not understand what they said, or they us, yet we found means to make them understand that we were seafaring men and strangers, and that we were in distress for want of provisions.

The first proof we had of their kindness was, that as soon as they saw us come on shore and begin to make our habitation, one of their captains or kings, for we knew not what to call them, came down with five or six men and some women, and brought us five goats and two young fat steers, and gave them to us for nothing; and when we went to offer them anything, the captain or the king would not let any of them touch it, or take anything of us. About two hours after came another king, or captain, with forty or fifty men after him. We began to be afraid of him, and laid hands upon our weapons; but he perceiving it, caused two men to go before him, carrying two long poles in their hands, which they held upright, as high as they could, which we presently perceived was a signal of peace; and these two poles they set up afterwards, sticking them up in the ground; and when the king and his men came to these two poles, they struck all their lances up in the ground, and came on unarmed, leaving their lances, as also their bows and arrows, behind them.

This was to satisfy us that they were come as friends, and we were glad to see it, for we had no mind to quarrel with them if we could help it. The captain of this gang seeing some of our men making up their huts, and that they did it but bunglingly, he beckoned to some of his men to go and help us. Immediately fifteen or sixteen of them came and mingled among us, and went to work for us; and indeed, they were better workmen than we were, for they run up three or four huts for us in a moment, and much handsomer done than ours.

After this they sent us milk, plantains, pumpkins, and abundance of roots and greens that were very good, and then took their leave, and would not take anything from us that we had. One of our men offered the king or captain of these men a dram, which he drank and was mightily pleased with it, and held out his hand for another, which we gave him; and in a word, after this, he hardly failed coming to us two or three times a week, always bringing us something or other; and one time sent us seven head of black cattle, some of which we cured and dried as before.

And here I cannot but remember one thing, which afterwards stood us in great stead, viz., that the flesh of their goats, and their beef also, but especially the former, when we had dried and cured it, looked red, and ate hard and firm, as dried beef in Holland; they were so pleased with it, and it was such a dainty to them, that at any time after they would trade with us for it, not knowing, or so much as imagining what it was; so that for ten or twelve pounds' weight of smoke-dried beef, they would give us a whole bullock, or cow, or anything else we could desire.

Here we observed two things that were very material to us, even essentially so; first, we found they had a great deal of earthenware here, which they made use of many ways as we did; particularly they had long, deep earthen pots, which they used to sink into the ground, to keep the water which they drunk cool and pleasant; and the other was, that they had larger canoes than their neighbours had.

By this we were prompted to inquire if they had no larger vessels than those we saw there, or if any other of the inhabitants had not such. They signified presently that they had no larger boats than that they showed us; but that on the other side of the island they had larger boats, and that with decks upon them, and large sails; and this made us resolve to coast round the whole island to see them; so we prepared and victualed our canoe for the voyage, and, in a word, went to sea for the third time.

It cost us a month or six weeks' time to perform this voyage, in which time we went on shore several times for water and provisions, and found the natives always very free and courteous; but we were surprised one morning early, being at the extremity of the northernmost part of the island, when one of our men cried out, "A sail! a sail!" We presently saw a vessel a great way out at sea; but after we had looked at it with our perspective glasses, and endeavoured all we could to make out what it was, we could not tell what to think of it; for it was neither ship, ketch, galley, galliot, or like anything that we had ever seen before; all that we could make of it was, that it went from us, standing out to sea. In a word, we soon lost sight of it, for we were in no condition to chase anything, and we never saw it again; but, by all that we could perceive of it, from what we saw of such things afterwards, it was some

Arabian vessel, which had been trading to the coast of Mozambique, or Zanzibar, the same place where we afterwards went, as you shall hear.

I kept no journal of this voyage, nor indeed did I all this while understand anything of navigation, more than the common business of a foremast-man; so I can say nothing to the latitudes or distances of any places we were at, how long we were going, or how far we sailed in a day; but this I remember, that being now come round the island, we sailed up the eastern shore due south, as we had done down the western shore due north before.

Nor do I remember that the natives differed much from one another, either in stature or complexion, or in their manners, their habits, their weapons, or indeed in anything; and yet we could not perceive that they had any intelligence one with another; but they were extremely kind and civil to us on this side, as well as on the other.

We continued our voyage south for many weeks, though with several intervals of going on shore to get provisions and water. At length, coming round a point of land which lay about a league further than ordinary into the sea, we were agreeably surprised with a sight which, no doubt, had been as disagreeable to those concerned, as it was pleasant to us. This was the wreck of an European ship, which had been cast away upon the rocks, which in that place run a great way into the sea.

We could see plainly, at low water, a great deal of the ship lay dry; even at high water, she was not entirely covered; and that at most she did not lie above a league from the shore. It will easily be believed that our curiosity led us, the wind and weather also permitting, to go directly to her, which we did without any difficulty, and presently found that it was a Dutch-built ship, and that she could not have been very long in that condition, a great deal of the upper work of her stern remaining firm, with the mizzen-mast standing. Her stern seemed to be jammed in between two ridges of the rock, and so remained fast, all the fore part of the ship having been beaten to pieces.

We could see nothing to be gotten out of the wreck that was worth our while; but we resolved to go on shore, and stay some time thereabouts, to see if perhaps we might get any light into the story of her; and we were not without hopes that we might hear something more particular about her men, and perhaps find some of them on shore there, in the same condition that we were in, and so might increase our company.

It was a very pleasant sight to us when, coming on shore, we saw all the marks and tokens of a ship-carpenter's yard; as a launch-block and cradles, scaffolds and planks, and pieces of planks, the remains of the building a ship or vessel; and, in a word, a great many things that fairly invited us to go about the same work; and we soon came to understand that the men belonging to the ship that was lost had saved themselves on shore, perhaps in their boat, and had built themselves a bark or sloop, and so were gone to sea again; and, inquiring of the natives which way they went, they pointed to the south and south-west, by which we could easily understand they were gone away to the Cape of Good Hope.

Nobody will imagine we could be so dull as not to gather from hence that we might take the same method for our escape; so we resolved first, in general, that we would try if possible to build us a boat of one kind or other, and go to sea as our fate should direct.

In order to this our first work was to have the two carpenters search about to see what materials the Dutchmen had left behind them that might be of use; and, in particular, they found one that was very useful, and which I was much employed about, and that was a pitch-kettle, and a little pitch in it.

When we came to set close to this work we found it very laborious and difficult, having but few tools, no ironwork, no cordage, no sails; so that, in short, whatever we built, we were obliged to be our own smiths, rope-makers, sail-makers, and indeed to practice twenty trades that we knew little or nothing of. However, necessity was the spur to invention, and we did many things which before we thought impracticable, that is to say, in our circumstances.

After our two carpenters had resolved upon the dimensions of what they would build, they set us all to work, to go off in our boats and split up the wreck of the old ship, and to bring away everything we could; and particularly that, if possible, we should bring away the mizzen-mast, which was left standing, which with much difficulty we effected, after above twenty days' labour of fourteen of our men.

At the same time we got out a great deal of ironwork, as bolts, spikes, nails, &c., all of which our artist, of whom I have spoken already, who was now grown a very dexterous smith, made us nails and hinges for our rudder, and spikes such as we wanted.

But we wanted an anchor, and if we had had an anchor, we could not have made a cable; so we contented ourselves with making some ropes with the help of the natives, of such stuff as they made their mats of, and with these we made such a kind of cable or tow-line as was sufficient to fasten our vessel to the shore, which we contented ourselves with for that time.

To be short, we spent four months here, and worked very hard too; at the end of which time we launched our frigate, which, in a few words, had many defects, but yet, all things considered, it was as well as we could expect it to be.

In short, it was a kind of sloop, of the burthen of near eighteen or twenty tons; and had we had masts and sails, standing and running rigging, as is usual in such cases, and other conveniences, the vessel might have carried us wherever we could have had a mind to go; but of all the materials we wanted, this was the worst, viz., that we had no tar or pitch to pay the seams and secure the bottom; and though we did what we could, with tallow and oil, to make a mixture to supply that part, yet we could not bring it to answer our end fully; and when we launched her into the water, she was so leaky, and took in the water so fast, that we thought all our labour had been lost, for we had much ado to make her swim; and as for pumps, we had none, nor had we any means to make one.

But at length one of the natives, a black Negro-man, showed us a tree, the wood of which being put into the fire, sends forth a liquid that is as glutinous and almost as strong as tar, and of which, by boiling, we made a sort of stuff which served us for pitch, and this answered our end effectually; for we perfectly made our vessel sound and tight, so that we wanted no pitch or tar at all. This secret has stood me in stead upon many occasions since that time in the same place.

Our vessel being thus finished, out of the mizzen-mast of the ship we made a very good mast to her, and fitted our sails to it as well as we could; then we made a rudder and tiller, and, in a word, everything that our present necessity called upon us for; and having victualed her, and put as much fresh water on board as we thought we wanted, or as we knew how to stow (for we were yet without casks), we put to sea with a fair wind.

We had spent near another year in these rambles, and in this piece of work; for it was now, as our men said, about the beginning of our February, and the sun went from us apace, which was much to our satisfaction, for the heats were exceedingly violent. The wind, as I said, was fair; for, as I have since learned, the winds generally spring up to the eastward, as the sun goes from them to the north.

Our debate now was, which way we should go, and never were men so irresolute; some were for going to the east, and stretching away directly for the coast of Malabar; but others, who considered more seriously the length of that voyage, shook their heads at the proposal, knowing very well that neither our provisions, especially of water, or our vessel, were equal to such a run as that is, of near 2000 miles without any land to touch at in the way.

These men, too, had all along had a great mind to a voyage for the mainland of Africa, where they said we should have a fair cast for our lives, and might be sure to make ourselves rich, which way so ever we went, if we were but able to make our way through, whether by sea or by land.

Besides, as the case stood with us, we had not much choice for our way; for, if we had resolved for the east, we were at the wrong season of the year, and must have stayed till April or May before we had gone to sea. At length, as we had the wind at S.E. and E.S.E., and fine promising weather, we came all into the first proposal, and resolved for the coast of Africa; nor were we long in disputing as to our coasting the island which we were upon, for we were now upon the wrong side of the island for the voyage we intended; so we stood away to the north, and, having rounded the cape, we hauled away southward, under the lee of the island, thinking to reach the west point of land, which, as I observed before, runs out so far towards the coast of Africa, as would have shortened our run almost 100 leagues. But when we had sailed about thirty leagues, we found the winds variable under the shore, and right against us, so we concluded to stand over directly, for then we had the wind fair, and our vessel was but very ill fated to lie near the wind, or any way indeed but just before it.

Having resolved upon it, therefore, we put into the shore to furnish ourselves again with fresh water and other provisions, and about the latter end of March, with more courage than discretion, more resolution than judgment, we launched for the main coast of Africa.

As for me, I had no anxieties about it, so that we had but a view of reaching some land or other, I cared not what or where it was to be, having at this time no views of what was before me, nor much thought of what might or might not befall me; but with as little consideration as any one can be supposed to have at my age, I consented to everything that was proposed, however hazardous the thing itself, however improbable the success.

The voyage, as it was undertaken with a great deal of ignorance and desperation, so really it was not carried on with much resolution or judgment; for we knew no more of the course we were to steer than this, that it was anywhere about the west, within two or three points N. or S., and as we had no compass with us but a little brass pocket compass, which one of our men had more by accident than otherwise, so we could not be very exact in our course.

However, as it pleased God that the wind continued fair at S.E. and by E., we found that N.W. by W., which was right afore it, was as good a course for us as any we could go, and thus we went on.

The voyage was much longer than we expected; our vessel also, which had no sail that was proportioned to her, made but very little way in the sea, and sailed heavily. We had, indeed, no great adventures happened in this voyage, being out of the way of everything that could offer to divert us; and as for seeing any vessel, we had not the least occasion to hail anything in all the voyage; for we saw not one vessel, small or great, the sea we were upon being entirely out of the way of all commerce; for the people of Madagascar knew no more of the shores of Africa than we did, only that there was a country of lions, as they call it, that way.

We had been eight or nine days under sail, with a fair wind, when, to our great joy, one of our men cried out "Land!" We had great reason to be glad of the discovery, for we had not water enough left for above two or three days more, though at a short allowance. However, though it was early in the morning when we discovered it, we made it near night before we reached it, the wind slackening almost to a calm, and our ship being, as I said, a very dull sailor.

We were sadly baulked upon our coming to the land, when we found that, instead of the mainland of Africa, it was only a little island, with no inhabitants upon it, at least none that we could find; nor any cattle, except a few goats, of which we killed three only. However, they served us for fresh meat, and we found very good water; and it was fifteen days more before we reached the main, which, however, at last we arrived at, and which was most essential to us, as we came to it just as all our provisions were spent. Indeed, we may say they were spent first, for we had but a pint of water a day to each man for the last two days. But, to our great joy, we saw the land, though at a great distance, the evening before, and by a pleasant gale in the night were by morning within two leagues of the shore.

We never scrupled going ashore at the first place we came at, though, had we had patience, we might have found a very fine river a little farther north. However, we kept our frigate on float by the help of two great poles, which we fastened into the ground to moor her, like poles; and the little weak ropes, which, as I said, we had made of matting, served us well enough to make the vessel fast.

As soon as we had viewed the country a little, got fresh water, and furnished ourselves with some victuals, which we found very scarce here, we went on board again with our stores. All we got for provision was some fowls that we killed, and a kind of wild buffalo or bull, very small, but good meat; I say, having got these things on board, we resolved to sail along the coast, which lay N.N.E., till we found some creek or river, that we might run up into the country, or some town or people; for we had reason enough to know the place was inhabited, because we several times saw fires in the night, and smoke in the day, every way at a distance from us.

At length we came to a very large bay, and in it several little creeks or rivers emptying themselves into the sea, and we ran boldly into the first creek we came at; where, seeing some huts and wild people about them on the shore, we ran our vessel into a little cove on the north side of the creek, and held up a long pole, with a white bit of cloth on it, for a signal of peace to them. We found they understood us presently, for they came flocking to us, men, women, and children, most of them, of both sexes, stark naked. At first they stood wondering and staring at us, as if we had been monsters, and as if they had been frighted; but we found they inclined to be familiar with us afterwards. The first thing we did to try them, was, we held up our hands to our mouths, as if we were to drink, signifying that we wanted water. This they understood presently, and three of their women and two boys ran away up the land, and came back in about half a quarter of an hour, with several pots, made of earth, pretty enough, and baked, I suppose, in the sun; these they brought us full of water, and set them down near the sea-shore, and there left them, going back a little, that we might fetch them, which we did.

Some time after this, they brought us roots and herbs, and some fruits which I cannot remember, and gave us; but as we had nothing to give them, we found them not so free as the people in Madagascar were. However, our cutler went to work, and, as he had saved some iron out of the wreck of the ship, he made abundance of toys, birds, dogs, pins, hooks, and rings; and we helped to file them, and make them bright for him, and when we gave them some of these, they brought us all sorts of provisions they had, such as goats, hogs, and cows, and we got victuals enough.

We were now landed upon the continent of Africa, the most desolate, desert, and inhospitable country in the world, even Greenland and Nova Zembla itself not excepted, with this difference only, that even the worst part of it we found inhabited, though, taking the nature and quality of some of the inhabitants, it might have been much better to us if there had been none.

And, to add to the exclamation I am making on the nature of the place, it was here that we took one of the rashest, and wildest, and most desperate resolutions that ever was taken by man, or any number of men, in the world; this was, to travel overland through the heart of the country, from the coast of Mozambique, on the east ocean, to the coast of Angola or Guinea, on the western or Atlantic Ocean, a continent of land of at least 1800 miles, in which journey we had excessive heats to support, unpassable deserts to go over, no carriages, camels, or beasts of any kind to carry our baggage, innumerable numbers of wild and ravenous beasts to encounter with, such as lions, leopards, tigers, lizards, and elephants; we had the equinoctial line to pass under, and, consequently, were in the very centre of the torrid zone; we had nations of savages to encounter with, barbarous and brutish to the last degree; hunger and thirst to struggle with, and, in one word, terrors enough to have daunted the stoutest hearts that ever were placed in cases of flesh and blood.

Yet, fearless of all these, we resolved to adventure, and accordingly made such preparations for our journey as the place we were in would allow us, and such as our little experience of the country seemed to dictate to us.

It had been some time already that we had been used to tread barefooted upon the rocks, the gravel, the grass, and the sand on the shore; but as we found the worst thing for our feet was the walking or traveling on the dry burning sands, within the country, so we provided ourselves with a sort of shoes, made of the skins of wild beasts, with the hair inward, and being dried in the sun, the outsides were thick and hard, and would last a great while. In short, as I called them, so I think the term very proper still, we made us gloves for our feet, and we found them very convenient and very comfortable.

We conversed with some of the natives of the country, who were friendly enough. What tongue they spoke I do not yet pretend to know.

We talked as far as we could make them understand us, not only about our provisions, but also about our undertaking, and asked them what country lay that way, pointing west with our hands. They told us but little to our purpose, only we thought, by all their discourse, that there were people to be found, of one sort or other, everywhere; that there were many great rivers, many lions and tigers, elephants, and furious wild cats (which in the end we found to be civet cats), and the like.

When we asked them if any one had ever traveled that way, they told us yes, some had gone to where the sun sleeps, meaning to the west, but they could not tell us who they were. When we asked for some to guide us, they shrunk up their shoulders as Frenchmen do when they are afraid to undertake a thing. When we asked them about the lions and wild creatures, they laughed, and let us know that they would do us no hurt, and directed us to a good way indeed to deal with them, and that was to make some fire, which would always fright them away; and so indeed we found it.

Upon these encouragements we resolved upon our journey, and many considerations put us upon it, which, had the thing itself been practicable, we were not so much to blame for as it might otherwise be supposed; I will name some of them, not to make the account too tedious.

First, we were perfectly destitute of means to work about our own deliverance any other way; we were on shore in a place perfectly remote from all European navigation; so that we could never think of being relieved, and fetched off by any of our own countrymen in that part of the world. Secondly, if we had adventured to have sailed on along the coast of Mozambique, and the desolate shores of Africa to the north, till we came to the Red Sea, all we could hope for there was to be taken by the Arabs, and be sold for slaves to the Turks, which to all of us was little better than death. We could not build anything of a vessel that would carry us over the great Arabian Sea to India, nor could we reach the Cape de Bona Speranza, the winds being too variable, and the sea in that latitude too tempestuous; but we all knew, if we could cross this continent of land, we might reach some of the great rivers that run into the Atlantic Ocean; and that, on the banks of any of those rivers, we might there build us canoes which would carry us down, if it were thousands of miles, so that we could want nothing but food, of which we were assured we might kill sufficient with our guns; and to add to the satisfaction of our deliverance, we concluded we might, every one of us, get a quantity of gold, which, if we came safe, would infinitely recompense us for our toil.

I cannot say that in all our consultations I ever began to enter into the weight and merit of any enterprise we went upon till now. My view before was, as I thought, very good, viz., that we should get into the Arabian Gulf, or the mouth of the Red Sea; and waiting for some vessel passing or repassing there, of which there is plenty, have seized upon the first we came at by force, and not only have enriched ourselves with her cargo, but have carried ourselves to what part of the world we had pleased; but when they came to talk to me of a march of 2000 or 3000 miles on foot, of wandering in deserts among lions and tigers, I confess my blood ran chill, and I used all the arguments I could to persuade them against it.

But they were all positive, and I might as well have held my tongue; so I submitted, and told them I would keep to our first law, to be governed by the majority, and we resolved upon our journey. The first thing we did was to take an observation, and see whereabouts in the world we were, which we did, and found we were in the latitude of 12 degrees 35 minutes south of the line. The next thing was to look on the charts, and see the coast of the country we aimed at, which we found to be from 8 to 11 degrees south latitude, if we went for the coast of Angola, or in 12 to 29 degrees north latitude, if we made for the river Niger, and the coast of Guinea.

Our aim was for the coast of Angola, which, by the charts we had, lying very near the same latitude we were then in, our course thither was due west; and as we were assured we should meet with rivers, we doubted not but that by their help we might ease our journey, especially if we could find means to cross the great lake, or inland sea, which the natives call Coalmucoa, out of which it is said the river Nile has its source or beginning; but we reckoned without our host, as you will see in the sequel of our story.

The next thing we had to consider was, how to carry our baggage, which we were first of all determined not to travel without; neither indeed was it possible for us to do so, for even our ammunition, which was absolutely necessary to us, and on which our subsistence, I mean for food, as well as our safety, and particularly our defence against wild beasts and wild men, depended, — I say, even our ammunition was a load too heavy for us to carry in a country where the heat was such that we should be load enough for ourselves.

We inquired in the country, and found there was no beast of burthen known among them, that is to say, neither horses or mules, or asses, camels, or dromedaries; the only creature they had was a kind of buffalo, or tame bull, such a one as we had killed; and that some of these they had brought so to their hand, that they taught them to go and come with their voices, as they called them to them, or sent them from them; that they made them carry burdens; and particularly that they would swim over rivers and lakes upon them, the creatures swimming very high and strong in the water.

But we understood nothing of the management of guiding such a creature, or how to bind a burthen upon them; and this last part of our consultation puzzled us extremely. At last I proposed a method for them, which, after some consideration, they found very convenient; and this was, to quarrel with some of the Negro natives, take ten or twelve of them prisoners, and binding them as slaves, cause them to travel with us, and make them carry our baggage; which I alleged would be convenient and useful many ways as well to show us the way, as to converse with other natives for us.

This counsel was not accepted at first, but the natives soon gave them reason to approve it, and also gave them an opportunity to put it in practice; for, as our little traffic with the natives was hitherto upon the faith of their first kindness, we found some knavery among them at last; for having bought some cattle of them for our toys, which, as I said, our cutler had contrived, one of our men differing with his chapman, truly they huffed him in their manner, and, keeping the things he had offered them for the cattle, made their fellows drive away the cattle before his face, and laugh at him. Our man crying out loud of this violence, and calling to some of us who were not far off, the Negro he was dealing with threw a lance at him, which came so true, that, if he had not with great agility jumped aside, and held up his hand also to turn the lance as it came, it had struck through his body; and, as it was, it wounded him in the arm; at which the man, enraged, took up his fusée, and shot the Negro through the heart.

The others that were near him, and all those that were with us at a distance, were so terribly frighted, first, at the flash of fire; secondly, at the noise; and thirdly, at seeing their countryman killed, that they stood like men stupid and amazed, at first, for some time; but after they were a little recovered from their fright, one of them, at a good distance from us, set up a sudden screaming noise, which, it seems, is the noise they make when they go to fight; and all the rest understanding what he meant, answered him, and ran together to the place where he was, and we not knowing what it meant, stood still, looking upon one another like a parcel of fools.

But we were presently undeceived; for, in two or three minutes more, we heard the screaming roaring noise go on from one place to another, through all their little towns; nay, even over the creek to the other side; and, on a sudden, we saw a naked multitude running from all parts to the place where the first man began it, as to a rendezvous; and, in less than an hour, I believe there was near 500 of them gotten together, armed some with bows and arrows, but most with lances, which they throw at a good distance, so nicely that they will strike a bird flying.

We had but a very little time for consultation, for the multitude was increasing every moment; and I verily believe, if we had stayed long, they would have been 10,000 together in a little time. We had nothing to do, therefore, but to fly to our ship or bark, where indeed we could have defended ourselves very well, or to advance and try what a volley or two of small shot would do for us.

We resolved immediately upon the latter, depending upon it that the fire and terror of our shot would soon put them to flight; so we drew up all in a line, and marched boldly up to them. They stood ready to meet us, depending, I suppose, to destroy us all with their lances; but before we came near enough for them to throw their lances, we halted, and, standing at a good distance from one another, to stretch our line as far as we could, we gave them a salute with our shot, which, besides what we wounded that we knew not of, knocked sixteen of them down upon the spot, and three more were so lamed, that they fell about twenty or thirty yards from them.

As soon as we had fired, they set up the horridest yell, or howling, partly raised by those that were wounded, and partly by those that pitied and condoled the bodies they saw lie dead, that I never heard anything like it before or since.

We stood stock still after we had fired, to load our guns again, and finding they did not stir from the place we fired among them again; we killed about nine of them at the second fire; but as they did not stand so thick as before, all our men did not fire, seven of us being ordered to reserve our charge, and to advance as soon as the other had fired, while the rest loaded again; of which I shall speak again presently.

As soon as we had fired the second volley, we shouted as loud as we could, and the seven men advanced upon them, and, coming about twenty yards nearer, fired again, and those that were behind having loaded again with all expedition, followed; but when they saw us advance, they ran screaming away as if they were bewitched.

When we came up to the field of battle, we saw a great number of bodies lying upon the ground, many more than we could suppose were killed or wounded; nay, more than we had bullets in our pieces when we fired; and we could not tell what to make of it; but at length we found how it was, viz., that they were frighted out of all manner of sense; nay, I do believe several of those that were really dead, were frighted to death, and had no wound about them.

Of those that were thus frighted, as I have said, several of them, as they recovered themselves, came and worshipped us (taking us for gods or devils, I know not which, nor did it much matter to us): some kneeling, some throwing themselves flat on the ground, made a thousand antic gestures, but all with tokens of the most profound submission. It presently came into my head, that we might now, by the law of arms, take as many prisoners as we would, and make them travel with us, and carry our baggage. As soon as I proposed it, our men were all of my mind; and accordingly we secured about sixty lusty young fellows, and let them know they must go with us; which they seemed very willing to do. But the next question we had among ourselves, was, how we should do to trust them, for we found the people not like those of Madagascar, but fierce, revengeful, and treacherous; for which reason we were sure that we should have no service from them but that of mere slaves; no subjection that would continue any longer than the fear of us was upon them, nor any labour but by violence.

Before I go any farther, I must hint to the reader, that from this time forward I began to enter a little more seriously into the circumstance I was in, and concerned myself more in the conduct of our affairs; for though my comrades were all older men, yet I began to find them void of counsel, or, as I now call it, presence of mind, when they came to the execution of a thing. The first occasion I took to observe this, was in their late engagement with the natives, when, though they had taken a good resolution to attack them and fire upon them, yet, when they had fired the first time, and found that the Negroes did not run as they expected, their hearts began to fail, and I am persuaded, if their bark had been near hand, they would every man have run away.

Upon this occasion I began to take upon me a little to hearten them up, and to call upon them to load again, and give them another volley, telling them that I would engage, if they would be ruled by me,

I'd make the Negroes run fast enough. I found this heartened them, and therefore, when they fired a second time, I desired them to reserve some of their shot for an attempt by itself, as I mentioned above.

Having fired a second time, I was indeed forced to command, as I may call it. "Now, seigniors," said I, "let us give them a cheer." So I opened my throat, and shouted three times, as our English sailors do on like occasions. "And now follow me," said I to the seven that had not fired, "and I'll warrant you we will make work with them," and so it proved indeed; for, as soon as they saw us coming, away they ran, as above.

From this day forward they would call me nothing but Seignior Capitanio; but I told them I would not be called seignior. "Well, then," said the gunner, who spoke good English, "you shall be called Captain Bob;" and so they gave me my title ever after.

Nothing is more certain of the Portuguese than this, take them nationally or personally, if they are animated and heartened up by anybody to go before, and encourage them by example, they will behave well enough; but if they have nothing but their own measures to follow, they sink immediately: these men had certainly fled from a parcel of naked savages, though even by flying they could not have saved their lives, if I had not shouted and hallooed, and rather made sport with the thing than a fight, to keep up their courage.

Nor was there less need of it upon several occasions hereafter; and I do confess I have often wondered how a number of men, who, when they came to the extremity, were so ill supported by their own spirits, had at first courage to propose and to undertake the most desperate and impracticable attempt that ever men went about in the world.

There were indeed two or three indefatigable men among them, by whose courage and industry all the rest were upheld; and indeed those two or three were the managers of them from the beginning; that was the gunner, and that cutler whom I call the artist; and the third, who was pretty well, though not like either of them, was one of the carpenters. These indeed were the life and soul of all the rest, and it was to their courage that all the rest owed the resolution they showed upon any occasion. But when those saw me take a little upon me, as above, they embraced me, and treated me with particular affection ever after.

This gunner was an excellent mathematician, a good scholar, and a complete sailor; and it was in conversing intimately with him that I learned afterwards the grounds of what knowledge I have since had in all the sciences useful for navigation, and particularly in the geographical part of knowledge.

Even in our conversation, finding me eager to understand and learn, he laid the foundation of a general knowledge of things in my mind, gave me just ideas of the form of the earth and of the sea, the situation of countries, the course of rivers, the doctrine of the spheres, the motion of the stars; and, in a word, taught me a kind of system of astronomy, which I afterwards improved.

In an especial manner, he filled my head with aspiring thoughts, and with an earnest desire after learning everything that could be taught me; convincing me, that nothing could qualify me for great undertakings, but a degree of learning superior to what was usual in the race of seamen; he told me, that to be ignorant was to be certain of a mean station in the world, but that knowledge was the first step to preferment. He was always flattering me with my capacity to learn; and though that fed my pride, yet, on the other hand, as I had a secret ambition, which just at that time fed itself in my mind, it prompted in me an insatiable thirst after learning in general, and I resolved, if ever I came back to Europe, and had anything left to purchase it, I would make myself master of all the parts of learning needful to the making of me a complete sailor; but I was not so just to myself afterwards as to do it when I had an opportunity.

But to return to our business; the gunner, when he saw the service I had done in the fight, and heard my proposal for keeping a number of prisoners for our march, and for carrying our baggage, turns to me before them all. "Captain Bob," says he, "I think you must be our leader, for all the success of this enterprise is owing to you." "No, no," said I, "do not compliment me; you shall be our Seignior Capitanio, you shall be general; I am too young for it." So, in short, we all agreed he should be our leader; but he would not accept of it alone, but would have me joined with him; and all the rest agreeing, I was obliged to comply.

The first piece of service they put me upon in this new command was as difficult as any they could think of, and that was to manage the prisoners; which, however, I cheerfully undertook, as you shall hear presently. But the immediate consultation was yet of more consequence; and that was, first, which way we should go; and secondly, how to furnish ourselves for the voyage with provisions.

There was among the prisoners one tall, well-shaped, handsome fellow, to whom the rest seemed to pay great respect, and who, as we

645

understood afterwards, was the son of one of their kings; his father was, it seems, killed at our first volley, and he wounded with a shot in his arm, and with another just on one of his hips or haunches. The shot in his haunch being in a fleshy part, bled much, and he was half dead with the loss of blood. As to the shot in his arm, it had broke his wrist, and he was by both these wounds quite disabled, so that we were once going to turn him away, and let him die; and, if we had, he would have died indeed in a few days more: but, as I found the man had some respect showed him, it presently occurred to my thoughts that we might bring him to be useful to us, and perhaps make him a kind of commander over them. So I caused our surgeon to take him in hand, and gave the poor wretch good words, that is to say, I spoke to him as well as I could by signs, to make him understand that we would make him well again.

This created a new awe in their minds of us, believing that, as we could kill at a distance by something invisible to them (for so our shot was, to be sure), so we could make them well again too. Upon this the young prince (for so we called him afterwards) called six or seven of the savages to him, and said something to them; what it was we know not, but immediately all the seven came to me, and kneeled down to me, holding up their hands, and making signs of entreaty, pointing to the place where one of those lay whom we had killed.

It was a long time before I or any of us could understand them; but one of them ran and lifted up a dead man, pointing to his wound, which was in his eyes, for he was shot into the head at one of his eyes. Then another pointed to the surgeon, and at last we found it out, that the meaning was, that he should heal the prince's father too, who was dead, being shot through the head, as above.

We presently took the hint, and would not say we could not do it, but let them know, the men that were killed were those that had first fallen upon us, and provoked us, and we would by no means make them alive again; and that, if any others did so, we would kill them too, and never let them live any more: but that, if he (the prince) would be willing to go with us, and do as we should direct him, we would not let him die, and would make his arm well. Upon this he bid his men go and fetch a long stick or staff, and lay on the ground. When they brought it, we saw it was an arrow; he took it with his left hand (for his other was lame with the wound), and, pointing up at the sun, broke the arrow in two, and set the point against his breast, and then gave it to me. This was, as I understood afterwards, wishing the sun, whom they worship, might shoot him into the breast with an arrow, if ever he failed to be my friend; and giving the point of the arrow to me was to be a testimony that I was the man he had sworn to: and never was Christian more punctual to an oath than he was to this, for he was a sworn servant to us for many a weary month after that.

When I brought him to the surgeon, he immediately dressed the wound in his haunch or buttock, and found the bullet had only grazed upon the flesh, and passed, as it were, by it, but it was not lodged in the part, so that it was soon healed and well again; but, as to his arm, he found one of the bones broken, which are in the fore-part from the wrist to the elbow; and this he set, and splintered it up, and bound his arm in a sling, hanging it about his neck, and making signs to him that he should not stir it; which he was so strict an observer of, that he set him down, and never moved one way or other but as the surgeon gave him leave.

I took a great deal of pains to acquaint this Negro what we intended to do, and what use we intended to make of his men; and particularly to teach him the meaning of what we said, especially to teach him some words, such as yes and no, and what they meant, and to inure him to our way of talking; and he was very willing and apt to learn anything I taught him.

It was easy to let him see that we intended to carry our provision with us from the first day; but he made signs to us to tell us we need not, for we should find provision enough everywhere for forty days. It was very difficult for us to understand how he expressed forty; for he knew no figures, but some words that they used to one another that they understood it by. At last one of the Negroes, by his order, laid forty little stones one by another, to show us how many days we should travel, and find provisions sufficient.

Then I showed him our baggage, which was very heavy, particularly our powder, shot, lead, iron, carpenters' tools, seamen's instruments, cases of bottles, and other lumber. He took some of the things up in his hand to feel the weight, and shook his head at them; so I told our people they must resolve to divide their things into small parcels, and make them portable; and accordingly they did so, by which means we were fain to leave all our chests behind us, which were eleven in number.

Then he made signs to us that he would procure some buffaloes, or young bulls, as I called them, to carry things for us, and made signs, too, that if we were weary, we might be carried too; but that we slighted, only were willing to have the creatures, because, at last, when they could serve us no farther for carriage, we might eat them all up if we had any occasion for them.

I then carried him to our bark, and showed him what things we had here. He seemed amazed at the sight of our bark, having never seen anything of that kind before, for their boats are most wretched things, such as I never saw before, having no head or stern, and being made only of the skins of goats, sewed together with dried guts of goats and sheep, and done over with a kind of slimy stuff like rosin and oil, but of a most nauseous, odious smell; and they are poor miserable things for boats, the worst that any part of the world ever saw; a canoe is an excellent contrivance compared to them.

But to return to our boat. We carried our new prince into it, and helped him over the side, because of his lameness. We made signs to him that his men must carry our goods for us, and showed him what we had; he answered, "Si, Seignior," or, "Yes, sir" (for we had taught him that word and the meaning of it), and taking up a bundle, he made signs to us, that when his arm was well he would carry some for us.

I made signs again to tell him, that if he would make his men carry them, we would not let him carry anything. We had secured all the prisoners in a narrow place, where we had bound them with mat cords, and set up stakes like a palisado round them; so, when we carried the prince on shore, we went with him to them, and made signs to him to ask them if they were willing to go with us to the country of lions. Accordingly he made a long speech to them, and we could understand by it that he told them, if they were willing, they must say, "Si, Seignior," telling them what it signified. They immediately answered, "Si, Seignior," and clapped their hands, looking up to the sun, which, the prince signified to us, was swearing to be faithful. But as soon as they had said so, one of them made a long speech to the prince; and in it we perceived, by his gestures, which were very antic, that they desired something from us, and that they were in great concern about it. So I asked him, as well as I could, what it was they desired of us; he told us by signs that they desired we should clap our hands to the sun (that was, to swear) that we would not kill them, that we would give them chiaruck, that is to say, bread, would not starve them, and would not let the lions eat them. I told him we would promise all that; then he pointed to the sun, and clapped his hands, signing to me that I should do so too, which I did; at which all the prisoners fell flat on the ground, and rising up again, made the oddest, wildest cries that ever I heard.

I think it was the first time in my life that ever any religious thought affected me; but I could not refrain some reflections, and almost tears, in considering how happy it was that I was not born among such creatures as these, and was not so stupidly ignorant and barbarous; but this soon went off again, and I was not troubled again with any qualms of that sort for a long time after.

When this ceremony was over, our concern was to get some provisions, as well for the present subsistence of our prisoners as ourselves; and making signs to our prince that we were thinking upon that subject, he made signs to me that, if I would let one of the prisoners go to his town, he should bring provisions, and should bring some beasts to carry our baggage. I seemed loth to trust him, and supposing that he would run away, he made great signs of fidelity, and with his own hands tied a rope about his neck, offering me one end of it, intimating that I should hang him if the man did not come again. So I consented, and he gave him abundance of instructions, and sent him away, pointing to the light of the sun, which it seems was to tell him at what time he must be back.

The fellow ran as if he was mad, and held it till he was quite out of sight, by which I supposed he had a great way to go. The next morning, about two hours before the time appointed, the black prince, for so I always called him, beckoning with his hand to me, and hallooing after his manner, desired me to come to him, which I did, when, pointing to a little hill about two miles off, I saw plainly a little drove of cattle, and several people with them; those, he told me by signs, were the man he had sent, and several more with him, and cattle for us.

Accordingly, by the time appointed, he came quite to our huts, and brought with him a great many cows, young runts, about sixteen goats, and four young bulls, taught to carry burdens.

This was a supply of provisions sufficient; as for bread, we were obliged to shift with some roots which we had made use of before. We then began to consider of making some large bags like the soldiers' knapsacks, for their men to carry our baggage in, and to make it easy to them; and the goats being killed, I ordered the skins to be spread in the sun, and they were as dry in two days as could be desired; so we found means to make such little bags as we wanted, and began to divide our baggage into them. When the black prince found what they were for, and how easy they were of carriage when we put them on, he smiled a little, and sent away the man again to fetch skins, and he brought two natives more with him, all loaded with skins better cured than ours, and of other kinds, such as we could not tell what names to give them.

These two men brought the black prince two lances, of the sort they use in their fights, but finer than ordinary, being made of black smooth wood, as fine as ebony, and headed at the point with the end of a long tooth of some creature — we could not tell of what creature; the head was so firm put on, and the tooth so strong, though no bigger than my thumb, and sharp at the end, that I never saw anything like it in any place in the world.

The prince would not take them till I gave him leave, but made signs that they should give them to me; however, I gave him leave to take them himself, for I saw evident signs of an honourable just principle in him.

We now prepared for our march, when the prince coming to me, and pointing towards the several quarters of the world, made signs to know which way we intended to go; and when I showed him, pointing to the west, he presently let me know there was a great river a little further to the north, which was able to carry our bark many leagues into the country due west. I presently took the hint, and inquired for the mouth of the river, which I understood by him was above a day's march, and, by our estimation, we found it about seven leagues further. I take this to be the great river marked by our chart-makers at the northmost part of the coast of Mozambique, and called there Quilloa.

Consulting thus with ourselves, we resolved to take the prince, and as many of the prisoners as we could stow in our frigate, and go about by the bay into the river; and that eight of us, with our arms, should march by land to meet them on the river side; for the prince, carrying us to a rising ground, had showed us the river very plain, a great way up the country, and in one place it was not above six miles to it.

It was my lot to march by land, and be captain of the whole caravan. I had eight of our men with me, and seven-and-thirty of our prisoners, without any baggage, for all our luggage was yet on board. We drove the young bulls with us; nothing was ever so tame, so willing to work, or carry anything. The Negroes would ride upon them four at a time, and they would go very willingly. They would eat out of our hand, lick our feet, and were as tractable as a dog.

We drove with us six or seven cows for food; but our Negroes knew nothing of curing the flesh by salting and drying it till we showed them the way, and then they were mighty willing to do so as long as we

650

had any salt to do it with, and to carry salt a great way too, after we found we should have no more.

It was an easy march to the river side for us that went by land, and we came thither in a piece of a day, being, as above, no more than six English miles; whereas it was no less than five days before they came to us by water, the wind in the bay having failed them, and the way, by reason of a great turn or reach in the river, being about fifty miles about.

We spent this time in a thing which the two strangers, which brought the prince the two lances, put into the head of the prisoners, viz., to make bottles of the goats' skins to carry fresh water in, which it seems they knew we should come to want; and the men did it so dexterously, having dried skins fetched them by those two men, that before our vessel came up, they had every man a pouch like a bladder, to carry fresh water in, hanging over their shoulders by a thong made of other skins, about three inches broad, like the sling of a fusée.

Our prince, to assure us of the fidelity of the men in this march, had ordered them to be tied two and two by the wrist, as we handcuff prisoners in England; and made them so sensible of the reasonableness of it, that he made them do it themselves, appointing four of them to bind the rest; but we found them so honest, and particularly so obedient to him, that after we were gotten a little further off of their own country, we set them at liberty, though, when he came to us, he would have them tied again, and they continued so a good while.

All the country on the bank of the river was a high land, no marshy swampy ground in it; the verdure good, and abundance of cattle feeding upon it wherever we went, or which way so ever we looked; there was not much wood indeed, at least not near us; but further up we saw oak, cedar, and pine-trees, some of which were very large.

The river was a fair open channel, about as broad as the Thames below Gravesend, and a strong tide of flood, which we found held us about sixty miles; the channel deep, nor did we find any want of water for a great way. In short, we went merrily up the river with the flood and the wind blowing still fresh at E. and E.N.E. We stemmed the ebb easily also, especially while the river continued broad and deep; but when we came past the swelling of the tide, and had the natural current of the river to go against, we found it too strong for us, and began to think of quitting our bark; but the prince would by no means agree to that, for, finding we had on board pretty good store of roping made of mats and flags, which I described before, he ordered all the prisoners which were on shore to come and take hold of those ropes, and tow us along by the shore side; and as we hoisted our sail too, to ease them, the men ran along with us at a very great rate.

In this manner the river carried us up, by our computation, near 200 miles, and then it narrowed apace, and was not above as broad as the Thames is at Windsor, or thereabouts; and, after another day, we came to a great waterfall or cataract, enough to fright us, for I believe the whole body of water fell at once perpendicularly down a precipice above sixty foot high, which made noise enough to deprive men of their hearing, and we heard it above ten miles before we came to it.

Here we were at a full stop, and now our prisoners went first on shore; they had worked very hard and very cheerfully, relieving one another, those that were weary being taken into the bark. Had we had canoes or any boats which might have been carried by men's strength we might have gone two hundred miles more up this river in small boats, but our great boat could go no farther.

All this way the country looked green and pleasant, and was full of cattle, and some people we saw, though not many; but this we observed now, that the people did no more understand our prisoners here than we could understand them; being, it seems, of different nations and of different speech. We had yet seen no wild beasts, or, at least, none that came very near us, except two days before we came to the waterfall, when we saw three of the most beautiful leopards that ever were seen, standing upon the bank of the river on the north side, our prisoners being all on the other side of the water. Our gunner espied them first, and ran to fetch his gun, putting a ball extraordinary in it; and coming to me, "Now, Captain Bob," says he, "where is your prince?" So I called him out. "Now," says he, "tell your men not to be afraid; tell them they shall see that thing in his hand speak in fire to one of those beasts, and make it kill itself."

The poor Negroes looked as if they had been all going to be killed, notwithstanding what their prince said to them, and stood staring to expect the issue, when on a sudden the gunner fired; and as he was a very good marksman, he shot the creature with two slugs, just in the head. As soon as the leopard felt herself struck, she reared up on her two hind-legs, bolt upright, and throwing her forepaws about in the air, fell backward, growling and struggling, and immediately died; the other two, frighted with the fire and the noise, fled, and were out of sight in an instant.

But the two frighted leopards were not in half the consternation that our prisoners were; four or five of them fell down as if they had been shot; several others fell on their knees, and lifted up their hands to us; whether to worship us, or pray us not to kill them, we did not know; but we made signs to their prince to encourage them, which he did, but it was with much ado that he brought them to their senses. Nay, the prince, notwithstanding all that was said to prepare him for it, yet when the piece went off, he gave a start as if he would have leaped into the river.

When we saw the creature killed, I had a great mind to have the skin of her, and made signs to the prince that he should send some of his men over to take the skin off. As soon as he spoke but a word, four of them, that offered themselves, were untied, and immediately they jumped into the river, and swam over, and went to work with him. The prince having a knife that we gave him, made four wooden knives so clever, that I never saw anything like them in my life; and in less than an hour's time they brought me the skin of the leopard, which was a monstrous great one, for it was from the ears to the tale about seven foot, and near five foot broad on the back, and most admirably spotted all over. The skin of this leopard I brought to London many years after.

We were now all upon a level as to our traveling, being unshipped, for our bark would swim no farther, and she was too heavy to carry on our backs; but as we found the course of the river went a great way farther, we consulted our carpenters whether we could not pull the bark in pieces, and make us three or four small boats to go on with. They told us we might do so, but it would be very long a-doing; and that, when we had done, we had neither pitch or tar to make them sound to keep the water out, or nails to fasten the plank. But one of them told us that as soon as he could come at any large tree near the river, he would make us a canoe or two in a quarter of the time, and which would serve us as well for all the uses we could have any occasion for as a boat; and such, that if we came to any waterfalls, we might take them up, and carry them for a mile or two by land upon our shoulders.

Upon this we gave over the thoughts of our frigate, and hauling her into a little cove or inlet, where a small brook came into the main river, we laid her up for those that came next, and marched forward. We spent indeed two days dividing our baggage, and loading our tame buffaloes and our Negroes. Our powder and shot, which was the thing we were most careful of, we ordered thus: — First, the powder we divided into little leather bags, that is to say, bags of dried skins, with the hair inward, that the powder might not grow damp; and then we put those bags into other bags, made of bullocks' skins, very thick and hard, with the hair outward, that no wet might come in; and this succeeded so well, that in the greatest rains we had, whereof some were very violent and very long, we always kept our powder dry. Besides these bags, which held our chief magazine, we divided to every one a quarter of a pound of powder, and half a pound of shot, to carry always about us; which, as it was enough for our present use, so we were willing to have no weight to carry more than was absolutely necessary, because of the heat.

We kept still on the bank of the river, and for that reason had but very little communication with the people of the country; for, having also our bark stored with plenty of provisions, we had no occasion to look abroad for a supply; but now, when we came to march on foot, we were obliged often to seek out for food. The first place we came to on the river, that gave us any stop, was a little Negro town, containing about fifty huts, and there appeared about 400 people, for they all came out to see us, and wonder at us. When our Negroes appeared the inhabitants began to fly to arms, thinking there had been enemies coming upon them; but our Negroes, though they could not speak their language, made signs to them that they had no weapons, and were tied two and two together as captives, and that there were people behind who came from the sun, and that could kill them all, and make them alive again, if they pleased; but that they would do them no hurt, and came with peace. As soon as they understood this they laid down their lances, and bows and arrows, and came and stuck twelve large stakes in the ground as a token of peace, bowing themselves to us in token of submission. But as soon as they saw white men with beards, that is to say, with mustachios, they ran screaming away, as in a fright.

We kept at a distance from them, not to be too familiar; and when we did appear it was but two or three of us at a time. But our prisoners made them understand that we required some provisions of them; so they brought us some black cattle, for they have abundance of cows and buffaloes all over that side of the country, as also great numbers of deer. Our cutler, who had now a great stock of things of his handiwork, gave them some little knick-knacks, as plates of silver and of iron, cut diamond fashion, and cut into hearts and into rings, and they were mightily pleased. They also brought several fruits and roots, which we did not understand, but our Negroes fed heartily on them, and after we had seen them eat them, we did so too.

Having stocked ourselves here with flesh and root as much as we could well carry, we divided the burdens among our Negroes, appointing about thirty to forty pounds weight to a man, which we thought indeed was load enough in a hot country; and the Negroes did not at all repine at it, but would sometimes help one another when they began to be weary, which did happen now and then, though not often; besides, as most of their luggage was our provision, it lightened every day, like Aesop's basket of bread, till we came to get a recruit. — Note, when we loaded them we untied their hands, and tied them two and two together by one foot.

The third day of our march from this place our chief carpenter desired us to halt, and set up some huts, for he had found out some trees that he liked, and resolved to make us some canoes; for, as he told me, he knew we should have marching enough on foot after we left the river, and he was resolved to go no farther by land than needs must.

We had no sooner given orders for our little camp, and given leave to our Negroes to lay down their loads, but they fell to work to build our huts; and though they were tied as above, yet they did it so nimbly as surprised us. Here we set some of the Negroes quite at liberty, that is to say, without tying them, having the prince's word passed for their fidelity; and some of these were ordered to help the carpenters, which they did very handily, with a little direction, and others were sent to see whether they could get any provisions near hand; but instead of provisions, three of them came in with two bows and arrows, and five lances. They could not easily make us understand how they came by them, only that they had surprised some Negro women, who were in some huts, the men being from home, and they had found the lances and bows in the huts, or houses, the women and children flying away at the sight of them, as from robbers. We seemed very angry at them, and made the prince ask them if they had not killed any of the women or children, making them believe that, if they had killed anybody, we would make them kill themselves too; but they protested their innocence, so we excused them. Then they brought us the bows and arrows and lances; but, at a motion of their black prince, we gave them back the bows and arrows, and gave them leave to go out to see what they could kill for food; and here we gave them the laws of arms, viz., that if any man appeared to assault them, or shoot at them to offer any violence to them, they might kill them; but that they should not offer to kill or hurt any that offered them peace, or laid down their weapons, nor any women or children, upon any occasion whatsoever. These were our articles of war.

These two fellows had not been gone out above three or four hours, but one of them came running to us without his bow and arrows, hallooing and whooping a great while before he came at us, "Okoamo, okoamo!" which, it seems, was, "Help, help!" The rest of the Negroes rose up in a hurry, and by twos, as they could, ran forward towards their fellows, to know what the matter was. As for me, I did not understand it, nor any of our people; the prince looked as if something unlucky had fallen out, and some of our men took up their arms to be ready on occasion. But the Negroes soon discovered the thing, for we saw four of them presently after coming along with a great load of meat upon their backs. The case was, that the two who went out with their bows and arrows, meeting with a great herd of deer in the plain, had been so nimble as to shoot three of them, and then one of them came running to us for help to fetch them away. This was the first venison we had met with in all our march, and we feasted upon it very plentifully; and this was the first time we began to prevail with our prince to eat his meat dressed our way; after which his men were prevailed with by his example, but before that, they ate most of the flesh they had quite raw.

We wished now we had brought some bows and arrows out with us, which we might have done; and we began to have so much confidence in our Negroes, and to be so familiar with them, that we oftentimes let them go, or the greatest part of them, untied, being well assured they would not leave us, and that they did not know what course to take without us; but one thing we resolved not to trust them with, and that was the charging our guns: but they always believed our guns had some heavenly power in them, that would send forth fire and smoke, and speak with a dreadful noise, and kill at a distance whenever we bid them.

In about eight days we finished three canoes, and in them we embarked our white men and our baggage, with our prince, and some of the prisoners. We also found it needful to keep some of ourselves always on shore, not only to manage the Negroes, but to defend them from enemies and wild beasts. Abundance of little incidents happened upon this march, which it is impossible to crowd into this account; particularly, we saw more wild beasts now than we did before, some elephants, and two or three lions, none of which kinds we had seen any of before; and we found our Negroes were more afraid of them a great deal than we were; principally, because they had no bows and arrows, or lances, which were the particular weapons they were bred up to the exercise of.

But we cured them of their fears by being always ready with our firearms. However, as we were willing to be sparing of our powder, and the killing of any of the creatures now was no advantage to us, seeing their skins were too heavy for us to carry, and their flesh not good to eat, we resolved therefore to keep some of our pieces uncharged and only primed; and causing them to flash in the pan, the beasts, even the lions themselves, would always start and fly back when they saw it, and immediately march off.

We passed abundance of inhabitants upon this upper part of the river, and with this observation, that almost every ten miles we came to a separate nation, and every separate nation had a different speech, or else their speech had differing dialects, so that they did not understand one another. They all abounded in cattle, especially on the river-side; and the eighth day of this second navigation we met with a little Negro town, where they had growing a sort of corn like rice, which ate very sweet; and, as we got some of it of the people, we made very good cakes of bread of it, and, making a fire, baked them on the ground, after the fire was swept away, very well; so that hitherto we had no want of provisions of any kind that we could desire.

Our Negroes towing our canoes, we traveled at a considerable rate, and by our own account could not go less than twenty or twenty-five English miles a day, and the river continuing to be much of the same breadth and very deep all the way, till on the tenth day we came to another cataract; for a ridge of high hills crossing the whole channel of the river, the water came tumbling down the rocks from one stage to another in a strange manner, so that it was a continued link of cataracts from one to another, in the manner of a cascade, only that the falls were sometimes a quarter of a mile from one another, and the noise confused and frightful.

We thought our voyaging was at a full stop now; but three of us, with a couple of our Negroes, mounting the hills another way, to view the course of the river, we found a fair channel again after about half a mile's march, and that it was like to hold us a good way further. So we set all hands to work, unloaded our cargo, and hauled our canoes on shore, to see if we could carry them.

Upon examination we found that they were very heavy; but our carpenters, spending but one day's work upon them, hewed away so much of the timber from their outsides as reduced them very much, and yet they were as fit to swim as before. When this was done, ten men with poles took up one of the canoes and made nothing to carry it. So we ordered twenty men to each canoe, that one ten might relieve the other; and thus we carried all our canoes, and launched them into the water again, and then fetched our luggage and loaded it all again into the canoes, and all in an afternoon; and the next morning early we moved forward again. When we had towed about four days more, our gunner, who was our pilot, began to observe that we did not keep our right course so exactly as we ought, the river winding away a little towards the north, and gave us notice of it accordingly. However, we were not willing to lose the advantage of water-carriage, at least not till we were forced to it; so we jogged on, and the river served us for about threescore miles further; but then we found it grew very small and shallow, having passed the mouths of several little brooks or rivulets which came into it; and at length it became but a brook itself.

We towed up as far as ever our boats would swim, and we went two days the farther — having been about twelve days in this last part of the river — by lightening the boats and taking our luggage out, which we made the Negroes carry, being willing to ease ourselves as long as we could; but at the end of these two days, in short, there was not water enough to swim a London wherry.

We now set forward wholly by land, and without any expectation of more water-carriage. All our concern for more water was to be sure to have a supply for our drinking; and therefore upon every hill that we came near we clambered up to the highest part to see the country before us, and to make the best judgment we could which way to go to keep the lowest grounds, and as near some stream of water as we could.

The country held verdant, well grown with trees, and spread with rivers and brooks, and tolerably well with inhabitants, for about thirty days' march after our leaving the canoes, during which time things went pretty well with us; we did not tie ourselves down when to march and when to halt, but ordered those things as our convenience and the health and ease of our people, as well our servants as ourselves, required.

About the middle of this march we came into a low and plain country, in which we perceived a greater number of inhabitants than in any other country we had gone through; but that which was worse for us, we found them a fierce, barbarous, treacherous people, and who at first looked upon us as robbers, and gathered themselves in numbers to attack us.

Our men were terrified at them at first, and began to discover an unusual fear, and even our black prince seemed in a great deal of confusion; but I smiled at him, and showing him some of our guns, I asked him if he thought that which killed the spotted cat (for so they called the leopard in their language) could not make a thousand of those naked creatures die at one blow? Then he laughed, and said, yes, he believed it would. "Well, then," said I, "tell your men not to be afraid of these people, for we shall soon give them a taste of what we can do if they pretend to meddle with us." However, we considered we were in the middle of a vast country, and we knew not what numbers of people and nations we might be surrounded with, and, above all, we knew not how much we might stand in need of the friendship of these that we were now among, so that we ordered the Negroes to try all the methods they could to make them friends.

Accordingly the two men who had gotten bows and arrows, and two more to whom we gave the prince's two fine lances, went foremost, with five more, having long poles in their hands; and after them ten of our men advanced toward the Negro town that was next to us, and we all stood ready to succour them if there should be occasion.

When they came pretty near their houses our Negroes hallooed in their screaming way, and called to them as loud as they could. Upon their calling, some of the men came out and answered, and immediately after the whole town, men, women, and children, appeared; our Negroes, with their long poles, went forward a little, and stuck them all in the ground, and left them, which in their country was a signal of peace, but the other did not understand the meaning of that. Then the two men with bows laid down their bows and arrows, went forward unarmed, and made signs of peace to them, which at last the other began to understand; so two of their men laid down their bows and arrows, and came towards them. Our men made all the signs of friendship to them that they could think of, putting their hands up to their mouths as a sign that they wanted provisions to eat; and the other pretended to be pleased and friendly, and went back to their fellows and talked with them a while, and they came forward again, and made signs that they would bring some provisions to them before the sun set; and so our men came back again very well satisfied for that time.

But an hour before sunset our men went to them again, just in the same posture as before, and they came according to their appointment, and brought deer's flesh, roots, and the same kind of corn, like rice, which I mentioned above; and our Negroes, being furnished with such toys as our cutler had contrived, gave them some of them, which they seemed infinitely pleased with, and promised to bring more provisions the next day.

Accordingly the next day they came again, but our men perceived they were more in number by a great many than before. However, having sent out ten men with firearms to stand ready, and our whole army being in view also, we were not much surprised; nor was the treachery of the enemy so cunningly ordered as in other cases, for they might have surrounded our Negroes, which were but nine, under a show of peace; but when they saw our men advance almost as far as the place where they were the day before, the rogues snatched up their bows and arrows and came running upon our men like so many furies, at which our ten men called to the Negroes to come back to them, which they did with speed enough at the first word, and stood all behind our men. As they fled, the other advanced, and let fly near a hundred of their arrows at them, by which two of our Negroes were wounded, and one we thought had been killed. When they came to the five poles that our men had stuck in the ground, they stood still awhile, and gathering about the poles, looked at them, and handled them, as wondering what they meant. We then, who were drawn up behind all, sent one of our number to our ten men to bid them fire among them while they stood so thick, and to put some small shot into their guns besides the ordinary charge, and to tell them that we would be up with them immediately.

Accordingly they made ready; but by the time they were ready to fire, the black army had left their wandering about the poles, and began to stir as if they would come on, though seeing more men stand at some distance behind our Negroes, they could not tell what to make of us; but if they did not understand us before, they understood us less afterwards, for as soon as ever our men found them to begin to move forward they fired among the thickest of them, being about the distance of 120 yards, as near as we could guess.

It is impossible to express the fright, the screaming and yelling of those wretches upon this first volley. We killed six of them, and wounded eleven or twelve, I mean as we knew of; for, as they stood thick, and the small shot, as we called it, scattered among them, we had reason to believe we wounded more that stood farther off, for our small shot was made of bits of lead and bits of iron, heads of nails, and such things as our diligent artificer, the cutler, helped us to.

As to those that were killed and wounded, the other frighted creatures were under the greatest amazement in the world, to think what should hurt them, for they could see nothing but holes made in their bodies they knew not how. Then the fire and noise amazed all their women and children, and frighted them out of their wits, so that they ran staring and howling about like mad creatures.

However, all this did not make them fly, which was what we wanted, nor did we find any of them die as it were with fear, as at first; so we resolved upon a second volley, and then to advance as we did before. Whereupon our reserved men advancing, we resolved to fire only three men at a time, and move forward like an army firing in platoon; so, being all in a line, we fired, first three on the right, then three on the left, and so on; and every time we killed or wounded some of them, but still they did not fly, and yet they were so frighted that they used none of their bows and arrows, or of their lances; and we thought their numbers increased upon our hands, particularly we thought so by the noise. So I called to our men to halt, and bid them pour in one whole volley and then shout, as we did in our first fight, and so run in upon them and knock them down with our muskets.

But they were too wise for that too, for as soon as we had fired a whole volley and shouted, they all ran away, men, women, and children, so fast that in a few moments we could not see one creature of them except some that were wounded and lame, who lay wallowing and screaming here and there upon the ground as they happened to fall.

Upon this we came up to the field of battle, where we found we had killed thirty-seven of them, among which were three women, and had wounded about sixty-four, among which were two women; by wounded I mean such as were so maimed as not to be able to go away, and those our Negroes killed afterwards in a cowardly manner in cold blood, for which we were very angry, and threatened to make them go to them if they did so again.

There was no great spoil to be got, for they were all stark naked as they came into the world, men and women together, some of them having feathers stuck in their hair, and others a kind of bracelet about their necks, but nothing else; but our Negroes got a booty here, which we were very glad of, and this was the bows and arrows of the vanquished, of which they found more than they knew what to do with, belonging to the killed and wounded men; these we ordered them to pick up, and they were very useful to us afterwards. After the fight, and our Negroes had gotten bows and arrows, we sent them out in parties to see what they could get, and they got some provisions; but, which was better than all the rest, they brought us four more young bulls, or buffaloes, that had been brought up to labour and to carry burdens. They knew them, it seems, by the burdens they had carried having galled their backs, for they have no saddles to cover them with in that country.

Those creatures not only eased our Negroes, but gave us an opportunity to carry more provisions; and our Negroes loaded them very hard at this place with flesh and roots, such as we wanted very much afterwards.

In this town we found a very little young leopard, about two spans high; it was exceeding tame, and purred like a cat when we stroked it with our hands, being, as I suppose, bred up among the Negroes like a house-dog. It was our black prince, it seems, who, making his tour among the abandoned houses or huts, found this creature there, and making much of him, and giving a bit or two of flesh to him, the creature followed him like a dog; of which more hereafter.

Among the Negroes that were killed in this battle there was one who had a little thin bit or plate of gold, about as big as a sixpence, which hung by a little bit of a twisted gut upon his forehead, by which we supposed he was a man of some eminence among them; but that was not all, for this bit of gold put us upon searching very narrowly if there was not more of it to be had thereabouts, but we found none at all.

From this part of the country we went on for about fifteen days, and then found ourselves obliged to march up a high ridge of mountains, frightful to behold, and the first of the kind that we met with; and having no guide but our little pocket-compass, we had no advantage of information as to which was the best or the worst way, but was obliged to choose by what we saw, and shift as well as we could. We met with several nations of wild and naked people in the plain country before we came to those hills, and we found them much more tractable and friendly than those devils we had been forced to fight with; and though we could learn little from these people, yet we understood by the signs they made that there was a vast desert beyond these hills, and, as our Negroes called them, much lion, much spotted cat (so they called the leopard); and they signed to us also that we must carry water with us. At the last of these nations we furnished ourselves with as much provisions as we could possibly carry, not knowing what we had to suffer, or what length we had to go; and, to make our way as familiar to us as possible, I proposed that of the last inhabitants we could find we should make some prisoners and carry them with us for guides over the desert, and to assist us in carrying provision, and, perhaps, in getting it too. The advice was too necessary to be slighted; so finding, by our dumb signs to the inhabitants, that there were some people that dwelt at the foot of the mountains on the other side before we came to the desert itself, we resolved to furnish ourselves with guides by fair means or foul.

Here, by a moderate computation, we concluded ourselves 700 miles from the sea-coast where we began. Our black prince was this day set free from the sling his arm hung in, our surgeon having perfectly restored it, and he showed it to his own countrymen quite well, which made them greatly wonder. Also our two Negroes began to recover, and their wounds to heal apace, for our surgeon was very skilful in managing their cure.

Having with infinite labour mounted these hills, and coming to a view of the country beyond them, it was indeed enough to astonish as stout a heart as ever was created. It was a vast howling wilderness — not a tree, a river, or a green thing to be seen; for, as far as the eye could look, nothing but a scalding sand, which, as the wind blew, drove about in clouds enough to overwhelm man and beast. Nor could we see any end of it either before us, which was our way, or to the right hand or left; so that truly our men began to be discouraged, and talk of going back again. Nor could we indeed think of venturing over such a horrid place as that before us, in which we saw nothing but present death.

I was as much affected at the sight as any of them; but, for all that, I could not bear the thoughts of going back again. I told them we had marched 700 miles of our way, and it would be worse than death to think of going back again; and that, if they thought the desert was not passable, I thought we should rather change our course, and travel south till we came to the Cape of Good Hope, or north to the country that lay along the Nile, where, perhaps, we might find some way or other over to the west sea; for sure all Africa was not a desert.

Our gunner, who, as I said before, was our guide as to the situation of places, told us that he could not tell what to say to going for the Cape, for it was a monstrous length, being from the place where we now were not less than 1500 miles; and, by his account, we were now come a third part of the way to the coast of Angola, where we should meet the western ocean, and find ways enough for our escape home. On the other hand, he assured us, and showed us a map of it, that, if we went northward, the western shore of Africa went out into the sea above 1000 miles west, so that we should have so much and more land to travel afterwards; which land might, for aught we knew, be as wild, barren, and desert as this. And therefore, upon the whole, he proposed that we should attempt this desert, and perhaps we should not find it so long as we feared; and however, he proposed that we should see how far our provisions would carry us, and, in particular, our water; and we should venture no further than half so far as our water would last; and if we found no end of the desert, we might come safely back again.

This advice was so reasonable that we all approved of it; and accordingly we calculated that we were able to carry provisions for forty-two days, but that we could not carry water for above twenty days, though we were to suppose it to stink, too, before that time expired. So that we concluded that, if we did not come at some water in ten days' time, we would return; but if we found a supply of water, we could then travel twenty-one days; and, if we saw no end of the wilderness in that time, we would return also.

With this regulation of our measures, we descended the mountains, and it was the second day before we quite reached the plain; where, however, to make us amends, we found a fine little rivulet of very good water, abundance of deer, a sort of creature like a hare, but not so nimble, but whose flesh we found very agreeable. But we were deceived in our intelligence, for we found no people; so we got no more prisoners to assist us in carrying our baggage.

The infinite number of deer and other creatures which we saw here, we found was occasioned by the neighbourhood of the waste or desert, from whence they retired hither for food and refreshment. We stored ourselves here with flesh and roots of divers kinds, which our Negroes understood better than we, and which served us for bread; and with as much water as (by the allowance of a quart a day to a man for our Negroes, and three pints a day a man for ourselves, and three quarts a day each for our buffaloes) would serve us twenty days; and thus loaded for a long miserable march, we set forwards, being all sound in health and very cheerful, but not alike strong for so great a fatigue; and, which was our grievance, were without a guide.

In the very first entrance of the waste we were exceedingly discouraged, for we found the sand so deep, and it scalded our feet so much with the heat, that after we had, as I may call it, waded rather than walked through it about seven or eight miles, we were all heartily tired and faint; even the very Negroes laid down and panted like creatures that had been pushed beyond their strength.

Here we found the difference of lodging greatly injurious to us; for, as before, we always made us huts to sleep under, which covered us from the night air, which is particularly unwholesome in those hot countries. But we had here no shelter, no lodging, after so hard a march; for here were no trees, no, not a shrub near us; and, which was still more frightful, towards night we began to hear the wolves howl, the lions bellow, and a great many wild asses braying, and other ugly noises which we did not understand.

Upon this we reflected upon our indiscretion, that we had not, at least, brought poles or stakes in our hands, with which we might have, as it were, palisadoed ourselves in for the night, and so we might have slept secure, whatever other inconveniences we suffered. However, we found a way at last to relieve ourselves a little; for first we set up the lances and bows we had, and endeavoured to bring the tops of them as near to one another as we could, and so hung our coats on the top of them, which made us a kind of sorry tent. The leopard's skin, and a few other skins we had put together, made us a tolerable covering, and thus we laid down to sleep, and slept very heartily too, for the first night; setting, however, a good watch, being two of our own men with their fusées, whom we relieved in an hour at first, and two hours afterwards. And it was very well we did this, for they found the wilderness swarmed with raging creatures of all kinds, some of which came directly up to the very enclosure of our tent. But our sentinels were ordered not to alarm us with firing in the night, but to flash in the pan at them, which they did, and found it effectual, for the creatures went off always as soon as they saw it, perhaps with some noise or howling, and pursued such other game as they were upon.

If we were tired with the day's travel, we were all as much tired with the night's lodging. But our black prince told us in the morning he would give us some counsel, and indeed it was very good counsel. He told us we should be all killed if we went on this journey, and through this desert, without some covering for us at night; so he advised us to march back again to a little river-side where we lay the night before, and stay there till we could make us houses, as he called them, to carry with us to lodge in every night. As he began a little to understand our speech, and we very well to understand his signs, we easily knew what he meant, and that we should there make mats (for we remembered that we saw a great deal of matting or bass there, that the natives make mats of) — I say, that we should make large mats there for covering our huts or tents to lodge in at night.

We all approved this advice, and immediately resolved to go back that one day's journey, resolving, though we carried less provisions, we would carry mats with us to cover us in the night. Some of the nimblest of us got back to the river with more ease than we had traveled it the day before; but, as we were not in haste, the rest made a halt, encamped another night, and came to us the next day.

In our return of this day's journey, our men that made two days of it met with a very surprising thing, that gave them some reason to be careful how they parted company again. The case was this: — The second day in the morning, before they had gone half a mile, looking behind them they saw a vast cloud of sand or dust rise in the air, as we see sometimes in the roads in summer when it is very dusty and a large drove of cattle are coming, only very much greater; and they could easily perceive that it came after them; and it came on faster as they went from it. The cloud of sand was so great that they could not see what it was that raised it, and concluded that it was some army of enemies that pursued them; but then considering that they came from the vast uninhabited wilderness, they knew it was impossible any nation or people that way should have intelligence of them or the way of their march; and therefore, if it was an army, it must be of such as they were, traveling that way by accident. On the other hand, as they knew that there were no horses in the country, and that they came on so fast, they concluded that it must be some vast collection of wild beasts, perhaps making to the hill country for food or water, and that they should be all devoured or trampled under foot by their multitude.

Upon this thought, they very prudently observed which way the cloud seemed to point, and they turned a little out of their way to the north, supposing it might pass by them. When they were about a quarter of a mile, they halted to see what it might be. One of the Negroes, a nimbler fellow than the rest, went back a little, and came in a few minutes running as fast as the heavy sands would allow, and by signs gave them to know that it was a great herd, or drove, or whatever it might be called, of vast monstrous elephants.

As it was a sight our men had never seen, they were desirous to see it, and yet a little uneasy at the danger too; for though an elephant is a heavy unwieldy creature, yet in the deep sand, which is nothing at all to them, they marched at a great rate, and would soon have tired our people, if they had had far to go, and had been pursued by them.

Our gunner was with them, and had a great mind to have gone close up to one of the outermost of them, and to have clapped his piece to his ear, and to have fired into him, because he had been told no shot would penetrate them; but they all dissuaded him, lest upon the noise they should all turn upon and pursue us; so he was reasoned out of it, and let them pass, which, in our people's circumstances, was certainly the right way.

They were between twenty and thirty in number, but prodigious great ones; and though they often showed our men that they saw them, yet they did not turn out of their way, or take any other notice of them than, as we might say, just to look at them. We that were before saw the cloud of dust they raised, but we had thought it had been our own caravan, and so took no notice; but as they bent their course one point of the compass, or thereabouts, to the southward of the east, and we went due east, they passed by us at some little distance; so that we did not see them, or know anything of them, till evening, when our men came to us and gave us this account of them. However, this was a useful experiment for our future conduct in passing the desert, as you shall hear in its place.

We were now upon our work, and our black prince was head surveyor, for he was an excellent mat-maker himself, and all his men understood it, so that they soon made us near a hundred mats; and as every man, I mean of the Negroes, carried one, it was no manner of load, and we did not carry an ounce of provisions the less. The greatest burthen was to carry six long poles, besides some shorter stakes; but the Negroes made an advantage of that, for carrying them between two, they made the luggage of provisions which they had to carry so much the lighter, binding it upon two poles, and so made three couple of them. As soon as we saw this, we made a little advantage of it too; for having three or four bags, called bottles (I mean skins to carry water), more than the men could carry, we got them filled, and carried them this way, which was a day's water and more, for our journey.

Having now ended our work, made our mats, and fully recruited our stores of all things necessary, and having made us abundance of small ropes of matting for ordinary use, as we might have occasion, we set forward again, having interrupted our journey eight days in all, upon this affair. To our great comfort, the night before we set out there fell a very violent shower of rain, the effects of which we found in the sand; though the heat of one day dried the surface as much as before, yet it was harder at bottom, not so heavy, and was cooler to our feet, by which means we marched, as we reckoned, about fourteen miles instead of seven, and with much more ease.

When we came to encamp, we had all things ready, for we had fitted our tent, and set it up for trial, where we made it; so that, in less than an hour, we had a large tent raised, with an inner and outer apartment, and two entrances. In one we lay ourselves, in the other our Negroes, having light pleasant mats over us, and others at the same time under us. Also we had a little place without all for our buffaloes, for they deserved our care, being very useful to us, besides carrying forage and water for themselves. Their forage was a root, which our black prince directed us to find, not much unlike a parsnip, very moist and nourishing, of which there was plenty wherever we came, this horrid desert excepted.

When we came the next morning to decamp, our Negroes took down the tent, and pulled up the stakes; and all was in motion in as little time as it was set up. In this posture we marched eight days, and yet could see no end, no change of our prospect, but all looking as wild and dismal as at the beginning. If there was any alteration, it was that the sand was nowhere so deep and heavy as it was the first three days. This we thought might be because, for six months of the year the winds blowing west (as for the other six they blow constantly east), the sand was driven violently to the side of the desert where we set out, where the mountains lying very high, the easterly monsoons, when they blew, had not the same power to drive it back again; and this was confirmed by our finding the like depth of sand on the farthest extent of the desert to the west.

It was the ninth day of our travel in this wilderness, when we came to the view of a great lake of water; and you may be sure this was a particular satisfaction to us, because we had not water left for above two or three days more, at our shortest allowance; I mean allowing water for our return, if we had been driven to the necessity of it. Our water had served us two days longer than expected, our buffaloes having found, for two or three days, a kind of herb like a broad flat thistle, though without any prickle, spreading on the ground, and growing in the sand, which they ate freely of, and which supplied them for drink as well as forage.

The next day, which was the tenth from our setting out, we came to the edge of this lake, and, very happily for us, we came to it at the south point of it, for to the north we could see no end of it; so we passed by it and traveled three days by the side of it, which was a great comfort to us, because it lightened our burthen, there being no need to carry water when we had it in view. And yet, though here was so much water, we found but very little alteration in the desert; no trees, no grass or herbage, except that thistle, as I called it, and two or three more plants, which we did not understand, of which the desert began to be pretty full.

But as we were refreshed with the neighbourhood of this lake of water, so we were now gotten among a prodigious number of ravenous inhabitants, the like whereof, it is most certain, the eye of man never saw; for as I firmly believe that never man nor body of men passed this desert since the flood, so I believe there is not the like collection of fierce, ravenous, and devouring creatures in the world; I mean not in any particular place.

For a day's journey before we came to this lake, and all the three days we were passing by it, and. for six or seven days' march after it, the ground was scattered with elephants' teeth in such a number as is incredible; and as some of them have lain there for some hundreds of years, so, seeing the substance of them scarce ever decays, they may lie there, for aught I know, to the end of time. The size of some of them is, it seems, to those to whom I have reported it, as incredible as the number; and I can assure you there were several so heavy as the strongest man among us could not lift. As to number, I question not but there are enough to load a thousand sail of the biggest ships in the world, by which I may be understood to mean that the quantity is not to be conceived of; seeing that as they lasted in view for above eighty miles' traveling, so they might continue as far to the right hand, and to the left as far, and many times as far, for aught we knew; for it seems the number of elephants hereabouts is prodigiously great. In one place in particular we saw the head of an elephant, with several teeth in it, but one of the biggest that ever I saw; the flesh was consumed, to be sure, many hundred years before, and all the other bones; but three of our strongest men could not lift this skull and teeth; the great tooth, I believe, weighed at least three hundredweight; and this was particularly remarkable to me, that I observed the whole skull was as good ivory as the teeth, and, I believe, altogether weighed at least six hundredweight; and though I do not know but, by the same rule, all the bones of the elephant may be ivory, yet I think there is this just objection against it from the example before me, that then all the other bones of this elephant would have been there as well as the head.

I proposed to our gunner, that, seeing we had traveled now fourteen days without intermission, and that we had water here for our refreshment, and no want of food yet, nor any fear of it, we should rest our people a little, and see, at the same time, if perhaps we might kill some creatures that were proper for food. The gunner, who had more forecast of that kind than I had, agreed to the proposal, and added, why might we not try to catch some fish out of the lake? The first thing we had before us was to try if we could make any hooks, and this indeed put our artificer to his trumps; however, with some labour and difficulty, he did it, and we catched fresh fish of several kinds. How they came there, none but He that made the lake and all the world knows; for, to be sure, no human hands ever put any in there, or pulled any out before.

We not only catched enough for our present refreshment, but we dried several large fishes, of kinds which I cannot describe, in the sun, by which we lengthened out our provision considerably; for the heat of the sun dried them so effectually without salt that they were perfectly cured, dry, and hard, in one day's time.

We rested ourselves here five days; during which time we had abundance of pleasant adventures with the wild creatures, too many to relate. One of them was very particular, which was a chase between a she-lion, or lioness, and a large deer; and though the deer is naturally a very nimble creature, and she flew by us like the wind, having, perhaps, about 300 yards the start of the lion, yet we found the lion, by her strength, and the goodness of her lungs, got ground of her. They passed by us within about a quarter of a mile, and we had a view of them a great way, when, having given them over, we were surprised, about an hour after, to see them come thundering back again on the other side of us, and then the lion was within thirty or forty yards of her; and both straining to the extremity of their speed, when the deer, coming to the lake, plunged into the water, and swam for her life, as she had before run for it.

The lioness plunged in after her, and swam a little way, but came back again; and when she was got upon the land she set up the most hideous roar that ever I heard in my life, as if done in the rage of having lost her prey.

We walked out morning and evening constantly; the middle of the day we refreshed ourselves under our tent. But one morning early we saw another chase, which more nearly concerned us than the other; for our black prince, walking by the side of the lake, was set upon by a vast, great crocodile, which came out of the lake upon him; and though he was very light of foot, yet it was as much as he could do to get away. He fled amain to us, and the truth is, we did not know what to do, for we were told no bullet would enter her; and we found it so at first, for though three of our men fired at her, yet she did not mind them; but my friend the gunner, a venturous fellow, of a bold heart, and great presence of mind, went up so near as to thrust the muzzle of his piece into her mouth, and fired, but let his piece fall, and ran for it the very moment he had fired it. The creature raged a great while, and spent its fury upon the gun, making marks upon the very iron with its teeth, but after some time fainted and died.

Our Negroes spread the banks of the lake all this while for game, and at length killed us three deer, one of them very large, the other two very small. There was water-fowl also in the lake, but we never came near enough to them to shoot any; and as for the desert, we saw no fowls anywhere in it but at the lake.

We likewise killed two or three civet cats; but their flesh is the worst of carrion. We saw abundance of elephants at a distance, and observed they always go in very good company, that is to say, abundance of them together, and always extended in a fair line of battle; and this, they say, is the way they defend themselves from their enemies; for if lions or tigers, wolves or any creatures, attack them, they being drawn in a line, sometimes reaching five or six miles in length, whatever comes in their way is sure to be trod under foot, or beaten in pieces with their trunks, or lifted up in the air with their trunks; so that if a hundred lions or tigers were coming along, if they meet a line of elephants, they will always fly back till they see room to pass by the right hand or the left; and if they did not, it would be impossible for one of them to escape; for the elephant, though a heavy creature, is yet so dexterous and nimble with his trunk, that he will not fail to lift up the heaviest lion, or any other wild creature, and throw him up in the air quite over his back, and then trample him to death with his feet. We saw several lines of battle thus; we saw one so long that indeed there was no end of it to be seen, and I believe there might be 2000 elephants in row or line. They are not beasts of prey, but live upon the herbage of the field, as an ox does; and it is said, that though they are so great a creature, yet that a smaller quantity of forage supplies one of them than will suffice a horse.

The numbers of this kind of creature that are in those parts are inconceivable, as may be gathered from the prodigious quantity of teeth

671

which, as I said, we saw in this vast desert; and indeed we saw a hundred of them to one of any other kind.

One evening we were very much surprised. We were most of us laid down on our mats to sleep, when our watch came running in among us, being frighted with the sudden roaring of some lions just by them, which, it seems, they had not seen, the night being dark, till they were just upon them. There was, as it proved, an old lion and his whole family, for there was the lioness and three young lions, besides the old king, who was a monstrous great one. One of the young ones — who were good, large, well-grown ones too — leaped up upon one of our Negroes, who stood sentinel, before he saw him, at which he was heartily frighted, cried out, and ran into the tent. Our other man, who had a gun, had not presence of mind at first to shoot him, but struck him with the butt-end of his piece, which made him whine a little, and then growl at him fearfully; but the fellow retired, and, we being all alarmed, three of our men snatched up their guns, ran to the tent door, where they saw the great old lion by the fire of his eyes, and first fired at him, but, we supposed, missed him, or at least did not kill him; for they went all off, but raised a most hideous roar, which, as if they had called for help, brought down a prodigious number of lions, and other furious creatures, we know not what, about them, for we could not see them; but there was a noise, and yelling and howling, and all sorts of such wilderness music on every side of us, as if all the beasts of the desert were assembled to devour us.

We asked our black prince what we should do with them. "Me go," says he, "and fright them all." So he snatches up two or three of the worst of our mats, and getting one of our men to strike some fire, he hangs the mat up at the end of a pole, and set it on fire, and it blazed abroad a good while; at which the creatures all moved off, for we heard them roar, and make their bellowing noise at a great distance. "Well," says our gunner, "if that will do, we need not burn our mats, which are our beds to lay under us, and our tilting to cover us. Let me alone," says he. So he comes back into our tent, and falls to making some artificial fireworks and the like; and he gave our sentinels some to be ready at hand upon occasion, and particularly he placed a great piece of wild-fire upon the same pole that the mat had been tied to, and set it on fire, and that burnt there so long that all the wild creatures left us for that time.

However, we began to be weary of such company; and, to be rid of them, we set forward again two days sooner than we intended. We found now, that though the desert did not end, nor could we see any appearance of it, yet that the earth was pretty full of green stuff of one sort or another, so that our cattle had no want; and secondly, that there were several little rivers which ran into the lake, and so long as the country continued low, we found water sufficient, which eased us very much in our carriage, and we went on still sixteen days more without yet coming to any appearance of better soil. After this we found the country rise a little, and by that we perceived that the water would fail us; so, for fear of the worst, we filled our bladder-bottles with water. We found the country rising gradually thus for three days continually, when, on the sudden, we perceived that, though we had mounted up insensibly, yet that we were on the top of a very high ridge of hills, though not such as at first.

When we came to look down on the other side of the hills, we saw, to the great joy of all our hearts, that the desert was at an end; that the country was clothed with green, abundance of trees, and a large river; and we made no doubt but that we should find people and cattle also; and here, by our gunner's account, who kept our computations, we had marched about 400 miles over this dismal place of horror, having been four-and-thirty days a-doing of it, and consequently were come about 1100 miles of our journey.

We would willingly have descended the hills that night, but it was too late. The next morning we saw everything more plain, and rested ourselves under the shade of some trees, which were now the most refreshing things imaginable to us, who had been scorched above a month without a tree to cover us. We found the country here very pleasant, especially considering that we came from; and we killed some deer here also, which we found very frequent under the cover of the woods. Also we killed a creature like a goat, whose flesh was very good to eat, but it was no goat; we found also a great number of fowls like partridge, but something smaller, and were very tame; so that we lived here very well, but found no people, at least none that would be seen, no, not for several days' journey; and to allay our joy, we were almost every night disturbed with lions and tigers; elephants, indeed, we saw none here.

In three days' march we came to a river, which we saw from the hills, and which we called the Golden River; and we found it ran northward, which was the first stream we had met with that did so. It ran with a very rapid current, and our gunner, pulling out his map, assured me that this was either the river Nile, or run into the great lake out of which the river Nile was said to take its beginning; and he brought out his charts and maps, which, by his instruction, I began to understand very well, and told me he would convince me of it, and indeed he seemed to make it so plain to me that I was of the same opinion.

But I did not enter into the gunner's reason for this inquiry, not in the least, till he went on with it farther, and stated it thus: — "If this is the river Nile, why should not we build some more canoes, and go down this stream, rather than expose ourselves to any more deserts and scorching sands in quest of the sea, which when we are come to, we shall be as much at a loss how to get home as we were at Madagascar?"

The argument was good, had there been no objections in the way of a kind which none of us were capable of answering; but, upon the whole, it was an undertaking of such a nature that every one of us thought it impracticable, and that upon several accounts; and our surgeon, who was himself a good scholar and a man of reading, though not acquainted with the business of sailing, opposed it, and some of his reasons, I remember, were such as these: — First, the length of the way, which both he and the gunner allowed, by the course of the water, and turnings of the river, would be at least 4000 miles. Secondly, the innumerable crocodiles in the river, which we should never be able to escape. Thirdly, the dreadful deserts in the way; and lastly, the approaching rainy season, in which the streams of the Nile would be so furious, and rise so high — spreading far and wide over all the plain country — that we should never be able to know when we were in the channel of the river and when not, and should certainly be cast away, overset, or run aground so often that it would be impossible to proceed by a river so excessively dangerous.

This last reason he made so plain to us that we began to be sensible of it ourselves, so that we agreed to lay that thought aside, and proceed in our first course, westwards towards the sea; but, as if we had been loth to depart, we continued, by way of refreshing ourselves, to loiter two days upon this river, in which time our black prince, who delighted much in wandering up and down, came one evening and brought us several little bits of something, he knew not what, but he found it felt heavy and looked well, and showed it to me as what he thought was some rarity. I took not much notice of it to him, but stepping out and calling the gunner to me I showed it to him, and told him what I thought, viz., that it was certainly gold. He agreed with me in that, and also in what followed, that we would take the black prince out with us the next day, and make him show us where he found it; that if there was any quantity to be found we would tell our company of it, but if there was but little we would keep counsel, and have it to ourselves.

But we forgot to engage the prince in the secret, who innocently told so much to all the rest, as that they guessed what it was, and came to us to see. When we found it was public, we were more concerned to prevent their suspecting that we had any design to conceal it, and openly telling our thoughts of it, we called our artificer, who agreed presently that it was gold; so I proposed that we should all go with the prince to the place where he found it, and if any quantity was to be had, we would lie here some time and see what we could make of it.

Accordingly we went every man of us, for no man was willing to be left behind in a discovery of such a nature. When we came to the place we found it was on the west side of the river, not in the main river, but in another small river or stream which came from the west, and ran into the other at that place. We fell to raking in the sand, and washing it in our hands; and we seldom took up a handful of sand but we washed some little round lumps as big as a pin's head, or sometimes as big as a grape stone, into our hands; and we found, in two or three hours' time, that every one had got some, so we agreed to leave off, and go to dinner.

While we were eating, it came into my thoughts that while we worked at this rate in a thing of such nicety and consequence, it was ten to one if the gold, which was the make-bait of the world, did not, first or last, set us together by the ears, to break our good articles and our understanding one among another, and perhaps cause us to part companies, or worse; I therefore told them that I was indeed the youngest man in the company, but as they had always allowed me to give my opinion in things, and had sometimes been pleased to follow my advice, so I had something to propose now, which I thought would be for all our advantages, and I believed they would all like it very well. I told them we were in a country where we all knew there was a great deal of gold, and that all the world sent ships thither to get it; that we did not indeed know where it was, and so we might get a great deal, or a little, we did not know whether; but I offered it to them to consider whether it would not be the best way for us, and to preserve the good harmony and friendship that had been always kept among us, and which was so absolutely necessary to our safety, that what we found should be brought together to one common stock, and be equally divided at last, rather than to run the hazard of any difference which might happen among us from any one's having found more or less than another. I told them, that if we were all upon one bottom we should all apply ourselves heartily to the work; and, besides that, we might then set our Negroes all to work for us, and receive equally the fruit of their labour and of our own, and being all exactly alike sharers, there could be no just cause of quarrel or disgust among us.

They all approved the proposal, and every one jointly swore, and gave their hands to one another, that they would not conceal the least grain of gold from the rest; and consented that if any one or more should be found to conceal any, all that he had should be taken from him and divided among the rest; and one thing more was added to it by our gunner, from considerations equally good and just, that if any one of us, by any play, bet, game, or wager, won any money or gold, or the value of any, from another, during our whole voyage, till our return quite to Portugal, he should be obliged by us all to restore it again on the penalty of being disarmed and turned out of the company, and of having no relief from us on any account whatever. This was to prevent wagering and playing for money, which our men were apt to do by several means and at several games, though they had neither cards nor dice.

Having made this wholesome agreement, we went cheerfully to work, and showed our Negroes how to work for us; and working up the stream on both sides, and in the bottom of the river, we spent about three weeks' time dabbling in the water; by which time, as it lay all in our way, we had gone about six miles, and not more; and still the higher we went, the more gold we found; till at last, having passed by the side of a hill, we perceived on a sudden that the gold stopped, and that there was not a bit taken up beyond that place. It presently occurred to my mind, that it must then be from the side of that little hill that all the gold we found was worked down.

Upon this, we went back to the hill, and fell to work with that. We found the earth loose, and of a yellowish loamy colour, and in some places a white hard kind of stone, which, in describing since to some of our artists, they tell me was the spar which is found by ore, and surrounds it in the mine. However, if it had been all gold, we had no instrument to force it out; so we passed that. But scratching into the loose earth with our fingers, we came to a surprising place, where the earth, for the quantity of two bushels, I believe, or thereabouts, crumbled down with little more than touching it, and apparently showed us that there was a great deal of gold in it. We took it all carefully up, and washing it in the water, the loamy earth washed away, and left the gold dust free in our hands; and that which was more remarkable was, that, when this loose earth was all taken away, and we came to the rock or hard stone, there was not one grain of gold more to be found.

At night we all came together to see what we had got; and it appeared we had found, in that day's heap of earth, about fifty pounds' weight of gold dust, and about thirty-four pounds' weight more in all the rest of our works in the river.

It was a happy kind of disappointment to us, that we found a full stop put to our work; for, had the quantity of gold been ever so small, yet, had any at all come, I do not know when we should have given over; for, having rummaged this place, and not finding the least grain of gold in any other place, or in any of the earth there, except in that loose parcel, we went quite back down the small river again, working it over and over again, as long as we could find anything, how small so ever; and we did get six or seven pounds more the second time. Then we went into the first river, and tried it up the stream and down the stream, on the one side and on the other. Up the stream we found nothing, no, not a grain; down the stream we found very little, not above the quantity of half an ounce in two miles' working; so back we came again to the Golden River, as we justly called it, and worked it up the stream and down the stream twice more apiece, and every time we found some gold, and perhaps might have done so if we had stayed there till this time; but the quantity was at last so small, and the work so much the harder, that we agreed by consent to give it over, lest we should fatigue ourselves and our Negroes so as to be quite unfit for our journey.

When we had brought all our purchase together, we had in the whole three pounds and a half of gold to a man, share and share alike, according to such a weight and scale as our ingenious cutler made for us to weigh it by, which indeed he did by guess, but which, as he said, he was sure was rather more than less, and so it proved at last; for it was near two ounces more than weight in a pound. Besides this, there was seven or eight pounds' weight left, which we agreed to leave in his hands, to work it into such shapes as we thought fit, to give away to such people as we might yet meet with, from whom we might have occasion to buy provisions, or even to buy friendship, or the like; and particularly we gave about a pound to our black prince, which he hammered and worked by his own indefatigable hand, and some tools our artificer lent him, into little round bits, as round almost as beads, though not exact in shape, and drilling holes through them, put them all upon a string, and wore them about his black neck, and they looked very well there, I assure you; but he was many months a-doing it. And thus ended our first golden adventure.

We now began to discover what we had not troubled our heads much about before, and that was, that, let the country be good or bad that we were in, we could not travel much further for a considerable time. We had been now five months and upwards in our journey, and the seasons began to change; and nature told us, that, being in a climate that had a winter as well as a summer, though of a different kind from what our country produced, we were to expect a wet season, and such as we should not be able to travel in, as well by reason of the rain itself, as of the floods which it would occasion wherever we should come; and though we had been no strangers to those wet seasons in the island of Madagascar, yet we had not thought much of them since we began our travels; for, setting out when the sun was about the solstice, that is, when it was at the greatest northern distance from us, we had found the benefit of it in our travels. But now it drew near us apace, and we found it began to rain; upon which we called another general council, in which we debated our present circumstances, and, in particular, whether we should go forward, or seek for a proper place upon the bank of our Golden River, which had been so lucky to us, to fix our camp for the winter.

Upon the whole, it was resolved to abide where we were; and it was not the least part of our happiness that we did so, as shall appear in its place.

Having resolved upon this, our first measures were to set our Negroes to work, to make huts or houses for our habitation, and this they did very dexterously; only that we changed the ground where we at first intended it, thinking, as indeed it happened, that the river might reach it upon any sudden rain. Our camp was like a little town, in which our huts were in the centre, having one large one in the centre of them also, into which all our particular lodgings opened; so that none of us went into our apartments but through a public tent, where we all ate and drank together, and kept our councils and society; and our carpenters made us tables, benches, and stools in abundance, as many as we could make use of.

We had no need of chimneys, it was hot enough without fire; but yet we found ourselves at last obliged to keep a fire every night upon a particular occasion. For though we had in all other respects a very pleasant and agreeable situation, yet we were rather worse troubled with the unwelcome visits of wild beasts here than in the wilderness itself; for as the deer and other gentle creatures came hither for shelter and food, so the lions and tigers and leopards haunted these places continually for prey.

When first we discovered this we were so uneasy at it that we thought of removing our situation; but after many debates about it we resolved to fortify ourselves in such a manner as not to be in any danger from it; and this our carpenters undertook, who first palisaded our camp quite round with long stakes, for we had wood enough, which stakes were not stuck in one by another like pales, but in an irregular manner; a great multitude of them so placed that they took up near two yards in thickness, some higher, some lower, all sharpened at the top, and about a foot asunder: so that had any creature jumped at them, unless he had gone clean over, which it was very hard to do, he would be hung upon twenty or thirty spikes.

The entrance into this had larger stakes than the rest, so placed before one another as to make three or four short turnings which no four-footed beast bigger than a dog could possibly come in at; and that we might not be attacked by any multitude together, and consequently be alarmed in our sleep, as we had been, or be obliged to waste our ammunition, which we were very chary of, we kept a great fire every night without the entrance of our palisade, having a hut for our two sentinels to stand in free from the rain, just within the entrance, and right against the fire.

To maintain this fire we cut a prodigious deal of wood, and piled it up in a heap to dry, and with the green boughs made a second covering over our huts, so high and thick that it might cast the rain from the first, and keep us effectually dry.

We had scarcely finished all these works but the rain came on so fierce and so continued that we had little time to stir abroad for food, except indeed that our Negroes, who wore no clothes, seemed to make nothing of the rain; though to us Europeans, in those hot climates, nothing is more dangerous.

We continued in this posture for four months, that is to say, from the middle of June to the middle of October; for though the rains went off, at least the greatest violence of them, about the equinox, yet, as the sun was then just over our heads, we resolved to stay awhile till it passed a little to the southward.

During our encampment here we had several adventures with the ravenous creatures of that country; and had not our fire been always kept burning, I question much whether all our fence, though we strengthened it afterwards with twelve or fourteen rows of stakes or more, would have kept us secure. It was always in the night that we had the disturbance of them, and sometimes they came in such multitudes that we thought all the lions and tigers, and leopards and wolves of Africa were come together to attack us. One night, being clear moonshine, one of our men being upon the watch, told us that he verily believed he saw ten thousand wild creatures of one sort or another pass by our little camp, and ever as they saw the fire they sheered off, but were sure to howl or roar, or whatever it was, when they were past.

The music of their voices was very far from being pleasant to us, and sometimes would be so very disturbing that we could not sleep for it; and often our sentinels would call us that were awake to come and look at them. It was one windy, tempestuous night, after a rainy day, that we were indeed called up; for such innumerable numbers of devilish creatures came about us that our watch really thought they would attack us. They would not come on the side where the fire was; and though we thought ourselves secure everywhere else, yet we all got up and took to our arms. The moon was near the full, but the air full of flying clouds, and a strange hurricane of wind to add to the terror of the night; when, looking on the back part of our camp, I thought I saw a creature within our fortification, and so indeed he was, except his haunches, for he had taken a running leap, I suppose, and with all his might had thrown himself clear over our palisades, except one strong pile, which stood higher than the rest, and which had caught hold of him, and by his weight he had hanged himself upon it, the spike of the pile running into his hinder haunch or thigh, on the inside; and by that he hung, growling and biting the wood for rage. I snatched up a lance from one of the Negroes that stood just by me, and running to him, struck it three or four times into him, and dispatched him, being unwilling to shoot, because I had a mind to have a volley fired among the rest, whom I could see standing without, as thick as a drove of bullocks going to a fair. I immediately called our people out, and showed them the object of terror which I had seen, and, without any further consultation, fired a full volley among them, most of our pieces being loaded with two or three slugs or bullets apiece. It made a horrible clutter among them, and in general they all took to their heels, only that we could observe that some walked off with more gravity and majesty than others, being not so much frighted at the noise and fire; and we could perceive that some were left upon the ground struggling as for life, but we durst not stir out to see what they were.

Indeed they stood so thick, and were so near us, that we could not well miss killing or wounding some of them, and we believed they had certainly the smell of us, and our victuals we had been killing; for we had killed a deer, and three or four of those creatures like goats the day before; and some of the offal had been thrown out behind our camp, and this, we suppose, drew them so much about us; but we avoided it for the future.

Though the creatures fled, yet we heard a frightful roaring all night at the place where they stood, which we supposed was from some that were wounded, and as soon as day came we went out to see what execution we had done. And indeed it was a strange sight; there were three tigers and two wolves quite killed, besides the creature I had killed within our palisade, which seemed to be of an ill-gendered kind, between a tiger and a leopard. Besides this there was a noble old lion alive, but with both his fore-legs broke, so that he could not stir away, and he had almost beat himself to death with struggling all night, and we found that this was the wounded soldier that had roared so loud and given us so much disturbance. Our surgeon, looking at him, smiled. "Now," says he, "if I could be sure this lion would be as grateful to me as one of his majesty's ancestors was to Androcles, the Roman slave, I would certainly set both his legs again and cure him." I had not heard the story of Androcles, so he told it me at large; but as to the surgeon, we told him he had no way to know whether the lion would do so or not, but to cure him first and trust to his honour; but he had no faith, so to dispatch him and put him out of his torment, he shot him in the head and killed him, for which we called him the king-killer ever after.

Our Negroes found no less than five of these ravenous creatures wounded and dropped at a distance from our quarters; whereof, one was a wolf, one a fine spotted young leopard, and the other were creatures that we knew not what to call them.

We had several more of these gentlefolks about after that, but no such general rendezvous of them as that was any more; but this ill effect it had to us, that it frighted the deer and other creatures from our neighbourhood, of whose company we were much more desirous, and which were necessary for our subsistence. However, our Negroes went out every day a-hunting, as they called it, with bow and arrow, and they scarce ever failed of bringing us home something or other; and particularly we found in this part of the country, after the rains had fallen some time, abundance of wild fowl, such as we have in England, duck, teal, widgeon, etc.; some geese, and some kinds that we had never seen before; and we frequently killed them. Also we catched a great deal of fresh fish out of the river, so that we wanted no provision. If we wanted anything, it was salt to eat with our fresh meat; but we had a little left, and we used it sparingly; for as to our Negroes, they could not taste it, nor did they care to eat any meat that was seasoned with it.

The weather began now to clear up, the rains were down, and the floods abated, and the sun, which had passed our zenith, was gone to the southward a good way; so we prepared to go on our way.

It was the 12th of October, or thereabouts, that we began to set forward; and having an easy country to travel in, as well as to supply us with provisions, though still without inhabitants, we made more dispatch, traveling sometimes, as we calculated it, twenty or twenty-five miles a day; nor did we halt anywhere in eleven days' march, one day excepted, which was to make a raft to carry us over a small river, which, having swelled with the rains, was not yet quite down.

When we were past this river, which, by the way, ran to the northward too, we found a great row of hills in our way. We saw, indeed, the country open to the right at a great distance; but, as we kept true to our course, due west, we were not willing to go a great way out of our way, only to shun a, few hills. So we advanced; but we were surprised when, being not quite come to the top, one of our company, who, with two Negroes, was got up before us, cried out, "The sea! the sea!" and fell a-dancing and jumping, as signs of joy.

The gunner and I were most surprised at it, because we had but that morning been calculating that we must have yet above 1000 miles on the sea side, and that we could not expect to reach it till another rainy season would be upon us; so that when our man cried out, "The sea," the gunner was angry, and said he was mad.

But we were both in the greatest surprise imaginable, when, coming to the top of the hill, and though it was very high, we saw nothing but water, either before us or to the right hand or the left, being a vast sea, without any bounds but the horizon.

We went down the hill full of confusion of thought, not being able to conceive whereabouts we were or what it must be, seeing by all our charts the sea was yet a vast way off.

It was not above three miles from the hills before we came to the shore, or water-edge of this sea, and there, to our further surprise, we found the water fresh and pleasant to drink; so that, in short, we knew not what course to take. The sea, as we thought it to be, put a full stop to our journey (I mean westward), for it lay just in the way. Our next question was, which hand to turn to, to the right hand or the left, but this was soon resolved; for, as we knew not the extent of it, we considered that our way, if it had been the sea really, must be on the north, and therefore, if we went to the south now, it must be just so much out of our way at last. So, having spent a good part of the day in our surprise at the thing, and consulting what to do, we set forward to the north.

We traveled upon the shore of this sea full twenty-three days before we could come to any resolution about what it was; at the end of which, early one morning, one of our seamen cried out, "Land!" and it was no false alarm, for we saw plainly the tops of some hills at a very great distance, on the further side of the water, due west; but though this satisfied us that it was not the ocean, but an inland sea or lake, yet we saw no land to the northward, that is to say, no end of it, but were obliged to travel eight days more, and near 100 miles farther, before we came to the end of it, and then we found this lake or sea ended in a very great river which ran N. or N. by E., as the other river had done which I mentioned before.

My friend the gunner, upon examining, said that he believed that he was mistaken before, and that this was the river Nile, but was still of the mind that we were of before, that we should not think of a voyage into Egypt that way; so we resolved upon crossing this river, which, however, was not so easy as before, the river being very rapid and the channel very broad.

It cost us, therefore, a week here to get materials to waft ourselves and cattle over this river; for though here were stores of trees, yet there was none of any considerable growth sufficient to make a canoe.

During our march on the edge of this bank we met with great fatigue, and therefore traveled a fewer miles in a day than before, there being such a prodigious number of little rivers that came down from the hills on the east side, emptying themselves into this gulf, all which waters were pretty high, the rains having been but newly over.

In the last three days of our travel we met with some inhabitants, but we found they lived upon the little hills and not by the water-side; nor were we a little put to it for food in this march, having killed nothing for four or five days but some fish we caught out of the lake, and that not in such plenty as we found before.

683

But, to make us some amends, we had no disturbance upon all the shores of this lake from any wild beasts; the only inconveniency of that kind was, that we met an ugly, venomous, deformed kind of a snake or serpent in the wet grounds near the lake, that several times pursued us as if it would attack us; and if we struck or threw anything at it, it would raise itself up and hiss so loud that it might be heard a great way. It had a hellish ugly deformed look and voice, and our men would not be persuaded but it was the devil, only that we did not know what business Satan could have there, where there were no people.

It was very remarkable that we had now traveled 1000 miles without meeting with any people in the heart of the whole continent of Africa, where, to be sure, never man set his foot since the sons of Noah spread themselves over the face of the whole earth. Here also our gunner took an observation with his forestaff, to determine our latitude, and he found now, that having marched about thirty-three days northward, we were in 6 degrees 22 minutes south latitude.

After having with great difficulty got over this river, we came into a strange wild country that began a little to affright us; for though the country was not a desert of dry scalding sand as that was we had passed before, yet it was mountainous, barren, and infinitely full of most furious wild beasts, more than any place we had passed yet. There was indeed a kind of coarse herbage on the surface, and now and then a few trees, or rather shrubs. But people we could see none, and we began to be in great suspense about victuals, for we had not killed a deer a great while, but had lived chiefly upon fish and fowl, always by the water-side, both which seemed to fail us now; and we were in the more consternation, because we could not lay in a stock here to proceed upon, as we did before, but were obliged to set out with scarcity, and without any certainty of a supply.

We had, however, no remedy but patience; and having killed some fowls and dried some fish, as much as, with short allowance, we reckoned would last us five days, we resolved to venture, and venture we did; nor was it without cause that we were apprehensive of the danger, for we traveled the five days and met neither with fish nor fowl, nor four-footed beast, whose flesh was fit to eat, and we were in a most dreadful apprehension of being famished to death. On the sixth day we almost fasted, or, as we may say, we ate up all the scraps of what we had left, and at night lay down supperless upon our mats, with heavy hearts, being obliged the eighth day to kill one of our poor faithful servants, the buffaloes that carried our baggage. The flesh of this creature was very good, and so sparingly did we eat of it that it lasted us all three days and a half, and was just spent; and we were on the point of killing another when we saw before us a country that promised better, having high trees and a large river in the middle of it.

This encouraged us, and we quickened our march for the riverside, though with empty stomachs, and very faint and weak; but before we came to this river we had the good hap to meet with some young deer, a thing we had long wished for. In a word, having shot three of them, we came to a full stop to fill our bellies, and never gave the flesh time to cool before we ate it; nay, it was much we could stay to kill it and had not eaten it alive, for we were, in short, almost famished.

Through all that inhospitable country we saw continually lions, tigers, leopards, civet cats, and abundance of kinds of creatures that we did not understand; we saw no elephants, but every now and then we met with an elephant's tooth lying on the ground, and some of them lying, as it were, half buried by the length of time that they had lain there.

When we came to the shore of this river, we found it ran northerly still, as all the rest had done, but with this difference, that as the course of the other rivers were N. by E. or N.N.E., the course of this lay N.W.N.

On the farther bank of this river we saw some sign of inhabitants, but met with none for the first day; but the next day we came into an inhabited country, the people all Negroes, and stark naked, without shame, both men and women.

We made signs of friendship to them, and found them a very frank, civil, and friendly sort of people. They came to our Negroes without any suspicion, nor did they give us any reason to suspect them of any villainy, as the others had done; we made signs to them that we were hungry, and immediately some naked women ran and fetched us great quantities of roots, and of things like pumpkins, which we made no scruple to eat; and our artificer showed them some of his trinkets that he had made, some of iron, some of silver, but none of gold. They had so much judgment as to choose that of silver before the iron; but when we showed them some gold, we found they did not value it so much as either of the other.

For some of these things they brought us more provisions, and three living creatures as big as calves, but not of that kind; neither did we ever see any of them before; their flesh was very good; and after that they brought us twelve more, and some smaller creatures like hares; all which were very welcome to us, who were indeed at a very great loss for provisions.

We grew very intimate with these people, and indeed they were the civilest and most friendly people that we met with at all, and mightily pleased with us; and, which was very particular, they were much easier to be made to understand our meaning than any we had met with before.

At last we began to inquire our way, pointing to the west. They made us understand easily that we could not go that way, but they pointed to us that we might go north-west, so that we presently understood that there was another lake in our way, which proved to be true; for in two days more we saw it plain, and it held us till we passed the equinoctial line, lying all the way on our left hand, though at a great distance.

Traveling thus northward, our gunner seemed very anxious about our proceedings; for he assured us, and made me sensible of it by the maps which he had been teaching me out of, that when we came into the latitude of six degrees, or thereabouts, north of the line, the land trended away to the west to such a length that we should not come at the sea under a march of above 1500 miles farther westward than the country we desired to go to. I asked him if there were no navigable rivers that we might meet with, which, running into the west ocean, might perhaps carry us down their stream, and then, if it were 1500 miles, or twice 1500 miles, we might do well enough if we could but get provisions.

Here he showed me the maps again, and that there appeared no river whose stream was of any such a length as to do any kindness, till we came perhaps within 200 or 300 miles of the shore, except the Rio Grande, as they call it, which lay farther northward from us, at least 700 miles; and that then he knew not what kind of country it might carry us through; for he said it was his opinion that the heats on the north of the line, even in the same latitude, were violent, and the country more desolate, barren, and barbarous, than those of the south; and that when we came among the Negroes in the north part of Africa, next the sea, especially those who had seen and trafficked with the Europeans, such as Dutch, English, Portuguese, Spaniards, etc., they had most of them been so ill-used at some time or other that they would certainly put all the spite they could upon us in mere revenge.

Upon these considerations he advised us that, as soon as we had passed this lake, we should proceed W.S.W., that is to say, a little inclining to the south, and that in time we should meet with the great river Congo, from whence the coast is called Congo, being a little north of Angola, where we intended at first to go.

I asked him if ever he had been on the coast of Congo. He said, yes, he had, but was never on shore there. Then I asked him how we should get from thence to the coast where the European ships came, seeing, if the land trended away west for 1500 miles, we must have all that shore to traverse before we could double the west point of it.

He told me it was ten to one but we should hear of some European ships to take us in, for that they often visited the coast of Congo and Angola, in trade with the Negroes; and that if we could not, yet, if we could but find provisions, we should make our way as well along the sea-shore as along the river, till we came to the Gold Coast, which, he said, was not above 400 or 500 miles north of Congo, besides the turning of the coast west about 300 more; that shore being in the latitude of six or seven degrees; and that there the English, or Dutch, or French had settlements or factories, perhaps all of them.

I confess I had more mind, all the while he argued, to have gone northward, and shipped ourselves in the Rio Grande, or, as the traders call it, the river Negro or Niger, for I knew that at last it would bring us down to the Cape de Verd, where we were sure of relief; whereas, at the coast we were going to now, we had a prodigious way still to go, either by sea or land, and no certainty which way to get provisions but by force; but for the present I held my tongue, because it was my tutor's opinion.

But when, according to his desire, we came to turn southward, having passed beyond the second great lake, our men began all to be uneasy, and said we were now out of our way for certain, for that we were going farther from home, and that we were indeed far enough off already.

But we had not marched above twelve days more, eight whereof were taken up in rounding the lake, and four more south-west, in order to make for the river Congo, but we were put to another full stop, by entering a country so desolate, so frightful, and so wild, that we knew not what to think or do; for, besides that it appeared as a terrible and boundless desert, having neither woods, trees, rivers, or inhabitants, so even the place where we were was desolate of inhabitants, nor had we any way to gather in a stock of provisions for the passing of this desert, as we did before at our entering the first, unless we had marched back four days to the place where we turned the head of the lake.

Well, notwithstanding this, we ventured; for, to men that had passed such wild places as we had done, nothing could seem too desperate to undertake. We ventured, I say, and the rather because we saw very high mountains in our way at a great distance, and we imagined, wherever there were mountains there would be springs and rivers; where rivers there would be trees and grass; where trees and grass there would be cattle; and where cattle, some kind of inhabitants. At last, in consequence of this speculative philosophy, we entered this waste, having a great heap of roots and plants for our bread, such as the Indians gave us, a very little flesh or salt, and but a little water.

We traveled two days towards those hills, and still they seemed as far off as they did at first, and it was the fifth day before we got to them; indeed, we traveled but softly, for it was excessively hot; and we were much about the very equinoctial line, we hardly knew whether to the south or the north of it.

As we had concluded, that where there were hills there would be springs, so it happened; but we were not only surprised, but really frighted, to find the first spring we came to, and which looked admirably clear and beautiful, to be salt as brine. It was a terrible disappointment to us, and put us under melancholy apprehensions at first; but the gunner, who was of a spirit never discouraged, told us we should not be disturbed at that, but be very thankful, for salt was a bait we stood in as much need of as anything, and there was no question but we should find fresh water as well as salt; and here our surgeon stepped in to encourage us, and told us that if we did not know he would show us a way how to make that salt water fresh, which indeed made us all more cheerful, though we wondered what he meant.

Meantime our men, without bidding, had been seeking about for other springs, and found several; but still they were all salt; from whence we concluded that there was a salt rock or mineral stone in those mountains, and perhaps they might be all of such a substance; but still I wondered by what witchcraft it was that our artist the surgeon would make this salt water turn fresh, and I longed to see the experiment, which was indeed a very odd one; but he went to work with as much assurance as if he had tried it on the very spot before.

He took two of our large mats and sewed them together, and they made a kind of a bag four feet broad, three feet and a half high, and about a foot and a half thick when it was full.

He caused us to fill this bag with dry sand and tread it down as close as we could, not to burst the mats. When thus the bag was full within a foot, he sought some other earth and filled up the rest with it, and still trod all in as hard as he could. When he had done, he made a hole in the upper earth about as broad as the crown of a large hat, or something bigger about, but not so deep, and bade a Negro fill it with water, and still as it shrunk away to fill it again, and keep it full. The bag he had placed at first across two pieces of wood, about a foot from the ground; and under it he ordered some of our skins to be spread that would hold water. In about an hour, and not sooner, the water began to come dropping through the bottom of the bag, and, to our great surprise, was perfectly fresh and sweet, and this continued for several hours; but in the end the water began to be a little brackish. When we told him that, "Well, then," said he, "turn the sand out, and fill it again." Whether he did this by way of experiment from his own fancy, or whether he had seen it done before, I do not remember.

The next day we mounted the tops of the hills, where the prospect was indeed astonishing, for as far as the eye could look, south, or west, or northwest, there was nothing to be seen but a vast howling wilderness, with neither tree nor river, nor any green thing. The surface we found, as the part we passed the day before, had a kind of thick moss upon it, of a blackish dead colour, but nothing in it that looked like food, either for man or beast.

Had we been stored with provisions to have entered for ten or twenty days upon this wilderness, as we were formerly, and with fresh water, we had hearts good enough to have ventured, though we had been obliged to come back again, for if we went north we did not know but we might meet with the same; but we neither had provisions, neither were we in any place where it was possible to get them. We killed some wild ferine creatures at the foot of these hills; but, except two things, like to nothing that we ever saw before, we met with nothing that was fit to eat. These were creatures that seemed to be between the kind of a buffalo and a deer, but indeed resembled neither; for they had no horns, and had great legs like a cow, with a fine head, and the neck like a deer. We killed also, at several times, a tiger, two young lions, and a wolf; but, God be thanked, we were not so reduced as to eat carrion.

Upon this terrible prospect I renewed my motion of turning northward, and making towards the river Niger or Rio Grande, then to turn west towards the English settlements on the Gold Coast; to which every one most readily consented, only our gunner, who was indeed our best guide, though he happened to be mistaken at this time. He moved that, as our coast was now northward, so we might slant away north-west, that so, by crossing the country, we might perhaps meet with some other river that run into the Rio Grande northward, or down to the Gold Coast southward, and so both direct our way and shorten the labour; as also because, if any of the country was inhabited and fruitful, we should probably find it upon the shore of the rivers, where alone we could be furnished with provisions.

This was good advice, and too rational not to be taken; but our present business was, what to do to get out of this dreadful place we were in. Behind us was a waste, which had already cost us five days' march, and we had not provisions for five days left to go back again the same way. Before us was nothing but horror, as above; so we resolved, seeing the ridge of the hills we were upon had some appearance of fruitfulness, and that they seemed to lead away to the northward a great way, to keep under the foot of them on the east side, to go on as far as we could, and in the meantime to look diligently out for food.

Accordingly we moved on the next morning; for we had no time to lose, and, to our great comfort, we came in our first morning's march to very good springs of fresh water; and lest we should have a scarcity again, we filled all our bladder bottles and carried it with us. I should also have observed that our surgeon, who made the salt water fresh, took the opportunity of those salt springs, and made us the quantity of three or four pecks of very good salt.

In our third march we found an unexpected supply of food, the hills being full of hares. They were of a kind something different from ours in England, larger and not as swift of foot, but very good meat. We shot several of them, and the little tame leopard, which I told you we took at the Negro town that we plundered, hunted them like a dog, and killed us several every day; but she would eat nothing of them unless we gave it her, which, indeed, in our circumstance, was very obliging. We salted them a little and dried them in the sun whole, and carried a strange parcel along with us. I think it was almost three hundred, for we did not know when we might find any more, either of these or any other food. We continued our course under these hills very comfortably for eight or nine days, when we found, to our great satisfaction, the country beyond us began to look with something of a better countenance. As for the west side of the hills, we never examined it till this day, when three of our company, the rest halting for refreshment, mounted the hills again to satisfy their curiosity, but found it all the same, nor could they see any end of it, no, not to the north, the way we were going; so the tenth day, finding the hills made a turn, and led as it were into the vast desert, we left them and continued our course north, the country being very tolerably full of woods, some waste, but not tediously long, till we came, by our gunner's observation, into the latitude of eight degrees five minutes, which we were nineteen days more in performing.

All this way we found no inhabitants, but abundance of wild ravenous creatures, with which we became so well acquainted now that really we did not much mind them. We saw lions and tigers and leopards every night and morning in abundance; but as they seldom came near us, we let them go about their business: if they offered to come near us, we made false fire with any gun that was uncharged, and they would walk off as soon as they saw the flash.

We made pretty good shift for food all this way; for sometimes we killed hares, sometimes some fowls, but for my life I cannot give names to any of them, except a kind of partridge, and another that was like our turtle. Now and then we began to meet with elephants again in great numbers; those creatures delighted chiefly in the woody part of the country.

This long-continued march fatigued us very much, and two of our men fell sick, indeed, so very sick that we thought they would have died; and one of our Negroes died suddenly. Our surgeon said it was an apoplexy, but he wondered at it, he said, for he could never complain of his high feeding. Another of them was very ill; but our surgeon with much ado persuading him, indeed it was almost forcing him to be let blood, he recovered.

We halted here twelve days for the sake of our sick men, and our surgeon persuaded me and three or four more of us to be let blood during the time of rest, which, with other things he gave us, contributed very much to our continued health in so tedious a march and in so hot a climate.

In this march we pitched our matted tents every night, and they were very comfortable to us, though we had trees and woods to shelter us in most places. We thought it very strange that in all this part of the country we yet met with no inhabitants; but the principal reason, as we found afterwards, was, that we, having kept a western course first, and then a northern course, were gotten too much into the middle of the country and among the deserts; whereas the inhabitants are principally found among the rivers, lakes, and lowlands, as well to the south-west as to the north.

What little rivulets we found here were so empty of water, that except some pits, and little more than ordinary pools, there was scarcely any water to be seen in them; and they rather showed that during the rainy months they had a channel, than that they had really running water in them at that time, by which it was easy for us to judge that we had a great way to go; but this was no discouragement so long as we had but provisions, and some seasonable shelter from the violent heat, which indeed I thought was much greater now than when the sun was just over our heads.

Our men being recovered, we set forward again, very well stored with provisions, and water sufficient, and bending our course a little to the westward of the north, traveled in hopes of some favourable stream which might bear a canoe; but we found none till after twenty days' travel, including eight days' rest; for our men being weak, we rested very often, especially when we came to places which were proper for our purpose, where we found cattle, fowl, or anything to kill for our food. In those twenty days' march we advanced four degrees to the northward, besides some meridian distance westward, and we met with abundance of elephants, and with a good number of elephants' teeth scattered up and down, here and there, in the woody grounds especially, some of which were very large. But they were no booty to us; our business was provisions, and a good passage out of the country; and it had been much more to our purpose to have found a good fat deer, and to have killed it for our food, than a hundred ton of elephants' teeth; and yet, as you shall presently hear, when we came to begin our passage by water, we once thought to have built a large canoe, on purpose to have loaded it with ivory; but this was when we knew nothing of the rivers, nor knew anything how dangerous and how difficult a passage it was we were likely to have in them, nor had considered the weight of carriage to lug them to the rivers where we might embark.

At the end of twenty days' travel, as above, in the latitude of three degrees sixteen minutes, we discovered in a valley, at some distance from us, a pretty tolerable stream, which we thought deserved the name of a river, and which ran its course N.N.W., which was just what we wanted. As we had fixed our thoughts upon our passage by water, we took this for the place to make the experiment, and bent our march directly to the valley.

There was a small thicket of trees just in our way, which we went by, thinking no harm, when on a sudden one of our Negroes was dangerously wounded with an arrow shot into his back, slanting between his shoulders. This put us to a full stop; and three of our men, with two Negroes, spreading the wood, for it was but a small one, found a Negro with a bow, but no arrow, who would have escaped, but our men that discovered him shot him in revenge of the mischief he had done; so we lost the opportunity of taking him prisoner, which, if we had done, and sent him home with good usage, it might have brought others to us in a friendly manner.

Going a little farther, we came to five Negro huts or houses, built after a different manner from any we had seen yet; and at the door of one of them lay seven elephants' teeth, piled up against the wall or side of the hut, as if they had been provided against a market. Here were no men, but seven or eight women, and near twenty children. We offered them no incivility of any kind, but gave them every one a bit of silver beaten out thin, as I observed before, and cut diamond fashion, or in the shape of a bird, at which the women were overjoyed, and brought out to us several sorts of food, which we did not understand, being cakes of a meal made of roots, which they bake in the sun, and which ate very well. We went a little way farther and pitched our camp for that night, not doubting but our civility to the women would produce some good effect when their husbands might come home.

Accordingly, the next morning the women, with eleven men, five young boys, and two good big girls, came to our camp. Before they came quite to us, the women called aloud, and made an odd screaming noise to bring us out; and accordingly we came out, when two of the women, showing us what we had given them, and pointing to the company behind, made such signs as we could easily understand signified friendship. When the men advanced, having bows and arrows, they laid them down on the ground, scraped and threw sand over their heads, and turned round three times with their hands laid up upon the tops of their heads. This, it seems, was a solemn vow of friendship. Upon this we beckoned them with our hands to come nearer; then they sent the boys and girls to us first, which, it seems, was to bring us more cakes of bread and some green herbs to eat, which we received, and took the boys up and kissed them, and the little girls too; then the men came up close to us, and sat them down on the ground, making signs that we should sit down by them, which we did. They said much to one another, but we could not understand them, nor could we find any way to make them understand us, much less whither we were going, or what we wanted, only that we easily made them understand we wanted victuals; whereupon one of the men, casting his eyes about him towards a rising ground that was about half a mile off, started up as if he was frighted, flew to the place where they had laid down their bows and arrows, snatched up a bow and two arrows, and ran like a racehorse to the place. When he came there, he let fly both his arrows, and comes back again to us with the same speed. We, seeing he came with the bow, but without the arrows, were the more inquisitive; but the fellow, saying nothing to us, beckons to one of our Negroes to come to him, and we bid him go; so he led him back to the place, where lay a kind of deer, shot with two arrows, but not quite dead, and between them they brought it down to us. This was for a gift to us, and was very welcome, I assure you, for our stock was low. These people were all stark naked.

The next day there came about a hundred men to us, and women making the same awkward signals of friendship, and dancing, and showing themselves very well pleased, and anything they had they gave us. How the man in the wood came to be so butcherly and rude as to shoot at our men, without making any breach first, we could not imagine; for the people were simple, plain, and inoffensive in all our other conversation with them.

From hence we went down the banks of the little river I mentioned, and where, I found, we should see the whole nation of Negroes, but whether friendly to us or not, that we could make no judgment of yet.

The river was no use to us, as to the design of making canoes, a great while; and we traversed the country on the edge of it about five days more, when our carpenters, finding the stream increased, proposed to pitch our tents, and fall to work to make canoes; but after we had begun the work, and cut down two or three trees, and spent five days in the labour, some of our men, wandering further down the river, brought us word that the stream rather decreased than increased, sinking away into the sands, or drying up by the heat of the sun, so that the river appeared not able to carry the least canoe that could be any way useful to us; so we were obliged to give over our enterprise and move on.

In our further prospect this way, we marched three days full west, the country on the north side being extraordinary mountainous, and more parched and dry than any we had seen yet; whereas, in the part which looks due west, we found a pleasant valley running a great way between two great ridges of mountains. The hills looked frightful, being entirely bare of trees or grass, and even white with the dryness of the sand; but in the valley we had trees, grass, and some creatures that were fit for food, and some inhabitants.

We passed by some of their huts or houses, and saw people about them, but they ran up into the hills as soon as they saw us. At the end of this valley we met with a peopled country, and at first it put us to some doubt whether we should go among them, or keep up towards the hills northerly; and as our aim was principally as before, to make our way to the river Niger, we inclined to the latter, pursuing our course by the compass to the N.W. We marched thus without interruption seven days more, when we met with a surprising circumstance much more desolate and disconsolate than our own, and which, in time to come, will scarce seem credible.

We did not much seek the conversing, or acquainting ourselves with the natives of the country, except where we found the want of them for our provision, or their direction for our way; so that, whereas we found the country here begin to be very populous, especially towards our left hand, that is, to the south, we kept at the more distance northerly, still stretching towards the west.

In this tract we found something or other to kill and eat, which always supplied our necessity, though not so well as we were provided in our first setting out; being thus, as it were, pushing to avoid a peopled country, we at last came to a very pleasant, agreeable stream of water, not big enough to be called a river, but running to the N.N.W., which was the very course we desired to go.

On the farthest bank of this brook, we perceived some huts of Negroes, not many, and in a little low spot of ground, some maize, or Indian corn, growing, which intimated presently to us, that there were some inhabitants on that side less barbarous than what we had met with in other places where we had been.

As we went forward, our whole caravan being in a body, our Negroes, who were in the front, cried out, that they saw a white man! We were not much surprised at first, it being, as we thought, a mistake of the fellows, and asked them what they meant; when one of them stepped to me, and pointing to a hut on the other side of the hill, I was astonished to see a white man indeed, but stark naked, very busy near the door of his hut, and stooping down to the ground with something in his hand, as if he had been at some work; and his back being towards us, he did not see us.

I gave notice to our Negroes to make no noise, and waited till some more of our men were come up, to show the sight to them, that they might be sure I was not mistaken; and we were soon satisfied of the truth, for the man, having heard some noise, started up, and looked full at us, as much surprised, to be sure, as we were, but whether with fear or hope, we then knew not.

As he discovered us, so did the rest of the inhabitants belonging to the huts about him, and all crowded together, looking at us at a distance, a little bottom, in which the brook ran, lying between us; the white man, and all the rest, as he told us afterwards, not knowing well whether they should stay or run away. However, it presently came into my thoughts, that if there were white men among them, it would be much easier to make them understand what we meant as to peace or war, than we found it with others; so tying a piece of white rag to the end of a stick, we sent two Negroes with it to the bank of the water, carrying the pole up as high as they could; it was presently understood, and two of their men and the white man came to the shore on the other side.

However, as the white man spoke no Portuguese, they could understand nothing of one another but by signs; but our men made the white man understand that they had white men with them too, at which they said the white man laughed. However, to be short, our men came back, and told us they were all good friends, and in about an hour four of our men, two Negroes, and the black prince, went to the river-side, where the white man came to them.

They had not been half a quarter of an hour, but a Negro came running to me, and told me the white man was Inglese, as he called him; upon which I ran back, eagerly enough, you may be sure, with him, and found, as he said, that he was an Englishman; upon which he embraced me very passionately, the tears running down his face. The first surprise of his seeing us was over before we came, but any one may conceive it by the brief account he gave us afterwards of his very unhappy circumstances, and of so unexpected a deliverance, such as perhaps never happened to any man in the world, for it was a million to one odds that ever he could have been relieved; nothing but an adventure that never was heard or read of before could have suited his case, unless Heaven, by some miracle that never was to be expected, had acted for him.

He appeared to be a gentleman, not an ordinary-bred fellow, seaman, or labouring man; this showed itself in his behaviour in the first moment of our conversing with him, and in spite of all the disadvantages of his miserable circumstances.

He was a middle-aged man, not above thirty-seven or thirty-eight, though his beard was grown exceedingly long, and the hair of his head and face strangely covered him to the middle of his back and breast; he was white, and his skin very fine, though discoloured, and in some places blistered, and covered with a brown blackish substance, scurfy, scaly, and hard, which was the effect of the scorching heat of the sun; he was stark naked, and had been so, as he told us, upwards of two years.

He was so exceedingly transported at our meeting with him, that he could scarce enter into any discourse at all with us that day; and when he could get away from us for a little, we saw him walking alone, and showing all the most extravagant tokens of an ungovernable joy; and even afterwards he was never without tears in his eyes for several days, upon the least word spoken by us of his circumstances, or by him of his deliverance.

We found his behaviour the most courteous and endearing I ever saw in any man whatever, and most evident tokens of a mannerly, well-bred person appeared in all things he did or said, and our people were exceedingly taken with him. He was a scholar and a mathematician; he could not speak Portuguese indeed, but he spoke Latin to our surgeon, French to another of our men, and Italian to a third.

He had no leisure in his thoughts to ask us whence we came, whither we were going, or who we were; but would have it always as an answer to himself, that to be sure, wherever we were a-going, we came from Heaven, and were sent on purpose to save him from the most wretched condition that ever man was reduced to.

Our men pitching their camp on the bank of a little river opposite to him, he began to inquire what store of provisions we had, and how we proposed to be supplied. When he found that our store was but small, he said he would talk with the natives, and we should have provisions enough; for he said they were the most courteous, good-natured part of the inhabitants in all that part of the country, as we might suppose by his living so safe among them.

The first things this gentleman did for us were indeed of the greatest consequence to us; for, first, he perfectly informed us where we were, and which was the properest course for us to steer; secondly, he put us in the way how to furnish ourselves effectually with provisions; and thirdly, he was our complete interpreter and peacemaker with all the natives, who now began to be very numerous about us, and who were a more fierce and politic people than those we had met with before; not so easily terrified with our arms as those, and not so ignorant as to give their provisions and corn for our little toys, such as, I said before, our artificer made; but as they had frequently traded and conversed with the Europeans on the coast, or with other Negro nations that had traded and been concerned with them, they were the less ignorant and the less fearful, and consequently nothing was to be had from them but by exchange for such things as they liked.

This I say of the Negro natives, which we soon came among; but as to these poor people that he lived among, they were not much acquainted with things, being at the distance of above 300 miles from the coast; only that they found elephants' teeth upon the hills to the north, which they took and carried about sixty or seventy miles south, where other trading Negroes usually met them, and gave them beads, glass, shells, and cowries, for them, such as the English and Dutch and other traders furnish them with from Europe.

We now began to be more familiar with our new acquaintance; and first, though we made but a sorry figure as to clothes ourselves, having neither shoe, or stocking, or glove, or hat among us, and but very few shirts, yet as well as we could we clothed him; and first, our surgeon having scissors and razors, shaved him, and cut his hair; a hat, as I say, we had not in all our stores, but he supplied himself by making himself a cap of a piece of a leopard-skin, most artificially. As for shoes or stockings, he had gone so long without them that he cared not even for the buskins and foot-gloves we wore, which I described above.

As he had been curious to hear the whole story of our travels, and was exceedingly delighted with the relation, so we were no less to know, and pleased with, the account of his circumstances, and the history of his coming to that strange place alone, and in that condition which we found him in, as above. This account of his would indeed be in itself the subject of an agreeable history, and would be as long and diverting as our own, having in it many strange and extraordinary incidents; but we cannot have room here to launch out into so long a digression: the sum of his history was this: ——

He had been a factor for the English Guinea Company at Sierra Leone, or some other of their settlements which had been taken by the French, where he had been plundered of all his own effects, as well as of what was entrusted to him by the company. Whether it was that the company did not do him justice in restoring his circumstances, or in further employing him, he quitted their service, and was employed by those called separate traders, and being afterwards out of employ there also, traded on his own account; when, passing unwarily into one of the company's settlements, he was either betrayed into the hands of some of the natives, or, somehow or other, was surprised by them. However, as they did not kill him, he found means to escape from them at that time, and fled to another nation of the natives, who, being enemies to the other, entertained him friendly, and with them he lived some time; but not liking his quarters or his company, he fled again, and several times changed his landlords: sometimes was carried by force, sometimes hurried by fear, as circumstances altered with him (the variety of which deserves a history by itself), till at last he had wandered beyond all possibility of return, and had taken up his abode where we found him, where he was well received by the petty king of the tribe he lived with; and he, in return, instructed them how to value the product of their labour, and on what terms to trade with those Negroes who came up to them for teeth.

As he was naked, and had no clothes, so he was naked of arms for his defence, having neither gun, sword, staff, or any instrument of war about him, no, not to guard himself against the attacks of a wild beast, of which the country was very full. We asked him how he came to be so entirely abandoned of all concern for his safety? He answered, that to him, that had so often wished for death, life was not worth defending; and that, as he was entirely at the mercy of the Negroes, they had much the more confidence in him, seeing he had no weapons to hurt them. As for wild beasts, he was not much concerned about that, for he scarce ever went from his hut; but if he did, the Negro king and his men went all with him, and they were all armed with bows and arrows, and lances, with which they would kill any of the ravenous creatures, lions as well as others; but that they seldom came abroad in the day; and if the Negroes wander anywhere in the night, they always build a hut for themselves, and make a fire at the door of it, which is guard enough.

We inquired of him what we should next do towards getting to the seaside. He told us we were about one hundred and twenty English leagues from the coast, where almost all the European settlements and factories were, and which is called the Gold Coast; but that there were so many different nations of Negroes in the way, that it was ten to one if we were not either fought with continually, or starved for want of provisions; but that there were two other ways to go, which, if he had had any company to go with him, he had often contrived to make his escape by. The one was to travel full west, which, though it was farther to go, yet was not so full of people, and the people we should find would be so much the civiler to us, or be so much the easier to fight with; or that the other way was, if possible, to get to the Rio Grande, and go down the stream in canoes. We told him, that was the way we had resolved on before we met with him; but then he told us there was a prodigious desert to go over, and as prodigious woods to go through, before we came to it, and that both together were at least twenty days' march for us, travel as hard as we could.

We asked him if there were no horses in the country, or asses, or even bullocks or buffaloes, to make use of in such a journey, and we showed him ours, of which we had but three left. He said no, all the country did not afford anything of that kind.

He told us that in this great wood there were immense numbers of elephants; and upon the desert, great multitudes of lions, lynxes, tigers, leopards, &c.; and that it was to that wood and that desert that the Negroes went to get elephants' teeth, where they never failed to find a great number.

We inquired still more, and particularly the way to the Gold Coast, and if there were no rivers to ease us in our carriage; and told him, as to the Negroes fighting with us, we were not much concerned at that; nor were we afraid of starving, for if they had any victuals among them, we would have our share of it; and, therefore, if he would venture to show us the way, we would venture to go; and as for himself, we told him we would live and die together — there should not a man of us stir from him.

He told us, with all his heart, if we resolved it, and would venture, we might be assured he would take his fate with us, and he would endeavour to guide us in such a way as we should meet with some friendly savages who would use us well, and perhaps stand by us against some others, who were less tractable; so, in a word, we all resolved to go full south for the Gold Coast.

The next morning he came to us again, and being all met in council, as we may call it, he began to talk very seriously with us, that since we were now come, after a long journey, to a view of the end of our troubles, and had been so obliging to him as to offer to carry him with us, he had been all night revolving in his mind what he and we all might do to make ourselves some amends for all our sorrows; and first, he said, he was to let me know that we were just then in one of the richest parts of the world, though it was really otherwise but a desolate, disconsolate wilderness; "for," says he, "there is not a river but runs gold — not a desert but without ploughing bears a crop of ivory. What mines of gold, what immense stores of gold, those mountains may contain, from whence these rivers come, or the shores which these waters run by, we know not, but may imagine that they must be inconceivably rich, seeing so much is washed down the stream by the water washing the sides of the land, that the quantity suffices all the traders which the European world send thither." We asked him how far they went for it, seeing the ships only trade upon the coast. He told us that the Negroes on the coast search the rivers up for the length of 150 or 200 miles, and would be out a month, or two, or three at a time, and always come home sufficiently rewarded; "but," says he, "they never come thus far, and yet hereabouts is as much gold as there." Upon this he told us that he believed he might have gotten a hundred pounds' weight of gold since he came thither, if he had employed himself to look and work for it; but as he knew not what to do with it, and had long since despaired of being ever delivered from the misery he was in, he had entirely omitted it. "For what advantage had it been to me," said he, "or what richer had I been, if I had a ton of gold dust, and lay and wallowed in it? The richness of it," said he, "would not give me one moment's felicity, nor relieve me in the present exigency. Nay," says he, "as you all see, it would not buy me clothes to cover me, or a drop of drink to save me from perishing. It is of no value here," says he; "there are several people among these huts that would weigh gold against a few glass beads or a cockle-shell, and give you a handful of gold-dust for a handful of cowries." N.B. — These are little shells which our children call blackamoors' teeth.

When he had said thus he pulled out a piece of an earthen pot baked hard in the sun. "Here," says he, "is some of the dirt of this country, and if I would I could have got a great deal more;" and, showing it to us, I believe there was in it between two and three pounds weight of gold-dust, of the same kind and colour with that we had gotten already, as before. After we had looked at it a while, he told us, smiling, we were his deliverers, and all he had, as well as his life, was ours; and therefore, as this would be of value to us when we came to our own country, so he desired we would accept of it among us; and that was the only time that he had repented that he had picked up no more of it.

I spoke for him, as his interpreter, to my comrades, and in their names thanked him; but, speaking to them in Portuguese, I desired them to defer the acceptance of his kindness to the next morning; and so I did, telling him we would further talk of this part in the morning; so we parted for that time.

When he was gone I found they were all wonderfully affected with his discourse, and with the generosity of his temper, as well as the magnificence of his present, which in another place had been

701

extraordinary. Upon the whole, not to detain you with circumstances, we agreed that, seeing he was now one of our number, and that as we were a relief to him in carrying him out of the dismal condition he was in, so he was equally a relief to us, in being our guide through the rest of the country, our interpreter with the natives, and our director how to manage with the savages, and how to enrich ourselves with the wealth of the country; that, therefore, we would put his gold among our common stock, and every one should give him as much as would make his up just as much as any single share of our own, and for the future we would take our lot together, taking his solemn engagement to us, as we had before one to another, that we would not conceal the least grain of gold we found one from another.

In the next conference we acquainted him with the adventures of the Golden River, and how we had shared what we got there, so that every man had a larger stock than he for his share; that, therefore, instead of taking any from him, we had resolved every one to add a little to him. He appeared very glad that we had met with such good success, but would not take a grain from us, till at last, pressing him very hard, he told us, that then he would take it thus: — that, when we came to get any more, he would have so much out of the first as should make him even, and then we would go on as equal adventurers; and thus we agreed.

He then told us he thought it would not be an unprofitable adventure if, before we set forward, and after we had got a stock of provisions, we should make a journey north to the edge of the desert he had told us of, from whence our Negroes might bring every one a large elephant's tooth, and that he would get some more to assist; and that, after a certain length of carriage, they might be conveyed by canoes to the coast, where they would yield a very great profit.

I objected against this on account of our other design we had of getting gold-dust; and that our Negroes, who we knew would be faithful to us, would get much more by searching the rivers for gold for us than by lugging a great tooth of a hundred and fifty pounds weight a hundred miles or more, which would be an insufferable labour to them after so hard a journey, and would certainly kill them.

He acquiesced in the justice of this answer, but fain would have had us gone to see the woody part of the hill and the edge of the desert, that we might see how the elephants' teeth lay scattered up and down there; but when we told him the story of what we had seen before, as is said above, he said no more.

We stayed here twelve days, during which time the natives were very obliging to us, and brought us fruits, pompions, and a root like carrots, though of quite another taste, but not unpleasant neither, and some guinea-fowls, whose names we did not know. In short, they brought us plenty of what they had, and we lived very well, and we gave them all such little things as our cutler had made, for he had now a whole bag full of them.

On the thirteenth day we set forward, taking our new gentleman with us. At parting, the Negro king sent two savages with a present to him of some dried flesh, but I do not remember what it was, and he gave him again three silver birds which our cutler helped him to, which I assure you was a present for a king.

We traveled now south, a little west, and here we found the first river for above 2000 miles' march, whose waters run south, all the rest running north or west. We followed this river, which was no bigger than a good large brook in England, till it began to increase its water. Every now and then we found our Englishman went down as it were privately to the water, which was to try the land; at length, after a day's march upon this river, he came running up to us with his hands full of sand, and saying, "Look here." Upon looking we found that a good deal of gold lay spangled among the sand of the river. "Now," says he, "I think we may begin to work;" so he divided our Negroes into couples and set them to work, to search and wash the sand and ooze in the bottom of the water where it was not deep.

In the first day and a quarter our men all together had gathered a pound and two ounces of gold or thereabouts, and as we found the quantity increased the farther we went, we followed it about three days, till another small rivulet joined the first, and then searching up the stream, we found gold there too; so we pitched our camp in the angle where the rivers joined, and we diverted ourselves, as I may call it, in washing the gold out of the sand of the river, and in getting provisions.

Here we stayed thirteen days more, in which time we had many pleasant adventures with the savages, too long to mention here, and some of them too homely to tell of, for some of our men had made something free with their women, which, had not our new guide made peace for us with one of their men at the price of seven fine bits of silver, which our artificer had cut out into the shapes of lions, and fishes, and birds, and had punched holes to hang them up by (an inestimable treasure), we must have gone to war with them and all their people.

All the while we were busy washing gold-dust out of the rivers, and our Negroes the like, our ingenious cutler was hammering and cutting, and he was grown so dexterous by use that he formed all manner of images. He cut out elephants, tigers, civet cats, ostriches, eagles, cranes, fowls, fishes, and indeed whatever he pleased, in thin plates of hammered gold, for his silver and iron were almost all gone.

At one of the towns of these savage nations we were very friendly received by their king, and as he was very much taken with our workman's toys, he sold him an elephant cut out of a gold plate as thin as a sixpence at an extravagant rate. He was so much taken with it that he would not be quiet till he had given him almost a handful of gold-dust, as they call it; I suppose it might weigh three-quarters of a pound; the piece of gold that the elephant was made of might be about the weight of a pistole, rather less than more. Our artist was so honest, though the labour and art were all his own, that he brought all the gold and put it into our common stock; but we had, indeed, no manner of reason in the least to be covetous, for, as our new guide told us, we that were strong enough to defend ourselves, and had time enough to stay (for we were none of us in haste), might in time get together what quantity of gold we pleased, even to an hundred pounds weight each man if we thought fit; and therefore he told us, though he had as much reason to be sick of the country as any of us, yet if we thought to turn our march a little to the south-east, and pitch upon a place proper for our headquarters, we might find provisions plenty enough, and extend ourselves over the country among the rivers for two or three years to the right and left, and we should soon find the advantage of it.

The proposal, however good as to the profitable part of it, suited none of us, for we were all more desirous to get home than to be rich, being tired of the excessive fatigue of above a year's continual wandering among deserts and wild beasts.

However, the tongue of our new acquaintance had a kind of charm in it, and used such arguments, and had so much the power of persuasion, that there was no resisting him. He told us it was preposterous not to take the fruit of all our labours now we were come to the harvest; that we might see the hazard the Europeans run with ships and men, and at great expense, to fetch a little gold, and that we, that were in the centre of it, to go away empty-handed was unaccountable; that we were strong enough to fight our way through whole nations, and might make our journey afterward to what part of the coast we pleased, and we should never forgive ourselves when we

704

came to our own country to see we had 500 pistoles in gold, and might as easily have had 5000 or 10,000, or what we pleased; that he was no more covetous than we, but seeing it was in all our powers to retrieve our misfortunes at once, and to make ourselves easy for all our lives, he could not be faithful to us, or grateful for the good we had done him, if he did not let us see the advantage we had in our hands; and he assured us he would make it clear to our own understanding, that we might in two years' time, by good management and by the help of our Negroes, gather every man a hundred pounds weight of gold, and get together perhaps two hundred ton of teeth; whereas, if once we pushed on to the coast and separated, we should never be able to see that place again with our eyes, or do any more than sinners did with heaven, — wish themselves there, but know they can never come at it.

Our surgeon was the first man that yielded to his reasoning, and after him the gunner; and they too, indeed, had a great influence over us, but none of the rest had any mind to stay, nor I neither, I must confess; for I had no notion of a great deal of money, or what to do with myself, or what to do with it if I had it. I thought I had enough already, and all the thoughts I had about disposing of it, if I came to Europe, was only how to spend it as fast as I could, buy me some clothes, and go to sea again to be a drudge for more.

However, he prevailed with us by his good words at last to stay but for six months in the country, and then, if we did resolve to go, he would submit; so at length we yielded to that, and he carried us about fifty English miles south-east, where we found several rivulets of water, which seemed to come all from a great ridge of mountains, which lay to the north-east, and which, by our calculation, must be the beginning that way of the great waste, which we had been forced northward to avoid.

Here we found the country barren enough, but yet we had by his direction plenty of food; for the savages round us, upon giving them some of our toys, as I have so often mentioned, brought us in whatever they had; and here we found some maize, or Indian wheat, which the Negro women planted, as we sow seeds in a garden, and immediately our new provider ordered some of our Negroes to plant it, and it grew up presently, and by watering it often, we had a crop in less than three months' growth.

As soon as we were settled, and our camp fixed, we fell to the old trade of fishing for gold in the rivers mentioned above, and our English gentleman so well knew how to direct our search, that we scarce ever lost our labour.

One time, having set us to work, he asked if we would give him leave, with four or five Negroes, to go out for six or seven days to seek his fortune, and see what he could discover in the country, assuring us whatever he got should be for the public stock. We all gave him our consent, and lent him a gun; and two of our men desiring to go with him, they took then six Negroes with them, and two of our buffaloes that came with us the whole journey; they took about eight days' provision of bread with them, but no flesh, except about as much dried flesh as would serve them two days.

They traveled up to the top of the mountains I mentioned just now, where they saw (as our men afterwards vouched it to be) the same desert which we were so justly terrified at when we were on the farther side, and which, by our calculation, could not be less than 300 miles broad and above 600 miles in length, without knowing where it ended.

The journal of their travels is too long to enter upon here. They stayed out two-and-fifty days, when they brought us seventeen pound and something more (for we had no exact weight) of gold-dust, some of it in much larger pieces than any we had found before, besides about fifteen ton of elephants' teeth, which he had, partly by good usage and partly by bad, obliged the savages of the country to fetch, and bring down to him from the mountains, and which he made others bring with him quite down to our camp. Indeed, we wondered what was coming to us when we saw him attended with above 200 Negroes; but he soon undeceived us, when he made them all throw down their burdens on a heap at the entrance of our camp.

Besides this, they brought two lions' skins, and five leopards' skins, very large and very fine. He asked our pardon for his long stay, and that he had made no greater a booty, but told us he had one excursion more to make, which he hoped should turn to a better account.

So, having rested himself and rewarded the savages that brought the teeth for him with some bits of silver and iron cut out diamond fashion, and with two shaped like little dogs, he sent them away mightily pleased.

The second journey he went, some more of our men desired to go with him, and they made a troop of ten white men and ten savages, and the two buffaloes to carry their provisions and ammunition. They took the same course, only not exactly the same track, and they stayed thirty-two days only, in which time they killed no less than fifteen leopards, three lions, and several other creatures, and brought us home four-and-twenty pound some ounces of gold-dust, and only six elephants' teeth, but they were very great ones.

Our friend the Englishman showed us that now our time was well bestowed, for in five months which we had stayed here, we had gathered so much gold-dust that, when we came to share it, we had five pound and a quarter to a man, besides what we had before, and besides six or seven pound weight which we had at several times given our artificer to make baubles with. And now we talked of going forward to the coast to put an end to our journey; but our guide laughed at us then. "Nay, you can't go now," says he, "for the rainy season begins next month, and there will be no stirring then." This we found, indeed, reasonable, so we resolved to furnish ourselves with provisions, that we might not be obliged to go abroad too much in the rain, and we spread ourselves some one way and some another, as far as we cared to venture, to get provisions; and our Negroes killed us some deer, which we cured as well as we could in the sun, for we had now no salt.

By this time the rainy months were set in, and we could scarce, for above two months, look out of our huts. But that was not all, for the rivers were so swelled with the land-floods, that we scarce knew the little brooks and rivulets from the great navigable rivers. This had been a very good opportunity to have conveyed by water, upon rafts, our elephants' teeth, of which we had a very great pile; for, as we always gave the savages some reward for their labour, the very women would bring us teeth upon every opportunity, and sometimes a great tooth carried between two; so that our quantity was increased to about two-and-twenty ton of teeth.

As soon as the weather proved fair again, he told us he would not press us to any further stay, since we did not care whether we got any more gold or no; that we were indeed the first men he ever met with in his life that said they had gold enough, and of whom it might be truly said, that, when it lay under our feet, we would not stoop to take it up. But, since he had made us a promise, he would not break it, nor press us to make any further stay; only he thought he ought to tell us that now was the time, after the land-flood, when the greatest quantity of gold was found; and that, if we stayed but one month, we should see thousands of savages spread themselves over the whole country to wash the gold out of the sand, for the European ships which would come on the coast; that they do it then, because the rage of the floods always works down a great deal of gold out of the hills; and, if we took the advantage to be there before them, we did not know what extraordinary things we might find.

This was so forcible, and so well argued, that it appeared in all our faces we were prevailed upon; so we told him we would all stay: for though it was true we were all eager to be gone, yet the evident prospect of so much advantage could not well be resisted; that he was greatly mistaken, when he suggested that we did not desire to increase our store of gold, and in that we were resolved to make the utmost use of the advantage that was in our hands, and would stay as long as any gold was to be had, if it was another year.

He could hardly express the joy he was in on this occasion; and the fair weather coming on, we began, just as he directed, to search about the rivers for more gold. At first we had but little encouragement, and began to be doubtful; but it was very plain that the reason was, the water was not fully fallen, or the rivers reduced to their usual channel; but in a few days we were fully requited, and found much more gold than at first, and in bigger lumps; and one of our men washed out of the sand a piece of gold as big as a small nut, which weighed, by our estimation — for we had no small weights — almost an ounce and a half.

This success made us extremely diligent; and in little more than a month we had altogether gotten near sixty pound weight of gold; but after this, as he told us, we found abundance of the savages, men, women, and children, hunting every river and brook, and even the dry land of the hills for gold; so that we could do nothing like then, compared to what we had done before.

But our artificer found a way to make other people find us in gold without our own labour; for, when these people began to appear, he had a considerable quantity of his toys, birds, beasts, &c., such as before, ready for them; and the English gentleman being the interpreter, he brought the savages to admire them; so our cutler had trade enough, and, to be sure, sold his goods at a monstrous rate; for he would get an ounce of gold, sometimes two, for a bit of silver, perhaps of the value of a groat; nay, if it were iron and if it was of gold, they would not give the more for it; and it was incredible almost to think what a quantity of gold he got that way.

In a word, to bring this happy journey to a conclusion, we increased our stock of gold here, in three months' stay more, to such a degree that, bringing it all to a common stock, in order to share it, we divided almost four pound weight again to every man; and then we set forward for the Gold Coast, to see what method we could find out for our passage into Europe.

There happened several remarkable incidents in this part of our journey, as to how we were, or were not, received friendly by the several nations of savages through which we passed; how we delivered one Negro king from captivity, who had been a benefactor to our new guide; and now our guide, in gratitude, by our assistance, restored him to his kingdom, which, perhaps, might contain about 300 subjects; how he entertained us; and how he made his subjects go with our Englishmen, and fetch all our elephants' teeth which we had been obliged to leave behind us, and to carry them for us to the river, the name of which I forgot, where we made rafts, and in eleven days more came down to one of the Dutch settlements on the Gold Coast, where we arrived in perfect health, and to our great satisfaction. As for our cargo of teeth, we sold it to the Dutch factory, and received clothes and other necessaries for ourselves, and such of our Negroes as we thought fit to keep with us; and it is to be observed, that we had four pound of gunpowder left when we ended our journey. The Negro prince we made perfectly free, clothed him out of our common stock, and gave him a pound and a half of gold for himself, which he knew very well how to manage; and here we all parted after the most friendly manner possible. Our Englishman remained in the Dutch factory some time, and, as I heard afterwards, died there of grief; for he having sent a thousand pounds sterling over to England, by the way of Holland, for his refuge at his return to his friends, the ship was taken by the French and the effects all lost.

The rest of my comrades went away, in a small bark, to the two Portuguese factories, near Gambia, in the latitude of fourteen; and I, with two Negroes which I kept with me, went away to Cape Coast Castle, where I got passage for England, and arrived there in September; and thus ended my first harvest of wild oats; the rest were not sowed to so much advantage.

I had neither friend, relation, nor acquaintance in England, though it was my native country; I had consequently no person to trust with what I had, or to counsel me to secure or save it; but, falling into ill company, and trusting the keeper of a public-house in Rotherhithe with a great part of my money, and hastily squandering away the rest, all that great sum, which I got with so much pains and hazard, was gone in little more than two years' time; and, as I even rage in my own thoughts to reflect upon the manner how it was wasted, so I need record no more; the rest merits to be concealed with blushes, for that it was spent in all kinds of folly and wickedness. So this scene of my life may be said to have begun in theft, and ended in luxury; a sad setting-out, and a worse coming home.

About the year —— —— I began to see the bottom of my stock, and that it was time to think of further adventures; for my spoilers, as I call them, began to let me know, that as my money declined, their respect would ebb with it, and that I had nothing to expect of them further than as I might command it by the force of my money, which, in short, would not go an inch the further for all that had been spent in their favour before.

This shocked me very much, and I conceived a just abhorrence of their ingratitude; but it wore off; nor had I met with any regret at the wasting so glorious a sum of money as I brought to England with me.

I next shipped myself, in an evil hour to be sure, on a voyage to Cadiz, in a ship called the —— —— , and in the course of our voyage, being on the coast of Spain, was obliged to put into the Groin, by a strong southwest wind.

Here I fell into company with some masters of mischief; and, among them, one, forwarder than the rest, began an intimate confidence with me, so that we called one another brothers, and communicated all our circumstances to one another. His name was Harris. This fellow came to me one morning, asking me if I would go on shore, and I agreed; so we got the captain's leave for the boat, and went together. When we were together, he asked me if I had a mind for an adventure that might make amends for all past misfortunes. I told him, yes, with all my heart; for I did not care where I went, having nothing to lose, and no one to leave behind me.

He then asked me if I would swear to be secret, and that, if I did not agree to what he proposed, I would nevertheless never betray him. I readily bound myself to that, upon the most solemn imprecations and curses that the devil and both of us could invent.

He told me, then, there was a brave fellow in the other ship, pointing to another English ship which rode in the harbour, who, in concert with some of the men, had resolved to mutiny the next morning, and run away with the ship; and that, if we could get strength enough among our ship's company, we might do the same. I liked the proposal very well, and he got eight of us to join with him, and he told us, that as soon as his friend had begun the work, and was master of the ship, we should be ready to do the like. This was his plot; and I, without the least hesitation, either at the villainy of the fact or the difficulty of performing it, came immediately into the wicked conspiracy, and so it went on among us; but we could not bring our part to perfection.

Accordingly, on the day appointed, his correspondent in the other ship, whose name was Wilmot, began the work, and, having seized the captain's mate and other officers, secured the ship, and gave the signal to us. We were but eleven in our ship, who were in the conspiracy, nor could we get any more that we could trust; so that, leaving the ship, we all took the boat, and went off to join the other.

Having thus left the ship I was in, we were entertained with a great deal of joy by Captain Wilmot and his new gang; and, being well prepared for all manner of roguery, bold, desperate (I mean myself), without the least checks of conscience for what I was entered upon, or for anything I might do, much less with any apprehension of what might be the consequence of it; I say, having thus embarked with this crew, which at last brought me to consort with the most famous pirates of the age, some of whom have ended their journals at the gallows, I think the giving an account of some of my other adventures may be an agreeable piece of story; and this I may venture to say beforehand, upon the word of a pirate, that I shall not be able to recollect the full, no, not by far, of the great variety which has formed one of the most reprobate schemes that ever man was capable to present to the world.

I that was, as I have hinted before, an original thief, and a pirate, even by inclination before, was now in my element, and never undertook anything in my life with more particular satisfaction.

Captain Wilmot (for so we are now to call him) being thus possessed of a ship, and in the manner as you have heard, it may be easily concluded he had nothing to do to stay in the port, or to wait either the attempts that might be made from the shore, or any change that might happen among his men. On the contrary, we weighed anchor the same tide, and stood out to sea, steering away for the Canaries. Our ship had twenty-two guns, but was able to carry thirty; and besides, as she was fitted out for a merchant-ship only, she was not furnished either with ammunition or small-arms sufficient for our design, or for the occasion we might have in case of a fight. So we put into Cadiz, that is to say, we came to an anchor in the bay; and the captain, and one whom we called young Captain Kidd, who was the gunner, [landed,] and some of the men who could best be trusted, among whom was my comrade Harris, who was made second mate, and myself, who was made a lieutenant. Some bales of English goods were proposed to be carried on shore with us for sale, but my comrade, who was a complete fellow at his business, proposed a better way for it; and having been in the town before, told us, in short, that he would buy what powder and bullet, small-arms, or anything else we wanted, on his own word, to be paid for when they came on board, in such English goods as we had there. This was much the best way, and accordingly he and the captain went on shore by themselves, and having made such a bargain as they found for their turn, came away again in two hours' time, and bringing only a butt of wine and five casks of brandy with them, we all went on board again.

The next morning two *barcos longos* came off to us, deeply laden, with five Spaniards on board them, for traffic. Our captain sold them good pennyworths, and they delivered us sixteen barrels of powder, twelve small rundlets of fine powder for our small-arms, sixty muskets, and twelve fusées for the officers; seventeen ton of cannon-ball, fifteen barrels of musket-bullets, with some swords and twenty good pair of pistols. Besides this, they brought thirteen butts of wine (for we, that were now all become gentlemen, scorned to drink the ship's beer), also sixteen puncheons of brandy, with twelve barrels of raisins and twenty chests of lemons; all which we paid for in English goods; and, over and above, the captain received six hundred pieces of eight in money. They would have come again, but we would stay no longer.

From hence we sailed to the Canaries, and from thence onward to the West Indies, where we committed some depredation upon the Spaniards for provisions, and took some prizes, but none of any great value, while I remained with them, which was not long at that time; for, having taken a Spanish sloop on the coast of Carthagena, my friend made a motion to me, that we should desire Captain Wilmot to put us into the sloop, with a proportion of arms and ammunition, and let us try what we could do; she being much fitter for our business than the great ship, and a better sailor. This he consented to, and we appointed our rendezvous at Tobago, making an agreement, that whatever was taken by either of our ships should be shared among the ship's company of both; all which we very punctually observed, and joined our ships again, about fifteen months after, at the island of Tobago, as above.

We cruised near two years in those seas, chiefly upon the Spaniards; not that we made any difficulty of taking English ships, or Dutch, or French, if they came in our way; and particularly, Captain Wilmot attacked a New England ship bound from the Madeiras to

712

Jamaica, and another bound from New York to Barbados, with provisions; which last was a very happy supply to us. But the reason why we meddled as little with English vessels as we could, was, first, because, if they were ships of any force, we were sure of more resistance from them; and, secondly, because we found the English ships had less booty when taken, for the Spaniards generally had money on board, and that was what we best knew what to do with. Captain Wilmot was, indeed, more particularly cruel when he took any English vessel, that they might not too soon have advice of him in England; and so the men-of-war have orders to look out for him. But this part I bury in silence for the present.

We increased our stock in these two years considerably, having taken 60,000 pieces of eight in one vessel, and 100,000 in another; and being thus first grown rich, we resolved to be strong too, for we had taken a brigantine built at Virginia, an excellent sea-boat, and a good sailor, and able to carry twelve guns; and a large Spanish frigate-built ship, that sailed incomparably well also, and which afterwards, by the help of good carpenters, we fitted up to carry twenty-eight guns. And now we wanted more hands, so we put away for the Bay of Campeachy, not doubting we should ship as many men there as we pleased; and so we did.

Here we sold the sloop that I was in; and Captain Wilmot keeping his own ship, I took the command of the Spanish frigate as captain, and my comrade Harris as eldest lieutenant, and a bold enterprising fellow he was, as any the world afforded. One culverdine was put into the brigantine, so that we were now three stout ships, well manned, and victualed for twelve months; for we had taken two or three sloops from New England and New York, laden with flour, peas, and barreled beef and pork, going for Jamaica and Barbados; and for more beef we went on shore on the island of Cuba, where we killed as many black cattle as we pleased, though we had very little salt to cure them.

Out of all the prizes we took here we took their powder and bullet, their small-arms and cutlasses; and as for their men, we always took the surgeon and the carpenter, as persons who were of particular use to us upon many occasions; nor were they always unwilling to go with us, though for their own security, in case of accidents, they might easily pretend they were carried away by force; of which I shall give a pleasant account in the course of my other expeditions.

We had one very merry fellow here, a Quaker, whose name was William Walters, whom we took out of a sloop bound from

713

Pennsylvania to Barbados. He was a surgeon, and they called him doctor; but he was not employed in the sloop as a surgeon, but was going to Barbados to get a berth, as the sailors call it. However, he had all his surgeon's chests on board, and we made him go with us, and take all his implements with him. He was a comic fellow indeed, a man of very good solid sense, and an excellent surgeon; but, what was worth all, very good-humoured and pleasant in his conversation, and a bold, stout, brave fellow too, as any we had among us.

I found William, as I thought, not very averse to go along with us, and yet resolved to do it so that it might be apparent he was taken away by force, and to this purpose he comes to me. "Friend," says he, "thou sayest I must go with thee, and it is not in my power to resist thee if I would; but I desire thou wilt oblige the master of the sloop which I am on board to certify under his hand, that I was taken away by force and against my will." And this he said with so much satisfaction in his face, that I could not but understand him. "Ay, ay," says I, "whether it be against your will or no, I'll make him and all the men give you a certificate of it, or I'll take them all along with us, and keep them till they do." So I drew up a certificate myself, wherein I wrote that he was taken away by main force, as a prisoner, by a pirate ship; that they carried away his chest and instruments first, and then bound his hands behind him and forced him into their boat; and this was signed by the master and all his men.

Accordingly I fell a-swearing at him, and called to my men to tie his hands behind him, and so we put him into our boat and carried him away. When I had him on board, I called him to me. "Now, friend," says I, "I have brought you away by force, it is true, but I am not of the opinion I have brought you away so much against your will as they imagine. Come," says I, "you will be a useful man to us, and you shall have very good usage among us." So I unbound his hands, and first ordered all things that belonged to him to be restored to him, and our captain gave him a dram.

"Thou hast dealt friendly by me," says he, "and I will be plain with thee, whether I came willingly to thee or not. I shall make myself as useful to thee as I can, but thou knowest it is not my business to meddle when thou art to fight." "No, no," says the captain, "but you may meddle a little when we share the money." "Those things are useful to furnish a surgeon's chest," says William, and smiled, "but I shall be moderate."

In short, William was a most agreeable companion; but he had the better of us in this part, that if we were taken we were sure to be hanged, and he was sure to escape; and he knew it well enough. But, in short, he was a sprightly fellow, and fitter to be captain than any of us. I shall have often an occasion to speak of him in the rest of the story.

Our cruising so long in these seas began now to be so well known, that not in England only, but in France and Spain, accounts had been made public of our adventures, and many stories told how we murdered the people in cold blood, tying them back to back, and throwing them into the sea; one half of which, however, was not true, though more was done than is fit to speak of here.

The consequence of this, however, was, that several English men-of-war were sent to the West Indies, and were particularly instructed to cruise in the Bay of Mexico, and the Gulf of Florida, and among the Bahama islands, if possible, to attack us. We were not so ignorant of things as not to expect this, after so long a stay in that part of the world; but the first certain account we had of them was at Honduras, when a vessel coming in from Jamaica told us that two English men-of-war were coming directly from Jamaica thither in quest of us. We were indeed as it were embayed, and could not have made the least shift to have got off, if they had come directly to us; but, as it happened, somebody had informed them that we were in the Bay of Campeachy, and they went directly thither, by which we were not only free of them, but were so much to the windward of them, that they could not make any attempt upon us, though they had known we were there.

We took this advantage, and stood away for Carthagena, and from thence with great difficulty beat it up at a distance from under the shore for St. Martha, till we came to the Dutch island of Curacoa, and from thence to the island of Tobago, which, as before, was our rendezvous; which, being a deserted, uninhabited island, we at the same time made use of for a retreat. Here the captain of the brigantine died, and Captain Harris, at that time my lieutenant, took the command of the brigantine.

Here we came to a resolution to go away to the coast of Brazil, and from thence to the Cape of Good Hope, and so for the East Indies; but Captain Harris, as I have said, being now captain of the brigantine, alleged that his ship was too small for so long a voyage, but that, if Captain Wilmot would consent, he would take the hazard of another cruise, and he would follow us in the first ship he could take. So we appointed our rendezvous to be at Madagascar, which was done by my recommendation of the place, and the plenty of provisions to be had there.

Accordingly, he went away from us in an evil hour; for, instead of taking a ship to follow us, he was taken, as I heard afterwards, by an English man-of-war, and being laid in irons, died of mere grief and anger before he came to England. His lieutenant, I have heard, was afterwards executed in England for a pirate; and this was the end of the man who first brought me into this unhappy trade.

We parted from Tobago three days after, bending our course for the coast of Brazil, but had not been at sea above twenty-four hours, when we were separated by a terrible storm, which held three days, with very little abatement or intermission. In this juncture Captain Wilmot happened, unluckily, to be on board my ship, to his great mortification; for we not only lost sight of his ship, but never saw her more till we came to Madagascar, where she was cast away. In short, after having in this tempest lost our fore-topmast, we were forced to put back to the isle of Tobago for shelter, and to repair our damage, which brought us all very near our destruction.

We were no sooner on shore here, and all very busy looking out for a piece of timber for a topmast, but we perceived standing in for the shore an English man-of-war of thirty-six guns. It was a great surprise to us indeed, because we were disabled so much; but, to our great good fortune, we lay pretty snug and close among the high rocks, and the man-of-war did not see us, but stood off again upon his cruise. So we only observed which way she went, and at night, leaving our work, resolved to stand off to sea, steering the contrary way from that which we observed she went; and this, we found, had the desired success, for we saw him no more. We had gotten an old mizzen-topmast on board, which made us a jury fore-topmast for the present; and so we stood away for the isle of Trinidad, where, though there were Spaniards on shore, yet we landed some men with our boat, and cut a very good piece of fir to make us a new topmast, which we got fitted up effectually; and also we got some cattle here to eke out our provisions; and calling a council of war among ourselves, we resolved to quit those seas for the present, and steer away for the coast of Brazil.

The first thing we attempted here was only getting fresh water, but we learnt that there lay the Portuguese fleet at the bay of All Saints, bound for Lisbon, ready to sail, and only waited for a fair wind. This made us lie by, wishing to see them put to sea, and, accordingly as they were with or without convoy, to attack or avoid them.

It sprung up a fresh gale in the evening at S.W. by W., which, being fair for the Portugal fleet, and the weather pleasant and agreeable, we heard the signal given to unmoor, and running in under the island of Si — -, we hauled our mainsail and foresail up in the brails, lowered the topsails upon the cap, and clewed them up, that we might lie as snug as we could, expecting their coming out, and the next morning saw the whole fleet come out accordingly, but not at all to our satisfaction, for they consisted of twenty-six sail, and most of them ships of force, as well as burthen, both merchantmen and men-of-war; so, seeing there was no meddling, we lay still where we were also, till the fleet was out of sight, and then stood off and on, in hopes of meeting with further purchase.

It was not long before we saw a sail, and immediately gave her chase; but she proved an excellent sailor, and, standing out to sea, we saw plainly she trusted to her heels — that is to say, to her sails. However, as we were a clean ship, we gained upon her, though slowly, and had we had a day before us, we should certainly have come up with her; but it grew dark apace, and in that case we knew we should lose sight of her.

Our merry Quaker, perceiving us to crowd still after her in the dark, wherein we could not see which way she went, came very dryly to me. "Friend Singleton," says he, "dost thee know what we are a-doing?" Says I, "Yes; why, we are chasing yon ship, are we not?" "And how dost thou know that?" says he, very gravely still. "Nay, that's true," says I again; "we cannot be sure." "Yes, friend," says he, "I think we may be sure that we are running away from her, not chasing her. I am afraid," adds he, "thou art turned Quaker, and hast resolved not to use the hand of power, or art a coward, and art flying from thy enemy."

"What do you mean?" says I (I think I swore at him). "What do you sneer at now? You have always one dry rub or another to give us."

"Nay," says he, "it is plain enough the ship stood off to sea due east, on purpose to lose us, and thou mayest be sure her business does not lie that way; for what should she do at the coast of Africa in this latitude, which should be as far south as Congo or Angola? But as soon as it is dark, that we would lose sight of her, she will tack and stand away west again for the Brazil coast and for the bay, where thou knowest she was going before; and are we not, then, running away from her? I am greatly in hopes, friend," says the dry, gibing creature, "thou wilt turn Quaker, for I see thou art not for fighting."

"Very well, William," says I; "then I shall make an excellent pirate." However, William was in the right, and I apprehended what he meant immediately; and Captain Wilmot, who lay very sick in his cabin, overhearing us, understood him as well as I, and called out to me that William was right, and it was our best way to change our course, and stand away for the bay, where it was ten to one but we should snap her in the morning.

Accordingly we went about-ship, got our larboard tacks on board, set the top-gallant sails, and crowded for the bay of All Saints, where we came to an anchor early in the morning, just out of gunshot of the forts; we furled our sails with rope-yarns, that we might haul home the sheets without going up to loose them, and, lowering our main and fore-yards, looked just as if we had lain there a good while.

In two hours afterwards we saw our game standing in for the bay with all the sail she could make, and she came innocently into our very mouths, for we lay still till we saw her almost within gunshot, when, our foremost gears being stretched fore and aft, we first ran up our yards, and then hauled home the topsail sheets, the rope-yarns that furled them giving way of themselves; the sails were set in a few minutes; at the same time slipping our cable, we came upon her before she could get under way upon the other tack. They were so surprised that they made little or no resistance, but struck after the first broadside.

We were considering what to do with her, when William came to me. "Hark thee, friend," says he, "thou hast made a fine piece of work of it now, hast thou not, to borrow thy neighbour's ship here just at thy neighbour's door, and never ask him leave? Now, dost thou not think there are some men-of-war in the port? Thou hast given them the alarm sufficiently; thou wilt have them upon thy back before night, depend upon it, to ask thee wherefore thou didst so."

"Truly, William," said I, "for aught I know, that may be true; what, then, shall we do next?" Says he, "Thou hast but two things to do: either to go in and take all the rest, or else get thee gone before they come out and take thee; for I see they are hoisting a topmast to yon great ship, in order to put to sea immediately, and they won't be long before they come to talk with thee, and what wilt thou say to them when they ask thee why thou borrowedst their ship without leave?"

As William said, so it was. We could see by our glasses they were all in a hurry, manning and fitting some sloops they had there, and a large man-of-war, and it was plain they would soon be with us. But we were not at a loss what to do; we found the ship we had taken was laden with nothing considerable for our purpose, except some cocoa, some sugar, and twenty barrels of flour; the rest of her cargo was hides; so we took out all we thought fit for our turn, and, among the rest, all her ammunition, great shot, and small-arms, and turned her off. We also took a cable and three anchors she had, which were for our purpose, and some of her sails. She had enough left just to carry her into port, and that was all.

Having done this, we stood on upon the Brazil coast, southward, till we came to the mouth of the river Janeiro. But as we had two days the wind blowing hard at S.E. and S.S.E., we were obliged to come to an anchor under a little island, and wait for a wind. In this time the Portuguese had, it seems, given notice over land to the governor there, that a pirate was upon the coast; so that, when we came in view of the port, we saw two men-of-war riding just without the bar, whereof one, we found, was getting under sail with all possible speed, having slipped her cable on purpose to speak with us; the other was not so forward, but was preparing to follow. In less than an hour they stood both fair after us, with all the sail they could make.

Had not the night come on, William's words had been made good; they would certainly have asked us the question what we did there, for we found the foremost ship gained upon us, especially upon one tack, for we plied away from them to windward; but in the dark losing sight of them, we resolved to change our course and stand away directly for sea, not doubting that we should lose them in the night.

Whether the Portuguese commander guessed we would do so or no, I know not; but in the morning, when the daylight appeared, instead of having lost him, we found him in chase of us about a league astern; only, to our great good fortune, we could see but one of the two. However, this one was a great ship, carried six-and-forty guns, and an admirable sailor, as appeared by her outsailing us; for our ship was an excellent sailor too, as I have said before.

When I found this, I easily saw there was no remedy, but we must engage; and as we knew we could expect no quarter from those scoundrels the Portuguese, a nation I had an original aversion to, I let Captain Wilmot know how it was. The captain, sick as he was, jumped up in the cabin, and would be led out upon the deck (for he was very weak) to see how it was. "Well," says he, "we'll fight them!"

Our men were all in good heart before, but to see the captain so brisk, who had lain ill of a calenture ten or eleven days, gave them double courage, and they went all hands to work to make a clear ship and be ready. William, the Quaker, comes to me with a kind of a smile. "Friend," says he, "what does yon ship follow us for?" "Why," says I, "to fight us, you may be sure." "Well," says he, "and will he come up with us, dost thou think?" "Yes," said I, "you see she will." "Why, then, friend," says the dry wretch, "why dost thou run from her still, when thou seest she will overtake thee? Will it be better for us to be overtaken farther off than here?" "Much as one for that," says I; "why, what would you have us do?" "Do!" says he; "let us not give the poor man more trouble than needs must; let us stay for him and hear what he has to say to us." "He will talk to us in powder and ball," said I. "Very well, then," says he, "if that be his country language, we must talk to him in the same, must we not? or else how shall he understand us?" "Very well, William," says I, "we understand you." And the captain, as ill as he was, called to me, "William's right again," says he; "as good here as a league farther." So he gives a word of command, "Haul up the main-sail; we'll shorten sail for him."

Accordingly we shortened sail, and as we expected her upon our lee-side, we being then upon our starboard tack, brought eighteen of our guns to the larboard side, resolving to give him a broadside that should warm him. It was about half-an-hour before he came up with us, all which time we luffed up, that we might keep the wind of him, by which he was obliged to run up under our lee, as we designed him; when we got him upon our quarter, we edged down, and received the fire of five or six of his guns. By this time you may be sure all our hands were at their quarters, so we clapped our helm hard a-weather, let go the lee-braces of the maintop sail, and laid it a-back, and so our ship fell athwart the Portuguese ship's hawse; then we immediately poured in our broadside, raking them fore and aft, and killed them a great many men.

The Portuguese, we could see, were in the utmost confusion; and not being aware of our design, their ship having fresh way, ran their bowsprit into the fore part of our main shrouds, as that they could not easily get clear of us, and so we lay locked after that manner. The enemy could not bring above five or six guns, besides their small-arms, to bear upon us, while we played our whole broadside upon him.

In the middle of the heat of this fight, as I was very busy upon the quarter-deck, the captain calls to me, for he never stirred from us, "What the devil is friend William a-doing yonder?" says the captain; "has he any business upon, deck?" I stepped forward, and there was friend William, with two or three stout fellows, lashing the ship's bowsprit fast to our mainmast, for fear they should get away from us; and every now and then he pulled a bottle out of his pocket, and gave the men a dram to encourage them. The shot flew about his ears as thick as may be supposed in such an action, where the Portuguese, to give them their due, fought very briskly, believing at first they were sure of their game, and trusting to their superiority; but there was William, as composed, and in as perfect tranquillity as to danger, as if he had been over a bowl of punch, only very busy securing the matter, that a ship of forty-six guns should not run away from a ship of eight-and-twenty.

This work was too hot to hold long; our men behaved bravely: our gunner, a gallant man, shouted below, pouring in his shot at such a rate, that the Portuguese began to slacken their fire; we had dismounted several of their guns by firing in at their forecastle, and raking them, as I said, fore and aft. Presently comes William up to me. "Friend," says he, very calmly, "what dost thou mean? Why dost thou not visit thy neighbour in the ship, the door being open for thee?" I understood him immediately, for our guns had so torn their hull, that we had beat two port-holes into one, and the bulk-head of their steerage was split to pieces, so that they could not retire to their close quarters; so I gave the word immediately to board them. Our second lieutenant, with about thirty men, entered in an instant over the forecastle, followed by some more with the boatswain, and cutting in pieces about twenty-five men that they found upon the deck, and then throwing some grenadoes into the steerage, they entered there also; upon which the Portuguese cried quarter presently, and we mastered the ship, contrary indeed to our own expectation; for we would have compounded with them if they would have sheered off: but laying them athwart the hawse at first, and following our fire furiously, without giving them any time to get clear of us and work their ship; by this means, though they had six-and-forty guns, they were not able to fight above five or six, as I said above, for we beat them immediately from their guns in the forecastle, and killed them abundance of men between decks, so that when we entered they had hardly found men enough to fight us hand to hand upon their deck.

The surprise of joy to hear the Portuguese cry quarter, and see their ancient struck, was so great to our captain, who, as I have said, was reduced very weak with a high fever, that it gave him new life. Nature conquered the distemper, and the fever abated that very night; so that in two or three days he was sensibly better, his strength began to come, and he was able to give his orders effectually in everything that was material, and in about ten days was entirely well and about the ship.

In the meantime I took possession of the Portuguese man-of-war; and Captain Wilmot made me, or rather I made myself, captain of her for the present. About thirty of their seamen took service with us, some of which were French, some Genoese; and we set the rest on shore the next day on a little island on the coast of Brazil, except some wounded men, who were not in a condition to be removed, and whom we were bound to keep on board; but we had an occasion afterwards to dispose of them at the Cape, where, at their own request, we set them on shore.

Captain Wilmot, as soon as the ship was taken, and the prisoners stowed, was for standing in for the river Janeiro again, not doubting but we should meet with the other man-of-war, who, not having been able to find us, and having lost the company of her comrade, would certainly be returned, and might be surprised by the ship we had taken, if we carried Portuguese colours; and our men were all for it.

But our friend William gave us better counsel, for he came to me, "Friend," says he, "I understand the captain is for sailing back to the Rio Janeiro, in hopes to meet with the other ship that was in chase of thee yesterday. Is it true, dost thou intend it?" "Why, yes," says I, "William, pray why not?" "Nay," says he, "thou mayest do so if thou wilt." "Well, I know that too, William," said I, "but the captain is a man will be ruled by reason; what have you to say to it?" "Why," says William gravely, "I only ask what is thy business, and the business of all the people thou hast with thee? Is it not to get money?" "Yes, William, it is so, in our honest way." "And wouldest thou," says he, "rather have money without fighting, or fighting without money? I mean which wouldest thou have by choice, suppose it to be left to thee?" "O William," says I, "the first of the two, to be sure." "Why, then," says he, "what great gain hast thou made of the prize thou hast taken now, though it has cost the lives of thirteen of thy men, besides some hurt? It is true thou hast got the ship and some prisoners; but thou wouldest have had twice the booty in a merchant-ship, with not one quarter of the fighting; and how dost thou know either what force or what number of men may be in the other ship, and what loss thou mayest suffer, and what gain it shall be to thee if thou take her? I think, indeed, thou mayest much better let her alone."

"Why, William, it is true," said I, "and I'll go tell the captain what your opinion is, and bring you word what he says." Accordingly in I went to the captain and told him William's reasons; and the captain was of his mind, that our business was indeed fighting when we could not help it, but that our main affair was money, and that with as few blows as we could. So that adventure was laid aside, and we stood along shore again south for the river De la Plata, expecting some purchase thereabouts; especially we had our eyes upon some of the Spanish ships from Buenos Ayres, which are generally very rich in silver, and one such prize would have done our business. We plied about here, in the latitude of —— —— south, for near a month, and nothing offered; and here we began to consult what we should do next, for we had come to no resolution yet. Indeed, my design was always for the Cape de Bona Speranza, and so to the East Indies. I had heard some flaming stories of Captain Avery, and the fine things he had done in the Indies, which were doubled and doubled, even ten thousand fold; and from taking a great prize in the Bay of Bengal, where he took a lady, said to be the Great Mogul's daughter, with a great quantity of jewels about her, we had a story told us, that he took a Mogul ship, so the foolish sailors called it, laden with diamonds.

I would fain have had friend William's advice whither we should go, but he always put it off with some quaking quibble or other. In short, he did not care for directing us neither; whether he made a piece of conscience of it, or whether he did not care to venture having it come against him afterwards or no, this I know not; but we concluded at last without him.

We were, however, pretty long in resolving, and hankered about the Rio de la Plata a long time. At last we spied a sail to windward, and it was such a sail as I believe had not been seen in that part of the world a great while. It wanted not that we should give it chase, for it stood directly towards us, as well as they that steered could make it; and even that was more accident of weather than anything else, for if the wind had chopped about anywhere they must have gone with it. I leave any man that is a sailor, or understands anything of a ship, to judge what a figure this ship made when we first saw her, and what we could imagine was the matter with her. Her maintop-mast was come by the board about six foot above the cap, and fell forward, the head of the topgallant-mast hanging in the fore-shrouds by the stay; at the same time the parrel of the mizzen-topsail-yard by some accident giving way, the mizzen-topsail-braces (the standing part of which being fast to the main-topsail shrouds) brought the mizzen-topsail, yard and all, down with it, which spread over part of the quarter-deck like an awning; the fore-topsail was hoisted up two-thirds of the mast, but the sheets were flown; the fore-yard was lowered down upon the forecastle, the sail loose, and part of it hanging overboard. In this manner she came down upon us with the wind quartering. In a word, the figure the whole ship made was the most confounding to men that understood the sea that ever was seen. She had no boat, neither had she any colours out.

When we came near to her, we fired a gun to bring her to. She took no notice of it, nor of us, but came on just as she did before. We fired again, but it was all one. At length we came within pistol-shot of one another, but nobody answered nor appeared; so we began to think that it was a ship gone ashore somewhere in distress, and the men having forsaken her, the high tide had floated her off to sea. Coming nearer to her, we ran up alongside of her so close that we could hear a noise within her, and see the motion of several people through her ports.

Upon this we manned out two boats full of men, and very well armed, and ordered them to board her at the same minute, as near as they could, and to enter one at her fore-chains on the one side, and the other amidships on the other side. As soon as they came to the ship's side, a surprising multitude of black sailors, such as they were, appeared upon deck, and, in short, terrified our men so much that the boat which was to enter her men in the waist stood off again, and durst not board her; and the men that entered out of the other boat, finding the first boat, as they thought, beaten off, and seeing the ship full of men, jumped all back again into their boat, and put off, not knowing what the matter was. Upon this we prepared to pour in a broadside upon her; but our friend William set us to rights again here; for it seems he guessed how it was sooner than we did, and coming up to me (for it was our ship that came up with her), "Friend," says he, "I am of opinion that thou art wrong in this matter, and thy men have been wrong also in their conduct. I'll tell thee how thou shalt take this ship, without making use of those things called guns." "How can that be, William?" said I. "Why," said he, "thou mayest take her with thy helm; thou seest they keep no steerage, and thou seest the condition they are in; board her with thy ship upon her lee quarter, and so enter her from the ship. I am persuaded thou wilt take her without fighting, for there is some mischief has befallen the ship, which we know nothing of."

In a word, it being a smooth sea, and little wind, I took his advice, and laid her aboard. Immediately our men entered the ship, where we found a large ship, with upwards of 600 Negroes, men and women, boys and girls, and not one Christian or white man on board.

I was struck with horror at the sight; for immediately I concluded, as was partly the case, that these black devils had got loose, had murdered all the white men, and thrown them into the sea; and I had no sooner told my mind to the men, but the thought so enraged them that I had much ado to keep my men from cutting them all in pieces. But William, with many persuasions, prevailed upon them, by telling them that it was nothing but what, if they were in the Negroes' condition, they would do if they could; and that the Negroes had really the highest injustice done them, to be sold for slaves without their consent; and that the law of nature dictated it to them; that they ought not to kill them, and that it would be willful murder to do it.

This prevailed with them, and cooled their first heat; so they only knocked down twenty or thirty of them, and the rest ran all down between decks to their first places, believing, as we fancied, that we were their first masters come again.

It was a most unaccountable difficulty we had next; for we could not make them understand one word we said, nor could we understand one word ourselves that they said. We endeavoured by signs to ask them whence they came; but they could make nothing of it. We pointed to the great cabin, to the round-house, to the cook-room, then to our faces, to ask if they had no white men on board, and where they were gone; but they could not understand what we meant. On the other hand, they pointed to our boat and to their ship, asking questions as well as they could, and said a thousand things, and expressed themselves with great earnestness; but we could not understand a word of it all, or know what they meant by any of their signs.

We knew very well they must have been taken on board the ship as slaves, and that it must be by some European people too. We could easily see that the ship was a Dutch-built ship, but very much altered, having been built upon, and, as we supposed, in France; for we found two or three French books on board, and afterwards we found clothes, linen, lace, some old shoes, and several other things. We found among the provisions some barrels of Irish beef, some Newfoundland fish, and several other evidences that there had been Christians on board, but saw no remains of them. We found not a sword, gun, pistol, or weapon of any kind, except some cutlasses; and the Negroes had hid them below where they lay. We asked them what was become of all the small-arms, pointing to our own and to the places where those belonging to the ship had hung. One of the Negroes understood me presently, and beckoned to me to come upon the deck, where, taking my fusée, which

I never let go out of my hand for some time after we had mastered the ship — I say, offering to take hold of it, he made the proper motion of throwing it into the sea; by which I understood, as I did afterwards, that they had thrown all the small-arms, powder, shot, swords, &c., into the sea, believing, as I supposed, those things would kill them, though the men were gone.

After we understood this we made no question but that the ship's crew, having been surprised by these desperate rogues, had gone the same way, and had been thrown overboard also. We looked all over the ship to see if we could find any blood, and we thought we did perceive some in several places; but the heat of the sun, melting the pitch and tar upon the decks, made it impossible for us to discern it exactly, except in the round-house, where we plainly saw that there had been much blood. We found the scuttle open, by which we supposed that the captain and those that were with him had made their retreat into the great cabin, or those in the cabin had made their escape up into the round-house.

But that which confirmed us most of all in what had happened was that, upon further inquiry, we found that there were seven or eight of the Negroes very much wounded, two or three of them with shot, whereof one had his leg broken and lay in a miserable condition, the flesh being mortified, and, as our friend William said, in two days more he would have died. William was a most dexterous surgeon, and he showed it in this cure; for though all the surgeons we had on board both our ships (and we had no less than five that called themselves bred surgeons, besides two or three who were pretenders or assistants) — though all these gave their opinions that the Negro's leg must be cut off, and that his life could not be saved without it; that the mortification had touched the marrow in the bone, that the tendons were mortified, and that he could never have the use of his leg if it should be cured, William said nothing in general, but that his opinion was otherwise, and that he desired the wound might be searched, and that he would then tell them further. Accordingly he went to work with the leg; and, as he desired that he might have some of the surgeons to assist him, we appointed him two of the ablest of them to help, and all of them to look on, if they thought fit.

William went to work his own way, and some of them pretended to find fault at first. However, he proceeded and searched every part of the leg where he suspected the mortification had touched it; in a word, he cut off a great deal of mortified flesh, in all which the poor fellow felt no pain. William proceeded till he brought the vessels which he had cut to bleed, and the man to cry out; then he reduced the splinters of the bone, and, calling for help, set it, as we call it, and bound it up, and laid the man to rest, who found himself much easier than before.

At the first opening the surgeons began to triumph; the mortification seemed to spread, and a long red streak of blood appeared from the wound upwards to the middle of the man's thigh, and the surgeons told me the man would die in a few hours. I went to look at it, and found William himself under some surprise; but when I asked him how long he thought the poor fellow could live, he looked gravely at me, and said, "As long as thou canst; I am not at all apprehensive of his life," said he, "but I would cure him, if I could, without making a cripple of him." I found he was not just then upon the operation as to his leg, but was mixing up something to give the poor creature, to repel, as I thought, the spreading contagion, and to abate or prevent any feverish temper that might happen in the blood; after which he went to work again, and opened the leg in two places above the wound, cutting out a great deal of mortified flesh, which it seemed was occasioned by the bandage, which had pressed the parts too much; and withal, the blood being at the time in a more than common disposition to mortify, might assist to spread it.

Well, our friend William conquered all this, cleared the spreading mortification, and the red streak went off again, the flesh began to heal, and matter to run; and in a few days the man's spirits began to recover, his pulse beat regular, he had no fever, and gathered strength daily; and, in a word, he was a perfect sound man in about ten weeks, and we kept him amongst us, and made him an able seaman. But to return to the ship: we never could come at a certain information about it, till some of the Negroes which we kept on board, and whom we taught to speak English, gave the account of it afterwards, and this maimed man in particular.

We inquired, by all the signs and motions we could imagine, what was become of the people, and yet we could get nothing from them. Our lieutenant was for torturing some of them to make them confess, but William opposed that vehemently; and when he heard it was under consideration he came to me. "Friend," says he, "I make a request to thee not to put any of these poor wretches to torment." "Why, William," said I, "why not? You see they will not give any account of what is become of the white men." "Nay," says William, "do not say so; I suppose they have given thee a full account of every particular of it." "How so?" says I; "pray what are we the wiser for all their jabbering?" "Nay," says William, "that may be thy fault, for aught I know; thou wilt not punish the poor men because they cannot speak English; and perhaps they never heard a word of English before. Now, I may very well suppose that they have given thee a large account of everything; for thou seest with what earnestness, and how long, some of them have talked to thee; and if thou canst not understand their language, nor they thine, how can they help that? At the best, thou dost but suppose that they have not told thee the whole truth of the story; and, on the contrary, I suppose they have; and how wilt thou decide the question, whether thou art right or whether I am right? Besides, what can they say to thee when thou askest them a question upon the torture, and at the same time they do not understand the question, and thou dost not know whether they say ay or no?"

It is no compliment to my moderation to say I was convinced by these reasons; and yet we had all much ado to keep our second lieutenant from murdering some of them, to make them tell. What if they had told? He did not understand one word of it; but he would not be persuaded but that the Negroes must needs understand him when he asked them whether the ship had any boat or no, like ours, and what was become of it.

But there was no remedy but to wait till we made these people understand English, and to adjourn the story till that time. The case was thus: where they were taken on board the ship, that we could never understand, because they never knew the English names which we give to those coasts, or what nation they were who belonged to the ship, because they knew not one tongue from another; but thus far the Negro I examined, who was the same whose leg William had cured, told us, that they did not speak the same language as we spoke, nor the same our Portuguese spoke; so that in all probability they must be French or Dutch.

Then he told us that the white men used them barbarously; that they beat them unmercifully; that one of the Negro men had a wife and two Negro children, one a daughter, about sixteen years old; that a white man abused the Negro man's wife, and afterwards his daughter, which, as he said, made all the Negro men mad; and that the woman's husband was in a great rage; at which the white man was so provoked that he threatened to kill him; but, in the night, the Negro man, being loose, got a great club, by which he made us understand he meant a handspike, and that when the same Frenchman (if it was a Frenchman) came among them again, he began again to abuse the Negro man's wife, at which the Negro, taking up the handspike, knocked his brains out at one blow; and then taking the key from him with which he usually unlocked the handcuffs which the Negroes were fettered with, he set about a hundred of them at liberty, who, getting up upon the deck by the same scuttle that the white men came down, and taking the man's cutlass who was killed, and laying hold of what came next them, they fell upon the men that were upon the deck, and killed them all, and afterwards those they found upon the forecastle; that the captain and his other men, who were in the cabin and the round-house, defended themselves with great courage, and shot out at the loopholes at them, by which he and several other men were wounded, and some killed; but that they broke into the round-house after a long dispute, where they killed two of the white men, but owned that the two white men killed eleven of their men before they could break in; and then the rest, having got down the scuttle into the great cabin, wounded three more of them.

That, after this, the gunner of the ship having secured himself in the gun-room, one of his men hauled up the long-boat close under the stern, and putting into her all the arms and ammunition they could come at, got all into the boat, and afterwards took in the captain, and those that were with him, out of the great cabin. When they were all thus embarked, they resolved to lay the ship aboard again, and try to recover it. That they boarded the ship in a desperate manner, and killed at first all that stood in their way; but the Negroes being by this time all loose, and having gotten some arms, though they understood nothing of powder and bullet, or guns, yet the men could never master them. However, they lay under the ship's bow, and got out all the men they had left in the cook-room, who had maintained themselves there, notwithstanding all the Negroes could do, and with their small-arms killed between thirty and forty of the Negroes, but were at last forced to leave them.

They could give me no account whereabouts this was, whether near the coast of Africa, or far off, or how long it was before the ship fell into our hands; only, in general, it was a great while ago, as they called it; and, by all we could learn, it was within two or three days after they had set sail from the coast. They told us that they had killed about thirty of the white men, having knocked them on the head with crows and handspikes, and such things as they could get; and one strong Negro killed three of them with an iron crow, after he was shot twice through the body; and that he was afterwards shot through the head by the captain himself at the door of the round-house, which he had split

729

open with the crow; and this we supposed was the occasion of the great quantity of blood which we saw at the round-house door.

The same Negro told us that they threw all the powder and shot they could find into the sea, and they would have thrown the great guns into the sea if they could have lifted them. Being asked how they came to have their sails in such a condition, his answer was, "They no understand; they no know what the sails do;" that was, they did not so much as know that it was the sails that made the ship go, or understand what they meant, or what to do with them. When we asked him whither they were going, he said they did not know, but believed they should go home to their own country again. I asked him, in particular, what he thought we were when we first came up with them? He said they were terribly frighted, believing we were the same white men that had gone away in their boats, and were come again in a great ship, with the two boats with them, and expected they would kill them all.

This was the account we got out of them, after we had taught them to speak English, and to understand the names and use of the things belonging to the ship which they had occasion to speak of; and we observed that the fellows were too innocent to dissemble in their relation, and that they all agreed in the particulars, and were always in the same story, which confirmed very much the truth of what they said.

Having taken this ship, our next difficulty was, what to do with the Negroes. The Portuguese in the Brazils would have bought them all of us, and been glad of the purchase, if we had not showed ourselves enemies there, and been known for pirates; but, as it was, we durst not go ashore anywhere thereabouts, or treat with any of the planters, because we should raise the whole country upon us; and, if there were any such things as men-of-war in any of their ports, we should be as sure to be attacked by them, and by all the force they had by land or sea.

Nor could we think of any better success if we went northward to our own plantations. One while we determined to carry them all away to Buenos Ayres, and sell them there to the Spaniards; but they were really too many for them to make use of; and to carry them round to the South Seas, which was the only remedy that was left, was so far that we should be no way able to subsist them for so long a voyage.

At last, our old, never-failing friend, William, helped us out again, as he had often done at a dead lift. His proposal was this, that he should go as master of the ship, and about twenty men, such as we could best trust, and attempt to trade privately, upon the coast of

Brazil, with the planters, not at the principal ports, because that would not be admitted.

We all agreed to this, and appointed to go away ourselves towards the Rio de la Plata, where we had thought of going before, and to wait for him, not there, but at Port St Pedro, as the Spaniards call it, lying at the mouth of the river which they call Rio Grande, and where the Spaniards had a small fort and a few people, but we believe there was nobody in it.

Here we took up our station, cruising off and on, to see if we could meet any ships going to or coming from the Buenos Ayres or the Rio de la Plata; but we met with nothing worth notice. However, we employed ourselves in things necessary for our going off to sea; for we filled all our water-casks, and got some fish for our present use, to spare as much as possible our ship's stores.

William, in the meantime, went away to the north, and made the land about the Cape de St Thomas; and betwixt that and the isles De Tuberon he found means to trade with the planters for all his Negroes, as well the women as the men, and at a very good price too; for William, who spoke Portuguese pretty well, told them a fair story enough, that the ship was in scarcity of provisions, that they were driven a great way out of their way, and indeed, as we say, out of their knowledge, and that they must go up to the northward as far as Jamaica, or sell there upon the coast. This was a very plausible tale, and was easily believed; and, if you observe the manner of the Negroes' sailing, and what happened in their voyage, was every word of it true.

By this method, and being true to one another, William passed for what he was — I mean, for a very honest fellow; and by the assistance of one planter, who sent to some of his neighbour planters, and managed the trade among themselves, he got a quick market; for in less than five weeks William sold all his Negroes, and at last sold the ship itself, and shipped himself and his twenty men, with two Negro boys whom he had left, in a sloop, one of those which the planters used to send on board for the Negroes. With this sloop Captain William, as we then called him, came away, and found us at Port St Pedro, in the latitude of 32 degrees 30 minutes south.

Nothing was more surprising to us than to see a sloop come along the coast, carrying Portuguese colours, and come in directly to us, after we were assured he had discovered both our ships. We fired a gun, upon her nearer approach, to bring her to an anchor, but immediately she fired five guns by way of salute, and spread her English ancient.

Then we began to guess it was friend William, but wondered what was the meaning of his being in a sloop, whereas we sent him away in a ship of near 300 tons; but he soon let us into the whole history of his management, with which we had a great deal of reason to be very well satisfied. As soon as he had brought the sloop to an anchor, he came aboard of my ship, and there he gave us an account how he began to trade by the help of a Portuguese planter, who lived near the seaside; how he went on shore and went up to the first house he could see, and asked the man of the house to sell him some hogs, pretending at first he only stood in upon the coast to take in fresh water and buy some provisions; and the man not only sold him seven fat hogs, but invited him in, and gave him, and five men he had with him, a very good dinner; and he invited the planter on board his ship, and, in return for his kindness, gave him a Negro girl for his wife.

This so obliged the planter that the next morning he sent him on board, in a great luggage-boat, a cow and two sheep, with a chest of sweetmeats and some sugar, and a great bag of tobacco, and invited Captain William on shore again; that, after this, they grew from one kindness to another; that they began to talk about trading for some Negroes; and William, pretending it was to do him service, consented to sell him thirty Negroes for his private use in his plantation, for which he gave William ready money in gold, at the rate of five-and-thirty moidores per head; but the planter was obliged to use great caution in the bringing them on shore; for which purpose he made William weigh and stand out to sea, and put in again, about fifty miles farther north, where at a little creek he took the Negroes on shore at another plantation, being a friend's of his, whom, it seems, he could trust.

This remove brought William into a further intimacy, not only with the first planter, but also with his friends, who desired to have some of the Negroes also; so that, from one to another, they bought so many, till one overgrown planter took 100 Negroes, which was all William had left, and sharing them with another planter, that other planter chaffered with William for ship and all, giving him in exchange a very clean, large, well-built sloop of near sixty tons, very well furnished, carrying six guns; but we made her afterwards carry twelve guns. William had 300 moidores of gold, besides the sloop, in payment for the ship; and with this money he stored the sloop as full as she could hold with provisions, especially bread, some pork, and about sixty hogs alive; among the rest, William got eighty barrels of good gunpowder, which was very much for our purpose; and all the provisions which were in the French ship he took out also.

This was a very agreeable account to us, especially when we saw that William had received in gold coined, or by weight, and some Spanish silver, 60,000 pieces of eight, besides a new sloop, and a vast quantity of provisions.

We were very glad of the sloop in particular, and began to consult what we should do, whether we had not best turn off our great Portuguese ship, and stick to our first ship and the sloop, seeing we had scarce men enough for all three, and that the biggest ship was thought too big for our business. However, another dispute, which was now decided, brought the first to a conclusion. The first dispute was, whither we should go. My comrade, as I called him now, that is to say, he that was my captain before we took this Portuguese man-of-war, was for going to the South Seas, and coasting up the west side of America, where we could not fail of making several good prizes upon the Spaniards; and that then, if occasion required it, we might come home by the South Seas to the East Indies, and so go round the globe, as others had done before us.

But my head lay another way. I had been in the East Indies, and had entertained a notion ever since that, if we went thither, we could not fail of making good work of it, and that we might have a safe retreat, and good beef to victual our ship, among my old friends the natives of Zanzibar, on the coast of Mozambique, or the island of St Lawrence. I say, my thoughts lay this way; and I read so many lectures to them all of the advantages they would certainly make of their strength by the prizes they would take in the Gulf of Mocha, or the Red Sea, and on the coast of Malabar, or the Bay of Bengal, that I amazed them.

With these arguments I prevailed on them, and we all resolved to steer away S.E. for the Cape of Good Hope; and, in consequence of this resolution, we concluded to keep the sloop, and sail with all three, not doubting, as I assured them, but we should find men there to make up the number wanting, and if not, we might cast any of them off when we pleased.

We could do no less than make our friend William captain of the sloop which, with such good management, he had brought us. He told us, though with much good manners, he would not command her as a frigate; but, if we would give her to him for his share of the Guinea ship, which we came very honestly by, he would keep us company as a victualer, if we commanded him, as long as he was under the same force that took him away.

We understood him, so gave him the sloop, but upon condition that he should not go from us, and should be entirely under our command. However, William was not so easy as before; and, indeed, as we afterwards wanted the sloop to cruise for purchase, and a right thorough-paced pirate in her, so I was in such pain for William that I could not be without him, for he was my privy counselor and companion upon all occasions; so I put a Scotsman, a bold, enterprising, gallant fellow, into her, named Gordon, and made her carry twelve guns and four petereroes, though, indeed, we wanted men, for we were none of us manned in proportion to our force.

We sailed away for the Cape of Good Hope the beginning of October 1706, and passed by, in sight of the Cape, the 12th of November following, having met with a great deal of bad weather. We saw several merchant-ships in the roads there, as well English as Dutch, whether outward bound or homeward we could not tell; be it what it would, we did not think fit to come to an anchor, not knowing what they might be, or what they might attempt against us, when they knew what we were. However, as we wanted fresh water, we sent the two boats belonging to the Portuguese man-of-war, with all Portuguese seamen or Negroes in them, to the watering-place, to take in water; and in the meantime we hung out a Portuguese ancient at sea, and lay by all that night. They knew not what we were, but it seems we passed for anything but really what we was.

Our boats returning the third time loaden, about five o'clock next morning, we thought ourselves sufficiently watered, and stood away to the eastward; but, before our men returned the last time, the wind blowing an easy gale at west, we perceived a boat in the grey of the morning under sail, crowding to come up with us, as if they were afraid we should be gone. We soon found it was an English long-boat, and that it was pretty full of men. We could not imagine what the meaning of it should be; but, as it was but a boat, we thought there could be no great harm in it to let them come on board; and if it appeared they came only to inquire who we were, we would give them a full account of our business, by taking them along with us, seeing we wanted men as much as anything. But they saved us the labour of being in doubt how to dispose of them; for it seems our Portuguese seamen, who went for water, had not been so silent at the watering-places as we thought they would have been. But the case, in short, was this: Captain — — (I

734

forbear his name at present, for a particular reason), captain of an East India merchant-ship, bound afterwards for China, had found some reason to be very severe with his men, and had handled some of them very roughly at St Helena; insomuch, that they threatened among themselves to leave the ship the first opportunity, and had long wished for that opportunity. Some of these men, it seems, had met with our boat at the watering-place, and inquiring of one another who we were, and upon what account, whether the Portuguese seamen, by faltering in their account, made them suspect that we were out upon the cruise, or whether they told it in plain English or no (for they all spoke English enough to be understood), but so it was, that as soon as ever the men carried the news on board, that the ships which lay by to the eastward were English, and that they were going upon the *account*, which, by they way, was a sea term for a pirate; I say, as soon as ever they heard it, they went to work, and getting all things ready in the night, their chests and clothes, and whatever else they could, they came away before it was day, and came up with us about seven o'clock.

When they came by the ship's side which I commanded we hailed them in the usual manner, to know what and who they were, and what their business. They answered they were Englishmen, and desired to come on board. We told them they might lay the ship on board, but ordered they should let only one man enter the ship till the captain knew their business, and that he should come without any arms. They said, Ay, with all their hearts.

We presently found their business, and that they desired to go with us; and as for their arms, they desired we would send men on board the boat, and that they would deliver them all to us, which was done. The fellow that came up to me told me how they had been used by their captain, how he had starved the men, and used them like dogs, and that, if the rest of the men knew they should be admitted, he was satisfied two-thirds of them would leave the ship. We found the fellows were very hearty in their resolution, and jolly brisk sailors they were; so I told them I would do nothing without our admiral, that was the captain of the other ship; so I sent my pinnace on board Captain Wilmot, to desire him to come on board. But he was indisposed, and being to leeward, excused his coming, but left it all to me; but before my boat was returned, Captain Wilmot called to me by his speaking-trumpet, which all the men might hear as well as I; thus, calling me by my name, "I hear they are honest fellows; pray tell them they are all welcome, and make them a bowl of punch."

735

As the men heard it as well as I, there was no need to tell them what the captain said; and, as soon as the trumpet had done, they set up a huzza, that showed us they were very hearty in their coming to us; but we bound them to us by a stronger obligation still after this, for when we came to Madagascar, Captain Wilmot, with consent of all the ship's company, ordered that these men should have as much money given them out of the stock as was due to them for their pay in the ship they had left; and after that we allowed them twenty pieces of eight a man bounty money; and thus we entered them upon shares, as we were all, and brave stout fellows they were, being eighteen in number, whereof two were midshipmen, and one a carpenter.

It was the 28th of November, when, having had some bad weather, we came to an anchor in the road off St Augustine Bay, at the south-west end of my old acquaintance the isle of Madagascar. We lay here awhile and trafficked with the natives for some good beef; though the weather was so hot that we could not promise ourselves to salt any of it up to keep; but I showed them the way which we practiced before, to salt it first with saltpetre, then cure it by drying it in the sun, which made it eat very agreeably, though not so wholesome for our men, that not agreeing with our way of cooking, viz., boiling with pudding, brewis, &c., and particularly this way, would be too salt, and the fat of the meat be rusty, or dried away so as not to be eaten.

This, however, we could not help, and made ourselves amends by feeding heartily on the fresh beef while we were there, which was excellent, good and fat, every way as tender and as well relished as in England, and thought to be much better to us who had not tasted any in England for so long a time.

Having now for some time remained here, we began to consider that this was not a place for our business; and I, that had some views a particular way of my own, told them that this was not a station for those who looked for purchase; that there were two parts of the island which were particularly proper for our purposes; first, the bay on the east side of the island, and from thence to the island Mauritius, which was the usual way which ships that came from the Malabar coast, or the coast of Coromandel, Fort St George, &c., used to take, and where, if we waited for them, we ought to take our station.

But, on the other hand, as we did not resolve to fall upon the European traders, who were generally ships of force and well manned, and where blows must be looked for; so I had another prospect, which I promised myself would yield equal profit, or perhaps greater, without any of the hazard and difficulty of the former; and this was the Gulf of Mocha, or the Red Sea.

I told them that the trade here was great, the ships rich, and the Strait of Babelmandel narrow; so that there was no doubt but we might cruise so as to let nothing slip our hands, having the seas open from the Red Sea, along the coast of Arabia, to the Persian Gulf, and the Malabar side of the Indies.

I told them what I had observed when I sailed round the island in my former progress; how that, on the northernmost point of the island, there were several very good harbours and roads for our ships; that the natives were even more civil and tractable, if possible, than those where we were, not having been so often ill-treated by European sailors as those had in the south and east sides; and that we might always be sure of a retreat, if we were driven to put in by any necessity, either of enemies or weather.

They were easily convinced of the reasonableness of my scheme; and Captain Wilmot, whom I now called our admiral, though he was at first of the mind to go and lie at the island Mauritius, and wait for some of the European merchant-ships from the road of Coromandel, or the Bay of Bengal, was now of my mind. It is true we were strong enough to have attacked an English East India ship of the greatest force, though some of them were said to carry fifty guns; but I represented to him that we were sure to have blows and blood if we took them; and, after we had done, their loading was not of equal value to us, because we had no room to dispose of their merchandise; and, as our circumstances stood, we had rather have taken one outward-bound East India ship, with her ready cash on board, perhaps to the value of forty or fifty thousand pounds, than three homeward-bound, though their loading would at London be worth three times the money, because we knew not whither to go to dispose of the cargo; whereas the ships from London had abundance of things we knew how to make use of besides their money, such as their stores of provisions and liquors, and great quantities of the like sent to the governors and factories at the English settlements for their use; so that, if we resolved to look for our own country ships, it should be those that were outward-bound, not the London ships homeward.

All these things considered, brought the admiral to be of my mind entirely; so, after taking in water and some fresh provisions where we lay, which was near Cape St Mary, on the south-west corner of the island, we weighed and stood away south, and afterwards S.S.E., to

737

round the island, and in about six days' sail got out of the wake of the island, and steered away north, till we came off Port Dauphin, and then north by east, to the latitude of 13 degrees 40 minutes, which was, in short, just at the farthest part of the island; and the admiral, keeping ahead, made the open sea fair to the west, clear of the whole island; upon which he brought to, and we sent a sloop to stand in round the farthest point north, and coast along the shore, and see for a harbour to put into, which they did, and soon brought us an account that there was a deep bay, with a very good road, and several little islands, under which they found good riding, in ten to seventeen fathom water, and accordingly there we put in.

However, we afterwards found occasion to remove our station, as you shall hear presently. We had now nothing to do but go on shore, and acquaint ourselves a little with the natives, take in fresh water and some fresh provisions, and then to sea again. We found the people very easy to deal with, and some cattle they had; but it being at the extremity of the island, they had not such quantities of cattle here. However, for the present we resolved to appoint this for our place of rendezvous, and go and look out. This was about the latter end of April.

Accordingly we put to sea, and cruised away to the northward, for the Arabian coast. It was a long run, but as the winds generally blow trade from the S. and S.S.E. from May to September, we had good weather; and in about twenty days we made the island of Socotra, lying south from the Arabian coast, and E.S.E. from the mouth of the Gulf of Mocha, or the Red Sea.

Here we took in water, and stood off and on upon the Arabian shore. We had not cruised here above three days, or thereabouts, but I spied a sail, and gave her chase; but when we came up with her, never was such a poor prize chased by pirates that looked for booty, for we found nothing in her but poor, half-naked Turks, going a pilgrimage to Mecca, to the tomb of their prophet Mahomet. The junk that carried them had no one thing worth taking away but a little rice and some coffee, which was all the poor wretches had for their subsistence; so we let them go, for indeed we knew not what to do with them.

The same evening we chased another junk with two masts, and in something better plight to look at than the former. When we came on board we found them upon the same errand, but only that they were people of some better fashion than the other; and here we got some plunder, some Turkish stores, a few diamonds in the ear-drops of five or six persons, some fine Persian carpets, of which they made their saffras to lie upon, and some money; so we let them go also.

We continued here eleven days longer, and saw nothing but now and then a fishing-boat; but the twelfth day of our cruise we spied a ship: indeed I thought at first it had been an English ship, but it appeared to be an European freighted for a voyage from Goa, on the coast of Malabar, to the Red Sea, and was very rich. We chased her, and took her without any fight, though they had some guns on board too, but not many. We found her manned with Portuguese seamen, but under the direction of five merchant Turks, who had hired her on the coast of Malabar of some Portugal merchants, and had laden her with pepper, saltpetre, some spices, and the rest of the loading was chiefly calicoes and wrought silks, some of them very rich.

We took her and carried her to Socotra; but we really knew not what to do with her, for the same reasons as before; for all their goods were of little or no value to us. After some days we found means to let one of the Turkish merchants know, that if he would ransom the ship we would take a sum of money and let them go. He told me that if I would let one of them go on shore for the money they would do it; so we adjusted the value of the cargo at 30,000 ducats. Upon this agreement, we allowed the sloop to carry him on shore, at Dofar, in Arabia, where a rich merchant laid down the money for them, and came off with our sloop; and on payment of the money we very fairly and honestly let them go.

Some days after this we took an Arabian junk, going from the Gulf of Persia to Mocha, with a good quantity of pearl on board. We gutted him of the pearl, which it seems was belonging to some merchants at Mocha, and let him go, for there was nothing else worth our taking.

We continued cruising up and down here till we began to find our provisions grow low, when Captain Wilmot, our admiral, told us it was time to think of going back to the rendezvous; and the rest of the men said the same, being a little weary of beating about for above three months together, and meeting with little or nothing compared to our great expectations; but I was very loth to part with the Red Sea at so cheap a rate, and pressed them to tarry a little longer, which at my instance they did; but three days afterwards, to our great misfortune, understood that, by landing the Turkish merchants at Dofar, we had alarmed the coast as far as the Gulf of Persia, so that no vessel would stir that way, and consequently nothing was to be expected on that side.

I was greatly mortified at this news, and could no longer withstand the importunities of the men to return to Madagascar. However, as the wind continued still to blow at S.S.E. by S., we were obliged to stand away towards the coast of Africa and the Cape Guardafui, the winds being more variable under the shore than in the open sea.

Here we chopped upon a booty which we did not look for, and which made amends for all our waiting; for the very same hour that we made land we spied a large vessel sailing along the shore to the southward. The ship was of Bengal, belonging to the Great Mogul's country, but had on board a Dutch pilot, whose name, if I remember right, was Vandergest, and several European seamen, whereof three were English. She was in no condition to resist us. The rest of her seamen were Indians of the Mogul's subjects, some Malabars and some others. There were five Indian merchants on board, and some Armenians. It seems they had been at Mocha with spices, silks, diamonds, pearls, calico, &c., such goods as the country afforded, and had little on board now but money in pieces of eight, which, by the way, was just what we wanted; and the three English seamen came along with us, and the Dutch pilot would have done so too, but the two Armenian merchants entreated us not to take him, for that he being their pilot, there was none of the men knew how to guide the ship; so, at their request, we refused him; but we made them promise he should not be used ill for being willing to go with us.

We got near 200,000 pieces of eight in this vessel; and, if they said true, there was a Jew of Goa, who intended to have embarked with them, who had 200,000 pieces of eight with him, all his own; but his good fortune, springing out of his ill fortune, hindered him, or he fell sick at Mocha, and could not be ready to travel, which was the saving of his money.

There was none with me at the taking this prize but the sloop, for Captain Wilmot's ship proving leaky, he went away for the rendezvous before us, and arrived there the middle of December; but not liking the port, he left a great cross on shore, with directions written on a plate of lead fixed to it, for us to come after him to the great bays at Mangahelly, where he found a very good harbour; but we learned a piece of news here that kept us from him a great while, which the admiral took offence at; but we stopped his mouth with his share of 200,000 pieces of eight to him and his ship's crew. But the story which interrupted our coming to him was this. Between Mangahelly and another point, called Cape St Sebastian, there came on shore in the night an European ship, and whether by stress of weather or want of a pilot I know not, but the ship stranded and could not be got off.

We lay in the cove or harbour, where, as I have said, our rendezvous was appointed, and had not yet been on shore, so we had not seen the directions our admiral had left for us.

Our friend William, of whom I have said nothing a great while, had a great mind one day to go on shore, and importuned me to let him have a little troop to go with him, for safety, that they might see the country. I was mightily against it for many reasons; but particularly I told him he knew the natives were but savages, and they were very treacherous, and I desired him that he would not go; and, had he gone on much farther, I believe I should have downright refused him, and commanded him not to go.

But, in order to persuade me to let him go, he told me he would give me an account of the reason why he was so importunate. He told me, the last night he had a dream, which was so forcible, and made such an impression upon his mind, that he could not be quiet till he had made the proposal to me to go; and if I refused him, then he thought his dream was significant; and if not, then his dream was at an end.

His dream was, he said, that he went on shore with thirty men, of which the coxswain, he said, was one, upon the island; and that they found a mine of gold, and enriched them all. But this was not the main thing, he said, but that the same morning he had dreamed so, the coxswain came to him just then, and told him that he dreamed he went on shore on the island of Madagascar, and that some men came to him and told him they would show him where he should get a prize which would make them all rich.

These two things put together began to weigh with me a little, though I was never inclined to give any heed to dreams; but William's importunity turned me effectually, for I always put a great deal of stress upon his judgment; so that, in short, I gave them leave to go, but I charged them not to go far off from the sea-coast; that, if they were forced down to the seaside upon any occasion, we might perhaps see them, and fetch them off with our boats.

They went away early in the morning, one-and-thirty men of them in number, very well armed, and very stout fellows; they traveled all the day, and at night made us a signal that all was well, from the top of a hill, which we had agreed on, by making a great fire.

Next day they marched down the hill on the other side, inclining towards the seaside, as they had promised, and saw a very pleasant valley before them, with a river in the middle of it, which, a little farther below them, seemed to be big enough to bear small ships; they marched apace towards this river, and were surprised with the noise of a piece going off, which, by the sound, could not be far off. They listened long, but could hear no more; so they went on to the river-side, which was a very fine fresh stream, but widened apace, and they kept on by the banks of it, till, almost at once, it opened or widened into a good large creek or harbour, about five miles from the sea; and that which was still more surprising, as they marched forward, they plainly saw in the mouth of the harbour, or creek, the wreck of a ship.

The tide was up, as we call it, so that it did net appear very much above the water, but, as they made downwards, they found it grow bigger and bigger; and the tide soon after ebbing out, they found it lay dry upon the sands, and appeared to be the wreck of a considerable vessel, larger than could be expected in that country.

After some time, William, taking out his glass to look at it more nearly, was surprised with hearing a musket-shot whistle by him, and immediately after that he heard the gun, and saw the smoke from the other side; upon which our men immediately fired three muskets, to discover, if possible, what or who they were. Upon the noise of these guns, abundance of men came running down to the shore from among the trees; and our men could easily perceive that they were Europeans, though they knew not of what nation; however, our men hallooed to them as loud as they could, and by-and-by they got a long pole, and set it up, and hung a white shirt upon it for a flag of truce. They on the other side saw it, by the help of their glasses, too, and quickly after our men see a boat launch off from the shore, as they thought, but it was from another creek, it seems; and immediately they came rowing over the creek to our men, carrying also a white flag as a token of truce.

It is not easy to describe the surprise, or joy and satisfaction, that appeared on both sides, to see not only white men, but Englishmen, in a place so remote; but what then must it be when they came to know one another, and to find that they were not only countrymen but comrades, and that this was the very ship that Captain Wilmot, our admiral, commanded, and whose company we had lost in the storm at Tobago, after making an agreement to rendezvous at Madagascar!

They had, it seems, got intelligence of us when they came to the south part of the island, and had been a-roving as far as the Gulf of Bengal, when they met Captain Avery, with whom they joined, took several rich prizes, and, amongst the rest, one ship with the Great

Mogul's daughter, and an immense treasure in money and jewels; and from thence they came about the coast of Coromandel, and afterwards that of Malabar, into the Gulf of Persia, where they also took some prize, and then designed for the south part of Madagascar; but the winds blowing hard at S.E. and S.E. by E., they came to the northward of the isle, and being after that separated by a furious tempest from the N.W., they were forced into the mouth of that creek, where they lost their ship. And they told us, also, that they heard that Captain Avery himself had lost his ship also not far off.

When they had thus acquainted one another with their fortunes, the poor overjoyed men were in haste to go back to communicate their joy to their comrades; and, leaving some of their men with ours, the rest went back, and William was so earnest to see them that he and two more went back with them, and there he came to their little camp where they lived. There were about a hundred and sixty men of them in all; they had got their guns on shore, and some ammunition, but a good deal of their powder was spoiled; however, they had raised a fair platform, and mounted twelve pieces of cannon upon it, which was a sufficient defence to them on that side of the sea; and just at the end of the platform they had made a launch and a little yard, and were all hard at work, building another little ship, as I may call it, to go to sea in; but they put a stop to this work upon the news they had of our being come in.

When our men went into their huts, it was surprising, indeed, to see the vast stock of wealth they had got, in gold and silver and jewels, which, however, they told us was a trifle to what Captain Avery had, wherever he was gone.

It was five days we had waited for our men, and no news of them; and indeed I gave them over for lost, but was surprised, after five days' waiting, to see a ship's boat come rowing towards us along shore. What to make of it I could not tell, but was at least better satisfied when our men told me they heard them halloo and saw them wave their caps to us.

In a little time they came quite up to us; and I saw friend William stand up in the boat and make signs to us; so they came on board; but when I saw there were but fifteen of our one-and-thirty men, I asked him what had become of their fellows. "Oh," says William, "they are all very well; and my dream is fully made good, and the coxswain's too."

This made me very impatient to know how the case stood; so he told us the whole story, which indeed surprised us all. The next day we weighed, and stood away southerly to join Captain Wilmot and ship at Mangahelly, where we found him, as I said, a little chagrined at our stay; but we pacified him afterwards with telling him the history of William's dream, and the consequence of it.

In the meantime the camp of our comrades was so near Mangahelly, that our admiral and I, friend William, and some of the men, resolved to take the sloop and go and see them, and fetch them all, and their goods, bag and baggage, on board our ship, which accordingly we did, and found their camp, their fortifications, the battery of guns they had erected, their treasure, and all the men, just as William had related it; so, after some stay, we took all the men into the sloop, and brought them away with us.

It was some time before we knew what was become of Captain Avery; but after about a month, by the direction of the men who had lost their ship, we sent the sloop to cruise along the shore, to find out, if possible, where they were; and in about a week's cruise our men found them, and particularly that they had lost their ship, as well as our men had lost theirs, and that they were every way in as bad a condition as ours.

It was about ten days before the sloop returned, and Captain Avery with them; and this was the whole force that, as I remember, Captain Avery ever had with him; for now we joined all our companies together, and it stood thus: — We had two ships and a sloop, in which we had 320 men, but much too few to man them as they ought to be, the great Portuguese ship requiring of herself near 400 men to man her completely. As for our lost, but now found comrade, her complement of men was 180, or thereabouts; and Captain Avery had about 300 men with him, whereof he had ten carpenters with him, most of which were taken aboard the prize they had taken; so that, in a word, all the force Avery had at Madagascar, in the year 1699, or thereabouts, amounted to our three ships, for his own was lost, as you have heard; and never had any more than about 1200 men in all.

It was about a month after this that all our crews got together, and as Avery was unshipped, we all agreed to bring our own company into the Portuguese man-of-war and the sloop, and give Captain Avery the Spanish frigate, with all the tackles and furniture, guns and ammunition, for his crew by themselves; for which they, being full of wealth, agreed to give us 40,000 pieces of eight.

It was next considered what course we should take. Captain Avery, to give him his due, proposed our building a little city here, establishing ourselves on shore, with a good fortification and works proper to defend ourselves; and that, as we had wealth enough, and could increase it to what degree we pleased, we should content ourselves to retire here, and bid defiance to the world. But I soon convinced him that this place would be no security to us, if we pretended to carry on our cruising trade; for that then all the nations of Europe, and indeed of that part of the world, would be engaged to root us out; but if we resolved to live there as in retirement, and plant in the country as private men, and give over our trade of pirating, then, indeed, we might plant and settle ourselves where we pleased. But then, I told him, the best way would be to treat with the natives, and buy a tract of land of them farther up the country, seated upon some navigable river, where boats might go up and down for pleasure, but not ships to endanger us; that thus planting the high ground with cattle, such as cows and goats, of which the country also was full, to be sure we might live here as well as any men in the world; and I owned to him I thought it was a good retreat for those that were willing to leave off and lay down, and yet did not care to venture home and be hanged; that is to say, to run the risk of it.

Captain Avery, however he made no positive discovery of his intentions, seemed to me to decline my notion of going up into the country to plant; on the contrary, it was apparent he was of Captain Wilmot's opinion, that they might maintain themselves on shore, and yet carry on their cruising trade too; and upon this they resolved. But, as I afterwards understood, about fifty of their men went up the country, and settled themselves in an inland place as a colony. Whether they are there still or not, I cannot tell, or how many of them are left alive; but it is my opinion they are there still, and that they are considerably increased, for, as I hear, they have got some women among them, though not many; for it seems five Dutch women and three or four little girls were taken by them in a Dutch ship, which they afterwards took going to Mocha; and three of those women, marrying some of these men, went with them to live in their new plantation. But of this I speak only by hearsay.

As we lay here some time, I found our people mightily divided in their notions; some were for going this way, and some that, till at last I began to foresee they would part company, and perhaps we should not have men enough to keep together to man the great ship; so I took Captain Wilmot aside, and began to talk to him about it, but soon perceived that he inclined himself to stay at Madagascar, and having got a vast wealth for his own share, had secret designs of getting home some way or other.

I argued the impossibility of it, and the hazard he would run, either of falling into the hands of thieves and murderers in the Red Sea, who would never let such a treasure as his pass their hands, or of his falling into the hands of the English, Dutch, or French, who would certainly hang him for a pirate. I gave him an account of the voyage I had made from this very place to the continent of Africa, and what a journey it was to travel on foot.

In short, nothing could persuade him, but he would go into the Red Sea with the sloop, and where the children of Israel passed through the sea dry-shod, and, landing there, would travel to Grand Cairo by land, which is not above eighty miles, and from thence he said he could ship himself, by the way of Alexandria, to any part of the world.

I represented the hazard, and indeed the impossibility, of his passing by Mocha and Jiddah without being attacked, if he offered it by force, or plundered, if he went to get leave; and explained the reasons of it so much and so effectually, that, though at last he would not hearken to it himself, none of his men would go with him. They told him they would go anywhere with him to serve him, but that this was running himself and them into certain destruction, without any possibility of avoiding it, or probability of answering his end. The captain took what I said to him quite wrong, and pretended to resent it, and gave me some buccaneer words upon it; but I gave him no return to it but this: that I advised him for his advantage; that if he did not understand it so, it was his fault, not mine; that I did not forbid him to go, nor had I offered to persuade any of the men not to go with him, though it was to their apparent destruction.

However, warm heads are not easily cooled. The captain was so eager that he quitted our company, and, with most part of his crew, went over to Captain Avery, and sorted with his people, taking all the treasure with him, which, by the way, was not very fair in him, we having agreed to share all our gains, whether more or less, whether absent or present.

Our men muttered a little at it, but I pacified them as well as I could, and told them it was easy for us to get as much, if we minded our hits; and Captain Wilmot had set us a very good example; for, by the same rule, the agreement of any further sharing of profits with them was at an end. I took this occasion to put into their heads some part of my further designs, which were, to range over the eastern sea, and see if we could not make ourselves as rich as Mr. Avery, who, it was true, had gotten a prodigious deal of money, though not one-half of what was said of it in Europe.

Our men were so pleased with my forward, enterprising temper, that they assured me that they would go with me, one and all, over the whole globe, wherever I would carry them; and as for Captain Wilmot, they would have nothing more to do with him. This came to his ears, and put him into a great rage, so that he threatened, if I came on shore, he would cut my throat.

I had information of it privately, but took no notice of it at all; only I took care not to go unprovided for him, and seldom walked about but in very good company. However, at last Captain Wilmot and I met, and talked over the matter very seriously, and I offered him the sloop to go where he pleased, or, if he was not satisfied with that, I offered to take the sloop and leave him the great ship; but he declined both, and only desired that I would leave him six carpenters, which I had in our ship more than I had need of, to help his men to finish the sloop that was begun before we came thither, by the men that lost their ship. This I consented readily to, and lent him several other hands that were useful to them; and in a little time they built a stout brigantine, able to carry fourteen guns and 200 men.

What measures they took, and how Captain Avery managed afterwards, is too long a story to meddle with here; nor is it any of my business, having my own story still upon my hands.

We lay here, about these several simple disputes, almost five months, when, about the latter end of March, I set sail with the great ship, having in her forty-four guns and 400 men, and the sloop, carrying eighty men. We did not steer to the Malabar coast, and so to the Gulf of Persia, as was first intended, the east monsoons blowing yet too strong, but we kept more under the African coast, where we had the wind variable till we passed the line, and made the Cape Bassa, in the latitude of four degrees ten minutes; from thence, the monsoons beginning to change to the N.E. and N.N.E., we led it away, with the wind large, to the Maldives, a famous ledge of islands, well known by all the sailors who have gone into those parts of the world; and, leaving these islands a little to the south, we made Cape Comorin, the southernmost land of the coast of Malabar, and went round the isle of Ceylon. Here we lay by a while to wait for purchase; and here we saw three large English East India ships going from Bengal, or from Fort St

George, homeward for England, or rather for Bombay and Surat, till the trade set in.

We brought to, and hoisting an English ancient and pendant, lay by for them, as if we intended to attack them. They could not tell what to make of us a good while, though they saw our colours; and I believe at first they thought us to be French; but as they came nearer to us, we let them soon see what we were, for we hoisted a black flag, with two cross daggers in it, on our main-top-mast head, which let them see what they were to expect.

We soon found the effects of this; for at first they spread their ancients, and made up to us in a line, as if they would fight us, having the wind off shore, fair enough to have brought them on board us; but when they saw what force we were of, and found we were cruisers of another kind, they stood away from us again, with all the sail they could make. If they had come up, we should have given them an unexpected welcome, but as it was, we had no mind to follow them; so we let them go, for the same reasons which I mentioned before.

But though we let them pass, we did not design to let others go at so easy a price. It was but the next morning that we saw a sail standing round Cape Comorin, and steering, as we thought, the same course with us. We knew not at first what to do with her, because she had the shore on her larboard quarter, and if we offered to chase her, she might put into any port or creek, and escape us; but, to prevent this, we sent the sloop to get in between her and the land. As soon as she saw that, she hauled in to keep the land aboard, and when the sloop stood towards her she made right ashore, with all the canvas she could spread.

The sloop, however, came up with her and engaged her, and found she was a vessel of ten guns, Portuguese built, but in the Dutch traders' hands, and manned by Dutchmen, who were bound from the Gulf of Persia to Batavia, to fetch spices and other goods from thence. The sloop's men took her, and had the rummaging of her before we came up. She had in her some European goods, and a good round sum of money, and some pearl; so that, though we did not go to the gulf for the pearl, the pearl came to us out of the gulf, and we had our share of it. This was a rich ship, and the goods were of very considerable value, besides the money and the pearl.

We had a long consultation here what we should do with the men, for to give them the ship, and let them pursue their voyage to Java, would be to alarm the Dutch factory there, who are by far the strongest in the Indies, and to make our passage that way impracticable; whereas we resolved to visit that part of the world in our way, but were not willing to pass the great Bay of Bengal, where we hoped for a great deal of purchase; and therefore it behooved us not to be waylaid before we came there, because they knew we must pass by the Straits of Malacca, or those of Sunda; and either way it was very easy to prevent us.

While we were consulting this in the great cabin, the men had had the same debate before the mast; and it seems the majority there were for pickling up the poor Dutchmen among the herrings; in a word, they were for throwing them all into the sea. Poor William, the Quaker, was in great concern about this, and comes directly to me to talk about it. "Hark thee," says William, "what wilt thou do with these Dutchmen that thou hast on board? Thou wilt not let them go, I suppose," says he. "Why," says I, "William, would you advise me to let them go?" "No," says William, "I cannot say it is fit for thee to let them go; that is to say, to go on with their voyage to Batavia, because it is not for thy turn that the Dutch at Batavia should have any knowledge of thy being in these seas." "Well, then," says I to him, "I know no remedy but to throw them overboard. You know, William," says I, "a Dutchman swims like a fish; and all our people here are of the same opinion as well as I." At the same time I resolved it should not be done, but wanted to hear what William would say. He gravely replied, "If all the men in the ship were of that mind, I will never believe that thou wilt be of that mind thyself, for I have heard thee protest against cruelty in all other cases." "Well, William," says I, "that is true; but what then shall we do with them?" "Why," says William, "is there no way but to murder them? I am persuaded thou canst not be in earnest." "No, indeed, William," says I, "I am not in earnest; but they shall not go to Java, no, nor to Ceylon, that is certain." "But," says William, "the men have done thee no injury at all; thou hast taken a great treasure from them; what canst thou pretend to hurt them for?" "Nay, William," says I, "do not talk of that; I have pretence enough, if that be all; my pretence is, to prevent doing me hurt, and that is as necessary a piece of the law of self-preservation as any you can name; but the main thing is, I know not what to do with them, to prevent their prating."

While William and I were talking, the poor Dutchmen were openly condemned to die, as it may be called, by the whole ship's company; and so warm were the men upon it, that they grew very clamorous; and when they heard that William was against it, some of them swore they should die, and if William opposed it, he should drown along with them.

But, as I was resolved to put an end to their cruel project, so I found it was time to take upon me a little, or the bloody humour might grow too strong; so I called the Dutchmen up, and talked a little with them. First, I asked them if they were willing to go with us. Two of them offered it presently; but the rest, which were fourteen, declined it. "Well, then," said I, "where would you go?" They desired they should go to Ceylon. No, I told them I could not allow them to go to any Dutch factory, and told them very plainly the reasons of it, which they could not deny to be just. I let them know also the cruel, bloody measures of our men, but that I had resolved to save them, if possible; and therefore I told them I would set them on shore at some English factory in the Bay of Bengal, or put them on board any English ship I met, after I was past the Straits of Sunda or of Malacca, but not before; for, as to my coming back again, I told them I would run the venture of their Dutch power from Batavia, but I would not have the news come there before me, because it would make all their merchant-ships lay up, and keep out of our way.

It came next into our consideration what we should do with their ship; but this was not long resolving; for there were but two ways, either to set her on fire, or to run her on shore, and we chose the last. So we set her foresail with the tack at the cat-head, and lashed her helm a little to starboard, to answer her head-sail, and so set her agoing, with neither cat or dog in her; and it was not above two hours before we saw her run right ashore upon the coast, a little beyond the Cape Comorin; and away we went round about Ceylon, for the coast of Coromandel.

We sailed along there, not in sight of the shore only, but so near as to see the ships in the road at Fort St David, Fort St George, and at the other factories along that shore, as well as along the coast of Golconda, carrying our English ancient when we came near the Dutch factories, and Dutch colours when we passed by the English factories. We met with little purchase upon this coast, except two small vessels of Golconda, bound across the bay with bales of calicoes and muslins and wrought silks, and fifteen bales of romals, from the bottom of the bay, which were going, on whose account we knew not, to Acheen, and to other ports on the coast of Malacca. We did not inquire to what place in particular; but we let the vessels go, having none but Indians on board.

In the bottom of the bay we met with a great junk belonging to the Mogul's court, with a great many people, passengers as we supposed them to be: it seems they were bound for the river Hooghly or Ganges, and came from Sumatra. This was a prize worth taking indeed; and we got so much gold in her, besides other goods which we did not meddle with — pepper in particular — that it had like to have put an end to our cruise; for almost all my men said we were rich enough, and desired to go back again to Madagascar. But I had other things in my head still, and when I came to talk with them, and set friend William to talk with them, we put such further golden hopes into their heads that we soon prevailed with them to let us go on.

My next design was to leave all the dangerous straits of Malacca, Singapore, and Sunda, where we could expect no great booty, but what we might light on in European ships, which we must fight for; and though we were able to fight, and wanted no courage, even to desperation, yet we were rich too, and resolved to be richer, and took this for our maxim, that while we were sure the wealth we sought was to be had without fighting, we had no occasion to put ourselves to the necessity of fighting for that which would come upon easy terms.

We left, therefore, the Bay of Bengal, and coming to the coast of Sumatra, we put in at a small port, where there was a town, inhabited only by Malays; and here we took in fresh water, and a large quantity of good pork, pickled up and well salted, notwithstanding the heat of the climate, being in the very middle of the torrid zone, viz., in three degrees fifteen minutes north latitude. We also took on board both our vessels forty hogs alive, which served us for fresh provisions, having abundance of food for them, such as the country produced, such as guams, potatoes, and a sort of coarse rice, good for nothing else but to feed the swine. We killed one of these hogs every day, and found them to be excellent meat. We took in also a monstrous quantity of ducks, and cocks and hens, the same kind as we have in England, which we kept for change of provisions; and if I remember right, we had no less than two thousand of them; so that at first we were pestered with them very much, but we soon lessened them by boiling, roasting, stewing, &c., for we never wanted while we had them.

My long-projected design now lay open to me, which was to fall in amongst the Dutch Spice Islands, and see what mischief I could do there. Accordingly, we put out to sea the 12th of August, and passing the line on the 17th, we stood away due south, leaving the Straits of Sunda and the isle of Java on the east, till we came to the latitude of eleven degrees twenty minutes, when we steered east and E.N.E., having easy gales from the W.S.W. till we came among the Moluccas, or Spice Islands.

We passed those seas with less difficulty than in other places, the winds to the south of Java being more variable, and the weather good, though sometimes we met with squally weather and short storms; but when we came in among the Spice Islands themselves we had a share of the monsoons, or trade-winds, and made use of them accordingly.

The infinite number of islands which lie in these seas embarrassed us strangely, and it was with great difficulty that we worked our way through them; then we steered for the north side of the Philippines, when we had a double chance for purchase, viz., either to meet with the Spanish ships from Acapulco, on the coast of New Spain, or we were certain not to fail of finding some ships or junks of China, who, if they came from China, would have a great quantity of goods of value on board, as well as money; or if we took them going back, we should find them laden with nutmegs and cloves from Banda and Ternate, or from some of the other islands.

We were right in our guesses here to a title, and we steered directly through a large outlet, which they call a strait, though it be fifteen miles broad, and to an island they call Dammer, and from thence N.N.E. to Banda. Between these islands we met with a Dutch junk, or vessel, going to Amboyna: we took her without much trouble, and I had much ado to prevent our men murdering all the men, as soon as they heard them say they belonged to Amboyna: the reasons I suppose any one will guess.

We took out of her about sixteen ton of nutmegs, some provisions, and their small-arms, for they had no great guns, and let the ship go: from thence we sailed directly to the Banda Island, or Islands, where we were sure to get more nutmegs if we thought fit. For my part, I would willingly have got more nutmegs, though I had paid for them, but our people abhorred paying for anything; so we got about twelve ton more at several times, most of them from shore, and only a few in a small boat of the natives, which was going to Gilolo. We would have traded openly, but the Dutch, who have made themselves masters of all those islands, forbade the people dealing with us, or any strangers whatever, and kept them so in awe that they durst not do it; so we could indeed have made nothing of it if we had stayed longer, and therefore resolved to be gone for Ternate, and see if we could make up our loading with cloves.

Accordingly we stood away north, but found ourselves so entangled among innumerable islands, and without any pilot that understood the channel and races between them, that we were obliged to give it over, and resolved to go back again to Banda, and see what we could get among the other islands thereabouts.

The first adventure we made here had like to have been fatal to us all, for the sloop, being ahead, made the signal to us for seeing a sail, and afterwards another, and a third, by which we understood she saw three sail; whereupon we made more sail to come up with her, but on a sudden were gotten among some rocks, falling foul upon them in such a manner as frighted us all very heartily; for having, it seems, but just water enough, as it were to an inch, our rudder struck upon the top of a rock, which gave us a terrible shock, and split a great piece off the rudder, and indeed disabled it so that our ship would not steer at all, at least not so as to be depended upon; and we were glad to hand all our sails, except our fore-sail and main-topsail, and with them we stood away to the east, to see if we could find any creek or harbour where we might lay the ship on shore, and repair our rudder; besides, we found the ship herself had received some damage, for she had some little leak near her stern-post, but a great way under water.

By this mischance we lost the advantages, whatever they were, of the three sail of ships, which we afterwards came to hear were small Dutch ships from Batavia, going to Banda and Amboyna, to load spice, and, no doubt, had a good quantity of money on board.

Upon the disaster I have been speaking of you may very well suppose that we came to an anchor as soon as we could, which was upon a small island not far from Banda, where, though the Dutch keep no factory, yet they come at the season to buy nutmegs and mace. We stayed there thirteen days; but there being no place where we could lay the ship on shore, we sent the sloop to cruise among the islands, to look out for a place fit for us. In the meantime we got very good water here, some provisions, roots, and fruits, and a good quantity of nutmegs and mace, which we found ways to trade with the natives for, without the knowledge of their masters, the Dutch.

At length our sloop returned; having found another island where there was a very good harbour, we ran in, and came to an anchor. We immediately unbent all our sails, sent them ashore upon the island, and set up seven or eight tents with them; then we unrigged our top-masts, and cut them down, hoisted all our guns out, our provisions and loading, and put them ashore in the tents. With the guns we made two small batteries, for fear of a surprise, and kept a look-out upon the hill. When we were all ready, we laid the ship aground upon a hard sand, the upper end of the harbour, and shored her up on each side. At low water she lay almost dry, so we mended her bottom, and stopped the leak, which was occasioned by straining some of the rudder irons with the shock which the ship had against the rock.

Having done this, we also took occasion to clean her bottom, which, having been at sea so long, was very foul. The sloop washed and tallowed also, but was ready before us, and cruised eight or ten days among the islands, but met with no purchase; so that we began to be tired of the place, having little to divert us but the most furious claps of thunder that ever were heard or read of in the world.

We were in hopes to have met with some purchase here among the Chinese, who, we had been told, came to Ternate to trade for cloves, and to the Banda Isles for nutmegs; and we would have been very glad to have loaded our galleon, or great ship, with these two sorts of spice, and have thought it a glorious voyage; but we found nothing stirring more than what I have said, except Dutchmen, who, by what means we could not imagine, had either a jealousy of us or intelligence of us, and kept themselves close in their ports.

I was once resolved to have made a descent at the island of Dumas, the place most famous for the best nutmegs; but friend William, who was always for doing our business without fighting, dissuaded me from it, and gave such reasons for it that we could not resist; particularly the great heats of the season, and of the place, for we were now in the latitude of just half a degree south. But while we were disputing this point we were soon determined by the following accident: — We had a strong gale of wind at S.W. by W., and the ship had fresh way, but a great sea rolling in upon us from the N.E., which we afterwards found was the pouring in of the great ocean east of New Guinea. However, as I said, we stood away large, and made fresh way, when, on the sudden, from a dark cloud which hovered over our heads, came a flash, or rather blast, of lightning, which was so terrible, and quivered so long among us, that not I only, but all our men, thought the ship was on fire. The heat of the flash, or fire, was so sensibly felt in our faces, that some of our men had blisters raised by it on their skins, not immediately, perhaps, by the heat, but by the poisonous or noxious particles which mixed themselves with the matter inflamed. But this was not all; the shock of the air, which the fracture in the clouds made, was such that our ship shook as when a broadside is fired; and her motion being checked, as it were at once, by a repulse superior to the force that gave her way before, the sails all flew back in a moment, and the ship lay, as we might truly say, thunder-struck. As the blast from the cloud was so very near us, it was but a few moments after the flash that the terriblest clap of thunder followed that was ever heard by mortals. I firmly believe a blast of a hundred thousand barrels of gunpowder could not have been greater to our hearing; nay, indeed, to some of our men it took away their hearing.

It is not possible for me to describe, or any one to conceive, the terror of that minute. Our men were in such a consternation, that not a man on board the ship had presence of mind to apply to the proper duty of a sailor, except friend William; and had he not run very nimbly, and with a composure that I am sure I was not master of, to let go the fore-sheet, set in the weather-brace of the fore-yard, and haul down the top-sails, we had certainly brought all our masts by the board, and perhaps have been overwhelmed in the sea.

As for myself, I must confess my eyes were open to my danger, though not the least to anything of application for remedy. I was all amazement and confusion, and this was the first time that I can say I began to feel the effects of that horror which I know since much more of, upon the just reflection on my former life. I thought myself doomed by Heaven to sink that moment into eternal destruction; and with this peculiar mark of terror, viz., that the vengeance was not executed in the ordinary way of human justice, but that God had taken me into His immediate disposing, and had resolved to be the executer of His own vengeance.

Let them alone describe the confusion I was in who know what was the case of [John] Child, of Shadwell, or Francis Spira. It is impossible to describe it. My soul was all amazement and surprise. I thought myself just sinking into eternity, owning the divine justice of my punishment, but not at all feeling any of the moving, softening tokens of a sincere penitent; afflicted at the punishment, but not at the crime; alarmed at the vengeance, but not terrified at the guilt; having the same gust to the crime, though terrified to the last degree at the thought of the punishment, which I concluded I was just now going to receive.

But perhaps many that read this will be sensible of the thunder and lightning, that may think nothing of the rest, or rather may make a jest of it all; so I say no more of it at this time, but proceed to the story of the voyage. When the amazement was over, and the men began to come to themselves, they fell a-calling for one another, every one for his friend, or for those he had most respect for; and it was a singular satisfaction to find that nobody was hurt. The next thing was to inquire if the ship had received no damage, when the boatswain, stepping forward, found that part of the head was gone, but not so as to endanger the bowsprit; so we hoisted our top-sails again, hauled aft the fore-sheet, braced the yards, and went our course as before. Nor can I deny but that we were all somewhat like the ship; our first astonishment being a little over, and that we found the ship swim again, we were soon the same irreligious, hardened crew that we were before, and I among the rest.

As we now steered, our course lay N.N.E., and we passed thus, with a fair wind, through the strait or channel between the island of Gilolo and the land of Nova Guinea, when we were soon in the open sea or ocean, on the south-east of the Philippines, being the great Pacific, or South Sea, where it may be said to join itself with the vast Indian Ocean.

As we passed into these seas, steering due north, so we soon crossed the line to the north side, and so sailed on towards Mindanao and Manilla, the chief of the Philippine Islands, without meeting with any purchase till we came to the northward of Manilla, and then our trade began; for here we took three Japanese vessels, though at some distance from Manilla. Two of them had made their market, and were going home with nutmegs, cinnamon, cloves, &c., besides all sorts of European goods, brought with the Spanish ships from Acapulco. They had together eight-and-thirty ton of cloves, and five or six ton of nutmegs, and as much cinnamon. We took the spice, but meddled with very little of the European goods, they being, as we thought, not worth our while; but we were very sorry for it soon after, and therefore grew wiser upon the next occasion.

The third Japanese was the best prize to us; for he came with money, and a great deal of gold uncoined, to buy such goods as we mentioned above. We eased him of his gold, and did him no other harm, and having no intention to stay long here, we stood away for China.

We were at sea above two months upon this voyage, beating it up against the wind, which blew steadily from the N.E., and within a point or two one way or other; and this indeed was the reason why we met with the more prizes in our voyage.

We were just gotten clear of the Philippines, and we purposed to go to the isle of Formosa, but the wind blew so fresh at N.N.E. that there was no making anything of it, and we were forced to put back to Laconia, the most northerly of those islands. We rode here very secure, and shifted our situation, not in view of any danger, for there was none, but for a better supply of provisions, which we found the people very willing to supply us with.

There lay, while we remained here, three very great galleons, or Spanish ships, from the south seas; whether newly come in or ready to sail we could not understand at first; but as we found the China traders began to load and set forward to the north, we concluded the Spanish ships had newly unloaded their cargo, and these had been buying; so we doubted not but we should meet with purchase in the rest of the voyage, neither, indeed, could we well miss of it.

We stayed here till the beginning of May, when we were told the Chinese traders would set forward; for the northern monsoons end about the latter end of March or beginning of April; so that they are sure of fair winds home. Accordingly we hired some of the country boats, which are very swift sailors, to go and bring us word how affairs stood at Manilla, and when the China junks would sail; and by this intelligence we ordered our matters so well, that three days after we set sail we fell in with no less than eleven of them; out of which, however, having by misfortune of discovering ourselves, taken but three, we contented ourselves and pursued our voyage to Formosa. In these three vessels we took, in short, such a quantity of cloves, nutmegs, cinnamon, and mace, besides silver, that our men began to be of my opinion, — that we were rich enough; and, in short, we had nothing to do now but to consider by what methods to secure the immense treasure we had got.

I was secretly glad to hear that they were of this opinion, for I had long before resolved, if it were possible, to persuade them to think of returning, having fully perfected my first projected design of rummaging among the Spice Islands; and all those prizes, which were exceeding rich at Manilla, was quite beyond my design.

But now I had heard what the men said, and how they thought we were very well, I let them know by friend William, that I intended only to sail to the island of Formosa, where I should find opportunity to turn our spices and Europe goods into ready money, and that then I would tack about for the south, the northern monsoons being perhaps by that time also ready to set in. They all approved of my design, and willingly went forward; because, besides the winds, which would not permit until October to go to the south, I say, besides this, we were now a very deep ship, having near two hundred ton of goods on board, and particularly, some very valuable; the sloop also had a proportion.

With this resolution we went on cheerfully, when, within about twelve days' sail more, we made the island Formosa, at a great distance, but were ourselves shot beyond the southernmost part of the island, being to leeward, and almost upon the coast of China. Here we were a little at a loss, for the English factories were not far off, and we might be obliged to fight some of their ships, if we met with them; which, though we were able enough to do, yet we did not desire it on many accounts, and particularly because we did not think it was our business to have it known who we were, or that such a kind of people as we had been seen on the coast. However, we were obliged to keep to the northward, keeping as good an offing as we could with respect to the coast of China.

We had not sailed long but we chased a small Chinese junk, and having taken her, we found she was bound to the island of Formosa, having no goods on board but some rice and a small quantity of tea; but she had three Chinese merchants in her; and they told us that they were going to meet a large vessel of their country, which came from Tonquin, and lay in a river in Formosa, whose name I forgot; and they were going to the Philippine Islands, with silks, muslins, calicoes, and such goods as are the product of China, and some gold; that their business was to sell their cargo, and buy spices and European goods.

This suited very well with our purpose; so I resolved now that we would leave off being pirates and turn merchants; so we told them what goods we had on board, and that if they would bring their supercargoes or merchants on board, we would trade with them. They were very willing to trade with us, but terribly afraid to trust us; nor was it an unjust fear, for we had plundered them already of what they had. On the other hand, we were as diffident as they, and very uncertain what to do; but William the Quaker put this matter into a way of barter. He came to me and told me he really thought the merchants looked like fair men, that meant honestly. "And besides," says William, "it is their interest to be honest now, for, as they know upon what terms we got the goods we are to truck with them, so they know we can afford good pennyworths; and in the next place, it saves them going the whole voyage, so that the southerly monsoons yet holding, if they traded with us, they could immediately return with their cargo to China;" though, by the way, we afterwards found they intended for Japan; but that was all one, for by this means they saved at least eight months' voyage. Upon these foundations, William said he was satisfied we might trust them; "for," says William, "I would as soon trust a man whose interest

758

binds him to be just to me as a man whose principle binds himself." Upon the whole, William proposed that two of the merchants should be left on board our ship as hostages, and that part of our goods should be loaded in their vessel, and let the third go with it into the port where their ship lay; and when he had delivered the spices, he should bring back such things as it was agreed should be exchanged. This was concluded on, and William the Quaker ventured to go along with them, which, upon my word, I should not have cared to have done, nor was I willing that he should, but he went still upon the notion that it was their interest to treat him friendly.

In the meantime, we came to an anchor under a little island in the latitude of 23 degrees 28 minutes, being just under the northern tropic, and about twenty leagues from the island. Here we lay thirteen days, and began to be very uneasy for my friend William, for they had promised to be back again in four days, which they might very easily have done. However, at the end of thirteen days, we saw three sail coming directly to us, which a little surprised us all at first, not knowing what might be the case; and we began to put ourselves in a posture of defence; but as they came nearer us, we were soon satisfied, for the first vessel was that which William went in, who carried a flag of truce; and in a few hours they all came to an anchor, and William came on board us with a little boat, with the Chinese merchant in his company, and two other merchants, who seemed to be a kind of brokers for the rest.

Here he gave us an account how civilly he had been used; how they had treated him with all imaginable frankness and openness; that they had not only given him the full value of his spices and other goods which he carried, in gold, by good weight, but had loaded the vessel again with such goods as he knew we were willing to trade for; and that afterwards they had resolved to bring the great ship out of the harbour, to lie where we were, that so we might make what bargain we thought fit; only William said he had promised, in our name, that we should use no violence with them, nor detain any of the vessels after we had done trading with them. I told him we would strive to outdo them in civility, and that we would make good every part of his agreement; in token whereof, I caused a white flag likewise to be spread at the poop of our great ship, which was the signal agreed on.

As to the third vessel which came with them, it was a kind of bark of the country, who, having intelligence of our design to traffic, came off to deal with us, bringing a great deal of gold and some provisions, which at that time we were very glad of.

In short, we traded upon the high seas with these men, and indeed we made a very good market, and yet sold thieves' pennyworths too. We sold here about sixty ton of spice, chiefly cloves and nutmegs, and above two hundred bales of European goods, such as linen and woolen manufactures. We considered we should have occasion for some such things ourselves, and so we kept a good quantity of English stuffs, cloth, baize, &c., for ourselves. I shall not take up any of the little room I have left here with the further particulars of our trade; it is enough to mention, that, except a parcel of tea, and twelve bales of fine China wrought silks, we took nothing in exchange for our goods but gold; so that the sum we took here in that glittering commodity amounted to above fifty thousand ounces good weight.

When we had finished our barter, we restored the hostages, and gave the three merchants about the quantity of twelve hundredweight of nutmegs, and as many of cloves, with a handsome present of European linen and stuff for themselves, as a recompense for what we had taken from them; so we sent them away exceedingly well satisfied.

Here it was that William gave me an account, that while he was on board the Japanese vessel, he met with a kind of religious, or Japan priest, who spoke some words of English to him; and, being very inquisitive to know how he came to learn any of those words, he told him that there was in his country thirteen Englishmen; he called them Englishmen very articulately and distinctly, for he had conversed with them very frequently and freely. He said that they were all that were left of two-and-thirty men, who came on shore on the north side of Japan, being driven upon a great rock in a stormy night, where they lost their ship, and the rest of their men were drowned; that he had persuaded the king of his country to send boats off to the rock or island where the ship was lost, to save the rest of the men, and to bring them on shore, which was done, and they were used very kindly, and had houses built for them, and land given them to plant for provision; and that they lived by themselves.

He said he went frequently among them, to persuade them to worship their god (an idol, I suppose, of their own making), which, he said, they ungratefully refused; and that therefore the king had once or twice ordered them all to be put to death; but that, as he said, he had prevailed upon the king to spare them, and let them live their own way, as long as they were quiet and peaceable, and did not go about to withdraw others from the worship of the country.

I asked William why he did not inquire from whence they came. "I did," said William; "for how could I but think it strange," said he, "to hear him talk of Englishmen on the north side of Japan?" "Well," said I, "what account did he give of it?" "An account," said William, "that will surprise thee, and all the world after thee, that shall hear of it, and which makes me wish thou wouldst go up to Japan and find them out." "What do you mean?" said I. "Whence could they come?" "Why," says William, "he pulled out a little book, and in it a piece of paper, where it was written, in an Englishman's hand, and in plain English words, thus; and," says William, "I read it myself: — 'We came from Greenland, and from the North Pole.'" This, indeed, was amazing to us all, and more so to those seamen among us who knew anything of the infinite attempts which had been made from Europe, as well by the English as the Dutch, to discover a passage that way into those parts of the world; and as William pressed as earnestly to go on to the north to rescue those poor men, so the ship's company began to incline to it; and, in a word, we all came to this, that we would stand in to the shore of Formosa, to find this priest again, and have a further account of it all from him. Accordingly, the sloop went over; but when they came there, the vessels were very unhappily sailed, and this put an end to our inquiry after them, and perhaps may have disappointed mankind of one of the most noble discoveries that ever was made, or will again be made, in the world, for the good of mankind in general; but so much for that.

William was so uneasy at losing this opportunity, that he pressed us earnestly to go up to Japan to find out these men. He told us that if it was nothing but to recover thirteen honest poor men from a kind of captivity, which they would otherwise never be redeemed from, and where, perhaps, they might, some time or other, be murdered by the barbarous people, in defence of their idolatry, it were very well worth our while, and it would be, in some measure, making amends for the mischiefs we had done in the world; but we, that had no concern upon us for the mischiefs we had done, had much less about any satisfactions to be made for it, so he found that kind of discourse would weigh very little with us. Then he pressed us very earnestly to let him have the sloop to go by himself, and I told him I would not oppose it; but when he came to the sloop none of the men would go with him; for the case was plain, they had all a share in the cargo of the great ship, as well as in that of the sloop, and the richness of the cargo was such that they would not leave it by any means; so poor William, much to his mortification, was obliged to give it over. What became of those thirteen men, or whether they are not there still, I can give no account of.

We are now at the end of our cruise; what we had taken was indeed so considerable, that it was not only enough to satisfy the most covetous and the most ambitious minds in the world, but it did indeed satisfy us, and our men declared they did not desire any more. The next motion, therefore, was about going back, and the way by which we should perform the voyage, so as not to be attacked by the Dutch in the Straits of Sunda.

We had pretty well stored ourselves here with provisions, and it being now near the return of the monsoons, we resolved to stand away to the southward; and not only to keep without the Philippine Islands, that is to say, to the eastward of them, but to keep on to the southward, and see if we could not leave not only the Moluccas, or Spice Islands, behind us, but even Nova Guinea and Nova Hollandia also; and so getting into the variable winds, to the south of the tropic of Capricorn, steer away to the west, over the great Indian Ocean.

This was indeed at first a monstrous voyage in its appearance, and the want of provisions threatened us. William told us in so many words, that it was impossible we could carry provisions enough to subsist us for such a voyage, and especially fresh water; and that, as there would be no land for us to touch at where we could get any supply, it was a madness to undertake it.

But I undertook to remedy this evil, and therefore desired them not to be uneasy at that, for I knew that we might supply ourselves at Mindanao, the most southerly island of the Philippines.

Accordingly, we set sail, having taken all the provisions here that we could get, the 28th of September, the wind veering a little at first from the N.N.W. to the N.E. by E., but afterwards settled about the N.E. and the E.N.E. We were nine weeks in this voyage, having met with several interruptions by the weather, and put in under the lee of a small island in the latitude of 16 degrees 12 minutes, of which we never knew the name, none of our charts having given any account of it: I say, we put in here by reason of a strange tornado or hurricane, which brought us into a great deal of danger. Here we rode about sixteen days, the winds being very tempestuous and the weather uncertain. However, we got some provisions on shore, such as plants and roots, and a few hogs. We believed there were inhabitants on the island, but we saw none of them.

From hence, the weather settling again, we went on and came to the southernmost part of Mindanao, where we took in fresh water and some cows, but the climate was so hot that we did not attempt to salt up any more than so as to keep a fortnight or three weeks; and away we stood southward, crossing the line, and, leaving Gillolo on the starboard side, we coasted the country they call New Guinea, where, in the latitude of eight degrees south, we put in again for provisions and water, and where we found inhabitants; but they fled from us, and were altogether inconversable. From thence, sailing still southward, we left all behind us that any of our charts and maps took any notice of, and went on till we came to the latitude of seventeen degrees, the wind continuing still north-east.

Here we made land to the westward, which, when we had kept in sight for three days, coasting along the shore for the distance of about four leagues, we began to fear we should find no outlet west, and so should be obliged to go back again, and put in among the Moluccas at last; but at length we found the land break off, and go trending away to the west sea, seeming to be all open to the south and south-west, and a great sea came rolling out of the south, which gave us to understand that there was no land for a great way.

In a word, we kept on our course to the south, a little westerly, till we passed the south tropic, where we found the winds variable; and now we stood away fair west, and held it out for about twenty days, when we discovered land right ahead, and on our larboard bow; we made directly to the shore, being willing to take all advantages now for supplying ourselves with fresh provisions and water, knowing we were now entering on that vast unknown Indian Ocean, perhaps the greatest sea on the globe, having, with very little interruption of islands, a continued sea quite round the globe.

We found a good road here, and some people on shore; but when we landed, they fled up the country, nor would they hold any correspondence with us, nor come near us, but shot at us several times with arrows as long as lances. We set up white flags for a truce, but they either did not or would not understand it; on the contrary, they shot our flag of truce through several times with their arrows, so that, in a word, we never came near any of them.

We found good water here, though it was something difficult to get at it, but for living creatures we could see none; for the people, if they had any cattle, drove them all away, and showed us nothing but themselves, and that sometimes in a threatening posture, and in number

763

so great, that made us suppose the island to be greater than we first imagined. It is true, they would not come near enough for us to engage with them, at least not openly; but they came near enough for us to see them, and, by the help of our glasses, to see that they were clothed and armed, but their clothes were only about their lower and middle parts; that they had long lances, half pikes, in their hands, besides bows and arrows; that they had great high things on their heads, made, as we believed, of feathers, and which looked something like our grenadiers' caps in England.

When we saw them so shy that they would not come near us, our men began to range over the island, if it was such (for we never surrounded it), to search for cattle, and for any of the Indian plantations, for fruits or plants; but they soon found, to their cost, that they were to use more caution than that came to, and that they were to discover perfectly every bush and every tree before they ventured abroad in the country; for about fourteen of our men going farther than the rest, into a part of the country which seemed to be planted, as they thought, for it did but seem so, only I think it was overgrown with canes, such as we make our cane chairs with — I say, venturing too far, they were suddenly attacked with a shower of arrows from almost every side of them, as they thought, out of the tops of the trees.

They had nothing to do but to fly for it, which, however, they could not resolve on, till five of them were wounded; nor had they escaped so, if one of them had not been so much wiser or thoughtfuler than the rest, as to consider, that though they could not see the enemy, so as to shoot at them, yet perhaps the noise of their shot might terrify them, and that they should rather fire at a venture. Accordingly, ten of them faced about, and fired at random anywhere among the canes.

The noise and the fire not only terrified the enemy, but, as they believed, their shot had luckily hit some of them; for they found not only that the arrows, which came thick among them before, ceased, but they heard the Indians halloo, after their way, to one another, and make a strange noise, more uncouth and inimitably strange than any they had ever heard, more like the howling and barking of wild creatures in the woods than like the voice of men, only that sometimes they seemed to speak words.

They observed also, that this noise of the Indians went farther and farther off, so that they were satisfied the Indians fled away, except on one side, where they heard a doleful groaning and howling, and where it continued a good while, which they supposed was from some or other of them being wounded, and howling by reason of their wounds; or killed, and others howling over them: but our men had enough of making discoveries; so they did not trouble themselves to look farther, but resolved to take this opportunity to retreat. But the worst of their adventure was to come; for as they came back, they passed by a prodigious great trunk of an old tree; what tree it was, they said, they did not know, but it stood like an old decayed oak in a park, where the keepers in England take a stand, as they call it, to shoot a deer; and it stood just under the steep side of a great rock, or hill, that our people could not see what was beyond it.

As they came by this tree, they were of a sudden shot at, from the top of the tree, with seven arrows and three lances, which, to our great grief, killed two of our men, and wounded three more. This was the more surprising, because, being without any defence, and so near the trees, they expected more lances and arrows every moment; nor would flying do them any service, the Indians being, as appeared, very good marksmen. In this extremity, they had happily this presence of mind, viz., to run close to the tree, and stand, as it were, under it; so that those above could not come at, or see them, to throw their lances at them. This succeeded, and gave them time to consider what to do; they knew their enemies and murderers were above; they heard them talk, and those above knew those were below; but they below were obliged to keep close for fear of their lances from above. At length, one of our men, looking a little more strictly than the rest, thought he saw the head of one of the Indians just over a dead limb of the tree, which, it seems, the creature sat upon. One man immediately fired, and leveled his piece so true that the shot went through the fellow's head; and down he fell out of the tree immediately, and came upon the ground with such force, with the height of his fall, that if he had not been killed with the shot, he would certainly have been killed with dashing his body against the ground.

This so frightened them, that, besides the howling noise they made in the tree, our men heard a strange clutter of them in the body of the tree, from whence they concluded they had made the tree hollow, and were got to hide themselves there. Now, had this been the case, they were secure enough from our men, for it was impossible any of our men could get up the tree on the outside, there being no branches to climb by; and, to shoot at the tree, that they tried several times to no purpose, for the tree was so thick that no shot would enter it. They made no doubt, however, but that they had their enemies in a trap, and that a small siege would either bring them down, tree and all, or starve them out; so they resolved to keep their post, and send to us for help. Accordingly, two of them came away to us for more hands, and particularly desired that some of our carpenters might come with tools, to help to cut down the tree, or at least to cut down other wood and set fire to it; and that, they concluded, would not fail to bring them out.

Accordingly, our men went like a little army, and with mighty preparations for an enterprise, the like of which has scarce been ever heard, to form the siege of a great tree. However, when they came there, they found the task difficult enough, for the old trunk was indeed a very great one, and very tall, being at least two-and-twenty feet high, with seven old limbs standing out every way from the top, but decayed, and very few leaves, if any, left on it.

William the Quaker, whose curiosity led him to go among the rest, proposed that they should make a ladder, and get upon the top, and then throw wild-fire into the tree, and smoke them out. Others proposed going back, and getting a great gun out of the ship, which would split the tree in pieces with the iron bullets; others, that they should cut down a great deal of wood, and pile it up round the tree, and set it on fire, and burn the tree, and the Indians in it.

These consultations took up our people no less than two or three days, in all which time they heard nothing of the supposed garrison within this wooden castle, nor any noise within. William's project was first gone about, and a large strong ladder was made, to scale this wooden tower; and in two or three hours' time it would have been ready to mount, when, on a sudden, they heard the noise of the Indians in the body of the tree again, and a little after, several of them appeared at the top of the tree, and threw some lances down at our men; one of which struck one of our seamen a-top of the shoulder, and gave him such a desperate wound, that the surgeons not only had a great deal of difficulty to cure him, but the poor man endured such horrible torture, that we all said they had better have killed him outright. However, he was cured at last, though he never recovered the perfect use of his arm, the lance having cut some of the tendons on the top of the arm, near the shoulder, which, as I supposed, performed the office of motion to the limb before; so that the poor man was a cripple all the days of his life. But to return to the desperate rogues in the tree; our men shot at them, but did not find they had hit them, or any of them; but as soon as ever they shot at them, they could hear them huddle down into the trunk of the tree again, and there, to be sure, they were safe.

Well, however, it was this which put by the project of William's ladder; for when it was done, who would venture up among such a troop of bold creatures as were there, and who, they supposed, were desperate by their circumstances? And as but one man at a time could go up, they began to think it would not do; and, indeed, I was of the opinion (for about this time I was come to their assistance) that going up the ladder would not do, unless it was thus, that a man should, as it were, run just up to the top, and throw some fireworks into the tree, and come down again; and this we did two or three times, but found no effect of it. At last, one of our gunners made a stink-pot, as we called it, being a composition which only smokes, but does not flame or burn; but withal the smoke of it is so thick, and the smell of it so intolerably nauseous, that it is not to be suffered. This he threw into the tree himself, and we waited for the effect of it, but heard or saw nothing all that night or the next day; so we concluded the men within were all smothered; when, on a sudden, the next night we heard them upon the top of the tree again shouting and hallooing like madmen.

We concluded, as anybody would, that this was to call for help, and we resolved to continue our siege; for we were all enraged to see ourselves so baulked by a few wild people, whom we thought we had safe in our clutches; and, indeed, never were there so many concurring circumstances to delude men in any case we had met with. We resolved, however, to try another stink-pot the next night, and our engineer and gunner had got it ready, when, hearing a noise of the enemy on the top of the tree, and in the body of the tree, I was not willing to let the gunner go up the ladder, which, I said, would be but to be certain of being murdered. However, he found a medium for it, and that was to go up a few steps, and, with a long pole in his hand, to throw it in upon the top of the tree, the ladder being standing all this while against the top of the tree; but when the gunner, with his machine at the top of his pole, came to the tree, with three other men to help him, behold the ladder was gone.

This perfectly confounded us; and we now concluded the Indians in the tree had, by this piece of negligence, taken the opportunity, and come all down the ladder, made their escape, and had carried away the ladder with them. I laughed most heartily at my friend William, who, as I said, had the direction of the siege, and had set up a ladder for the garrison, as we called them, to get down upon, and run away. But when daylight came, we were all set to rights again; for there stood our ladder, hauled up on the top of the tree, with about half of it in the hollow of the tree, and the other half upright in the air. Then we began to laugh at the Indians for fools, that they could not as well have found their way down by the ladder, and have made their escape, as to have pulled it up by main strength into the tree.

We then resolved upon fire, and so to put an end to the work at once, and burn the tree and its inhabitants together; and accordingly we went to work to cut wood, and in a few hours' time we got enough, as we thought, together; and, piling it up round the bottom of the tree, we set it on fire, waiting at a distance to see when, the gentlemen's quarters being too hot for them, they would come flying out at the top. But we were quite confounded when, on a sudden, we found the fire all put out by a great quantity of water thrown upon it. We then thought the devil must be in them, to be sure. Says William, "This is certainly the cunningest piece of Indian engineering that ever was heard of; and there can be but one thing more to guess at, besides witchcraft and dealing with the devil, which I believe not one word of," says he; "and that must be, that this is an artificial tree, or a natural tree artificially made hollow down into the earth, through root and all; and that these creatures have an artificial cavity underneath it, quite into the hill, or a way to go through, and under the hill, to some other place; and where that other place is, we know not; but if it be not our own fault, I'll find the place, and follow them into it, before I am two days older." He then called the carpenters, to know of them if they had any large saws that would cut through the body; and they told him they had no saws that were long enough, nor could men work into such a monstrous old stump in a great while; but that they would go to work with it with their axes, and undertake to cut it down in two days, and stock up the root of it in two more. But William was for another way, which proved much better than all this; for he was for silent work, that, if possible, he might catch some of the fellows in it. So he sets twelve men to it with large augers, to bore great holes into the side of the tree, to go almost through, but not quite through; which holes were bored without noise, and when they were done he filled them all with gunpowder, stopping strong plugs, bolted crossways, into the holes, and then boring a slanting hole, of a less size, down into the greater hole, all of which were filled with powder, and at once blown up. When they took fire, they made such a noise, and tore and split up the tree in so many places, and in such a manner, that we could see plainly such another blast would demolish it; and so it did. Thus at the second time we could, at two or three places, put our hands in them, and discovered a cheat,

768

namely, that there was a cave or hole dug into the earth, from or through the bottom of the hollow, and that it had communication with another cave farther in, where we heard the voices of several of the wild folks, calling and talking to one another.

When we came thus far we had a great mind to get at them; and William desired that three men might be given him with hand-grenadoes; and he promised to go down first, and boldly he did so; for William, to give him his due, had the heart of a lion.

They had pistols in their hands, and swords by their sides; but, as they had taught the Indians before by their stink-pots, the Indians returned them in their own kind; for they made such a smoke come up out of the entrance into the cave or hollow, that William and his three men were glad to come running out of the cave, and out of the tree too, for mere want of breath; and indeed they were almost stifled.

Never was a fortification so well defended, or assailants so many ways defeated. We were now for giving it over, and particularly I called William, and told him I could not but laugh to see us spinning out our time here for nothing; that I could not imagine what we were doing; that it was certain that the rogues that were in it were cunning to the last degree, and it would vex anybody to be so baulked by a few naked ignorant fellows; but still it was not worth our while to push it any further, nor was there anything that I knew of to be got by the conquest when it was made, so that I thought it high time to give it over.

William acknowledged what I said was just, and that there was nothing but our curiosity to be gratified in this attempt; and though, as he said, he was very desirous to have searched into the thing, yet he would not insist upon it; so we resolved to quit it and come away, which we did. However, William said before we went he would have this satisfaction of them, viz., to burn down the tree and stop up the entrance into the cave. And while doing this the gunner told him he would have one satisfaction of the rogues; and this was, that he would make a mine of it, and see which way it had vent. Upon this he fetched two barrels of powder out of the ships, and placed them in the inside of the hollow of the cave, as far in as he durst go to carry them, and then filling up the mouth of the cave where the tree stood, and ramming it sufficiently hard, leaving only a pipe or touch-hole, he gave fire to it, and stood at a distance to see which way it would operate, when on a sudden he found the force of the powder burst its way out among some bushes on the other side the little hill I mentioned, and that it came roaring out there as out of the mouth of a cannon. Immediately running thither, we saw the effects of the powder.

First, we saw that there was the other mouth of the cave, which the powder had so torn and opened, that the loose earth was so fallen in again that nothing of shape could be discerned; but there we saw what was become of the garrison of the Indians, too, who had given us all this trouble, for some of them had no arms, some no legs, some no head; some lay half buried in the rubbish of the mine — that is to say, in the loose earth that fell in; and, in short, there was a miserable havoc made in them all; for we had good reason to believe not one of them that were in the inside could escape, but rather were shot out of the mouth of the cave, like a bullet out of a gun.

We had now our full satisfaction of the Indians; but, in short, this was a losing voyage, for we had two men killed, one quite crippled, and five more wounded; we spent two barrels of powder, and eleven days' time, and all to get the understanding how to make an Indian mine, or how to keep garrison in a hollow tree; and with this wit, bought at this dear price, we came away, having taken in some fresh water, but got no fresh provisions.

We then considered what we should do to get back again to Madagascar. We were much about the latitude of the Cape of Good Hope, but had such a very long run, and were neither sure of meeting with fair winds nor with any land in the way, that we knew not what to think of it. William was our last resort in this case again, and he was very plain with us. "Friend," says he to Captain Wilmot, "what occasion hast thou to run the venture of starving, merely for the pleasure of saying thou hast been where nobody has been before? There are a great many places nearer home, of which thou mayest say the same thing at less expense. I see no occasion thou hast of keeping thus far south any longer than till you are sure you are to the west end of Java and Sumatra; and then thou mayest stand away north towards Ceylon, and the coast of Coromandel and Madras, where thou mayest get both fresh water and fresh provisions; and to that part it is likely we may hold out well enough with the stores we have already."

This was wholesome advice, and such as was not to be slighted; so we stood away to the west, keeping between the latitude of 31 and 35, and had very good weather and fair winds for about ten days' sail; by which time, by our reckoning, we were clear of the isles, and might run away to the north; and if we did not fall in with Ceylon, we should at least go into the great deep Bay of Bengal.

But we were out in our reckoning a great deal; for, when we had stood due north for about fifteen or sixteen degrees, we met with land again on our starboard bow, about three leagues' distance; so we came to an anchor about half a league from it, and manned out our boats to see what sort of a country it was. We found it a very good one; fresh water easy to come at, but no cattle that we could see, or inhabitants; and we were very shy of searching too far after them, lest we should make such another journey as we did last; so that we let rambling alone, and chose rather to take what we could find, which was only a few wild mangoes, and some plants of several kinds, which we knew not the names of.

We made no stay here, but put to sea again, N.W. by N., but had little wind for a fortnight more, when we made land again; and standing in with the shore, we were surprised to find ourselves on the south shore of Java; and just as we were coming to an anchor we saw a boat, carrying Dutch colours, sailing along-shore. We were not solicitous to speak with them, or any other of their nation, but left it indifferent to our people, when they went on shore, to see the Dutchmen or not to see them; our business was to get provisions, which, indeed, by this time were very short with us.

We resolved to go on shore with our boats in the most convenient place we could find, and to look out a proper harbour to bring the ship into, leaving it to our fate whether we should meet with friends or enemies; resolving, however, not to stay any considerable time, at least not long enough to have expresses sent across the island to Batavia, and for ships to come round from thence to attack us.

We found, according to our desire, a very good harbour, where we rode in seven fathom water, well defended from the weather, whatever might happen; and here we got fresh provisions, such as good hogs and some cows; and that we might lay in a little store, we killed sixteen cows, and pickled and barreled up the flesh as well as we could be supposed to do in the latitude of eight degrees from the line.

We did all this in about five days, and filled our casks with water; and the last boat was coming off with herbs and roots, we being unmoored, and our fore-topsail loose for sailing, when we spied a large ship to the northward, bearing down directly upon us. We knew not what she might be, but concluded the worst, and made all possible haste to get our anchor up, and get under sail, that we might be in a readiness to see what she had to say to us, for we were under no great concern for one ship, but our notion was, that we should be attacked by three or four together.

By the time we had got up our anchor and the boat was stowed, the ship was within a league of us, and, as we thought, bore down to engage us; so we spread our black flag, or ancient, on the poop, and the bloody flag at the top-mast-head, and having made a clear ship, we stretched away to the westward, to get the wind of him.

They had, it seems, quite mistaken us before, expecting nothing of an enemy or a pirate in those seas; and, not doubting but we had been one of their own ships, they seemed to be in some confusion when they found their mistake, so they immediately hauled upon a wind on the other tack, and stood edging in for the shore, towards the easternmost part of the island. Upon this we tacked, and stood after him with all the sail we could, and in two hours came almost within gunshot. Though they crowded all the sail they could lay on, there was no remedy but to engage us, and they soon saw their inequality of force. We fired a gun for them to bring to; so they manned out their boat, and sent to us with a flag of truce. We sent back the boat, but with this answer to the captain, that he had nothing to do but to strike and bring his ship to an anchor under our stern, and come on board us himself, when he should know our demands; but that, however, since he had not yet put us to the trouble of forcing him, which we saw we were able to do, we assured them that the captain should return again in safety, and all his men, and that, supplying us with such things as we should demand, his ship should not be plundered. They went back with this message, and it was some time after they were on board before they struck, which made us begin to think they refused it; so we fired a shot, and in a few minutes more we perceived their boat put off; and as soon as the boat put off the ship struck and came to an anchor, as was directed.

When the captain came on board, we demanded an account of their cargo, which was chiefly bales of goods from Bengal for Bantam. We told them our present want was provisions, which they had no need of, being just at the end of their voyage; and that, if they would send their boat on shore with ours, and procure us six-and-twenty head of black cattle, threescore hogs, a quantity of brandy and arrack, and three hundred bushels of rice, we would let them go free.

As to the rice, they gave us six hundred bushels, which they had actually on board, together with a parcel shipped upon freight. Also, they gave us thirty middling casks of very good arrack, but beef and pork they had none. However, they went on shore with our men, and bought eleven bullocks and fifty hogs, which were pickled up for our occasion; and upon the supplies of provision from shore, we dismissed them and their ship.

We lay here several days before we could furnish ourselves with the provisions agreed for, and some of the men fancied the Dutchmen were contriving our destruction; but they were very honest, and did what they could to furnish the black cattle, but found it impossible to supply so many. So they came and told us ingenuously, that, unless we could stay a while longer, they could get no more oxen or cows than those eleven, with which we were obliged to be satisfied, taking the value of them in other things, rather than stay longer there. On our side, we were punctual with them in observing the conditions we had agreed on; nor would we let any of our men so much as go on board them, or suffer any of their men to come on board us; for, had any of our men gone on board, nobody could have answered for their behaviour, any more than if they had been on shore in an enemy's country.

We were now victualed for our voyage; and, as we mattered not purchase, we went merrily on for the coast of Ceylon, where we intended to touch, to get fresh water again, and more provisions; and we had nothing material offered in this part of the voyage, only that we met with contrary winds, and were above a month in the passage.

We put in upon the south coast of the island, desiring to have as little to do with the Dutch as we could; and as the Dutch were lords of the country as to commerce, so they are more so of the sea-coast, where they have several forts, and, in particular, have all the cinnamon, which is the trade of that island.

We took in fresh water here, and some provisions, but did not much trouble ourselves about laying in any stores, our beef and hogs, which we got at Java, being not yet all gone by a good deal. We had a little skirmish on shore here with some of the people of the island, some of our men having been a little too familiar with the homely ladies of the country; for homely, indeed, they were, to such a degree, that if our men had not had good stomachs that way, they would scarce have touched any of them.

I could never fully get it out of our men what they did, they were so true to one another in their wickedness, but I understood in the main, that it was some barbarous thing they had done, and that they had like to have paid dear for it, for the men resented it to the last degree, and gathered in such numbers about them, that, had not sixteen more of our men, in another boat, come all in the nick of time, just to

773

rescue our first men, who were but eleven, and so fetch them off by main force, they had been all cut off, the inhabitants being no less than two or three hundred, armed with darts and lances, the usual weapons of the country, and which they are very dexterous at the throwing, even so dexterous that it was scarce credible; and had our men stood to fight them, as some of them were bold enough to talk of, they had been all overwhelmed and killed. As it was, seventeen of our men were wounded, and some of them very dangerously. But they were more frighted than hurt too, for every one of them gave themselves over for dead men, believing the lances were poisoned. But William was our comfort here too; for, when two of our surgeons were of the same opinion, and told the men foolishly enough that they would die, William cheerfully went to work with them, and cured them all but one, who rather died by drinking some arrack punch than of his wound; the excess of drinking throwing him into a fever.

We had enough of Ceylon, though some of our people were for going ashore again, sixty or seventy men together, to be revenged; but William persuaded them against it; and his reputation was so great among the men, as well as with us that were commanders, that he could influence them more than any of us.

They were mighty warm upon their revenge, and they would go on shore, and destroy five hundred of them. "Well," says William, "and suppose you do, what are you the better?" "Why, then," says one of them, speaking for the rest, "we shall have our satisfaction." "Well, and what will you be the better for that?" says William. They could then say nothing to that. "Then," says William, "if I mistake not, your business is money; now, I desire to know, if you conquer and kill two or three thousand of these poor creatures, they have no money, pray what will you get? They are poor naked wretches; what shall you gain by them? But then," says William, "perhaps, in doing this, you may chance to lose half-a-score of your own company, as it is very probable you may. Pray, what gain is in it? and what account can you give the captain for his lost men?" In short, William argued so effectually, that he convinced them that it was mere murder to do so; and that the men had a right to their own, and that they had no right to take them away; that it was destroying innocent men, who had acted no otherwise than as the laws of nature dictated; and that it would be as much murder to do so, as to meet a man on the highway, and kill him, for the mere sake of it, in cold blood, not regarding whether he had done any wrong to us or no.

These reasons prevailed with them at last, and they were content to go away, and leave them as they found them. In the first skirmish they killed between sixty and seventy men, and wounded a great many more; but they had nothing, and our people got nothing by it, but the loss of one man's life, and the wounding sixteen more, as above.

But another accident brought us to a necessity of further business with these people, and indeed we had like to have put an end to our lives and adventures all at once among them; for, about three days after our putting out to sea from the place where we had that skirmish, we were attacked by a violent storm of wind from the south, or rather a hurricane of wind from all the points southward, for it blew in a most desperate and furious manner from the S.E. to the S.W., one minute at one point, and then instantly turning about again to another point, but with the same violence; nor were we able to work the ship in that condition, so that the ship I was in split three top-sails, and at last brought the main-top-mast by the board; and, in a word, we were once or twice driven right ashore; and one time, had not the wind shifted the very moment it did, we had been dashed in a thousand pieces upon a great ledge of rocks which lay off about half-a-league from the shore; but, as I have said, the wind shifting very often, and at that time coming to the E.S.E., we stretched off, and got above a league more sea-room in half-an-hour. After that, it blew with some fury S.W. by S., then S.W. by W., and put us back again a great way to the eastward of the ledge of rocks, where we found a great opening between the rocks and the land, and endeavoured to come to an anchor there, but we found there was no ground fit to anchor in, and that we should lose our anchors, there being nothing but rocks. We stood through the opening, which held about four leagues. The storm continued, and now we found a dreadful foul shore, and knew not what course to take. We looked out very narrowly for some river or creek or bay, where we might run in, and come to an anchor, but found none a great while. At length we saw a great headland lie out far south into the sea, and that to such a length, that, in short, we saw plainly that, if the wind held where it was, we could not weather it, so we ran in as much under the lee of the point as we could, and came to an anchor in about twelve fathom water.

But the wind veering again in the night, and blowing exceedingly hard, our anchors came home, and the ship drove till the rudder struck against the ground; and had the ship gone half her length farther she had been lost, and every one of us with her. But our sheet-anchor held its own, and we heaved in some of the cable, to get clear of the ground

775

we had struck upon. It was by this only cable that we rode it out all night; and towards morning we thought the wind abated a little; and it was well for us that it was so, for, in spite of what our sheet-anchor did for us, we found the ship fast aground in the morning, to our very great surprise and amazement.

When the tide was out, though the water here ebbed away, the ship lay almost dry upon a bank of hard sand, which never, I suppose, had any ship upon it before. The people of the country came down in great numbers to look at us and gaze, not knowing what we were, but gaping at us as at a great sight or wonder at which they were surprised, and knew not what to do.

I have reason to believe that upon the sight they immediately sent an account of a ship being there, and of the condition we were in, for the next day there appeared a great man; whether it was their king or no I know not, but he had abundance of men with him, and some with long javelins in their hands as long as half-pikes; and these came all down to the water's edge, and drew up in a very good order, just in our view. They stood near an hour without making any motion; and then there came near twenty of them, with a man before them carrying a white flag. They came forward into the water as high as their waists, the sea not going so high as before, for the wind was abated, and blew off the shore.

The man made a long oration to us, as we could see by his gestures; and we sometimes heard his voice, but knew not one word he said. William, who was always useful to us, I believe was here again the saving of all our lives. The case was this: The fellow, or what I might call him, when his speech was done, gave three great screams (for I know not what else to say they were), then lowered his white flag three times, and then made three motions to us with his arm to come to him.

I acknowledge that I was for manning out the boat and going to them, but William would by no means allow me. He told me we ought to trust nobody; that, if they were barbarians, and under their own government, we might be sure to be all murdered; and, if they were Christians, we should not fare much better, if they knew who we were; that it was the custom of the Malabars to betray all people that they could get into their hands, and that these were some of the same people; and that, if we had any regard to our own safety, we should not go to them by any means. I opposed him a great while, and told him I thought he used to be always right, but that now I thought he was not; that I was no more for running needless risks than he or any one else;

776

but I thought all nations in the world, even the most savage people, when they held out a flag of peace, kept the offer of peace made by that signal very sacredly; and I gave him several examples of it in the history of my African travels, which I have here gone through in the beginning of this work, and that I could not think these people worse than some of them. And, besides, I told him our case seemed to be such that we must fall into somebody's hands or other, and that we had better fall into their hands by a friendly treaty than by a forced submission, nay, though they had indeed a treacherous design; and therefore I was for a parley with them.

"Well, friend," says William very gravely, "if thou wilt go I cannot help it; I shall only desire to take my last leave of thee at parting, for, depend upon it, thou wilt never see us again. Whether we in the ship may come off any better at last I cannot resolve thee; but this I will answer for, that we will not give up our lives idly, and in cool blood, as thou art going to do; we will at least preserve ourselves as long as we can, and die at last like men, not like fools, trepanned by the wiles of a few barbarians."

William spoke this with so much warmth, and yet with so much assurance of our fate, that I began to think a little of the risk I was going to run. I had no more mind to be murdered than he; and yet I could not for my life be so faint-hearted in the thing as he. Upon which I asked him if he had any knowledge of the place, or had ever been there. He said, No. Then I asked him if he had heard or read anything about the people of this island, and of their way of treating any Christians that had fallen into their hands; and he told me he had heard of one, and he would tell me the story afterward. His name, he said, was Knox, commander of an East India ship, who was driven on shore, just as we were, upon this island of Ceylon, though he could not say it was at the same place, or whereabouts; that he was beguiled by the barbarians, and enticed to come on shore, just as we were invited to do at that time; and that, when they had him, they surrounded him, and eighteen or twenty of his men, and never suffered them to return, but kept them prisoners, or murdered them, he could not tell which; but they were carried away up into the country, separated from one another, and never heard of afterwards, except the captain's son, who miraculously made his escape, after twenty years' slavery.

I had no time then to ask him to give the full story of this Knox, much less to hear him tell it me; but, as it is usual in such cases, when one begins to be a little touched, I turned short with him. "Why then, friend William," said I, "what would you have us do? You see what condition we are in, and what is before us; something must be done, and that immediately." "Why," says William, "I'll tell thee what thou shalt do; first, cause a white flag to be hanged out, as they do to us, and man out the longboat and pinnace with as many men as they can well stow, to handle their arms, and let me go with them, and thou shalt see what we will do. If I miscarry, thou mayest be safe; and I will also tell thee, that if I do miscarry, it shall be my own fault, and thou shalt learn wit by my folly."

I knew not what to reply to him at first; but, after some pause, I said, "William, William, I am as both you should be lost as you are that I should; and if there be any danger, I desire you may no more fall into it than I. Therefore, if you will, let us all keep in the ship, fare alike, and take our fate together."

"No, no," says William, "there's no danger in the method I propose; thou shalt go with me, if thou thinkest fit. If thou pleasest but to follow the measures that I shall resolve on, depend upon it, though we will go off from the ships, we will not a man of us go any nearer them than within call to talk with them. Thou seest they have no boats to come off to us; but," says he, "I rather desire thou wouldst take my advice, and manage the ships as I shall give the signal from the boat, and let us concert that matter together before we go off."

Well, I found William had his measures in his head all laid beforehand, and was not at a loss what to do at all; so I told him he should be captain for this voyage, and we would be all of us under his orders, which I would see observed to a title.

Upon this conclusion of our debates, he ordered four-and-twenty men into the long-boat, and twelve men into the pinnace, and the sea being now pretty smooth, they went off, being all very well armed. Also he ordered that all the guns of the great ship, on the side which lay next the shore, should be loaded with musket-balls, old nails, stubs, and such-like pieces of old iron, lead, and anything that came to hand; and that we should prepare to fire as soon as ever we saw them lower the white flag and hoist up a red one in the pinnace.

With these measures fixed between us, they went off towards the shore, William in the pinnace with twelve men, and the long-boat coming after him with four-and-twenty more, all stout resolute fellows, and very well armed. They rowed so near the shore as that they might speak to one another, carrying a white flag, as the other did, and offering a parley. The brutes, for such they were, showed themselves very courteous; but finding we could not understand them, they fetched an old Dutchman, who had been their prisoner many years, and set him to speak to us. The sum and substance of his speech was, that the king of the country had sent his general down to know who we were, and what our business was. William stood up in the stern of the pinnace, and told him, that as to that, he, that was an European, by his language and voice, might easily know what we were, and our condition; the ship being aground upon the sand would also tell him that our business there was that of a ship in distress; so William desired to know what they came down for with such a multitude, and with arms and weapons, as if they came to war with us.

He answered, they might have good reason to come down to the shore, the country being alarmed with the appearance of ships of strangers upon the coast; and as our vessels were full of men, and as we had guns and weapons, the king had sent part of his military men, that, in case of any invasion upon the country, they might be ready to defend themselves, whatsoever might be the occasion.

"But," says he, "as you are men in distress, the king has ordered his general, who is here also, to give you all the assistance he can, and to invite you on shore, and receive you with all possible courtesy." Says William, very quick upon him, "Before I give thee an answer to that, I desire thee to tell me what thou art, for by thy speech thou art an European." He answered presently, he was a Dutchman. "That I know well," says William, "by thy speech; but art thou a native Dutchman of Holland, or a native of this country, that has learned Dutch by conversing among the Hollanders, who we know are settled upon this island?"

"No," says the old man, "I am a native of Delft, in the province of Holland, in Europe."

"Well," says William, immediately, "but art thou a Christian or a heathen, or what we call a renegado?"

"I am," says he, "a Christian." And so they went on, in a short dialogue, as follows: —

William. Thou art a Dutchman, and a Christian, thou sayest; pray, art thou a freeman or a servant?

Dutchman. I am a servant to the king here, and in his army.

W. But art thou a volunteer, or a prisoner?

D. Indeed I was a prisoner at first, but am at liberty now, and so am a volunteer.

W. That is to say, being first a prisoner, thou hast liberty to serve them; but art thou so at liberty that thou mayest go away, if thou pleasest, to thine own countrymen?

D. No, I do not say so; my countrymen live a great way off, on the north and east parts of the island, and there is no going to them without the king's express license.

W. Well, and why dost thou not get a license to go away?

D. I have never asked for it.

W. And, I suppose, if thou didst, thou knowest thou couldst not obtain it.

D. I cannot say much as to that; but why do you ask me all these questions?

W. Why, my reason is good; if thou art a Christian and a prisoner, how canst thou consent to be made an instrument to these barbarians, to betray us into their hands, who are thy countrymen and fellow-Christians? Is it not a barbarous thing in thee to do so?

D. How do I go about to betray you? Do I not give you an account how the king invites you to come on shore, and has ordered you to be treated courteously and assisted?

W. As thou art a Christian, though I doubt it much, dost thou believe the king or the general, as thou callest it, means one word of what he says?

D. He promises you by the mouth of his great general.

W. I don't ask thee what he promises, or by whom; but I ask thee this: Canst thou say that thou believest he intends to perform it?

D. How can I answer that? How can I tell what he intends?

W. Thou canst tell what thou believest.

D. I cannot say but he will perform it; I believe he may.

W. Thou art but a double-tongued Christian, I doubt. Come, I'll ask thee another question: Wilt thou say that thou believest it, and that thou wouldst advise me to believe it, and put our lives into their hands upon these promises?

D. I am not to be your adviser.

W. Thou art perhaps afraid to speak thy mind, because thou art in their power. Pray, do any of them understand what thou and I say? Can they speak Dutch?

D. No, not one of them; I have no apprehensions upon that account at all.

W. Why, then, answer me plainly, if thou art a Christian: Is it safe for us to venture upon their words, to put ourselves into their hands, and come on shore?

D. You put it very home to me. Pray let me ask you another question: Are you in any likelihood of getting your ship off, if you refuse it?

W. Yes, yes, we shall get off the ship; now the storm is over we don't fear it.

D. Then I cannot say it is best for you to trust them.

W. Well, it is honestly said.

D. But what shall I say to them?

W. Give them good words, as they give us.

D. What good words?

W. Why, let them tell the king that we are strangers, who were driven on his coast by a great storm; that we thank him very kindly for his offer of civility to us, which, if we are further distressed, we will accept thankfully; but that at present we have no occasion to come on shore; and besides, that we cannot safely leave the ship in the present condition she is in; but that we are obliged to take care of her, in order to get her off; and expect, in a tide or two more, to get her quite clear, and at an anchor.

D. But he will expect you to come on shore, then, to visit him, and make him some present for his civility.

W. When we have got our ship clear, and stopped the leaks, we will pay our respects to him.

D. Nay, you may as well come to him now as then.

W. Nay, hold, friend; I did not say we would come to him then: you talked of making him a present, that is to pay our respects to him, is it not?

D. Well, but I will tell him that you will come on shore to him when your ship is got off.

W. I have nothing to say to that; you may tell him what you think fit.

D. But he will be in a great rage if I do not.

W. Who will he be in a great rage at?

D. At you.

W. What occasion have we to value that?

D. Why, he will send all his army down against you.

W. And what if they were all here just now? What dost thou suppose they could do to us?

D. He would expect they should burn your ships and bring you all to him.

W. Tell him, if he should try, he may catch a Tartar.

D. He has a world of men.

W. Has he any ships?

D. No, he has no ships.

W. Nor boats?

D. No, nor boats.

W. Why, what then do you think we care for his men? What canst thou do now to us, if thou hadst a hundred thousand with thee?

D. Oh! they might set you on fire.

W. Set us a-firing, thou meanest; that they might indeed; but set us on fire they shall not; they may try, at their peril, and we shall make mad work with your hundred thousand men, if they come within reach of our guns, I assure thee.

D. But what if the king gives you hostages for your safety?

W. Whom can he give but mere slaves and servants like thyself, whose lives he no more values than we an English hound?

D. Whom do you demand for hostages?

W. Himself and your worship.

D. What would you do with him?

W. Do with him as he would do with us — cut his head off.

D. And what would you do with me?

W. Do with thee? We would carry thee home into thine own country; and, though thou deservest the gallows, we would make a man and a Christian of thee again, and not do by thee as thou wouldst have done by us — betray thee to a parcel of merciless, savage pagans, that know no God, nor how to show mercy to man.

D. You put a thought in my head that I will speak to you about to-morrow.

Thus they went away, and William came on board, and gave us a full account of his parley with the old Dutchman, which was very diverting, and to me instructing; for I had abundance of reason to acknowledge William had made a better judgment of things than I.

It was our good fortune to get our ship off that very night, and to bring her to an anchor at about a mile and a half farther out, and in deep water, to our great satisfaction; so that we had no need to fear the Dutchman's king, with his hundred thousand men; and indeed we had some sport with them the next day, when they came down, a vast prodigious multitude of them, very few less in number, in our imagination, than a hundred thousand, with some elephants; though, if it had been an army of elephants, they could have done us no harm; for we were fairly at our anchor now, and out of their reach. And indeed we thought ourselves more out of their reach than we really were; and it was ten thousand to one that we had not been fast aground again, for the wind blowing off shore, though it made the water smooth where we lay, yet it blew the ebb farther out than usual, and we could easily perceive the sand, which we touched upon before, lay in the shape of a half-moon, and surrounded us with two horns of it, so that we lay in the middle or centre of it, as in a round bay, safe just as we were, and in deep water, but present death, as it were, on the right hand and on the left, for the two horns or points of the sand reached out beyond where our ship lay near two miles.

On that part of the sand which lay on our east side, this misguided multitude extended themselves; and being, most of them, not above their knees, or most of them not above ankle-deep in the water, they as it were surrounded us on that side, and on the side of the mainland, and a little way on the other side of the sand, standing in a half-circle, or rather three-fifths of a circle, for about six miles in length. The other horn, or point of the sand, which lay on our west side, being not quite so shallow, they could not extend themselves upon it so far.

They little thought what service they had done us, and how unwittingly, and by the greatest ignorance, they had made themselves pilots to us, while we, having not sounded the place, might have been lost before we were aware. It is true we might have sounded our new harbour before we had ventured out, but I cannot say for certain whether we should or not; for I, for my part, had not the least suspicion of what our real case was; however, I say, perhaps, before we had weighed, we should have looked about us a little. I am sure we ought to have done it; for, besides these armies of human furies, we had a very leaky ship, and all our pumps could hardly keep the water from growing upon us, and our carpenters were overboard, working to find out and stop the wounds we had received, heeling her first on the one side, and then on the other; and it was very diverting to see how, when our men heeled the ship over to the side next the wild army that stood on the east horn of the sand, they were so amazed, between fright and joy, that it put them into a kind of confusion, calling to one another, hallooing and skreeking, in a manner that it is impossible to describe.

While we were doing this, for we were in a great hurry you may be sure, and all hands at work, as well at the stopping our leaks as repairing our rigging and sails, which had received a great deal of damage, and also in rigging a new main-top-mast and the like; — I say, while we were doing all this, we perceived a body of men, of near a thousand, move from that part of the army of the barbarians that lay at the bottom of the sandy bay, and came all along the water's edge, round the sand, till they stood just on our broadside east, and were within about half-a-mile of us. Then we saw the Dutchman come forward nearer to us, and all alone, with his white flag and all his motions, just as before, and there he stood.

Our men had but just brought the ship to rights again as they came up to our broadside, and we had very happily found out and stopped the worst and most dangerous leak that we had, to our very great satisfaction; so I ordered the boats to be hauled up and manned as they were the day before, and William to go as plenipotentiary. I would have gone myself if I had understood Dutch, but as I did not, it was to no purpose, for I should be able to know nothing of what was said but from him at second-hand, which might be done as well afterwards. All the instructions I pretended to give William was, if possible, to get the old Dutchman away, and, if he could, to make him come on board.

Well, William went just as before, and when he came within about sixty or seventy yards of the shore, he held up his white flag as the Dutchman did, and turning the boat's broadside to the shore, and his men lying upon their oars, the parley or dialogue began again thus: —

William. Well, friend, what dost thou say to us now?

Dutchman. I come of the same mild errand as I did yesterday.

W. What! dost thou pretend to come of a mild errand with all these people at thy back, and all the foolish weapons of war they bring with them? Prithee, what dost thou mean?

D. The king hastens us to invite the captain and all his men to come on shore, and has ordered all his men to show them all the civility they can.

W. Well, and are all those men come to invite us ashore?

D. They will do you no hurt, if you will come on shore peaceably.

W. Well, and what dost thou think they can do to us, if we will not?

D. I would not have them do you any hurt then, neither.

W. But prithee, friend, do not make thyself fool and knave too. Dost not thou know that we are out of fear of all thy army, and out of danger of all that they can do? What makes thee act so simply as well as so knavishly?

D. Why, you may think yourselves safer than you are; you do not know what they may do to you. I can assure you they are able to do you a great deal of harm, and perhaps burn your ship.

W. Suppose that were true, as I am sure it is false; you see we have more ships to carry us off (pointing to the sloop).

[N.B. — Just at this time we discovered the sloop standing towards us from the east, along the shore, at about the distance of two leagues, which was to our particular satisfaction, she having been missing thirteen days.]

D. We do not value that; if you had ten ships, you dare not come on shore, with all the men you have, in a hostile way; we are too many for you.

W. Thou dost not, even in that, speak as thou meanest; and we may give thee a trial of our hands when our friends come up to us, for thou hearest they have discovered us.

[Just then the sloop fired five guns, which was to get news of us, for they did not see us.]

D. Yes, I hear they fire; but I hope your ship will not fire again; for, if they do, our general will take it for breaking the truce, and will make the army let fly a shower of arrows at you in the boat.

W. Thou mayest be sure the ship will fire that the other ship may hear them, but not with ball. If thy general knows no better, he may begin when he will; but thou mayest be sure we will return it to his cost.

D. What must I do, then?

W. Do! Why, go to him, and tell him of it beforehand, then; and let him know that the ship firing is not at him nor his men; and then come again, and tell us what he says.

D. No; I will send to him, which will do as well.

W. Do as thou wilt, but I believe thou hadst better go thyself; for if our men fire first, I suppose he will be in a great wrath, and it may be at thee; for, as to his wrath at us, we tell thee beforehand we value it not.

D. You slight them too much; you know not what they may do.

W. Thou makest as if these poor savage wretches could do mighty things: prithee, let us see what you can all do, we value it not; thou mayest set down thy flag of truce when thou pleasest, and begin.

D. I had rather make a truce, and have you all part friends.

W. Thou art a deceitful rogue thyself, for it is plain thou knowest these people would only persuade us on shore to entrap and surprise us; and yet thou that art a Christian, as thou callest thyself, would have us come on shore and put our lives into their hands who know nothing that belongs to compassion, good usage, or good manners. How canst thou be such a villain?

D. How can you call me so? What have I done to you, and what would you have me do?

W. Not act like a traitor, but like one that was once a Christian, and would have been so still, if you had not been a Dutchman.

D. I know not what to do, not I. I wish I were from them; they are a bloody people.

W. Prithee, make no difficulty of what thou shouldst do. Canst thou swim?

D. Yes, I can swim; but if I should attempt to swim off to you, I should have a thousand arrows and javelins sticking in me before I should get to your boat.

W. I'll bring the boat close to thee, and take thee on board in spite of them all. We will give them but one volley, and I'll engage they will all run away from thee.

D. You are mistaken in them, I assure you; they would immediately come all running down to the shore, and shoot fire-arrows at you, and set your boat and ship and all on fire about your ears.

W. We will venture that if thou wilt come off.

D. Will you use me honourably when I am among you?

W. I'll give thee my word for it, if thou provest honest.

D. Will you not make me a prisoner?

W. I will be thy surety, body for body, that thou shalt be a free man, and go whither thou wilt, though I own to thee thou dost not deserve it.

Just at this time our ship fired three guns to answer the sloop and let her know we saw her, who immediately, we perceived, understood it, and stood directly for the place. But it is impossible to express the confusion and filthy vile noise, the hurry and universal disorder, that was among that vast multitude of people upon our firing off three guns. They immediately all repaired to their arms, as I may call it; for to say they put themselves into order would be saying nothing.

Upon the word of command, then, they advanced all in a body to the seaside, and resolving to give us one volley of their fire-arms (for such they were), immediately they saluted us with a hundred thousand of their fire-arrows, every one carrying a little bag of cloth dipped in brimstone, or some such thing, which, flying through the air, had nothing to hinder it taking fire as it flew, and it generally did so.

I cannot say but this method of attacking us, by a way we had no notion of, might give us at first some little surprise, for the number was so great at first, that we were not altogether without apprehensions that they might unluckily set our ship on fire, so that William resolved immediately to row on board, and persuade us all to weigh and stand out to sea; but there was no time for it, for they immediately let fly a volley at the boat, and at the ship, from all parts of the vast crowd of people which stood near the shore. Nor did they fire, as I may call it, all at once, and so leave off; but their arrows being soon notched upon their bows, they kept continually shooting, so that the air was full of flame.

I could not say whether they set their cotton rag on fire before they shot the arrow, for I did not perceive they had fire with them, which, however, it seems they had. The arrow, besides the fire it carried with it, had a head, or a peg, as we call it, of bone; and some of sharp flint stone; and some few of a metal, too soft in itself for metal, but hard enough to cause it to enter, if it were a plank, so as to stick where it fell.

William and his men had notice sufficient to lie close behind their waste-boards, which, for this very purpose, they had made so high that they could easily sink themselves behind them, so as to defend themselves from anything that came point-blank (as we call it) or upon a line; but for what might fall perpendicularly out of the air they had no guard, but took the hazard of that. At first they made as if they would row away, but before they went they gave a volley of their fire-arms, firing at those which stood with the Dutchman; but William ordered them to be sure to take their aim at others, so as to miss him, and they did so.

There was no calling to them now, for the noise was so great among them that they could hear nobody, but our men boldly rowed in nearer to them, for they were at first driven a little off, and when they came nearer, they fired a second volley, which put the fellows into great confusion, and we could see from the ship that several of them were killed or wounded.

We thought this was a very unequal fight, and therefore we made a signal to our men to row away, that we might have a little of the sport as well as they; but the arrows flew so thick upon them, being so near

787

the shore, that they could not sit to their oars, so they spread a little of their sail, thinking they might sail along the shore, and lie behind their waste-board; but the sail had not been spread six minutes till it had five hundred fire-arrows shot into it and through it, and at length set it fairly on fire; nor were our men quite out of the danger of its setting the boat on fire, and this made them paddle and shove the boat away as well as they could, as they lay, to get farther off.

By this time they had left us a fair mark at the whole savage army; and as we had sheered the ship as near to them as we could, we fired among the thickest of them six or seven times, five guns at a time, with shot, old iron, musket-bullets, &c.

We could easily see that we made havoc among them, and killed and wounded abundance of them, and that they were in a great surprise at it; but yet they never offered to stir, and all this while their fire-arrows flew as thick as before.

At last, on a sudden their arrows stopped, and the old Dutchman came running down to the water-side all alone, with his white flag, as before, waving it as high as he could, and making signals to our boat to come to him again.

William did not care at first to go near him, but the man continuing to make signals to him to come, at last William went; and the Dutchman told him that he had been with the general, who was much mollified by the slaughter of his men, and that now he could have anything of him.

"Anything!" says William; "what have we to do with him? Let him go about his business, and carry his men out of gunshot, can't he?"

"Why," says the Dutchman, "but he dares not stir, nor see the king's face; unless some of your men come on shore, he will certainly put him to death."

"Why, then," says William, "he is a dead man; for if it were to save his life, and the lives of all the crowd that is with him, he shall never have one of us in his power. But I'll tell thee," said William, "how thou shalt cheat him, and gain thy own liberty too, if thou hast any mind to see thy own country again, and art not turned savage, and grown fond of living all thy days among heathens and savages."

"I would be glad to do it with all my heart," says he; "but if I should offer to swim off to you now, though they are so far from me, they shoot so true that they would kill me before I got half-way."

"But," says William, "I'll tell thee how thou shalt come with his consent. Go to him, and tell him I have offered to carry you on board, to try if you could persuade the captain to come on shore, and that I would not hinder him if he was willing to venture."

The Dutchman seemed in a rapture at the very first word. "I'll do it," says he; "I am persuaded he will give me leave to come."

Away he runs, as if he had a glad message to carry, and tells the general that William had promised, if he would go on board the ship with him, he would persuade the captain to return with him. The general was fool enough to give him orders to go, and charged him not to come back without the captain; which he readily promised, and very honestly might.

So they took him in, and brought him on board, and he was as good as his word to them, for he never went back to them any more; and the sloop being come to the mouth of the inlet where we lay, we weighed and set sail; but, as we went out, being pretty near the shore, we fired three guns, as it were among them, but without any shot, for it was of no use to us to hurt any more of them. After we had fired, we gave them a cheer, as the seamen call it; that is to say, we hallooed, at them, by way of triumph, and so carried off their ambassador. How it fared with their general, we know nothing of that.

This passage, when I related it to a friend of mine, after my return from those rambles, agreed so well with his relation of what happened to one Mr. Knox, an English captain, who some time ago was decoyed on shore by these people, that it could not but be very much to my satisfaction to think what mischief we had all escaped; and I think it cannot but be very profitable to record the other story (which is but short) with my own, to show whoever reads this what it was I avoided, and prevent their falling into the like, if they have to do with the perfidious people of Ceylon. The relation is as follows: —

The island of Ceylon being inhabited for the greatest part by barbarians, which will not allow any trade or commerce with any European nation, and inaccessible by any travelers, it will be convenient to relate the occasion how the author of this story happened to go into this island, and what opportunities he had of being fully acquainted with the people, their laws and customs, that so we may the better depend upon the account, and value it as it deserves, for the rarity as well as the truth of it; and both these the author gives us a brief relation of in this manner. His words are as follows:

In the year 1657, the *Anne* frigate, of London, Captain Robert Knox, commander, on the 21st day of January, set sail out of the Downs, in the service of the honourable East India Company of

England, bound for Fort St George, upon the coast of Coromandel, to trade for one year from port to port in India; which having performed, as he was lading his goods to return for England, being in the road of Masulipatam, on the 19th of November 1659, there happened such a mighty storm, that in it several ships were cast away, and he was forced to cut his mainmast by the board, which so disabled the ship, that he could not proceed in his voyage; whereupon Cottiar, in the island of Ceylon, being a very commodious bay, fit for her present distress, Thomas Chambers, Esq., since Sir Thomas Chambers, the agent at Fort St George, ordered that the ship should take in some cloth and India merchants belonging to Porto Novo, who might trade there while she lay to set her mast, and repair the other damages sustained by the storm. At her first coming thither, after the Indian merchants were set ashore, the captain and his men were very jealous of the people of that place, by reason the English never had any commerce or dealing with them; but after they had been there twenty days, going ashore and returning again at pleasure, without any molestation, they began to lay aside all suspicious thoughts of the people that dwelt thereabouts, who had kindly entertained them for their money.

By this time the king of the country had notice of their arrival, and, not being acquainted with their intents, he sent down a dissauva, or general, with an army, to them, who immediately sent a messenger to the captain on board, to desire him to come ashore to him, pretending a letter from the king. The captain saluted the message with firing of guns, and ordered his son, Robert Knox, and Mr. John Loveland, merchant of the ship, to go ashore, and wait on him. When they were come before him, he demanded who they were, and how long they should stay. They told him they were Englishmen, and not to stay above twenty or thirty days, and desired permission to trade in his Majesty's port. His answer was, that the king was glad to hear the English were come into his country, and had commanded him to assist them as they should desire, and had sent a letter to be delivered to none but the captain himself. They were then twelve miles from the seaside, and therefore replied, that the captain could not leave his ship to come so far; but if he pleased to go down to the seaside, the captain would wait on him to receive the letter; whereupon the dissauva desired them to stay that day, and on the morrow he would go with them; which, rather than displease him in so small a matter, they consented to. In the evening the dissauva sent a present to the captain of cattle and fruits, &c., which, being carried all night by the messengers, was delivered to him in the morning, who told him withal that his men were coming down with the dissauva, and desired his company on shore against his coming, having a letter from the king to deliver into his own hand. The captain, mistrusting nothing, came on shore with his boat, and, sitting under a tamarind tree, waited for the dissauva. In the meantime the native soldiers privately surrounded him and the seven men he had with him, and seizing them, carried them to meet the dissauva, bearing the captain on a hammock on their shoulders.

The next day the long-boat's crew, not knowing what had happened, came on shore to cut down a tree to make cheeks for the mainmast, and were made prisoners after the same manner, though with more violence, because they were more rough with them, and made resistance; yet they were not brought to the captain and his company, but quartered in another house in the same town.

The dissauva having thus gotten two boats and eighteen men, his next care was to gain the ship; and to that end, telling the captain that he and his men were only detained because the king intended to send letters and a present to the English nation by him, desired he would send some men on board his ship to order her to stay; and because the ship was in danger of being fired by the Dutch if she stayed long in the bay, to bring her up the river. The captain did not approve of the advice, but did not dare to own his dislike; so he sent his son with the order, but with a solemn conjuration to return again, which he accordingly did, bringing a letter from the company in the ship, that they would not obey the captain, nor any other, in this matter, but were resolved to stand on their own defence. This letter satisfied the dissauva, who thereupon gave the captain leave to write for what he would have brought from the ship, pretending that he had not the king's order to release them, though it would suddenly come.

The captain seeing he was held in suspense, and the season of the year spending for the ship to proceed on her voyage to some place, sent order to Mr. John Burford, the chief mate, to take charge of the ship, and set sail to Porto Novo, from whence they came, and there to follow the agent's order.

And now began that long and sad captivity they all along feared. The ship being gone, the dissauva was called up to the king, and they were kept under guards a while, till a special order came from the king to part them, and put one in a town, for the conveniency of their maintenance, which the king ordered to be at the charge of the country. On September 16, 1660, the captain and his son were placed in a town called Bonder Coswat, in the country of Hotcurly, distant from the city of Kandy northward thirty miles, and from the rest of the English a full day's journey. Here they had their provisions brought them twice a day, without money, as much as they could eat, and as good as the country yielded. The situation of the place was very pleasant and commodious; but that year that part of the land was very sickly by agues and fevers, of which many died. The captain and his son after some time were visited with the common distemper, and the captain, being also loaded with grief for his deplorable condition, languished more than three months, and then died, February 9, 1661.

Robert Knox, his son, was now left desolate, sick, and in captivity, having none to comfort him but God, who is the Father of the fatherless, and hears the groans of such as are in captivity; being alone to enter upon a long scene of misery and calamity; oppressed with weakness of body and grief of soul for the loss of his father, and the remediless trouble that he was like to endure; and the first instance of it was in the burial of his father, for he sent his black boy to the people of the town, to desire their assistance, because they understood not their language; but they sent him only a rope, to drag him by the neck into the woods, and told him that they would offer him no other help, unless he would pay for it. This barbarous answer increased his trouble for his father's death, that now he was like to lie unburied, and be made a prey to the wild beasts in the woods; for the ground was very hard, and they had not tools to dig with, and so it was impossible for them to bury him; and having a small matter of money left him, viz., a pagoda and a gold ring, he hired a man, and so buried him in as decent a manner as their condition would permit.

His dead father being thus removed out of his sight, but his ague continuing, he was reduced very low, partly by sorrow and partly by his disease. All the comfort he had was to go into the wood and fields with a book, either the "Practice of Piety" or Mr. Rogers's "Seven Treatises," which were the only two books he had, and meditate and read, and sometimes pray; in which his anguish made him often invert Elijah's petition, — that he might die, because his life was a burden to him. God, though He was pleased to prolong his life, yet He found a way to lighten his grief, by removing his ague, and granting him a desire which above all things was acceptable to him. He had read his two books over so often that he had both almost by heart; and though they were both pious and good writings, yet he longed for the truth from the original fountain, and thought it his greatest unhappiness that he had not a Bible, and did believe that he should never see one again; but, contrary to his expectation, God brought him one after this manner. As he was fishing one day with his black boy, to catch some fish to relieve his hunger, an old man passed by them, and asked his boy whether his master could read; and when the boy had answered yes, he told him that he had gotten a book from the Portuguese, when they left Colombo; and, if his master pleased, he would sell it him. The boy told his master, who bade him go and see what book it was. The boy having served the English some time, knew the book, and as soon as he got it into his hand, came running to him, calling out before he came to him, "It is the Bible!" The words startled him, and he flung down his angle to meet him, and, finding it was true, was mightily rejoiced to see it; but he was afraid he should not have enough to purchase it, though he was resolved to part with all the money he had, which was but one pagoda, to buy it; but his black boy persuading him to slight it, and leave it to him to buy it, he at length obtained it for a knit cap.

This accident he could not but look upon as a great miracle, that God should bestow upon him such an extraordinary blessing, and bring him a Bible in his own native language, in such a remote part of the world, where His name was not known, and where it was never heard of that an Englishman had ever been before. The enjoyment of this mercy was a great comfort to him in captivity, and though he wanted no bodily convenience that the country did afford; for the king, immediately after his father's death, had sent an express order to the people of the towns, that they should be kind to him, and give him good victuals; and after he had been some time in the country, and understood the language, he got him good conveniences, as a house and gardens; and falling to husbandry, God so prospered him, that he had plenty, not only for himself, but to lend others; which being, according to the custom of the country, at 50 per cent. a year, much enriched him: he had also goats, which served him for mutton, and hogs and hens. Notwithstanding this, I say, for he lived as fine as any of their noblemen, he could not so far forget his native country as to be contented to dwell in a strange land, where there was to him a famine of God's word and sacraments, the want of which made all other things to be of little value to him; therefore, as he made it his daily and fervent prayer to God, in His good time, to restore him to both, so, at length, he, with one Stephen Rutland, who had lived with him two years before, resolved to make their escape, and, about the year 1673, meditated all secret ways to compass it. They had before taken up a way of peddling about the country, and buying tobacco, pepper, garlic, combs, and all sorts of iron ware, and carried them into those parts of the country where they wanted them; and now, to promote their design, as they went with their commodities from place to place, they discoursed with the country people (for they could now speak their language well) concerning the ways and inhabitants, where the isle was thinnest and fullest inhabited, where and how the watches lay from one country to another, and what commodities were proper for them to carry into all parts; pretending that they would furnish themselves with such wares as the respective places wanted. None doubted but what they did was upon the account of trade, because Mr. Knox was so well seated, and could not be supposed to leave such an estate, by traveling northward, because that part of the land was least inhabited; and so, furnishing themselves with such wares as were vendible in those parts, they set forth, and steered their course towards the north part of the islands, knowing very little of the ways, which were generally intricate and perplexed, because they have no public roads, but a multitude of little paths from one town to another, and those often changing; and for white men to inquire about the ways was very dangerous, because the people would presently suspect their design.

At this time they traveled from Conde Uda as far as the country of Nuwarakalawiya, which is the furthermost part of the king's dominions, and about three days' journey from their dwelling. They were very thankful to Providence that they had passed all difficulties so far, but yet they durst not go any farther, because they had no wares left to traffic with; and it being the first time they had been absent so long from home, they feared the townsmen would come after them to seek for them; and so they returned home, and went eight or ten times into those parts with their wares, till they became well acquainted both with the people and the paths.

In these parts Mr. Knox met his black boy, whom he had turned away divers years before. He had now got a wife and children, and was very poor; but being acquainted with these quarters, he not only took directions of him, but agreed with him, for a good reward, to conduct him and his companions to the Dutch. He gladly undertook it, and a time was appointed between them; but Mr. Knox being disabled by a grievous pain, which seized him on his right side, and held him five days that he could not travel, this appointment proved in vain; for though he went as soon as he was well, his guide was gone into another country about his business, and they durst not at that time venture to run away without him.

These attempts took up eight or nine years, various accidents hindering their designs, but most commonly the dry weather, because they feared in the woods they should be starved with thirst, all the country being in such a condition almost four or five years together for lack of rain.

On September 22, 1679, they set forth again, furnished with knives and small axes for their defence, because they could carry them privately and send all sorts of wares to sell as formerly, and all necessary provisions, the moon being twenty-seven days old, that they might have light to run away by, to try what success God Almighty would now give them in seeking their liberty. Their first stage was to Anuradhapoora, in the way to which lay a wilderness, called Parraoth Mocolane, full of wild elephants, tigers, and bears; and because it is the utmost confines of the king's dominions, there is always a watch kept.

In the middle of the way they heard that the governor's officers of these parts were out to gather up the king's revenues and duties, to send them up to the city; which put them into no small fear, lest, finding them, they should send them back again; whereupon they withdrew to the western parts of Ecpoulpot, and sat down to knitting till they heard the officers were gone. As soon as they were departed, they went onwards of their journey, having got a good parcel of cotton-yarn to knit caps with, and having kept their wares, as they pretended, to exchange for dried flesh, which was sold only in those lower parts. Their way lay necessarily through the governor's yard at Kalluvilla, who dwells there on purpose to examine all that go and come. This greatly distressed them, because he would easily suspect they were out of their bounds, being captives; however, they went resolutely to his house, and meeting him, presented him with a small parcel of tobacco and betel; and, showing him their wares, told him they came to get dried flesh to carry back with them. The governor did not suspect them, but told them he was sorry they came in so dry a time, when no deer were to be catched, but if some rain fell, he would soon supply them. This answer pleased them, and they seemed contented to stay; and accordingly, abiding with him two or three days, and no rain falling, they presented the governor with five or six charges of gunpowder, which is a rarity among them; and leaving a bundle at his house, they desired him to shoot them some deer, while they made a step to Anuradhapoora. Here also they were put in a great fright by the coming of certain soldiers from the king to the governor, to give him orders to set a secure guard at the watches, that no suspicious persons might pass, which, though it was only intended to prevent the flight of the relations of certain nobles whom the king had clapped up, yet they feared they might wonder to see white men here, and so send them back again; but God so ordered it that they were very kind to them and left them to their business, and so they got safe to Anuradhapoora. Their pretence was dried flesh, though they knew there was none to be had; but their real business was to search the way down to the Dutch, which they stayed three days to do; but finding that in the way to Jaffnapatam, which is one of the Dutch ports, there was a watch which could hardly be passed, and other inconveniences not surmountable, they resolved to go back, and take the river Malwatta Oya, which they had before judged would be a probable guide to lead them to the sea; and, that they might not be pursued, left Anuradhapoora just at night, when the people never travel for fear of wild beasts, on Sunday, October 12, being stored with all things needful for their journey, viz., ten days' provision, a basin to boil their provision in, two calabashes to fetch water in, and two great tallipat leaves for tents, with jaggery, sweetmeats, tobacco, betel, tinder-boxes, and a deerskin for shoes, to keep their feet from thorns, because to them they chiefly trusted. Being come to the river, they struck into the woods, and kept by the side of it; yet not going on the sand (lest their footsteps should be discerned), unless forced, and then going backwards.

Being gotten a good way into the wood, it began to rain; wherefore they erected their tents, made a fire, and refreshed themselves against the rising of the moon, which was then eighteen days old; and having tied deerskins about their feet, and eased themselves of their wares, they proceeded on their journey. When they had traveled three or four hours with difficulty, because the moon gave but little light among the thick trees, they found an elephant in their way before them, and because they could not scare him away, they were forced to stay till morning; and so they kindled a fire, and took a pipe of tobacco. By the light they could not discern that ever anybody had been there, nothing being to be seen but woods; and so they were in great hopes that they were past all danger, being beyond all inhabitants; but they were mistaken, for the river winding northward, brought them into the midst of a parcel of towns, called Tissea Wava, where, being in danger of being seen, they were under a mighty terror; for had the people found them, they would have beat them, and sent them up to the king; and, to avoid it, they crept into a hollow tree, and sat there in mud and wet till it began to grow dark, and then betaking themselves to their legs, traveled till the darkness of night stopped them. They heard voices behind them, and feared it was somebody in pursuit of them; but at length, discerning it was only an hallooing to keep the wild beasts out of the corn, they pitched their tents by the river, and having boiled rice and roasted meat for their suppers, and satisfied their hunger, they committed themselves to God's keeping, and laid them down to sleep.

The next morning, to prevent the worst, they got up early and hastened on their journey; and though they were now got out of all danger of the tame Chiangulays, they were in great danger of the wild ones, of whom those woods were full; and though they saw their tents, yet they were all gone, since the rains had fallen, from the river into the woods; and so God kept them from that danger, for, had they met the wild men, they had been shot.

Thus they traveled from morning till night several days, through bushes and thorns, which made their arms and shoulders, which were naked, all of a gore blood. They often met with bears, hogs, deer, and wild buffaloes; but they all ran away as soon as they saw them. The river was exceedingly full of alligators; in the evening they used to pitch their tents, and make great fires both before and behind them, to affright the wild beasts; and though they heard the voices of all sorts, they saw none.

On Thursday, at noon, they crossed the river Coronda, which parts the country of the Malabars from the king's, and on Friday, about nine or ten in the morning, came among the inhabitants, of whom they were as much afraid as of the Chiangulays before; for, though the Wanniounay, or prince of this people, payeth tribute to the Dutch out of fear, yet he is better affected to the King of Kandy, and, if he had took them, would have sent them up to their old master; but not knowing any way to escape, they kept on their journey by the river-side by day, because the woods were not to be traveled by night for thorns and wild beasts, who came down then to the river to drink. In all the Malabar country they met with only two Brahmins, who treated them very civilly; and for their money, one of them conducted them till they came into the territories of the Dutch, and out of all danger of the King of Kandy, which did not a little rejoice them; but yet they were in no small trouble how to find the way out of the woods, till a Malabar, for the lucre of a knife, conducted them to a Dutch town, where they found guides to conduct them from town to town, till they came to the fort called Aripo, where they arrived Saturday, October 18, 1679, and there thankfully adored God's wonderful providence, in thus completing their deliverance from a long captivity of nineteen years and six months.

I come now back to my own history, which grows near a conclusion, as to the travels I took in this part of the world. We were now at sea, and we stood away to the north for a while, to try if we could get a market for our spice, for we were very rich in nutmegs, but we ill knew what to do with them; we durst not go upon the English coast, or, to speak more properly, among the English factories to trade; not that we were afraid to fight any two ships they had, and, besides that, we knew that, as they had no letters of mark, or of reprisals from the government, so it was none of their business to act offensively, no, not though we were pirates. Indeed, if we had made any attempt upon them, they might have justified themselves in joining together to resist, and assisting one another to defend themselves; but to go out of their business to attack a pirate ship of almost fifty guns, as we were, it was plain that it was none of their business, and consequently it was none of our concern, so we did not trouble ourselves about it; but, on the other hand, it was none of our business to be seen among them, and to have the news of us carried from one factory to another, so that whatever design we might be upon at another time, we should be sure to be prevented and discovered. Much less had we any occasion to be seen among any of the Dutch factories upon the coast of Malabar; for, being fully laden with the spices which we had, in the sense of their trade, plundered them of, it would have told them what we were, and all that we had been doing; and they would, no doubt, have concerned themselves all manner of ways to have fallen upon us.

The only way we had for it was to stand away for Goa, and trade, if we could, for our spices, with the Portuguese factory there. Accordingly, we sailed almost thither, for we had made land two days before, and being in the latitude of Goa, were standing in fair for Margaon, on the head of Salsat, at the going up to Goa, when I called to the men at the helm to bring the ship to, and bid the pilot go away N.N.W., till we came out of sight of the shore, when William and I called a council, as we used to do upon emergencies, what course we should take to trade there and not be discovered; and we concluded at length that we would not go thither at all, but that William, with such trusty fellows only as could be depended upon, should go in the sloop to Surat, which was still farther northward, and trade there as merchants with such of the English factory as they could find to be for their turn.

To carry this with the more caution, and so as not to be suspected, we agreed to take out all her guns, and put such men into her, and no other, as would promise us not to desire or offer to go on shore, or to enter into any talk or conversation with any that might come on board; and, to finish the disguise to our mind, William documented two of our men, one a surgeon, as he himself was, and the other, a ready-witted fellow, an old sailor, that had been a pilot upon the coast of New England, and was an excellent mimic; these two William dressed up like two Quakers, and made them talk like such. The old pilot he made go captain of the sloop, and the surgeon for doctor, as he was, and himself supercargo. In this figure, and the sloop all plain, no curled work upon her (indeed she had not much before), and no guns to be seen, away he went for Surat.

I should, indeed, have observed, that we went, some days before we parted, to a small sandy island close under the shore, where there was a good cove of deep water, like a road, and out of sight of any of the factories, which are here very thick upon the coast. Here we shifted the loading of the sloop, and put into her such things only as we had a mind to dispose of there, which was indeed little but nutmegs and cloves, but chiefly the former; and from thence William and his two Quakers, with about eighteen men in the sloop, went away to Surat, and came to an anchor at a distance from the factory.

William used such caution that he found means to go on shore himself, and the doctor, as he called him, in a boat which came on board them to sell fish, rowed with only Indians of the country, which boat he afterwards hired to carry him on board again. It was not long that they were on shore, but that they found means to get acquaintance with some Englishmen, who, though they lived there, and perhaps were the company's servants at first, yet appeared then to be traders for themselves, in whatever coast business especially came in their way; and the doctor was made the first to pick acquaintance; so he recommended his friend, the supercargo, till, by degrees, the merchants were as fond of the bargain as our men were of the merchants, only that the cargo was a little too much for them.

However, this did not prove a difficulty long with them, for the next day they brought two more merchants, English also, into their bargain, and, as William could perceive by their discourse, they resolved, if they bought them, to carry them to the Gulf of Persia upon their own accounts. William took the hint, and, as he told me afterwards, concluded we might carry them there as well as they. But this was not William's present business; he had here no less than three-and-thirty ton of nuts and eighteen ton of cloves. There was a good quantity of mace among the nutmegs, but we did not stand to make much allowance. In short, they bargained, and the merchants, who would gladly have bought sloop and all, gave William directions, and two men for pilots, to go to a creek about six leagues from the factory, where they brought boats, and unloaded the whole cargo, and paid William very honestly for it; the whole parcel amounting, in money, to about thirty-five thousand pieces of eight, besides some goods of value, which William was content to take, and two large diamonds, worth about three hundred pounds sterling.

When they paid the money, William invited them on board the sloop, where they came; and the merry old Quaker diverted them exceedingly with his talk, and "thee'd" them and "thou'd" them till he made them so drunk that they could not go on shore for that night.

They would fain have known who our people were, and whence they came; but not a man in the sloop would answer them to any question they asked, but in such a manner as let them think themselves bantered and jested with. However, in discourse, William said they were able men for any cargo we could have brought them, and that they would have bought twice as much spice if we had had it. He ordered the merry captain to tell them that they had another sloop that lay at Margaon, and that had a great quantity of spice on board also; and that, if it was not sold when he went back (for that thither he was bound), he would bring her up.

Their new chaps were so eager, that they would have bargained with the old captain beforehand. "Nay, friend," said he, "I will not trade with thee unsight and unseen; neither do I know whether the master of the sloop may not have sold his loading already to some merchants of Salsat; but if he has not when I come to him, I think to bring him up to thee."

The doctor had his employment all this while, as well as William and the old captain, for he went on shore several times a day in the Indian boat, and brought fresh provisions for the sloop, which the men had need enough of. He brought, in particular, seventeen large casks of arrack, as big as butts, besides smaller quantities, a quantity of rice, and abundance of fruits, mangoes, pompions, and such things, with fowls and fish. He never came on board but he was deep laden; for, in short, he bought for the ship as well as for themselves; and, particularly, they half-loaded the ship with rice and arrack, with some hogs, and six or seven cows, alive; and thus, being well victualed, and having directions for coming again, they returned to us.

William was always the lucky welcome messenger to us, but never more welcome to us than now; for where we had thrust in the ship, we could get nothing, except a few mangoes and roots, being not willing to make any steps into the country, or make ourselves known till we had news of our sloop; and indeed our men's patience was almost tired, for it was seventeen days that William spent upon this enterprise, and well bestowed too.

When he came back we had another conference upon the subject of trade, namely, whether we should send the best of our spices, and other goods we had in the ship, to Surat, or whether we should go up to the Gulf of Persia ourselves, where it was probable we might sell them as well as the English merchants of Surat. William was for going ourselves, which, by the way, was from the good, frugal, merchant-like temper of the man, who was for the best of everything; but here I overruled William, which I very seldom took upon me to do; but I told him, that, considering our circumstances, it was much better for us to sell all our cargoes here, though we made but half-price of them, than to go with them to the Gulf of Persia, where we should run a greater risk, and where people would be much more curious and inquisitive into things than they were here, and where it would not be so easy to manage them, seeing they traded freely and openly there, not by stealth, as those men seemed to do; and, besides, if they suspected anything, it would be much more difficult for us to retreat, except by mere force, than here, where we were upon the high sea as it were, and could be gone whenever we pleased, without any disguise, or, indeed, without the least appearance of being pursued, none knowing where to look for us.

My apprehensions prevailed with William, whether my reasons did or no, and he submitted; and we resolved to try another ship's loading to the same merchants. The main business was to consider how to get off that circumstance that had exposed them to the English merchants, namely that it was our other sloop; but this the old Quaker pilot undertook; for being, as I said, an excellent mimic himself, it was the easier for him to dress up the sloop in new clothes; and first, he put on all the carved work he had taken off before; her stern, which was painted of a dumb white or dun colour before, all flat, was now all lacquered and blue, and I know not how many gay figures in it; as to her quarter, the carpenters made her a neat little gallery on either side; she had twelve guns put into her, and some petereroes upon her gunnel, none of which were there before; and to finish her new habit or appearance, and make her change complete, he ordered her sails to be altered; and as she sailed before with a half-sprit, like a yacht, she sailed now with square-sail and mizzen-mast, like a ketch; so that, in a word, she was a perfect cheat, disguised in everything that a stranger could be supposed to take any notice of that had never had but one view, for they had been but once on board.

In this mean figure the sloop returned; she had a new man put into her for captain, one we knew how to trust; and the old pilot appearing only as a passenger, the doctor and William acting as the supercargoes, by a formal procuration from one Captain Singleton, and all things ordered in form.

We had a complete loading for the sloop; for, besides a very great quantity of nutmegs and cloves, mace, and some cinnamon, she had on board some goods which we took in as we lay about the Philippine Islands, while we waited as looking for purchase.

William made no difficulty of selling this cargo also, and in about twenty days returned again, freighted with all necessary provisions for our voyage, and for a long time; and, as I say, we had a great deal of other goods: he brought us back about three-and-thirty thousand pieces of eight, and some diamonds, which, though William did not pretend to much skill in, yet he made shift to act so as not to be imposed upon, the merchants he had to deal with, too, being very fair men.

They had no difficulty at all with these merchants, for the prospect they had of gain made them not at all inquisitive, nor did they make the least discovery of the sloop; and as to the selling them spices which were fetched so far from thence, it seems it was not so much a novelty there as we believed, for the Portuguese had frequently vessels which came from Macao in China, who brought spices, which they bought of the Chinese traders, who again frequently dealt among the Dutch Spice Islands, and received spices in exchange for such goods as they carried from China.

This might be called, indeed, the only trading voyage we had made; and now we were really very rich, and it came now naturally before us to consider whither we should go next. Our proper delivery port, as we ought to have called it, was at Madagascar, in the Bay of Mangahelly; but William took me by myself into the cabin of the sloop one day, and told me he wanted to talk seriously with me a little; so we shut ourselves in, and William began with me.

"Wilt thou give me leave," says William, "to talk plainly with thee upon thy present circumstances, and thy future prospect of living? and wilt thou promise, on thy word, to take nothing ill of me?"

"With all my heart," said I. "William, I have always found your advice good, and your designs have not only been well laid, but your counsel has been very lucky to us; and, therefore, say what you will, I promise you I will not take it ill."

"But that is not all my demand," says William; "if thou dost not like what I am going to propose to thee, thou shalt promise me not to make it public among the men."

"I will not, William," says I, "upon my word;" and swore to him, too, very heartily.

"Why, then," says William, "I have but one thing more to article with thee about, and that is, that thou wilt consent that if thou dost not approve of it for thyself, thou wilt yet consent that I shall put so much of it in practice as relates to myself and my new comrade doctor, so that it be nothing to thy detriment and loss."

"In anything," says I, "William, but leaving me, I will; but I cannot part with you upon any terms whatever."

"Well," says William, "I am not designing to part from thee, unless it is thy own doing. But assure me in all these points, and I will tell my mind freely."

So I promised him everything he desired of me in the solemnest manner possible, and so seriously and frankly withal, that William made no scruple to open his mind to me.

"Why, then, in the first place," says William, "shall I ask thee if thou dost not think thou and all thy men are rich enough, and have really gotten as much wealth together (by whatsoever way it has been gotten, that is not the question) as we all know what to do with?"

"Why, truly, William," said I, "thou art pretty right; I think we have had pretty good luck."

"Well, then," says William, "I would ask whether, if thou hast gotten enough, thou hast any thought of leaving off this trade; for most people leave off trading when they are satisfied of getting, and are rich enough; for nobody trades for the sake of trading; much less do men rob for the sake of thieving."

"Well, William," says I, "now I perceive what it is thou art driving at. I warrant you," says I, "you begin to hanker after home."

"Why, truly," says William, "thou hast said it, and so I hope thou dost too. It is natural for most men that are abroad to desire to come

803

home again at last, especially when they are grown rich, and when they are (as thou ownest thyself to be) rich enough, and so rich as they know not what to do with more if they had it."

"Well, William," said I, "but now you think you have laid your preliminary at first so home that I should have nothing to say; that is, that when I had got money enough, it would be natural to think of going home. But you have not explained what you mean by home, and there you and I shall differ. Why, man, I am at home; here is my habitation; I never had any other in my lifetime; I was a kind of charity school boy; so that I can have no desire of going anywhere for being rich or poor, for I have nowhere to go."

"Why," says William, looking a little confused, "art not thou an Englishman?"

"Yes," says I, "I think so: you see I speak English; but I came out of England a child, and never was in it but once since I was a man; and then I was cheated and imposed upon, and used so ill that I care not if I never see it more."

"Why, hast thou no relations or friends there?" says he; "no acquaintance — none that thou hast any kindness or any remains of respect for?"

"Not I, William," said I; "no more than I have in the court of the Great Mogul."

"Nor any kindness for the country where thou wast born?" says William.

"Not I, any more than for the island of Madagascar, nor so much neither; for that has been a fortunate island to me more than once, as thou knowest, William," said I.

William was quite stunned at my discourse, and held his peace; and I said to him, "Go on, William; what hast thou to say farther? for I hear you have some project in your head," says I; "come, let's have it out."

"Nay," says William, "thou hast put me to silence, and all I had to say is overthrown; all my projects are come to nothing, and gone."

"Well, but, William," said I, "let me hear what they were; for though it is so that what I have to aim at does not look your way, and though I have no relation, no friend, no acquaintance in England, yet I do not say I like this roving, cruising life so well as never to give it over. Let me hear if thou canst propose to me anything beyond it."

"Certainly, friend," says William, very gravely, "there is something beyond it;" and lifting up his hands, he seemed very much affected, and

I thought I saw tears stand in his eyes; but I, that was too hardened a wretch to be moved with these things, laughed at him. "What!" says I, "you mean death, I warrant you: don't you? That is beyond this trade. Why, when it comes, it comes; then we are all provided for."

"Ay," says William, "that is true; but it would be better that some things were thought on before that came."

"Thought on!" says I; "what signifies thinking of it? To think of death is to die, and to be always thinking of it is to be all one's life long a-dying. It is time enough to think of it when it comes."

You will easily believe I was well qualified for a pirate that could talk thus. But let me leave it upon record, for the remark of other hardened rogues like myself, — my conscience gave me a pang that I never felt before when I said, "What signifies thinking of it?" and told me I should one day think of these words with a sad heart; but the time of my reflection was not yet come; so I went on.

Says William very seriously, "I must tell thee, friend, I am sorry to hear thee talk so. They that never think of dying, often die without thinking of it."

I carried on the jesting way a while farther, and said, "Prithee, do not talk of dying; how do we know we shall ever die?" and began to laugh.

"I need not answer thee to that," says William; "it is not my place to reprove thee, who art commander over me here; but I would rather thou wouldst talk otherwise of death; it is a coarse thing."

"Say anything to me, William," said I; "I will take it kindly." I began now to be very much moved at his discourse.

Says William (tears running down his face), "It is because men live as if they were never to die, that so many die before they know how to live. But it was not death that I meant when I said that there was something to be thought of beyond this way of living."

"Why, William," said I, "what was that?"

"It was repentance," says he.

"Why," says I, "did you ever know a pirate repent?"

At this he startled a little, and returned, "At the gallows I have [known] one before, and I hope thou wilt be the second."

He spoke this very affectionately, with an appearance of concern for me.

"Well, William," says I, "I thank you; and I am not so senseless of these things, perhaps, as I make myself seem to be. But come, let me hear your proposal."

"My proposal," says William, "is for thy good as well as my own. We may put an end to this kind of life, and repent; and I think the fairest occasion offers for both, at this very time, that ever did, or ever will, or, indeed, can happen again."

"Look you, William," says I; "let me have your proposal for putting an end to our present way of living first, for that is the case before us, and you and I will talk of the other afterwards. I am not so insensible," said I, "as you may think me to be. But let us get out of this hellish condition we are in first."

"Nay," says William, "thou art in the right there; we must never talk of repenting while we continue pirates."

"Well," says I, "William, that's what I meant; for if we must not reform, as well as be sorry for what is done, I have no notion what repentance means; indeed, at best I know little of the matter; but the nature of the thing seems to tell me that the first step we have to take is to break off this wretched course; and I'll begin there with you, with all my heart."

I could see by his countenance that William was thoroughly pleased with the offer; and if he had tears in his eyes before, he had more now; but it was from quite a different passion; for he was so swallowed up with joy he could not speak.

"Come, William," says I, "thou showest me plain enough thou hast an honest meaning; dost thou think it practicable for us to put an end to our unhappy way of living here, and get off?"

"Yes," says he, "I think it very practicable for me; whether it is for thee or no, that will depend upon thyself."

"Well," says I, "I give you my word, that as I have commanded you all along, from the time I first took you on board, so you shall command me from this hour, and everything you direct me I'll do."

"Wilt thou leave it all to me? Dost thou say this freely?"

"Yes, William," said I, "freely; and I'll perform it faithfully."

"Why, then," says William, "my scheme is this: We are now at the mouth of the Gulf of Persia; we have sold so much of our cargo here at Surat, that we have money enough; send me away for Bassorah with the sloop, laden with the China goods we have on board, which will make another good cargo, and I'll warrant thee I'll find means, among the English and Dutch merchants there, to lodge a quantity of goods and money also as a merchant, so as we will be able to have recourse to it again upon any occasion, and when I come home we will

806

contrive the rest; and, in the meantime, do you bring the ship's crew to take a resolution to go to Madagascar as soon as I return."

I told him I thought he need not go so far as Bassorah, but might run into Gombroon, or to Ormuz, and pretend the same business.

"No," says he, "I cannot act with the same freedom there, because the Company's factories are there, and I may be laid hold of there on pretence of interloping."

"Well, but," said I, "you may go to Ormuz, then; for I am loth to part with you so long as to go to the bottom of the Persian Gulf." He returned, that I should leave it to him to do as he should see cause.

We had taken a large sum of money at Surat, so that we had near a hundred thousand pounds in money at our command, but on board the great ship we had still a great deal more.

I ordered him publicly to keep the money on board which he had, and to buy up with it a quantity of ammunition, if he could get it, and so to furnish us for new exploits; and, in the meantime, I resolved to get a quantity of gold and some jewels, which I had on board the great ship, and place them so that I might carry them off without notice as soon as he came back; and so, according to William's directions, I left him to go the voyage, and I went on board the great ship, in which we had indeed an immense treasure.

We waited no less than two months for William's return, and indeed I began to be very uneasy about William, sometimes thinking he had abandoned me, and that he might have used the same artifice to have engaged the other men to comply with him, and so they were gone away together; and it was but three days before his return that I was just upon the point of resolving to go away to Madagascar, and give him over; but the old surgeon, who mimicked the Quaker and passed for the master of the sloop at Surat, persuaded me against that, for which good advice and apparent faithfulness in what he had been trusted with, I made him a party to my design, and he proved very honest.

At length William came back, to our inexpressible joy, and brought a great many necessary things with him; as, particularly, he brought sixty barrels of powder, some iron shot, and about thirty ton of lead; also he brought a great deal of provisions; and, in a word, William gave me a public account of his voyage, in the hearing of whoever happened to be upon the quarter-deck, that no suspicions might be found about us.

After all was done, William moved that he might go up again, and that I would go with him; named several things which we had on board that he could not sell there; and, particularly, told us he had been obliged to leave several things there, the caravans being not come in; and that he had engaged to come back again with goods.

This was what I wanted. The men were eager for his going, and particularly because he told them they might load the sloop back with rice and provisions; but I seemed backward to going, when the old surgeon stood up and persuaded me to go, and with many arguments pressed me to it; as, particularly, if I did not go, there would be no order, and several of the men might drop away, and perhaps betray all the rest; and that they should not think it safe for the sloop to go again if I did not go; and to urge me to it, he offered himself to go with me.

Upon these considerations I seemed to be over-persuaded to go, and all the company seemed to be better satisfied when I had consented; and, accordingly, we took all the powder, lead, and iron out of the sloop into the great ship, and all the other things that were for the ship's use, and put in some bales of spices and casks or frails of cloves, in all about seven ton, and some other goods, among the bales of which I had conveyed all my private treasure, which, I assure you, was of no small value, and away I went.

At going off I called a council of all the officers in the ship to consider in what place they should wait for me, and how long, and we appointed the ship to stay eight-and-twenty days at a little island on the Arabian side of the Gulf, and that, if the sloop did not come in that time, they should sail to another island to the west of that place, and wait there fifteen days more, and that then, if the sloop did not come, they should conclude some accident must have happened, and the rendezvous should be at Madagascar.

Being thus resolved, we left the ship, which both William and I, and the surgeon, never intended to see any more. We steered directly for the Gulf, and through to Bassorah, or Balsara. This city of Balsara lies at some distance from the place where our sloop lay, and the river not being very safe, and we but ill acquainted with it, having but an ordinary pilot, we went on shore at a village where some merchants live, and which is very populous, for the sake of small vessels riding there.

Here we stayed and traded three or four days, landing all our bales and spices, and indeed the whole cargo that was of any considerable value, which we chose to do rather than go up immediately to Balsara till the project we had laid was put in execution.

After we had bought several goods, and were preparing to buy several others, the boat being on shore with twelve men, myself,

William, the surgeon, and one fourth man, whom we had singled out, we contrived to send a Turk just at the dusk of the evening with a letter to the boatswain, and giving the fellow a charge to run with all possible speed, we stood at a small distance to observe the event. The contents of the letter were thus written by the old doctor: —

"BOATSWAIN THOMAS, — We are all betrayed. For God's sake make off with the boat, and get on board, or you are all lost. The captain, William the Quaker, and George the reformade are seized and carried away: I am escaped and hid, but cannot stir out; if I do I am a dead man. As soon as you are on board cut or slip, and make sail for your lives. Adieu. — R.S."

We stood undiscovered, as above, it being the dusk of the evening, and saw the Turk deliver the letter, and in three minutes we saw all the men hurry into the boat and put off, and no sooner were they on board than they took the hint, as we supposed, for the next morning they were out of sight, and we never heard tale or tidings of them since.

We were now in a good place, and in very good circumstances, for we passed for merchants of Persia.

It is not material to record here what a mass of ill-gotten wealth we had got together: it will be more to the purpose to tell you that I began to be sensible of the crime of getting of it in such a manner as I had done; that I had very little satisfaction in the possession of it; and, as I told William, I had no expectation of keeping it, nor much desire; but, as I said to him one day walking out into the fields near the town of Bassorah, so I depended upon it that it would be the case, which you will hear presently.

We were perfectly secured at Bassorah, by having frighted away the rogues, our comrades; and we had nothing to do but to consider how to convert our treasure into things proper to make us look like merchants, as we were now to be, and not like freebooters, as we really had been.

We happened very opportunely here upon a Dutchman, who had traveled from Bengal to Agra, the capital city of the Great Mogul, and from thence was come to the coast of Malabar by land, and got shipping, somehow or other, up the Gulf; and we found his design was to go up the great river to Bagdad or Babylon, and so, by the caravan, to Aleppo and Scanderoon. As William spoke Dutch, and was of an agreeable, insinuating behaviour, he soon got acquainted with this Dutchman, and discovering our circumstances to one another, we found he had considerable effects with him; and that he had traded long in that country, and was making homeward to his own country; and that he had servants with him; one an Armenian, whom he had taught to speak Dutch, and who had something of his own, but had a mind to travel into Europe; and the other a Dutch sailor, whom he had picked up by his fancy, and reposed a great trust in him, and a very honest fellow he was.

This Dutchman was very glad of an acquaintance, because he soon found that we directed our thoughts to Europe also; and as he found we were encumbered with goods only (for we let him know nothing of our money), he readily offered us his assistance to dispose of as many of them as the place we were in would put off, and his advice what to do with the rest.

While this was doing, William and I consulted what to do with ourselves and what we had; and first, we resolved we would never talk seriously of our measures but in the open fields, where we were sure nobody could hear; so every evening, when the sun began to decline and the air to be moderate we walked out, sometimes this way, sometimes that, to consult of our affairs.

I should have observed that we had new clothed ourselves here, after the Persian manner, with long vests of silk, a gown or robe of English crimson cloth, very fine and handsome, and had let our beards grow so after the Persian manner that we passed for Persian merchants, in view only, though, by the way, we could not understand or speak one word of the language of Persia, or indeed of any other but English and Dutch; and of the latter I understood very little.

However, the Dutchman supplied all this for us; and as we had resolved to keep ourselves as retired as we could, though there were several English merchants upon the place, yet we never acquainted ourselves with one of them, or exchanged a word with them; by which means we prevented their inquiry of us now, or their giving any intelligence of us, if any news of our landing here should happen to come, which, it was easy for us to know, was possible enough, if any of our comrades fell into bad hands, or by many accidents which we could not foresee.

It was during my being here, for here we stayed near two months, that I grew very thoughtful about my circumstances; not as to the danger, neither indeed were we in any, but were entirely concealed and unsuspected; but I really began to have other thoughts of myself, and of the world, than ever I had before.

William had struck so deep into my unthinking temper with hinting to me that there was something beyond all this; that the present time was the time of enjoyment, but that the time of account approached; that the work that remained was gentler than the labour past, viz., repentance, and that it was high time to think of it; — I say these, and such thoughts as these, engrossed my hours, and, in a word, I grew very sad.

As to the wealth I had, which was immensely great, it was all like dirt under my feet; I had no value for it, no peace in the possession of it, no great concern about me for the leaving of it.

William had perceived my thoughts to be troubled and my mind heavy and oppressed for some time; and one evening, in one of our cool walks, I began with him about the leaving our effects. William was a wise and wary man, and indeed all the prudentials of my conduct had for a long time been owing to his advice, and so now all the methods for preserving our effects, and even ourselves, lay upon him; and he had been telling me of some of the measures he had been taking for our making homeward, and for the security of our wealth, when I took him very short. "Why, William," says I, "dost thou think we shall ever be able to reach Europe with all this cargo that we have about us?"

"Ay," says William, "without doubt, as well as other merchants with theirs, as long as it is not publicly known what quantity or of what value our cargo consists."

"Why, William," says I, smiling, "do you think that if there is a God above, as you have so long been telling me there is, and that we must give an account to Him, — I say, do you think, if He be a righteous Judge, He will let us escape thus with the plunder, as we may call it, of so many innocent people, nay, I might say nations, and not call us to an account for it before we can get to Europe, where we pretend to enjoy it?"

William appeared struck and surprised at the question, and made no answer for a great while; and I repeated the question, adding that it was not to be expected.

After a little pause, says William, "Thou hast started a very weighty question, and I can make no positive answer to it; but I will state it thus: first, it is true that, if we consider the justice of God, we have no reason to expect any protection; but as the ordinary ways of Providence are out of the common road of human affairs, so we may hope for mercy still upon our repentance, and we know not how good He may be to us; so we are to act as if we rather depended upon the last, I mean the merciful part, than claimed the first, which must produce nothing but judgment and vengeance."

"But hark ye, William," says I, "the nature of repentance, as you have hinted once to me, included reformation; and we can never reform; how, then, can we repent?"

"Why can we never reform?" says William.

"Because," said I, "we cannot restore what we have taken away by rapine and spoil."

"It is true," says William, "we never can do that, for we can never come to the knowledge of the owners."

"But what, then, must be done with our wealth," said I, "the effects of plunder and rapine? If we keep it, we continue to be robbers and thieves; and if we quit it we cannot do justice with it, for we cannot restore it to the right owners."

"Nay," says William, "the answer to it is short. To quit what we have, and do it here, is to throw it away to those who have no claim to it, and to divest ourselves of it, but to do no right with it; whereas we ought to keep it carefully together, with a resolution to do what right with it we are able; and who knows what opportunity Providence may put into our hands to do justice, at least, to some of those we have injured? So we ought, at least, to leave it to Him and go on. As it is, without doubt our present business is to go to some place of safety, where we may wait His will."

This resolution of William was very satisfying to me indeed, as, the truth is, all he said, and at all times, was solid and good; and had not William thus, as it were, quieted my mind, I think, verily, I was so alarmed at the just reason I had to expect vengeance from Heaven upon me for my ill-gotten wealth, that I should have run away from it as the devil's goods, that I had nothing to do with, that did not belong to me, and that I had no right to keep, and was in certain danger of being destroyed for.

However, William settled my mind to more prudent steps than these, and I concluded that I ought, however, to proceed to a place of safety, and leave the event to God Almighty's mercy. But this I must leave upon record, that I had from this time no joy of the wealth I had got. I looked upon it all as stolen, and so indeed the greatest part of it was. I looked upon it as a hoard of other men's goods, which I had robbed the innocent owners of, and which I ought, in a word, to be hanged for here, and damned for hereafter. And now, indeed, I began sincerely to hate myself for a dog; a wretch that had been a thief and a murderer; a wretch that was in a condition which nobody was ever in; for I had robbed, and though I had the wealth by me, yet it was impossible I should ever make any restitution; and upon this account it ran in my head that I could never repent, for that repentance could not be sincere without restitution, and therefore must of necessity be damned. There was no room for me to escape. I went about with my heart full of these thoughts, little better than a distracted fellow; in short, running headlong into the dreadfulest despair, and premeditating nothing but how to rid myself out of the world; and, indeed, the devil, if such things are of the devil's immediate doing, followed his work very close with me, and nothing lay upon my mind for several days but to shoot myself into the head with my pistol.

I was all this while in a vagrant life, among infidels, Turks, pagans, and such sort of people. I had no minister, no Christian to converse with but poor William. He was my ghostly father or confessor, and he was all the comfort I had. As for my knowledge of religion, you have heard my history. You may suppose I had not much; and as for the Word of God, I do not remember that I ever read a chapter in the Bible in my lifetime. I was little Bob at Bussleton, and went to school to learn my Testament.

However, it pleased God to make William the Quaker everything to me. Upon this occasion, I took him out one evening, as usual, and hurried him away into the fields with me, in more haste than ordinary; and there, in short, I told him the perplexity of my mind, and under what terrible temptations of the devil I had been; that I must shoot myself, for I could not support the weight and terror that was upon me.

"Shoot yourself!" says William; "why, what will that do for you?"

"Why," says I, "it will put an end to a miserable life."

"Well," says William, "are you satisfied the next will be better?"

"No, no," says I; "much worse, to be sure."

"Why, then," says he, "shooting yourself is the devil's motion, no doubt; for it is the devil of a reason, that, because thou art in an ill case, therefore thou must put thyself into a worse."

This shocked my reason indeed. "Well, but," says I, "there is no bearing the miserable condition I am in."

"Very well," says William; "but it seems there is some bearing a worse condition; and so you will shoot yourself, that you may be past remedy?"

"I am past remedy already," says I.

"How do you know that?" says he.

"I am satisfied of it," said I.

"Well," says he, "but you are not sure; so you will shoot yourself to make it certain; for though on this side death you cannot be sure you will be damned at all, yet the moment you step on the other side of time you are sure of it; for when it is done, it is not to be said then that you will be, but that you are damned."

"Well, but," says William, as if he had been between jest and earnest, "pray, what didst thou dream of last night?"

"Why," said I, "I had frightful dreams all night; and, particularly, I dreamed that the devil came for me, and asked me what my name was; and I told him. Then he asked me what trade I was. 'Trade?' says I; 'I am a thief, a rogue, by my calling: I am a pirate and a murderer, and ought to be hanged.' 'Ay, ay,' says the devil, 'so you do; and you are the man I looked for, and therefore come along with me.' At which I was most horribly frighted, and cried out so that it waked me; and I have been in horrible agony ever since."

"Very well," says William; "come, give me the pistol thou talkedst of just now."

"Why," says I, "what will you do with it?"

"Do with it!" says William. "Why, thou needest not shoot thyself; I shall be obliged to do it for thee. Why, thou wilt destroy us all."

"What do you mean, William?" said I.

"Mean!" said he; "nay, what didst thou mean, to cry out aloud in thy sleep, 'I am a thief, a pirate, a murderer, and ought to be hanged'? Why, thou wilt ruin us all. 'Twas well the Dutchman did not understand English. In short, I must shoot thee, to save my own life. Come, come," says he, "give me thy pistol."

I confess this terrified me again another way, and I began to be sensible that, if anybody had been near me to understand English, I had been undone. The thought of shooting myself forsook me from that time; and I turned to William, "You disorder me extremely, William," said I; "why, I am never safe, nor is it safe to keep me company. What shall I do? I shall betray you all."

"Come, come, friend Bob," says he, "I'll put an end to it all, if you will take my advice."

"How's that?" said I.

"Why, only," says he, "that the next time thou talkest with the devil, thou wilt talk a little softlier, or we shall be all undone, and you too."

This frighted me, I must confess, and allayed a great deal of the trouble of mind I was in. But William, after he had done jesting with me, entered upon a very long and serious discourse with me about the nature of my circumstances, and about repentance; that it ought to be attended, indeed, with a deep abhorrence of the crime that I had to charge myself with; but that to despair of God's mercy was no part of repentance, but putting myself into the condition of the devil; indeed, that I must apply myself with a sincere, humble confession of my crime, to ask pardon of God, whom I had offended, and cast myself upon His mercy, resolving to be willing to make restitution, if ever it should please God to put it in my power, even to the utmost of what I had in the world. And this, he told me, was the method which he had resolved upon himself; and in this, he told me, he had found comfort.

I had a great deal of satisfaction in William's discourse, and it quieted me very much; but William was very anxious ever after about my talking in my sleep, and took care to lie with me always himself, and to keep me from lodging in any house where so much as a word of English was understood.

However, there was not the like occasion afterward; for I was much more composed in my mind, and resolved for the future to live a quite different life from what I had done. As to the wealth I had, I looked upon it as nothing; I resolved to set it apart to any such opportunity of doing justice as God should put into my hand; and the miraculous opportunity I had afterwards of applying some parts of it to preserve a ruined family, whom I had plundered, may be worth reading, if I have room for it in this account.

With these resolutions I began to be restored to some degree of quiet in my mind; and having, after almost three months' stay at Bassorah, disposed of some goods, but having a great quantity left, we hired boats according to the Dutchman's direction, and went up to Bagdad, or Babylon, on the river Tigris, or rather Euphrates. We had a very considerable cargo of goods with us, and therefore made a great figure there, and were received with respect. We had, in particular, two-and-forty bales of Indian stuffs of sundry sorts, silks, muslins, and fine chintz; we had fifteen bales of very fine China silks, and seventy packs or bales of spices, particularly cloves and nutmegs, with other goods. We were bid money here for our cloves, but the Dutchman advised us not to part with them, and told us we should get a better price at Aleppo, or in the Levant; so we prepared for the caravan.

We concealed our having any gold or pearls as much as we could, and therefore sold three or four bales of China silks and Indian calicoes, to raise money to buy camels and to pay the customs which are taken at several places, and for our provisions over the deserts.

I traveled this journey, careless to the last degree of my goods or wealth, believing that, as I came by it all by rapine and violence, God would direct that it should be taken from me again in the same manner; and, indeed, I think I might say I was very willing it should be so. But, as I had a merciful Protector above me, so I had a most faithful steward, counsellor, partner, or whatever I might call him, who was my guide, my pilot, my governor, my everything, and took care both of me and of all we had; and though he had never been in any of these parts of the world, yet he took the care of all upon him; and in about nine-and-fifty days we arrived from Bassorah, at the mouth of the river Tigris or Euphrates, through the desert, and through Aleppo to Alexandria, or, as we call it, Scanderoon, in the Levant.

Here William and I, and the other two, our faithful comrades, debated what we should do; and here William and I resolved to separate from the other two, they resolving to go with the Dutchman into Holland, by the means of some Dutch ship which lay then in the road. William and I told them we resolved to go and settle in the Morea, which then belonged to the Venetians.

It is true we acted wisely in it not to let them know whither we went, seeing we had resolved to separate; but we took our old doctor's directions how to write to him in Holland, and in England, that we might have intelligence from him on occasion, and promised to give him an account how to write to us, which we afterwards did, as may in time be made out.

We stayed here some time after they were gone, till at length, not being thoroughly resolved whither to go till then, a Venetian ship touched at Cyprus, and put in at Scanderoon to look for freight home. We took the hint, and bargaining for our passage, and the freight of our goods, we embarked for Venice, where, in two-and-twenty days, we arrived safe, with all our treasure, and with such a cargo, take our goods and our money and our jewels together, as, I believed, was never brought into the city by two single men, since the state of Venice had a being.

We kept ourselves here *incognito* for a great while, passing for two Armenian merchants still, as we had done before; and by this time we had gotten so much of the Persian and Armenian jargon, which they talked at Bassorah and Bagdad, and everywhere that we came in the country, as was sufficient to make us able to talk to one another, so as not to be understood by anybody, though sometimes hardly by ourselves.

Here we converted all our effects into money, settled our abode as for a considerable time, and William and I, maintaining an inviolable friendship and fidelity to one another, lived like two brothers; we neither had or sought any separate interest; we conversed seriously and gravely, and upon the subject of our repentance continually; we never changed, that is to say, so as to leave off our Armenian garbs; and we were called, at Venice, the two Grecians.

I had been two or three times going to give a detail of our wealth, but it will appear incredible, and we had the greatest difficulty in the world how to conceal it, being justly apprehensive lest we might be assassinated in that country for our treasure. At length William told me he began to think now that he must never see England any more, and that indeed he did not much concern himself about it; but seeing we had gained so great wealth, and he had some poor relations in England, if I was willing, he would write to know if they were living, and to know what condition they were in, and if he found such of them were alive as he had some thoughts about, he would, with my consent, send them something to better their condition.

I consented most willingly; and accordingly William wrote to a sister and an uncle, and in about five weeks' time received an answer from them both, directed to himself, under cover of a hard Armenian name that he had given himself, viz., Signore Constantine Alexion of Ispahan, at Venice.

It was a very moving letter he received from his sister, who, after the most passionate expressions of joy to hear he was alive, seeing she had long ago had an account that he was murdered by the pirates in the West Indies, entreats him to let her know what circumstances he was in; tells him she was not in any capacity to do anything considerable for him, but that he should be welcome to her with all her heart; that she was left a widow, with four children, but kept a little shop in the Minories, by which she made shift to maintain her family; and that she had sent him five pounds, lest he should want money, in a strange country, to bring him home.

I could see the letter brought tears out of his eyes as he read it; and, indeed, when he showed it to me, and the little bill for five pounds, upon an English merchant in Venice, it brought tears out of my eyes too.

After we had been both affected sufficiently with the tenderness and kindness of this letter, he turns to me; says he, "What shall I do for this poor woman?" I mused a while; at last says I, "I will tell you what you shall do for her. She has sent you five pounds, and she has four children, and herself, that is five; such a sum, from a poor woman in her circumstances, is as much as five thousand pounds is to us; you shall send her a bill of exchange for five thousand pounds English money, and bid her conceal her surprise at it till she hears from you again; but bid her leave off her shop, and go and take a house somewhere in the country, not far off from London, and stay there, in a moderate figure, till she hears from you again."

"Now," says William, "I perceive by it that you have some thoughts of venturing into England."

"Indeed, William," said I, "you mistake me; but it presently occurred to me that you should venture, for what have you done that you may not be seen there? Why should I desire to keep you from your relations, purely to keep me company?"

William looked very affectionately upon me. "Nay," says he, "we have embarked together so long, and come together so far, I am resolved I will never part with thee as long as I live, go where thou wilt, or stay where thou wilt; and as for my sister," said William, "I cannot send her such a sum of money, for whose is all this money we have? It is most of it thine."

"No, William," said I, "there is not a penny of it mine but what is yours too, and I won't have anything but an equal share with you, and therefore you shall send it to her; if not, I will send it."

"Why," says William, "it will make the poor woman distracted; she will be so surprised she will go out of her wits."

"Well," said I, "William, you may do it prudently; send her a bill backed of a hundred pounds, and bid her expect more in a post or two, and that you will send her enough to live on without keeping shop, and then send her more."

Accordingly William sent her a very kind letter, with a bill upon a merchant in London for a hundred and sixty pounds, and bid her comfort herself with the hope that he should be able in a little time to send her more. About ten days after, he sent her another bill of five hundred and forty pounds; and a post or two after, another for three hundred pounds, making in all a thousand pounds; and told her he would send her sufficient to leave off her shop, and directed her to take a house as above.

He waited then till he received an answer to all the three letters, with an account that she had received the money, and, which I did not expect, that she had not let any other acquaintance know that she had received a shilling from anybody, or so much as that he was alive, and would not till she had heard again.

When he showed me this letter, "Well, William," said I, "this woman is fit to be trusted with life or anything; send her the rest of the five thousand pounds, and I'll venture to England with you, to this woman's house, whenever you will."

In a word, we sent her five thousand pounds in good bills; and she received them very punctually, and in a little time sent her brother word that she had pretended to her uncle that she was sickly and could not carry on the trade any longer, and that she had taken a large house about four miles from London, under pretence of letting lodgings for her livelihood; and, in short, intimated as if she understood that he intended to come over to be *incognito*, assuring him he should be as retired as he pleased.

This was opening the very door for us that we thought had been effectually shut for this life; and, in a word, we resolved to venture, but to keep ourselves entirely concealed, both as to name and every other circumstance; and accordingly William sent his sister word how kindly he took her prudent steps, and that she had guessed right that he desired to be retired, and that he obliged her not to increase her figure, but live private, till she might perhaps see him.

He was going to send the letter away. "Come, William," said I, "you shan't send her an empty letter; tell her you have a friend coming with you that must be as retired as yourself, and I'll send her five thousand pounds more."

So, in short, we made this poor woman's family rich; and yet, when it came to the point, my heart failed me, and I durst not venture; and for William, he would not stir without me; and so we stayed about two years after this, considering what we should do.

You may think, perhaps, that I was very prodigal of my ill-gotten goods, thus to load a stranger with my bounty, and give a gift like a prince to one that had been able to merit nothing of me, or indeed know me; but my condition ought to be considered in this case; though I had money to profusion, yet I was perfectly destitute of a friend in the world, to have the least obligation or assistance from, or knew not either where to dispose or trust anything I had while I lived, or whom to give it to if I died.

When I had reflected upon the manner of my getting of it, I was sometimes for giving it all to charitable uses, as a debt due to mankind, though I was no Roman Catholic, and not at all of the opinion that it would purchase me any repose to my soul; but I thought, as it was got by a general plunder, and which I could make no satisfaction for, it was due to the community, and I ought to distribute it for the general good. But still I was at a loss how, and where, and by whom to settle this charity, not daring to go home to my own country, lest some of my comrades, strolled home, should see and detect me, and for the very spoil of my money, or the purchase of his own pardon, betray and expose me to an untimely end.

Being thus destitute, I say, of a friend, I pitched thus upon William's sister; the kind step of hers to her brother, whom she thought to be in distress, signifying a generous mind and a charitable disposition; and having resolved to make her the object of my first bounty, I did not doubt but I should purchase something of a refuge for myself, and a kind of a centre, to which I should tend in my future actions; for really a man that has a subsistence, and no residence, no place that has a magnetic influence upon his affections, is in one of the most odd, uneasy conditions in the world, nor is it in the power of all his money to make it up to him.

It was, as I told you, two years and upwards that we remained at Venice and thereabout, in the greatest hesitation imaginable, irresolute and unfixed to the last degree. William's sister importuned us daily to come to England, and wondered we should not dare to trust her, whom we had to such a degree obliged to be faithful; and in a manner lamented her being suspected by us.

At last I began to incline; and I said to William, "Come, brother William," said I (for ever since our discourse at Bassorah I called him brother), "if you will agree to two or three things with me, I'll go home to England with all my heart."

Says William, "Let me know what they are."

"Why, first," says I, "you shall not disclose yourself to any of your relations in England but your sister — no, not one; secondly, we will not shave off our mustachios or beards" (for we had all along worn our beards after the Grecian manner), "nor leave off our long vests, that we may pass for Grecians and foreigners; thirdly, that we shall never speak

English in public before anybody, your sister excepted; fourthly, that we will always live together and pass for brothers."

William said he would agree to them all with all his heart, but that the not speaking English would be the hardest, but he would do his best for that too; so, in a word, we agreed to go from Venice to Naples, where we converted a large sum of money into bales of silk, left a large sum in a merchant's hands at Venice, and another considerable sum at Naples, and took bills of exchange for a great deal too; and yet we came with such a cargo to London as few American merchants had done for some years, for we loaded in two ships seventy-three bales of thrown silk, besides thirteen bales of wrought silks, from the duchy of Milan, shipped at Genoa, with all which I arrived safely; and some time after I married my faithful protectress, William's sister, with whom I am much more happy than I deserve.

And now, having so plainly told you that I am come to England, after I have so boldly owned what life I have led abroad, it is time to leave off, and say no more for the present, lest some should be willing to inquire too nicely after your old friend CAPTAIN BOB.